PENGUIN  CLASSICS

THE LATER ROMAN EMPIRE

ADVISORY EDITOR: BETTY RADICE

AMMIANUS MARCELLINUS was the last great Roman historian. He was not a professional man of letters but an army officer of Greek origin born at Antioch and contemporary with the events described in what remains of his work. He set himself the task of continuing the histories of Tacitus from AD 96 down to his own day. The first thirteen of his thirty-one books are lost: the remainder describe a period of only twenty-five years (AD 354–378) and the reigns of the emperors Constantius, Julian, Jovian, Valentinian and Valens, for which he is a prime authority. He was a pagan and an admirer of the apostate Julian, to whose career about half the surviving books are devoted. But his treatment of Christianity is free from prejudice and his impartiality and good judgement have been generally recognized. His style is sometimes bizarre, but in all the essential qualities of an historian he deserves the praise accorded to him by Gibbon and is well able to stand comparison with Livy and Tacitus.

WALTER HAMILTON was an Honorary Fellow of Magdalene College, Cambridge, where he was also Master from 1967 until 1978. He was born in 1908 and was a Scholar of Trinity College, Cambridge, where he gained first class honours in both parts of the classical Tripos. He was a fellow of Trinity College and a University Lecturer at Cambridge, and taught at Eton before becoming Headmaster of Westminster School (1950–57) and of Rugby School (1957–66). He has also translated Plato's *Symposium*, the *Gorgias*, *Phaedrus* and *Letters VII and VIII* for Penguin Classics. Walter Hamilton died in 1988.

ANDREW WALLACE-HADRILL was born in 1951. He was a Scholar of Corpus Chistie College, Oxford, where he gained first class honours in Classical Moderations and Greats together with the Hertford, Craven and Ireland Scholarships. He was Fellow and Classical Lecturer of Magdalene College, Cambridge (1976–83), then Lecturer in Ancient

History at Leicester University and is now Professor of Classics at Reading University. His books include *Suetonius: the Scholar and his Caesars,* and he has edited *Patronage in Ancient Society* and has published papers on a wide range of Roman themes.

AMMIANUS MARCELLINUS

THE LATER ROMAN EMPIRE
(A.D. 354–378)

Selected and translated by
Walter Hamilton
with an Introduction and Notes by
Andrew Wallace-Hadrill

PENGUIN BOOKS

PENGUIN BOOKS

Published by the Penguin Group
Penguin Books Ltd, 80 Strand, London WC2R 0RL, England
Penguin Putnam Inc., 375 Hudson Street, New York, New York 10014, USA
Penguin Books Australia Ltd, 250 Camberwell Road, Camberwell, Victoria 3124, Australia
Penguin Books Canada Ltd, 10 Alcorn Avenue, Toronto, Ontario, Canada M4V 3B2
Penguin Books India (P) Ltd, 11 Community Centre, Panchsheel Park, New Delhi – 110 017, India
Penguin Books (NZ) Ltd, Cnr Rosedale and Airborne Roads, Albany, Auckland, New Zealand
Penguin Books (South Africa) (Pty) Ltd, 24 Sturdee Avenue, Rosebank 2196, South Africa

Penguin Books Ltd, Registered Offices: 80 Strand, London WC2R 0RL, England

www.penguin.com

This translation first published 1986
17

Translation copyright © Walter Hamilton, 1986
Introduction and Notes copyright © Andrew Wallace-Hadrill, 1986
All rights reserved

Printed in England by Clays Ltd, St Ives plc
Filmset in Monophoto 10/12pt Ehrhardt

In affectionate memory of Betty Radice,
who commissioned and approved this translation.

CONTENTS

CONTENTS

PREFACE

This volume contains in translation the major part of the extant books (14–31) of the histories of Ammianus Marcellinus, which cover the years A.D. 354–378. To keep within the bounds of a single Penguin volume some selection has been necessary, and the reader should be aware that this leaves a slightly unbalanced impression of Ammianus' writing. Cuts have fallen most heavily on passages which do not affect the coherence of the narrative. One result is that the reign of Julian is more fully represented than those of Valentinian and Valens, which fall into a number of self-contained episodes. But the chief sacrifice has been a number of Ammianus' celebrated digressions, mostly those on geography and natural phenomena. Some of these would be frankly tedious to a modern reader, but the digression was an integral feature of Ammianus' approach to historical writing (cf. Introduction, § 23), and we have tried to retain enough material of this type to give some idea of his method and the remarkable range of his interests. The omitted passages constitute about one fifth of the whole, and every omission is indicated in the text.

The text of Ammianus, for which we have to rely almost entirely upon a single ninth-century manuscript, is disfigured by many corruptions and lacunae, though fortunately the passages in which the meaning is seriously in doubt are comparatively few. The translator has not found it possible to follow any single modern editor implicitly. He has used his own judgement in the choice of readings, but has consulted throughout the new Teubner edition of W. Seyfarth, the volumes of the Budé series as far as they at present extend, and the Loeb edition of J. C. Rolfe. Passages where the corruption is hopeless and it is necessary to resort to conjecture are *printed in italics*, as are also the chapter headings, abbreviated in most cases from those in the manuscripts, which are themselves the work of an early editor. In effect, all words in italics are editorial.

Ammianus' style is characterized briefly in the Introduction (§ 24).

Here the translator need only add that it is such that any attempt at a close rendering in modern English would be unreadable. But he has tried to preserve what he can of the flavour of Ammianus' style, both in his occasional sublimities and in his not infrequent lapses into pomposity and even absurdity.

The subject-matter of Ammianus is diverse and wide-ranging, and the reader may often feel in need of explanation. Unfortunately, there is still no good historical commentary in English to which he can be referred. We have tried to provide what help is possible in the limited space available. It was not possible, nor in our view desirable, to provide comment in the Notes on all points of detail: for instance, Ammianus' frequent mythological and historical allusions can be readily identified by consulting any standard work of reference (the *Oxford Classical Dictionary*, or the Penguin *Who's Who in the Ancient World*). Instead the Notes concentrate on more general features of the author's approach to his material in the form of a running commentary by chapters or groups of chapters. The identification of the surprisingly large number of individuals who recur at scattered points in the histories will be made easier by the Notes on Persons.

Geographical names present a special problem. Consistency would dictate the use of ancient forms throughout, but to retain Londinium or Mediolanum or Argentorate for London or Milan or Strasbourg would be merely irritating to the reader. In general, therefore, modern names are used in the text where they are well known and their identity certain, but ancient forms are added in brackets at least on first appearance. Ancient names are used in the maps, but cross-references in the Geographical Key will eliminate any difficulty.

This volume is the fruit of cooperation over a number of years. Though each of us has separate responsibility for the translation and the explanatory material, we read and discussed each other's work at every stage; and we were rewarded to discover that our respect for and enjoyment of Ammianus grew progressively in the course of our work. We are also indebted in various ways to several friends, none of whom, of course, can be held responsible for our errors. The Introduction was greatly improved by the comments of Peter Garnsey and Michael Wallace-Hadrill, and both Introduction and Notes by those of John Matthews (we regret that we did not have the further benefit of John Matthews's major forthcoming book on Ammianus). Jamie Masters took on the donkey-work of map-making, and Michael Whitby helped to locate a number of place-names. Typing was cheerfully undertaken by Janet Bradford, Alwynne Gardner, and especially Jo Wallace-Hadrill (who suffered Ammianus in more ways than this).

One outstanding debt is acknowledged in the dedication. The wise advice and encouragement of Betty Radice were of enormous value to us during the preparation of the book. She had read the translation, but did not live to see the volume through the press. We cannot emphasize too strongly our sense of loss and our gratitude.

March 1985   W. H.
                                                             A. W-H.

INTRODUCTION

I.

It is not without the most sincere regret that I must now take leave of an accurate and faithful guide, who has composed the history of his own times without indulging the prejudices and passions which usually affect the mind of a contemporary.

Gibbon's affectionate farewell to Ammianus (*Decline and Fall*, vol. 3, ch. 26, p. 122, ed. Bury) reflects the admiration he felt for Rome's last great historian. Not that Gibbon was blind to Ammianus' failings, which provoked some of his most caustic asides. He frequently censures 'the vices of his style, the disorder and perplexity of his narrative' (vol. 3, ch. 26, p. 111); 'those turgid metaphors, those false ornaments, that perpetually disfigure the style of Ammianus' (vol. 3, ch. 26, p. 104); he finds fault with his selection of material: 'his superfluous prolixity is disagreeably balanced by his unseasonable brevity' (vol. 3, ch. 26, p. 96); and he contrasts unfavourably with Tacitus 'the coarse and undistinguishing pencil of Ammianus' (vol. 3, ch. 25, p. 19). But though these features irked Gibbon, as they may still irk the modern reader, the history as a whole made a profound impact on Gibbon's picture of late antiquity and his conception of Rome in 'decline'. This history is more than a narrative of the twenty-five eventful years that culminated in the disastrous defeat of the Romans at Adrianople in 378. Ammianus presents an evocation of the late Roman world of extraordinary vividness and variety, suffused with a sense of admiration for and continuity with the classical Roman past. It is by no means the only valid perspective; but it remains still of central importance in any attempt to reconstruct late antiquity, and present-day historians pay tribute to Ammianus' value no less handsomely than Gibbon.

AMMIANUS' LIFE

2. There is a strong autobiographical streak in the histories of Ammianus Marcellinus, which allows us to grasp at least the essentials of his background. He describes himself as 'a former soldier and a Greek' in the closing paragraph of his work, though we should not be deceived by the mock-modest tone of this description. Born in *c.* A.D. 330 towards the end of the reign of Constantine, he was a native of Antioch on the Orontes, capital of Syria, 'the jewel of the East' (22.9), one of the four major cities of the empire. The city is well known to us through the prolific letters and orations of the professor of rhetoric Libanius, who knew, if he did not teach, Ammianus. Antioch was important both as a cultural and as an administrative centre. We meet it repeatedly in Ammianus' pages: here the Caesar Gallus holds court and disgraces himself (14.7–9); here Julian prepares his invasion of Persia and quarrels dramatically with the populace (22.9–14); here too take place the gruesome trials for treason and magic under Valens which the author recalls with a shudder (29.1–2). The city was ruled by a Greek-speaking elite of landowners (the peasantry spoke Syriac); the richer families were obliged in theory to shoulder the financial burdens of membership of the city council. To this class (the 'curial class') Ammianus' family must have belonged, though we have no details. One of the major tensions of the period was caused by the tendency for members of such local aristocracies of the cities of the empire to escape local obligations, particularly through service in the imperial army and administration. The sharp protests of Ammianus against Julian's unsuccessful attempts to reverse this process and remove the privileged status of former imperial officials indicate where his own interests lay (22.9). His own service would have given him such privileged status.

3. The normal avenue of promotion for a highly educated young man, like the majority of Libanius' pupils, was the imperial bureaucracy. Somewhat unusually, Ammianus entered the army. But he was no ordinary soldier. Already in his twenties we find him as a staff officer, a *protector domesticus*. Posts in this elite corps were highly sought after, achieved through favour and influence. They normally involved attendance on the emperor (though officers might be detached, as was Ammianus, to serve on the staff of another commander) and this was marked by the rare privilege of permission 'to kiss the imperial purple'. When the emperor Julian died, leaving his army stranded in Persia,

the officers (including Ammianus) cast round desperately for a new emperor, and the candidate on whom their choice eventually fell, the relatively young Jovian, was the senior officer of the corps, and a son of a distinguished general. Ammianus' own credentials were perhaps not so impressive; but he certainly moved in high circles, close to the seat of power. Like several of the major historians of antiquity, he belonged to the number of those who might have been (but in fact were not) important figures in the history of their times.

4. Ammianus certainly gives full exposure to the events in which he was personally involved. In the surviving portion of his narrative (the first half is lost) he first emerges on the staff of the general Ursicinus in 354 (14.9). He is ferociously loyal to his commanding officer, and scathing about the motives of the imperial court in relieving him of the command of the forces in the East and recalling him (14.11). In the next year he and Ursicinus were dispatched on the dangerous mission of deceiving and murdering the usurper Silvanus in Gaul: a vivid if not wholly creditable episode (15.5). In its aftermath Julian, the key figure of Ammianus' whole history, was appointed to the command in Gaul as Caesar (355). For the next year Ursicinus and Ammianus remained in Gaul (16.2); the historian's admiration for Julian stems partly from personal contact with his hero which presumably goes back to this period. But in 357 Ursicinus was reappointed to the Eastern command and Ammianus followed him, still too young to be promoted tribune (16.10). For the next six years Ammianus was separated from Julian's triumphant career. Instead, however, he was involved in important events nearer to his native Antioch. In 359 the Persians launched a formidable invasion of Mesopotamia (18.7), and Ammianus' account of his personal experiences in the unhappy resistance to this invasion makes for the most gripping moments in all his narrative: the near escape of the staff from capture, and the reconnaissance visit to the Persian satrap of Corduene, by chance an old Antiochene student and friend of Ammianus (18.6); the chance encounter with the renegade Roman Antoninus, who advised the invading forces (18.8); the long siege of Amida and his hair-raising escape from its sack (19.1–8). After this (359) the historian was involved in no important events – or none that he cared to recall – until in 363 he joined the Persian expedition of Julian, now emperor. His silence about his own part in the intervening years need not mean that he left active service; but he had hardly covered himself with glory in 359 and may have been passed over for

the more important assignments. It is not until Julian's army is advancing down the Euphrates that 'we' reappears in the narrative (23.5). For a second time the campaign in which Ammianus took part proved a disastrous failure; after the death of Julian, the unfortunate Jovian was forced to cede territory to the Persians in order to preserve the remnants of the stranded expeditionary force. Ammianus attacks Jovian bitterly for this humiliation (25.7), but there was little else that could have been done. After the army's dismal return to base, Ammianus again disappears from the narrative; it is reasonable to infer that he left the service and returned to Antioch. He was there in 371 when a wave of treason trials swept the city, and was at least in some personal danger: 'we all crept about at that time in a Cimmerian darkness' (29.2).

CIRCUMSTANCES OF COMPOSITION

5. It was not simply as a veteran officer and a Greek of Antioch that Ammianus wrote. For he wrote in Latin and he wrote in Rome. He could well, like his contemporary Eunapius of Sardis, have written in Greek. There was certainly a market among men like Libanius and his friends for a history in Greek from a pagan point of view, particularly one that centred on the hellenophile Julian. This is what Eunapius but not Ammianus gave them. So Roman is Ammianus' vision that he thought it tragic that Julian's body was not buried by the waters of the Tiber (25.10); Julian had never seen Rome, and Libanius' suggestion of Athens as a burial place was far more appropriate. It is a notable fact of literary history that the last great Latin history was written by a Greek (paralleled by the fact that the last great Latin epic was written by the Greek Claudian).

6. When and why Ammianus moved to Rome is not something he discloses. But he was not the only one who felt the drawing-power of Rome at this period. Libanius complains at the rising prestige of Latin studies in Antioch, and even claims that students were leaving Antioch to pursue their studies in Italy in such numbers that he almost gave up teaching. Distinguished Antiochenes also took up residence in Rome, like Hypatius who held the prefecture (below, § 8). There may have been personal reasons that made Antioch uncomfortable for Ammianus: perhaps he was affected by the treason trials of 371 (it sounds at least as if he could have burnt his library in fear, 29.2) or perhaps he suffered

in some private legal dispute, at the hands of the advocates against whom he fulminates with bitter incoherence (30.4). Be that as it may, the first clear sign of his presence in Rome is in the context of a food shortage, probably in 384. Foreigners were expelled from the city to relieve pressure, and, to the historian's indignation, exception was made for ballet-dancers but not for men of learning. It sounds as if he had been personally involved. How long before 384 he arrived is uncertain. He travelled widely, had visited Egypt (17.4), Sparta (26.10) and possibly Thrace (31.7), though the observation that a battlefield of 377 was even now 'white with bones' (a Virgilian phrase) need not be personal observation. What is certain is that he gave readings of his history and published it in Rome, for a letter of Libanius written in 392 congratulates him on the good press he had received. It was in Latin-speaking circles, as the author intended, that the history had found ready ears.

7. Rome made a deep impact on Ammianus' history. He held the Eternal City in high admiration (below, § 38) and, despite its relative insignificance in historical developments, he manages to keep it before the reader's eye through his regular reports on the prefectures of Rome, with their brilliant portrait gallery of the grandees who held the post. This material could hardly have been gathered except on the spot. Who, then, were Ammianus' contacts? It was once assumed that he belonged to the circle of the great pagan orator Symmachus, whose letters remain one of the best sources for the social and cultural life of the period. This circle (at least as recreated some time later in Macrobius' *Saturnalia*) included Nicomachus Flavianus, who himself wrote *Annales*, and Vettius Agorius Praetextatus, editor of Livy. This belief has been justly challenged. In two unforgettable digressions (14.6, 28.4) Ammianus launches a withering satirical attack on the vanity and philistinism of the Roman aristocracy: they have no stomach for any literature more taxing than superficial imperial biographies or the *Satires* of Juvenal. The attack is hard to reconcile with membership of a literary circle of the most prominent aristocrats of the day. If, as seems likely, Symmachus was himself the prefect who allowed men of learning to be expelled from Rome while dancing-girls remained, Ammianus can have had little to thank him for.

8. Contacts and protectors Ammianus must have had. How else could he afford to speak out so fearlessly against one of the most potent clans of the day, the Anicii (16.8, 27.11)? But his closest links may have

been among fellow-outsiders of his own age-group who had retired to
Rome. Eutherius, the former imperial chamberlain, was one such. Not
only does Ammianus single him out among all eunuchs for praise, but
he comments specifically on his memory (16.7). Another man of whom
he speaks with unusual warmth is his fellow-Antiochene Hypatius.
Once brother-in-law of an emperor, he had suffered in the treason trials
at Antioch in the early 370s; but had retrieved his position to become
prefect of Rome in 379, and subsequently praetorian prefect in Italy
(29.2). A useful contact could have been Aurelius Victor, a man of
letters who ingratiated himself with Julian by publishing an abbreviated
history up to his reign and who served as prefect of Rome in 389 (cf.
21.10). Eupraxius of Mauretania, the quaestor of Valentinian who is
praised for his fearless defence of justice (27.6 and 7) sounds like another
contact. Other friends might be sought among those officers who in 363
sat down together and tried to pick up the pieces left by the death of
Julian (25.5), or among the many others, in Gaul, on the Eastern frontier
or in Antioch, with whom Ammianus' career brought him into contact.
In the end we can only guess. He knew enough of the senatorial
aristocracy of Rome to have decided opinions about the merits of its
leading members; yet he viewed it as an outsider.

9. The contemporary scene which formed the background to the
composition of Ammianus' history was a rapidly changing one, and the
crisis of conflict between paganism and Christianity was coming to a
head just as he published. He will have first conceived his history, with
its heavy emphasis on the figure of Julian, in the reign of Valentinian
and his brother Valens. Whatever the faults of Valentinian, he did
pursue a policy of religious toleration or non-interference (30.9). By the
time that Ammianus was giving readings of excerpts preliminary to
publication, the mood had sharply changed. Theodosius, a baptized
Catholic, had thrown the weight of imperial authority behind his
Church, and Ambrose had established his extraordinary dominance
over the imperial court at Milan. In 388 Theodosius marched on Italy
to overthrow the usurper Magnus Maximus, and in the next year made
a ceremonial entry into Rome, the first imperial visit since that of
Constantius in 357, unforgettably described by Ammianus. To concili-
ate the Roman aristocracy, Theodosius appointed two leading pagans,
Nicomachus Flavianus and Symmachus, to high office. But Ambrose
reinforced his terrifying moral ascendancy, and in 391 Flavianus as
prefect of Italy found himself having to enforce Theodosius' new law

banning all pagan sacrifice and cult. This declaration of war on paganism led later in the year to a bloody riot in Alexandria and the destruction of the temple of Serapis, praised by Ammianus as one of the wonders of the world (22.16). It was in the general context of these developments that the publication celebrated by Libanius took place. Ammianus includes a reference to the city prefecture of the historian Aurelius Victor in 389; but says nothing in his description of the temple of Serapis of its destruction. If he published in 390 or 391, it would take a little while for news of his success to reach Libanius in 392.

10. The dramatic hardening of Theodosius' heart against paganism in 391 was followed by a reaction. The next year Valentinian II died in suspicious circumstances, and his army commander, the barbarian Arbogast, put the imperial secretary Eugenius in his place. Between 392 and 394 Eugenius held court in Milan; and to the standard of this former professor of rhetoric the less prudent members of the pagan cause, led by Nicomachus Flavianus, rallied. Theodosius refused to acknowledge the usurper and was forced to march west a second time; in August 394 he was victorious at the battle of the river Frigidus, though he did not long survive his victory and died in January 395. Was Ammianus still writing as these developments took place? He implies at the beginning of Book 26 that his last six books, covering the reigns of Valentinian and Valens, were an afterthought. Since Libanius in 392 was urging him to follow up his success by a continuation of his history, many scholars believe that these books were a second instalment, published between 392 and the death of Theodosius. The death of Valentinian II had the added convenience of removing any inhibitions about writing the history of the father of a living emperor. And a conspicuous feature of the last books is the blatant panegyric of the elder Theodosius, father of Theodosius I, the other living emperor. On the other hand, the latest reference to a contemporary event in these books is to the consulship of Neoterius in 390 (26.5), and there are good reasons for supposing that these books too were published during Theodosius' first visit to the West, and before the usurpation of Eugenius.

11. We cannot yet pronounce conclusively on the precise date(s) of publication, but for understanding Ammianus that is not of decisive importance. Before publication there were years of thinking and writing. The years during which his histories took shape, the late 380s and perhaps early 390s, were ones of acute religious and ideological conflict,

in which the interpretation of the past, and particularly of the immediate past, was an integral part of the controversy. It was this atmosphere of tension and the need to re-evaluate the past that lay behind the first publication of a serious work of history in Latin at Rome since Tacitus' *Annals* more than two and a half centuries before.

THE SCOPE OF THE HISTORIES

12. In his closing words Ammianus indicates the starting-point of his work: the accession of Nerva in 96. In some ways this is a surprising revelation. The books that survive (14–31) cover events within the author's own lifetime, a mere twenty-five years between 354 and Adrianople. The first thirteen books thus had 257 years to cover. Some have found this contrast hard to swallow, and maintain that there must have been two separate works, one covering the 'ancient' history from Nerva onwards, the other contemporary events, perhaps from the death of Constantine onwards. This suggestion is mistaken, for it misses the close relationship that exists for Ammianus between the distant and the immediate past.

13. Even within the surviving books the tempo of narration changes, and these changes of tempo indicate much about what the author is doing. Twelve books (14–25) cover less than that number of years, between 354 and 363; but the pace of the last six books is much brisker, running over fifteen years down to 378. Even within those first twelve the tempo changes, in that Julian's brief two-year reign as sole Augustus occupies four books by itself, three of which are devoted to the three months of the Persian expedition. The figure of Julian is in fact the heart of the history; the period from his appointment as Caesar to his death forms the core – Books 15 to 25, beginning and ending on round numbers. What precedes Book 15 is in a sense a prelude; what follows Book 25 is marked off as a postlude, an afterthought.

14. No history of Julian's reign could open abruptly with his elevation to Caesar in 355. At the very least it would be necessary to provide the background of conflict within the dynasty going back to the death of the great Constantine in 337. He left behind him not only three sons, Constantine, Constantius and Constans, but a clutch of nephews, Dalmatius and Hannibalian, sons of his brother Dalmatius, and Gallus and Julian, sons of Julius Constantius. In addition there were two

sisters, Anastasia and Eutropia, married to the senators Optatus and Nepotian. Constantine divided the empire between his nephews Dalmatius and Hannibalian and his own sons. The troops, hardly spontaneously, declared that none but the sons of Constantine should rule, and proceeded to massacre his brothers, brothers-in-law and nephews. Only Gallus and Julian were saved from the carnage by their age and were eventually locked away in a remote fortress in Asia Minor to keep them out of trouble. The two survivors played no part in public events until Constantius brought them in turn out of isolation to act as his Caesars. But there were major developments that Ammianus needed on any count to discuss. First, there was the gradual elimination of Constantius' brothers that left him eventually in sole power, a series of civil wars culminating in the defeat of Constans' murderer Magnentius in 353 (probably described in Book 13). Secondly, there was a succession of offensives by the Persians in the East, the repeated sieges of Nisibis (in 338, 346 and 350) and the costly battle of Singara; these troubles Ammianus certainly needed to narrate in preparation for the Persian campaigns in which he was personally involved and on which he lavishes such attention (the best part of three books each on the Persian invasion of 359 and on Julian's campaign of 363).

15. It is a plausible guess that the beginning of Book 10 marked a turning-point in Ammianus' narrative, and that this was Constantine's death. If so, he had four books in which to cover the events of sixteen years, a somewhat brisker pace than that of the last six books. But then, that would leave nine books for 240 years, a breathless rush indeed. Why was it worth while to go back so far so fast?

16. The superficial answer is that Tacitus' *Annals* ended with the death of Domitian in 96 and that Ammianus wanted (as was common among ancient historians) to write a continuation of the last major history in the same language. If he had chosen to write in his native Greek, the situation would have been very different. Cassius Dio, Dexippus, and Eunapius between them provided a continuous account of Roman history up to the present. But a Latin reader had apparently nothing better to rely on than often frivolous imperial biographies and the elementary historical summaries recently produced by Eutropius and Aurelius Victor. In nine books, however, Ammianus can have done little to fill the gap, nor was that his intention. Rather he needed to bridge the gap with the early empire in order to put the present in perspective. Like many of his contemporaries he saw in the Greco–

Roman past a model and standard against which to measure the present. This comes out clearly in his use of *exempla* – examples and comparisons drawn from the classical past against which again and again the actions of the present are judged. He rightly saw the history of Rome as a continuum and wished to restore the thread of continuity.

17. But there was a particular advantage in starting with Nerva, one which Gibbon exploited in the same spirit. He could open his tale with a Golden Age in which the progress of Rome might be felt to have reached its high point. Trajan's conquest of Dacia and Mesopotamia brought the empire to its widest extent; peace and the rule of justice seemed to be established as never before; and the glory of Rome was reflected in the magnificence of its monuments, among them the Forum of Trajan, a creation which, so Ammianus claimed, had no match on earth (16.10). The tragedy of Rome, from the viewpoint of Ammianus, was that in the period following the death of Marcus Aurelius, who achieved the ideal of the philosopher-king, the Golden Age lost its lustre. And the achievement of Julian was that he restored the old gleam. His account of Julian verges on panegyric; and the highest praise is to say that Julian combined the virtues of Titus, Trajan, Pius and Marcus (16.1). By conquest, justice, and respect for the values of the past Julian gave reason to hope that the Golden Age would return: Astraea, in traditional imagery the banished goddess of justice, would walk again among mortals (22.10, 25.4, and cf. 14.11). The sequel is a story of disappointed hopes. Valentinian, that staunch defender of the frontiers, might also have been a Trajan or Marcus if only his virtues had not been sullied by deplorable vices (30.9).

THE TEXTURE OF THE HISTORY

18. The form and content of Ammianus' history is in many ways highly traditional: deliberately so. He was harking back to a tradition which linked him to Tacitus on the Latin side, and to Herodotus and Thucydides on the Greek. This meant going against certain contemporary trends. After Tacitus, imperial biography had come to dominate the Latin field. Suetonius had been imitated by the frivolous Marius Maximus whose popularity with the Roman aristocracy so irritated Ammianus; and this tradition culminated at just about the time Ammianus published in the spoof collection of emperors' lives known to us

as the *Historia Augusta* (*Lives of the Later Caesars* in the Penguin Classics). Inevitably there is a strong element of imperial biography in Ammianus. His account is shaped round the reigns of emperors; he pays much attention to the personality of the ruler; and he marks the ruler's death by an extended assessment of his character and reign. But in this respect he is much closer to Tacitus, or the Greek historian Cassius Dio, than he is to Suetonius; and he does what the biographers did not, by providing detailed narratives of campaigns, while omitting such details as biographers relished, like the itemization of emperors' diets. Here he is unlike his contemporary Eunapius, who scoffed at chronology, and organized his history round the persons of the rulers, as we learn from one of the surviving fragments of his histories.

19. Panegyric was another flourishing contemporary tradition from which Ammianus distanced himself. History was supposed to be non-partisan, and generally Ammianus lived up, formally at least, to this ideal (below, § 31). The exceptions make this clearer. He candidly admits that his account of Julian will be almost panegyrical (16.1). Almost, but not quite. He employs some of the standard tricks of the panegyrist's arsenal, like that of amplifying the glory of his hero's achievements by comparing him with heroes of the past. His necrology on Julian is close to panegyric indeed: he praises Julian for the four virtues which every schoolchild was instructed to include in an encomium, and then adds further virtues which Cicero had used in a formal panegyric of Pompey (25.4). Even so, he does what the panegyrist should on no account do, and persistently criticizes Julian's failings. In fact his account of the campaigns of the elder Theodosius is more truly panegyrical. And it is clear that he writes like this not out of admiration but because in the circumstances no other course was prudent.

20. Biographical or panegyrical at times, Ammianus remains firmly an historian in the ancient sense. He narrates the public affairs of the state. A large proportion of his narrative concerns wars, and above all the Persian Wars in which he had been involved. He is also concerned with the imperial court, with accessions and deaths, intrigues and usurpations. War is not the only activity of government he cares about: the administration of justice, or rather its abuse, is a favourite theme; and (unlike Tacitus) he shows a healthy interest in problems of taxation. The City of Rome traditionally bulked large in Roman histories: Livy and Tacitus tend to alternate their accounts between Rome and theatres of action outside. This must be one reason why Ammianus includes

regular reports on the prefecture of Rome. But the difference shows clearly enough, for the parochial nature of Roman affairs is not disguised and these chapters form little more than an interlude between chapters on matters that affected the whole empire.

21. One dimension almost wholly absent from this traditionalist historian is the history of the Christian Church. It is not that he is shy of mentioning Christianity. When the rioting between supporters of rival candidates for the papacy leaves 137 dead in Rome, he can give a splendid account of this incident (27.3). What catches his eye is the secular dimensions of the occasion. But the doctrinal wrangles of the Church are simply irrelevant to his purpose. He discusses the condemnation of Athanasius and the consequent deposition of his supporter pope Liberius, to comment adversely on the injustice of Constantius' conduct in the affair (15.7); he does not, however, explain the distinction between Orthodox and Arian, nor does he mention (for instance) the significance of Valens' Arianism. Constantius' concern with synods earns his hot disapproval, for it hamstrung the public post (21.16); he has evident sympathy with Julian's observation that no beasts are so savage as are Christians to each other in their doctrinal controversies (22.5). But even had he approved of synods, it is unlikely he would have admitted them to his history. Church history formed a quite distinct tradition. For that matter, Eusebius and his successors ignored the history of the state except as indispensable background. Each side, historian and Church historian, continued to avoid poaching on the other's preserve, and each to its detriment.

22. History and Church history were poles apart in form as well as content. One feature of Eusebius, and also as it happens of imperial biography, was the use and citation of documents, authentic or purportedly so. There was room for controversy and a scholarly tone could be appropriate. But ancient historical writing tended to adopt an elevated stylistic tone incompatible with the quotation of documents. Ammianus subscribes to this convention, and to the linked convention of the set-piece speech whereby the historian attributed to the characters the words he felt appropriate to the historical circumstances. But, just as in his handling of Rome, Ammianus knows how to adapt a convention to suit the realities of his day. An 'adlocution' to the troops was an imperial prerogative; and of the dozen set-piece speeches in his pages, all but one are formal imperial adlocutions.

23. The digression was another traditional feature of ancient histori-

cal writing, but Ammianus uses it on a scale unparalleled since the father of history, Herodotus. For us his digressions may seem bewildering – in number, length and diversity of subject-matter, ranging from geographical and ethnographical descriptions through social satire to a hotch-potch of technical themes, siege engines (23.4), the obelisk (17.4), the calendar (26.1), the plague (19.4), the causes of earthquakes (17.7), the eclipse (20.3), or the rainbow (20.11). There are delights in these digressions, like the picture of the Gallic wife who enters the fray on her husband's behalf with arms flailing like a catapult (15.12), or like his observations in a miniature digression on the mating of the date-palm (24.3). But by and large they seem to modern taste excessive and out of place. It is the more important to try to grasp what Ammianus was doing. First, he was giving an educated fourth-century audience what it wanted. Contemporary rhetorical education set much store by the excursus as a sort of virtuoso cadenza, a factor which has been invoked to explain the no less prolix excursuses in Augustine's theological writing. Ammianus, like Herodotus, was at one level an entertainer, and the audiences of his readings probably relished the digression. Secondly, the digression serves an important dramatic function, of slowing down the tempo and so underlining the importance of the immediately following narrative. It is no coincidence that the digressions cluster in the books on Julian, above all in the lead-up to his Persian campaigns in Books 22 and 23. Here digressions occupy more than half the text. They are sparse, by contrast, in the more swiftly moving account of the house of Valentinian. But as important as these literary considerations is the function the digression serves in putting Roman history in perspective. Herodotus was driven to the digression by the nature of his subject-matter, the clash between the Greek world (itself composed of numerous communities with diverse traditions) with the Eastern world. Thucydides' history, relatively parochial in scope, could largely dispense with the digression. In Ammianus again we have the sense of the diversity both of the peoples and terrains of the empire and of the barbarian peoples that beset it. The geographical digressions evoke a picture of the Roman world and its neighbours, even if it is only loosely related to contemporary reality, being partly the product of book-learning (his main declared source on Gaul was some four centuries out of date), partly of stereotyping and fantasy (his nomads, Huns or Saracens, bear an uncanny generic similarity, while the notion that the Huns half cooked their meat by placing it under their saddles is a typical piece of learned invention). More abstruse to our taste are the scientific digressions. But just as Ammianus seeks to place the actions of armies in the context of the world in which they operate, or by his historical examples to place contemporary events in the context of the Greco–Roman past, so his scientific digressions place the actions of men in the context of the natural order. This natural order may impinge on the history of man through an eclipse, an earthquake, even a rainbow; its eternity provides a reference-point for the transitory nature of human vanities, as when Constantius terms himself 'Our Eternity' (15.1); and more precisely through the art of prognostication it provides indications of the course of human events, for Ammianus has no doubt that man and nature are both directed by the divine will (21.1). In each case the key to understanding is provided for Ammianus by scholarly learning; and the rationalistic level at which he explains natural phenomena is linked to the pragmatic way he approaches human history.

24. Ammianus, like other historians of antiquity, meant his work to be more than an assemblage of information. It is a work of art. We can describe it as 'rhetorical' in that it appeals to the canons of taste inculcated by the contemporary schools of rhetoric. Ammianus' style is no easy one – this much is apparent even in translation. It is complex, overloaded, often tortuous; sometimes brilliant, sometimes, as Gibbon complained, simply in bad taste. It used to be thought that the author had difficulty with the Latin language. A native Greek speaker, he was supposed to have picked up a smattering of Latin in the camp, and to have found composition in Latin a struggle, so producing a very artificial style. But in fact he is likely enough to have had an early acquaintance with Latin; his knowledge of Latin literature is very considerable; and if what he wrote was an artificial literary language remote from the spoken Latin of the day, this is equally true of all literary authors of the period, as comparison with Symmachus or the panegyrists shows.

25. His text is the product of careful working, rich in imagery, dense with borrowings from earlier literature, particularly earlier histories and epic poetry. One result is a heavy use of literary stereotypes. Not only do his nomad tribes resemble each other; one siege is very much like another; judicial persecutions take the same outrageous form whether in the Antioch of 354 or the Rome of the 370s, and the agents of government, Paul 'the Chain' or the basilisk Maximin, are cast in the same odious mould; even emperors show a predictable mixture of

arrogance, credulity and bestiality. Behind them all lie literary models. Yet to say this is not to question the author's integrity. He drew on models because that was, for him, the only way to do his subject justice. Take his picture of the battle of Strasbourg (16.12). A tiresome proportion of this lengthy narrative is patently derived from the author's imagination and reading, and not from factual accounts of the event. His picture of the carnage of barbarians, some with 'their heads severed by pikes as massive as beams, so that they hung merely by the throat', others slipping in their comrades' blood, could – and does – occur in any epic. It required no hard information to evoke a river choked with corpses, stained with blood, 'lost in wonder at this strange addition to its waters'; more relevant is knowledge of Achilles' slaughter of the Trojans on the banks of the Scamander or the fate of Thucydides' Athenians in the river Assinarus near Syracuse. But Ammianus is not inventing with intent to deceive, as a well-read audience would understand. It is because he sees Strasbourg as a battle of crucial historical importance, as the one which confirmed the stature of Julian, that he needs to endow it with full epic grandeur.

26. The same episode exemplifies the strong dramatic quality of his history. 'The scene now resembled a stage show, when the curtain reveals some wonderful spectacle.' This image is a recurrent one. It reflects Ammianus' desire to involve his reader as the audience of a play is involved. The nemesis of Gallus comes complete with visions of Furies (14.11). He wishes (and frequently succeeds in his intention) to present the past vividly and to stir the reader to reaction. Only an insensitive reader will feel no sense of horror at the conduct of a Gallus, no sense of just retribution at his death.

27. In addition to a keen sense of the dramatic, Ammianus has an exceptionally fine eye for visual detail. During the Persian expedition, his eye was caught by the works of art in the royal pleasure parks; and he observed, accurately, the obsession of Iranian art with scenes of slaughter and of battle (24.6). At his best, Ammianus can conjure up scenes of powerful imaginative impact: the intrepid prefect Leontius plunging into an angry mob to seize the ringleader Petrus Valvomeres (15.7); the pageant of Constantius' entry into Rome (16.10); or that finest of imperial death-scenes, Valentinian carried off in an apoplexy of rage with a barbarian embassy (30.6).

28. Allusions to classical literature, sometimes explicit but often not, enrich the text at numerous points. The authors whom he cites, both

Greek (Homer, Theognis, Simonides, Plato, Demosthenes, etc.) and Latin (Cicero, Virgil, Sallust, Terence, etc.), would have been the standard school-texts of the day. In addition he makes undeclared use of collections of sayings and anecdotes, like those of Valerius Maximus or Plutarch, which were also a standby for the schools of rhetoric. Two authors are of outstanding importance to Ammianus, as they were to Augustine, Virgil and Cicero. Central to the educational curriculum throughout the imperial period, they formed the essential items of the intellectual baggage of the educated man of late antiquity. Ammianus uses the two in slightly different ways. Frequent Virgilian echoes elevate the literary texture of the history to epic level; so at Book 15 the second half of the work, with its focus on Julian, is introduced by an allusion to Virgil's introduction to the second half of the *Aeneid*. Cicero provides Ammianus with a model for prose style (re-interpreted according to the canons of late antique taste): but more than this, he is cited to give authority to the author's judgements. So when Ammianus criticizes Valentinian for his savageness in punishment, he backs up his own reflections on the proper role of the ruler with a quotation from Cicero (30.8). This dual role of classical allusions is of general application: they both enhance the literary quality of his work and give it authority.

29. What of the sources for the historical information in Ammianus? Book-learning lies behind his classical allusions and more specifically behind the digressions. Some have inferred that he derived his narrative too from other historians, whether perhaps the *Annals* (now lost) of the pagan aristocrat Nicomachus Flavianus, or the Greek histories of Eunapius (now only fragmentarily preserved), or perhaps from some other now unknown historian. It is not helpful to generalize about this issue. There are numerous different components of Ammianus' history, and they are likely to derive from the full spectrum of sources, ranging from previous histories, through consultation of witnesses and documents, to the author's own experience. For Julian, Ammianus consulted the emperor's own writings, including probably his account of the battle of Strasbourg; he also is likely to have used the memoirs of Julian's doctor Oribasius, either directly or through Eunapius. For some battles he will have drawn on official reports, though he knew better than to put faith in the boastful publicity of Constantius (16.12). There can be no doubt that he conducted extensive interviews with eye-witnesses, as he claims (15.1); this was in any case the normal method of the historian in antiquity when writing of the recent past.

Following ancient convention he conceals the identities of his informants, and it is only occasionally that we can guess at some of them (above,
§ 8). Finally his own experiences made a considerable contribution, as
is obvious in the account of the assassination of Silvanus or the siege of
Amida. Two disadvantages are linked with eye-witness accounts. First,
human memory, especially that of an old man, plays strange tricks. It
is sobering to discover that Ammianus' own memory of the topography
of Amida, which he once knew intimately, is demonstrably false on
nearly every count (19.9, with note). Secondly, participants are likely
to have marked views about the personalities of others involved in the
events. Ammianus has a distinct tendency to make heroes or villains of
the characters who feature in his pages, and in this he reflects the
prejudices of his informants where he does not reflect his own.

VALUES IN AMMIANUS

30. The intellectual world into which Ammianus was born was dominated by the assault of Christianity, aggressive and intolerant, against
the old classical traditions. His native Antioch, despite the efforts of
Libanius, had become a centre of theological discourse; and, even
in the Rome to which he migrated, numerous members of the old
aristocracy, alert to the potential of the new faith for extending their
bases of power, duly accommodated their beliefs. Pagans (as the
Christians described the adherents of the vast and disparate assortment
of cults other than their own) were now on the defensive. Julian offered
the next generation a powerful symbol of resistance to the victory of
'the Galileans'. In Rome, monuments and funerary inscriptions indicate
a self-conscious 'pagan revival' in the second part of the fourth century,
at least in certain circles. In 394, at a date very close to that of the
publication of Ammianus' history, there was fought the last Roman
civil war in which the opposing forces advertised allegiance to 'paganism'
and 'Christianity'. Against this background, it becomes urgent to relate
the opinions and values of Ammianus to contemporary debate.

31. Yet his stated opinions reveal hardly a trace of bigotry of any
sort. He has often earned high praise for impartiality, from Gibbon to
the present day. In the view of A. H. M. Jones, he excels even Tacitus
'in breadth of view and impartiality of judgment' (*Later Roman Empire*,
1010). This is a compliment which would have pleased him, for he was

insistent on the time-worn principle that the historian should adopt no partisan viewpoint (see, for example, 30.8). Any attempt to make him out a polemicist soon founders: on all the great controversial issues of the day he is deliberately ambiguous or evasive. One famous incident is instructive. For anyone in contact with senatorial circles in the Rome of Theodosius, one of the great issues was the removal of the altar of Victory from the senate-house. The duel, gentlemanly but passionate, between Symmachus and Ambrose symbolizes the struggle over the survival of pagan values and traditions in a Christian state. It is astonishing to observe that Ammianus in his memorable description of the visit of Constantius to Rome in 357 quite omits to mention what in retrospect must have seemed a most significant feature of this visit – the first removal of the altar (16.10).

32. This silence is consistent with his handling of Christianity in general. He underplays the historical importance of the Church (§ 21), but he does not, as do some pagan writers, pretend that it does not exist. The action he narrates takes place often enough against a backdrop of Christian chapels, festivals, priests and bishops; so Silvanus the usurper is killed, as it happens, on his way to morning prayers in a chapel (15.5). The detail, known to the author from his personal involvement, is merely incidental. In the few passages where he lingers over ecclesiastical affairs, he breathes no word of criticism of the Christian faith itself: a 'plain and simple religion', even if Constantius perverted it with senseless doctrinal controversy (21.16); a faith 'which preaches only justice and mercy', though that human snake, bishop George of Alexandria, forgot it (22.11). Ammianus reserves his scathing condemnation for the conduct of individuals, like Constantius, George, or the rival papal candidates who betray too clearly their worldly ambitions, and abandon the model of more modest provincial bishops who 'demonstrate to the supreme god and his true worshippers the purity and modesty of their lives' (27.3). Moreover, he conspicuously avoids subscribing to rumours designed to defame Christians. A bishop of Bezabde was rumoured to have used the opportunity of negotiations with the Persians to betray his city, but Ammianus scotches the tale (20.7). More impressive, when it comes to the narrative of Julian's death he makes no mention of the story (circulated by Libanius among others) that the fatal wound was dealt by a Christian within the ranks (25.3), even though he knew there was a rumour that Julian fell to a Roman thrust (25.6).

33. A similar studied impartiality affects his portrait of Julian. Of course Julian is the hero and centrepiece of his history. But in making judgement he balances praise with criticism, and we may even feel that beside the rather wooden panegyric the criticisms are penetrating, even devastating. They strike at the heart of Julian's policies: twice he is blamed for forcing men to serve on their local councils (22.9 and 25.4), though this was a prerequisite for the renaissance of city life and the restriction of central administration; his zeal for animal sacrifice was excessive, expensive and demoralized the bloated troops (22.12); his pose as citizen-emperor was affectation in pursuit of cheap popularity (22.7); his purge of palace staff was unphilosophical (22.4); while the attempt to exclude Christians from teaching was a mistake 'which should be buried in lasting oblivion' (22.10). This last remark is immediately followed by his account of bishop George's attempt to incite a mob to burn a pagan temple (22.11). In both cases Ammianus implies that it is the incitement of hatred between pagan and Christian that is wrong.

34. His anti-controversialism is thus a matter of principle. This is borne out by his emphatic commendation of the emperor Valentinian's policy of religious toleration, the clearest statement he makes on this question (30.9). But principle coincided with prudence. An historian giving readings of his work in Rome (as Libanius reveals) had to cater for a mixed audience. Among the aristocracy, pagan and Christian lived together on easy social terms; and though Ammianus might satirize philistines (in a longstanding Roman tradition), partisan polemic on religious matters was more sensitive and embarrassing. Nor is it clear how much a writer could have got away with in the early 390s. The heavy-handedness of the praise Ammianus gives the elder Theodosius surely does suggest that the opinions of 'the most Christian' emperor had to be taken into account. And an historian who wished his works to survive would do well to allow for the likely prejudices of future generations.

35. For however impartial Ammianus may be, particularly at the level of explicit judgements, he leaves the reader in no doubt of his profound pagan conviction. This much is transparent in his long excursus on prognostication, in which he not only expounds the rational basis of a practice banned by Christian emperors, but does so in terminology that betrays awareness of Neoplatonist thought (21.1). Omens and portents surround his narrative; a standard feature indeed of

classical historiography, yet in context they are more than conventional. The gloomy portents that attend Julian's invasion of Persia show that the diviners were right in opposition to the philosophers who supported the invasion (23.5). Valens' treason trials at Antioch, with their distinctly anti-pagan overtones, are described with horror; yet Ammianus not only concedes that prognostication and magic had been used to foretell Valens' successor, but shows these prognostications to be proved true by events (29.1). Behind prognostications lies a world densely populated with pagan gods. Adrastia, the spirit of justice, who from her magnificent entry in the nemesis of Gallus (14.11) stalks Ammianus' pages, cannot be reduced to a metaphor. It is hard to extract a coherent philosophy from his references to 'fate', 'fortune' and 'the divine power', but the underlying assumptions are patently un-Christian. His attitude to the religions of Persia and Egypt is revealing: the land of the Chaldaeans where authentic divination (i.e. astrology) was developed is the 'nurse of ancient philosophy', and the practices of the Magi, developed from Chaldaean lore by Zoroaster, are described on the authority of Plato as 'the most uncorrupted cult of the divine' (23.6, omitted in the present translation). But Egypt above all is the 'cradle' of religion, the source of knowledge of the divine and of prognostication, and the inspiration of Pythagoras and Plato, even of Roman law (22.16). He enthuses about Alexandria as an intellectual centre, noting that it produced Ammonius Saccas the teacher of Plotinus, but omitting to note that it was the seat of that architect of Orthodox theology, Athanasius. Ammianus' 'holy men' are pagan ones: the trio of Hermes Trismegistus, Apollonius of Tyana and Plotinus round off the account of outstanding men to whom the faculty had been granted of perceiving their guardian spirits – and this to explain a sign of the death of the Christian Constantius (21.14).

36. One feature which may strike the modern reader is the way in which the author distances himself from Christian ideas and practices. Christians are 'they' and their institutions are frequently glossed by periphrases: Athanasius had been deposed by 'an assembly of the adherents of the same faith, meeting as what they call a synod' (15.7); we meet similar explanations or circumlocutions for martyrs (22.11), Epiphany (21.2) and nuns (18.10). Such expressions are partly misleading. Ammianus is affected by the stylistic conventions of his genre, and since Christian technicalities had no place in the tradition of classical historiography, it was right and proper to introduce them with an apology. The same consideration 'explains' his restraint in introducing

Christian subject-matter at all: since the genre defined the subject of history as war and the affairs of the state, ecclesiastical affairs are only mentioned where they directly impinge on secular affairs. These observations are true and important. But that is not an end to the matter. In choosing at the end of the fourth century to revive the classical tradition of secular history, Ammianus chose a genre which kept Christianity at the periphery. It offered a structure suitable for carrying an essentially pagan view of the world.

37. Just what Ammianus' personal beliefs and philosophies were is a question of merely biographical interest. What the reader of his history wants to discover is the degree to which pagan values actually shape the presentation of the past in his text. It is at this level, rather than that of explicit judgements, that the influence of paganism may be felt at its deepest. The text is informed with a sense of respect for the past and its values – seen, for instance, in the use of *exempla*, or the use of Nerva's death as a starting-point, or the citations of Cicero or Plato, or the use of digressions to rummage among ancient texts of learning and science. Pagan religious beliefs are part and parcel of this respect for the past. The hoary antiquity of the pagan gods is striking: religious lore emerges from its cradles in Persia and Egypt in the distant mists of time. Its antiquity is the guarantee of paganism (Christianity, whatever the merits of its moral doctrines, was a newcomer). Conversely, the pagan gods provide spiritual sanction for the respect for the past. Ammianus' paganism is thus bound up with his sense of history. Julian too, though he failed to read the signs and so failed in his invasion (a failure which it was hard for a pagan to forgive), restored traditional cult as part of his sense of respect for tradition. This is why his reign, for all its brevity and inadequacies, is of sufficient moment to become the pivotal element in the structure of the history as a whole.

38. Central to this value system is the city of Rome itself. We have seen how the reports on the prefectures of Rome both reflect the importance attached to the city in traditional historiography and show up its actual parochiality (above, § 20). The value of Rome to Ammianus is essentially symbolic. 'Most sacred', 'the home of the empire and of all that is good', it is the physical expression of the past glory of the state. This is why the pride of Constantius collapses in the face of the monuments of Rome: he cannot even imitate Trajan's horse, for he cannot build a suitable stable (16.10). Rome has indeed grown old; but unlike Florus, who used the image of the ages of man to explain the

cessation of imperial expansion, Ammianus is positive about Rome's old age. She has grown old and entrusted management of her affairs to her children the Caesars; but old age is in itself venerable: 'everywhere the authority of its senators is paid the respect due to their grey hairs, and the name of the Roman people is an object of reverence and awe' (14.6). This is what makes the conduct of its inhabitants outrageous: they compromise the integrity of the symbol.

39. With the city and its gods are conjoined the ancient virtues which made the *res publica* great, exemplified through the names of great heroes. Julian is the model of good government because he embodies the traditional ideals; other emperors are good or bad in so far as they measure up to the same standards. Justice is a cardinal principle: Julian's reign almost brought back a Golden Age and the return of Justice from her refuge in the skies as the constellation Virgo (22.10, 25.4). With his dying words Julian defines the purpose of the just ruler as the safety and welfare of his subjects (25.3), a principle of which Valens seemingly remained in shocking ignorance (29.2). Julian's exemplary attention to jurisdiction (18.1, 22.10) contrasts with the negligence of Valens, who allowed himself to be talked into delegating this function to others, so opening the door to corruption and accelerating the ruin of the state (30.4). Julian's success in lightening the crushing burden of taxation (17.3) is matched by criticism of Constantius (21.16) and praise for Valentinian (30.9) on this score; it is a serious criticism of Constantius that his synods had overburdened the public transport system (21.16), for the expense of the postal service to the taxpayer 'had ruined countless homes' (19.11). Defence of the frontiers against Rome's enemies is the supreme service to the state, by which Julian proves himself; Valentinian too, for all his lamentable cruelty, gets full credit for fighting the barbarian (30.8–9); but Constantius, despite his campaigns, is character-ized as successful only in civil wars (21.16).

40. Service of the *res publica* is the ideal, and preference of private advantage to public interest the reason why emperors and (no less important) their subordinates constantly betray it. Jovian betrays the state and surrenders Nisibis out of a selfish desire to protect his own power (25.9). Constantius' minions corrupt his policies and judgement by their intrigues; it is the fact that the chamberlain Eusebius has his eye on the Antiochene property of Ursicinus that leads him to deprive the East of the general Rome needs (18.4). The potent Petronius Probus was driven into his string of offices and fiscal abuses by the greed of

his numerous dependants (27.11). The workings of corruption are brilliantly exposed in the affair of Lepcis (28.6): the local commander refuses to aid the city against barbarians unless an extortionate price is paid; and when the people of Lepcis complain to the emperor, redress of their wrongs is baulked by the connections of the guilty governor with the marshal of the court, and by the weakness of the investigator sent to the city, who by accepting bribes exposes himself to blackmail.

41. Ammianus' analysis of contemporary malaise is thus a pragmatic one. He is not so incautious as to blame Christianity for disaster: the calamity of Adrianople is brought on Rome not by Valens' persecution of Catholics (as Orosius believed) but by the greed of the officers who traded dog-meat for slaves with the starving barbarian horde (31.4). It is corruption, not Christianity, for which he criticizes Probus or Strategius Musonianus. The answers to which the ex-soldier points are not religious and ideological but practical: vigorous defence of the frontiers; protection of the taxpayer, especially the peasant, by eradicating the corruption of officials; the fair administration of justice, by giving the accused, whether a poisoner or a bishop, a fair hearing, and not succumbing to whispers; the control of superfluous extravagance at court, and so on. It is this strong pragmatic bent which has recommended Ammianus to historians from Gibbon to Jones. But at the same time we may recognize the religious underpinning of this analysis. It is by reference to the ideals of the ancient Roman tradition that he supports his case; and at a time when Christians sought to displace these ideals with their own novel system of values, this use of the past is both pagan and covertly polemical. To defeat the pagan, as Augustine appreciated, it was necessary not only to ridicule his gods but to undermine his respect for the Roman past itself.

FURTHER READING

GENERAL BACKGROUND

For a narrative history of the late empire, there is nothing to beat Edward Gibbon's *Decline and Fall of the Roman Empire*, cited here in the 1896 edition of J. B. Bury. The major modern work is the magisterial survey of A. H. M. Jones, *The Later Roman Empire 284–602* (1964) (= Jones, *Later Roman Empire*). For a different perspective, see P. R. L. Brown, *The World of Late Antiquity* (1971).

On the spiritual conflict central to the history of the period, there is an important collection of essays edited by A. Momigliano, *The Conflict between Paganism and Christianity in the Fourth Century* (1963); also seminal is P. R. L. Brown, *Religion and Society in the Age of St Augustine* (1972); for a new view, see R. MacMullen, *Christianising the Roman Empire* (1984). The main sources are collected in translation and well introduced by B. Croke and J. Harries, *Religious Conflict in Fourth-Century Rome* (1982).

For the period of which Ammianus writes, there are two biographies of Julian: G. W. Bowersock, *Julian the Apostate* (1978) and R. Browning, *The Emperor Julian* (1976). For the earlier fourth century, see D. Bowder, *The Age of Constantine and Julian* (1978). A study is still needed of the reign of Valentinian; though A. Alföldi, *A Conflict of Ideas in the Late Roman Empire* (1952), is concerned with the reign, his views need modification. J. F. Matthews, *Western Aristocracies and Imperial Court A.D. 364–425* (1975) is important for the politics of this reign and the reigns under which Ammianus wrote. For a fine study of the city which formed Ammianus' background, see J. H. W. G. Liebeschuetz, *Antioch: City and Imperial Administration in the Later Roman Empire* (1972).

For an atlas of the empire, particularly strong on this period, see T. Cornell and J. Matthews, *Atlas of the Roman World* (1982).

AMMIANUS

There are two good (and brief) monographs in English: E. A. Thompson, *The Historical Work of Ammianus Marcellinus* (1947) and R. C. Blockley, *Ammianus Marcellinus. A Study of his Historiography and Political Thought* (1975).

Valuable essays on the historian are: A. Momigliano, 'The lonely historian Ammianus Marcellinus' in his *Essays in Ancient and Modern Historiography* (1977), 127–40; J. Matthews, 'Ammianus Marcellinus' in *Ancient Writers: Greece and Rome*, vol. 2, ed. T. J. Luce (1982), 1117–38; also by the same author, 'Ammianus' historical evolution' in *History and Historians in Late Antiquity*, ed. B. Croke and A. Emmett (1984), 30–41 (this collection has several pieces relevant to Ammianus). We look forward to John Matthews's forthcoming book on Ammianus.

SPECIAL ASPECTS

On the date of composition of the history and its relationship to the collection of imperial biographies inappropriately called the 'Historia Augusta', see R. Syme, *Ammianus and the Historia Augusta* (1968) with criticisms by A. Cameron, *Journal of Roman Studies* 61 (1971), 259–62. On his sources of information and contacts: W. R. Chalmers, 'Eunapius, Ammianus Marcellinus and Zosimus on Julian's Persian expedition', *Classical Quarterly* n.s. 10 (1960), 152–60; A. Cameron, 'The Roman friends of Ammianus', *Journal of Roman Studies* 54 (1964), 15–28. On Ammianus as a writer, E. Auerbach, 'The arrest of Peter Valvomeres' in *Mimesis: the Representation of Reality in Western Literature* (1953), 50–76. On aspects of military history: H. T. Rowell, *Ammianus Marcellinus, Soldier-Historian of the Later Roman Empire* (1967); G. A. Crump, *Ammianus Marcellinus as a Military Historian* (1975); N. J. E. Austin, *Ammianus on Warfare: An Investigation into Ammianus' Military Knowledge* (1979). On the elusive topic of Ammianus' attitude to Christianity: A. and A. Cameron, 'Christianity and tradition in the historiography of the late Empire', *Classical Quarterly* n.s. 14 (1964), 306–28; E. D. Hunt, 'Christians and Christianity in Ammianus', *Classical Quarterly* n.s. 35 (1985), 186–200.

It is valuable to contrast Ammianus with pagan historians writing in Greek about the same period. Zosimus, *Historia Nova* is translated by J. Buchanan and H. Davis (1967). The fragments of Eunapius (and others) are now collected and translated by R. C. Blockley, *The Fragmentary Classicising Historians of the Later Roman Empire*, vol. 2 (1983). Eunapius' *Lives of the Philosophers and Sophists*, a work of pagan hagiography, is translated by W. C. Wright in the Loeb edition, Philostratus and Eunapius, *The Lives of the Sophists*. Julian's own writings are translated by the same author in the same series (three volumes). Church historians, notably Socrates, are translated in *A Select Library of Nicene and Post-Nicene Fathers*, ed. P. Schaff (1890–1900).

The scholarly bibliography (particularly by continental scholars) has been systematically surveyed by K. Rosen, *Ammianus Marcellinus* (*Erträge der Forschung*, vol. 183, 1982).

Family Tree of Constantine the Great

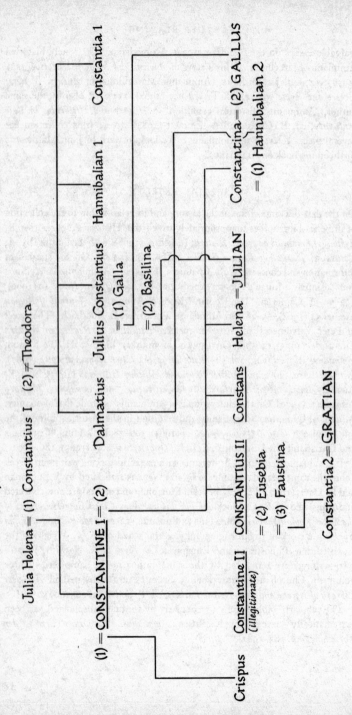

EMPORERS are underlined
CENTRAL CHARACTERS in *Ammianus* are in capitals

INTRODUCTORY NOTE

After the death of Constantine the Great in 337 the empire was divided between his three sons, Constantine, Constantius, and Constans. The rest of his family were massacred by the troops, with the exception of Gallus and Julian, the two young sons of his half-brother, Julius Constantius, who were kept in confinement (for the relationships, see Family Tree, p. 38). Constantine died in 340 fighting against Constans; Constans was assassinated in 350 and his power was seized by the usurper Magnentius. In 351 Constantius elevated Gallus to the rank of Caesar, and left him in control of the East, his own original share in the division of the empire, while he marched against Magnentius. He defeated the usurper initially at the battle of Mursa in 351, but it was not until the summer of 353 that he finally eliminated opposition and brought the whole empire under his control. The surviving narrative picks up at this point, and opens at Antioch, in the winter of 353–4. Note that up to Book 26 (A.D. 365) Ammianus' narrative is arranged by separate years, usually marked off by the names of the consuls at the beginning of a new year. In Books 27–30 events are grouped by longer periods of time and the chronology is less clear.

BOOK 14

1. The cruelty of the Caesar Gallus.

When this arduous campaign reached its end both sides were exhausted: their morale had been sapped by its manifold dangers and difficulties; but before the trumpets had ceased to bray or the troops taken up their winter quarters cruel fortune let loose upon the state the squalls of another storm, which arose from the many fearful misdeeds of the Caesar Gallus. Gallus in his early manhood had risen at a bound from what seemed a hopeless depth of misery to the height of power, and, going beyond the limits of the authority granted to him, was causing universal mischief by his excessive harshness. His pride was inflated by his kinship with the imperial house and by the fact that he shared the name of Constantius, and it appeared that only lack of strength kept him from embarking on hostilities against the author of his prosperity. His savage nature found a sharp spur in his wife, who had been previously married by her father Constantine to his nephew, king Hannibalian; as sister of the emperor her pride was swollen beyond measure; she was a Fury in mortal form, incessantly adding fuel to her husband's rage, and as thirsty for human blood as he. Time made the pair more expert in inflicting harm; adroit secret dealers in backstairs gossip, versed in the evil trade of exaggerating slight rumours, brought them the false reports that they wished to hear, and innocent people were charged with aspiring to the throne or practising black arts. Notorious above lesser cases, once their tyranny no longer stopped short at minor crimes, was the sudden and wicked death of Clematius, a prominent native of Alexandria; the story went that his mother-in-law, who lusted after him but found herself unable to seduce him, gained entrance to the palace through a back door, and by the present of a valuable necklace to the queen procured the despatch of a death-warrant to Honoratus, at that time count of the East; by this means

Clematius, an utterly innocent man, was put to death without being allowed to open his mouth or speak.

After this act of wickedness, which, now that cruelty had been given free rein, aroused fears that it would be repeated in other cases, a number of people were found guilty and condemned through mere misty suspicion. Of these some were put to death; others suffered confiscation of their property and were driven into exile from their homes; left with no resource but complaints and tears they supported life on the charity of others, and when what had been a just constitutional government was transformed into a bloody despotism many rich and noble houses shut their doors. In the past savage emperors had often preserved the appearance of legality by preferring charges against their victims in the courts of law, but now even a counterfeit accusation was felt to be superfluous; as one mischief was heaped upon another whatever the implacable Caesar had resolved was immediately put into effect, as if it had all the force of a deliberate legal decision. A further device was to station in all the quarters of Antioch a number of unknown persons, whose very insignificance shielded them from suspicion, and whose task it was to report what they heard. These people, mingling clandestinely and as it were en passant with parties of men of standing and infiltrating into wealthy houses in the guise of people in want, took back whatever information they could pick up to the palace, to which they were secretly admitted by a back door; they were careful to observe a common policy, which was to invent a part of their report, to make the worst of any known facts by exaggeration, and to suppress any remarks favourable to the Caesar, which in many cases were extorted from unwilling speakers by fear of trouble to come. It sometimes happened that what the father of a family had whispered to his wife in the furthest corner of his house, with no confidential servant present, became known on the following day to the prince, as if it had been revealed by Amphiaraus or Marcius, the famous seers of old. In consequence, men began to fear even the walls which were the only witnesses of their secrets. The obstinacy of Gallus in investigating matters of this kind was increased by the influence of the queen, who was pushing her husband headlong to destruction; it should have been her part to bring him by feminine mildness and sensible advice back to the paths of truth and kindness, like the wife of the fierce emperor Maximin, whose story I have already told in my account of the Gordians.

Finally Gallus had the audacity to embark on a new and disastrous course which gave rise to grave scandal; it is said that Gallienus disgraced himself utterly by sometimes pursuing it at Rome. Taking with him a few attendants armed with hidden weapons, Gallus used to roam in the evening about the streets and eating-houses, asking everybody in Greek, of which he had a thorough knowledge, what they thought of the Caesar. He was bold enough to do this in a city where the brightness of the street lighting makes night as clear as day. At last, when he had been frequently recognized, he realized that he would make himself conspicuous if he went out, and after that he was seen in public only in the daytime and for reasons which he considered of sufficient importance. All this grieved many people to the heart.

Certainly Thalassius, at that time praetorian prefect at court, a man of overbearing nature himself, who saw many people being put in danger by Gallus' increasingly hasty temper, did nothing to assuage the Caesar's anger by experienced advice, as high officials have sometimes done in other cases; instead he roused him to madness by opposition and unseasonable reproaches. At the same time he sent frequent exaggerated reports of his behaviour to the emperor, and for some reason which is not clear made no secret of the fact that he was doing so. By this means the Caesar's savage temper was further exacerbated; he raised on high, so to speak, the banner of self-will, and was carried away, without regard for the safety either of himself or others, by an irreversible momentum like that of a rushing river to overturn the obstacles which lay in his path.

Chapters on the brigands of Isauria (2), an unsuccessful attempt by the Persians to capture Batnae (3), and the habits of the Saracens (4) are omitted.

5. *The adherents of Magnentius are tortured* (A.D. 354).

While this was happening in the East, Constantius was spending the winter at Arles (Arelate), where on 10 October, which marked the end of the thirtieth year of his reign, he gave shows on a grand scale in the theatre and the circus. The weight of his arbitrary rule now fell more heavily, and he accepted as clear and established any doubtful or false charge; one example of this was his causing Gerontius, an adherent of Magnentius, to be tortured and afterwards to suffer the pains of banishment. As an ailing body is liable to be severely shaken even by slight indisposition, so Constantius' narrow and sensitive mind treated the slightest rumour as evidence of an actual or projected attempt on his life, and made his victory an occasion of mourning by the slaughter of the innocent. Any military officer or civil dignitary or person of standing among his fellows who was even faintly suspected of having favoured the opposing side was loaded with chains and dragged away like a wild animal; no pressure from a personal enemy was needed; the fact that he had been named or reported upon or brought to court was enough to ensure that he was condemned to death or deprived of his property or banished to a lonely island.

At any hint of an encroachment upon his authority, the emperor's harsh and irritable temper, prone in any case to entertain baseless suspicions, was further excited by the flattery of his bloodthirsty courtiers; they magnified every incident and pretended to feel unbounded grief at the dangers threatening the safety of a sovereign, on the thread of whose life, as they hypocritically declared, the fate of the whole world hung. So we are told that Constantius, unlike even inexorable emperors in the past, never ordered the sentence on anyone condemned on these or similar charges to be revoked once the warrant had been formally presented. And whereas in other men this taste for slaughter sometimes loses its force as they grow older, in Constantius it became more violent, because the flatterers around him were always rekindling the fire of his stubborn temper.

Among these flatterers the notary Paul was pre-eminent. He was a native of Spain, with a smooth inscrutable face, and an extraordinary capacity for scenting hidden perils. He had been sent to Britain to fetch certain officers who had been bold enough to join Magnentius' conspiracy; when he found them unable to resist he went far beyond his instructions, and descending like a sudden torrent upon the persons and estates of many people spread ruin and destruction in various forms. Loading the limbs of free-born men with chains and subjecting some to the degradation of handcuffs, he stitched together a patchwork of charges far removed from the truth. This led to a wicked deed which has stamped an indelible mark of shame upon the reign of Constantius. Martinus, the pro-prefect who governed these provinces, was deeply grieved at the troubles of the innocent and made frequent pleas that those who were free from all guilt should be spared. When these proved vain he threatened to resign, hoping that this at any rate would deter the malicious inquisitor from exposing to evident danger men who were wedded to peace. Paul, believing that this was a clog upon his activity and being a master in the dreadful art of weaving intrigues, from which he got the nickname of 'the Chain', involved the governor himself, who was still defending his subordinates, in the common peril. He insisted that Martinus together with some tribunes and several others should be taken under arrest to the imperial court, with the result that Martinus in the face of imminent disaster assaulted Paul, and lacking the strength to inflict a fatal wound thrust the sword that he had drawn into his own side. This was the wretched end to which an upright governor came in his attempt to relieve the miserable plight of many of his people. After these atrocious acts Paul returned to the emperor's quarters steeped in blood and bringing with him a number of prisoners almost crushed with chains, whom he had reduced to squalid misery. On their arrival the rack was put in order and the executioner got ready his hooks and instruments of torture. Of these prisoners many suffered loss of property, others exile, some death. It is difficult to call to mind anyone who was acquitted in Constantius' reign, once so much as a whisper had set the machinery of punishment in motion

6. The faults of the senate and people of Rome.

At this time the government of the Eternal City was in the hands of Orfitus, a man whose overbearing behaviour went beyond the proper limits of the office of urban prefect which he held. He was shrewd and had a thorough knowledge of the law, but he was deficient in the polish which a liberal education normally produces in a man of his rank. During his administration there were serious riots over shortage of wine, which often provokes violent disturbances among a population accustomed to consume it greedily.

If any foreigner should happen to read this work, I suppose that he may wonder why, when it has occasion to speak of events at Rome, it should confine itself to riots and taverns and similar sordid subjects. I will give a brief summary of the reasons, which will not as far as I can help it depart from the truth.

At the time when Rome, a city destined to endure as long as the human race survives, was beginning its ascent to world-wide renown, valour and good fortune, which are so often at variance, conspired in an unbreakable bond to assist the steps by which it rose to glory. If either had failed Rome would never have reached the height of greatness. From its first infancy to the end of its childhood, a period comprising some three hundred years, the Roman people were engaged in wars close to its walls; next, in its adolescence, after various grievous struggles, it penetrated beyond the Alps and the sea; in its early and its mature manhood it won laurels of victory in every part of the great globe; finally, when it was verging on old age and owed its occasional victories only to its reputation, it gave itself over to a more peaceful way of life. The venerable city, having set its foot on the proud necks of savage peoples and given them laws to serve as the eternal foundation and guarantee of liberty, took the course which a thrifty, wise, and rich parent takes with his children, and handed over to the Caesars the administration of its heritage. Although the tribes and centuries of the voters have long been inactive, and electoral contests have been superseded by a calm which recalls the time of Numa, Rome is accepted in every region of the world as mistress and queen; everywhere the authority of its senators is paid the respect due to their grey hairs, and the name of the Roman people is an object of reverence and awe.

Nevertheless the majesty of these assemblies is damaged by the disorderly frivolity of a few, who do not bear in mind where they were born and behave as if they were licensed to indulge in vice and debauchery. As the poet Simonides says, if a man is to live a life of perfect happiness he needs above all a country of which he can be proud. Of these few some set their hearts upon statues, believing that in this way their fame will be secured for ever, as if there were more satisfaction to be gained from senseless bronze figures than from the consciousness of a well-spent life. They have these statues covered in gold leaf, a privilege first granted to Acilius Glabrio for his skill and courage in defeating king Antiochus. But Cato the censor showed how much finer it is to despise these vanities and to set one's steps on what the bard of Ascra calls the steep path to true glory. When he was asked why, unlike many others, he had no statue, Cato replied: 'I would rather have good men wondering why I have not deserved a statue than grumbling because I have been given one: that would be much worse.'

Others think that the height of glory is to be found in unusually high carriages and an ostentatious style of dress; they sweat under the burden of cloaks which they attach to their necks and fasten at the throat. These being of very fine texture are easily blown about, and they *contrive* by frequent movements, especially of the left hand, to show off their long

46

fringes and display the garments beneath, which are embroidered with various animal figures. Others again, with an appearance of deep gravity, hold forth unasked on the immense extent of their family property, multiplying in imagination the annual produce of their fertile lands, which extend, they boastfully declare, from farthest east to farthest west. They presumably do not know that their ancestors, who were responsible for the expansion of Rome, did not owe their distinction to riches, but overcame all obstacles by their valour in fierce wars, in which, as far as wealth or style of living or dress was concerned, they were indistinguishable from common soldiers. This is why a collection had to be made to defray the funeral expenses of the famous Valerius Publicola, why the destitute wife and children of Regulus were maintained by subscriptions from her husband's friends, why the daughter of Scipio received a dowry from the state, because the nobles were ashamed that a girl in her bloom should be left to wither in the absence of her indigent father.

But nowadays, if you come as a respectable stranger from the provinces to pay a first call on a man who prides himself on his ample means, you will be received like a long-lost friend. You will be asked so many questions that you are driven to invent the answers, and you will be so surprised to find an important personage who has never seen you before paying earnest attention to your slender claims that you will be sorry that you did not visit Rome ten years earlier to enjoy such exceptional favour. If, relying on this friendly reception, you repeat your visit the next day, you will find yourself left standing like an unknown and unwelcome intruder, while the man who was so encouraging yesterday takes a long time to decide who you are and where you come from. Finally, however, you are recognized and included in his circle of dependants. But if after that you wait upon him without a break for three years and then absent yourself for as many days, you will be back in the same position; he will not ask where you have been, and unless you take yourself off, poor fellow, you will spend your whole life paying vain homage to this booby. Moreover, when at suitable intervals preparations are put in hand for a tedious and unwholesome dinner or the distribution of the customary clients' dole, it is a matter of anxious debate whether, except for those who are owed a return of hospitality, anyone from abroad should be invited, and if, after full consideration, it is decided that they should, the man who is asked will be one who haunts the houses of racing drivers or is a professor of gambling or pretends to knowledge of some more recondite mystery. Men of learning and sobriety are shunned as bringers of bad luck who have nothing to contribute. In addition, the footmen are in the habit of selling invitations of this kind for a fee, and pass off as guests at these charitable distributions and entertainments some people of low origin and obscure station.

Not to be tedious, I will pass over the high living which wastes men's substance and the various temptations in which luxury involves them, and turn to another subject. Some, regardless of the risk, gallop their horses at the speed of the public post through the open spaces and paved streets of the city, hell for leather, as the phrase goes; behind them come their slaves in crowds like a gang of highwaymen, and, in the words of the comic poet, not even the jester is left at home. Many ladies copy them, racing through all quarters of the city with covered heads and in closed litters. And as skilful generals in a pitched battle place in the van their best units in close order, next, light-armed troops, behind them javelin men, and finally a reserve, ready to reinforce any weak spot, so the stewards of a city household, whose rank is marked by a wand in their right hand, show the same care in discharging their task. As at the word of command, all those employed in weaving march next to the carriage; then comes the smoke-begrimed kitchen staff; after them the rest of the slaves indiscriminately together with the idle populace of the neighbourhood; finally a crowd of eunuchs, young and old, with ghastly complexions and distorted features. Anyone who sees wherever he goes troops of these maimed creatures must curse the memory of queen Semiramis of old, who was the first to castrate young males, laying violent hands as it were upon nature and wresting her from her ordained course, since it is nature who in our very infancy implants in us the original source of our seed, and points out by a kind of unwritten law the means by which we are to propagate our race.

In this state of things the few houses which once had the reputation of being centres of serious culture are now given over to the trivial pursuits of passive idleness, and echo with the sound of singing accompanied by wind instruments or the twangling of strings. Men put themselves to school to the singer instead of the philosopher, to the theatrical producer rather than the teacher of oratory. The libraries are like tombs, permanently shut; men manufacture water-organs and lutes the size of carriages and flutes and heavy properties for theatrical performances.

Lastly, the ultimate disgrace, not long ago, when foreigners were banished in headlong haste from the city because a famine was expected, no respite whatever was granted to professors of the liberal arts, though very few in number, while at the same time the hangers-on of actresses and those who posed as such for the occasion, together with three thousand dancers with their choruses and the same number of dancing instructors, were allowed to remain without even being questioned. Wherever you turn your eyes you can see any number of women with curled ringlets, old enough, if they were married, to be mothers of three, skimming the floor with their feet to the point of exhaustion and launching themselves into the bird-like evolutions by which they represent the countless scenes which form the imaginary content of theatrical pieces. There can be no doubt that formerly, when every good quality found a dwelling in Rome, many of the grandees tried by various acts of kindness to keep among them strangers of good birth, like the Lotus-Eaters in Homer who tempted new arrivals with their delicious fruit. Now, however, some are so swollen with empty pride that they despise anyone born outside the city walls. Childless people and bachelors are the only exception; it is hardly credible what attention in various forms is lavished at Rome upon those without children. And since, as you might expect in the capital of the world, the inhabitants are peculiarly subject to severe epidemics of a kind which the whole medical profession is powerless to cure, they have thought of a way of preserving their health. No one visits a friend who is sick, and the more nervous minority adopt a further efficient precaution: when they send a servant to ask how the sufferer is they do not let him return home until he has taken a bath, so frightened are they of infection at second hand. Yet, although they are so careful in this respect, some who are crippled, if they are asked to a wedding where there is a prospect of having their palm greased, will find the strength to go as far as Spoleto (Spoletium). Such are the manners of the upper classes.

Of the lowest and poorest class, some spend the night in bars, others shelter under the awnings of the theatres, which were first erected by Catulus when he was aedile in imitation of the luxury of Campania. They hold quarrelsome gambling sessions, at which they make ugly noises by breathing loudly through the nose; or else – and this is their prime passion – they wear themselves out from dawn to dusk, wet or fine, in detailed discussion of the merits and demerits of horses and their drivers. It is most extraordinary to see a horde of people hanging in burning excitement on the outcome of a chariot race. Things like this prevent anything worthy of serious mention happening at Rome. So I must return to my main theme.

7. Outrageous and cruel behaviour of Gallus.

The Caesar, whose recklessness had now taken a wider scope, which made him hateful to all respectable people, henceforth threw aside all restraint, and made his oppression felt through all the regions of the East, sparing neither officials nor city worthies nor members of the populace. Finally, maddened by an unwisely blunt answer to a suggestion by him of a sudden and ill-timed price freeze in the face of an impending famine, he issued a single decree for the execution of all the leading members of the senate of Antioch; and they would have perished to a man but for the inflexible resistance of Honoratus, at that time count of the East. Another plain and obvious indication of his cruel nature was the pleasure which he took in gladiatorial shows; he sometimes watched as many as six or seven fights with fascinated attention, and was as happy at the sight of boxers killing one another in bloody combat as if he had made a great financial coup. His propensity for inflicting harm, easily aroused at any time, was further stimulated by a worthless woman, who was admitted to the palace at her own request and revealed the existence of a secret conspiracy against him by some soldiers of the lowest rank. Constantina, loudly proclaiming her joy that her husband's safety was assured, rewarded the woman, placed her in a carriage, and sent her out by the main gate of the palace, so that others might be tempted by her example to lay information about similar or even graver crimes.

Soon after, when Gallus was about to set out for Hierapolis, in order to give at least the appearance of taking part in a campaign, the people of Antioch humbly besought him to remove the fear of famine with which a combination of difficulties appeared to threaten them. Unlike other rulers whose widely extended power often enables them to relieve local distresses, Gallus made no arrangements and gave no orders for the transport of food from neighbouring provinces; instead he handed over Theophilus, the governor of Syria, who was standing at his side, to the panic-stricken mob, repeating more than once that no one would lack victuals unless the governor willed it so. This increased the boldness of the rabble; maddened with hunger as the shortage of provisions grew worse, they set fire to the grand house of one Eubulus, who enjoyed a great reputation among his fellows, and treated the governor as a man delivered over to them by imperial decree; they belaboured him with feet and fists till he was half dead, and then finished the wretched man off by tearing him in pieces. After this deplorable murder everyone saw in the destruction of this one man a model of the danger in which he stood, and feared that this recent example portended a similar fate for himself. At the same time Serenian, a former military commander, whose ineptitude had led, as I have already related, to the sacking of Celseis in Phoenicia, was brought to trial in due form on a charge of treason and in some mysterious way secured a verdict of acquittal; it was plainly proved that he had caused forbidden spells to be cast upon a cap of liberty which he wore, and had sent his servant with it to inquire of an oracle whether, as he hoped, the imperial power was surely and certainly destined to be his. So the same period saw a double misfortune; Theophilus, who was innocent, was the victim of a fearful outrage, and Serenian, who deserved universal execration, got off scot-free, though the strength of public opinion almost resulted in a demonstration.

Constantius, hearing of these events as they occurred and having been informed of some particulars by Thalassius, who, he learnt, had now died a natural death, wrote to the Caesar in mild terms and little by little deprived him of his backing. He pretended to be alarmed that the military, who are apt to be mutinous when they are unemployed, might form a conspiracy against Gallus' life, and bade him content himself with the detachments of his palace and personal guards together with the troops known as Scutarii and Gentiles. He also gave instructions to Domitian, who had been promoted from the treasury to the position of praetorian prefect, that on his arrival in Syria he should put gentle and respectful pressure on Gallus to hasten to Italy, to which he had been repeatedly summoned. Domitian proceeded by forced marches on his mission, but when he reached Antioch, instead of visiting the Caesar as he ought, he passed close by the doors of the palace and betook himself in solemn state to his official residence. There he remained for some time, giving his health as a reason for not entering the palace or appearing in public; in fact he was employing his seclusion in working out a scheme for the Caesar's destruction and adding superfluous details to the periodic reports which he sent to the emperor. Finally he was summoned to attend the Caesar's council, where without the slightest preface he began with these rash and ill-considered words:

'Obey the emperor's orders and set off, Caesar; I warn you that if you delay I shall have supplies for you and your court cut off at once.' After this insolent speech, he went off in a huff and was never seen in Gallus' presence again, though he was often sent for. The Caesar, resenting this harsh and unworthy treatment, had the prefect arrested by some guards whom he could trust. When he heard of this Montius, who was then quaestor, a man of excitable disposition but not given to extremes, made a public-spirited attempt to compose matters; he sent for the leaders of the palace guards and in a mild speech warned them of the impropriety and mischief of these proceedings, adding, however, in a reproachful tone that if they were set on this course they had better begin by overthrowing the statues of Constantius; they would then be in a position to contemplate putting the prefect to death with an easier mind.

At this news Gallus, like a snake wounded by a spear or stone, anticipated the worst, and, grasping at any means of saving himself, assembled all who carried arms, and addressed the astonished throng with snarls and grins of rage as follows: 'I need your help, my brave men, in a danger which is threatening us all. Montius, with unprecedented arrogance, has made a speech which amounts to an accusation that I am a rebel in revolt against the majesty of the emperor; he is angered, no doubt, because, to teach him a lesson, I have ordered the arrest of an insolent prefect who pretends not to know what protocol requires.' On the instant, the soldiery, eager as ever for any pretext for violence, attacked Montius, who lived nearby, tied the legs of the frail and ailing old man with rough ropes, and without a moment's delay dragged him off spread-eagled to the prefect's residence. In the same fit of fury they threw Domitian headlong downstairs, tied him up in the same way, and carried their victims bound together in a riotous rush through the wide streets of the city. Finally, when joints and limbs were dislocated, they trampled on the dead bodies till they were mutilated beyond recognition, and, having glutted their rage, threw them into the river. In the execution of this wicked enterprise they had been inflamed to madness by the sudden appearance of one Luscus, the city treasurer, who, howling like the leader of a gang of porters, incited them with repeated shouts to finish what they had begun. For this he was not long after burnt alive.

When Montius was at the last gasp in the hands of his butchers he called in reproach more than once upon Epigonus and Eusebius, without any indication of their position or rank. So an eager search was made for men with these names, and to keep the pot boiling the philosopher Epigonus of Cilicia and the ranting speaker Eusebius of Emesa, nicknamed Pittacas, were arrested, although the people Montius meant were not these, but two tribunes in charge of arsenals, who had promised him arms if there were any sign of a revolution. During these same days Apollinaris, the son-in-law of Domitian, who until recently had been marshal of the court and had then been sent by his father-in-law to Mesopotamia, was making strict inquiries among the troops whether they had received any secret message from Gallus which gave evidence of some deep-laid design. When he heard what had happened at Antioch he slipped away through Lesser Armenia and made for Constantinople, from which he was brought back by a detachment of guards and kept under close arrest.

In the course of these events it came to light that a royal robe had been secretly woven at Tyre, though it was not clear who had commissioned it or for whose use it was intended. So the then ruler of the province, who was the father of Apollinaris and bore the same name, was arrested as an accessory, and many others were collected from a number of cities and loaded with accusations of an outrageous kind.

And now, when the approach of intestine disaster was being heralded in trumpet-tones, the frenzy of Gallus, whose disturbed mind could no longer apprehend the truth, began to emerge from its hitherto latent state; no formal inquiry was made into the reliability of charges imputed or invented, no distinction drawn between innocent and guilty; justice was exiled, so to speak, from the courts; no voice was raised in defence, as prescribed by law; throughout the eastern provinces the executioner played his role as the agent of rapine, and the death penalty and confiscation were everywhere in evidence. These provinces I think it now an opportune moment to enumerate, apart from Mesopotamia, which I have already described in my account of the Parthian war, and Egypt, which I must defer to another time.

A description of the Eastern provinces is omitted (8).

9. Further history of Gallus.

In the midst of these various disasters Ursicinus, to whose staff I had been attached by the emperor's order, was summoned from Nisibis, where he was in command, and compelled to preside over the investigation of capital charges. This was much against his will, and he protested loudly against the packs of flatterers who yelped around him; he had always shown himself a brave soldier and commander of soldiers, but he was a complete stranger to the strife of the courts. Fearing for his own safety when he saw himself associated with venal prosecutors and judges who emerged like wild beasts from the same dens, he kept Constantius informed by private letters of what was happening both in public and behind the scenes, and begged him to send such assistance as would intimidate the Caesar and serve to deflate his notoriously swollen pride. But this excessive caution brought Ursicinus into a worse snare, as I shall tell later; his enemies concocted a serious intrigue to poison Constantius' mind, and Constantius, though in general a mild ruler, was cruel and implacable if some nobody brought this sort of thing to his ears, and became in these circumstances quite unlike himself.

When the day for these fatal trials arrived the master of cavalry took his seat on the bench in the character of a judge, assisted by assessors who were briefed in advance of the course which things were to take, and surrounded by shorthand writers who kept the Caesar informed by up-to-date reports of the questions asked and the answers given. The cruel orders of the prince and the influence of the queen, who from time to time thrust out her face from behind a curtain, caused many to perish without being allowed to refute the charges or make any defence. The first persons put on trial, Epigonus and Eusebius, were condemned simply on account of the coincidence of their names. As I have already said, Montius at the point of death had incriminated under these names two officials of the arsenal who had promised him assistance in a projected undertaking. Epigonus, who, it became clear, had nothing of the philosopher about him but his dress, first tried supplication, but in vain; then, when his sides were furrowed by torture and death was before his eyes, he made a shameful confession that he had been a party to a non-existent plot, though he had never heard or seen anything and was completely ignorant of public affairs. Eusebius, on the other hand, boldly denied the charges and stood his ground even on the rack, exclaiming loudly that this was a den of thieves, not a court of justice. His knowledge of the law enabled him to press his demand to be faced by his accuser and given a proper trial, but when he heard of this the Caesar treated his free speech as insolence and ordered him to be put to the question as an impudent slanderer. Mangled to such a degree that there was nothing left to torture, begging justice from heaven, and smiling defiantly, he remained unshaken and was condemned to death with his wretched companion, without being reduced to accuse either himself or another, without either confessing or being convicted. He was brought to the scaffold with his spirit unbroken, reviling the wickedness of the times and following the example of the old Stoic Zeno, who, when he had been tortured for a long time to extort a false confession, tore his tongue from its roots and flung it, bloody spittle and all, in the eyes of the king of Cyprus who was examining him.

Next the affair of the royal robe was investigated, and after the workers in purple had been tortured and had admitted the making of a short sleeveless tunic a man named Maras was brought forward, who was what the Christians call a deacon. A letter from him in Greek was produced, addressed to the manager of the factory at Tyre, which pressed for the rapid completion of a piece of work but gave no indication of its nature. Maras too was tortured almost to death without any confession being obtained from him. So the scope of the examination was widened to include people of various classes, but certain things remained in doubt and it was recognized that some charges had been brought without sufficient evidence. Finally, when many had perished, the two Apollinares, father and son, were condemned to banishment, and when they arrived at an estate which they owned called Craterae, about twenty-four miles from Antioch, their legs were broken, according to orders, and they were put to death. Their execution did nothing to abate the ferocity of Gallus; on the contrary, like a lion who has tasted human flesh, he went on to hunt out other prey of the same kind. These cases, however, I shall not relate individually, for fear of exceeding the limit which I have set myself, an error which must certainly be avoided.

10. Constantius grants peace to the Alamanni.

While the East was enduring these prolonged misfortunes Constantius in his own seventh and the Caesar's third consulship moved at the beginning of the warm season from Arles to Valence (Valentia), intending to take the field against the brothers Gundomad and Vadomar, kings of the Alamanni, whose frequent raids were devastating the frontier regions of Gaul. He was kept there some time waiting for supplies from Aquitaine, the arrival of which was delayed by unusually heavy spring rains and swollen rivers. During this interval a staff-officer called Herculanus reached the court; he was the son of the former master of cavalry Hermogenes, who, as I have already told, was torn to pieces by the mob in a riot at Constantinople. He brought an accurate account of the behaviour of Gallus and his wife, but Constantius, though full of grief for the past and fear for the future, kept his disquiet at bay as long as he could. Meanwhile the troops, who were all assembled at Châlon (Cabyllona), chafed at the delay, all the more because they were on short commons, their usual supplies not having yet arrived. This brought Rufinus, at that time praetorian prefect, into great danger. To pacify the army and to explain the reason why its supplies were held up, he was obliged to go in person to visit the troops, whose surliness was increased by shortage of food and who in any case are traditionally rough and brutal in their behaviour to civil functionaries. This was a clever and deliberate plot to bring about the death of Gallus' uncle, whose power was such that it was thought that it might encourage his nephew in his fatal ambitions. But Rufinus discharged his task with such loyalty that this design was deferred, and the grand chamberlain Eusebius was sent to Châlon with money, which he distributed secretly among the authors of the agitation. This quieted the unrest of the troops and saved the life of the prefect. Shortly afterwards supplies arrived in abundance and the army moved from its camp on the appointed day.

After a difficult march over roads which were mostly blocked by snow the army reached Augst (Rauraci) on the banks of the Rhine, but the superior force of the Alamannic host, which let loose upon them a hail of missiles, prevented them from building a bridge of boats. The apparent impossibility of crossing took the emperor by surprise, and he was anxiously debating his next step when unexpectedly a guide presented himself who knew the country, and in return for a reward pointed out by night a ford where the river was passable. While the enemy's attention was concentrated on another place our army might have crossed at this point before anyone was aware and gone on to ravage the whole region, had not a few men of the same race, who had attained high rank in our army, sent a secret warning to their compatriots. That at any rate was what some believed, and suspicion fell on Latinus, count of the household troops, Agilo, the superintendent of the stables, and Scudilo, the general of the Scutarii, all men who were held in high respect as pillars of the state. The barbarians, however, took the decision which the circumstances required; either because the auspices happened to be unfavourable or because they were forbidden to join battle on religious grounds, they relaxed the unbending spirit which stiffened their resistance and sent some of their chief men to beg pardon for their wrongdoing and to ask for peace. The envoys of the kings were detained and the matter privately debated for some time; finally, when it was generally agreed that it would be advantageous to grant peace on the reasonable conditions proposed, the emperor decided to address his assembled troops on the situation. Taking his place on the platform used for such occasions and surrounded by a retinue of high officials, he spoke to the following effect:

'None of you, I hope, will feel surprise if, after undergoing the toil of so long a march and accumulating supplies in such abundance, at a moment when my confidence in you has brought me to the verge of barbarian territory, I seem suddenly to change my plan and adopt a more peaceful course. If each of you will take thought according to his rank and capacity he will find it to be true that, whereas any individual soldier, however strong and vigorous his frame, concentrates solely on the preservation of himself and his own life, *a conscientious commander who must consult the interest of all equally is aware that the safety of those for whom he is responsible cannot be separated from his own*; he should therefore seize eagerly as heaven-sent favours any opportunities of relief that the circumstances admit. So I will show you in a word, my trusty comrades, why I have assembled you all here, and ask you to lend a favourable ear to my brief explanation. It is always a simple matter to set forth the truth.

'The kings and peoples of the Alamanni, seeing with fear the height of glory you have attained, which report has spread in glowing terms to the inhabitants of the most distant quarters, have sent these spokesmen to ask with bowed heads for forgiveness of their past offences and for peace. This request I have considered with all due caution and deliberation and with an eye to our advantage, and I believe that there are many reasons why, if I have your approval, it should be granted. First, it will enable us to avoid the chances and changes of war; second, we have the promise of their help instead of their enmity; next, we shall secure without bloodshed the abatement of those fits of ferocity which have often proved destructive to our provinces; finally, we must reflect that there are more ways than one of beating an enemy; he can either fall in battle overcome by weight of arms or he can take the safer course of submitting voluntarily to the yoke before the trumpets sound, discovering by experience that the victors are lacking neither in courage against the defiant nor in mercy to the submissive. In short, you are the judges and I await your decision, believing myself, as a peace-loving prince, that it is best to behave with restraint when luck has come our way. I am sure that such a wise decision will not be ascribed to lack of spirit on our part, but to moderation and humanity.'

No sooner had he ended than the whole army fell in with his wishes, praised his judgement, and gave their voice for peace. What specially moved them was the knowledge acquired in several campaigns that it was only in civil strife that the emperor's guardian angel kept a watchful eye on him, and that his foreign wars had generally ended in disaster. So a treaty was made according to the forms observed by the Alamanni, and when this had been done the emperor departed to spend the winter at Milan (Mediolanum).

11. The Caesar Gallus is sent for by Constantius and executed.

Here, free from the weight of other cares, Constantius addressed his mind to the knotty problem posed by the Caesar, an obstacle in his path which it would need all his strength to remove. In many discussions held secretly at night with his nearest associates he debated how this might be achieved by force or fraud before Gallus' increasing confidence caused him to embark on a more persistent course of disruption. Finally it was decided to send him a mild letter, summoning him to Milan on the ground that he was needed for very urgent public business; in this way he could be deprived of support and put to death without let or hindrance. This plan was opposed by several groups of fickle courtiers, among whom was Arbitio, an ardent intriguer, and Eusebius the grand chamberlain, who was even more given to mischief; they objected that it would be dangerous to leave Ursicinus in the East after the Caesar's departure, with no one to check any ambitious designs that he might entertain. They were supported by the rest of the eunuchs in the royal service, whose greed at that time passed all human bounds, and who found in the course of their private attendance on the emperor opportunities of fostering fictitious accusations by mysterious whispers. The gallant officer was almost crushed by the implacable hatred of his enemies; they put about a rumour that his grown sons, who were popular on account of their looks and youth, were being groomed for supreme power, and that their reputation for versatility in the management of arms and for physical agility in the daily military exercises was part of this plan. It was suggested that Gallus' naturally savage temper had been excited to acts of violence by agents placed about him for this purpose, so that when he had earned the detestation of all classes the trappings of imperial power might be transferred to the sons of the master of cavalry.

While this and similar talk assailed the harassed emperor's ears, which were always open to gossip of this kind, he wavered between various courses, but concluded in the end that the best plan open to him was to begin by sending for Ursicinus in the most honorific terms, alleging that in the present crisis he urgently needed to consult him about the additional forces required to break the threatened attack of the Parthian peoples. To avert any suspicion on the part of Ursicinus, count Prosper was sent to act as his deputy till he returned. So when this letter arrived, together with leave to use the imperial posting system, we hurried to Milan with all possible speed.

The next thing was to induce the Caesar to hasten his own departure, and to remove any suspicion Constantius urged his sister, Gallus' wife, to come to him, pretending with many professions of affection that he had long desired a visit from her. Though she feared his cruel nature and hesitated, she set out in the hope that as he was her brother she would be able to soften him, but when she reached the post station in Bithynia called Caeni Gallicani she was carried off by a sudden fever. Her death left her husband a prey to anxiety about his best course; he realized that he had lost his chief support, and in his difficult and confused situation one thought alone occupied his distracted mind, that Constantius, who relied entirely upon his own judgement, would admit no excuse and grant no forgiveness for his errors, but being inclined, as he was, to destroy his kindred, would spread a secret snare for him and punish him with death if he caught him off his guard. In these straits, expecting the worst if he relaxed his vigilance, he came to a secret decision to lay claim to supreme power, if he saw an opening; he had, however, a double reason for fearing that he would be betrayed by those nearest to him, first because they dreaded his cruel and capricious temper, and second, because they were overawed by the better luck of Constantius in civil warfare. In the midst of these great and crushing anxieties he received incessant letters from the emperor advising and entreating his presence, and obliquely hinting that the empire neither could nor should be divided, but that everyone must contribute what he could to its support in its present tottering state, an allusion presumably to the devastation of the Gallic provinces. By way of precedent from the not very distant past, Constantius added that Diocletian and his colleague had employed the Caesars as adjutants who were despatched hither and thither about the empire and had no fixed place of residence, and that on one occasion in Syria, when the Augustus was angry, Galerius in his purple had marched on foot in front of his carriage for nearly a mile.

Last of a number of envoys came Scudilo, tribune of the Scutarii, who under a blunt exterior concealed consummate skill in the art of persuasion. By a mixture of flattery and lies he succeeded where all others had failed in enticing Gallus to set out, constantly assuring him with an appearance of sincerity that his cousin was burning with eagerness to see him, that his gentleness and mildness were such that he would pardon anything that he had done amiss, and that he would associate him with himself in the empire and make him his partner in the tasks which had to be undertaken in the long-exhausted provinces of the North. It is a commonplace that when fate lays its hand upon a man his perceptions are dulled and blunted; Gallus was encouraged by these blandishments to hope for better things, and, leaving Antioch under an evil star, jumped, as the old proverb puts it, from the frying-pan into the fire. On reaching Constantinople he held games in the hippodrome, as if he were perfectly safe and secure, and placed the crown on the head of the charioteer Thorax, who was the winner.

At this news Constantius' rage passed all bounds. To prevent Gallus in his anxiety for his future from attempting to secure his safety by stirring up revolutionary movements along his route, he deliberately removed from their posts all the troops stationed in the towns which the Caesar had to pass through. At that moment Taurus, who was travelling to Armenia to take up the post of quaestor, passed through Constantinople without troubling to address Gallus or visit him. But other persons arrived by the emperor's orders, ostensibly to take up various posts but in reality to keep Gallus under observation and prevent him making any move; among them was Leontius, afterwards urban prefect, who came as quaestor, Lucillian, appointed count of the bodyguard, and a tribune of the Scutarii called Bainobaudes.

After a long march over level ground Gallus reached Adrianople, a city in the neighbourhood of Mount Haemus previously called Uscudama. There he stopped to rest for twelve days, and learnt that the Theban legions, who were wintering in towns nearby, had sent some of their number with strong assurances of loyalty to advise him to remain where he was. *Stationed as they were in large numbers in the locality*, they were confident of their own strength, but the constant vigilance of those around him prevented Gallus from snatching any opportunity of seeing them or hearing their errand. Since letter after letter arrived urging his departure, he made use of ten vehicles of the imperial post in accordance with the emperor's instructions, and, leaving behind all his retinue except a few whom he had brought to wait on him in his bedroom and at table, he yielded to pressure and hastened his journey, covered with dust and frequently reproaching himself with tears and curses for his own rashness, which had brought him down and placed him at the mercy of the lowest of the low. At this time, whenever nature granted him the respite of sleep, his senses were assailed by the shrieks of terrifying spectres, and hosts of his victims, headed by Domitian and Montius, seemed in his dream to be seizing him and delivering him into the clutches of the Furies. When the soul is set free from its ties with the body it remains ceaselessly active, and summons up, from the subconscious thoughts and anxieties which harass men's minds, visions of the night, which we Greeks call phantoms.

So, as his miserable lot opened before him, the path on which he was fated to lose both his power and his life, he proceeded without a stop and with many relays of horses to Poetovio, a town in Noricum. Here the whole truth of the plot against him was at last revealed. Count Barbatio, who had commanded his bodyguard, suddenly appeared, together with the secret agent Apodemius; he brought with him picked troops who were bound to the emperor by past favours and whose loyalty he was confident would be proof against either bribes or pity.

Henceforward all pretence was laid aside. Barbatio, after surrounding with armed men all that part of the palace which lay outside the walls, entered as night was falling, stripped the Caesar of his royal apparel, and dressed him in the tunic and cloak of a common soldier, assuring him, however, with repeated oaths that he had the emperor's authority to tell him that he would suffer nothing further. Then, with the order 'Stand up at once', he set him before he knew what was happening in a private carriage and conveyed him to a place in Istria near the town of Pola, where I am told that Crispus the son of Constantine was formerly put to death. There he was kept in close confinement, half-dead with fear of his approaching fate, till he was visited by Eusebius, at that time grand chamberlain, Pentadius, a notary, and Mallobaudes, a tribune of the guards; they had orders from the emperor to question him in detail on the reasons which had led him to order the death of each of his victims at Antioch. Gallus, with a face as white as that of Adrastus, had just strength enough to reply that most of them had been massacred at the instance of his wife Constantina; he was ignorant, no doubt, of the wise answer given by Alexander the Great to his mother when she was urging him to put to death an innocent person, and in the hope of getting what she wanted reminded him that she had carried him for nine months in her womb. 'Ask some other boon, my good mother; no benefit can be put in the balance with the life of a man.'

When this was reported to the emperor his anger and indignation became inexorable; he saw that his only means of ensuring his own safety lay in the destruction of Gallus. So he sent Serenian, who, as I have already said, had escaped a charge of treason by a sort of sleight of hand, together with Pentadius the notary and Apodemius the security agent, with orders to carry out the execution, and Gallus, with his hands tied like a highwayman, was beheaded. His head and face were mutilated, and the man who so short a time before had been an object of dread to cities and provinces was left lying a hideous corpse upon the ground.

But the justice of the powers above kept its unsleeping eye on both sides alike. Gallus was brought down by his own wicked deeds, but, guilty though he was, both the men who led him into a fatal snare by their lies and cajolery were cut off not long after by an agonizing death. Scudilo was attacked by an abscess of the liver and died vomiting up his lungs; Barbatio, who had over a long period been inventing false charges against Gallus, fell victim to a whispering campaign. The suggestion that he had higher ambitions than the supreme command of the infantry led to his condemnation. So by an unlamented death he made reparation to the spirit of the Caesar whom his treachery had destroyed.

These and countless other events of this kind are brought to pass from time to time (would that it were invariably so) by the operation of Adrastia, who punishes evil and rewards good deeds and whom we also call Nemesis. She is the sublime manifestation of a powerful divinity dwelling, men believe, above the orbit of the moon. Others define her as the personification of a protective power, exercising a general surveillance over the destinies of individuals, and represented in the theogonies of old as the daughter of Justice, who from her unseen eternal throne looks down upon all things on earth. Queen over all causation and arbiter and umpire of all events, she controls the urn from which men's lots are cast and regulates their vicissitudes of fortune, often bringing their enterprises to a different end from that which they designed and confounding their various actions by the changes which she imposes. It is she, too, who binds the vainly swelling pride of mortal men in the indissoluble chain of necessity, and casts, as she alone can, her weight into the scale by which they rise or fall; at one moment she bears down upon the stiff necks of the proud and takes away their strength, at another she raises the good out of the dust and exalts them to prosperity. The myths of antiquity endowed her with wings so that all might understand that she appears with the speed of a bird; they put a rudder in her hand and a wheel beneath her feet to signify that she runs through all the elements and governs the universe.

Such was the way in which Gallus, who had himself become weary of life, came to an untimely end at the age of twenty-eight after a reign of four years. He was born in Etruria at Massa Veternensis; his father was Constantius, brother of the emperor Constantine, and his mother Galla, the sister of Rufinus and Cerealis, who both attained the distinction of the consulship and a prefecture. He was a man of remarkably good looks, with a fine frame and well-proportioned limbs. His hair was blond and soft, and his beard, though at first a delicate down, gave him a look of authority beyond his years. In character the difference between him and his sober brother Julian was as great as between Domitian and Titus, the sons of Vespasian. After reaching the highest place that fortune can give he experienced the caprice by which she makes a mockery of human life, at one moment exalting men to the sky and at the next plunging them into the depths of hell. Of this there are innumerable examples, some of which I will briefly touch upon. This same fickle and changeable fortune raised Agathocles from the trade of a potter to be king of Sicily, and set Dionysius, once the terror of nations, to preside over an elementary school at Corinth. She brought Andriscus of Adramyttium, a man born in a fuller's shop, to a position in which he could usurp the name of Philip, and taught the legitimate son of Perseus to earn his living by the trade of a blacksmith. She delivered Mancinus, after he had held supreme command, into the hands of the people of Numantia, she abandoned Veturius and Claudius to the tender mercies of the Samnites and Corsicans respectively, and she subjected Regulus to the cruelty of the Carthaginians. Through the injustice of fortune Pompey, whose glorious exploits had earned him the title of Great, was murdered in Egypt at the behest of eunuchs, while a convict called Eunus achieved the command of fugitive slaves in Sicily. How many Romans of high birth prostrated themselves at the feet of Viriathus or Spartacus while this mistress of the world looked on. How many heads at which the peoples of the earth trembled have fallen by the fatal hand of the executioner. One man is thrown into prison, another is raised to power beyond his hopes, a third is cast down from the highest pinnacle of greatness. To try to fathom the variety and frequency of such events would be as foolish as to try to number the sands of the sea or to calculate the weight of mountains.

BOOK 15

1. Constantius' reactions to the death of Gallus.

Using my best efforts to find out the truth, I have set out, in the order in which they occurred, events which I was able to observe myself or discover by thorough questioning of contemporaries who took part in them. The rest, which will occupy the pages that follow, I shall execute to the best of my ability in a more polished style, and I shall pay no heed to the criticism which some make of a work which they think too long. Brevity is only desirable when it cuts short tedious irrelevance without subtracting from our knowledge of the past.

Hardly had Gallus been stripped of his imperial dress in Noricum when Apodemius, who was a firebrand all his life, snatched up the Caesar's shoes, and, driving so hard with constant relays of horses that he destroyed some by the way, arrived first with the news at Milan. He threw the shoes down at Constantius' feet as if they were the spoils of a fallen Parthian king. At this sudden announcement that what had seemed so desperate and difficult a matter had been brought to a successful end with the utmost ease, the high court officials, concentrating in a customary act of adulation their desire to stand well with the emperor, extolled to the skies the valour and good fortune of Constantius, at whose nod two princes, to wit Vetranio and Gallus, had been cashiered, though at different times, like common soldiers. Constantius, intoxicated by this carefully compounded flattery and firmly convinced that henceforth he would be immune from all the ills that flesh is heir to, departed so far from the path of moderation as sometimes to use the words 'Our Eternity' in dictating letters and to style himself 'master of the world' when writing in his own hand. Such expressions, if they had been applied to him by others, should have aroused high indignation in a man who constantly declared that he was using his utmost endeavours to frame his life and character on the model of citizen emperors. Even if he had been reigning over the innumerable

worlds of Democritus, of which Anaxarchus encouraged Alexander the
Great to dream, reading or listening should have taught him to reflect
that, according to the unanimous opinion of scholars, the circumference
of the whole earth, which seems to us immense, is no more than a tiny
point in comparison with the vastness of the universe.

2. *Ursicinus and Julian accused of treason.*

Once the fallen Caesar had come to this miserable end, the trumpet
rang out for a struggle in the courts of law, and Ursicinus was charged
with treason. He was exposed increasingly to the jealousy which dogs
all good men, and in particular he had to encounter the difficulty that
the emperor was deaf to all reasonable and credible arguments for the
defence, but lent a ready ear to the secret whispers of those who
insinuated that the name of Constantius was forgotten through all the
regions of the East, and that men were clamouring both in private and
in public for the officer in question as the only commander who could
put fear into the Persians. In the face of this the noble hero remained
unshaken; he took care not to adopt too humble a posture, while he
groaned inwardly that an innocent man could be placed in such danger;
what particularly saddened him was that the friends who previously
thronged about him had deserted to the stronger side, like the lictors
who transfer their attendance from the holders of office to their
successors when custom requires it. He had in addition to sustain the
enmity of Arbitio, who was plotting against him under a cloak of good
will and who frequently referred to him openly as 'my gallant colleague'.
Arbitio was a past master in the art of entrapping a man of upright life
in a fatal snare, and at that moment he enjoyed great power. He was
like a snake which lies hidden in a hole in the ground watching for
individual passers-by whom it then suddenly attacks; even *when he had
attained high* military command he was consumed with jealousy of the
prosperity of others, and stained his conscience by his insatiable appetite
for inflicting injury, though he himself had been neither injured nor
even provoked. So after long deliberation with the emperor in the
presence of a few accomplices a decision was reached to carry off
Ursicinus on the following night out of sight of the troops and put him
to death without a trial, a fate like that which we are told befell Domitius
Corbulo, who had defended the provinces with loyalty and prudence
during the vile times of Nero. This was arranged and the agents

appointed to carry out the plan were waiting for the hour to strike, when the emperor softened, and gave orders that the execution of this wicked deed should be deferred for further consideration.

The engines of defamation were next turned against Julian, the famous future emperor, who had recently been fetched to Milan; his enemies asserted that he was guilty on two counts, first, that in pursuit of a liberal education he had left the estate of Macellum in Cappadocia and made his way into the province of Asia, and, second, that he had seen his brother Gallus when the latter was passing through Constantinople. Julian rebutted both charges and proved that in neither case had he acted without orders, but he would have perished at the instance of an abominable clique of toadies had not the empress Eusebia by some divine inspiration taken his part. He was escorted to Como, a town near Milan, and after a short stay there was allowed to go to Greece in accordance with his passionate desire to improve his mind.

In the wake of these events some developments took place which might be ascribed to the operation of a favourable providence; some punishments were justly inflicted, and in other cases the prosecution ran into the sand. But some rich men obtained the protection of those in power and by clinging to them like ivy to high trees bought themselves off at enormous expense, whereas poor men who had little or nothing with which to purchase their safety were condemned out of hand. So truth was overshadowed by lies and in some cases falsehood passed for truth.

At the same period Gorgonius, who had been the Caesar's chamberlain, and who by his own confession had shared and sometimes prompted his outrages, got off scot free, because the eunuchs combined to smother justice under a tissue of lies.

3. Punishment of Gallus' adherents.

While this was happening at Milan, parties of military personnel together with a number of court functionaries were brought from the East to Aquileia. Drooping in their chains and almost at their last gasp, they cursed their continued existence under such a load of complicated misery. They were accused of being the agents of the savage tyranny of Gallus, responsible, it was believed, for Domitian and Montius being torn in pieces and others subsequently driven over the brink of destruction. Arbitio, together with Eusebius, at that time chamberlain, was sent to try them; both these were men of careless arrogance, equally capable of injustice and cruelty. Without any thorough investigation, without drawing any distinction between innocent and guilty, they sentenced some to exile after being beaten or tortured, reduced others to the ranks, and condemned the rest to capital punishment. Then, having filled the cemeteries with corpses, they returned as if from a successful campaign, and reported their exploits to the emperor, who in these and similar cases never failed to show himself inflexible and severe.

From this time onward Constantius, as if determined utterly to reverse what fate ordained, opened his mind more eagerly than ever to the intriguers who surrounded him. So there suddenly sprang up a host of rumour-mongers, who attacked like wild beasts men at the summit of an honourable career, and afterwards rich and poor indiscriminately. Unlike the brothers from Cibyra employed by Verres, who fawned upon the judgement-seat of a single governor, these men spread mischief over the members of the whole state. Easily the most notorious among them were Paul and Mercury, the latter a Persian by origin, the former a native of Dacia. Paul was a notary, Mercury had risen from attendance at the emperor's table to be a supervisor of his finances. Paul, as I said earlier, was known by the nickname of 'the Chain' because of his skill in linking slanders together to form an unbreakable whole; he spent his efforts in an astonishing variety of tricks, like some wrestlers who show superlative cleverness in the bouts of the ring. Mercury, on the other hand, was called the 'Count of Dreams'. His speciality was to insinuate himself into dinner-parties and similar gatherings, like a fierce dog which conceals its savage disposition by humbly wagging its tail. Then, if anyone mentioned to a friend that he had seen something in a dream, when nature roams unchecked, Mercury used his poisonous skill to paint it in the worst colours, and poured it into the receptive ear of the emperor, with the result that the person in question was treated as guilty of an unforgivable offence and subjected to a serious criminal charge. Such incidents were magnified by common rumour, till at last, so far from publishing their dreams, people were reluctant to admit in the presence of strangers that they had slept at all, and some learned persons regretted that they had not been born in the region of Mount Atlas, where dreams are said to be unknown. But how that may be we must leave to the experts in such matters.

While judicial investigations and punishments were taking such dreadful forms, Illyricum was the scene of another calamity, which began with empty words and ended by bringing many people into danger. At a dinner given at Sirmium by Africanus, the governor of Lower Pannonia, some of the guests, believing that no one was there to betray them, spoke freely in their cups of their disgust at the existing regime; others assured them that signs were not wanting that the change which they longed for was at hand; and some with inconceivable folly announced that it was foretold in prophecies handed down in their families.

Among the party was a secret agent called Gaudentius, whose stupidity was equalled by his impetuosity. He reported the incident as a serious matter to Rufinus, at that time head of the praetorian prefect's staff, a man always eager for extreme measures and notorious for his inveterate badness of heart. Rufinus flew as if on wings to court, and inflamed the emperor, who was always accessible to suspicions of this kind, to such a degree that without any pause for thought he gave orders for Africanus and all his guests at the fatal meal to be taken up and carried off. This success encouraged the baleful informer, whose appetite, as is the way with men, was strongest for forbidden fruit, to ask for and obtain a prolongation of his existing office for two years. Teutomeres, a staff-officer, was sent with a colleague to seize the offenders, and brought them all in chains in accordance with his orders. But when they reached Aquileia the tribune Marinus, a former drill-master but at that time unattached, a man of fiery disposition who had originated the fatal conversation, finding himself alone in an inn while arrangements for the journey were being made, plunged into his side a knife that lay to hand, disembowelled himself, and died on the spot. The rest were taken to Milan and tortured; they confessed that they had made some rash remarks at dinner and were sentenced to imprisonment, though with some faint hope of eventual release. The officers, however, were condemned to exile on the ground that they were privy to the suicide of Marinus, but were pardoned at the intercession of Arbitio.

4. Campaign of Constantius against the Lentienses.

When this affair was concluded war was declared on the Lentienses *and another Alamannic tribe* on account of their frequent and widespread raids across the Roman frontier. The emperor set out on this campaign, and reached the district of Raetia called Campi Canini, where after long discussion it was decided that honour as well as expediency would be satisfied if *Constantius remained there* with part of the army, while the master of the cavalry, Arbitio, made his way with a stronger force along the shores of Lake Constance, ready to give immediate battle to the barbarians. I will describe the nature of the terrain, as far as is consistent with my design.

The Rhine, which *rises* with a prodigious head of water in the recesses of lofty mountains, makes its way without being joined by any tributaries over high cliffs, like the Nile pouring headlong down its cataracts. Its waters are so abundant that it would be navigable from its very source, were it not that it resembles a torrent rather than a stream. When it reaches level ground it runs between high banks till it enters the vast round lake of Constance which the neighbouring Raetians call Brigantia. This is nearly sixty miles long and about the same in width; access to it is barred by thick, rough forests, except where the disciplined valour of the old Romans has made a broad road in spite of the obstacles posed by barbarians, terrain, and climate.

The river bursts into the lake in a loud welter of foam, and passes through its calm and sluggish waters as if they were an eternally hostile element, from which it is separated by a clear dividing line. Then without augmentation or diminution of its original volume, it leaves the lake with name and strength unchanged, and without suffering any further contact merges at last with the waters of the ocean. What is particularly remarkable is that the lake is not disturbed by the rushing stream passing through it, nor the river impeded by the mud of the lake bottom, but the two bodies of water cannot mingle. If it were not for the evidence of one's own eyes one would suppose that no power would suffice to keep them apart. In the same way the Alpheus, which rises in Arcadia, cuts its way through the Ionian sea, according to the myth, in its longing to reach the neighbourhood of its beloved fountain of Arethusa.

Arbitio, though he knew the difficulties involved in opening a campaign, did not wait for the return of scouts sent to report the approach of the barbarians, but fell into an ambush and was brought to a halt by this sudden catastrophe. The enemy sprang upon him without warning, and recklessly launched every kind of weapon at whatever target they could find; resistance was impossible, and the only hope of escape lay in rapid flight. So our men, with no aim but to avoid being wounded, dispersed in all directions and presented their backs to the foe. Most of them, however, who had scattered along narrow paths and escaped under cover of darkness, recovered their strength when day returned and rejoined their units. In this melancholy and unexpected disaster a large number of men and ten tribunes were lost.

On the following day the Alamanni, encouraged by this success, advanced more boldly upon the Roman entrenchments; the light was veiled in morning mist as they ran hither and thither with drawn swords, grinding their teeth and shouting boastful threats. Suddenly the Scutarii made a sally, and finding themselves repulsed and brought to a standstill by the opposing hordes called with one voice on their comrades to join the fight. The majority were still terrified by the disaster that they had just experienced, and Arbitio, believing that the result would be dangerous, was hesitating, when three tribunes leapt forward: Arintheus, acting commander of the heavy-armed guards, Seniauchus, who was in charge of a squadron of the household cavalry, and Bappo, an officer of the Veterans. These with the troops under them, making the common cause their own, like the Decii of old, fell on the enemy like a torrent and put them to a disgraceful rout; it was not a pitched battle but a succession of quick skirmishes. The ranks of the enemy were broken and they were scattered; finding their attempts to escape hindered by their armour, they cast it away, and exposed themselves unprotected to be cut down by a rain of blows from swords and lances. In many cases man and horse lay dead on the ground together, with the rider apparently still fast on the back of his mount. At the sight of this all who were hesitating to join in the fight threw caution to the winds; trampling on heaps of bodies and drenched with the blood of the slain, they completed the destruction of the barbarian host, except for those who escaped death by flight. At this successful outcome of the battle the emperor returned joyful and triumphant to pass the winter at Milan.

5. Silvanus proclaimed Augustus and murdered.

While things were in this disturbed state the provinces suffered damage on a similar scale from a storm of fresh disasters. This would have caused universal and total ruin had not Fortune, which governs the fates of men, put a rapid end to an exceptionally formidable uprising. Long neglect had exposed the provinces of Gaul to the miseries of slaughter, pillage, and fire; the barbarians plundered at will and no help came, till at last the emperor sent the master of infantry Silvanus, who was thought capable of redressing the situation. Arbitio used his best efforts to bring about this appointment; his aim was to impose on his absent rival, *whose continued survival he resented, the burden of a dangerous task*.

A man called Dynamius, superintendent of the imperial baggage train, in order to advertise his intimacy with Silvanus, had asked him for letters of introduction to his friends. Silvanus, suspecting nothing, naively granted his request, but Dynamius kept the letters, intending in due course to put them to a mischievous use. So while the general in question was traversing Gaul in the service of the state and repelling the barbarians, who had now lost their confidence and courage, Dynamius, in whom restless activity went along with cunning and long practice in intrigue, devised an act of wicked fraud. According to an unconfirmed report, the praetorian prefect Lampadius was his accomplice in this plot together with Eusebius, formerly treasurer of the privy purse, who was nicknamed 'Glutton', and Aedesius, previously keeper of the records; these two had been invited to the investiture of the consuls at the instance of the prefect, whose close friends they were. The lines of writing in the letters were obliterated by a sponge, leaving only the signature, over which a text quite different from the original was written. In this Silvanus appeared to be indirectly begging his friends, both court officials and private individuals (among them were Tuscus Albinus and several others), to support him in his attempts to gain a higher position and in the near future the imperial throne. This bundle of fictitious documents designed to destroy an innocent man was placed by Dynamius in the hands of the prefect, and by him presented secretly in a private interview to the emperor, who was always eager to examine evidence of this kind and with whom *the prefect hoped to increase his influence* by his unsleeping devotion to his master's safety. When this clever patchwork was read to the emperor's secret council, orders were given that the tribunes should be put under surveillance and the private persons mentioned in the letters brought from the provinces. But Malarich, the commander of the Gentiles, shocked by the injustice of these proceedings, assembled his colleagues and protested loudly that it was wrong that men devoted to the imperial service should be sacrificed to the machinations of a cabal: he asked that he himself should be despatched at once to fetch Silvanus, who was certainly not guilty of what was imputed to him by these ruthless conspirators; he would leave his relations as hostages, and Mallobaudes, the commander of the heavy brigade of guards, would give security for his return. Alternatively, he begged that he should be allowed to stand bail himself, while Mallobaudes hastened to Gaul to carry out the task which he himself had offered to undertake. He declared that he was quite sure that if an outsider were sent, Silvanus, who was temperamentally nervous even when there was nothing to alarm him, would be likely to disturb the peace. This suggestion met the needs of the situation, but Malarich might as well have spoken to the winds. Arbitio carried a proposal that Apodemius, the bitter and inveterate enemy of all good men, should be sent with a letter to fetch Silvanus. Apodemius *cared so little what might happen* that when he arrived in Gaul he departed from his instructions; instead of seeing Silvanus and presenting the letter of recall, he remained there, employing the local agent of the privy purse to ride roughshod over the dependants and slaves of the master of infantry, as if he were already outlawed and on the brink of execution.

In the meantime, however, while people were waiting for Silvanus' arrival and Apodemius was disturbing the peace, Dynamius, in an attempt to add credibility to his monstrous forgery, composed a letter tallying with what he had sent to the emperor through the prefect, and sent it in the names of Silvanus and Malarich to the superintendent of the arsenal at Cremona; he was addressed as a fellow-conspirator and told to get everything ready without delay. On reading this the superintendent, not knowing what it meant – indeed he could not remember that the writers of the letter had ever held any confidential communication with him – sent the letter itself by the bearer who had brought it in charge of a soldier to Malarich, begging him to say what he wanted plainly and not in riddles; he was, he said, too unsophisticated and simple a person to understand obscure hints. When the letter suddenly came into the hands of Malarich, who was still in a state of deep depression, deploring his own fate and that of his fellow-countryman Silvanus, he took a bolder line; he appealed to the Franks, of whom a large number at that time had influence in the palace, and raised a great clamour over the discovery of a conspiracy and the detection of a fraud manifestly aimed at their lives. At this the emperor decided that the matter should be thoroughly investigated by his council and the senior officers sitting together. When the court met, Florentius son of Nigrinian, the acting master of the offices, found on careful examination of the documents traces of the original writing and discerned what was in fact the truth, that the earlier text had been tampered with, and something very different from what Silvanus had dictated had been written over it with the design of producing a patchwork of lies. The cloud of intrigue was thus dissipated, and the emperor, receiving a faithful report of the facts, gave orders that the prefect should be dismissed from his post and brought to trial, but by the united efforts of a crowd of friends he was acquitted. Eusebius, however, the former treasurer of the privy purse, admitted under torture that he was a party to the plot. Aedesius, who persistently denied any knowledge whatever of the affair, got off unscathed. So the matter ended in the acquittal of all those against whom information had been laid. Dynamius, indeed, was treated as if he had highly distinguished himself, and was promoted to be governor of Etruria and Umbria with the title of Corrector.

Meanwhile Silvanus, who was at Cologne (Colonia Agrippina), heard by frequent reports from his friends of the efforts which Apodemius was making to undermine him. Knowing the sensitive disposition of the fickle emperor and fearing that he might be destroyed in his absence without a trial, he found himself in great difficulties and thought of throwing himself upon the mercy of the barbarians. He was prevented from doing so by Laniogaisus, at that time a tribune, who, as I have previously related, was the only person who stayed with Constans when he was dying; he was then serving as one of that emperor's personal guards. Laniogaisus warned Silvanus that his fellow-countrymen the Franks would either kill him or take a bribe to betray him. So Silvanus, realizing that his present situation offered no hope of safety, was driven to adopt extreme measures. He became gradually bolder in his talk with his senior officers, and, when he had excited them by the promise of a great reward, he seized as a makeshift the purple which adorned the standards and banners of the troops, and assumed the imperial power. While this was happening in Gaul there came to Milan as night was falling an unexpected message, which left no doubt that Silvanus, aiming higher than the mastership of infantry, had seduced his army and been proclaimed Augustus. This unexpected blow struck Constantius like a thunderbolt; a council was called late at night and all the dignitaries hastened to the palace. No one had the presence of mind or readiness of tongue to suggest what should be done, till at last people began to speak under their breath of Ursicinus as a man of outstanding military distinction who had been the innocent victim of grave injustice. He was accorded the unusual honour of being summoned by the master of ceremonies in person, and when he entered the council he was offered the purple to kiss much more graciously than ever before. (Diocletian was the emperor who first introduced this foreign and kingly form of obeisance; before him, we are told, the emperors were always greeted in the same way as holders of other high offices.) So the man who a short time before had been accused by his ill-wishers of swallowing up the East and attempting to usurp the supreme power through his sons now became the wisest of generals, the great comrade-in-arms of the emperor Constantine, the only man to be looked to to put out the fire, for reasons which were sound but nevertheless concealed an ulterior motive. Great efforts were certainly to be made to crush that stout rebel Silvanus, but if they failed, Ursicinus, into whose soul the iron had entered deeply, would be utterly destroyed, and a very formidable stumbling-block thus removed. Accordingly, when preparations were being made to hasten Ursicinus' departure, and that general was eager to refute the charges against him, he was forestalled by the emperor, who said in mild tones that this was not the moment to embark on a defence which was bound to be controversial; on the contrary, the difficulties pressing upon them, which must be mitigated before they grew worse, made it urgently necessary that the parties should resume their former harmonious relations.

A complicated discussion was held, in which the chief point debated was how Silvanus could be induced to think that the emperor was still in ignorance of what he had done. The best way of strengthening his confidence seemed to be to send a graciously worded letter, telling him that Ursicinus was to relieve him and that he should return in full enjoyment of his authority. When this was settled Ursicinus received orders to set out. He was accompanied, at his own request, by some tribunes and ten officers of the general staff to help in meeting the needs of the situation. Among the latter were my colleague Verinian and myself; all the rest were chosen by the emperor. Ursicinus set out with us in attendance, and for much of the way each of us was preoccupied solely by fear for his own safety. We were like condemned criminals thrown before fierce wild beasts; nevertheless we reflected that there is this at least to be said for misfortune, that it can give place only to something better, and we dwelt with admiration on the saying of Cicero, which seems to come from the very heart of truth and which runs as follows: 'Although the state most to be desired is the permanent continuance of undisturbed good fortune, nevertheless such a smooth course of life does not provide so piquant a sensation as a change to better things from misery and disaster.'

We proceeded therefore by forced marches, since our commander was anxious to appear in the suspected district before any rumour of the usurpation could spread through Italy. But for all our haste we were betrayed by common report, which flew before us on the wind, and when we reached Cologne we found a situation beyond our strength. A multitude had flocked in from all sides to support the enterprise so timidly begun, and in the face of this concentration of forces it seemed best that our general should change his tactics and accommodate himself to the intentions and wishes of the upstart emperor, whose confidence would be increased by these deceptive indications of an accession of strength. A pretence of falling in with his wishes in various ways would make him relax his precautions and trick him into thinking that he had no enemy to fear. But to bring our project to a successful conclusion was no easy matter; it required nice calculation to ensure that our designs upon him ripened at the right moment and were neither premature nor belated; if they came to light at the wrong time we should all undoubtedly suffer a common sentence of death.

Our general, however, was graciously received. The very nature of our business compelled him to incline his head, and he had to make a solemn obeisance to the man whose grasping ambition had led him to assume the purple, but he was treated as a distinguished and intimate friend. The ease with which he obtained access to Silvanus and the high place assigned to him at the royal table put him in so privileged a position that from that moment he was taken into confidential consultation on the most important matters. Silvanus was aggrieved because, while others had been advanced to the consulship and high dignities beyond their deserts, he and Ursicinus alone, after careers of great and continuous toil in the public service, had been treated with such contempt; the one, after being cruelly harassed by the judicial examination of his friends in a base dispute, had been summoned to be tried for treason, and the other had been brought back from the East and abandoned to the hatred of his enemies. This was his constant theme both privately and in public. Such talk alarmed us, because it was accompanied by clamorous complaints from the troops all around; they bewailed their destitute condition and were on fire to break through the passes of the Cottian Alps with the least possible delay.

In this state of perplexity we cast about in secret for a plan likely to effect our purpose, and at last, after many changes of mind from nervousness, we settled that we should use all our efforts to find discreet agents who could be sworn to secrecy, and who would work upon the minds of the Bracchiati and Cornuti, troops whose loyalty was apt to waver and who could be influenced in any direction by a handsome bribe. Some common soldiers, whose very obscurity made them suitable for our purpose, acted as intermediaries in the hope of a reward, and when the matter was arranged a band of armed men sallied out just as dawn was reddening the sky. They killed the guards, and, gaining confidence from this, as happens in moments of crisis, made their way into the palace, dragged Silvanus, who was on his way to a Christian service, from the shrine in which the panic-stricken man had taken refuge, and butchered him with repeated sword-thrusts.

Such was the end of a commander of no small merit, who was driven by fear of the slanders in which a hostile clique had ensnared him in his absence to adopt extreme measures in self-defence. He had a claim on the gratitude of Constantius for bringing his troops over to his side in the nick of time before the battle of Mursa, and he could point also to the services of his father Bonitus, who, though a Frank, had often played a gallant part on Constantine's side in the civil war against the adherents of Licinius, but he feared Constantius' uncertain and fickle temper. A further circumstance is that before any of this happened in Gaul the people in the Circus Maximus at Rome shouted aloud, 'Silvanus is vanquished!' Whether this was because of some report or from a premonition of the future is uncertain. The news that Silvanus, as I have related, had been killed at Cologne was received by the emperor with unutterable joy. Confirmed in his arrogance and pride he ascribed this too to his lucky star. Like Domitian before him he always hated heroes, and tried to get the better of them by any sort of opposition. So far from praising Ursicinus' adroit discharge of his mission, he even wrote that he had embezzled from the treasury in Gaul, which no one had touched. By way of investigating this he ordered Remigius, who at that time was in charge of finance at the headquarters of the commander-in-chief, to be narrowly questioned; this was the Remigius who much later, in the reign of Valentinian, hanged himself because of the scandal of the mission from Tripolis. When this was over, Constantius was exalted to the skies and adulated as the disposer of the fates of men in the extravagant language of his toadies, whose numbers he increased himself by the contempt with which he drove from him those unversed in this art. In the same way we read that Croesus drove Solon headlong from his kingdom because he did not know how to flatter; and Dionysius threatened the poet Philoxenus with death because, when the tyrant was reciting his own absurd and clumsy verses, Philoxenus alone listened in silence while the rest of the audience applauded. This pernicious custom is the nurse of vice. Praise should be welcome to the ears of the great only if an opening is also sometimes given to censure what has been done amiss.

6. *The execution of Silvanus' adherents.*

The restoration of control was followed by the usual trials, and many people suffered as criminals in chains and bondage. The hellish informer Paul came forward bubbling over with joy to exercise his poisonous arts with greater freedom, and, when the council and officers met at the emperor's command to investigate the affair, Proculus, a member of Silvanus' household, was put on the rack. He was frail and ailing, and it was feared that the effect of cruel torture on his feeble frame would be to make him incriminate a heterogeneous crowd of people. In the event, however, quite the reverse happened. By his own account of the matter he remembered a dream which forbade him to persecute an innocent man, and though he was tortured almost to death he did not betray the name of a single person, but steadfastly maintained that Silvanus alone was responsible for an enterprise to which he had been driven not by ambition but by necessity. For this he produced powerful evidence, asserting convincingly that a number of people could testify that four days before he assumed the imperial insignia Silvanus had made a payment to the troops in Constantius' name and exhorted them to be brave and loyal. It was clear that, if he had been contemplating at that time the assumption of a higher rank, he would have distributed so large a sum in his own name. After Proculus, Poemenius suffered the fate of the condemned; he was dragged to execution and perished. Poemenius, as I have previously related, had been chosen as the people's champion when Trier (Treveri) closed its gates against the Caesar Decentius. In addition, the counts Asclepiodotus, Lutto, and Maudio were put to death together with a number of others, who fell victims to the inflexible and tortuous methods then in use in an investigation of this sort.

7. Rome: prefecture of Leontius (A.D. 355–6).

In the midst of this storm of death and the collective executions to which it gave rise Leontius, the prefect of the Eternal City, gave many proofs of his excellence as a judge. He heard cases promptly and decided them impartially, and he was of a kindly nature, though some thought him severe and too much inclined to condemn in order to preserve his authority. The first incident that occasioned a demonstration against him was most trivial and insignificant. Orders had been given for the arrest of a charioteer called Philoromus, who was a particular pet of the mob; they followed him and launched a fearsome attack upon the prefect in the belief that he would be too timid to resist. Leontius, however, stood his ground; he set his constables upon the crowd, seized some persons and had them racked, and finally, without anyone daring to protest or oppose him, condemned them to exile on an island. A few days later the mob rioted again with its habitual violence over an alleged shortage of wine, and collected at a much-frequented spot called the Septemzodium, where the emperor Marcus built a Nymphaeum in a pretentious style. The prefect deliberately made his way to this place, in spite of the earnest entreaties of his civil and military attendants not to expose himself to an insolent and threatening crowd, still seething from the excitement of the previous incident. He was a hard man to frighten and kept straight on, with the result that part of his escort abandoned him, although he was running into manifest danger. Seated in his carriage apparently unmoved and fixing his keen gaze on the gangs of rioters as if they were so many snakes, he had to endure a storm of abuse, till finally he recognized a very tall, red-haired man towering above the rest and asked him if he had been rightly told that his name was Peter Valvomeres. When the man replied truculently that it was, Leontius, who already knew of him as the ringleader of the rioters, gave orders that he should be hoisted up to be flogged with his hands tied behind him. There was a shout of protest, but when Peter was seen trussed up his yells for help from his fellows proved vain; the whole mob, a moment before so tightly packed, scattered through the various quarters of the city and vanished, and the worst of the troublemakers, having been flogged as quietly as if he were in a prison cell, was banished to Picenum. There at a later date he had the audacity to rape a girl of good family, and was sentenced to death by the governor Patruinus.

During Leontius' administration Liberius the Christian bishop was summoned to appear before the imperial tribunal; his offence was resistance to the orders of the emperor and the decision of a majority of his brother bishops in a matter on which I will briefly touch. Athanasius, then bishop of Alexandria, who was persistently rumoured to have thoughts above his station and to be prying into matters outside his province, had been deposed from his office by an assembly of the adherents of the same faith, meeting as what they call a synod. It was alleged that, being deeply versed in the interpretation of oracular sayings and of the flight of birds, he had on several occasions foretold future events; he was also charged with other practices inconsistent with the principles of the faith of which he was the guardian. Liberius shared the views of his brethren, but when he was ordered by the emperor to sign the decree removing Athanasius from his priestly office he obstinately refused; he declared that it was entirely wrong to condemn a man unseen and unheard, and openly defied the emperor's wishes. Constantius, who was always hostile to Athanasius, knew that the sentence had been carried out, but was extremely eager to have it confirmed by the higher authority of the bishop of the Eternal City. Failing in this object, he just managed to have Liberius deported under cover of night. This was a matter of great difficulty because of the strong affection in which he was held by the public at large.

8. *Julian appointed Caesar.*

Events at Rome were as I have just related. But Constantius was disturbed by frequent messages about the desperate state of Gaul, which the barbarians were reducing to utter destruction unopposed. After long internal debate on how best to repel these troubles while he himself remained in Italy, which he wished to do because he thought it dangerous to remove to a distant region, he came at last to the right decision, and resolved to associate with himself in the imperial power his cousin Julian, whom he had recently sent for from Achaea, and who was still wearing his student's dress. When under the pressure of impending trouble he communicated his decision to his closest associates and declared openly, which he had never done before, that he could not sustain the burden of such heavy and repeated crises by himself any longer, they tried to turn his head by the flattery which they knew only too well how to apply, and maintained that there was no difficulty which his surpassing valour and the luck that raised him almost to the stars would not overcome, as it always had in the past. Several of them, who had a bad conscience about Julian, added that the title of Caesar should be avoided in future, and reminded Constantius of what had happened in the case of Gallus. Their persistent efforts encountered the solitary opposition of the empress; whether because she feared a journey to distant parts or because her native sagacity led her to consult the interest of the state, she urged that preference should be given to a kinsman above any other. So after much bandying of the matter in inconclusive discussions the emperor's decision stood; he dismissed further argument as pointless and resolved to confer the imperial power upon Julian. Julian came when he was sent for, and on the appointed day the emperor took his place on a high platform surrounded by eagles and standards in the presence of all the troops that were available. Taking Julian by the right hand, he addressed the assembly in calm tones as follows:

'We come before you, gallant guardians of the state, to plead a cause which is common to us all, and which it needs little short of unanimous resolution to defend. Before submitting it to your impartial judgement I will give a brief explanation. Since the death of the rebel usurpers, whose designs were inspired by rage and madness, the barbarians, as if to appease those unhallowed spirits with an offering of Roman blood, have disturbed the peace of our frontier and are ranging wantonly through Gaul, relying on the fact that harsh necessity requires our presence at the other end of the world. If, while there is still time, this mischief which is creeping forward over adjacent territory is countered by steps which have your and our united support, the swelling pride of these peoples will subside, and the frontiers of the empire will remain unviolated. It is for you to strengthen by your approval the hope for the future which I am nursing. You see before you Julian, who is as you know our cousin, and who is endeared to us as much by his tried discretion as by the bond of kinship; a young man, moreover, of conspicuously active temper. Him I desire to advance to the rank of Caesar, a proposal which needs to be ratified by your approval also, if you think fit.' Constantius was about to continue when the assembled troops respectfully interrupted, proclaiming with a kind of prevision of the future that this was a revelation of the will of God rather than of any human mind. The emperor remained motionless till they were silent, and then resumed his speech with increased confidence. 'Your joyful acclamations show that I have your approval. Let then this young man, in whom strength is matched by composure, and whose sober conduct I ask you to imitate rather than praise, come forward to receive an honour which can cause no surprise. The excellence of his disposition, fostered by a good education, is fully attested by the fact that my choice has fallen upon him. Now therefore, with the blessing of Heaven, I will put upon him the imperial robe.' With these words he clothed Julian in the purple of his ancestors, and declared him Caesar to the joy of the troops. Then, while Julian stood before him dejected and wearing a slight frown, he addressed him thus:

'Most beloved brother, you have attained while still young the distinction marked out for you by your ancestry, and this, I admit, increases my own glory, since to bestow power almost equal to my own upon a noble kinsman gives me a juster claim to be exalted than my power itself. Be then my partner in toil and danger, take upon yourself the government of Gaul, and bring relief to its afflicted regions by your generous treatment. If you have to meet the enemy in battle, post yourself firmly by the standards, watch for the right moment to encourage your men to an act of daring, keep up their spirit in the fight by taking the lead, though with circumspection. If they are in disorder, support them with reinforcements; calmly rebuke the slack, show yourself to heroes and cowards alike an impartial witness of their deeds. Go forth then in this hard time of trial to command men whose valour matches your own. We will help one another with undeviating mutual affection; we will wage war simultaneously, and if God grants our prayer we will reign together, equals in righteousness and mildness, over a world at peace. I shall feel that you are with me everywhere, and in whatever you undertake I shall not fail you. In a word, go, go with all speed, taking with you our united prayers, to defend with unsleeping vigilance a post to which you have been appointed, so to speak, by the state in person.'

At this conclusion none could keep silent; all the troops clashed their shields against their knees with a fearsome din. (This indicates complete approval, whereas to strike one's shield with one's spear is a sign of rage and grief.) With few exceptions they expressed prodigious joy at the choice of the Augustus, and evinced proper admiration for the Caesar, as he stood there blazing in the imperial purple. Gazing long and earnestly at eyes at once delightful and awe-inspiring, and a face to which animation added charm, they tried to deduce what sort of man he would prove to be; it was as if they were examining those old books which interpret physical characteristics as a revelation of the spirit within. To preserve the respect owed to the higher rank of the emperor, their applause of Julian neither exceeded nor fell short of what was due; in fact their sentiments were valued as expressions of critical judgement rather than soldierly enthusiasm. Finally, Julian took his seat with the emperor in his carriage and was conveyed to the palace, whispering to himself this line from Homer: 'Wrapped in death's purple by all-powerful fate.'

This took place on 6 November in the consulship of Arbitio and Lollianus. A few days later the Caesar was united in marriage to Helena, the unmarried sister of Constantius, and on 1 December, when all arrangements needed for an early departure had been made, he set out with a small suite. He was escorted by the Augustus as far as a spot marked by two columns between Laumellum and Pavia (Ticinum), from which he marched straight to Turin (Taurini). There he was shocked to receive bad news, which had reached the imperial court shortly before, but had been deliberately suppressed so as not to upset the preparations. It was that Cologne, the famous city of Lower Germany, had been taken by storm and destroyed by large forces of barbarians after an obstinate siege. This heavy blow went to Julian's heart; it seemed the first presage of disasters to come, and he was often to be heard complaining to himself that all he had achieved by his elevation was the prospect of perishing with more work on his hands. When he reached Vienne (Vienna), people of all ages and classes ran to greet his arrival as an answer to their prayers; they believed in his lucky star, and when they caught sight of him in the distance the whole population, reinforced from the country round about, went before him, chanting the praises of the gracious commander who would bring them prosperity. They gazed the more eagerly on his royal pomp because he was a lawful prince; they saw in his arrival the remedy for all their troubles, and felt that a guardian angel had appeared to shed light on their lamentable situation. It was on this occasion that a blind old woman asked who had arrived, and being told that it was the Caesar Julian, cried out: 'This is the man who will restore the temples of the gods.'

9. *The origin of the Gauls.*

Now, since, in the words of the sublime poet of Mantua, 'I am undertaking a grander task, and a grander theme opens before me', this seems the right moment to describe the regions and the topography of Gaul. Otherwise, by mixing matters of which some readers are ignorant with my account of fierce engagements and the varying fortunes of war, I may seem like those careless sailors who are driven in the midst of a storm at sea to patch up the damaged sails and rigging which they might have put in order in a period of calm. Early writers, in discussing the origin of the Gauls, have left us with very imperfect knowledge, but at a later date Timagenes, writing in his own tongue with all the thoroughness of a Greek, put together long-forgotten information from a variety of books. I shall rely on his authority and set this out clearly and distinctly in a manner free from all obscurity. Some writers have maintained that the first peoples known in these parts were indigenous, and were called Celts after a much-loved king, and Galatae, the Greek name for Gauls, after his mother; others assert that they were of Dorian origin, and followed an older Hercules to settle in regions bordering on the sea. The Druids declare that part of the population was in fact indigenous, but was joined by newcomers from remote islands and the country beyond the Rhine, who had been driven from their homes by frequent wars and the encroachments of a stormy sea. Others say that after the sack of Troy a few of those who were scattered everywhere in their flight from the Greeks occupied this region, which was then uninhabited. The inhabitants themselves strongly support a story which I have myself seen inscribed upon their monuments, that Hercules the son of Amphitryon made a hasty journey to destroy the cruel tyrants Geryon and Tauriscus, who were oppressing Spain and Gaul respectively, and that when he had overcome them both he formed unions with some women of good birth by whom he had several children, who gave their own names to the territories which they ruled. In fact, however, a people of Asiatic origin left Phocaea to escape the oppression of Harpalus, a satrap of king Cyrus, and came to Italy by sea; some of them founded Velia in Lucania, others Marseilles (Massilia) in the territory of Vienne, and in subsequent years as their strength increased a considerable number of other towns. I must, however, abstain from giving a variety of theories, since this is often cloying to the reader.

With the advance of civilization in these parts a taste for serious studies developed, encouraged by bards, seers, and Druids. The bards recited the exploits of heroes in epic verse, accompanied by the sweet strains of the lyre; the seers turned their attention to the skies and endeavoured to explain the mysteries of nature; while the Druids, who were of higher intellect, formed themselves into brotherhoods of the kind recommended by Pythagoras, rose above human concerns, which they despised, to the investigation of hidden and profound matters, and proclaimed the immortality of the soul.

Chapters on the geography of the Alps and Gaul (10 and 11) are omitted. See Map A.

12. *The character of the Gauls.*

Almost all Gauls are tall and fair-skinned, with reddish hair. Their savage eyes make them fearful objects; they are eager to quarrel and excessively truculent. When in the course of a dispute any of them calls in his wife, a creature with gleaming eyes much stronger than her husband, they are more than a match for a whole group of foreigners; especially when the woman, with swollen neck and gnashing teeth, swings her great white arms and begins to deliver a rain of punches mixed with kicks, like missiles launched by the twisted strings of a catapult. The voices of most sound alarming and menacing, whether they are angry or the reverse, but all alike are clean and neat, and throughout the whole region, and especially in Aquitaine, you will hardly find a man or woman, however poor, who is dirty and in rags, as you would elsewhere. They are fit for service in war at any age; old men embark upon a campaign with as much spirit as those in their prime; their limbs are hardened by the cold and by incessant toil, and there is no danger that they are not ready to defy. No one here ever cuts off his thumb to escape military service, as happens in Italy, where they have a special name for such malingerers (*murci*). As a race they are given to drink, and are fond of a number of liquors that resemble wine; some of the baser sort wander about aimlessly in a fuddled state of perpetual intoxication, a condition which Cato described as a kind of self-induced madness. There seems then to be some truth in what Cicero said in his defence of Fonteius, that 'henceforth the Gauls will take their drink with water, a practice which they used to think equivalent to taking poison'.

These regions, and especially those bordering on Italy, were gradually brought under the sway of Rome without much effort. The first attempt upon them was made by Fulvius; after that their strength was impaired by Sextius in several minor battles; finally they were thoroughly tamed by Fabius Maximus, whose success in defeating the tough tribe of the Allobroges completed the business and earned him the name of Allobrogicus. The whole of Gaul, except, as Sallust tells us, for the inaccessible marshy districts, was subdued by Caesar after ten years of fluctuating warfare, and attached to Rome by a treaty of perpetual alliance. I have allowed myself too long a digression, and I must now return to my main theme.

13. Development in the East.

After the cruel death of Domitian, Musonian succeeded him as prae-torian prefect in the government of the East. His command of both Greek and Latin won him a reputation which led to a career of unexpected distinction. Constantine, being in need of an interpreter in the course of his strict investigation into Manichaeism and similar heresies, had Musonian recommended to him as a suitable person, and appointed him to the post. His skilful discharge of this duty caused the emperor to change his name to Musonian (he was previously called Strategius), and from this beginning he rose through a number of career posts to the rank of prefect. He was a man of discretion whose rule the provinces found acceptable, and his manner was mild and urbane, but he seized any opportunity of gratifying a sordid love of gain, especially in judicial cases, where it is particularly disgraceful. This clearly manifested itself among other instances in the trials which followed the death of Theophilus, the governor of Syria, who was abandoned by the Caesar Gallus to be torn in pieces by a mob of rioters; a number of poor men who were known to have been elsewhere at the time of the incident were condemned, whereas the wealthy originators of this foul crime bought themselves off by the loss of their property.

Musonian was rivalled by Prosper, who was in command of the troops as deputy to the master of cavalry, who was still in Gaul. He was an arrant coward, who, as the comic poet (*Plautus*) says, thought it superfluous to employ art in his thievery and plundered openly.

These two were in league together, and enriched themselves by putting opportunities of profit in each other's way. Meanwhile the

Persian generals near the rivers, whose king was detained at the other end of his realm, kept our frontier in a state of turmoil by their predatory raids. They boldly invaded Armenia and on several occasions Mesopotamia, while the Roman commanders were engaged in despoiling their own subjects.

BOOK 16

1. Praise of the Caesar Julian (A.D. 356).

While fate was weaving this intricate web of events in the Roman world, the Caesar at Vienne, whom the Augustus had taken as his colleague in his own eighth consulship, was dreaming – such was his native energy – of the din of battle and the slaughter of the barbarians, and getting ready to restore the shattered fragments of the province, if fortune would only grant him a favourable wind. The great improvements which his valour and good luck enabled him to bring about in Gaul surpass many of the heroic actions of former times, and I shall therefore describe them one by one in due order. I intend to employ all the resources of my modest talent in the hope that they will prove adequate for the purpose. My narrative, which is not a tissue of clever falsehoods but an absolutely truthful account based on clear evidence, will not fall far short of a panegyric, because it seems that the life of this young man was guided by some principle which raised him above the ordinary and accompanied him from his illustrious cradle to his last breath. By a series of rapid steps he attained such distinction both at home and abroad that in sagacity he was reckoned the reincarnation of Titus the son of Vespasian, in the glorious outcome of his campaigns very like Trajan, as merciful as Antoninus, and in his striving after truth and perfection the equal of Marcus Aurelius, on whom he endeavoured to model his own actions and character. We are told by Cicero that great achievements are like trees, in the height of which we take more pleasure than in their roots and trunks; similarly the origins of this gifted nature were obscured by a number of overclouding circumstances, but ought in fact to be more regarded than his later wonderful exploits, seeing that he was brought up in seclusion like Erechtheus by Minerva, and that it was not from a soldier's tent but from the quiet shades of the Academy that he was drawn into the dust of battle, overthrew the

Germans, and, by spilling the blood of their ferocious kings or making them prisoners, brought peace to the valley of the freezing Rhine.

2. *Julian attacks and defeats the Alamanni.*

While he was passing a busy winter in Vienne he heard through one of the rumours which flew ceaselessly about that the barbarians had made a surprise attack upon the ancient city of Autun (Augustodunum), whose walls were of great extent but crumbling with age, and that while the troops stationed there remained inactive a body of veterans who were on the alert had rushed to its defence; it often happens that sudden perils are averted by the courage of despair. So, without any relief from his anxieties and ignoring the servile flattery of his suite, who tried to turn his mind towards pleasure and luxury, he made all necessary preparations and on 24 June arrived at Autun, intending like a seasoned commander of proved strength and sagacity to attack the barbarians, who were scattered over the country, as soon as an opportunity offered. At a council of war to consider the safest route, held with the assistance of men who knew the terrain, diverse opinions were expressed, some asserting that he should go by Sedelaucum and Cora and others *recommending a different route*. When, however, some added that Silvanus, recently master of infantry, had with considerable difficulty taken 8,000 auxiliary troops by a way which provided a short-cut but was dangerous because it lay through dark woods, the Caesar was on fire to imitate the example of this bold general. To avoid delay he took with him only the cuirassiers and artillerymen, an inadequate escort for a commander, and reached Auxerre (Autessiodurum) by Silvanus' route.

After a short halt to refresh himself and his men (it was never his habit to pause for long) Julian made his way towards Troyes (Tricasae). The barbarians hurled themselves upon him in successive bands; in some cases, when their superior numbers alarmed him, he did no more than close his ranks and keep an eye on the enemy; at other times he won an easy victory by descending on them from a point of vantage; some gave themselves up in panic, the rest took to flight as best they could and were allowed to get away unharmed, because he was hindered from pursuit by the weight of his equipment. At last, as his confidence grew in resisting their attacks, he accomplished his hazardous march to Troyes, where his arrival was so unexpected that when he was practically knocking at the gates the inhabitants, who lived in dread of the host of the barbarians spread about the country, opened them only after serious hesitation. After a brief halt to rest his tired troops, believing that speed was essential he set off for Reims (Remi), where he had ordered his forces to concentrate and wait for him. Reims was under the command of Marcellus, Ursicinus' successor, and Ursicinus himself had received orders to remain in the same area till the end of the campaign. After canvassing a number of possibilities Julian decided to attack the Alamanni by way of Decem Pagi, and the troops marched in that direction in close order with unusual spirit. The day was damp and grey, so that it was difficult to see even at close range; the enemy had the advantage of local knowledge and taking a cross route attacked two legions which formed the rearguard of the Caesar's army; they would almost have annihilated them if a sudden shout had not brought the allied troops to the rescue. From that time Julian, thinking that he could not cross roads or rivers without risk of an ambush, became cautious and deliberate, qualities which are of particular advantage in great generals and often enable them to relieve and preserve their armies. So hearing that the barbarians had occupied and were living on the territories of Strasbourg (Argentorate), Brumath (Brotomagum), Rheinzabern (Tabernae), Seltz (Saliso), Speyer (Nemetae), Worms (Vangiones), and Mainz (Moguntiacum) – they avoid the actual towns as if they were tombs surrounded by nets – he first of all seized Brumath. While he was approaching it he was met by a body of Germans who offered battle. Julian drew up his forces in a crescent formation, so that when battle was joined the enemy found themselves threatened on both sides; some were taken prisoner, others were cut to pieces in the very heat of the action, and the remainder scattered and took refuge in flight.

3. Julian recovers Cologne.

After this there was no resistance, and Julian decided to recover Cologne, which had been destroyed before he arrived in Gaul. In all that region there is no city or fort to be seen, except that near Koblenz (Confluentes), which is called after the confluence of the Moselle and the Rhine, there is a town called Remagen (Rigomagum), and near Cologne itself a single fort. So once he had entered Cologne he did not stir out until the kings of the Franks were cowed into submission and he could conclude a peace which would bring advantage to the state for a time, until he could get the city strongly fortified. Then, encouraged by these first-fruits of victory, he departed by way of Trier to spend the winter at the convenient town of Sens (Senones). He had to carry on his shoulders, as they say, the burden of a spate of wars, and to divide his attention between a number of problems: how to get the troops who had abandoned their usual posts back to the places which were threatened, how to scatter the tribes which had conspired to injure the name of Rome, and how to ensure that the army which was to be dispersed in different directions should not lack provisions.

4. Julian is besieged by the Alamanni in Sens.

While he was anxiously weighing these matters he was attacked by a horde of the enemy hoping to capture the town, and the more confident of doing so because deserters had betrayed the fact that he had with him neither the Scutarii nor the Gentiles; these had been dispersed in various towns for the convenience of victualling. So he shut the gates and strengthened the walls where they were weak. Night and day he was to be seen in person with his men on the ramparts and battlements, grinding his teeth with rage because the small numbers of the troops with him frustrated all his efforts to break out. After a month the barbarians withdrew dispirited, complaining that it had been futile and foolish to think of besieging a town. But a disgraceful feature of this affair was that Marcellus, the master of cavalry, who was stationed nearby, neglected to come to the help of the Caesar in peril; quite apart from the presence of the prince, he should have intervened with his forces to deliver the city from the hardships of a siege. Once this anxiety was relieved, the Caesar devoted all his efforts to ensuring that after such protracted toil his men should enjoy a period of rest; it could be only short, but it would be enough to recruit their strength. The region was in so destitute a state after frequent devastation that it could supply little in the way of food, but even this difficulty was overcome by his unfailing energy; he succeeded in inspiring the men with higher hopes of success, and embarked with confidence on the execution of his numerous plans.

5. The merits of Julian.

In the first place he imposed upon himself and practised strict self-discipline – no mean achievement. He behaved as if he were bound by the sumptuary laws which the Romans copied from the rhetrai or law code of Lycurgus. These were long observed at Rome, and when they were falling into disuse were gradually revived by the dictator Sulla, who agreed with Democritus in thinking that 'fortune provides a man's table with luxuries, virtue with only a frugal meal'. This point was also stressed by Cato of Tusculum, whose frugal way of life earned him the name Censorius. 'Great worry about food,' he said, 'implies great indifference to virtue.' Finally, though he constantly read the instructions which Constantius had written out for him with his own hand, as if he were sending a younger relative to the university, and in which he made very liberal provision for the expense of the Caesar's table, Julian forbade such delicacies as pheasant and sow's womb and udders to be ordered and served for him, and contented himself with the cheap food of the common soldiers, whatever it might be.

Another feature of his routine was that he divided the night into three periods, and gave one to sleep, one to business, and one to study. This is said to have been the practice of Alexander the Great, but Julian showed much greater resolution. Alexander used to keep his arm outside his bed over a bronze basin and hold a silver ball in his hand, so that when sleep came upon him and relaxed his muscles he might be awakened by the sound of its fall. Julian, however, needed no artificial aid to wake him whenever he willed. He always rose half-way through the night, not from a bed of down with a coverlet of shot silk, but from a rug and coarse blanket which the common people call 'sisurna'. Then he prayed in private to Mercury, who according to the theologians is the intelligence of the universe and the cause of activity in slower minds. In these austere conditions he dealt in detail with public business, and when he had finished this hard and important task turned to the improvement of his mind. The eagerness with which he pursued the sublime knowledge of first principles and sought nourishment for his soul in its ascent to ever loftier regions defies exaggeration; his learned studies took him through all the departments of philosophy. But the full and perfect knowledge which he acquired in these matters did not cause him to neglect more mundane subjects; he gave a reasonable degree of attention to poetry and rhetoric, as is shown by the pure and dignified style of his speeches and letters, and also to the complexities of domestic and foreign history. Furthermore, he knew Latin well enough to be able to discourse in it. If it is true, as various writers report, that king Cyrus and Simonides the lyric poet and Hippias of Elis, the most acute of the sophists, owed their retentive memory to drinking certain medicines, we must believe that Julian in his early manhood emptied a whole cask of the mnemonic potion, if such a thing was to be found. This then is the evidence of purity and virtue which his nights provided.

But what filled his days – his brilliant and witty talk, his exertions in preparing for battle or on the actual field, his large-minded and liberal reforms in civil administration – shall be related in detail as occasion arises. Being a prince as well as a philosopher he had to practise the rudiments of military training, and when he found himself learning the Pyrrhic march-step to the sound of the fife he would often call out the name of Plato and repeat the old proverb: 'Pack-saddles are put on the ox: they are no fit burden for me.' Once on an official occasion some members of the secret service were brought with others to his presence to receive a gift of money, and one of them took it in his two cupped hands, not, as etiquette requires, in a fold of his tunic. 'Secret servicemen,' said the emperor, 'are better at seizing than receiving.' The parents of a girl who had been raped appealed to him, and, when he sentenced the perpetrator of the offence to banishment, complained that he was treating them unfairly in not punishing him with death. 'The law,' he replied, 'may blame my clemency, but an emperor of merciful disposition should be above the law.' When he was setting out on a campaign and many appealed to him to redress their wrongs, he would send them to the provincial governors for a hearing; when he returned he would ask what had happened in each case, and be led by his native mildness to modify the punishments inflicted. Finally, to say nothing of the victorious battles in which he routed the barbarians, who often fell fighting to the last, the benefits which he conferred on impoverished Gaul when it was at the last gasp are most clearly illustrated by this fact: when he first arrived, he found that twenty-five gold pieces per head were exacted by way of tribute; when he left, seven sufficed to satisfy all demands. This was like bright sunshine breaking through dark clouds, and was greeted everywhere with dances of joy. Lastly, we know that up to the end of his reign and of his life he observed the useful principle of not remitting arrears of tribute by what are called indulgences. He knew that by doing so he would benefit only the rich, since everyone is aware that the poor are compelled to pay the whole sum due at the very beginning of a tax period, with no possibility of relief.

But while he was putting into effect these methods of government,

which should serve as a model to all good rulers, the fury of the
barbarians burst out more violently than ever. They were like wild
beasts which have acquired the habit of stealing their prey through the
neglect of the shepherds; even when a stronger guard is substituted
they do not desist, but continue their attacks upon flocks and herds,
maddened by hunger and regardless of their own safety. Just so the
barbarians, having consumed what they had plundered, were driven by
famine to renew their raids; sometimes they carried off a prize, at other
times they perished before they could make a capture.

6. *The consular Arbitio is accused and acquitted.*

These were the events of that year in Gaul, where a doubtful prospect
ended in a favourable issue. But at the court of the Augustus, Arbitio
was the object of howls of envy; it was asserted that in the expectation
of reaching the summit of power he had already equipped himself with
the insignia of empire, and a count called Verissimus raised a hideous
clamour against him, declaring publicly that he was not content with
having risen from the ranks to high military command, that this to him
seemed a mere trifle, and that he was aiming at the imperial throne.
Arbitio was particularly hounded by one Dorus, a former military
surgeon; I have already related how, on being promoted under Magnentius to the charge of protecting the treasures of Rome, Dorus accused
Adelphius, the urban prefect, of nursing improper ambitions. The
affair of Arbitio came to court, and when all the formalities were
in train and people were waiting to hear the charge proved, the
chamberlains, as persistent rumour had it, suddenly intervened. Without discussion those who had been arrested as accomplices were
released, Dorus vanished, and Verissimus fell silent, as suddenly as an
actor when the curtain comes down.

7. *The grand chamberlain Eutherius defends Julian; eulogy of Eutherius.*

At the same period Constantius, learning by hearsay that Marcellus
had failed to succour the Caesar when he was besieged at Sens, dismissed
him from the service and ordered him home. Marcellus, labouring
under a sense of great grievance, set on foot an intrigue against Julian,
in the confident hope of gaining the ear of the Augustus, who was always
ready to entertain an accusation. So when Marcellus left the army

Eutherius the grand chamberlain was sent straight after him to expose any fiction that he might concoct. Marcellus did not know this and shortly afterwards arrived at Milan, where he stormed and raged before the council like the liar and all but maniac that he was. Emphasizing his words with violent gestures, he accused Julian of arrogance and alleged that he was already preening his wings for a higher flight. While he was giving free rein to these inventions, Eutherius asked and was granted admission; he was told to speak his mind, and showed in moderate and respectful terms that the truth had been overlaid with lies. The fact was that while Marcellus was procrastinating, it was thought deliberately, the Caesar by his energy and alertness had repelled the barbarians who were besieging him at Sens, and Eutherius was ready to stake his own life that as long as he lived Julian would be a faithful servant to the man to whom he owed his promotion.

In this context I feel impelled to add a brief account of this same Eutherius. It may perhaps sound incredible, because if even Numa Pompilius or Socrates were to speak well of a eunuch and back their statements with an oath they would be accused of departing from the truth. But roses grow in the midst of thorns, and among wild beasts there are some that grow tame; so I will run over briefly the principal facts that are established about him. He was born in Armenia. His parents were free, but at an early age he was captured by members of a neighbouring hostile tribe, who castrated him and sold him to some Roman merchants, by whom he was brought to Constantine's palace. There, as he grew up, he displayed rectitude and intelligence. He received an education suitable to his condition, and showed outstanding acuteness in the study and solution of abstruse and thorny problems; he had a prodigious memory, and was so eager to be of service and so full of sound judgement that if the emperor Constans had followed the honourable and upright course which Eutherius, who was then of mature age, urged upon him, he would have committed no faults, or at the worst only such as were venial. In his position as chamberlain he sometimes rebuked even Julian for being wedded to Asiatic manners and in consequence frivolous.

Soon after withdrawing into retirement he was again summoned to the palace. He was calm and unusually consistent, and he cultivated the virtues of loyalty and moderation to such a degree that he was never charged with the betrayal of a confidence, unless it were to save another's life, or with the passion for gain which the rest of the courtiers exhibited.

Hence it came about that when he afterwards retired to Rome, where
he fixed his residence in old age, he carried a clear conscience about
with him and was cherished and loved by people of all classes, whereas
in general men of his kind look out for a secret retreat in which to enjoy
their ill-gotten wealth, and hide like creatures who hate the light from
the eyes of the multitude of those whom they have wronged.

Turning over the copious records of the past, I have not found any
eunuch with whom I could compare him. There were some in old times
who were loyal and honest, though very few, but their characters were
spotted in other ways. Mixed with the acquired or natural good qualities
which any of them possessed was rapacity, or contemptibly brutal
manners, or a propensity to inflict harm, or excessive obsequiousness
to the great, or the haughtiness which arises from the possession of
power. But a man so armed at all points as Eutherius I confess that I
have never read or heard of, and in saying this I rely on the ample
evidence available in our time. If some minute antiquarian should cite
against me the example of Menophilus, the eunuch of Mithridates king
of Pontus, let me remind him that nothing is known about Menophilus
except his heroic behaviour in a desperate crisis. The king in question,
having lost a great battle against the Romans under Pompey, fled to the
kingdom of Colchis, and left his grown daughter Drypetina, who was
gravely ill, in the care of Menophilus at the castle of Sinoria. The girl
completely recovered under medical treatment, and Menophilus was
doing his utmost to protect her for her father, when Mallius Priscus,
one of Pompey's lieutenants, laid siege to the fortress in which she
was kept. Menophilus, realizing that the garrison was contemplating
surrender, and fearing that it would bring shame on her father if the
girl survived to be captured and raped, killed her and then plunged his
sword into his own vitals. Now let me return to the point from which
I digressed.

8. Denunciations and slanders at Constantius' court. Greed of the courtiers.

After Marcellus had been foiled, as I have told, and had returned
to Sofia (Serdica), his place of origin, many shocking crimes were
committed at the Augustus' court on the pretext of protecting his
imperial majesty. If anyone consulted a soothsayer because he had
heard a shrewmouse squeak or met a weasel or encountered any similar
omen, or if he used an old wives' charm to relieve pain, a practice which

even medical authority allows, he was denounced through some agency which he could not guess, brought to trial, and punished with death.

About this time a native of Salona called Danus was accused by his wife, who wished merely to frighten him, of some trivial offences. Somehow or other Rufinus, who had kept his position as head of the praetorian prefect's staff by his servility, got to know her – Rufinus, as I have said, was the man who transmitted information from the agent Gaudentius which led to the death of Africanus, governor of Pannonia, and his guests. With his usual boastful talk he shamefully seduced this light woman, and then cajoled her into a dangerous plot. He persuaded her to accuse her innocent husband of treason by weaving a tissue of lies, and to allege that he and some accomplices had stolen and were concealing a purple pall from the tomb of Diocletian. Having set on foot this plan to involve many people in ruin, Rufinus in the expectation of bettering himself flew to the emperor's court to open his usual campaign of slander. When the affair was known, Mavortius, a man of high integrity who was then praetorian prefect, received orders to conduct a strict inquiry in conjunction with Ursulus, count of the largesses, who was also a person of commendable severity. The matter was magnified after the fashion of the age, but though several people were put to torture nothing was discovered, and the judges were wavering and in two minds when at last stifled truth regained her breath. Under the pressure of necessity the woman confessed that Rufinus was the author of the whole intrigue, and did not even suppress the fact of her foul adultery; whereupon the judges consulted the statutes and came with one mind to the just decision that both criminals should be condemned to death. At this news Constantius flew into a passion of grief, as if he had lost the one man on whom his own safety depended. He despatched a body of express riders to command Ursulus in threatening terms to return to court. *When he arrived an attempt was made to prevent him from vindicating the truth*, but Ursulus paid no attention to those who stood in his way and burst boldly into the emperor's cabinet, where he set out the facts in plain words which came from his heart. This confident behaviour stopped the mouths of flatterers and saved the prefect and himself from serious danger.

An incident then occurred in Aquitaine which attracted attention outside that province. An old rascal was invited to a sumptuous and elegant banquet of the kind that often takes place in those parts. He noticed that the servants had arranged the covers of the couches in such a way that their broad borders presented an unbroken surface of purple, and that the same was true of the table cloths. So he grasped the front part of his own cloak in each hand and folded it inwards so as to give his whole get-up the appearance of an imperial robe. This act ruined a rich estate.

By a similar exercise of malice a secret agent in Spain, who was likewise invited to a dinner, on hearing the slaves who were bringing in the lights at evening utter the customary formula 'May we prevail', gave a sinister interpretation to this traditional phrase and thereby destroyed a noble house.

Incidents of this kind became more and more frequent because Constantius was very nervous and always expecting to be attacked. In this he resembled Dionysius the famous Sicilian tyrant, who was led by this same failing to have his daughters taught the barber's trade, because he would not trust anyone else to shave him. The same Dionysius also enclosed the little building in which he used to sleep with a deep ditch crossed by a collapsible bridge; when he went to bed he dismantled the planks and pins, and took them with him, to be reassembled when he was going out at daybreak.

Those who had influence at court sounded these warnings of unrest like so many trumpets, in the hope of incorporating the property of the condemned with their own and finding opportunities for large depredations on the estates of their neighbours. There is clear documentary evidence that Constantine was the first to whet the appetite of his staff, but it was Constantius who crammed them with the marrow of the provinces. Under him the leading men of all classes were consumed by a passion for riches which knew no bounds and recognized no legal or moral restraint. Among the civilian officials, Rufinus the praetorian prefect took first place; among the military, Arbitio the master of cavalry; there were also the grand chamberlain Eusebius and the quaestor . . . , and in Rome itself the family of the Anicii, whose younger members, in an attempt to rival their ancestors, refused to be content with much greater possessions than their forebears.

9. *Negotiations for peace with the Persians.*

In the East the Persians, abandoning their previous policy of hand-to-hand fighting for one of theft and robbery, kept driving off prizes of men and cattle. Sometimes they got away with their loot by a surprise attack; sometimes they lost it through their inferior numbers; occasionally they were prevented from even catching sight of a possible haul. Musonian, however, the praetorian prefect, a man, as I have already said, with many good qualities, but venal and easily turned from the path of truth by a bribe, tried to get wind of the Persian plans through agents expert in deception and subterfuge; his confidant in such matters was Cassian, duke of Mesopotamia, a hardened veteran of many dangerous campaigns. The two of them, once they were assured by the unanimous reports of their spies that Sapor was at the furthest limit of his realm, where it was costing him much bloodshed to keep certain hostile tribes at bay, used some unknown soldiers to make a secret approach to Tamsapor, who commanded the Persians on our frontier. They suggested that, if he had an opportunity, he should urge the king by letter to make peace at last with the Roman emperor; once this was done he would be secure on one front and free to deal with his permanent enemies. Tamsapor acquiesced, and in reliance on their good faith reported to his king that Constantius was engaged in very formidable wars and begged for peace. A long time elapsed before this message reached the territory of the Chionitae and Euseni, where Sapor was spending the winter.

10. Constantius makes a state visit to Rome (A.D.357).*

While these arrangements were being made in the East and in Gaul to meet the needs of the time, Constantius, behaving as if the temple of Janus were shut and all his enemies overthrown, conceived a strong desire to visit Rome and celebrate the fall of Magnentius by a triumph to which he had no title, since it had been won by the spilling of Roman blood. He had not overcome in person any race that made war on him; no news had arrived that any had been defeated by the valour of his generals; he had added nothing to the empire; he had never been seen fighting at the head of his men or even in the front rank in moments of crisis. His object was simply to display his gold-inlaid standards and his brilliant retinue in a procession of inordinate length before the eyes of a populace that was living in peace and neither expected nor wished to see any such show. Perhaps he was unaware that the attendance of lictors had been enough for some of the earlier emperors in time of

* See map, Monuments of Rome, p. 500.

peace, and that in the heat of war, which forbids inaction, one of them had entrusted himself to a small fishing-boat at the height of a raging storm, another had followed the example of the Decii and vowed to sacrifice his life for the state, a third had personally made his way into the enemy's camp with some common soldiers, and several, in a word, had distinguished themselves by heroic deeds and left a glorious memory to be cherished by their descendants.

So in the second prefecture of Orfitus, when large funds had been laid out on the trappings of the show, Constantius passed through Ocriculum in tremendous state, escorted by a formidable body of troops. It was almost as if a campaign were in prospect, and the sight attracted the unwavering gaze of all beholders. As he approached the city he let his eye dwell without expression on the senators paying their humble duty and the venerable images of the patrician families. It did not occur to him as it had to Cineas, the celebrated envoy of Pyrrhus, that he was beholding an assembly of kings; his thought was rather that here was a place of sanctuary for the whole world, and when he turned towards the populace he was amazed to see in what numbers people of every race had flocked to Rome. His own appearance might have been designed as a show of strength to overawe the Euphrates or the Rhine; a double line of standards went before him, and he himself was seated on a golden car gleaming with various precious stones, whose mingled radiance seemed to throw a sort of shimmering light. Behind the motley cavalcade that preceded him the emperor's person was surrounded by purple banners woven in the form of dragons and attached to the tops of gilded and jewelled spears; the breeze blew through their gaping jaws so that they seemed to be hissing with rage, and their voluminous tails streamed behind them on the wind. On each side marched a file of men-at-arms with shields and plumed helmets, whose shining breastplates cast a dazzling light. At intervals were mailed cavalrymen, the so-called Ironclads, wearing masks and equipped with cuirasses and belts of steel; they seemed more like statues polished by the hand of Praxiteles than living men. Their limbs were entirely covered by a garment of thin circular plates fitted to the curves of the body, and so cunningly articulated that it adapted itself to any movement the wearer needed to make.

The emperor was greeted with welcoming cheers, which were echoed from the hills and river-banks, but in spite of the din he exhibited no emotion, but kept the same impassive air as he commonly wore before his subjects in the provinces. Though he was very short he stooped when he passed under a high gate; otherwise he was like a dummy, gazing straight before him as if his head were in a vice and turning neither to right nor left. When a wheel jolted he did not nod, and at no point was he seen to spit or to wipe or rub his face or nose or to move his hand. All this was no doubt affectation, but he gave other evidence too in his personal life of an unusual degree of self-control, which one was given to believe belonged to him alone. As for his habit throughout his reign of never allowing any private person to share his carriage or be his colleague in the consulship, as many deified emperors have, and many other similar customs which his towering pride led him to observe as if they had all the sanctity of law, I will pass them by because I am conscious that I have reported them as they occurred.

As soon as he entered Rome, the home of empire and of all perfection, he went to the Rostra and looked with amazement at the Forum, that sublime monument of pristine power; wherever he turned he was dazzled by the concentration of wonderful sights. After addressing the nobility in the senate-house and the people from the tribune he entered the palace amid many demonstrations of good will, and tasted the happiness which he had promised himself. On several occasions, when he held races in the Circus, he was amused by the witty sallies of the people, who kept their traditional freedom of speech without any loss of respect, and he himself took care to observe the proper forms. He did not, for example, as he did in other cities, allow the length of the combats to depend on his own will, but followed the local custom and left them to finish in their various ways as events dictated.

When he surveyed the different regions of the city and its environs, lying along the slopes and on level ground within the circle of the seven hills, it seemed to him that whatever his eye first lit on took the palm. It might be the shrine of Tarpeian Jupiter, beside which all else is like earth compared to heaven, or the buildings of the baths as big as provinces, or the solid mass of stone from Tibur that forms the amphitheatre, with its top almost beyond the reach of human sight, or the Pantheon spread like a self-contained district under its high and lovely dome, or the lofty columns with spiral stairs to platforms which support the statues of former emperors, or the temple of Rome or the Forum of Peace, the theatre of Pompey or the Odeum or the Stadium, or any of the other sights of the Eternal City.

But when he came to the Forum of Trajan, a creation which in my view has no like under the cope of heaven and which even the gods themselves must agree to admire, he stood transfixed with astonishment, surveying the gigantic fabric around him; its grandeur defies description and can never again be approached by mortal men. So he abandoned all hope of attempting anything like it, and declared that he would and could imitate simply Trajan's horse, which stands in the middle of the court with the emperor on its back. Prince Hormisdas, the Persian defector I have previously mentioned, who was near Constantius, remarked with oriental subtlety: 'First, your majesty, you must have a similar stable built, if you can; the horse you propose to fashion should have as much space to range in as this which we see.' This same Hormisdas, being asked what he thought of Rome, replied that only one thing about it gave him pleasure, the discovery that there, too, men were mortal. The emperor then, after viewing many sights with awe and amazement, complained of the weakness or malice of common report, which tends to exaggerate everything, but is feeble in its description of the wonders of Rome. So after much deliberation he determined to add to the beauties of the city by setting up an obelisk in the Circus Maximus. I will describe its provenance and appearance in the proper place.

Meanwhile Constantius' sister Helena, the Caesar Julian's wife, who had been summoned to Rome with a show of affection, fell a victim to the arts of the empress Eusebia. Eusebia had been childless all her life, and she treacherously prevailed on Helena to take an unusual drug, which would have the effect of causing a miscarriage whenever she conceived. She had already made her lose a male child in Gaul. The device she then employed was to bribe the midwife to kill the baby as soon as it was born by cutting the umbilical cord too short. So carefully was it contrived that the bravest of men should be childless.

The emperor would have liked to stay longer in the grandest of all cities to enjoy unalloyed ease and pleasure, but he was alarmed by frequent reliable reports that the Suebi were attacking the two provinces of Raetia and the Quadi Valeria, and that the Sarmatians, who are particularly expert marauders, were devastating Upper Moesia and Lower Pannonia. This news caused him to leave Rome on 29 May, a month after his arrival, and to hurry into Illyricum by way of Trent (Tridentum). From Trent he sent Severus, a veteran of ripe experience in war, to succeed Marcellus, and ordered Ursicinus to rejoin him. Ursicinus was pleased to receive this order and came to Sirmium with his staff. After much debate about the possibility reported by Musonian of making peace with the Persians, Ursicinus was sent back to the East as commander-in-chief. The older members of our company were promoted to commands; the younger, of whom I was one, were told to attend on Ursicinus and be ready to perform any task that he imposed on us in the service of the state.

11. Campaign of Julian against the Alamanni.

The Caesar Julian passed a troubled winter at Sens. Then, in his own second and the Augustus' ninth consulship, at a time when he was exposed on all sides to noisy threats from the Germans, he marched briskly towards Reims. The omens were favourable, and what particularly encouraged him was that the command had now passed to Severus, who was neither factious nor arrogant and who had demonstrated his worth over a long period of service; he followed Julian, who was marching straight ahead, like an obedient soldier. From another direction Barbatio, who had been promoted master of infantry after the death of Silvanus, brought 25,000 men from Italy to Augst at the emperor's orders. Preparations had been made in pursuance of a deliberate plan to ensure that the Alamanni, who were being exceptionally aggressive and pushing their raids further than usual, should be squeezed into a narrow space by a pincer movement of our two armies and cut to pieces. While this plan was being translated into rapid action, the Laeti, a tribe quick to seize any opportunity of plunder, slipped unseen between our two armies and made a surprise attack on Lyons (Lugdunum). They would have sacked it and burned it to the ground if they had not been checked by finding the gates closed; whereupon they laid waste whatever they could find outside the town. At the news of this catastrophe the Caesar came to a quick decision to send three crack squadrons of light cavalry to watch the three routes by which he knew that the marauders must certainly make their escape. This move was successful; all who took these tracks were slaughtered and all their loot was recovered intact. Only those got away unharmed who made their way undisturbed past the rampart of Barbatio's camp. They were enabled to slip by because the tribune Bainobaudes and Valentinian the future emperor, who had been allotted this task with the squadrons under their command, were forbidden by Cella, the tribune of the Scutarii, who had joined the campaign as Barbatio's colleague, to guard the road by which they learnt that the Germans would withdraw. Not content with this, the master of infantry, who was a coward and indefatigable in disparaging Julian's exploits, knowing that the orders which he had given were injurious to the Roman cause (Cella confessed as much when he was charged with it), sent a false report to Constantius that these same two tribunes had been sent on the pretext of duty to tamper with the troops under his command. For this they were cashiered and returned home as civilians.

At the same period the barbarians who had settled on our side of the Rhine were alarmed by the approach of our forces. Some of them cut down enormous trees and cleverly blocked the roads, which were difficult in any case and naturally steep. Others occupied the islands with which the course of the Rhine is liberally studded, and hurled abuse at the Romans and the Caesar in a chorus of wild and doleful yells. Enraged by this and hoping to catch some of them, Julian asked Barbatio for seven of the vessels which he had procured in order to span the river by a bridge of boats, but Barbatio, determined that Julian should get nothing from him, burnt them all. Finally, Julian, learning from some scouts who had just been captured that since it was now high summer the river was fordable, encouraged a body of light-armed auxiliaries under Bainobaudes, the tribune of the Cornuti, to attempt an exploit which would bring them renown if luck was on their side. Wading through the shallows and at times supporting themselves on their shields and swimming, they reached a nearby island, where they landed and slaughtered everyone they found like sheep, without distinction of age or sex. Then, finding some empty boats, they went on in them, rickety though they were, and forced their way through a number of similar places. Finally, when they were sick of slaughter, they all returned safe with a rich haul of loot, though some was carried away by the force of the stream. On hearing of this the rest of the Germans, realizing that islands offered inadequate protection, conveyed their families and stores and primitive treasure to the further bank of the Rhine.

Julian next turned to the task of repairing the fortifications of the strong-point known as Saverne (Tres Tabernae) which the enemy had recently destroyed by a determined attack. Its rebuilding guaranteed that the Germans could no longer penetrate, as they had been used to do, into the heart of Gaul. He finished this work sooner than expected, and stocked it with a whole year's provision for the garrison which was to be stationed there. This was collected, not without some risk, from the enemies' crops, and, not content with this, he gathered food for twenty days for himself as well. The troops felt particular satisfaction in using what their own hands had won. They were deeply incensed because they had received nothing from a convoy recently sent to them. Barbatio had arrogantly appropriated part of this as it passed near him, and then heaped up and burnt what he did not want. Whether this was the effect of his own pride and folly, or whether it was the emperor's orders which led him to commit so many monstrous acts, is even now an unresolved question. A rumour, however, was generally current that Julian had been appointed, not to relieve the distresses of Gaul but to ensure his own destruction in a fierce war, while he was still supposed to be a novice, unlikely to be able to stand even the noise of arms.

While the fortifications of the camp were rapidly rising, and the troops were engaged partly in occupying advanced posts in the country about, partly in collecting corn with due precautions against an ambush, a host of barbarians, moving with such speed as to outstrip any news of their approach, made a sudden assault upon Barbatio and his army, which, as I have said, lay at a distance from the Gallic camp. They routed him and pursued him to Augst and as far beyond as they could, and then returned home after capturing the greater part of his baggage train together with its drivers. Barbatio, behaving as if his campaign had ended in success, distributed his troops in winter quarters and, true to form, returned to the court to frame some charge against the Caesar.

12. *Julian attacks and routs the barbarians at Strasbourg.*

When the news of this shameful stampede got abroad, Chnodomar and Vestralp, kings of the Alamanni, as well as Urius and Ursicinus together with Serapio and Suomar and Hortar, collected their whole strength together and advanced towards the city of Strasbourg, believing that the Caesar had retreated for fear of the worst, when in fact he was engaged at that moment in perfecting his defences. These chiefs held their heads high and acted with increased confidence because a deserter from the Scutarii, who had come over to them after the departure of his defeated general to avoid punishment for an offence, informed them that Julian was left with only thirteen thousand men, the number in fact of the troops that were with him. Their natural ferocity roused in them generally a mad lust for battle, and the repeated assertions of the deserter raised their confidence still higher. So they sent envoys to the Caesar to bid him in an imperious tone to evacuate the territory which they had won by their own valour at the point of the sword. But Julian, who did not know the meaning of fear, showed neither anger nor distress. He laughed at the insolence of the barbarians and detained their envoys till his fortifications were completed, adhering unfalteringly to the resolute stand which he had taken.

King Chnodomar, however, was causing universal turmoil and confusion, and making himself felt everywhere by his ceaseless activity. He was the first in any dangerous enterprise; his pride was overweening and was inflated by several successful exploits. He had defeated the Caesar Decentius in a battle fought on equal terms, he had destroyed and sacked many rich towns, and for a long time ranged at will through Gaul with none to oppose him. The recent flight of a Roman commander, who was his superior in numbers and strength, served to fortify his belief in himself. The Alamanni had learnt from the devices on the Roman shields that the men who had given ground before a small band of marauders were the same as those for fear of whom they had on several occasions scattered with heavy losses without joining battle. This situation was a source of great anxiety to the Caesar, who, after losing his partner in danger, found himself compelled by sheer necessity to encounter teeming tribes with few, though picked, troops.

Now, as the sky grew red with the rising sun and the trumpets brayed in unison, the infantry were set in motion at a slow pace. Their flank was covered by squadrons of cavalry, among whom were cuirassiers and mounted archers, a formidable arm of the service. The distance from the Romans' starting-point to the barbarians' entrenchment was reckoned to be fourteen leagues or twenty-one miles. So the Caesar, with a wise regard for the benefit and safety of his army, recalled the skirmishers who had gone ahead, and, giving the usual order for silence, gathered his men round him by companies and addressed them in the relaxed tone which was natural to him:

'Comrades, I will explain as briefly as possible that it is regard for our common safety and not any loss of heart which prompts me, your Caesar, to beg you, confident though you are in your stout and tried valour, to choose the path of caution rather than of haste and risk in meeting or repelling what we have to expect. It is right that warriors should be active and bold in situations of danger, but they should also, when occasion requires it, be obedient and deliberate. I will tell you briefly my opinion, and I hope that you will go along with it, in spite of your justifiable impatience. It is already nearly mid-day; we are tired by our march, and the paths which we have to take will be rough and dark; the moon is waning and there will be no stars to light up the night; the country before us is burnt up by the heat and entirely devoid of water. Even if these difficulties could be easily surmounted, what are we to do when we meet the attack of the enemy's hordes, who will be rested and refreshed by food and drink? What strength shall we have to encounter them when we are worn out by hunger, thirst, and toil? But even the most difficult problems have often been solved by the exercise of foresight, and more than once sound advice taken in good part has miraculously rectified a dangerous position. I propose therefore that we set a watch and rest here, where we are protected by a rampart and ditch; then, at first light, after an adequate allowance of sleep and food, let us, God willing, advance our eagles to triumph and our standards to victory.'

The troops did not allow him to finish what he was saying. Grinding their teeth and clashing their spears against their shields to show their eagerness for battle, they begged him to lead them against an enemy who was already in sight. They relied on the help of Heaven, on their own morale, and on the tried abilities of a general who was the favourite of fortune. As the event showed, some guardian angel must have inspired them to fight while he was there to assist them. Their enthusiasm was supported by the full approval of the higher command, and especially of Florentius the praetorian prefect. He urged that, though there was a risk in joining battle, that risk must be accepted while conditions were favourable and the barbarians were in one mass; if they dispersed it would be impossible to control the anger of the troops, whose native impetuosity made them apt to mutiny, and who would not, in his opinion, endure to see victory snatched from their grasp without resorting to desperate measures. A two-fold consideration which added to the confidence of our men was this. In the year just passed, when the Romans were ranging at large in the lands beyond the Rhine, no one appeared to defend his home or to offer resistance; the barbarians, having blocked all the paths with a dense barrier of felled trees, kept at a distance through all the miseries of a freezing winter, and when the emperor himself entered their territory they obtained terms of peace by humble entreaties without daring to resist or show themselves. But no one noticed that the situation had now changed. Previously they had

had to face destruction from three sides; the emperor was pressing them
on the Raetian front, the Caesar, who was nearest them, prevented them
from slipping away in any direction, and their neighbours, with whom
they had quarrelled, almost had their necks beneath their heel, so that
they were beset on all hands. Now, however, the emperor had made
peace with them and departed; they were on good terms with the
neighbouring tribes, with whom they had composed their quarrel; and
the disgraceful withdrawal of a Roman general had further whetted
their natural ferocity. In addition, the difficulties of the Romans were
compounded by the following circumstance. The two royal brothers
who were bound by the terms of the peace obtained from Constantius
in a previous year had not ventured to create a disturbance or make any
move. But shortly afterwards one of them, Gundomad, the stronger
and more trustworthy of the two, was treacherously murdered. All his
people threw in their lot with our enemies, and the subjects of Vadomar –
against his will, by his own account – at once joined forces with the
barbarians who were clamouring for war.

So, when all ranks from the highest to the lowest showed, without
any weakening whatever of their resolve, their feeling that this was the
right moment to fight, a standard-bearer suddenly shouted: 'Follow,
Caesar, the guidance of your lucky star. You are fortune's darling, and
in you we see that valour and judgement are at last combined. Give us
a lead, like the lucky and brave warrior that you are. With Heaven's
blessing you shall see what your men can do under the eye of a warlike
general who is inseparable from them, when their blood is up.' These
words put an end to all delay; the army moved forward and reached a
gently sloping hill, covered with crops already ripe, a short distance
only from the banks of the Rhine. On its top the enemy had stationed
three mounted scouts, who went off at a gallop to announce the sudden
approach of the Roman army. But one man on foot, who could not keep
up with them, was captured through the nimbleness of our men, and
revealed that the Germans had been crossing the river for three days
and nights. When our commanders saw them a short way off forming
themselves into dense wedges, they halted. The vanguard with their
standard-bearers and junior officers made as it were an impregnable
wall, and the enemy showed like caution and stood still in their
formations. When, as they had already been told by the deserter that I
have mentioned, they saw all our cavalry drawn up on our right flank,
they massed all their strongest mounted men on their own left flank,

interspersed with light-armed men on foot, whose use was dictated by considerations of safety. They knew that for all his skill a mounted warrior meeting one of our cuirassiers, and using one hand to hold his reins and shield and the other to brandish his spear, could inflict no harm on an opponent dressed in mail, whereas in the heat of the fight, when a man is occupied solely with the danger that stares him in the face, someone on foot, creeping along unnoticed close to the ground, can stab a horse in the flank, bring his rider headlong to the ground, and finish him off without difficulty. Having made these dispositions they also stationed troops in ambush on their right flank to effect a surprise.

All these warlike and savage tribes were led by Chnodomar and Serapio, whose power exceeded that of the other kings. Chnodomar, whose pernicious influence was responsible for the whole war, rode with a flame-coloured plume on his head before the left wing, where he thought the battle would be hottest. He was a bold fighter, confident in the strength of his own right arm, and his huge bulk towered aloft on his foaming steed, ready to hurl a javelin of appalling size. His gleaming armour marked him out from the rest, and his energy as a soldier was equalled by his pre-eminence as a commander. The right wing was led by Serapio, a young man whose cheeks still carried a growth of down but who was capable beyond his years. He was the son of Mederich, Chnodomar's brother, a man who had been utterly faithless all his life. He owed his name to the fact that his father, who was initiated into certain Greek mysteries during a long period as a hostage in Gaul, changed his son's name to Serapio from that of Agenarich, which he had been given at birth. These two were followed by the next most powerful kings, five in number, by ten princes and a long train of nobles, and by an army of 35,000 men drawn from various peoples, some of whom served as mercenaries and the rest in accordance with pacts of mutual assistance.

Now, while the trumpets were sounding their fearful note, Severus, who commanded the Roman left wing, came in his advance near trenches packed with troops; they had been hidden there with the idea of throwing everything into disarray by a sudden sally. Severus halted without any sign of fear, and, suspecting an ambush, neither withdrew nor attempted to advance further. The Caesar, whose spirit was equal to the gravest dangers, grasped the situation. He had with him an escort of 200 cavalry, as the importance of the occasion required, and he urged on the columns of infantry with words and gestures to lose no time in launching an attack at several points. He could not address them in a body because of the wide extent of the front and the large numbers involved; another reason for not doing so was fear of the odium which he would incur by adopting a course which the Augustus regarded as his own prerogative. So, without thought for his own safety, he flew along the lines within range of the enemy and encouraged his men, known and unknown alike, to deeds of valour with words like these: 'Now, comrades, the moment to fight has come, the moment which you and I have longed for, the moment to which you clamoured to be brought just now, when you impatiently called for battle.' Similarly, when he came to those who were posted behind the standards in the extreme rear, he shouted: 'Companions in arms, the long-hoped-for day is here when we must all wipe out previous stains and restore its proper glory to the majesty of Rome. These are the barbarians whose rage and unbridled folly have led them to meet our forces in an encounter which must end in their destruction.' Again, when he was making some adjustment in the battle order of other troops whose fighting skill was based on long experience, he encouraged them by saying: 'Up, my heroes; our courage shall dispel the disgrace inflicted on our cause; it was the thought of this which led me, after much hesitation, to accept the title of Caesar.' But to those who were clamouring for battle thoughtlessly, and who he saw might frustrate his plan by their impatience, he said: 'Do not, I beg you, impair the victory that awaits us by being too eager in pursuit of the enemy we have to rout, and do not give ground except in the last extremity. Be in no doubt that I shall leave all who flee to their fate, whereas nothing shall divide me from those who smite the enemy in the back, provided they show proper judgement and caution.'

With frequent repetition of words of this kind he deployed the greater part of his army opposite the front rank of the barbarians. Suddenly an indignant shout was heard among the infantry of the Alamanni. They demanded with one voice that the princes should abandon their horses and take their stand with them: they were afraid that in the event of defeat their leaders would have an easy means of escape and leave their wretched followers in the lurch. When he learned of this, Chnodomar at once jumped down from his mount, and the rest followed his example without hesitation. None of them doubted that victory would be theirs.

When the traditional signal to engage was sounded on both sides, a violent battle ensued. After a short exchange of missiles the Germans rushed forward with more haste than caution, brandishing their weapons and throwing themselves upon our squadrons of horse with horrible grinding of their teeth and more than their usual fury. Their hair streamed behind them and a kind of madness flashed from their eyes. Our men faced them stubbornly, protecting their heads with their shields, and trying to strike fear into the foe with drawn swords or the deadly javelins that they brandished. At the very crisis of the battle, when our cavalry were bravely regrouping and the infantry were stoutly protecting their flanks with a wall of serried shields, thick clouds of dust arose and the fight swayed this way and that. At one moment our men stood firm, at the next they gave way, and some of the most experienced fighters among the barbarians tried to force their foes backward by the pressure of their knees. Obstinately they struggled, hand to hand and shield to shield; the welkin rang with the shouts of the victors and the screams of the wounded. But while our left wing, moving in close order, had thrown back by main force the columns of Germans which assailed it, and was advancing in fury upon the barbarians, our cavalry on the right unexpectedly gave way in disorder. The first to flee, however, blocked the path of those who followed, and when they found themselves safe in the lap of the legions they halted and renewed the fight. What caused this incident was that, while their ranks were being re-dressed, the cuirassiers saw their commander slightly wounded and one of their comrades slipping over the neck of his horse, which sank under the weight of his armour. They then began to shift each for himself, and would have created total confusion by trampling on the infantry, had not the latter, who were drawn up in very close order, held their ground. The Caesar, seeing from a distance his cavalry turning to flight, put spurs to his horse and threw himself in their path. He was recognized by the purple dragon attached to the tip of a long lance and streaming on the wind like the cast skin of a snake, and the tribune of the squadron stopped and turned back, pale and trembling, to renew the fight. The Caesar took the course usual in moments of crisis, and addressed the men in terms of mild reproach: 'Where are we off to, my brave fellows? Don't you know that flight never saved anyone? It is simply a proof of the folly of a vain enterprise. Let us return to our comrades, and at least have a share in their glory, even though we have thoughtlessly abandoned them in their fight for our country.' This tactful speech brought them all back to their duty. Allowing for some differences, it followed the example set by Sulla in times past. In a pitched battle against Archelaus, the general of Mithridates, Sulla was becoming exhausted by the violence of the struggle and found himself deserted by all his troops. He rushed to the front rank, seized a standard, and hurled it towards the enemy. 'Be off,' he shouted, 'you whom I picked to share my danger, and when you are asked where you left your general answer truthfully: "fighting alone in Boeotia and shedding his blood for us all".'

Then the Alamanni, having defeated and scattered our cavalry, attacked the front line of our infantry, intending to break their will to resist and to put them to flight. But when they came to close quarters the issue remained long in doubt. The Cornuti and Bracchiati, veterans long experienced in war, intimidated the enemy by their bearing and put all their strength into their famous war-cry. This is a shout which they raise when a fight is actually at boiling-point; it begins with a low murmur and gradually increases in volume till it resounds like the sea dashing against a cliff. Volleys of javelins flew hissing through the air from both sides. A uniform cloud of dust arose and obscured the field, in which arms were hurtling against arms and bodies against bodies. The barbarians lost all order; their rage and fury blazed like fire, as they set themselves to cleave asunder with repeated sword-strokes the shields, closely interlaced in tortoise formation, which protected our men. Seeing what was happening the Batavians, a redoubtable body, came at the double together with the regiment called Kings to help their comrades, and to extricate them, if luck was on their side, from the desperate situation in which they were entrapped. The trumpets sounded a harsh note as they fought with redoubled energy. But the Alamanni, hurling themselves into the fight, strove like inspired madmen to destroy everything before them. Yet the hail of darts and javelins and the volleys of iron-tipped arrows did not slacken, although blade was clashing on blade in hand-to-hand conflict, breastplates were split asunder by sword-blows, and wounded men who still had some blood left rose from the ground to attempt some further exploit. In a sense it was a battle of equals. The Alamanni had the advantage of strength and height, the Romans of training and discipline. One side was wild and turbulent, the other deliberate and cautious. Our men relied on their courage, the enemy on their prodigious physique. Often, however, a Roman who had been overwhelmed by the weight of the enemy's arms would rise up again, while a barbarian whose legs had given way from fatigue would bend his left knee as he sank to the ground and continue to attack his foe, a proof of supreme resolution.

Suddenly there leapt forward, burning for the fight, a troop of notables which included even the kings. With their men behind them they burst upon our line and forced their way as far as the legion of Primani, which was stationed at the centre of our position, in the formation which is known as 'praetorian camp'. Here our troops were drawn up in close formation and in several ranks. They stood as firm as towers and renewed the battle with increased spirit. Taking care to avoid being wounded and covering themselves like gladiators, they plunged their swords into the barbarians' sides, which their wild rage left exposed. The enemy, who were ready to squander their lives for victory, tried repeatedly to find weak spots in the fabric of our line. As they perished one after another and the confidence of the Romans who were striking them down increased, fresh hosts took the place of the slain, till the incessant cries of the dying stupefied them with fear. Then at last they gave way under the stress of disaster and put all their energy into attempts at flight. In their haste to get away they took various paths, like the crew and passengers of a wreck in a storm at sea, who are eager to get to land wherever the wind carries them. Anyone who was present will vouch that they had more reason to pray than to hope for escape.

The favour of a beneficent providence was on our side. Our men hacked at the backs of the retreating foe, and when, as sometimes happened, their swords bent and they had nothing to strike with, they seized the weapons of the barbarians and thrust them into their vitals. None could be found whose rage was glutted with blood, none whose right hand grew weary with repeated slaughter, none who had pity on a man who begged for mercy. So a great number lay mortally wounded, praying for the relief of a speedy death. Others, half-dead and hardly able to breathe, sought to catch a last glimpse of the light with their dying eyes. Some had their heads severed by pikes as massive as beams, so that they hung merely by the throat; others, who had slipped in the blood of their comrades on the muddy and treacherous ground, were suffocated under the heaps of bodies which tumbled on them, and died without receiving any wound. At this highly successful outcome our victorious troops pressed on still more strongly: their weapons were blunted by incessant use, and gleaming helmets and shields rolled underfoot. At last the barbarians, driven to extremity and finding their escape blocked by high heaps of corpses, resorted to the only expedient left, the river which was almost touching their backs. Under the pressure tirelessly maintained by our troops in spite of the weight of their arms, some of the fugitives, believing that they could escape because they could swim, entrusted their lives to the waves. This caused the Caesar, who saw in a flash what was likely to ensue, to give peremptory orders, which were repeated by the tribunes and superior officers, forbidding any of our men to plunge into the eddying stream in over-eager pursuit of the foe. The order was obeyed and our men stood on the bank, transfixing the Germans with missiles of various kinds. Any of the latter who were quick enough to escape death in this form were carried to the bottom by the weight of their own bodies. The scene now resembled a stage show, when the curtain reveals some wonderful spectacle. Henceforth one could watch in perfect security some who could not swim clinging to strong swimmers, others floating like logs when they were left behind by their faster companions, others again being swept away and swallowed by the raging stream as if it had a personal spite against them. Some, supported on their shields, avoided the steep walls of water which met them by taking an oblique course, and after many a narrow escape succeeded in reaching the opposite bank. The discoloured river, foaming with barbarian blood, was lost in wonder at this strange addition to its waters.

Meanwhile king Chnodomar, finding a chance to escape by slipping through the heaps of slain with a few attendants, made his way in great haste to the camp which he had been bold enough to establish near the Roman fortifications of Tribunci and Concordia. His plan was to embark on some boats which he had long kept in readiness for an emergency, and hide himself in a secret refuge. Since he could reach his own territory only by crossing the Rhine, he hid his face for fear of recognition and retreated gradually. He was already near the bank and making a detour round an inlet flooded with marsh water, with the idea of crossing the river, when his horse slipped on the soft and sticky ground and threw him. Although he was fat and heavy he extricated himself at once and took refuge on a hill nearby. There he was recognized – the high station which he had occupied made it impossible for him to conceal his identity – and a cohort with its tribune came after him in breathless haste and surrounded his position on the wooded height. They acted with caution and did not attempt to break through, for fear of being caught in an ambush in the gloom of the thicket. At the sight of them Chnodomar was reduced to utter panic, and came out of the wood alone and gave himself up. His attendants to the number of 200, together with three very close friends, also surrendered, considering it a disgrace to survive their king or not to die for him if the occasion required it. Chnodomar, like all barbarians, was as submissive in disaster as he was the opposite in success; finding himself in another's power he was dragged along pale and dismayed, speechless from consciousness of his crimes, a different being from the man who after a course of wild and deplorable outrages trampled upon the ashes of Gaul and uttered a string of savage threats.

At the close of day, when the favour of heaven had brought the battle to this successful end, the troops reluctantly obeyed the signal to return and pitched their camp near the bank of the Rhine, where they were protected by several rows of pickets and able to enjoy food and sleep. The Romans had lost 243 men and four officers, Bainobaudes, tribune of the Cornuti, together with Laipso, Innocentius, who commanded the cuirassiers, and an unattached tribune whose name I do not know. Of the Alamanni, however, 6,000 bodies were counted lying on the field, not to mention the masses of dead carried off by the river, whose number cannot be reckoned. Julian, who had shown himself a man whose merits were above his position, and whose authority was based more on his deserts than on his rank, was now hailed as Augustus by the unanimous voice of the whole army. But he rebuked the troops for this thoughtless behaviour, and solemnly affirmed with an oath that this was an elevation which he neither expected nor desired. To add to the general joy at this happy outcome he ordered Chnodomar to be brought before him *in the presence of the assembled troops.* Chnodomar first bowed low and then prostrated himself on the ground in an attitude of supplication, begging for forgiveness in his native tongue. Julian told him to take heart. A few days later he was taken to the emperor's court and from there sent to Rome, where he fell into a lethargy and died in the barracks assigned to foreign troops on the Caelian Hill.

When all these efforts had been crowned by success some of Constantius' courtiers sought to please the emperor either by finding fault with Julian or by referring to him ironically as Victorinus, because in his modest reports of his conduct of his command he often mentioned that the Germans had been defeated. By frequent repetition of empty praise and a vain parade of facts which were obvious they inflated Constantius' natural self-conceit after their usual manner, ascribing to his lucky star any success in any corner of the world. This big talk by his toadies encouraged him to set forth in the edicts which he published then and later a number of arrogant lies; though he had not been present himself at an action, he often declared that he alone had fought and conquered and inclined a merciful ear to the entreaties of native kings. If, for example, while he was in Italy, one of his generals distinguished himself against the Persians, no mention would be made of him in a very long bulletin, but letters wreathed in laurel would be sent to extract money from the provinces, in which Constantius informed them with odious self-praise that he had fought in the front rank. Statements by him are still extant in the imperial records *which show his vainglorious habit* of praising himself to the sky. When this battle was fought near Strasbourg, from which he was forty days' march away, his account of the action stated that he had drawn up the order of battle, taken his place by the standards, put the barbarians to flight, and had Chnodomar brought before him. Disgraceful to relate, he said nothing of the glorious exploits of Julian, which he would have buried utterly in oblivion; but common report forbids the suppression of great achievements, however many people try to keep them in the shade.

BOOK 17

1. Julian campaigns beyond the Rhine.

At the end of these various operations the young favourite of Mars, relieved from anxiety now that peace was restored to the Rhine after the battle of Strasbourg, and concerned to save the bodies of the slain from being devoured by birds of prey, ordered all to be buried indiscriminately in a common grave. He also set free the envoys who, as I have said, brought him a truculent message before the battle, and returned to Saverne, from which he despatched the booty and all the prisoners to Metz (Mediomatrici) to be kept safe against his return. He himself intended to march to Mainz, with the idea of building a bridge, crossing the river, and seeking out the barbarians in their own territory now that none of them was left in ours. He found himself hindered by the protests of his troops, but his eloquence and the charm of his speech won them over to his will. Their affection was fired by experience of his quality, and made them willing followers of a man who had shared in all their toil, who had shown himself a superb general, and who, it was plain, was in the habit of imposing more hardship on himself than on his men. The appointed place was soon reached; a bridge was built, the river crossed, and the country of the enemy occupied. The barbarians, who supposed themselves to be in perfect safety and free at that moment from all possibility of being molested, were overwhelmed by this great feat. The destruction of others inspired anxious thoughts of what might be in store for themselves. So, to avoid the shock of the first onslaught, they pretended to sue for peace and sent envoys to affirm in set terms their intention of abiding by the existing agreement. Afterwards, however, for some unknown reason they changed their minds, and sent a second party in great haste to threaten our troops with war to the death unless we evacuated their territory.

On hearing reliable news of this, the Caesar in the early hours of the night embarked 800 men on small, swift boats *with orders to land some distance upstream* and destroy whatever they could find with fire and sword. This was followed at dawn by an advance uphill by our men, who were in good heart; the barbarians had been seen on the heights but none of them was found there. They had withdrawn at once before the threat of attack, and huge columns of smoke were seen at a distance which showed that our boat party had penetrated and was devastating the enemy's country. This stroke broke the Germans' spirit; they abandoned the confined and obscure positions in which they were lying in wait for our troops, and fled across the river Main (Moenus), to bring help to their kinsfolk. Then, as is apt to happen in moments of doubt or confusion, they were thrown into a panic on finding themselves caught between the approach of our cavalry and the onslaught of the boat party. Their knowledge of the terrain enabled them to get away quickly, and our troops, advancing without opposition, ransacked farms rich in livestock and produce. None was spared. Prisoners were taken from the houses, which were carefully built in Roman fashion, and all were then set on fire and burnt to the ground. After an advance of some ten miles our men reached a dark and dreary forest, where Julian paused for some time in doubt, because a deserter had informed him that a large force was lurking in some subterranean tunnels and a maze of trenches, ready to burst out at an appropriate moment. Our men, however, had the hardihood to make a resolute approach, only to find the paths blocked with felled oaks and ashes and a great mass of fir-trees. So they withdrew cautiously, scarcely able to contain their anger as they realized that further progress could only be made by a long and rough detour. Besides, they were nipped by the bitter air – the autumn equinox was past and hill and plain alike in those parts were covered with snow – and further effort involved great risk to no purpose. So they embarked on a notable work, and without meeting any opposition enthusiastically took in hand the repair of a fort which Trajan had established in the territory of the Alamanni and called by his own name, and which had recently been the object of violent attack. A garrison was stationed there to meet the needs of the moment and stores accumulated from the very heartland of the barbarians. The enemy, seeing this scheme for their destruction far advanced and greatly fearing the completion of the work, flocked hastily together and sent spokesmen to beg for peace in the most humble terms. This the Caesar, after mature deliberation, found many plausible reasons for granting for the space of ten months; no doubt it occurred to a man of his keen intelligence that a position which he had occupied unopposed beyond his hopes should be strengthened by catapults on its walls and strong defensive equipment. Relying on this agreement three of the most savage kings from among those who had sent help to the vanquished at Strasbourg came at last, though still in a state of some alarm, to take an oath according to their native ritual that they would make no disturbance, but would observe the truce up to the appointed day, since that was our will, and leave the fort unmolested. They further undertook to bring supplies of corn on their shoulders if the garrison informed them that there was a shortage, and they kept both these promises, because fear put a check on their treacherous disposition.

This notable war, which can stand comparison with the wars against the Carthaginians and Teutons, but which was brought to an end with very slight losses on the Roman side, gave the Caesar cause to rejoice in his success and good fortune. His detractors pretended that the motive for his gallant exploits was that he preferred to fall gloriously in battle rather than meet a criminal's death like his brother Gallus, which was what he expected. This theory would be plausible if he had not, even after the death of Constantius, persisted in the same course and added to his reputation by his wonderful achievements.

2. *Julian starves 600 marauding Franks into surrender.*

Things being thus firmly settled as far as circumstances allowed, Julian on his way to his winter quarters found that he had still a toilsome task to perform. The master of cavalry, Severus, on his march to Reims by way of Cologne and Juliers (Iuliacum), encountered some strong companies of Frankish skirmishers, who to the number of 600, as later emerged, were laying waste unprotected areas. They were encouraged to this bold action by the fact that the Caesar was busy in the remote haunts of the Alamanni; they supposed therefore that they could carry off a rich haul without opposition. Frightened by the return of the army, they occupied two forts which had long been abandoned, and defended themselves as best they could. Julian, disturbed by this unexpected event and divining what would be its outcome if he passed on without attacking the marauders, halted his troops and prepared to blockade the strongholds, which were on the bank of the river Meuse (Mosa). The fixed resolve and incredible obstinacy with which the

barbarians defended themselves protracted the siege for fifty-four days
during the months of December and January. Then the Caesar, whose
sagacity suggested to him that the barbarians might wait for a moonless
night and cross the frozen river, arranged for parties to patrol in light
cutters in both directions every night from dusk till dawn, so as to break
up the slabs of ice and destroy any chance of an easy escape. This device
reduced the defenders, who were worn out by hunger and lack of sleep,
to utter despair. They surrendered voluntarily and were immediately
sent to the court of the Augustus. A large force of Franks which had set
out to rescue them, hearing that they had been carried into captivity,
made no further effort and returned home. After this success the Caesar
returned to spend the winter at Paris.

3. Julian attempts to relieve the Gauls from oppressive taxation.

Our prudent leader, expecting that a large number of tribes would
combine against him in greater strength, had a heavy weight of anxiety
to sustain as he pondered the uncertain chances of war. Though the
respite he was enjoying was brief and full of business, he thought that
he could do something to alleviate the disastrous losses suffered by the
owners of land, and embarked upon a reform of the system of taxation.
Florentius, the praetorian prefect, after what he maintained was a
careful review of the figures, declared that he would make up the deficit
in the product of the normal poll-taxes by a special levy, but Julian,
who was knowledgeable about such matters, affirmed that he would
rather die than allow this to be done. He knew that the irremediable
damage inflicted by settlements or, to give them a truer name, unsettle-
ments of this kind had often brought provinces to utter poverty; the
very thing that, as will be shown later, completely ruined Illyricum.
The praetorian prefect protested that it was intolerable that he, to whom
the Augustus had entrusted supreme responsibility, should suddenly
be treated as unreliable, but Julian returned a soft answer and demonstrated by a detailed and accurate calculation that the product of the
taxes was not merely adequate but even in excess of what was required
for necessary public expenditure. Nevertheless, at a much later date a
proposal for a supplementary levy was submitted to him, but he would
not read or sign it, and threw it on the ground. On receiving a report
from the prefect the Augustus sent a letter warning Julian not to
undermine Florentius' credit by his interference, but Julian replied

that it was a matter for congratulation if the provincials, after being plundered on all sides, could produce the standard taxes; as for a supplement, even torture could not wring that from men in extreme want. The upshot was that through the resolution of one man no attempt was made thereafter to exact from the Gauls anything more than the normal dues. Finally, contrary to all precedent, the Caesar persuaded the prefect to hand over to him the administration of the second Belgic province, which was suffering from a variety of troubles. He stipulated that no official either of the prefect or of the governor should put pressure to pay upon anyone, with the result that all whom he had taken under his wing were so heartened by this relief that they paid what was due before the appointed day without waiting for any demand.

4. Constantius erects an obelisk in the Circus Maximus at Rome.*

While these first steps were being taken towards the rehabilitation of Gaul, and Orfitus was still serving his second term as urban prefect, an obelisk was set up in the Circus Maximus at Rome, and this seems a suitable moment to give a brief account of it. The city of (Egyptian) Thebes, founded in remote antiquity and once famous for its imposing walls and its hundred gates, was called by its builders 'hundred-gated Thebes' on that account, and has given its name to the province which still at the present day is called the Thebaid. At the time when Carthage was beginning to expand, Thebes was destroyed by Punic commanders in an unexpected assault. Later, after being rebuilt, it was attacked by Cambyses, king of Persia, a monarch who was a monster of greed all his life and whose object in invading Egypt was to seize the riches which aroused his envy without sparing even the offerings sacred to the gods. While he was running wildly about among his plundering troops he tripped in his loose robes and fell on his face; his dagger, which he wore on his right thigh, was shaken from its sheath by his sudden fall and inflicted on him a wound which was well-nigh mortal. Long afterwards Cornelius Gallus, who was procurator of Egypt in the reign of Octavian, ruined the city by peculation on a large scale. When he returned home he was put on trial for his thefts and for pillaging the province, and, fearing the fierce indignation of the nobles to whom the emperor had entrusted the investigation of the case, fell on his own sword. This

* See map, Monuments of Rome, p. 500.

Gallus was, if I am not mistaken, the poet whom Virgil celebrates almost with tears in the polished verses of his last eclogue.

In this city among the huge monuments and colossal statues in the likeness of the gods of Egypt I have seen many obelisks, some of them lying in fragments on the ground. They were hewn by early kings out of veins of stone for which they ransacked mountains at the ends of the earth, and dedicated by them to the gods of Heaven to commemorate the defeat of a foreign race or some other successful achievement of their reign. An obelisk is a very hard stone in the shape of a turning-post in the circus; it rises to a great height, gradually tapering to resemble a sunbeam; its four sides converge to a narrow point and are polished by the craftsman's hand. The innumerable characters called hieroglyphs which we see inscribed on every face owe their form to tradition handed down from the sages of early times. By carving many kinds of birds and beasts, some even of a different world from this, men left a record of the vows which the kings promised or performed in order that the memory of their exploits might be widely preserved among generations to come. The writing of the early Egyptians is not like ours, in which a fixed and simple series of letters expresses all the ideas of the human mind; for them a single character served to signify a single substantive or verb, and sometimes, indeed, a complete sentence. Two examples will serve for the moment to illustrate this. The word 'nature' is represented by a vulture because natural historians report that no males are to be found among these birds, and they use the symbol of a bee making honey to signify 'king', indicating in this way that in a ruler's nature sweetness should be combined with a sting. And so on.

The flatterers whose habit it was to inflate the pride of Constantius kept dinning into his ears that the emperor Octavian, who brought two Egyptian obelisks from Heliopolis and set up one in the Circus Maximus and the other in the Campus Martius, did not dare to disturb or move the one which was brought to Rome in our day because he was daunted by the difficulties presented by its size. But let me tell those who do not know that the reason why that early emperor left this obelisk untouched when he moved some others was that it was dedicated as a special offering to the Sun God and placed in the sacred precinct of a magnificent temple, to which access was forbidden. There it towered over the whole structure. Constantine, however, made small account of this and rightly supposed that he would be committing no sacrilege if he removed this wonderful object from one temple and dedicated it at Rome, which may be called the temple of the whole world. So he tore it from its foundations, but then let it lie for a long period on the ground while the necessary preparations were being made for its transport. It was brought down the Nile by water and landed at Alexandria, where a ship of unheard-of size, requiring 300 rowers, was built for it. After this preliminary work the emperor in question died, and enthusiasm for the enterprise dwindled. At last, however, the obelisk was embarked and conveyed oversea and up the Tiber, which might well fear that its estuary would prove unequal to the task of bringing to the walls of the city it had nurtured this gift from the Nile it hardly knew. The obelisk was landed at Vicus Alexandri, three miles below the city. There it was placed on a sledge, slowly dragged through the Ostian Gate and the Piscina Publica, and brought into the Circus Maximus. It only remained to set it upright, a task which seemed almost, if not totally, impossible. *Dangerously tall masts were erected*, which gave the impression of a forest of beams. To these were attached long, stout ropes which formed a network so dense that it hid the sky. The mountain of obelisk covered with inscribed figures was tied to the ropes and gradually hauled up through the empty air, where it hung suspended for a long time till at last the efforts of many thousand men turning what looked like millstones placed it in position in the middle of the Circus. It was surmounted by a bronze sphere gleaming with gold leaf, but this was at once struck by lightning and destroyed. It was replaced by the bronze replica of a torch, also covered in gold, which shines like a sheet of flame. Successive generations have brought other obelisks to Rome, of which one was set up on the Vatican, another in the gardens of Sallust, and two more before the mausoleum of Augustus.

A Greek translation of hieroglyphic inscriptions is omitted.

5. Fruitless negotiations between Constantius and Sapor by letters and envoys (A.D. 358).

In the consulship of Datianus and Cerealis, while the whole administration of Gaul was being conducted with vigour tempered by caution, and the memory of past reverses kept raids by the barbarians in check, the Persian king Sapor was still engaged with the peoples on his farthest borders. He had concluded a treaty of alliance with the Chionitae and

Gelani, the fiercest fighters of all, and was about to return to his capital, when he received the letter from Tamsapor which contained the news that the Roman emperor was begging for peace. Believing that such a proposal must be a sign that the strength of the empire was impaired, Sapor opened his mouth wider, and while accepting peace in principle accompanied it with harsh conditions. He sent a certain Narses to convey presents and a letter to Constantius. The tenor of this, which showed no abatement of his native arrogance, I understand to have been as follows:

'From Sapor, king of kings, partner of the stars, brother of the sun and moon, to my brother Constantius Caesar, greetings.

'I rejoice and am well pleased that you have at last returned to the right way and acknowledge what perfect justice requires, having learnt by experience what disasters have often resulted from an obstinate greed for the possessions of others. Since therefore the language of truth should be uninhibited and free and it becomes those in high places to speak as they feel, I shall express my intention succinctly, remembering that I have often repeated in the past what I am about to say. That the rule of my ancestors once extended to the Strymon and the borders of Macedonia is a fact to which even your own ancient records bear witness, and it is right that I should demand this territory, since (with due modesty be it spoken) my splendour and the catalogue of my illustrious qualities surpass those of the kings of old. But the rule of right is ever dear to me; I have been wedded to it from my youth up, and have never committed any action which I have had cause to repent. So now I owe it to myself to recover Armenia and Mesopotamia, of which my grandfather was deprived by deliberate deceit. Never will I accept the principle which your overweening pride leads you to enunciate, that all is fair in war that brings success, whether it be achieved by force or fraud. In a word, if you will be guided by good advice let go this small area, which has always been a source of trouble and bloodshed, and reign in peace over the rest of your realm. Have the wisdom to reflect that those who practise medicine sometimes cauterize and cut and even amputate parts of the body in order that the patient may enjoy the healthy use of the rest. Even some animals do the same; when they realize what it is that makes men eager to capture them, they abandon it spontaneously in order to live thereafter free from fear. This I emphatically declare, that if my envoys return empty-handed I shall at the end of winter mobilize all my forces and advance as far as prudence permits, relying for success on fortune and the justice of what I propose.'

To this letter the emperor after long deliberation sent in plain terms, as they say, the following considered reply:

'From Constantius, victor on land and sea, perpetual Augustus, to his brother, king Sapor, greetings.

'I am glad to hear of your well-being and am ready if you wish to be your friend, but I strongly reprobate your greed, which never abates and is always spreading over a wider area. You lay claim to Mesopotamia, and Armenia as well, and you advise me to lop off some members of a sound body to ensure its health hereafter. I must totally reject such a suggestion, which can never win my assent. Listen then to the plain unvarnished truth, which is not to be shaken by empty threats. My praetorian prefect, believing that he was acting in the public interest, used two insignificant intermediaries to enter into negotiations for peace with your general, without consulting me. We do not disown or repudiate his initiative, provided that it is consistent with dignity and honour and involves no breach of the respect due to our majesty. For us, at a time when a series of various achievements has shed glory on us (may no jealous ear be offended by this), when the usurpers have been destroyed and the whole Roman world is at our feet, it would be absurd and foolish to abandon possessions which we long held intact, even when we were confined within the narrow limits of the East. Let there be an end, pray, to the threats which it is your habit to launch at us. It is beyond all doubt that it is self-restraint, not lack of spirit, which has sometimes led us to accept rather than provoke battle, and to defend our territory, whenever we are attacked, with courage inspired by a clear conscience. Both experience and reading have taught us that, though Rome has on a few rare occasions suffered a reverse in a particular battle, it has never emerged the loser from an entire war.'

The mission was dismissed empty-handed, since no further response was possible to the unbridled greed of the king, but in a very few days it was followed by count Prosper, accompanied by Spectatus, a notary who held the rank of tribune, and, at the suggestion of Musonian, the philosopher Eustathius, a master of the art of persuasion. They carried a letter and gifts from the emperor, and their task was to secure by diplomacy a delay in Sapor's preparations, while our northern provinces were being fortified beyond the possibility of an attack.

6. *Barbatio repels an attack of the Juthungi on Raetia.*

In the midst of these uncertainties the Juthungi, a branch of the
Alamanni whose territory bordered upon the prefecture of Italy, broke
the treaty of peace which had been granted in response to their prayers,
and made a violent inroad into the Raetian provinces, even going so far
beyond their habit as to besiege fortified towns. Barbatio, who had been
promoted master of infantry in place of Silvanus, was sent with a strong
force to repel them. He was a coward but a ready speaker. Kindling the
enthusiasm of his troops, he inflicted a disastrous defeat on the foe;
their losses were such that only a handful, who took to flight in panic,
escaped with their lives and got back to their homes, full of weeping
and wailing. Nevitta, who was afterwards consul, is said to have taken
part in this battle in command of a troop of cavalry, and to have done
valiantly.

7. *Nicomedia is destroyed by an earthquake.*

At the same period there were terrible earthquakes in Macedonia, Asia,
and Pontus, which shook many towns and mountains with repeated
shocks. Among all these various catastrophes the destruction of Nicomedia, the metropolis of Bithynia, stood out, and I will give a brief and
truthful account of the calamity which occurred there.

At dawn on 24 August the sky, which a short time before had been
brilliantly clear, was covered by thick masses of black cloud. The sun's
light was blotted out, and visibility became so bad that even the nearest
objects disappeared and a dense and dirty fog spread itself over the
ground. Then, as if God most high were hurling his fatal thunderbolts
and summoning the winds from the four quarters of the sky, squalls of
immense violence ensued, at the impact of which groans from the
mountains and crashing from the smitten shore were audible. There
followed whirlwinds and waterspouts, accompanied by a terrifying
earthquake, which entirely overset the city and its environs. Since most
of the houses were built on slopes they fell on top of one another, and
the whole air rang with the prodigious noise of their fall. The hill-tops
echoed the various cries of people searching for their wives and children
and others close to them. At last, shortly after the second hour, the day,
which was now bright and clear, revealed the full extent of the carnage.
Some had perished under the sheer weight of the debris which had

fallen on them; some were buried up to the neck in heaps of rubble and died for lack of assistance, when they might have survived had there been anybody to help them; others hung transfixed on the sharp points of projecting timbers. The majority died at a single stroke, and where a moment before had been human beings nothing was to be seen but heaps of jumbled corpses. Some were imprisoned unhurt by the fallen roofs of their houses to await an agonizing death from starvation. This was the lot of Aristaenetus, who breathed his last after protracted suffering; he was governor of the recently created diocese which Constantius entitled 'Pietas' in honour of his wife Eusebia. Others who were crushed by the sudden overwhelming shock lie buried to this day under the same ruins. Some, whose skulls had been fractured or who had lost arms or legs, hovered between life and death, and were abandoned in spite of their loud cries for help from others who were in the same plight. The greater part of the buildings, both public and private, and of the inhabitants might have been saved, had not a sudden outbreak of fire, which spread for five days and nights, burnt up everything that could be consumed.

A section on the nature and types of earthquakes is omitted.

8. Campaign of Julian against the Franks.

The Caesar, wintering in Paris, was at pains to forestall any move by the Alamanni, who were not yet collected in one body but whose boldness and ferocity after their defeat at Strasbourg approached the point of madness. While he waited for the month of July, which marks the opening of the campaigning season in Gaul, Julian was a prey to long anxiety. He could not take the field till mild summer weather succeeded the frost and cold and allowed his supplies to be replenished from Aquitaine. But careful thought overcomes nearly all difficulties. After turning over various plans he decided that the only course was not to wait for high summer but to encounter the barbarians before he was expected. Once this was settled, he took rations for twenty days from the meal kept for consumption in the standing camps, baked it to ensure that it would keep, and loaded it in the form commonly known as biscuit on the backs of his men, who were willing enough to carry it. Relying on this provision he set out with favourable auspices as before, in the belief that five or six months would suffice to complete two urgent and necessary campaigns. His first objective was the Franks, those specifically who are usually called Salii; they had had the temerity in the past to settle themselves on Roman soil at Toxiandria. When he arrived at Tongres (Tungri) he was met by a deputation from this people, who supposed that they would find him still in winter quarters. They offered peace on condition that they should be left undisturbed and unmolested in what they regarded as their own territory, provided that they gave no trouble. After fully considering the matter Julian suggested some complicated conditions and sent them away with gifts; they were under the impression that he would remain in the same area till their return. But once they had gone he followed them in a flash, and sending his general Severus along the river fell suddenly on the whole body and smote them like a thunderbolt. Instead of resisting they fell to entreaties; so, using his victory as a favourable opportunity to show mercy, he accepted their surrender with their goods and families.

A like fate befell the Chamavi, who had dared to behave in a similar way. Julian fell on them with the same speed; some were slain, some were taken alive after a stout resistance and put in irons, others, who took to headlong flight, were allowed to reach their homes unharmed, in order to save the troops the labour of a long pursuit. Soon afterwards they sent envoys to petition on their behalf and to represent their interests. They prostrated themselves in Julian's presence, and were granted peace and permission to return home in safety.

9. Julian on the Meuse.

Since everything was going his way, Julian, who was always on the watch for any opportunity to place the security of the provinces on a firm basis, decided in the circumstances to repair three forts erected in a straight line overlooking the Meuse, which had been destroyed some time before by a determined barbarian attack. This was immediately effected, although it involved a short intermission of the campaign. To ensure the success of this wise plan by rapid action, he took part of the seventeen days' rations which the troops carried on their backs when they set out, and used it to provision these forts, believing that the deficiency could be made up from the crops of the Chamavi. But this proved a serious miscalculation. The crops were not yet ripe, and when the troops had used up what they had with them and could find nothing to eat anywhere they resorted to the direst threats and heaped insults and abuse upon Julian, calling him a degenerate Greek from Asia and a liar and a fool who pretended to be wise. In any body of troops there are always some remarkably ready talkers, and these made many noisy protests to the following effect:

'Where are you taking us, now that we have lost all hope of seeing better times? For a long while we have put up with all the hardships of snow and cruel biting frosts, and now, shame upon you, when the final destruction of the enemy is within our grasp, we are wasting away from hunger, the most ignominious of all deaths. Do not think us mutineers; our only object is to preserve our lives. We do not ask for gold or silver, which we have not touched or even seen for a long while. One might think from the way in which they have been kept from us that we were guilty of encountering all this toil and danger in order to injure our country.'

They had good cause to complain. From the day when Julian arrived, through all the course of their meritorious service in dangerous and critical times, the troops, though worn out by their labours in Gaul, had received neither pay nor gratuity, because Julian had no means whatever to pay them, and Constantius would not authorize the normal expenditure from public funds. That this policy was inspired by malice rather than meanness is shown by the fact that when the Caesar gave a small coin to a common soldier, who asked, as they often do, for money for a shave, he was assailed with insults and slander by Gaudentius, who was then a notary. This Gaudentius remained in Gaul for a long time to spy on Julian's conduct, and was afterwards put to death at his order, as I shall relate in its proper place.

10. Julian grants peace to the Alamannic kings Suomar and Hortar.

At length order was restored by soft words, and the Rhine was crossed by a bridge of boats. But when they set foot on the territory of the Alamanni the master of cavalry Severus, who had hitherto shown himself a spirited and active officer, suddenly lost his nerve. The man who had so often encouraged all and sundry to deeds of valour now argued against battle and showed himself a despicable coward. Perhaps he had a premonition of approaching death; we read in the books of Tages and Vegoe that people who are soon to be struck by lightning fall into such apathy that they cannot hear thunder or other loud noises. Severus' march was so uncharacteristically sluggish that he even threatened to kill his guides, who were advancing at a good speed, if they did not unanimously declare that they were totally ignorant of the locality. Intimidated by this prohibition from their commander, they made no further progress in any direction.

While things were at a standstill Suomar, a king of the Alamanni, unexpectedly presented himself together with his men. In the past he had been on fire to inflict loss on the Romans, but now he thought that to be allowed to keep what was his own was an advantage for which he could hardly hope. His expression and bearing were those of a suppliant; so he was kindly received and told to take heart and set his mind at rest. He entirely surrendered his independence and begged for peace on bended knee. This was granted together with an amnesty on condition that he handed over his prisoners and undertook to provide food for the troops whenever they needed it. He was to take receipts like a common contractor for whatever he supplied, and he was told that if he could not produce them on demand he would be liable again to the same requisition.

Once this matter had been properly settled without any difficulty, the next objective was the country of another king called Hortar. To reach this nothing was lacking but guides. The Caesar ordered Nestica, tribune of the Scutarii, and Charietto, a man of astonishing courage, to use their best endeavours to find and bring him a prisoner. No time was lost in seizing and sending to Julian a young Alamann, who promised that he would act as guide if his life were spared. He led the way and the troops followed, but they found the direct route blocked by a barrier built of tall trees. Finally, however, they reached their goal by a long and winding detour. But our men were so enraged that they burnt up the fields, carried off men and beasts, and cut to pieces without mercy any who offered resistance. The king was shattered by this disaster; the spectacle of desolation presented by the burnt villages of his land convinced him that he was on the verge of total ruin. So he too begged for pardon, and bound himself with an oath to obey Julian's orders and give back all his prisoners. Julian was particularly anxious for their release; the king, however, kept back most of them and surrendered only a few. When he heard of this Julian was justly indignant, and, when the king came to receive presents in the customary way, he would not release the four vassals on whose support and loyalty Hortar chiefly relied until all the prisoners were returned. When at last he was summoned to an interview with the Caesar, Hortar prostrated himself before him with fear in his eyes, and was so overcome by the sight of his conqueror that he accepted the harsh terms imposed on him. These were that, since after so many successes it was only fitting that the towns destroyed by the barbarians should be rebuilt, Hortar should provide wagons and materials for this from the resources of himself and his subjects. After promising to do so and invoking on his own head the punishment of death if he should be guilty of the least treachery, he was allowed to return to his own country. He could not be compelled to furnish corn like Suomar, because his lands had been so totally devastated that nothing could be found for him to provide.

Thus those kings, once inordinately swollen with pride, who had been in the habit of enriching themselves by plundering our people, bowed their necks to the Roman yoke, and obeyed the imperial commands without a murmur, as if they had been born and brought up among payers of tribute. At the conclusion of this affair the troops were dispersed to their usual posts and the Caesar returned to winter quarters.

11. Julian's successes depreciated at court.

When news of these events reached the court of Constantius, to whom the Caesar, like any other subordinate, was bound to submit a report of all his doings, all the most influential courtiers, past masters in the art of flattery, made fun of his well-conceived plans and the success which had attended them. Endless silly jokes were bandied about, such as 'he is more of a goat than a man' – an allusion to his wearing a beard – and 'his victories are becoming a bore'. 'Babbling mole', 'ape in purple', 'Greek dilettante' and other such names were applied to him, and by ringing the changes on these in the ears of the emperor, who was eager to hear this kind of talk, his enemies attempted to smother his good qualities under their shameless words. They attacked him as slack and timid and sedentary, and accused him of dressing up his reverses in fine language.

This was not the first example of such treatment. The most glorious actions are always the target of envy, and we read that in old times, too, malice invented, if it could not detect, faults and crimes in the greatest captains, who had given offence by the brilliance of their exploits. Cimon, the son of Miltiades, for example, who after many other successes destroyed a countless host of Persians at the battle of the river Eurymedon in Pamphylia and compelled that haughty people to sue humbly for peace, was accused of *drunkenness*. In the same way Scipio Aemilianus, whose unerring alertness brought about the destruction of two powerful cities bent on the ruin of Rome, was represented by his jealous rivals as a sleepy-head. Pompey's detractors also, whose malevolent scrutiny could find nothing in him to deserve blame, finally hit upon two ridiculous and trivial traits. One was his ingrained habit of scratching his head with one finger, the other that for a time he wore a white bandage upon his leg to hide an ugly ulcer. The first was said to be an effeminate gesture, the second a sign that he was intent on a revolutionary coup. It made no difference, they averred, on what part of his body he wore the emblem of royal dignity. Such was the futile argument employed by those who barked at the heels of a man whom we have the clearest proof to have had no equal as a hero and a patriot.

During these events Artemius, the vice-prefect at Rome, also discharged the functions of Bassus, who died a natural death shortly after being promoted urban prefect. His administration was marked by some violent disturbances, but nothing occurred in it which is worth reporting.

12. Successful campaigns of Constantius on the Danube against the Sarmatians and Quadi.

Meanwhile the Augustus was spending the winter at Sirmium, where he received from a succession of reports the serious news that the Sarmatians and Quadi, who were on good terms with one another because they were neighbours with a similar way of life and similar weapons, had joined forces and were making raids in detached bands into the Pannonias and Upper Moesia. These peoples, whose habits are more suited to brigandage than to open warfare, use long spears and breastplates made of pieces of polished horn attached like scales to a linen backing. Their horses are usually gelded to prevent their bolting in excitement if they see a mare, or plunging wildly when they are placed in ambush and betraying their riders by repeated whinnying. They cover enormous distances either in pursuit or in flight, riding horses that are swift and tractable and each leading another beast and sometimes two, so as to maintain the strength of their mounts by changing them and recruiting their energies by alternate periods of rest.

So after the spring equinox the emperor collected a strong force and took the field with good prospects of success. The river Danube was in flood owing to the melting of the snows, but Constantius crossed it at the most suitable spot on a bridge of boats and set about ravaging the territory of the barbarians. The speed of his march took them by surprise; they had not supposed that a hostile force could be mobilized so early in the year. When they saw it at their throats they did not dare to draw breath or make a stand, but dispersed in flight to avoid a destruction they had not foreseen. A large number were despatched because fear kept them rooted to the spot. Those who saved their lives by their speed hid themselves in obscure recesses of the mountains and watched the devastation of their country by the sword, when they might have rescued it if they had resisted as vigorously as they ran away. These events took place in that part of Sarmatia which faces the second province of Pannonia, while on the borders of Valeria also the lands of the barbarians were laid waste by a hurricane attack, in which our troops showed the same courage, and burned and despoiled all that lay in their path.

The Sarmatians, overwhelmed by this prodigious disaster, abandoned their policy of concealment and formed themselves into three parties to attack our men under pretence of suing for peace, so that they would have no chance of getting their weapons in order or avoiding wounds or even taking to flight, which is the last resource in a desperate situation. The Quadi, moreover, who had often been their inseparable partners in crime, came at once to share the perils of the Sarmatians. But even their ready courage availed nothing as they threw themselves into a situation of manifest danger. Many were killed, and those who survived made off by hill-paths with which they were familiar. Our men, whose morale was raised by this success, adopted a closer formation and advanced rapidly towards the realm of the Quadi, who, taught by their recent disaster to dread what lay in store for them, decided to beg humbly for peace. They believed that they could approach the emperor with confidence, because he was inclined to be lenient in cases such as theirs. On the day appointed for settling the terms, Zizais, a fine young man who was already of royal rank, drew up the Sarmatians in battle order to present their petition, and at the sight of the emperor threw away his weapons, flung himself prostrate on the ground, and lay apparently lifeless. He aroused greater pity because at the moment when he should have spoken fear choked his utterance; after several attempts, interrupted by sobs, he was hardly able to set forth his request.

At last he recovered himself and was told to rise. Kneeling, and with his voice once more under control, he begged forgiveness and pardon for his past offences. The multitude of his followers who were admitted to join in his petition remained dumb from fear as long as the fate of their superior hung in the balance, but, when he was told to stand up and gave them the long-awaited signal to add their entreaties to his, they all threw down their shields and spears and stretched out their arms in supplication, striving to outdo even their prince in the humility of their appeal. The latter had brought with him among the rest of the Sarmatians the vassal kings Rumo, Zinafer, and Fragiledus, and a number of notables, who hoped to be successful in a similar petition. Overjoyed that their lives were spared, they promised to atone for their acts of hostility by accepting harsh terms, and would gladly have put their own persons, together with their property, their wives and children, and the whole extent of their lands, at the disposal of the Romans. Justice, however, was tempered with mercy; they were told to keep their homes and fear nothing. So they gave up their prisoners, brought the hostages that were demanded of them, and promised prompt obedience to all orders in future.

Encouraged by this instance of clemency a prince called Arahar hurried to submit with all his men, and with him Usifer, a prominent noble. Both commanded forces of their countrymen, Arahar part of the Transiugitani and Quadi, and Usifer some of the Sarmatians, peoples bound in close union by neighbourhood and warlike spirit. The emperor kept the mass of their people at a distance for fear that they might suddenly rush to arms under pretence of concluding an agreement. He also separated the partners, and gave orders that the Sarmatian representatives should withdraw for a time while the case of Arahar and the Quadi was being considered. The latter presented themselves and stood with bowed heads like criminals, unable to justify their grave offences. Fearing that they might suffer the supreme penalty, they handed over the hostages that were demanded, a guarantee of good faith that they had never before been forced to give. When their case had been fairly and justly dealt with, Usifer was admitted to plead, though Arahar strongly protested, claiming that the terms which he had obtained should extend also to Usifer, who was his partner, though of inferior rank and accustomed to obey his orders. But after a discussion it was decided that the Sarmatians should be freed from an alien yoke, on the ground that they had always been dependants of Rome, and they gladly accepted the obligation to give hostages as a bond for keeping the peace. There followed a great influx of parties from native tribes with their kings, who, hearing that Arahar had got off unpunished, begged that the sword might be removed from their throats as well. They too obtained the peace which they asked on the same terms, and brought sooner than was expected sons of notables from the interior of their country to be handed over as hostages together with their Roman prisoners. The surrender of these had been stipulated, and they parted from them with as much grief as from their own kindred.

When this was settled the emperor turned his attention to the Sarmatians, who were more to be pitied than hated. The benefit which they gained on this occasion passes belief, and serves to justify the opinion of those who think that fate can be either defeated or determined by the power of a prince. The natives of this realm had once been powerful and renowned, but a secret conspiracy led to an armed uprising of their slaves, and, since with barbarians might is always right, the masters were overcome by the slaves, who were their equal in courage and their superior in numbers. The losers, whose judgement was impaired by panic, took refuge with a distant tribe called Victohali, believing that in their sad plight submission to those who would protect them was preferable to slavery to slaves. Now they deplored their situation, and having obtained pardon and protection from us asked for a guarantee of their freedom. The emperor was moved by their hard fate, and, calling them together and addressing them in mild terms in the presence of the whole army, bade them yield obedience to none but himself and the generals of Rome. Further, to give additional weight to the restoration of their freedom, he appointed Zizais their king. Even at that period Zizais was fitted to sustain the honours of a lofty station, and subsequent events showed him to be a man of his word. But no one was allowed to depart after this glorious outcome until our prisoners were returned in accordance with the stipulation.

After these operations on barbarian soil the camp was moved to Bregetio, in order that there too the embers of the war against the Quadi, who were still active in those parts, should be quenched in blood or tears. Their prince Vitrodorus, son of king Viduar, a subordinate chief called Agilimund, and other notables and judges who held sway over various tribes, once they saw our army in the heart of their native land, threw themselves at the feet of our troops, were pardoned, and carried out the orders they were given. They handed over their children as pledges for the performance of the conditions imposed on them, and drawing their swords, which to them are objects of religious reverence, swore that they would remain loyal.

13. Constantius forces the Limigantes to emigrate.

When these affairs had been brought to a successful conclusion, as I have reported, the interests of the state required the immediate transfer of our forces to deal with the Limigantes, the former slaves of the Sarmatians, whom it would have been a disgrace to leave unpunished for all the outrages that they had committed. When the Free Sarmatians broke their bounds the ex-slaves too, in apparent forgetfulness of the past, seized the opportunity thus presented to violate the Roman frontier, and joined forces for once in this treacherous attack with those who were both their masters and their enemies. Nevertheless, a decision was taken to inflict on them a milder punishment than the gravity of their offences merited, and to go no further than to transplant them to a distant region where they would be unable to molest our territory. But the consciousness of the crimes which they had committed over a long period made them fearful of danger. Believing that the weight of our offensive was about to be directed against them, they prepared to meet it with a mixture of fraud, force, and entreaty. The first appearance of our army, however, struck them like a thunderbolt. Fearing the worst, they begged for their lives, and promised annual tribute, a levy of their able-bodied men, and a supply of slaves. But their gestures and looks showed that they would refuse to migrate elsewhere if they were ordered to do so, because they relied on the natural strength of the region in which they had settled in safety after the expulsion of their masters.

This tract is watered by the Theiss (Parthiscus) in a winding course before it falls into the Danube. While it flows alone and unconfined it travels slowly through a long, broad plain, but near its mouth this is narrowed, so that those who dwell there are protected by the Danube from the Romans, and by the barrier of the Theiss itself from barbarian inroads. The ground besides is mostly marshy and flooded by the rivers when they rise, and being full of bogs and overgrown with osiers cannot be crossed without local knowledge. Moreover, there is an island near the confluence of the Theiss and Danube which the larger river winds round and separates from the land.

At the instance of the emperor the Limigantes crossed in all their native pride to our bank of the river, with no intention, as the event proved, of doing what they were told, but in order to avoid any appearance of being afraid of our troops. There they stood truculently, letting it be seen that their purpose in coming near was to reject any orders that they might be given. The emperor, who was aware of this possibility, had secretly divided his forces into a number of detachments, and by a swift manoeuvre encircled the stationary barbarians in a ring of his own troops. Then, taking his place with a few attendants on a raised mound, protected by his guards, he warned them in mild terms not to behave with violence. They wavered in a state of indecision between two opposite courses; rage was tempered by cunning, and they sought to disguise their hostile intentions under a show of entreaty. Intending to attack our men at close quarters, they purposely threw down their shields some way in front of them. This gave them an opportunity to advance gradually to recover them, and so gain ground without betraying their treacherous plan.

When evening was coming on and the waning light made further delay inadvisable, our men raised their standards and launched a fiery assault. The enemy, packed closely together, concentrated their attack on the emperor himself, and menaced him with savage looks and shouts where he stood, as I said, on a higher level. This mad behaviour was too much for the temper of our men; while the barbarians were fiercely threatening the emperor, the troops adopted a wedge formation (what is known in common soldiers' parlance as a 'pig's head'), and scattered the foe by a furious charge; on the right our infantry cut to pieces their warriors on foot, while on the left our cavalry engaged their agile horsemen. The praetorian cohort, whose task was to protect the person of the Augustus against attack, struck at the enemies' breasts while they resisted and then at their backs as they fled. The barbarians fell with their spirit unbroken, and showed by their fearful yells that death caused them less anguish than the triumph of our troops. In addition to the dead many lay hamstrung and were thus prevented from taking refuge in flight; others lost their right hands; some were unwounded but crushed by the weight of falling bodies; all bore their sufferings in deep silence. In all these various agonies no one asked for mercy or threw away his sword or begged to be put out of his misery. Shattered though they were they clung grimly to their weapons, considering it less of a disgrace to be vanquished by the strength of others than to suffer the reproaches of their own conscience; occasionally they were heard to complain that what had happened was sheer misfortune and not what they deserved. So in the course of half an hour the outcome of the fight was decided, and so many barbarians fell in a moment that nothing but the signs of victory showed that there had been a battle.

No sooner had the hostile tribes been overthrown than the families of the slain were dragged forth in droves from their humble huts, without distinction of age or sex, to exchange the proud independence of their former life for the degraded status of slaves. A brief space of time served to reveal piles of corpses and throngs of prisoners. So, excited by the heat of battle and the prospect of loot, our men betook themselves to the destruction of those who had fled from the fight or were lying concealed in their huts. Thirsting for barbarian blood they tore down the frail thatch and slaughtered those within; even a house built of the strongest timbers could not preserve its inmates from death. At last, when everything was on fire and there was nowhere left to hide, the survivors, finding every avenue of escape cut off, either refused to yield and perished in the flames or else came out and escaped one form of torment only to fall at the hands of their enemies. Some, however, escaped the sword and the raging fire and entrusted themselves to the depths of the river nearby, hoping to reach the further bank because they could swim. Some of these died by drowning; others were pierced by missiles and perished; so much blood was spilt that the whole stream foamed with it. Thus with the help of two elements the rage and courage of the victors destroyed the Sarmatians.

After this it was decided to deprive them all of any prospect of relief. So, when their homes had been burnt and their families carried off, orders were given to collect boats to hunt down those who were protected from our army by being on the further bank. The keenness of our men was given no time to cool. Light-armed troops were at once embarked in skiffs, and taking a course out of sight of the enemy seized the hideouts of the Sarmatians, who were deceived at first by the familiar appearance of the native boats that suddenly appeared. But when the gleam of arms revealed that what they feared was upon them they took refuge in marshy country, into which they were hotly pursued by our troops. Many were killed and a victory was won in a spot where it was believed impossible to keep one's footing or undertake any bold exploit.

After the dispersal and almost total destruction of the Amicenses, no time was lost in attacking the Picenses, who took their name from the adjacent region. The persistent rumours of the disasters which had overtaken their allies had put them on their guard; it was a difficult business to pursue their scattered bands and our men were hampered by ignorance of the terrain. So the Taifali and the Free Sarmatians were called upon to help in putting them down. Since the nature of the country necessitated a division of forces, our troops chose to operate in the region bordering on Moesia, while the Taifali dealt with the country nearest their own homes and the Free Sarmatians occupied the lands immediately opposite them.

The Limigantes, terrified by what had befallen those who had been defeated and killed, could not decide for some time whether to seek death or beg for terms. There were weighty precedents for following either course, but at last the influence of a meeting of elders prevailed and they resolved to surrender. The laurels of our various victories were augmented by the submission of men who had taken up arms to usurp their freedom, and the survivors among them, who had looked on their masters with contempt as beaten weaklings, bowed their heads in entreaty before superior force.

So under a safe-conduct the greater part of them abandoned their mountain fastnesses and flocked to the Roman camp, spreading over the broad plain with their parents and children and wives and whatever poor possessions the circumstances of their hasty flight allowed them to huddle together. Men who, as long as they mistook mad recklessness for freedom, one thought would rather have died than change their place of abode, now consented to obey orders and to remove to new homes, whose peace and security could not be troubled by wars or affected by rebellions. The conditions imposed were thought to have their full assent, and they remained quiet for a short time, but later their inborn wildness roused them to commit a fatal crime, as I shall relate in the appropriate place.

By the happy outcome of these events the defences of Illyricum were adequately reinforced in two ways, and the emperor brought to a successful end both the great tasks to which he had addressed himself. The disloyal Sarmatians *were crushed*, and the exiles, who were equally fickle but who seemed likely to behave with rather more respect, were at last brought back and re-established in their ancestral domains. And as a crowning mercy Constantius set over them a king who was not of low birth but the very prince whom they had previously chosen for themselves, a man of outstanding gifts of mind and body. After such a series of successes Constantius put all his fears behind him, and for the second time was greeted by the troops as Sarmaticus after his defeated foes. Shortly before his departure from the front he assembled all the cohorts, centuries, and maniples, and standing on a raised platform, surrounded by standards and eagles and a numerous suite of high-ranking officers, he addressed his army, which received him, as usual, with universal applause.

'The thought of our glorious success, the sweetest pleasure brave men can enjoy, prompts me to rehearse, so far as modesty permits, the changes for the better which, by the will of Heaven which has given us the victory, we have brought about by our loyal defence of the Roman state, both before the fighting and in the very heat of battle. What can be so honourable or so deserving of transmission to the memory of posterity as the exultation of a soldier in the success of his exertions and of a commander in the prudence of his plans?

'Illyricum was being overrun by the fury of our foes, whose foolish pride led them to think meanly of us while we were away defending Italy and Gaul. In a number of raids they devastated our farthest frontiers, crossing the rivers sometimes in dug-out canoes and some-times on foot. They did not pin their hopes on pitched battles to be won by force of arms, but on their usual surprise attacks, in which their cunning and versatility had made them formidable to our forebears from the earliest infancy of their race. Because we were at a distance we put up with this as long as we could, believing that comparatively slight losses could be checked by the activity of our generals. But when impunity encouraged them to further excesses, with frequent disastrous effects upon our provinces, we fortified the approaches to Raetia, took most careful measures to place the security of Gaul on a firm footing, and leaving nothing in our rear to cause alarm advanced into Pannonia, intending, if it pleased the Almighty, to redress a dangerous situation. Setting out fully prepared, as you know, in the middle of spring, we embarked on the massive task which awaited us. Our first object was to prevent the construction of an extempore bridge being frustrated by a storm of missiles. This caused us no difficulty; we saw and set foot on the enemy's soil, and though the Sarmatians tried to resist to the death we overthrew them without loss to ourselves, and crushed the Quadi as well, who came to the help of the Sarmatians and showed equal audacity in attacking our glorious legions. The grievous losses which they experienced in their raids and in their breathless attempts to offer a defiant resistance taught them what our valour could do. They threw away their weapons, put behind their backs to be bound the hands which had been armed for war, and realizing that their only hope lay in submission flung themselves at the feet of a merciful Augustus, whose battles, they well knew, were often crowned by victory.

'When this business was despatched we showed similar resolution in defeating the Limigantes. Many were killed, and others had to save themselves by taking refuge in the marshes. After this success the moment had come to show mercy. We have forced the Limigantes to move to far distant regions, where they can no longer constitute a threat to our people, and spared the lives of the greater number. As for the Free Sarmatians, we have placed them under the rule of Zizais, who we believe will be devoted and loyal. Rather than bring in a king from outside we think it better to elevate him, and the fact that the king assigned to them is a man whom they have themselves previously chosen and accepted will give him a further title to respect.

'So a single campaign has won for us and for the state a four-fold advantage. First, we have inflicted punishment on a body of guilty brigands; next, you will find an ample source of gain in the prisoners you have taken, and the spoils that the work of their own hands has won are a sufficient reward for brave men. We ourselves have sufficient wealth, in fact a great store of riches, if our toil and resolution have preserved the possessions of all intact; this to the mind of a good ruler is the happiest consequence of his success. Finally, as my personal share of the spoil, I am proud to have won for the second time the title of Sarmaticus, which your unanimous voice has conferred on me, and which, if I may say so without immodesty, is not undeserved.'

At the end of this speech the audience displayed more than usual enthusiasm. They were encouraged to hope for further gain, and burst into triumphant shouts in praise of the emperor, calling God to witness, as their custom is, that Constantius was invincible. Then they returned to their tents in high spirits, while the emperor was escorted back to his quarters. There he rested for two days and then returned to Sirmium like a conqueror, while the various units marched back to the stations assigned to them.

14. Roman envoys to Persia return empty-handed.

At this very time Prosper, Spectatus, and Eustathius, who had been sent to Persia, had an audience of the king on his return to Ctesiphon. They delivered the emperor's letter and gifts, and proposed that peace should be concluded on the basis of the existing position. Mindful of their instructions they made no concessions inconsistent with the interests and dignity of Rome, but insisted that a treaty of friendship should be based on the firm understanding that no steps would be taken to disturb the status of Armenia and Mesopotamia. After a long wait they found the king inflexibly resolved not to conclude a peace unless the sovereignty of these regions was transferred to him, and returned from their mission unsuccessful. Later count Lucillian, and Procopius, at that time a notary, were sent on the same errand to propose similar strong conditions. This was the Procopius who afterwards found himself constrained by harsh necessity to attempt a usurpation.

BOOK 18

1. Julian's reforms in Gaul (A.D. 359).

These were the events of one and the same year in different parts of the world. The brothers Eusebius and Hypatius were now elevated to the consulship, and the situation in Gaul had improved. Julian, whose prestige was much enhanced by his career of unbroken success and who was now in winter quarters at Paris, laid aside for the time his military preoccupations, and devoted equal attention to a number of measures for the welfare of the provinces in his charge. He was particularly concerned to prevent the burden of taxation pressing too heavily, power being abused to acquire the property of others, men participating in public affairs who were enriching themselves by the general distress, and departures from the rule of right by a judge going unpunished. This last abuse he was able to put right without difficulty by deciding in person disputes which were important in themselves or involved important persons, and by never allowing himself to be misled in distinguishing right from wrong. Many instances might be given of his admirable conduct in cases of this kind, but one will suffice to give a general indication of his way of acting and speaking. Numerius, who had recently been governor of Narbonese Gaul, was accused of embezzlement. His trial was thrown open to the public, and Julian showed unusual strictness in his examination. Numerius denied the charge, and his defence could not be shaken at any point. The lack of proof so infuriated Delphidius, who was attacking him violently in a fiery speech for the prosecution, that he exclaimed: 'Will anyone ever be found guilty, your highness, if denial is enough to secure acquittal?' Julian on the spur of the moment countered him with this shrewd rejoinder: 'Will anyone ever be acquitted if accusation is enough to secure conviction?' This is one instance among many of his humane behaviour.

2. Campaign by Julian in Germany.

Believing that some districts of Germany were hostile to him, and that their inhabitants would venture on outrages if they were not put down like the rest, Julian was about to embark on an urgent campaign, but was in a state of anxious indecision how to launch an offensive in sufficient force and with sufficient speed to anticipate rumours of his intention and take them by surprise, as soon as a reasonable opportunity presented itself. After turning over many possibilities he decided on a course whose efficacy was demonstrated by its result. Without anyone knowing, he sent an unattached tribune called Hariobaudes, a man of tried loyalty and courage, on what appeared to be a mission to king Hortar, with whom our relations were already on a peaceful footing. His ulterior design was that Hariobaudes, who had a thorough command of the native language, could then easily go on to the borders of those who were to be attacked and discover what they were about. Hariobaudes set off boldly to carry out these orders, while Julian himself mobilized his troops when the campaigning season opened and took the field. He decided, however, that before engaging in hostilities one thing above all imperatively demanded his attention. This was to enter and recover towns long since destroyed and abandoned, and repair their defences; also to build granaries in place of those which had been burnt, to store the corn regularly brought from Britain. In both these enterprises his speed exceeded all expectation. The granaries were quickly built and stored with ample supplies of food, and seven towns were reoccupied, Fort Hercules, Quadriburgium (?Qualburg), Tricensima (near Xanten), Novesium (Neuss), Bonna (Bonn), Antennacum (Andernach), and Vingo (Bingen), where by a stroke of good fortune the prefect Florentius suddenly made his appearance, bringing with him part of the army and enough provisions to last for a long time.

After this one vital task remained, the restoration of the walls of the reoccupied towns while it could be carried out without obstruction. This operation provided clear evidence that on this occasion the barbarians were ready to serve the interests of the empire from fear, and the Romans from love of their commander. The kings, in accordance with the agreement of the preceding year, sent a quantity of building material in their own carts, while the auxiliary troops, who always think such work beneath them, were so eager to respond to Julian's blandishments that they carried beams of fifty feet or more on their shoulders without complaint and were of the greatest service in the building operations.

While these works were rapidly going forward Hariobaudes returned from his reconnaissance and reported what he had learned. On his arrival the whole army made a forced march to Mainz. There Florentius and Lupicinus, Severus' successor, obstinately insisted that they should build a bridge and cross the river. But the Caesar firmly rejected this proposal, arguing that they should not set foot on the territory of the tribes with whom they had made peace; otherwise, if, as often happened, the troops in their brutal way destroyed whatever lay in their path, the treaties might come to an abrupt end.

All the Germans, however, who were the object of our attack tried, in view of the imminent danger in which they stood, to bully king Suomar, whom the previous treaty had made our friend, into preventing the Romans crossing, seeing that his territory adjoined the further bank of the Rhine. He declared that he could not resist single-handed, and the barbarians united in a single body and approached Mainz, determined to oppose a Roman crossing with all their might. So the Caesar's policy was doubly justified. He had urged not only that they should not violate the territory of the tribes that had submitted, but also that they should not throw away lives by attempting to build a bridge in the face of fierce opposition; *the right course was to march to a spot* particularly suitable for the construction of a bridge. The enemy were clever enough to divine his purpose, and followed slowly along the opposite bank. When they saw our forces pitch their tents they passed a sleepless night themselves, constantly on the alert to frustrate any attempt at a crossing. But when our troops reached the place we had in mind they stopped to rest, protected by a rampart and ditch, and the Caesar, after consulting with Lupicinus, ordered reliable officers to equip 300 light-armed men with stakes, without, however, giving them any hint of what they were to do or where they were to go. They were marshalled at dead of night and filled to capacity forty patrol boats, all that were then available; their orders were to float down stream in total silence with their oars out of the water, for fear that the splash might arouse the barbarians. So, while the enemy's attention was fixed on our camp-fires, these men, by their quickness and alertness, established a bridgehead on the opposite bank.

During the execution of this coup king Hortar, who was bound to us by treaty and had no thought of revolt but was also on friendly terms with his neighbours, had invited all the kings, princes, and chieftains to a feast, which he kept up after the custom of the country till long after midnight. As they were leaving the guests accidentally fell in with our men, who attacked but could not kill or capture any of them. They got away in the darkness on horseback, wherever their blind career carried them. But their lackeys and slaves who were following on foot were killed, except for those who escaped detection in the gloom.

When the news spread that a crossing had been forced by the Romans, who in this as in former campaigns thought that the hardest part of their work was done once the enemy was located, the kings and their peoples, who had been desperately intent on preventing the building of a bridge, were terror-struck and scattered in disorderly flight. The violence of their rage abated, and they hastened to remove their families and possessions out of harm's way. A bridge was at once built without any further difficulty, and sooner than their anxious foes expected our troops appeared on barbarian soil, and traversed the territory of king Hortar without inflicting any damage. But when they reached the lands of the kings who were still hostile they burnt and ravaged everything and ranged at will over the rebels' country. Firing the frail homes in which they sheltered, putting a host of people to the sword, enjoying the spectacle of numbers falling and others begging for mercy, they came at last to a region called Capellatii or Palas, where boundary stones used to mark the frontier between Romans and Burgundians. There they encamped, so that Macrianus and Hariobaudus might be received in a way which would not alarm them. These kings were brothers, who seeing destruction at hand had come in great agitation of mind to sue for peace. After them there arrived king Vadomar, whose domain lay opposite Augst; he produced a letter from Constantius in which he was warmly spoken of, and was given the kind reception proper for one who had been granted by the Augustus the status of a vassal of Rome. When Macrianus and his brother found themselves among the eagles and standards they were overwhelmed by the magnificent appearance of our armed forces, which they had never seen before, and begged mercy for their peoples. Vadomar, on the other hand, who lived near our frontier and was no stranger to us, admired our splendid field equipment, but remembered often seeing the like from his early youth.

Finally, after long debate it was unanimously decided that Macrianus and Hariobaudus should be granted peace. Vadomar, however, who had come to ensure his own safety but also as an intermediary to beg similar terms for kings Urius, Ursicinus, and Vestralp, could not be given an immediate answer. In view of the fickle nature of the barbarians there was a fear that those whom Vadomar represented might pluck up courage after the departure of our forces and refuse to abide by terms obtained through the agency of another. But after the burning of their homes and harvests and the death or capture of many of their people, these kings too sent envoys and begged as humbly for peace as if they had themselves been guilty of these offences against us. So they obtained peace on similar terms, one of which in particular they were required to fulfil at once, the surrender of all the prisoners they had taken in their frequent raids.

3. Execution of Barbatio and his wife.

While things were improving in Gaul under the providence of Heaven, a new storm arose at the court of the Augustus, which began with a trifle and ended in grief and tears. The house of Barbatio, who then commanded the infantry, was visited by a remarkable swarm of bees, which caused him to consult in great anxiety experts in the interpretation of omens. They replied that the swarm foreshadowed a great danger, plainly basing their interpretation on the fact that these insects, once they have made their homes and gathered their store of honey, can only be driven from their hives by smoke and the loud clash of cymbals. Barbatio's wife, whose name was Assyria, was an indiscreet and silly woman. After Barbatio had left for a campaign, seriously worried by the predictions which had been made to him, she succumbed to feminine folly and took into her confidence a maidservant whom she had acquired from the estate of Silvanus and who was an expert in cryptography. Through her she wrote an ill-judged letter to her husband, begging him almost with tears that when his hope of becoming emperor after the approaching death of Constantius was realized he would not cast her off and enter into a marriage with Eusebia, who was then empress and a woman of unusual personal beauty. The letter was sent in the greatest possible secrecy, but, when the army returned from the campaign, the maid took a copy of what she had written at her mistress's dictation, and carried the document in the early hours of the night to Arbitio, who received her eagerly. Arbitio, whose skill in framing a charge was unrivalled, relied on this evidence and reported it to the emperor. As usual, no time was lost in actively pursuing the affair. Barbatio confessed that he had received the letter, his wife was convicted on strong evidence of having written it, and both were beheaded. Their execution was followed by a wide-ranging inquisition in which many suffered, whether innocent or guilty. Among them was Valentinus, who had been promoted tribune from a position on the staff. He with several others was put to the torture more than once as accessory to the crime, of which he was in fact totally ignorant. He survived, however, and as compensation for the injuries he had suffered was advanced to the position of commander in Illyricum.

This Barbatio was a man of rough manners and vaulting ambition, who had incurred general hatred by his treacherous betrayal of the Caesar Gallus when he was in command of his guards, and because after the latter's death, elated by promotion to a higher rank, he formed similar plots against the Caesar Julian, and poured much malicious gossip into the receptive ears of the Augustus, to the great indignation of honourable men. He cannot have known the wise saying of old Aristotle, who, when he sent his pupil and kinsman Callisthenes on a mission to king Alexander, repeatedly enjoined him to speak as little as possible in the presence of a man in whose tongue lay the power of life and death, and then only in pleasant terms.

It need cause no surprise that men, whose minds we believe to be akin to the divine, can sometimes distinguish between what is likely to benefit them and the reverse, since even irrational animals protect themselves at times by observing dead silence. The following is a well-known example of this. When wild geese, in their migration from east to west to escape the heat, approach the Taurus mountains, where eagles are common, their fear of these formidable birds leads them to stop up their beaks with small stones, to prevent a cry escaping them, however hard-pressed. But when they have passed over these hills in rapid flight they let the stones fall, and so pursue their way free from fear.

4. Sapor prepares for war.

While great pains were being devoted to this inquiry at Sirmium, the dread trumpets of approaching danger were being sounded in the East. The king of Persia, reinforced by the wild peoples on whom he had imposed peace, and burning with superhuman eagerness to extend his realm, was preparing his armed forces and their commissariat.

Necromancy was invoked to assist his plans, and no method of divining the future left untried. He intended, when all his preparations were made, to launch a full-scale invasion at the beginning of spring.

When the first rumours of this were confirmed by reliable reports, overwhelming fear of imminent disaster kept everyone in suspense. The gang of courtiers, hammering day and night at the instigation of the eunuchs on the same anvil, to use the proverbial phrase, kept the image of Ursicinus before the mind of the timid and suspicious emperor like a kind of Gorgon's head, constantly repeating that, since for lack of better men he had been sent again to defend the East after the death of Silvanus, he was panting for a higher position. Several, moreover, attempted by persistent sickening flattery of this kind to purchase the favour of Eusebius the grand chamberlain, with whom, if the truth be told, Constantius had great influence, and who had a double reason for launching a bitter attack upon the master of cavalry. Ursicinus stood out above the rest as the only man who did without Eusebius' help, and he would not give up to Eusebius his house at Antioch, which the latter most importunately demanded from him. Like a snake bursting with venom which sends out a swarm of its little ones to do mischief when they can scarcely crawl, Eusebius dispatched his subordinates the moment they reached maturity to assail the reputation of the hero with malicious suggestions, which their attendance in private gave them the chance of insinuating into the ears of the credulous emperor in the childish and reedy voice of their kind. They promptly carried out their instructions. It is disgust with these creatures and their like that leads me to praise the early emperor Domitian, who, though he was unlike his father and brother and disgraced his memory by acts which merit undying detestation, nevertheless distinguished himself by one most welcome measure. He forbade under threat of severe penalties the castration of any boy within the bounds of the Roman jurisdiction. If he had not done so who could have endured the resulting swarms of eunuchs, since we can barely tolerate them in small numbers? Still, Eusebius proceeded with caution, pretending that if Ursicinus were recalled he might start a revolution; his real motive, however, was to bring him to the block as soon as a favourable opportunity presented itself.

While Ursicinus' enemies, a prey to anxiety, were playing a waiting game, we were making a short stay at Samosata, the famous capital of the former kingdom of Commagene. There we suddenly received repeated and consistent reports of a new commotion, which will be unfolded in the succeeding pages.

5. *Defection of Antoninus to Persia.*

There was a man called Antoninus who after making a fortune in trade had become a financial official in the service of the commander of Mesopotamia, and finally a staff-officer. He was a man of experience and intelligence and was very well known in that part of the world. He found himself involved in great losses through the greed of certain persons, and realizing that he was being more and more unfairly treated in his struggle against powerful interests, because those who were examining his case were inclined to show favour to the stronger side, he decided not to kick against the pricks but to adopt a more yielding and obsequious attitude. He acknowledged his debts, which had been collusively transferred to the imperial treasury, and then, with a monstrous project in mind, devoted himself to prying secretly into all the departments of state. He had a command of both languages which enabled him to examine the records and to note what forces were serving where and in what strength, and what would be their objective when they took the field; and he was indefatigable in his inquiries into the stocks of arms and provisions and other military supplies. When he had learnt the secrets of the whole East, while the greater part of the army and the money to pay it was distributed over Illyricum, where the emperor was detained by serious business, the appointed day drew near when he must pay the sum for which fear of violence had compelled him to give his bond. Seeing that danger threatened to crush him on all sides and that the treasury was putting such cruel pressure on him to pay in order to gratify another party, he took the prodigious step of attempting to desert to the Persians with his wife and children and all he held dear. To evade the frontier guards he bought cheap a property in Hiaspis, a district immediately bordering the Tigris. This device made him a landowner with a large staff, and no one dared to inquire why he visited the extreme limit of the Roman world. Through faithful friends who could swim he conducted a secret correspondence with Tamsapor, who was in charge of the defence of the whole region on the opposite bank and who was already known to him. Finally, assisted by a body of active men from the Persian camp, he embarked in boats at dead of night and was ferried across with all his loved ones, like Zopyrus, who made himself famous by betraying Babylon, though with the opposite intention.

When things had come to this pass in Mesopotamia the palace clique, with an eye to our destruction, kept up their old refrain, and at last found a handle for injuring our heroic general. The plan was contrived and pushed on by the gang of eunuchs, who are always savage and bitter, and who, because they lack family ties, lavish on wealth alone the affection due to a beloved child. It was decided that Sabinian, an elderly man of culture and wealth but no soldier, whose obscurity had hitherto kept him far from a senior appointment, should be sent to govern the East, while Ursicinus returned to the court to take over command of the infantry in succession to Barbatio. It was thought that the presence at home of a man whom they loudly averred was set on revolution would lay him open to formidable attack by his deadly enemies.

While the court of Constantius was the scene of doings fit for the brothel or the stage, and the distributors of bribes were sharing out among the houses of the influential the price of the office suddenly put on sale, Antoninus was conducted to the king's winter quarters and received with open arms. The honour of the tiara was conferred upon him; this entitles the wearer to be placed at the royal table, and to offer advice and bring forward his views in discussions of affairs of state. Henceforward Antoninus embarked upon his attack on Rome, not by dark and winding channels which need a pole or a tow-rope, so to speak, but under full sail. He worked upon the king, like Maharbal reproaching Hannibal for his slowness, by constantly asserting that though he could win victories he did not know how to use them. His training and wide experience in public life gained him an attentive hearing from a lively audience anxious to have its ears charmed. They listened to him like the Phaeacians in Homer, not with applause but with silent wonder, while he, going back forty years, reminded them that in spite of constant successes, especially at Hileia and Singara, where after a bitter battle by night, in which our troops were cut to pieces with enormous losses, hostilities were broken off as if a herald had interposed his sacred person, the Persians had not yet reached Edessa or the bridges over the Euphrates; whereas their military might and splendid successes ought to have given them the confidence to enlarge their realm *over the whole of Asia*, especially at a time when the best blood of Rome was being spilt on both sides in a prolonged civil war.

These and such as these were the arguments which the deserter, who kept sober himself, employed from time to time at the banquets at which, like the ancient Greeks, the Persians are in the habit of discussing military and other serious matters. He fired the eager king to take the field as soon as the winter was over, confident of success, and boldly promised for his own part to help in any way that was needed.

6. *Ursicinus is recalled from the East and then sent back. Adventures of Ammianus.*

Almost at the same moment Sabinian, bursting with pride at his unexpected appointment, arrived in Cilicia and delivered to his predecessor the emperor's letter. This invited Ursicinus to make all haste to the court to be invested with a higher honour, and this at a crisis which on any rational calculation would have demanded his presence in the East had he been in the furthest North, in view of his long experience in the service and his intimate knowledge of the Persian way of fighting. The people of the provinces were cut to the heart by this news; in the towns the magistrates and populace passed resolution after resolution with loud acclaim, and almost laid hands on him in their efforts to detain the man whom they looked on as the protector of them all. They remembered that when he was left to defend them with an inactive and apathetic force he had suffered no loss for ten years, and they feared for their safety when they discovered that he was to be removed at this critical moment and replaced by a man who was totally incompetent. Rumour, we believe beyond a shadow of doubt, flies through the air on the wings of the wind. The news of our situation which it carried brought the deliberations of the Persians to a head, and after much discussion it was decided on the proposition of Antoninus that, since Ursicinus had been removed and the new man was beneath contempt, they should not involve themselves in the dangers of siege operations but burst straight over the Euphrates and take by surprise the provinces which in all previous wars, except in the time of Gallienus, had been left untouched, and which had grown rich in the course of a long peace. In this enterprise Antoninus promised, God willing, to be a most useful guide. This proposal met with unanimous approval. Everyone busied himself in the rapid collection of what was needed, and the preparation of provisions, troops, weapons, and other military stores for the approaching campaign went on during the whole winter.

We, meanwhile, after a short stop on the nearer side of the Taurus, were hurrying towards Italy in obedience to our orders, and had nearly reached the river Maritza (Hebrus), which rises in the mountains of the Odrysae, when we received a letter from the emperor bidding us lose no time in returning to Mesopotamia, where we should have to undertake a dangerous enterprise without any staff, since the entire command had been transferred to another. This was designed by those who moulded the policy of the government for their mischievous ends, to ensure that if the Persians returned unsuccessful to their own territory the glory of the achievement should fall to the new commander, while if disaster ensued Ursicinus could be indicted for betraying his country. After much debate and with much hesitation we returned to find Sabinian full of self-importance. He was a man of middle height with a mean and narrow mind, so shamefully nervous that he could hardly bear the slight disturbance of a noisy party, still less the din of a battle.

Since, however, our scouts reported that the enemy was in a fever of preparation, and this was persistently confirmed by deserters, we left the little man yawning and marched in haste to make ready for the defence of Nisibis, fearing that the Persians might disguise their intention to besiege it and then fall upon it unaware. While the necessary measures were being pushed on inside the walls, smoky fires were seen flickering from the direction of the Tigris past the Moors' Fort and Sisara and the rest of the frontier country in an unbroken chain right up to the city, in such unusual numbers that it was clear that the enemy's raiding parties had broken through and crossed the river. We hurried on at full speed in case the roads should be blocked, but when we were two miles from the city we came upon a child crying in the middle of the road. He was a fine boy, apparently about eight years old, and was wearing a neck ornament. He told us that he was the son of a man of good family, and that his mother, panic-stricken at the approach of the enemy, had abandoned him because he was a clog on her flight. Our general pitied him, and on his orders I set the boy before me on my horse and took him back to the city, but I found the walls already invested and enemy parties scouring the neighbourhood.

Dreading to find myself involved in the miseries of a siege, I put the boy down in the shelter of a postern gate that was not entirely shut, and galloped back half dead with fear to rejoin our column, but I only just avoided capture. A troop of the enemy's horse was pursuing a tribune called Abdigild and his batman. The master got away but the servant was caught. At the moment when I darted by they were asking him who was the official who had left the city, and when they heard that it was Ursicinus, who had visited the city shortly before and was now making for Mount Izala, they killed their informant, got together more of their number in a single body, and pursued me unflaggingly. Thanks to the speed of my mount I kept in front of them, and found our men, who had turned their horses out to graze, taking their ease by the ramshackle fort of Amudis. I stretched out my arm, gathered up the edges of my cloak, and waved it in the air, to give the usual signal that the enemy was upon them. In their company I was carried along at their pace, although my horse was now almost dropping. Our alarm was increased by the full moon and the flatness of the country round, which was devoid of trees and bushes and covered only by short grass, so that if we were harder pressed we should have nowhere to hide. So we adopted the device of tying a lighted lantern securely on the back of a pack-animal, and turning it loose by itself without a driver towards the left, while we pursued our way towards the hills on our right. The idea was that the Persians would believe that this torch of tallow was lighting the slow progress of our general, and would take that road rather than any other. But for this trick we should have been surrounded and taken, and have fallen into the hands of the enemy.

Having escaped this danger we came to a wooded area called Meiacarire, which is planted with vines and fruit-trees and takes its name from its cold springs. All the inhabitants had disappeared, but lurking in a remote corner we found a single soldier, who was brought before our general. Suspicion was aroused by the inconsistent answers that he gave in his fright, and finally threats extracted from him the whole truth. He was a native of Gaul born at Paris and had served in a cavalry regiment, but to escape punishment for some offence had deserted to Persia. There he married and raised a family, and was so well thought of that he was employed as a spy, and often brought back reliable information from behind our lines. On the present occasion he had been sent by Tamsapor and Nohodares, the grandees in command of the raiding-parties, and was on his way back to report to them. When he had told us what he knew of the operations of the other side he was put to death.

This incident heightened our anxiety, and we hurried on as fast as we could to Amida, a town whose later calamities made it famous. There our scouts rejoined us, and brought a sheet of parchment written in code and hidden in a scabbard. It came from Procopius, who had been sent with count Lucillian on a mission to the Persians, as I have already said. The purport of the message, which was deliberately wrapped in obscure terms to prevent the dreadful consequences that would follow if its bearers were seized and its contents understood, was as follows:

'The envoys of the Greeks have been removed to a distance, and may be put to death. The aged king, not content with Hellespont, will throw bridges across the Granicus and the Rhyndacus and invade Asia with a vast host. He is easily roused to passion and very cruel, and his natural temper is being worked upon and inflamed by a man who is the successor of the former Roman emperor Hadrian. If Greece does not take steps in time, all will be utterly lost.'

The inner meaning of this was that the Persian king, under the influence of Antoninus, had crossed the Anzaba and the Tigris and was aiming at dominion over the whole East. When the message had been deciphered, a matter of great difficulty because of its extreme obscurity, a clever plan was formed.

Corduene, which was subject to Persia, was ruled at that time by a satrap who was known on Roman soil as Jovinian. He was a young man whose secret sympathies lay with us, because as a hostage in Syria he had succumbed to the charm of liberal studies and ardently desired to return to our land. I was sent to him together with a loyal centurion to discover more accurately what was happening. Our way lay through pathless mountains and steep gorges. On my arrival he recognized me and received me warmly, and I communicated to him in confidence why I was there. He sent me with a silent guide who knew the country to a high and rocky place a long way off, from which, if one's eyesight were good enough, the smallest object would be visible fifty miles away. We waited there two whole days, and at dawn on the third we saw the whole expanse of country below us, stretching to what we Greeks call the horizon, covered with columns of troops, headed by the king in gleaming robes. On his left was Grumbates, king of the Chionitae, a man in middle life and of withered frame, but renowned for his great spirit and many glorious victories. On the king's right was the king of the Albani, Grumbates' equal in rank and honour; behind them came various highly-placed generals, followed by a host of all ranks drawn from the flower of the neighbouring peoples and inured to hardship by long experience.

How far can the Greeks' love of the fabulous go? They are always talking of the town of Doriscus in Thrace and of the armies which were counted there by being enclosed regiment by regiment in a pen, whereas I, a cautious, or to tell the truth, a timid historian, refrain from exaggerating what has been placed beyond doubt by reliable evidence.

7. Sapor invades Mesopotamia.

Passing by Nineveh, the great city of Adiabene, the kings offered sacrifice in the middle of the bridge over the Anzaba, and finding the omens favourable crossed with great confidence. Judging that the rest of the host would take at least three days to penetrate our territory, we returned in haste to rest and recruit our strength with the hospitable satrap. Then, faster than might have been expected, we retraced our steps over the lonely wilderness, taking comfort from the thought that necessity left us no choice, and brought to our perplexed comrades the sure news that the kings, without making any detour, had crossed the river on a single bridge of boats. Dispatch riders were sent at once to Cassian, the general in Mesopotamia, and Euphronius, then governor of the province, with orders to compel the country folk to move with their families and all their livestock to places of safety. Carrhae was to be evacuated immediately, because of the weakness of its fortifications, and the whole country set on fire, to deprive the enemy of a source of fodder. No time was lost in carrying out these instructions, and once fire was applied the fury of the raging element so completely burnt up the young vegetation and the grain, which was already swelling on its yellow stalks, that from the banks of the Tigris to the Euphrates not a green thing was to be seen. At the same time many wild animals were burnt to death, especially lions, which infest that region to a fearful extent, and often meet their end or lose their sight in the following way. The reed-beds and thickets which fringe the rivers of Mesopotamia are the haunt of countless lions, which are always harmless during the mild winters that prevail there. But when the burning sun brings the torrid season and the country is scorched by the heat they are plagued by the sultry weather and by the hosts of midges which swarm all over that part of the world. These insects are attracted by the moistness and brightness of the lions' eyes and settle on the surface of their eyelids. Then the lions, driven mad by the irritation, either plunge into the rivers to escape the torture and are drowned, or else lose their sight by constantly scratching their eyes with their claws, and are driven to a frenzy of rage. But for this the whole of the East would be overrun by these creatures.

While the country was being burnt, as I have told, tribunes were sent with members of the staff to reinforce our bank of the Euphrates with strong points and sharp stakes and every kind of defensive device. At potential crossings, where the stream was free from eddies, they planted engines which hurl missiles.

While these hasty measures were being taken, Sabinian, the general so appropriately chosen to conduct a deadly war, at a time when the common danger required that not a moment should be lost, was leading a life of dissolute luxury among the cemeteries of Edessa, secure, I suppose, in the belief that the dead were in no position to disturb the peace. He was being entertained in an atmosphere of profound calm by a pyrrhic war-dance, in which the gestures of the participants were accompanied by music. This was a performance which augured ill in itself and particularly in such a place, since the course of events teaches us that all good men should avoid words and acts of this kind, which are a sad presage of troubles to come.

Meanwhile the kings passed by Nisibis without thinking it worth-while to halt. The fires were spreading through the variety of dry material which they found to feed on, and to avoid a shortage of fodder the Persians took their way through the grassy valleys at the foot of the mountains. When they came to the domain of Bebase, between which and the town of Constantina, a hundred miles away, the country is parched by perpetual drought, except for a trickle of water in the wells, they hesitated for some time about their best course. Finally they decided to trust to the endurance of their men and brave the desert, only to learn that the Euphrates, swollen with melted snow, had burst its banks over a wide area and could not be forded anywhere. Finding themselves unexpectedly frustrated they decided to embrace whatever opportunity chance threw in their way. In view of the danger of their position they held an emergency meeting and told Antoninus to give his opinion. He at once advised them to turn to the right and make a considerable detour through an area which could supply all their needs and which the Romans had left untouched in the belief that the enemy would take the direct route. He would show the way to the two fortified camps of Barzalo and Claudias, where the river, being still near its source and not yet augmented by tributaries, was shallow and narrow and easily fordable. This advice was adopted. Antoninus was told to guide them by the way he knew, and the whole army abandoned its projected route and followed his lead.

8. *Ammianus reaches Amida.*

Hearing reports of these movements from reliable scouts, we decided to hurry to Samosata, cross the river at that point, and break down the bridges at Zeugma and Capersana, trusting that fortune would enable us to repel the enemy's attack. But a dreadful disgrace befell us which would be better buried in complete oblivion. Some seven hundred horse in two squadrons had lately been sent from Illyricum to reinforce Mesopotamia. They were a feeble and cowardly lot, and were given the duty of keeping watch over the enemy's route. They were so afraid of being surprised at night that in the evening, when it was particularly necessary that every path should be guarded, they used to withdraw to a distance from the main roads. Tamsapor and Nohodar became aware of this, and took advantage of their drunken sleep to slip by unseen with a force of some twenty thousand Persians, who were hidden with their weapons behind some high ground in the neighbourhood of Amida.

We, as I said, were about to set off for Samosata and were on the march before it was fully light, when as we reached a point of vantage the gleam of shining arms struck our eyes. An excited shout proclaimed that the enemy was upon us, so in obedience to the usual signal we halted in close order. Prudence suggested that we should neither take flight, since our pursuers were in view, nor yet meet certain death by giving battle to an enemy who were our superior in numbers and cavalry. At last, when a clash became absolutely inevitable but while we were still in doubt about our tactics, some of our men were rash enough to run out in front of our line and were killed. Both sides pressed forward, and Antoninus, leading a troop spoiling for the fight, was recognized by Ursicinus, who denounced him in violent terms as a traitor and a criminal. Thereupon Antoninus took from his head the tiara which he wore as a badge of honour, sprang from his horse, and, bowing so low that his face almost touched the ground, addressed Ursicinus as his patron and master, at the same time clasping his hands behind his back, a gesture of supplication among the Assyrians. 'Forgive me,' he said, 'most noble count, for conduct which I know is criminal, but which springs from necessity, not from choice. It is the exactions of wicked men, as you know, which have ruined me; against their avarice even so great a man as you has been unable to defend my wretched self.' With these words he withdrew, not turning away but walking backwards respectfully till he was out of sight.

Some half an hour had passed thus when our rearguard, who occupied higher ground, shouted that they had seen another body of heavy cavalry behind us and that it was fast approaching. As often happens in such desperate circumstances we were in doubt which way we should or could face, and under the pressure of the vast throng we all scattered and took each the nearest way out. But in the course of this sauve-qui-peut our broken troops became involved with the enemy skirmishers. So we gave ourselves up for lost and made a brave fight of it as we were driven to the banks of the Tigris, which at that point are deeply undercut. Some were driven headlong over the edge, and stuck in the shallows, hampered by their armour; others were sucked down by eddies; a number kept up the fight against the enemy with varying success; while a few, terrified by the massed formations, made for the nearest spurs of the Taurus mountains. Among these was our general himself; he was recognized and surrounded by a crowd of assailants, but the speed of his horse enabled him to get away with the tribune Aiadelthes and a single groom.

I meanwhile had been separated from my comrades and was considering my best course, when I fell in with Verinian, a staff-officer whose thigh had been pierced by an arrow. While I was trying to pull it out at his earnest entreaty, I was surrounded by the foremost Persians and made for the town, crawling along out of breath. On the side on which we were attacked the approach to the town lay up a steep hill. This could be scaled only by a single narrow passage, *which was further constricted by large blocks quarried from the hills and set in close order to reduce the width of the path.* Here we remained motionless till the following morning, mixed with the Persians who were making the same strenuous effort to reach the higher ground. We were so tightly packed that the bodies of the dead remained upright in the press because there was no room for them to fall, and a soldier in front of me, whose head had been split into two equal halves by a powerful sword-stroke, was so hemmed in on all sides that his corpse stood there like a stump. Showers of missiles from every kind of engine flew from the battlements, but we were saved from these by being so near the walls. At last I made my way in through a postern, and found the town crammed with people of both sexes who had flocked in from the neighbourhood. It so happened that this was the very time at which an annual fair was held in the suburbs, so that the normal population was swollen by crowds of country folk. There was a confused babel of cries; some were lamenting their lost friends and others were mortally wounded; many were calling out the names of their nearest and dearest, whom they could not see by reason of the throng.

9. Description of Amida.

This town was once very small, but Constantius, while he was still Caesar and at the same time as he built another town called Antoninupolis, enclosed it with strong towers and walls to provide a safe place of refuge for the neighbourhood, and established it in an arsenal of engines to repel an assault. This made it a formidable stronghold, which he desired to have called after his own name. On its southern side it is washed by a bend of the Tigris, which rises nearby; where it faces the east it looks down on the plains of Mesopotamia; on the north it is close to the river Nymphaeus and overshadowed by the peaks of Taurus, which divide the peoples beyond the Tigris from Armenia; and on the west it borders on Gumathena, a rich and well-cultivated region in which there is a village called Abarne celebrated for its medicinal hot springs. In the heart of Amida itself there gushes out beneath the citadel an abundant spring, which is drinkable but sometimes stinks in hot and humid weather. The permanent garrison of the town consisted of the Legion V Parthica together with a respectable detachment of native horse. But at this time its strong defences were also manned by six further legions, which had forestalled the approach of the Persian host by forced marches. There were troops of Magnentius and Decentius, who at the conclusion of the civil war had been posted by the emperor on account of their disloyalty and bad discipline to the East, where there was no fear of any but a foreign enemy. There were also the men of Legions XXX and X Fortenses, together with the Skirmishers and Scouts under the command of Aelian, who was now a count. These last, while they were still raw recruits, had made a sally from Singara under the same officer, then only a staff-officer, and had slaughtered a

DESCRIPTION OF AMIDA

great number of Persians in their sleep, as I have related earlier. Finally, there were the greater part of the household archers, the name given to detachments of horse in which serve all the barbarians of free birth who are pre-eminent for skill in arms and physical strength.

10. Surrender of two Roman forts.

While the storm of the Persians' first offensive was causing this unexpected disturbance, the king with his own people and the others under his command turned to the right at Bebase in accordance with Antoninus' advice, and took the road by Horren and Meiacarire and Charcha as if he meant to leave Amida on one side. As he approached two Roman forts called Reman and Busan he was informed by some deserters that many people had removed their treasure to these places, believing that it would be safe within their high walls. He was told too that he would find there with valuable chattels a woman of great beauty with her little daughter; she was the wife of one Craugasius of Nisibis, whose birth, reputation, and influence had won him great respect among the worthies of that town. So Sapor, spurred on by greed to possess himself of others' property, felt no qualms about launching an assault, and the inhabitants, panic-stricken at the sight of his multifarious array, surrendered themselves and all those who had taken refuge with them. On the order to evacuate the place they at once gave up the keys, and once the gates were open all the treasure stored within was ransacked. Women were dragged out stupefied with fear and with their children clinging to them; even at their tender age they were fated to experience the bitterness of grief. The king, finding by inquiry which was the wife of Craugasius, ordered that she should be allowed to approach him without fear, though she expected that she would be offered violence. Her face was covered with a black veil that left only her lips exposed, and when the king saw her he gave her a courteous assurance that she might hope to be reunited with her husband and that her honour should remain unspotted. Hearing that her husband loved her passionately, he thought that he could use her to purchase the betrayal of Nisibis. Finding that there were also other women who had been consecrated to a life of virginity according to the rites of the Christians, the king ordered that they too should be kept inviolate and allowed to practise their accustomed worship without hindrance. This pretence of mildness was assumed for the occasion in the hope that all whom he had previously terrified by his dread cruelty would lay aside their fear and come over to him of their own accord, once they realized from these latest instances that he now intended to employ his great success with humanity and gentleness.

BOOK 19

1. *Preliminaries to siege of Amida.*

The king set off from this place, delighted to have reduced our men to the miseries of captivity and confident of further successes of the same kind. Three days' slow advance brought him to Amida. At the first gleam of dawn the landscape as far as the eye could reach was a-glitter with arms, and hill and plain covered with cavalry in coats of mail. Towering on his horse above the rest rode the king at the head of his whole army. He had exchanged his diadem for a helmet in the shape of a ram's head, of gold set with precious stones, and his splendour was enhanced by a train of high dignitaries and an escort drawn from various peoples. It was taken for granted that he would do no more than parley with the garrison, since he was in a hurry to be off elsewhere in accordance with Antoninus' advice. But Heaven, whose will it was that the troubles of the whole Roman state should be concentrated within the circuit of a single region, had inspired Sapor with such boundless confidence that he believed that the mere sight of him would be enough to strike panic into the besieged and reduce them to humble entreaties. So he rode up to the gates, accompanied by his royal escort, and had the hardihood to approach so near that even his features could be clearly seen. His trappings made him a target for arrows and other missiles, and he would have perished under them had not the dust hidden him from the sight of the marksmen, and preserved him, with the loss of part of his cloak which was torn off by a missile, to be the author of countless massacres at a later time. This experience caused him to treat his foes as if they had committed sacrilege. He declared that the master of so many kings and peoples had been subjected to unhallowed outrage, and devoted himself to preparations for the utter destruction of the city. But when his most distinguished generals begged him not to let his rage deflect him from the glorious enterprise he had taken in hand he allowed himself to be persuaded, and decided that on the following day the besieged should again be summoned to surrender.

At daybreak, therefore, Grumbates, king of the Chionitae, advanced boldly towards the walls with a body of stout men to carry out Sapor's errand. Seeing him within range a crack shot on the walls discharged his weapon, and the bolt went through the breastplate and breast of Grumbates' son, who was close to his father's side. He was a prince in early manhood who surpassed his peers in height and good looks. At his fall his countrymen scattered in flight, but shortly afterwards returned, rightly fearing that his body might be carried off, and roused a number of tribes to arms with their harsh cries. When these joined in, missiles flew from both sides like hail and a fierce fight ensued. This deadly struggle continued till nightfall, when the body, which it had been hard to protect among the heaps of slain and torrents of blood, was dragged away under cover of darkness, like the corpse of Achilles' friend Patroclus at Troy, over which his comrades fought bitterly. The king's court was saddened by this death, and all the notables joined with the father in his grief at so sudden a disaster. A truce was proclaimed, and the young man, who was greatly loved for his noble qualities, was mourned after the manner of his own people. He was carried out dressed in the armour he usually wore and placed on a great high catafalque, round which were ranged ten couches bearing the effigies of dead men, laid out with such care that they looked like bodies already buried. For seven days all the men, with their tent-mates or by companies, gave themselves up to feasting, accompanied by dances and the singing of dismal dirges. This was their way of lamenting their young prince. But the women beat their breasts in sorrow and wailed in their accustomed manner because the hope of their race had been cut off in its first bloom. They were like the worshippers of Venus who are often seen weeping at the sacred rites commemorating the death of Adonis, which in the mystery religions is held to symbolize the ripening of the harvest.

2. *Amida surrounded and assaulted.*

When the body had been burnt and the bones enclosed in a silver urn to be taken home and committed to the ground as his father decreed, a council of war was held, and it was decided to propitiate the spirit of the dead man by destroying and burning the city, since Grumbates refused to let them march onward leaving the shade of his only child unavenged. So after resting for two days and sending out large parties to ravage the rich farmlands, which lay unprotected as in time of peace, the Persians surrounded the city with a circle of shields five deep. On the morning of the third day the prospect in every direction as far as the eye could reach was filled by squadrons of horse with gleaming arms, as the various detachments advancing at a slow pace took the positions assigned to them by lot. The whole circuit of the walls was beset by the Persians. The eastern side, where the young prince had fallen with such fatal consequences for us, was occupied by the Chionitae; the Cuseni were posted on the south, the Albani watched on the north, and the Segestani, the fiercest warriors of all, were stationed opposite the western gate. These last were accompanied by lines of elephants, wrinkled monsters of enormous height, which advanced slowly loaded with armed men, a sight more dreadful than any other form of horror, as I have often declared.

Seeing such countless peoples, who had been gathered over a long period to set the Roman world ablaze, concentrated on our destruction, we abandoned all hope. From that moment the one thing we all longed for was to find a way of ending our lives with glory. From dawn to nightfall the enemy ranks stood motionless, as though rooted to the spot. Not a sound was heard, not even the neighing of a horse. Then they withdrew without breaking their formation and refreshed themselves with food and sleep, but when night was almost over the trumpets sounded and they again drew their awful ring round the city, expecting that it would soon fall. Hardly had Grumbates hurled a spear dipped in blood, according to his native custom and the practice of our envoys at the declaration of war, when the army with a clashing of weapons flew at our walls. Instantly the grim storm of war blew high, as the cavalry advanced at a gallop and threw themselves into the fight, and our men met them with keen and determined resistance.

There was much shattering of enemy heads under the crushing weight of the stones hurled by our engines. Others were pierced by arrows, some were transfixed by missiles and littered the ground with their bodies, while those who were wounded ran in headlong flight to rejoin their comrades. Nor were there fewer sights of woe and death inside the city. Dense clouds of arrows darkened the sky, and the siege engines which the Persians had acquired at the sack of Singara inflicted many wounds. The garrison, recovering their strength and returning to the fight from which they had withdrawn in relays, showed the greatest spirit, but fell when wounded with disastrous effect; either their torn bodies overset their neighbours as they rolled against them, or else, if they still lived with arrows in them, they called for help from those who had the skill to pull them out. So carnage was piled on carnage and prolonged to the end of the day; even the shades of evening did nothing to abate it, such was the obstinacy shown by both sides. Men watched through the night without laying aside their arms, and the hills re-echoed with the shouts which rose on either hand. Our men extolled the prowess of Constantius Caesar, 'lord of all things and of the world', while the Persians hailed Sapor as Saanshah and Peroz, titles which signify 'king of kings' and 'conqueror in war'.

Before dawn, at a call from the trumpets, the battle was renewed with undiminished intensity, and countless forces moved forward on all sides like birds of prey. Far and wide, wherever one looked, the plains and valleys revealed nothing but the flashing arms of fierce tribesmen. Then with a shout all rushed forward in a wild charge; a mighty volley of missiles was fired from the walls, and, as might be expected in so dense a throng, none of them missed its mark. In this desperate situation what inspired us, as I have said, was not the hope of saving our lives but a burning desire to die bravely. From dawn to dusk the struggle was waged with more fury than discretion, and neither side gained an advantage. Shouts of rage mingled with cries of fear, and the fight was so keen that hardly a man could stand his ground unwounded. At last night put an end to the slaughter. Both sides had suffered such losses that they allowed themselves a longer breathing-space, but even when we gained a chance to rest the continuous strain which we had undergone without sleep sapped our slight reserves of strength. We were terrified by the blood and the pale faces of the dying, to whom the shortage of space within the walls forbade us to pay even the last tribute of burial. The narrow circuit of the town contained seven legions, a heterogeneous crowd of strangers and citizens of both sexes, and a few other troops, amounting in all to 20,000 souls. Everyone tended his own wounds as best he could or as medical help was available; some of the seriously wounded gave up the ghost from loss of blood after a long struggle; others, mangled by sword-thrusts, were treated without success, and when they at last expired their dead bodies were thrown aside; in some cases of extensive injury the surgeons forbade any attempt at treatment, which would only inflict further useless pain;

a number who faced the hazard of pulling out the arrows endured torments that were worse than death.

3. Ursicinus' efforts to surprise the besiegers frustrated.

While the two sides were fighting so obstinately at Amida, Ursicinus, chagrined that he was dependent on the will of a man who was his superior officer, kept urging Sabinian, who was still lingering among his tombs, to get together all his light-armed troops and hurry to the scene by a hidden route which skirted the foot of the mountains. With these forces they would be able with any luck to cut off the enemy's pickets and fall on the detachments who watched at night round the long circuit of the walls, or at least by incessant pinpricks divert the foe from his dogged prosecution of the siege. Sabinian opposed the suggestion on the ground that it was dangerous. He produced a letter from the emperor which expressly enjoined that only operations which would involve no loss to the army should be attempted, but he kept hidden in his heart the instructions that had been dinned into him at court. These were that he should deprive his predecessor, who was thirsting for glory, of any opportunity of acquiring honour, even if it should be likely to redound to the advantage of the state. So eager were his enemies to prevent the hero from gaining reputation as the originator or partner of any memorable exploit, that they were prepared to sacrifice the provinces to attain this end. Ursicinus, shattered by this treatment, frequently sent us scouts, though none of them could easily enter the town because so strict a watch was kept. But all his helpful schemes could effect nothing. He was like a lion of huge size and grim aspect which does not dare to go to the rescue of its trapped whelps because it has lost its claws and teeth.

4. Epidemic at Amida.

But in the town, where the number of corpses lying in the streets was too great to allow them to be buried, our troubles were increased by an outbreak of plague, fomented by the rotting of worm-eaten bodies, the humid heat, and the feeble state to which the inhabitants were reduced. I will briefly explain the causes which give rise to this type of malady.

Scientists and eminent physicians tell us that infectious diseases are brought on by excess of cold or heat, or of moisture or dryness. That is why people who live in damp or marshy places suffer from coughs and ophthalmia and the like, whereas the inhabitants of hot countries are dehydrated by burning fever. Since fire is the most violent of the elements, drought is the quickest road to death. For this reason, when Greece was sweating through a ten years' war to prevent Paris escaping the penalty for breaking up a royal marriage, a pestilence of this kind raged among them, and many perished from the darts of Apollo, whom we may identify with the sun. And, as Thucydides reports, the severe type of sickness which disastrously afflicted Athens at the beginning of the Peloponnesian War arose in the torrid region of Ethiopia and gradually spread until it reached Athens.

Others assert that the air, like water, can be infected by the stench of dead bodies or the like and gravely affect men's health, or at any rate that minor illnesses are caused by a sudden change of air. There are also some who say that when the atmosphere is thickened by unusually dense exhalations from the earth it blocks the body's natural vents and sometimes causes death. That is why, as we know from Homer and many later instances, animals which, unlike men, have their heads permanently bent towards the ground, are the first to perish when such a pestilence breaks out.

The first type of pestilence, which causes the inhabitants of excessively dry regions to be visited by frequent fevers, is called endemic. The second, which occurs periodically and affects the sight and causes dangerous humours in the body, is epidemic. The third is plague, which also lasts only for a time, but brings death with lightning speed.

We were weakened by this destructive outbreak, and a few died from the excessive heat, which was made worse by the crowded conditions, but on the night after the tenth day a slight fall of rain dispelled the thick and stifling air, and we regained our health.

5. *Two attacks on Amida.*

Meanwhile the Persian was not inactive. Mantlets and penthouses were being erected round the city, and high towers faced with iron were going up. On the top of each of these was placed a piece of artillery to drive the defenders from the ramparts. At the same time skirmishing by slingers and archers went on without the slightest pause.

We had with us, as I have already said, two of Magnentius' legions which had recently arrived from Gaul. These were strong and active men, admirably suited to fighting in open country, but quite useless, indeed a positive nuisance, in the kind of warfare to which we were restricted. They were no help in working the artillery or constructing defensive works, and from time to time they made senseless sallies, from which after fighting with great boldness they returned with diminished numbers, having done about as much good, in the proverbial phrase, as a man throwing water single-handed on a large-scale fire. Finally, when the gates were barred and they could not get out against their officers' orders, they snarled like wild beasts. But in the days that followed they were conspicuously effective, as will be seen.

In a remote part of the southern wall, which commands the river Tigris, there was a tower rising to a great height, under which yawned a precipice so steep that one could not look down without fearful dizziness. An underground passage cut through the bowels of the rock led by cunningly constructed steps from the bottom of the cliff to the level of the city. Through this water could be brought in secretly from the bed of the river, and I have seen the same thing in all the fortified places in those parts which are flanked by streams. This dark passage was so steep that it was left unguarded, and through it a renegade townsman, who had deserted to the other side, conducted seventy Persian archers of proved skill and loyalty from the king's own troop. Taking advantage of this remote and silent spot these men climbed suddenly in single file at midnight to the third storey of the tower, where they lay in hiding. But in the morning they displayed a scarlet cloak, which was the signal for battle, and, seeing their own forces flooding towards the city on every side, emptied their quivers, flung them at their feet, and discharged their arrows with consummate skill and a concerted yell that set everything alight. Soon all the massed forces of the enemy were assaulting the city far more furiously than before. We were divided in mind whether to direct our resistance against the threat from above or on the host mounted on scaling ladders which already had the very battlements in its grasp. So we shared the work and moved five of the lighter engines to positions opposite the tower. These kept up a rapid fire of wooden projectiles, some of which transfixed two men at once; part of the force fell seriously wounded, others, in panic at the noise of the artillery, threw themselves down headlong and were dashed to pieces. All this was the work of a moment. The engines were then restored to their usual places, and our united efforts enabled us to defend the walls with rather more confidence. The

criminal act of the deserter added fuel to the fury of our men; they
hurled their various missiles with all their strength, as if they were
charging on level ground, with the result that towards noon the
tribesmen suffered a severe repulse, and made for their tents lamenting
the death of many of their number and in fear of further losses.

6. *A sally by the Gallic legions.*

The wind of fortune blew upon us somewhat more favourably, since
the day had passed without loss to us and disastrously for the enemy.
Its remaining hours we spent in rest and refreshment, but at dawn on
the morrow we saw from the citadel a countless host of captives being
taken to the enemy's territory from the fortress of Ziata. This was a
capacious place with walls more than a mile in perimeter, within which
a heterogeneous crowd had taken refuge. These same days had seen the
seizure and burning of other forts as well, from which several thousand
people were dragged along the road to slavery. Among them were many
feeble old men and aged women. When their strength gave out for
various reasons under the hardships of the long march and they lost
any desire to live, their calves or hams were severed and they were left
behind.

   When the Gallic troops saw this crowd of wretched creatures, they
gave way to an impulse which was intelligible enough but ill-timed.
They clamoured to be given a chance of engaging the enemy, and
threatened their officers and superiors with death if they persisted in
forbidding them. Like wild beasts maddened by the stench of carrion,
which hurl themselves against the revolving bars of their cages in an
effort to get out, these men hewed with their swords at the gates, which
were bolted, as I said before. They were desperately afraid that they
might lose their lives without having performed any notable exploit, if
the city fell, or alternatively that it might be said that they had done
nothing to justify their country's reputation for courage if it were saved.
They had, it is true, already made a number of sallies, but in trying to
hinder the erection of ramps they had themselves suffered losses equal
to those they inflicted.

   In our helpless state we could not see how to resist their fury. In the
end the best plan we could hit on, to which we won their grudging
assent, was this. Since they could no longer be restrained they should
be allowed after a short delay to attack the enemy's outposts, which

were almost within range of our missiles. If they broke through they
could continue their advance, since it was clear that if they were
successful they would create great havoc. While preparations for this
were being made, no effort was spared for the defence of the walls. We
vied with one another in working and keeping watch and in placing
engines to fire stones and javelins on every side. But a body of Persian
infantry succeeded in erecting two high ramps, and their preparations
for the final assault went slowly on. Our men countered them by
devoting prodigious efforts to the construction of two great earthworks
rising to the same height as those of the enemy and capable of sustaining
even the enormous weight of our fighting men.

Meanwhile the Gauls, refusing to wait any longer, emerged from a
postern gate armed with axes and swords, taking advantage of a dark
night – it was the night before the new moon – and praying for the
blessing of heaven upon their enterprise. As they drew near they actually
held their breath; then in close order they made a furious charge, killed
some of the pickets, and cut down the sentries outside the camp, who
were so far from expecting an attack that they had gone to sleep. They
even entertained a secret hope that if luck were with them they might
surprise the very quarters of the king. But, slight though it was, the
sound of their movements and the groans of the dying roused many of
the enemy from sleep. Each man raised the cry 'To arms!', while our
men stood rooted to the spot and dared not advance. It would have
been imprudent, now that those whom they sought to surprise were
awake, to rush into the obvious danger presented by the hordes of
furious Persians who were flocking to the fight from every side. The
Gauls stood their ground with unshaken strength and courage as long
as they could, hacking at the enemy with their swords, but when some
of their number had fallen or been wounded by the hail of arrows which
rained on them, and they realized that the converging battalions of the
foe were concentrating their whole weight on a single spot, they made
haste to withdraw. None of them, however, turned his back, and when
they could no longer sustain the pressure of the serried ranks facing
them they allowed themselves to be gradually pushed outside the
rampart as if they were marching in time to music. The blare of horns
from the Persian camp quickened their retreat. These were answered
by the sound of many trumpets from the city, as the gates were thrown
open to receive our men if they succeeded in getting so far. Our artillery
whirred without firing any shot, so that the commanders of the Persian

outposts, *who did not know what was going on behind them after their comrades were killed, might abandon their position* opposite the walls, and thus allow our brave men to be admitted unharmed.

These tactics enabled the Gauls to enter about daybreak, but with reduced numbers. Some were fatally, others slightly, wounded, and their total losses that night amounted to 400 men. If luck had not been against them they might have slain the king of Persia in his very tent, surrounded by a hundred thousand men, a mightier exploit than killing Rhesus and his Thracians in their sleep before the walls of Troy. After the destruction of the city the emperor caused statues in full armour to be set up in a public place at Edessa in honour of the drill-sergeants who had led them in this heroic action. These statues have remained intact to the present day.

When the battlefield was revealed in the light of day the bodies of grandees and satraps were found among the slain, and harsh cries and wails showed how fate had struck in different places. There was general mourning, and angry complaints were heard among the kings at the thought that the Romans had penetrated their outposts before the walls. A three-day truce was appointed by common consent, and this gave us also a breathing-space.

7. *Progress of the siege.*

Then the enemy, outraged and infuriated by this novel mishap, lost no more time. Since sheer force was having little success they decided to settle the matter by siege-works. So eager were they for battle that they were ready either to propitiate the spirits of the slain by the destruction of the city or to meet a glorious death.

The necessary measures were taken amid general enthusiasm, and as the morning star was rising various forms of siege-engine together with armoured towers were moved forward to the walls. On the high tops of these were pieces of artillery, which threw into confusion those who were active in defence at a lower level. When it was getting light, men in mail appeared, in such numbers as to obscure the entire view, and the serried ranks came on, not as previously in disorderly fashion, but at a slow pace regulated by trumpet calls. No one broke the ranks by running ahead; they advanced under cover of their mantlets, holding wicker hurdles in front of them. When they came within range the Persian infantry had difficulty in protecting themselves against the arrows shot from the walls by our machines, and adopted a more open order. Hardly a missile failed to find its mark; even the heavy cavalry wavered and gave ground, which put new heart into our men. But their artillery on the armoured towers prevailed against the defence below; their superior position brought them corresponding success and they caused much bloodshed. When evening fell there was a lull on both sides, but the greater part of the night was spent by us in trying to devise some way of countering this terrible threat.

After turning over many possibilities we adopted a plan which depended for success on rapid execution. This was to bring up four scorpions to return the fire from the towers. But while they were being carefully moved into positions exactly opposite, a very delicate operation, day dawned and brought us greater misery. It revealed formidable bodies of Persians supported by lines of elephants, whose noise and monstrous size make them the most frightful objects the human mind can conceive. But while we were beset on all sides by the combined pressure of armed men, siege-works, and wild beasts, round stones hurled from the battlements by the iron slings of our scorpions shattered the joints of the towers, and threw their artillery and those who worked it headlong down. Some died of the fall without being wounded, others were crushed by the weight of debris. The elephants, too, were forcibly repulsed. As soon as the firebrands which were thrown at them touched their bodies, they bolted and their mahouts lost control. But though we subsequently burned their siege-works the enemy gave us no rest. The Persian king himself, though he is never obliged to fight in person, was so incensed by these stormy setbacks that he rushed forward into the thick of the fray like a common soldier. This was a novel and quite unprecedented event. The number of his suite made him conspicuous even at a distance, and he was the target of a hail of missiles. After losing many of his attendants he withdrew, passing in turn through the lines of his disciplined troops, and at the end of the day, undaunted by the ghastly sight presented by the dead and wounded, he at last allowed a brief interval of rest.

8. *Amida taken by storm. Escape of Ammianus.*

Night had put an end to the fighting and allowed a brief sleep, but at the first gleam of day the king, bursting with rage and resentment and resolved to stick at nothing to achieve his object, launched his peoples against us. Since, as I have said, his siege-works had been burnt, he tried to carry on the fight by means of high ramps built close to the walls, while our men, who had spared no effort in heaping up a mound of earth on the inside, resisted with equal vigour in this critical situation.

For a long time the outcome of this bloody fight hung in the balance. The unremitting courage of the besieged set death at defiance, and the strife had reached a stage when only some unavoidable accident could decide the issue. Suddenly our mound, on which we had spent so much labour, fell forward as if struck by an earthquake; it filled the gap which yawned between the wall and the ramp outside like a causeway or bridge, and presented the enemy with a level surface over which they could pass unhindered. Most of our men were thrown down and crushed or gave up the struggle from exhaustion. Nevertheless there was a general rush to avert the danger caused by this sudden catastrophe, but in their haste men got in each other's way, whereas the spirit of the enemy rose with their success. The king called up all his forces to take part in the sack; hand-to-hand fighting ensued and torrents of blood were spilt on both sides. The trenches were filled with corpses, which provided a broader front for the attack, and when the furious inrush of the enemy's troops filled the city all hope of defence or escape was gone, and soldiers and civilians were slaughtered like sheep without distinction of sex.

As it was getting dark and while a crowd of our men was still keeping up the fight, hopeless though it was, I and two others hid in an obscure corner of the town and escaped through an unguarded postern under cover of night. My acquaintance with the desert and the pace kept up by my companions brought me at last ten miles from the city. There we stopped for a short rest and were about to go on, though I, being of free birth, was hardly equal to the unaccustomed effort of walking, when we encountered a terrible sight, which, however, gave me in my exhausted state a most welcome relief. It was a runaway horse, which a groom had mounted without saddle or bit. To keep himself on he had in the usual way tied the halter by which he was leading it tightly to his left hand. Then he was thrown and could not undo the knot, so he was torn limb from limb by being dragged over rough ground and through woods, until the weight of his body brought the tired beast to a stop. We caught the animal and I availed myself of his back to reach, though with difficulty, some natural hot springs impregnated with sulphur. My companions were still with me. We were parched with thirst and moving at a snail's pace looking for water, and we almost missed a deep well. It was too deep for us to climb down, and we had no ropes, but under the spur of necessity we tore our linen clothes into long strips and made a great line, to the end of which we attached a cap which one of us was wearing under his helmet. We let this down and it sucked up water like a sponge, so that we were easily able to quench our consuming thirst. From there we made a quick march to the Euphrates, intending to cross to the further bank in a ferry-boat which it had long been the custom to keep there for the transport of men and animals. But all at once we saw in the distance a troop of Roman cavalry with its standards flying in disorder before a host of Persians; we could not tell where they had sprung from to attack so suddenly in our rear. Judging by this phenomenon I believe that the famous 'earth-born' men did not emerge from the bosom of the earth but were endowed from birth with extraordinary swiftness. Because they appeared unexpectedly in divers places they were called the 'sown' men and were thought to have sprung from the ground, an example of the tendency of the ancients to legendary exaggeration. Alarmed by this spectacle and concluding that our only hope of safety lay in flight, we made for the higher mountains through woods and thickets, and finally reached Melitene, a town in Lesser Armenia. There we found our general, who was about to take the road, and in his train we returned unexpectedly to Antioch.

9. Defection of Craugasius.

Autumn was now far advanced and the cruel constellation of the Kids was above the horizon. This discouraged the Persians from advancing into the interior, and they began to think of returning home with their prisoners and loot. Amid the scenes of death and pillage which marked the destruction of the city, count Aelian and the officers who had for so long maintained the defence of our walls and inflicted such losses on the Persians suffered an abominable death on the gibbet. Jacobus and Caesius, paymasters on the staff of the master of cavalry, and other staff-officers were led into captivity with their hands tied behind their backs. Those who had come from across the Tigris were hunted down with particular care and slaughtered to a man, high and low alike.

But the wife of Craugasius, though no attempt was made on her virtue and she was treated with the respect due to a married woman of rank, was in despair at the thought of seeing another country without her husband, in spite of the prospect of a more exalted lot which present indications afforded. Thinking of her future and foreseeing what would happen, she was a prey to anxiety on two counts; separation from her husband and a second marriage were equally hateful to her. So she sent her servant, whose loyalty was above suspicion and who was familiar with the countryside of Mesopotamia, to make his way secretly over Mount Izala between the forts of Maride and Lorne to Nisibis. He was in her entire confidence and carried a message begging her husband to join her when he heard her news so that they could enjoy a happy life together. Charged with this errand and travelling light, the messenger made a quick journey over rough forested country and entered Nisibis. There he gave out that he had not seen his mistress, who might well be dead, and that he himself had seized a chance of escaping from the enemy camp. In these circumstances nobody took much notice of him, but he told Craugasius how things really stood and received from him a promise that he would gladly rejoin his wife if he could do so with safety. Then he went off to carry this joyful news to the woman, who on receiving it petitioned the king through his general Tamsapor that, if an opportunity arose before he left Roman territory, he would graciously take her husband under his protection.

The unexpected departure of the new arrival, who after returning to his former home had again vanished before anyone was aware, awoke the suspicions of the general Cassian and the other notables of Nisibis. They assailed Craugasius in the most threatening terms, insisting that the man had both come and gone on his instructions. Craugasius, fearing a charge of treason and haunted by the thought that the movements of the fugitive would bring to light the fact that his wife was still alive and was being most respectfully treated, pretended to be a suitor for the hand of another girl of high birth. On the pretext of making preparations for the wedding-feast he went to a house in the country eight miles from Nisibis; then he set spurs to his horse and galloped off to join a band of Persian marauders whom he knew to be in the neighbourhood. They received him with open arms, and when he told them who he was delivered him five days later to Tamsapor, who presented him to the king. He recovered his property and all his family as well as his wife, whom he had lost a few months before, and he enjoyed a position second only to Antoninus, though in the words of the famous poet (*Virgil*), 'he came in a bad second'. Antoninus owed his position to his natural talent and long experience, on which he could draw for viable plans in any undertaking; Craugasius was less sophisticated but equally well known. These events occurred not long after the fall of Amida.

The king, however, though he wore a carefree expression and was apparently delighted at the destruction of the city, was at heart violently disturbed by the reflection that the labours of several sieges had involved him in grievous sacrifices and that he had lost far more men than he had taken alive from us, or than we had lost in various encounters with him, at Nisibis, for example, more than once, and at Singara. At Amida likewise, which he had besieged with a vast host for seventy-three days, his losses amounted to 30,000 fighting men. This number was ascertained soon afterwards by Diascenes, a tribune and notary in the civil service, whose task was made easier by the fact that, whereas the corpses of our men soon fall to pieces and decompose, so that after four days they are unrecognizable, those of the Persians dry up like the trunks of trees, without putrefaction or deliquescence. This is the result of their more frugal diet and of the dry heat of their native lands.

10. Food riot at Rome.

While these storms were fast succeeding one another in the far East, the Eternal City was disturbed by fear of an approaching shortage of grain. The people, to whom the prospect of famine is the worst of all disasters, threatened the then urban prefect Tertullus with violence on several occasions. This was quite unreasonable, since it was no fault of his that the regular arrival of cargo-boats was hindered by rough weather at sea and strong contrary winds, which drove them into the nearest sheltered water and deterred them from risking the grave danger of entering the harbour of Augustus (Ostia). In these circumstances the prefect, who had often been harassed by riots and who was now faced with the threat of imminent destruction from the increasing fury of the mob, gave up hope of saving his life. But he had the wit to take his small sons and exhibit them to the populace, which for all its wild behaviour is apt to be moved by misfortune. 'These,' he said with tears, 'are your fellow-citizens, who will share your fate (which heaven forbid) unless our affairs take a happier turn. So if you think that by their destruction you can avert disaster they are at your disposal.' This pathetic speech soothed the mob, which is naturally inclined to compassion; it fell silent, and calmly awaited its fate. Soon afterwards, through the divine providence which has attended the growth of Rome from its cradle and guaranteed that it shall endure for ever, while Tertullus was sacrificing in the temple of Castor and Pollux at Ostia, the sea became smooth and the wind changed to a light southerly breeze. The ships entered harbour under full sail and replenished the warehouses with grain.

11. Attack on Constantius by the Limigantes.

While things were in this uncertain state, Constantius, whose seat of government was at Sirmium during the winter break in operations, was disturbed by alarming news of a serious nature. The very thing which he chiefly dreaded had occurred. The Limigantes of Sarmatia, who, as I have already told, had once driven their masters from their ancestral domains, had gradually abandoned the places which public policy had assigned to them in the previous year to prevent any outbreak to which their fickle nature might dispose them. They had occupied the regions adjoining our frontiers and were roaming at large in their native way, and if they were not repulsed general havoc would result.

The emperor, believing that any delay would very soon encourage them to show greater insolence, collected a large force of crack troops from all parts, and took the field before spring had fully come. Two considerations made him more eager to fight; first, that the army, which had reaped a rich harvest of loot in the previous summer, would be roused to exert itself effectively by hope of a similar result, and second, that under the rule of Anatolius, who was then praetorian prefect in Illyricum, supplies of all kinds had been collected even before they were needed and were pouring in without expense to anyone. It is an established fact that the northern provinces have never to this day been so prosperous under any other prefect. Anatolius showed benevolence and skill in the correction of abuses; with a fine show of confidence he relieved the provincials from the enormous expense of the imperial post service, which had ruined countless homes, and from the hardships of taxation. In fact the inhabitants of those parts might have lived thereafter happy and untroubled lives with all their grievances settled, but for the abominable refinements of taxation to which they were later exposed. These were magnified to a criminal extent by tax-farmers and tax-collectors alike, the former confident that they would be safe when everyone's resources were exhausted, and the latter hoping that the authorities would protect them in their business. This resulted in the outlawry or suicide of the wretched victims.

The emperor, as I said, set out splendidly equipped to relieve the pressure of the situation, and entered Valeria. This was once part of Pannonia, but had been made into a province and so named in honour of Valeria the daughter of Diocletian. Constantius posted his troops in tents along the banks of the Danube and watched the barbarians, who before his arrival had been planning under the guise of friendship to invade and lay waste Pannonia in the depths of winter, while the river could still be crossed anywhere because spring had not melted the snows, and while the frost would make it difficult for our troops to endure long periods in the open.

Two officers, each accompanied by an interpreter, were sent at once to the Limigantes to ask in mild terms why they had left the homes assigned to them when they sued for peace, and why they were roaming at large and threatening our frontiers in defiance of our prohibition. They were afraid to tell the truth and produced vain and hollow excuses, begging the emperor's pardon and entreating him to lay aside his anger and allow them to cross the river and come to him, so that they could put before him the hardships they were suffering. They added that if he pleased they were ready to move to some distant region within the Roman world, where they could be wrapped in lasting peace and devote themselves to the worship of the saving goddess of Quiet with the obligations and status of a tributary people.

When the officers reported this on their return, the emperor, delighted at the prospect of solving without effort a problem which he had thought intractable, decided to admit them to his presence in a body. He was on fire to enlarge his possessions, and his clique of flatterers fanned the flame. They never ceased to remind him that, when affairs beyond the frontier were composed and universal peace established, he would gain an accession of man-power and be in a position to levy strong bodies of recruits, seeing that the provincials will willingly compound for personal service by cash payments, the prospect of which has more than once done damage to the Roman state. Accordingly, an earthwork was thrown up at Acimincum with a high mound to serve as a tribunal, and at the suggestion of a surveyor called Innocentius some vessels with light-armed legionaries on board were sent to keep watch on the waters near the bank, so that if they saw any untoward movement among the barbarians they could attack them unexpectedly in the rear while their attention was concentrated elsewhere. Although the Limigantes were aware of these hasty precautions they remained standing with bowed head, affecting to be mere suppliants but with a far different design in their heart from what was indicated by their words and bearing.

When the emperor appeared on his elevated platform and was about to address them in mild terms as prospective obedient subjects, one of them in a fit of savagery flung his shoe at the tribunal, shouting 'marha, marha', which is their war-cry. Following his lead the disorderly crowd suddenly displayed a barbarian banner, and with wild yells attacked the very person of the emperor. Constantius, seeing from above the whole area filled by a throng of men running to and fro among the troops with drawn swords and spears, realized that destruction was at hand. There was no time to hesitate or delay, so, thrusting in among the mixed crowd of strangers and his own men, with nothing to indicate whether he was an officer or a common soldier, he mounted a swift horse and went off at a gallop. But a few of his attendants, who tried to stem the rush which was overwhelming them like a spreading fire, either died of wounds or were crushed by the mere weight of their assailants, and the royal chair with its golden cushions was torn to pieces without anyone attempting to save it.

Soon, however, when it was known that the emperor had barely escaped destruction and was still not out of the wood, the troops, realizing that he was still in danger, took it to be their first duty to help him. Contempt for the enemy increased their confidence, so, although the suddenness of the onslaught had caught them only half armed, they shouted their war-cry and plunged into the horde of barbarians, who were resolved to fight to the death. So eager were our men to wipe out the disgrace that had fallen on them and to wreak their wrath upon the treacherous foe that they cut down whatever came in their way. Living, dying, and dead were trampled upon without mercy, and before they were weary of shedding barbarian blood the dead lay piled in heaps. The pressure upon the rebels was such that some were slaughtered, others scattered in panic, of whom part, who tried to save their lives by vain entreaties, suffered repeated blows before they succumbed. When all had been wiped out and the trumpets sounded the recall, some of our men, but not many, were seen to have fallen. They had either been trampled to death in the fierce rush, or had met their appointed end because in their efforts to resist the fury of the enemy they left their sides exposed. The most notable death was that of Cella, commander of the Scutarii, who had been the first to rush into the thick of the Sarmatians at the beginning of the fight.

After this bloody affair Constantius took such measures as were urgently needed for the protection of the frontier and returned to Sirmium, triumphant over a treacherous foe. Then, after dispatching the business which called for immediate attention, he made for Constantinople, where he would be nearer to the East. His intention was to remedy the defeat suffered at Amida and to reinforce his army, so as to check the attacks of the Persian king with numbers that matched his own. It was clear that, unless he was repelled by divine providence and the devoted efforts of a large number, Sapor would leave Mesopotamia in his rear and launch an offensive over a wider area.

12. Treason trials.

In the midst of these troubles, however, as if in observance of a time-honoured custom, trumpet-tones proclaimed, as if it were a civil war, a series of faked charges of high treason, the pursuit and management of which were entrusted to the devilish notary Paul, whom I often have occasion to mention. He was an expert in the art of bloodshed, and looked for gain and profit from the rack or the executioner in the same way as a trainer of gladiators from the business of funeral games or the circus. His fixed and settled policy was to inflict harm, and in pursuit of it he did not shrink from fraud or hesitate to plant fatal charges upon innocent persons if it suited him to do so to keep his damnable trade going.

A slight and trivial incident gave him infinite material for extending his investigations. In the furthest part of the Thebaid there is a town called Abydos, where a god locally called Besa used to reveal the future through an oracle and was worshipped with traditional rites by the inhabitants of the surrounding regions. Some of those who consulted the oracle did so in person, others sent a letter by an intermediary containing an explicit statement of their requests. In consequence, records of their petitions on paper or parchment sometimes remained in the temple even after the replies had been given. Some of these documents were sent to the emperor out of malice. His small mind made him deaf to other matters, however serious, but on this point he was more sensitive than the proverbial ear-lobe, suspicious and petty. He burst into furious anger and ordered Paul to proceed at once to the East, conferring on him, as on an experienced commander of great distinction, authority to have cases brought to court as he saw fit. The hearing of the trials was put in the hands of Modestus, at that time count of the East, a man very suitable for business of this sort. Hermogenes of Pontus, who was then praetorian prefect, was passed over as being of too mild a temper.

In obedience to his orders Paul went panting off, full of deadly spite. The way was open to false accusations on a large scale, and people were brought from all over the world, gentle and simple alike. Some were crushed by the weight of their chains, others succumbed to the rigours of close confinement. The town of Scythopolis in Palestine was chosen to witness these cruel tortures. Two reasons made it seem particularly suitable; it was comparatively secluded, and it was also midway between Antioch and Alexandria, from which most of the victims were brought to be tried.

Among the first to be prosecuted was Simplicius, son of the former prefect and consul Philip. He was accused of having consulted the oracle about his chances of the empire. Constantius, who in such circumstances never allowed loyal service to atone for a fault or a mistake, expressly commanded that he should be put to the torture, but by some special providence he escaped with a whole skin and was condemned to exile in a specified place. Next was Parnasius, formerly prefect of Egypt, a man without guile; though he had to face a capital charge he also was banished. He had often been heard to say that when he left his birthplace and home at Patras in Achaea to obtain an official post he dreamed that he was escorted by a number of figures dressed like tragic actors. Then Andronicus, the celebrated scholar and poet, was brought to the bar, but, since nothing suspicious could be proved against him and he defended himself calmly and confidently, he was acquitted. The philosopher Demetrius also, nicknamed Cythras, a man of great age but sound in body and mind, was shown to have offered sacrifice to Besa on several occasions. He could not deny it, but maintained that, though he had observed this practice from early youth, his purpose was simply to propitiate the deity, not to inquire into his own prospects of advancement; nor did he know of anybody who made this his aim. So after a long time on the rack, during which he boldly and confidently adhered to his plea without the slightest variation, he was allowed to depart to his native city of Alexandria without further injury.

These, then, and a few others were saved from the last extremity by the justice of fate, which came to the aid of truth. But, as such charges spread more widely and there seemed no end to the complicated web, some people died on the rack and others suffered the further penalty of confiscation. Paul was the prompter in this theatre of cruelty, continually producing fresh material from his reserves of lies and mischief; one might almost say that the lives of all involved depended on his nod. Anyone who wore round his neck a charm against the quartan ague or some other complaint, or was accused by his ill-wishers of visiting a grave in the evening, was found guilty and executed as a sorcerer or as an inquirer into the horrors of men's tombs and the empty phantoms of the spirits which haunt them. The matter was treated as seriously as if a host of people had consulted Claros or the oaks of Dodona or the once famous oracle of Delphi with a view to the emperor's death. So the palace clique ingeniously contrived a foul form of flattery; they asserted that the emperor would be exempt from the ills common to humanity, and loudly declared that the never-failing providence which protected him had manifested itself in the destruction of those who plotted against him.

No man of sense would find fault with a strict inquiry into these matters. It cannot be denied that the life of a lawful prince, who is the bulwark and defence of the good and on whom the lives of others depend, ought to be protected by the united efforts of all. When strong measures are needed to defend his authority from violation, no one, however highly placed, was exempted by the laws of Cornelius (Sulla) from examination even on the rack. But it is not decent to give way to unbridled joy at such unhappy events; it makes men seem the subjects of despotism rather than of lawful authority. On the contrary, we should imitate Cicero, who said himself that when it was in his power to spare or to harm he looked for an excuse to pardon rather than punish; that is the mark of a dispassionate and prudent judge.

At this time Daphne, the delightful and gorgeous suburb of Antioch, saw the birth of a monster as frightful to describe as to behold. It was a child with two heads, two sets of teeth, a beard, four eyes, and two very small ears. The birth of this deformed creature portended an ugly development in the state. Prodigies of this kind often appear and signify events of various kinds, but since we no longer make them the occasion of a public rite of purification, as our forebears did, they pass over without anyone hearing or knowing of them.

A short chapter (13) on an Isaurian raid is omitted.

BOOK 20

1. *Lupicinus sent to Britain* (A.D. 360).

Such was the course of events in Illyricum and the East. But in Britain, during Constantius' tenth and Julian's third consulship, the wild tribes of the Scots and Picts broke their undertaking to keep peace, laid waste the country near the frontier, and caused alarm among the provincials, who were exhausted by the repeated disasters they had already suffered. The Caesar, who was spending the winter at Paris a prey to various anxieties, shrank from going in person like Constans on a previous occasion to help his subjects across the Channel; he was afraid of leaving Gaul without a ruler at the very time when the Alamanni were bent on fierce war. He decided therefore to send Lupicinus, at that time master of cavalry, to settle these troubles either by negotiation or by force. Lupicinus was a stout and experienced soldier, who was apt, however, to set up his horn on high and to talk in the style of a tragic hero. It was long a matter of debate whether his greed predominated over his cruelty or the reverse. Taking with him a light-armed force of Herulians and Batavians together with two units of Moesians, this commander reached Boulogne (Bononia) in the depths of winter. He embarked his troops on vessels which he collected, and sailed with a favourable wind to Richborough (Rutufiae) on the opposite shore. From there he marched to London (Londinium), intending to let the situation determine his strategy and to take the field as soon as possible.

2. *The fall of Ursicinus.*

Meanwhile Ursicinus, who after the fall of Amida had rejoined the emperor as master of infantry in succession to Barbatio, as I have said earlier, was met by detractors, who began by spreading malicious gossip in whispers and went on to bring false charges against him openly. The emperor fell in with them; his judgement was generally swayed by preconceived opinions and he lent a ready ear to intrigue. He appointed Arbitio and Florentius, the master of the offices, to conduct an inquiry into the causes of the fall of Amida. These two rejected the obvious and probable explanation that what had happened was due to the persistent inactivity of Sabinian. They were afraid that if they admitted evidence which clearly demonstrated this they would give offence to Eusebius the grand chamberlain. So they left the truth on one side and concentrated their attention on trivial and utterly irrelevant matters.

The accused, irritated by the unfairness of these proceedings, said: 'Although the emperor has a poor opinion of me, this affair is of such importance that its investigation and any punishment inflicted in consequence require the judgement of the prince himself. Let me tell him in words which will prove prophetic that, as long as he grieves over a false account of events at Amida and as long as he allows himself to be dictated to by eunuchs, even his presence in person with all the flower of his army will not avail next spring to prevent the dismemberment of Mesopotamia.'

This speech lost nothing in the telling from the malice of those who reported it, and when it reached Constantius his fury was unbounded. Without examining the matter further or allowing the details of which he was ignorant to be explained, he ordered the victim of slander to lay down his command and retire into private life. Agilo, a former tribune of the Gentiles and the Scutarii, was given an enormous step in rank and appointed in his place.

Chapter on eclipses (3) is omitted.

4. Reluctant acceptance by Julian of title of Augustus.

While Constantius was hurrying to reinforce the East, where, according to the concurring accounts of scouts and deserters, a Persian offensive was to be expected very shortly, he was nettled by reports of Julian's exploits, which were receiving wide publicity by oral circulation among various peoples. The tale went abroad of the glorious outcome of all his efforts, how he had overthrown several Alamannic kingdoms and restored towns in Gaul formerly sacked and destroyed by the barbarians, whom he had now reduced to the status of tributaries and tax-payers. Stung by accounts of this kind and fearing that they would be still further magnified, Constantius yielded to a suggestion made, it was

said, by the prefect Florentius, and sent the tribune and notary
Decentius to remove from Julian his Herulian and Batavian auxiliaries
together with the Celts and Petulantes and 300 picked men from each
of the other divisions of his army. The pretext for rapid action was that
they must be in a position to join the forces which would be mobilized
for the Persian war in early spring.

The responsibility for hastening the departure of the auxiliaries and
the detachments of three hundred was assigned to Lupicinus alone (it
was not yet known that he had crossed to Britain), but Sintula, who was
then in charge of the Caesar's stables, was ordered to pick the best men
from the Scutarii and Gentiles and bring them in person.

Julian kept quiet and acquiesced in this decision, submitting in
everything to the will of his more powerful colleague. On one point,
however, he could not hide his feelings or remain silent. He must ensure
that hardship was not inflicted on men who had left their homes across
the Rhine to join him on the express condition that they should never
be sent to serve beyond the Alps. He pointed out that once they knew
that this promise had been broken the barbarian volunteers who often
came over to us on these terms would be deterred from doing so. But
his words fell on deaf ears. Sintula snapped his fingers at the Caesar's
protest, and in accordance with the orders of the emperor picked the
strongest and most active of the light-armed troops and went off with
them full of hope of promotion.

Julian was in two minds what to do about the rest of the troops that
he had been ordered to send. The various anxieties which beset him
made it necessary to act with circumspection; he was exposed to pressure
on one side from the wild barbarians and on the other from the express
commands of the emperor. The absence of Lupicinus in particular
added to his perplexity, and in these circumstances he urged the prefect
Florentius to return to him. The latter had gone to Vienne some time
before, ostensibly to collect supplies, but in reality to be out of the way
of these military troubles. He kept in mind that it was the report which
he was reputed to have sent earlier that had inspired the withdrawal
from the defence of Gaul of seasoned regiments which had already
made themselves feared by the barbarians. So when he received Julian's
letter urging him in the strongest terms to come at once and give the
benefit of his advice, he most emphatically refused. What particularly
alarmed him was a clear statement in the letter that at a moment of
terrible crisis the place of the prefect was at his master's side. And

Julian added that if Florentius shirked his duty he would himself lay
down the insignia of rule, since he thought it more glorious to meet
death at the emperor's command than to have the ruin of the province
attributed to him. But he could not overcome the resolution of the
prefect, who persisted with the greatest obstinacy in his refusal to obey
these reasonable requests.

During the delay caused by Lupicinus' absence and the prefect's fear
of a mutiny, Julian, left through lack of advice in a state of indecision,
concluded in the end that his best course was to call out all the men
from their winter quarters, and made arrangements to hasten their
departure in a regular way. When this got about someone in the camp
of the Petulantes threw on the ground an anonymous broadsheet, which
among much else contained the following words: 'We are to be driven
off to the ends of the earth like condemned criminals while our nearest
and dearest, whom we have set free from their previous captivity after
desperate fighting, again become the slaves of the Alamanni.' When this
manifesto was brought to headquarters and read, Julian, acknowledging
the reasonableness of the complaint, gave orders that they should start
for the East with their families, and put at their disposal the wagons of
the public transport service. After long debate about their route the
notary Decentius suggested that they should all pass through Paris,
from which the Caesar himself had as yet made no move. This plan was
followed. On their arrival the Caesar met them in the outskirts of
the city, greeted those whom he knew personally with words of
congratulation, reminded them individually of their brave deeds, and
encouraged them in mild tones to lose no time in joining the emperor,
by whose ample power and munificence they would be rewarded in
proportion to their deserts. To confer further honour on them at their
departure on so long a journey he invited their leading men to dinner
and bade them make any request that they had in mind. After this
liberal entertainment two sad thoughts oppressed them as they went
away; through the unkindness of fortune they were losing not only their
native land but a beneficent ruler. With these sorrowful feelings they
retired to their quarters. But at nightfall they broke out into open revolt;
they gave way to the feelings roused in each of them to a different degree
by this unexpected event, took up arms, and rushed to the palace with
tremendous uproar. They surrounded it so that no one could escape,
and saluted Julian as Augustus with terrifying shouts, urgently demanding that he should come out to them. They had to wait till day broke,

but at last they compelled him to appear. When they saw him they redoubled their noise and acclaimed him Augustus with the most uncompromising unanimity.

Julian, however, resisted one and all firmly and resolutely. At one moment he showed displeasure, at the next he stretched out his arms in passionate entreaty, begging them not to spoil so many happy victories by behaving dishonourably or to let rashness and bad judgement give rise to civil war. When calm was at last restored, he addressed them in mild language as follows: 'Control your angry feelings for a time, I beg you. Your demands can easily be met without dissension or recourse to revolution. Since you are kept here by the spell of your native country and your fear of strange foreign lands, return at once to your quarters in the assurance that you will never have to cross the Alps against your will. Augustus is wise and open to reason, and I will justify your refusal to him to his complete satisfaction.'

In spite of this appeal the shouting continued on all sides, and finding it impossible to resist the uniform pressure of this loud uproar, with which some abuse was mingled, the Caesar was obliged to give way. He was placed on an infantry shield, raised aloft, and proclaimed Augustus without a dissentient voice. Then he was told to produce a diadem, and when he said that he had never had one they asked for a necklace or a head ornament of his wife's. When he protested that to wear a female trinket would be an inauspicious beginning, they searched about for a horse-trapping to crown him with, so that he might have some symbol, however mean, of his elevation. This too he rejected as unbecoming, and finally a man called Maurus, who was later a count and suffered a defeat at the pass of Succi, but who at that time was only an ensign in the Petulantes, took off his standard-bearer's collar and boldly placed it on Julian's head. Julian, finding that there was no way out and perceiving that continued resistance would place him in instant danger, promised each man five gold pieces and a pound of silver.

This event did nothing to relieve his anxiety. He was quick enough to foresee the consequences; he did not wear a diadem and was afraid to appear in public or to transact any of the urgent business which demanded his attention. Terrified by the change which had occurred he withdrew into seclusion, where he remained until one of the decurions of the palace, an important official, hastened to the camp of the Petulantes and Celts shouting at the top of his voice that a shameful crime had been committed and that the man whom they had proclaimed

Augustus on the previous day had been secretly put to death. At this news the troops, who were as easily roused by false tidings as by true, rushed in the disorderly way which is natural in an emergency to occupy the palace, some brandishing javelins, others waving drawn swords with threatening gestures. This fearful din struck panic into the sentries, together with their officers and the count in command of the household troops, who was called Excubitor. Dreading treachery from the fickle soldiery they scattered in fear of sudden death and vanished. Finding, however, that complete calm prevailed, the men in arms stood quiet for a time. When they were asked what had led to this sudden foolish commotion there was a long silence while they were still in doubt about the emperor's safety, and they would not disperse till they had been admitted to his council chamber and had seen him in all the splendour of his imperial robes.

5. *Julian's speech to the army.*

When they heard of these events the other troops, who had gone ahead, as I have related, under the command of Sintula, returned with him to Paris with their minds at rest. It was proclaimed that all should assemble next day in an open place, where the emperor appeared in greater state than usual and mounted the tribunal, surrounded by standards, eagles, and banners, and hedged in, to ensure his safety, by detachments of armed men. After a brief silence during which he surveyed all the eager and happy faces below him, he stirred their feelings with words simple enough for their understanding, which acted on them like a trumpet-call.

'I see before me men who have shown courage and loyalty in protecting me and the state, and have often risked their lives with me in defence of the provinces. Now that your deliberate decision has raised your Caesar to the pinnacle of supreme power, the difficulty of the situation urgently demands that I should touch briefly on a few matters, so that we can take such right and prudent steps as these changed circumstances require. I had hardly reached manhood when, as you know, I received the nominal dignity of the purple and was committed by the will of heaven to your protection. Since then I have never abandoned the high standards which I set myself. I have been seen taking my full share in all the toils you endured when the insolence of the native peoples broke its bounds, when cities were destroyed and countless thousands of men lost, and incalculable ruin was spreading over the few regions that still remained to some extent uninjured. There is no need, I think, to recapitulate how often we repelled with heavy losses the hitherto invincible Alamanni, in raw winter and under a bitter sky, when both land and sea are normally free from hostilities. But I cannot pass over in silence the events of that most happy day near Strasbourg, which may be said to have brought lasting freedom to the provinces of Gaul. While I was moving to and fro under a hail of missiles, you, relying on your strength and experience, withstood the sudden assault of the enemy host which poured over you like a dashing torrent. Some you laid low with the sword, others were drowned in the depths of the river, but few of our own men were left upon the field, and them we buried in a mood of panegyric rather than of grief. After such exploits as these your services to the state, which are already fully known among all peoples, will not, I think, go unrecognized by posterity, provided that you defend with courage and firmness against any adversity the man whom you have elevated to the summit of imperial dignity. And to forestall any breach in the proper order of things and to ensure that courage receives its due reward and that no places are pre-empted by secret intrigue, I declare in the presence of this honourable company that no promotion, either civil or military, shall be given through unmerited patronage, and that no man who tries to pull strings on behalf of another shall escape without dishonour.'

The lower ranks, who had gone without promotion or reward for a long time, were encouraged by this speech to hope for better things. They rose up, clashing their spears against their shields with a mighty din, and expressed with almost one voice their approval of the emperor's words and plans. In order not to lose a moment in upsetting so wise an arrangement the Petulantes and Celts begged Julian on behalf of their commissaries to confer on them the government of whatever provinces he pleased, but when their request was refused they withdrew without showing grief or resentment.

Julian, however, told his most intimate friends that on the night before he was proclaimed Augustus he saw in a dream a figure in the traditional shape of the Genius of Rome, which addressed him in a tone of reproach as follows: 'For a long time, Julian, I have been watching in secret at your door, desiring to place you in a higher position, but more than once I have departed feeling myself rebuffed. If I find no admission even now, when public opinion is unanimous, I shall go away dejected and sorrowful. Do not allow yourself to forget that I shall then dwell with you no longer.'

6. *Singara taken and destroyed by Sapor.*

During these exciting events in Gaul the king of Persia, on whose harsh temper Antoninus could work with redoubled force since the arrival of Craugasius, was on fire to seize Mesopotamia while Constantius and his army were occupied far away. He crossed the Tigris in regular array with greatly increased strength and proceeded to attack Singara, a town which in the view of the local commanders was amply furnished with troops and every necessary. Its defenders espied the enemy a long way off and hastened to close their gates. They distributed themselves on the towers and battlements, eager for the fight, collected stones and engines of war, and when everything was ready stood to arms, prepared to repel the enemy host if it dared to approach the walls.

Accordingly the king on his arrival made peaceful overtures through some of his principal officers, who were allowed to do their errrand but found that they could not bend the defenders to his will. One whole day was allowed to pass quietly, but on the next at first light a flame-coloured banner was raised to give the signal for an attack on the town from all sides. Some carried scaling-ladders, others erected siege-engines, while the main body, under the shelter of penthouses and mantlets, tried to find a way to undermine the foundations of the walls. On the other side the townsfolk on their high battlements hurled stones and every kind of missile at long range to thwart this bold attempt to force a way in.

The fighting went on indecisively for several days with great losses in killed and wounded on both sides. Finally, when the battle was at its height and evening was coming on, an exceptionally powerful ram was brought into play among many other engines. Its repeated blows battered the round tower at the place where, as I have related, the wall was breached in the previous siege. The people flocked to the spot and the fight continued at close quarters; combustibles of every kind were flung on all hands to set the threatening monster on fire, while both sides kept up an incessant bombardment with arrows and sling-shot. But the sharp head of the ram frustrated every attempt to stop it; it dug into the joints of the newly-built walls, where the mortar was still damp and had not set. While they were still fighting with fire and sword the tower collapsed and a way into the city lay open. The defence being disrupted by the appalling danger and the place left clear, the Persian troops with shouts and yells filled every part of the town without opposition. A very small number were killed indiscriminately; the rest were taken alive by Sapor's orders and transported to the farthest parts of Persia.

Two legions, the 1st Flavian and the 1st Parthian, were responsible for the defence of the city, supported by a number of natives and a body of horse, which found itself shut up there owing to the suddenness of the disaster. They were all, as I said, taken off in fetters, without any attempt at rescue from our side. In fact the greater part of our army was encamped an immense distance away to protect Nisibis; moreover, even in earlier times, no one had ever been able to bring help to Singara when it was in danger, because all the surrounding country was dried up from lack of water. The place had been fortified in days of old as a convenient outpost to obtain advance information of any sudden enemy movement, but in fact it had proved a liability to Rome, because it was taken on several occasions with the loss of its garrison.

7. Bezabde stormed and garrisoned by Sapor.

After destroying this town the king wisely left Nisibis on one side, no doubt remembering the reverses which he had often suffered there, and marched to the right across country to Bezabde, which its first founders also called Phaenicha. He hoped either to take it by force or to win over the defenders by tempting promises. Bezabde was a very strong fortress on a fairly high hill. It extended towards the bank of the Tigris, and where the ground was low and treacherous it was protected by a double wall. Three legions were assigned to its defence, the 2nd Flavian, the 2nd Armenian, and the 2nd Parthian, together with a number of archers and the Zabdiceni, in whose territory this town lay and who were then our subjects.

In the first assault the king himself, towering in gleaming armour above his accompanying ironsides, made a circuit of the fortress and was rash enough to approach the very lip of the trenches. He was the target of fierce fire from the artillery and the archers, but was protected by a close formation of shields held up tortoise-fashion and got away unscathed. For the moment he suppressed his rage and sent heralds in the usual way to urge the besieged in mild terms to think of their lives

and prospects, and to put an end to the siege by a timely surrender; let
them open their gates and come out and throw themselves on the mercy
of the conqueror of the world. The heralds came near, bringing with
them some men of free birth captured at Singara and known to the
besieged, who out of pity for them held their fire. No one hurled a
missile, but no answer was returned to the proposed terms of peace.

This breathing-space lasted for a whole day and night, but before
dawn on the following day the whole Persian force fiercely attacked the
defences, uttering loud threats, and advanced boldly up to the very
walls, where they met with strong resistance from the townspeople. A
large number of Parthians were wounded, because the ladders or wicker
hurdles which they held in front of them blinded them as they advanced,
but they inflicted losses on our men, whose crowded ranks were the
target for dense clouds of arrows. After sunset the combatants separated
with equal losses, but just before dawn next day the trumpets sounded
on either hand and the fight was renewed with even greater keenness.
Both sides fought most obstinately and suffered losses of equal magnitude.

The following day was devoted to rest by common consent; those
within the walls were in the most alarming position, and the Persians
had equal cause for fear. At this moment the head of the Christian
community signalled by nods and gestures that he wished to leave the
town, and on receiving an assurance that he would be allowed to return
unharmed he actually reached the king's headquarters. He was given
leave to say what he wanted and proceeded to urge the Persians in mild
terms to return home, saying that he feared that the severe losses which
each side had suffered would be the prelude to even greater disasters.
But his persistence in these and similar arguments was of no avail;
nothing could overcome the mad rage of the king, who swore that he
would not depart till he had destroyed the fortress. The bishop incurred
a suspicion, which in my opinion was ill-founded but obtained wide
currency, that he had had a secret meeting with Sapor, in which he had
pointed out which parts of the walls were weak on the inside and
therefore best to attack. What seemed to lend plausibility to this
suspicion was that after his visit the enemy deliberately directed his
engines against the danger spots where the walls were crumbling, as if
he were exultantly taking advantage of information about conditions
inside the town.

Though the narrowness of the paths made the approach to the walls more difficult and the rams prepared for the purpose could hardly be moved forward in the face of a hail of arrows and of rocks thrown by hand, the engines and scorpions kept up their work, the former hurling javelins and the latter showers of stones. At the same time, blazing baskets of wicker smeared with pitch and bitumen rolled in quick succession down the slopes. As a result the engines stuck fast as if rooted to the ground, and were set on fire by the combustibles resolutely hurled at them.

But in spite of this and of the heavy losses on both sides the besiegers were all the more eager to destroy the town before winter, though it was protected by huge fortifications as well as by its natural position. They believed that the king's fury could not be assuaged till this was achieved, and neither the profuse bloodshed nor the infliction of many mortal wounds deterred the survivors from encountering similar risks. In a long and destructive struggle they exposed themselves to extreme danger, as the further progress of the rams which were brought up was checked by the massive weight of the stones that fell on them and by various combustible devices. One ram, however, which was taller than the rest and which, being covered with soaked bull's hide, was less liable to be damaged by fire and shot, was slowly pushed forward by gigantic efforts right up to the wall, where it dug its huge snout into the joints of the masonry and so weakened a tower that it collapsed. As it went down with a mighty crash those who were standing on it shared its sudden fall, and were either dashed to pieces or buried in the ruins. They were overtaken by death in various bizarre forms, while the mass of the enemy could now climb up more safely and rushed into the town.

Then, while the ear-splitting din raised by the yelling Persians struck terror into the vanquished, fighting broke out at closer quarters inside the walls. The enemy's units and our own struggled hand to hand, and since both parties were packed tightly together with drawn swords no one who came in their way was spared. At last the besieged, after a long and obstinate resistance in the face of destruction, were broken by the pressure of overwhelming numbers and scattered in all directions. From that moment, the infuriated enemy put to the sword all that could be found. Infants were torn from the breast and slaughtered, together with their mothers. No one cared what he did, but in the midst of these atrocities the greed for loot proved stronger in that people even than the lust for blood. They loaded themselves with spoil of every kind, and taking with them a great swarm of prisoners returned to their tents triumphant.

The king was beside himself with joy. He had long been on fire to take so conveniently placed a fortress as Phaenicha, and he did not leave it till he had completely restored the shattered part of the walls, laid in a store of provisions, and furnished it with a garrison of men of high birth renowned for their skill in the arts of war. He was afraid, as it turned out with good reason, that the Romans would take the loss of so mighty a stronghold to heart and make a great effort to recover it.

This success increased his confidence. He felt that he had a good prospect of bringing off whatever he might undertake, so after capturing some unimportant fortified places he set himself to attack Virta, a fortress of great antiquity believed to have been built by Alexander of Macedon. It lay in the farthest part of Mesopotamia, but it was protected by walls built zigzag with salients and re-entrants, and various devices had been employed to make the approach extremely difficult. Sapor left nothing untried. He rang the changes on tempting promises and threats of torture. He made several attempts to build ramps and brought up siege-engines, but at last after suffering greater losses than he inflicted he had to abandon the enterprise as hopeless, and withdrew.

8. Letter of Julian to Constantius.

These were the events of that year between the Tigris and the Euphrates. Frequent reports kept Constantius informed of them, and fear of a Parthian invasion detained him for the winter at Constantinople, where he devoted himself to strengthening the eastern frontier by supplies of every sort. He got together arms and recruits and dispatched reinforcements of good troops to the legions, which had often distinguished themselves in pitched battles in the eastern campaigns. In addition he asked the Scythians for help with or without pay, intending when spring was well advanced to set out from Thrace and immediately occupy the threatened areas.

In the meantime Julian in his winter quarters at Paris was in a state of anxious suspense, dreading the consequences of the action which had been taken. Careful consideration convinced him that Constantius, who had the meanest opinion of him, would never acquiesce in what had happened. After weighing the dangers involved in setting a revolution on foot he decided to send envoys to inform Constantius of the situation and to take him a letter to the same effect, in which he set out openly what had occurred and what the next step ought to be. Nevertheless he believed that the emperor had already received the news from the reports of Decentius, who had returned some time earlier, and of the chamberlains who had recently left Gaul after bringing to the Caesar certain annual payments. In order not to give the impression that he had suddenly *thrown off his allegiance* he avoided any overbearing language. The tenor of his letter was as follows:

'For my part I have been consistently faithful to my undertakings, both in my conduct and in my observation of our agreement as long as it was possible; the evidence of events has demonstrated this on a number of occasions. Ever since you appointed me Caesar and sent me to encounter the horrid din of war I have been content with the delegated authority that you entrusted to me. Like a loyal servant I have brought to your ears frequent tidings that your wishes have been crowned with success. I have never laid stress on my own dangers, though the dispersion and confusion of the Germans provide ample evidence that I was the first to encounter the toils of war and the last to take rest from them. Allow me to say that if, as you think, a revolution has now taken place, it is because the troops, who have worn themselves out without reward in much hard fighting, have carried out a long-standing plan; they have protested against service under a commander of subordinate rank because they think that a Caesar cannot make any return for their incessant toil and frequent victories. Their resentment at failing to receive either promotion or annual pay was increased by the unexpected order that men who are accustomed to a cold climate should be transferred to the furthest parts of the East, separated from their wives and children, and marched off in a state of want and destitution. In consequence they assembled at night in a mood of unusual anger and surrounded the palace, shouting loudly and repeatedly "Julian Augustus". I was horrified, I admit, and withdrew. As long as I could I kept out of their way and tried to *gain time* by concealing myself. But when the disturbance showed no sign of abating I presented myself to them, protected, if I may say so, by the bulwark of a clear conscience and thinking that I could calm the tumult by my authority or by mild words. But their excitement increased to an extraordinary degree, and when I tried to overcome their persistence by entreaties they went so far as to rush upon me and threaten me with instant death. At last I gave way and acquiesced, thinking that if I were struck down someone else would perhaps be willing to be proclaimed emperor, and believing that in this way I could assuage the violence of their proceedings.

'This is the plain truth of what has happened and I beg you to receive it without resentment. Do not suppose that things fell out otherwise or listen to the pernicious whispers of malicious men who are in the habit of sowing dissension between emperors for their own profit. Reject flattery, which is the nurse of error, and have regard to justice, which is the highest of all virtues. Accept in good part the fair conditions which I propose, and be assured that they are in the interests of the Roman state and of ourselves, who are joined by ties of blood and by partnership in our high office. Forgive me; I am less anxious for the implementation of these reasonable requests than for your approval of their rightness and usefulness, and I shall be eager in the future as in the past to obey your instructions.

'I will give a brief summary of what needs to be done. I will supply Spanish horses for your chariots and some young men of the Laeti to be incorporated with the Gentiles and Scutarii; they are sons of barbarians born on this side of the Rhine or, if not that, of parents who came over to our side. This obligation I promise to discharge as long as I live, and I *may add that I am not merely willing but eager* to do so. Praetorian prefects of approved integrity and merit shall be appointed at your gracious pleasure, but the promotion of other civil and military staff together with that of my suite must properly be left to my discretion. It is folly, when it can be avoided, to attach to an emperor's person people of whose character and disposition he knows nothing.

'One thing, however, I must place beyond doubt. The Gauls, who have been the victims of perennial trouble and the most serious disasters, cannot be either cajoled or coerced into sending recruits into distant foreign parts. If they lose the flower of their manhood, the grief they feel for their past afflictions will turn to despair at the thought of the destruction awaiting them. Nor would it be politic to send auxiliaries from here to oppose the Parthian peoples at a time when the attacks of the barbarians are not yet checked and when these provinces, if you can bear to be told the truth, need strong reinforcements themselves from abroad to repair the incessant calamities which have befallen them.

'In urging these demands and requests I believe that I am acting for the good of the state. Not to take a higher line than befits my position, I may say that I know, I know for a certainty, that situations in which all has been given up for lost have been retrieved by the common efforts of emperors willing to make mutual concessions. The example of our forebears shows that rulers who have adopted such a course have somehow discovered how to live happily and prosperously and to leave to their latest posterity a grateful memory of their reign.'

Together with this letter Julian sent another, more confidential, to be delivered to Constantius in private. This was in more reproachful and biting terms, but I have not been able to examine it, nor, if I had, would it have been proper for me to publish it.

Men of standing were chosen for this errand: Pentadius, master of the offices, and Eutherius, who was then chamberlain. After delivering the letters they were to return with a full report of all they had seen, and they were authorized to act boldly in any contingency that might arise. The bad impression created by this coup had been increased by the flight of the prefect Florentius. Foreseeing the disturbance that would result from Constantius' demand for troops, for which he was commonly held responsible, he had withdrawn to Vienne, giving the needs of the commissariat as a pretext for leaving the Caesar, whom he had often treated rudely and consequently feared. When he heard that Julian had been proclaimed Augustus he had little or no hope and feared for his life, but being at a distance he extricated himself from the danger he dreaded; he abandoned his family and made his way by slow stages to Constantius. To demonstrate his own innocence he laid a number of charges of treason against Julian. After his departure the latter came to a prudent decision. Wishing it to be known that he would have spared Florentius even if he had stayed with him, he ordered his family to be conveyed in safety to the East with all his property and gave them permission to use the public post service.

9. Rejection of Julian's proposals by Constantius.

Florentius' family was followed no less speedily by the envoys bearing the letters I have mentioned, but their keenness to accomplish their journey met with obstacles when they encountered higher officials. After suffering long and serious delays in Italy and Illyricum they crossed the Bosphorus and proceeded by slow stages to Caesarea in Cappadocia, where they found Constantius still lingering. (Caesarea, which was formerly called Mazaca, is a well sited and populous city at the foot of Mount Argaeus.) They were admitted to the emperor's presence and submitted their letters, but when he heard them Constantius flew into a passion unusual even for him, and gave them such a baleful look that it put the fear of death into them. Then he told them to be gone without asking them any further question or allowing them to speak.

In spite of his burning anger, however, he found himself in a dilemma; should he send the troops whose loyalty he trusted against the Persians or against Julian? After much hesitation and debate he allowed himself to be swayed by the opinion of some who advised him for his good, and ordered a march towards the East. But he dismissed the envoys summarily, and at the same time ordered his quaestor Leonas to make haste to Gaul with a letter for Julian, in which he declared that he would accept none of the changes that had been made, and admonished Julian if he had any regard for the welfare of himself and his friends to lay aside his lofty pretensions and be content with the position of Caesar. To add force to his threats and to show confidence in the strength of his own position he promoted Nebridius, the Caesar's quaestor, to be praetorian prefect in place of Florentius and the notary Felix to be master of the offices. He also made some other appointments. He had already promoted Gomoarius to be master of troops in succession to Lupicinus before he heard anything of what had occurred.

Leonas reached Paris and was received as befitted a man of his rank and discretion. On the next day the prince appeared on the parade-ground with a throng of soldiers and townsfolk whom he had summoned for the occasion, took his place on a high tribunal to emphasize his position, and ordered the letter to be presented to him. The scroll which contained Constantius' message was unrolled and the reading began. But when it reached the passage in which Constantius expressed disapproval of all that had happened and declared that the power of a Caesar was enough for Julian, it was interrupted from all sides by terrifying shouts of 'Julian Augustus!'. This was the decision of both provincials and troops, and expressed the resolution of a community which had been rescued from disaster but which still feared a renewal of barbarian attacks.

Leonas returned unharmed with this news and a letter from Julian to the same effect. Of Constantius' nominees Nebridius alone was admitted to the prefecture, a step which Julian had already said would be in accordance with his wishes. As master of the offices he had already named Anatolius, previously in charge of petitions, and he had also made such other appointments as he thought politic and safe.

While all this was going on, Lupicinus, though he was away on service in Britain, was a cause for anxiety. He was an arrogant man with inflated ideas, and it was feared that if he heard the news from across the Channel he might attempt a coup. So a notary was sent to Boulogne to keep strict watch and prevent anyone from crossing the straits. The result of this ban was that Lupicinus returned before hearing what had happened and was powerless to create any disturbance.

10. Campaign of Julian against the Attuarian Franks.

After sending his envoys to Constantius, Julian, cheered by his elevation and his confidence in his men, and eager not to let things cool or appear slack or remiss, set out for the frontier of Lower Germany, fully equipped with everything required for the business in hand, and approached the town of Tricensima. Then he crossed the Rhine and suddenly appeared in the territory of a Frankish tribe called the Attuarii, a wild people who were at that time ranging freely over the frontiers of Gaul. He caught them off their guard when they were feeling completely secure from attack, because no emperor in their memory had entered their country owing to the roughness and difficulty of the approach. Julian had no trouble in defeating them. The greater part were captured or killed and the rest sued for peace at his pleasure. This he granted, believing it to be in the interest of the neighbouring settlers. Then he recrossed the Rhine as rapidly as he had come, carefully checked and improved the frontier defences, and reached Augst. He recovered the places which the barbarians had taken and were treating as their own, and after spending much trouble on their re-establishment went by way of Besançon (Vesontio) to pass the winter at Vienne.

11. Constantius' failure to recapture Bezabde.

This was the course of events in Gaul. While things there were being managed with such success and circumspection, Constantius sent for Arsaces king of Armenia, entertained him lavishly, and urged him most earnestly to remain our loyal friend. He had heard that the king of Persia had often tried by a mixture of fraud, threats, and intrigue to detach Arsaces from his alliance with Rome and bind him tightly to his own policy. The king declared most solemnly that he would rather lose his life than change his allegiance, and returned to his realm with his retinue loaded with gifts. Nor did he dare thereafter to violate any of his undertakings, so firmly was he attached to Constantius by many ties of gratitude, of which the strongest of all was that Constantius had given him to wife Olympias, the daughter of the former praetorian prefect Ablabius, who had been betrothed to his brother Constans.

After his departure Constantius left Cappadocia himself by way of Melitene, a town of Lesser Armenia, Lacotena, and Samosata, crossed the Euphrates, and reached Edessa. There he halted for some time to await the arrival of troops from all parts and an ample supply of provisions, and after the autumnal equinox he set out for Amida. When he arrived and saw the defences reduced to ashes, he wept and groaned aloud at the thought of the sufferings of the wretched city. The treasurer Ursulus, who happened to be with him, cried out in anguish: 'See with what courage our cities are defended by men whom the resources of the empire are denuded to supply with pay.' This piece of irony was remembered against him later by the crowd of soldiers who brought him to a violent end at Chalcedon.

From here Constantius advanced in close order to Bezabde, where he pitched his camp and fortified it by a rampart and deep ditch. He made a circuit of the walls on horseback at a safe distance and was informed by several people that the parts which had fallen into decay from age and neglect had been repaired and were now stronger than ever. Deciding to leave no preliminary to a fierce encounter undone, he sent discreet persons to offer alternative conditions; the garrison should either give up what was not theirs without bloodshed and return to their own people or submit to the rule of Rome and receive promotion and reward. These proposals were rejected with the native obstinacy to be expected from men of good birth inured to toil and danger, and every preparation was made for a siege.

Roused by the call of the trumpet our troops in close order attacked the town spiritedly on every side. The legions were packed in various tortoise formations, so that they could advance slowly but safely to undermine the walls, but a rain of missiles of all sorts poured on them as they came up, and broke the cohesion of the shields. The retreat was sounded and they withdrew. After a day's intermission a renewed attempt was made to scale the walls at dawn; the troops were now more elaborately protected and advanced with shouts on all sides. The garrison were hidden behind curtains of sacking to keep them from the enemies' view, but whenever occasion arose they thrust out their arms boldly and pelted the foe with stones and missiles. The wicker penthouses were making good progress and getting near the walls, when great jars and millstones and fragments of pillars fell from above. Their weight tore apart the protective devices and overwhelmed the assailants, who escaped only by the skin of their teeth.

So on the tenth day from the start of the siege, when our men's hopes were dashed and there was general dejection, it was decided to bring up a massive ram, which the Persians had once used to demolish Antioch and had then brought back and left at Carrhae. Its unexpected appearance and its cunning construction damped the spirits of the besieged, who were almost reduced to seek safety in surrender, but they plucked up heart and made ready to resist this menacing engine. From then on neither their courage nor their good judgement failed them. The ram was old and had been taken to pieces for ease of transport. Immense effort and ingenuity were expended in putting it together, and it was protected by the strongest possible mantlet, but the artillery kept up a hot fire of stones and sling-shot which destroyed large numbers on both sides. The earthworks rose steadily higher and the pressure of the siege grew fiercer every day. Many of our men fell because they were fighting under the emperor's eye and left off their helmets in the hope of being easily recognized and rewarded by him; this exposed them to the skill of the enemy's archers. After that, days and nights spent without sleep made both sides more cautious. When the earthworks had reached a great height the Persians, terrified by the huge ram, which was followed by other smaller rams, tried by every means in their power to set them all alight, and kept up a constant rain of firebrands and other incendiary missiles. But their efforts were vain, because most of the beams were covered with wetted hides and rags and others carefully coated with alum, so that fire fell on them without doing any damage. Although the Romans who bravely pushed the rams forward had a hard task to defend them, their eagerness to capture the town made them scorn even obvious dangers. On the other side the besieged, at a moment when the great ram was about to shatter a tower standing in its path, succeeded most cleverly in catching its projecting iron head, which was in fact shaped like a ram's head, in a very long noose on both sides. By this means they kept it from drawing back to renew its momentum and from battering the walls with a series of well-aimed blows, while at the same time they poured down boiling pitch. For a long time the engines which had been brought up stood passive under a hail of stones and missiles from the wall.

The earthworks were now raised yet higher, and the besieged, thinking that if they were not careful they would be destroyed, took an utterly reckless step. They rushed out in a sudden sally and attacked our foremost troops, hurling at the rams with all their might torches and iron pots filled with combustibles. But after a struggle whose issue was for a time in doubt, most of them were driven back inside the walls without gaining their objective. Then these same Persians took their stand on the battlements and were assailed from our mounds with arrows and sling-shot and fire-darts, which penetrated the defences of the towers but for the most part did no harm, because men were at hand to put out the fires.

By this time the numbers on both sides were reduced and the Persians were being pushed to extremities. A better plan was needed to save them, and more careful preparations were made for a sally. A sudden rush was made by a large force, which included more people carrying combustibles, and iron baskets full of fire and brushwood and other inflammable materials were hurled at the timbers. Clouds of black smoke obscured the view, the trumpets sounded for the fight, and the legions advanced at the double in battle order. The two sides engaged and the struggle was gradually reaching its height when suddenly all the engines except the great ram went up in flames. The ropes thrown from the walls which held the latter were severed, and heroic efforts just succeeded in withdrawing it half burnt.

Darkness put an end to the fighting, but our men were not left to rest for long. After a scanty allowance of food and sleep they were roused by their officers' orders. The engines were moved to a distance from the walls, and preparations were made for an attack at closer quarters from the high mounds which were now finished and overtopped the walls. Two ballistas were placed on top of each to deter the besieged from defending the battlements, and it was thought that they would inspire such fear that no one would dare so much as to look out. When all was ready our men launched an attack in three divisions just before dawn, the spikes of their helmets nodding grimly and many of them carrying ladders. Arms clashed and trumpets brayed while the fight continued with equal keenness and courage on both sides. But the Romans extended their front when they saw the Persians taking cover from the fire of the engines on the mounds; they attacked a tower with a ram and brought up ladders as well as spades, mattocks, and crowbars. A hot fire was kept up from both sides. The Persians, however, sustained the greater damage from the missiles flung by the ballistas, which sped straight to their mark from the man-made slopes. Believing that their last hour had come they rushed to their appointed doom. They divided their forces to meet the crisis, and, while some were left to defend the walls, a strong body opened a postern gate unobserved and rushed out, sword in hand. They were followed by others who carried fire in covered vessels. While the Romans were either pressing their advantage over those who gave ground or receiving the assault of those who dared to attack them, these men, stooping and creeping along, pushed their burning coals into the joints of one mound, which was built of the branches of various trees, and rushes, and bundles of cane. This dry material burst into flame and was consumed, while our men made a perilous withdrawal with their engines intact.

When the approach of evening put an end to the conflict and the armies parted for a brief rest, the emperor turned over different courses in his mind and was torn between them. On the one hand there were strong reasons for spending longer over the destruction of Phaenicha, a fort which had been erected to be an impregnable barrier against enemy inroads; on the other he was deterred by the lateness of the season. He decided to remain, but to keep hostilities at a moderate level, believing that the Persians would perhaps be driven to surrender by lack of food. But things turned out very differently from what he expected. When the fighting slackened, the rainy season set in; dripping clouds spread gloom and darkness over the sky, and the ground became so wet through continual rain that, in that region of rich soft turf, sticky mud disrupted everything. In addition, the incessant crash of thunder and lightning filled men's minds with fear. Besides this there were continual rainbows, a phenomenon of which I will give a brief explanation (*omitted*).

These and other such causes kept the emperor wavering between hope and fear. He was threatened by the approach of winter, and there was also the possibility of an ambush in that trackless region, beside the fear that his exasperated troops might mutiny. But what particularly stung him was the thought of returning empty-handed when the door of a rich house, so to speak, had been open before him.

So he abandoned his fruitless enterprise and returned to Syria to winter at Antioch, having suffered severe and grievous losses of which the effect would long be felt. It seemed to be ordained by the stars that when Constantius fought in person against the Persians he should always be worsted. That was why he kept hoping to win at least through his generals, as we remember sometimes happened.

BOOK 21

1. Julian at Vienne.

While Constantius was tied up in these difficult operations across the Euphrates, Julian at Vienne was occupied day and night in forming plans for the future, as far as his straitened resources allowed. He was growing in confidence, but what he could not determine was whether he should try by every means to bring Constantius to an agreement or seek to strike terror into him by getting his blow in first. Either course was hazardous. On the one hand Constantius was likely to prove a grim friend, and on the other he had generally emerged victorious in civil troubles. But what particularly exercised Julian was the example of his brother Gallus, who had been betrayed by his own ineptitude and the combined treachery and perjury of certain people. At moments, however, he braced himself to meet the urgent and complex situation, thinking it safer to show himself an open enemy to one whose actions a wise man could infer from his past conduct rather than fall into a trap baited by a false show of friendship. So he paid little heed to the letter which Constantius had sent by Leonas, and recognized none of the promotions which Constantius had made except that of Nebridius. He held games like an Augustus to celebrate five years of rule, and appeared in a magnificent diadem set with gleaming gems, whereas at the beginning of his reign he had taken and worn only a cheap crown like the president at an athletic meeting dressed in purple. At this time, too, he sent the remains of his dead wife Helena to Rome, to be buried on his property near the city on the road to Nomentum, where her sister Constantina, once the wife of Gallus, was also buried.

His desire to take the initiative against Constantius, now that Gaul was at peace, was sharpened and kindled by the inference that Constantius would shortly die; this he drew from various premonitory signs (in the interpretation of which he was skilled), and from dreams. And since this learned prince, whose curiosity embraced all forms of knowledge, has been charged by his enemies with practising black arts to divine the future, we must briefly consider how a wise man may acquire this by no means unimportant branch of learning.

The spirit which directs the eternal bodies that constitute the elements and which is always and everywhere active in its work of foresight allows us to share in the gift of divination through the knowledge that we pursue by various paths of learning, and the powers above, when they are propitiated by divers rites, impart words of prophecy to mortal men from the waters, so to speak, of a never-failing spring. These are said to be presided over by the goddess Themis, who is so named because she makes known beforehand what is ordained by the fixed decrees of fate (which in Greek are called 'tetheimena') and for this reason early theogonies gave her a place in the bed and on the throne of Jove, the life-giving force.

We do not owe auguries and auspices to the will of birds; they have no knowledge of the future, and no one would be such a fool as to say that they have. The truth is that their flight is directed by God, so that the noise of their beaks or the movement of their wings, whether gentle or violent, may show us what is to come. By these means a gracious deity loves to reveal impending events to men, either to reward their merits or out of pure affection for them.

In the same way those who inspect the entrails of beasts infer the course of events from the countless shapes which they take. There is a story that the discoverer of this form of knowledge was a man called Tages, who was seen to spring up suddenly from the ground somewhere in Etruria.

Coming events are also revealed by a burning sensation in men's hearts, which results in prophetic words. The natural philosophers say that our minds are, as it were, sparks sent out by the sun, which is the mind of the universe, and that when they are kindled into flame they become aware of the future. Hence the Sibyls often say that their hearts burn within them and that a great flame is consuming them. Much meaning, too, is to be found in the sound of voices and in various signs which we encounter, as well as in thunder and lightning and in the flashing track of meteors.

Our belief in dreams would be sure and unshakable were it not that their interpreters sometimes blunder. We are assured by Aristotle that dreams are certain and reliable when the dreamer is in a deep sleep, with the pupil of his eye looking straight before him and not directed to either side. Common folk in their foolishness sometimes ignorantly grumble and ask, 'If knowledge of the future is attainable, why did so-and-so not know that he would fall in battle, or another man that he would suffer this or that?' To them it is enough to reply that even a grammarian is sometimes guilty of a solecism, that a musician is sometimes out of tune, and a medical man ignorant of a remedy, but we have not on that account abandoned grammar, music, and medicine. Cicero, among his other fine sayings, has this: 'The gods give us signs of future events. If we go wrong about them it is not the divinity but men's interpretation that is at fault.' Now, not to digress too far and weary my reader, let me go back and set out the events which were foreseen.

2. Julian's pretence of Christianity.

While Julian was still at Paris in the position of Caesar, he was swinging his shield in various field-exercises when the pins by which it was secured gave way, and he was left with only the handle, which he continued to hold in his strong grasp. There was general fright among those present at what seemed a bad omen, but Julian said: 'Have no fear; I still have a firm grip of what I held.' Again, at Vienne, when he had gone to rest with a clear head, a shining form appeared to him at the dread hour of midnight while he was half awake and recited some Greek hexameters to him plainly several times. He relied on these as proof that he would have no further trouble. The lines were as follows:

> When Zeus has crossed Aquarius' broad domain,
> And Cronos reached the five-and-twentieth day
> Of Virgo, then Constantius, Asia's king,
> Shall end his life in pain and misery.

So for the moment Julian left things unchanged and dealt calmly and quietly with such business as arose, gradually strengthening his position so that his rise in dignity should be matched by an increase in might. To frustrate any opposition and win universal good will he pretended to adhere to the Christian religion, from which he had secretly apostatized long before. A few only were in his confidence, and knew that his heart was set on divination and augury and all the other practices followed by worshippers of the old gods. To conceal this for the time being he went to church on the holy-day which the Christians celebrate in January and call Epiphany, and departed after joining in their customary worship.

3. Raid by Vadomar on the Raetian frontier (A.D. 361).

During these events and just as spring was at hand, Julian was startled by an unexpected piece of news which caused him sadness and grief. He heard that raiding parties of the Alamanni had set out from Vadomar's territory, a region from which no trouble was expected since the conclusion of the treaty, and were devastating the borders of Raetia, stopping at nothing and ranging far and wide. To turn a blind eye to this would give occasion for a renewal of hostilities, so he sent count Libino with the Celts and Petulantes, who were with him in winter quarters, to take such steps as were needed to rectify the situation. Libino quickly reached the neighbourhood of Säckingen (Sanctio), but was seen from a distance by the barbarians, who had hidden themselves in the valleys in preparation for battle. Urging on his men, who were spoiling for a fight in spite of their numerical inferiority, Libino rashly attacked the Germans and was himself the first to fall when battle was joined. His death raised the confidence of the barbarians and fired the Romans to avenge their leader; so an obstinate struggle ensued, in which our men succumbed to the pressure of numbers and were put to flight with slight losses in killed and wounded.

Constantius, as I have already told, had made peace with this Vadomar and his brother Gundomad, who was likewise king. Then, after Gundomad's death, believing that Vadomar would be loyal to him, Constantius, if we are to believe an unsubstantiated rumour, entrusted him with the execution of a secret plan, and sent him written orders to behave as if the peace were at an end and to fall upon the regions nearest to him. His idea was that this would deter Julian from abandoning the defence of Gaul. Vadomar, if the story is to be credited, committed these and similar outrages in obedience to Constantius' behests; he had from his earliest youth been wonderfully adept at intrigue, as he showed later when he was governor in Phoenicia. But when the facts came to light he desisted from his activities. A notary whom he had sent to Constantius was arrested by the sentries, and on examination a letter was found on him in which, among other things, he had written: 'your Caesar is insubordinate'. But when he wrote to Julian he always addressed him as lord, Augustus, and god.

4. Vadomar arrested by Julian.

In this dangerous and doubtful situation, which he thought might develop into a fatal disaster, Julian concentrated entirely on a single object. This was to lose no time in seizing Vadomar by force when he was off his guard, so as to ensure his own safety and that of the provinces. To this end he formed the following plan. He sent to those parts the notary Philagrius, afterwards count of the East, whose judgement he trusted from previous experience, and among a number of other instructions which he was to execute according to the exigencies of the situation he gave him a sealed letter, which he was not to open or read unless Vadomar appeared on our side of the Rhine. Philagrius went as he was ordered, and when after his arrival he was occupied in business of various kinds Vadomar crossed the river, behaving as if it were a time of profound peace and he had nothing to fear and knew nothing of any untoward events. He visited the commander of the local troops and had a brief formal conversation with him; then, in order that no suspicion should be aroused at his departure, he actually accepted an invitation to a banquet, at which Philagrius also was to be one of the guests. As soon as Philagrius came in and saw the king he recalled the emperor's instructions, and on the plea of urgent and serious business returned to his quarters, where he read the letter, learned what he was to do, and at once went back and took his place among the rest. At the end of the meal he read out his orders, placed Vadomar under arrest, and handed him over to the commanding officer to be placed in strict confinement at headquarters. Vadomar's attendants, about whom Philagrius had no instructions, were compelled to return to their homes. The king himself was taken to the emperor's camp. Hearing that the notary had been intercepted, he abandoned all hope of pardon, but Julian without so much as reproaching him sent him off to Spain. The object which Julian particularly wished to secure was that when he left Gaul this frightful man should not be at liberty to disturb the provinces which he had been at such pains to pacify.

Julian's spirits were raised by his success in arresting sooner than he had hoped a king who caused him such anxiety on the eve of his departure for far countries. He did not, however, slacken his efforts, but prepared to attack the barbarians who, as I have said, had slain count Libino and some of his men in battle. To prevent their having notice of his approach and moving to a more remote spot, he crossed the Rhine at dead of night with the lightest-armed of his auxiliaries and surrounded them when they were completely off their guard. They were aroused by the clash of their enemies' arms, and while they were groping for their swords and spears Julian flew upon them and killed a number. Others, who begged for mercy and offered to give up their booty, he allowed to surrender. The rest who remained there were granted peace in return for a promise that they would cause no trouble in future.

5. *Julian's address to his troops.*

During these energetic proceedings Julian, realizing the dimensions of the civil strife he had aroused, and foreseeing with his usual sagacity that in a sudden coup nothing succeeds like speed, concluded that open revolt would be his safest course. He was doubtful, however, of the loyalty of his men, so after performing a secret rite to propitiate the goddess of war he caused the trumpets to sound the assembly throughout his army, and taking his place on a stone platform addressed them with obviously increased confidence in a louder voice than usual:

'Fellow-soldiers, I am sure that in view of the great events that have occurred you have been long looking forward in your hearts to this occasion, when consideration can be given to the events which we expect and proper precautions taken. A soldier who is inured to great and glorious deeds does better to listen than to speak, and a leader of proved integrity should have no thoughts but such as can properly meet with praise and approval. So without circumlocution I will put briefly before you what I have in mind, and I beg you to give me your kind attention while I do so.

'When by the will of Heaven I first came among you, a young and inexperienced man, I put an end to the frequent inroads of the Alamanni and Franks and to their uninterrupted enjoyment of a licence to plunder. By our joint efforts I made it possible for the armies of Rome to cross the Rhine at will, and I stood firm against clamorous reports and the armed aggression of strong tribes, relying on the sure foundation of your courage. The provinces of Gaul, which are now restored after so many disasters and a long series of grave losses, have seen the labours we have undergone and will hand down the story to posterity from generation to generation. But now that your imperative judgement and the needs of the times have raised me to the dignity of Augustus I have a loftier aim, which I hope to achieve with the help of God and yourselves, if fortune smiles upon our enterprise. I pride myself that in my relations with an army renowned for its good discipline and feats of arms I have shown moderation and calm off the field, and prudence and caution in the frequent wars which we have waged against the united forces of foreign peoples. Now, therefore, follow what I believe to be the best course, and let us forestall any trouble that awaits us by the most intimate union of hearts. The general situation is favourable to our designs and wishes. While the regions of Illyricum are still without reinforcements let us march unhindered and occupy the farthest parts of Dacia. Then we can consider in the light of our success what should be our next step. *Have confidence in your commander*, I beg you, give your unwavering and faithful adherence to this plan, and confirm it by an oath. I for my part will do my utmost to see that there is no rashness or slackness, and if anyone requires it I will pledge myself with a clear conscience never willingly to engage in any undertaking which is not in our common interest. One thing I beg and beseech you: see that none of you is carried away by the heat of the moment into inflicting harm on private persons. Bear in mind that the knowledge that the provinces have been kept safe and secure by your exemplary conduct has contributed as much to our glory as the countless defeats that we have inflicted upon our enemies.'

This speech by the emperor was received as if it were an oracle. The assembled troops were strongly moved and eager for a change. With one accord they raised terrifying shouts and clashed their shields with a frightful din, calling Julian a great and sublime leader, and, as they knew from experience, a successful conqueror of peoples and kings. When they were told formally to take the oath of allegiance they all held their swords to their throats and swore in set terms with fearful imprecations that they would undergo anything for him and even lay down their lives if needed. Their example was followed by the officers and all the close attendants of the emperor, who pledged their loyalty in similar terms. The only refusal came from Nebridius, who declared firmly but rashly that he could not by any means bind himself by an oath against Constantius, to whose kindness he was indebted for so many acts of favour. This so enraged the soldiers standing near that they set upon him and tried to kill him, but the emperor, at whose knees he had fallen, covered him with his cloak. When he returned to the palace Julian found Nebridius, who had got there before him, prostrate on the ground and begging him to relieve his fears by giving him his hand. Julian answered: 'If *you* touch my hand I shall have no mark of distinction to confer on my friends. But go where you will; no one shall harm you.' At these words Nebridius withdrew in safety to his house in Tuscany. After these preliminary steps, which the importance of the matter in hand required, Julian, who knew from experience the value in troubled times of a pre-emptive strike, gave written orders for a march towards Pannonia, set his army with its standards in motion, and boldly committed himself to whatever fortune might bring.

6. *Constantius at Antioch.*

It is now time to retrace my steps and to give a brief account of Constantius' conduct of affairs, both domestic and military, while he was wintering at Antioch during these events in Gaul. When an emperor returns from abroad a deputation of men of conspicuous distinction, which includes some prominent ex-tribunes, is appointed to greet him, and such a ceremonial reception took place on Constantius' arrival from Mesopotamia. An ex-tribune from Paphlagonia called Amphilochius, who there were good grounds for suspecting had sown the seeds of discord between the *emperor's* brothers when he was serving under Constans, had the audacity to present himself as if he had an equal right with the others to pay his respects. He was recognized and excluded, amid loud shouts that he was a stubborn traitor who should no longer be allowed to see the light of day. Constantius, however, showed unusual mildness. 'Do not,' he said, 'persecute a man who is, I believe, guilty, but who has not yet been clearly convicted. Remember that if he has committed any such crime my presence will ensure that he is punished by the judgement of his own conscience, which he cannot evade.' There the matter rested. On the next day in the circus this same man was in his usual place opposite the emperor, when a sudden shout was raised at the beginning of a long-awaited event and the railing on which he with a number of others was leaning gave way. They all fell to the ground, but, whereas the rest were only slightly hurt, Amphilochius suffered an internal injury and was found to have breathed his last. Constantius was overjoyed at this apparent confirmation of his ability to foresee the future.

At the same time he married a wife called Faustina. He had long since lost Eusebia, the sister of the ex-consuls Eusebius and Hypatius, a woman of outstanding beauty and excellence of character, whose kindness of heart was unaffected by her high rank. It was by her well-deserved favour, as I have related, that Julian was rescued from danger and proclaimed Caesar.

During this period attention was also given to the position of Florentius, who had left Gaul through fear of the revolution. He was appointed to succeed Anatolius, the praetorian prefect of Illyricum, who had lately died, and the insignia of the highest magistracy were conferred on him together with Taurus, the praetorian prefect of Italy.

Even so, preparations for foreign and civil war were pushed forward. The number of squadrons of cavalry was increased, and reinforcements for the legions enlisted with the same urgency. Levies were ordered throughout the provinces, and people of every rank and calling were harassed by requisitions of clothing, arms, and engines of war, not to speak of gold and silver, stores of provisions of all sorts, and different kinds of pack-animals. The king of Persia had been reluctantly obliged to return to his own country by the onset of winter, but it was feared that he would mount a more powerful attack when the weather became more open. Envoys were therefore sent with generous gifts to the kings and satraps beyond the Tigris to urge them to remain loyal to us and abstain from any kind of intrigue or treachery. Above all, Arsaces and Meribanes, kings of Armenia and Hiberia respectively, were wooed by gifts of splendid robes and presents of many other kinds, since it was feared that they could gravely injure the interests of Rome if at this critical moment they went over to the Persians.

In the midst of these pressing affairs Hermogenes died and was succeeded in the prefecture by Helpidius, a native of Paphlagonia. He was a man of mean appearance and no speaker, but straightforward and humane, so mild in fact that once, when Constantius ordered the torture of an innocent man, he calmly asked that he might be relieved of his office and the execution of the emperor's orders left to more suitable instruments of his will.

7. *Constantius in Mesopotamia.*

Constantius, perplexed by the difficulties which beset him, remained long in doubt whether he should attack Julian, who was still far away, or repel the Parthians, who were threatening to cross the Euphrates. At last, after frequent consultations with his generals, he decided to finish, or at any rate stabilize, the war which was nearer, and then, leaving no enemy to fear behind him, to traverse Illyricum and Italy in the expectation of running down Julian like a hunted animal at the very beginning of his enterprise. This was what he kept declaring to soothe the fears of his men. But to keep things on the boil and avoid any appearance of neglecting the war on the other front, and to spread the terror of his coming in all parts by giving the impression that he was on his way from the East, he sent the notary Gaudentius by sea to Africa, which he feared might be invaded in his absence. Africa is a region of importance to emperors in any circumstances, and Gaudentius, as I have indicated earlier, had spent some time in Gaul keeping an eye on the activities of Julian. Constantius had a double reason for hoping that Gaudentius would be prompt and obedient in the discharge of his mission: first, because he feared the other side, which he had offended, and, second, because he would be eager to seize this chance of ingratiating himself with Constantius, of whose ultimate victory he had no doubt, an opinion at that time confidently shared by everybody.

On his arrival Gaudentius, having informed count Cretio and the other commanders of what was on foot, in accordance with the emperor's orders assembled the best troops from all parts, transferred light-armed skirmishers from both provinces of Mauretania, and kept the closest guard on the coast opposite Aquitaine and Italy. Constantius' adoption of this policy was justified by the fact that while he was alive none of his enemies reached these shores, although the coast of Sicily from Marsala (Lilybaeum) to Cape Passaro (Pachynum) was occupied by a strong force ready to cross at once if they got the chance.

When Constantius had arranged these and other less important matters to what he thought the best advantage, he was informed by messengers and letters from his generals that the proud king of Persia had mobilized his forces and was encamped near the bank of the Tigris, though the precise point where he intended to break through was unknown. Stung by this news and thinking that he could best anticipate the coming offensive if he were nearer the theatre of war, Constantius concentrated his cavalry and the flower of his infantry, on which he relied, left his winter quarters at the earliest possible moment, crossed the Euphrates on a bridge of boats at Capersana, and made for Edessa, a well-supplied and strongly fortified city, where he waited for a time until scouts or deserters should bring him news of the enemy's movements.

8. Julian on the march.

Meanwhile Julian, after disposing of the business I have mentioned, left Augst. He sent Sallustius, who was promoted to the rank of prefect, back to Gaul, and appointed Germanian to succeed Nebridius. At the same time he made Nevitta master of cavalry, distrusting the old traitor Gomoarius, who he was told had betrayed his own emperor Vetranio when he was in command of the Scutarii. Jovius, whom I have mentioned in my account of Magnentius, was appointed quaestor, and Mamertinus placed in charge of the treasury. Dagalaif was put in command of the household troops, and a number of others of approved merit and loyalty were appointed to various military posts.

Julian intended to march through the Black Forest and along the roads near the Danube, but the suddenness with which events had developed gave him pause; he was afraid that his appearance with only a small following might appear contemptible and that he might have to encounter the resistance of large numbers. To forestall this danger he devised a clever plan. He divided his army, and sent part under Jovinus and Jovius to make a rapid march over the familiar roads of Italy, while the rest under the cavalry commander Nevitta were to advance through the middle of Raetia. By being dispersed in this way over different regions they would give the impression of vast numbers and spread alarm everywhere, a strategy employed by Alexander the Great and a number of other skilful generals after him, when circumstances required it. Orders were given that from the very start they should proceed cautiously and be ready to meet an enemy at any moment. At night they were to post sentries and keep watch, to avoid any danger of being surprised.

9. Collapse of opposition to Julian.

After making these dispositions according to his best judgement Julian marched forward as he had often done in penetrating barbarian country, relying on the unbroken series of his successes. Reaching a place below which he was told that the river was navigable, he embarked on boats, which he was lucky enough to find in considerable numbers, and was carried downstream without attracting much notice. This was possible because he was inured to hardship, and, having no need of luxuries but being able to make do with a scanty supply of ordinary food, could pass towns and fortresses without stopping. In this he exemplified the fine saying of the old king Cyrus, who, when he was asked by his host what food he should get ready, replied: 'Only bread, for I hope to dine near a stream.' Rumour, however, whose thousand tongues wonderfully exaggerate the truth, spread throughout Illyricum the report that Julian, puffed up with his success in defeating a host of kings and peoples in Gaul, was now approaching with a numerous army. This so terrified the praetorian prefect Taurus that he made a hasty retreat as if in the face of a foreign foe. He availed himself of the quick relays of the public post service to cross the Julian Alps, taking with him at the same time the prefect Florentius. Count Lucillian, however, who then commanded in those parts with his headquarters at Sirmium, was alarmed by some slight intelligence of Julian's movements. Acting on this he collected such troops as he could get together at short notice and prepared to oppose Julian's advance. But Julian rushed like a fireball or a blazing dart straight to his goal. The moon was waning, and the greater part of the night consequently dark, when he reached Bononea, nineteen miles from Sirmium. There he unexpectedly landed, and at once sent Dagalaif with some light-armed men to summon Lucillian, and to bring him by force if he offered resistance. The latter was still asleep when he was aroused by a confused noise and found himself surrounded by a ring of unknown men. Realizing what had happened and overawed by the imperial title, he most reluctantly obeyed the order. So the man who a moment before had been a proud and spirited commander now had to bow to another's will. He was mounted on the first beast that came to hand and brought to the emperor a wretched prisoner, almost out of his wits with fright. But as soon as he saw Julian and realized that he was to be given an opportunity of doing homage to the purple, he pulled himself together in the knowledge that he was safe. 'It is rash and reckless of your majesty,' he said, 'to venture with a few men into another's territory.' Julian answered with a bitter smile: 'Keep these wise words for Constantius. I have allowed you to touch my imperial robe not because I need your advice but to allay your fears.'

10. Surrender of Sirmium and seizure of Succi.

After disposing of Lucillian, Julian, thinking that nothing was to be gained by delay or inaction, and behaving with his usual boldness and confidence at a moment of danger, advanced at speed towards the city, counting on its surrender. As he approached its large and extensive suburbs he was met with lights and flowers and good wishes by a heterogeneous crowd of soldiers and others, who greeted him as 'Augustus' and 'Lord' and escorted him to the palace. Delighted by this success, which he regarded as an omen that his hopes would be fulfilled and that the example of so famous and populous a metropolis would ensure his reception as a saviour from Heaven in other cities also, he gratified the populace by devoting the next day to chariot races. But his impatience was such that when the third day dawned he marched out along the public highway and seized Succi without opposition. A garrison under the loyal Nevitta was posted to guard it, and this will be a convenient moment to describe the nature of the place.

The adjacent high ranges of Haemus and Rhodope, the former of which rises from the very bank of the Danube and the latter from the nearer side of the river Vardar (Axius), leave between their swelling hills a narrow pass, which separates Illyricum from Thrace. It overlooks large and famous cities on both sides, on one Sofia (Serdica) in the heart of Dacia and on the other Philippopolis in Thrace. It is as if nature foresaw that the surrounding peoples must come under the rule of Rome, and purposely contrived a gap, which originally opened obscurely between close-set hills, but in our great and glorious latter days has been made passable even by carriages, and has on occasion been blocked so effectively as to repel the attacks of great generals and peoples. The side which faces Illyricum has a gentle slope and is often easily surmounted, and one might almost say caught napping. But the side which commands Thrace falls sheer down. Rough paths on either hand make hard going, and the ascent is difficult even when unopposed. At the foot of these heights on both sides is a wide extent of plain, which on the upper side stretches as far as the Julian Alps, while on the lower the ground is so flat and open that it presents no obstacle to habitation as far as the straits and the sea of Marmora (Propontis).

After dealing with this urgent matter the emperor left the master of the horse at Succi and returned to Niš (Naissus), a prosperous town, from which he could without hindrance make such dispositions as would suit him. He had seen the historian Victor at Sirmium, and he now sent for him, appointed him governor of Lower Pannonia with the rank of consular, and awarded him the honour of a bronze statue. Victor was a man who was a model of respectability, and long afterwards was urban prefect. Julian, whose ambition now took a higher flight and who

believed that there was no possibility of reaching an accord with
Constantius, sent a bitter letter reviling him to the senate. In this he set
out Constantius' faults and made certain specific charges. It was read
in the senate-house while Tertullus was still prefect. The nobility gave
a fine example of self-confidence and generous feeling by shouting
unanimously: 'We expect you to show respect to the man who has made
you what you are.'

On this occasion Julian attacked the reputation of Constantine also
by describing him as an innovator and a destroyer of hallowed laws and
traditions, and openly reproached him for being the first to promote
barbarians to the honour of the consulship. This was a tasteless and
irresponsible act on the part of Julian, who, instead of studying to avoid
the very fault which he so hotly reprobated, shortly afterwards made
Nevitta the colleague of Mamertinus in the consulship. Nevitta, so far
from being the equal in distinction, experience, and renown of those
on whom Constantine had conferred the highest magistracy, was
uncultivated and rather boorish and, what was even less tolerable, cruel
in the conduct of his high office.

11. Seizure of Aquileia on Constantius' behalf.

While Julian's attention was occupied by these important and worrying
affairs he received unexpected and alarming news of a monstrous plot
hatched by certain persons, which would impede his dashing progress
unless it were promptly nipped in the bud. I will give a brief account
of this.

Julian had found at Sirmium two of Constantius' legions and a cohort
of archers, of whose loyalty he entertained doubts. He therefore
despatched them to Gaul on the pretext that they were urgently needed
there. Dreading the prospect of the long march and of the fierce and
persistent hostility of the Germans, they moved slowly with mutiny in
mind; in this they were prompted and abetted by Nigrinus, a native of
Mesopotamia, who commanded a squadron of cavalry. The plot was
matured in clandestine meetings and kept a profound secret. When
they reached Aquileia, a prosperous city fortified by strong walls, they
suddenly closed the gates, an act of defiance in which they were
supported by the native population, which was still over-awed by the
name of Constantius. They blocked the entrances, posted armed men
on the towers and ramparts, and made preparations for a coming

struggle. In the meantime they lived a free and easy life, and their daring action encouraged the Italians round about to espouse the cause of Constantius, whom they supposed to be still alive.

12. Siege and surrender of Aquileia.

Julian received this news while he was still at Niš and free from any apprehension of a hostile movement in his rear. He had heard and read that Aquileia was a city which had survived several sieges without ever being destroyed or surrendered, and this made him the more eager to win it either by stratagem or by the arts of diplomacy before anything worse happened. So he ordered the master of cavalry, Jovinus, who was advancing over the Alps and had entered Noricum, to return at once and find some means of extinguishing the conflagration which had broken out. Also, to leave nothing undone, he gave instructions that any household or legionary troops that passed through Niš should be kept there to render what help they could.

Shortly after making these arrangements he heard of the death of Constantius, and crossed Thrace and entered Constantinople. There he learned from several sources that the siege of Aquileia would take time but need cause no anxiety. He therefore assigned Immo with some other members of his staff to this task, and transferred Jovinus to deal with more pressing problems elsewhere.

Once a double line of heavy infantry had been drawn round Aquileia, the generals were unanimous in thinking that it would be best to induce its defenders to surrender by a mixture of threats and fair words. But several exchanges served only to harden the resolution of the besieged, and negotiations were broken off without result. There was nothing for it now but battle. Both sides recruited their strength with food and sleep, and at dawn were roused by the trumpets to the business of mutual slaughter, which they set about with loud shouts and more spirit than discretion. The attackers, pushing in front of them penthouses and closely-woven hurdles, advanced slowly and cautiously and tried to undermine the walls with a multitude of iron tools. Many carried ladders made to match the height of the walls, but when they had all but reached them some were thrown down and crushed by a hail of stones and others transfixed by whistling darts. The resultant retreat carried with it all the rest, whose ardour for the fight was damped by fear of meeting a similar fate.

This first encounter raised the spirits of the besieged and encouraged them to hope for further success and to think that what remained to be done was comparatively easy. Full of confidence, they placed engines in suitable positions and without relaxing their efforts kept up their watch-keeping and the other precautions necessary for their safety. The engineers on the other side, though alarmed by the dangers which faced them, were ashamed to appear slack or inactive, and, seeing that a frontal assault had met with so little success, transferred their efforts to the methods of a regular siege. Since the river Natesio, which flows close by the city, left no space suitable for the deployment of rams and other engines or for digging mines, a device was adopted as admirable as anything contrived in old times. Without a moment's delay wooden towers were constructed high enough to overtop the enemy's ramparts, and each of these was placed on a platform made by fastening three ships tightly together. The tops of the towers were occupied by men-at-arms whose united efforts were to dislodge the opposition in a hand-to-hand fight, while at a lower level light-armed troops issued from the bowels of the towers and tried to cross on small portable bridges which they had put together for the purpose. The idea behind this joint operation was that while the two parties above were exchanging a fire of missiles and stones those who had crossed by the bridges should effect a breach in the wall without interference, and open a way into the heart of the city. This clever plan, however, came to nothing. As the towers approached they were showered with fire-darts soaked in pitch as well as with reeds and brushwood and various other combustibles, and the rapid spread of the flames, combined with the weight of the men who had a precarious footing on them, caused them to totter and fall into the river. Some of the men on their tops were killed by shot from catapults. The troops on foot, left in the lurch by the disaster of their friends on the ships, were crushed by huge stones, except for a few who saved themselves by their speed in spite of the obstacles in their path. Finally, when the fight had lasted till evening, the usual order was given to break off, and the two sides parted and passed the rest of the day with very different feelings. The doleful cries of the besiegers lamenting the deaths of their comrades encouraged their opponents to hope that they would get the upper hand, though they too had a few losses to mourn. Nevertheless there was no relaxation of effort. One whole night was allowed to restore the men's energy with food and rest, but at dawn the trumpet roused them and the fight was renewed. Some held their shields above their heads to facilitate their movements, others rushed forward with ladders on their shoulders as before, and all exposed their breasts to every kind of weapon. A number tried to break the iron bars of the gates, and were themselves attacked with fire or perished under a shower of stones from the walls. Yet others, who made a bold attempt to cross the ditch, were taken at a disadvantage by the sudden emergence of men from posterns and either paid for their rashness with their lives or withdrew wounded. Their opponents had a safe line of retreat, and while they were lying in wait were completely sheltered by a turf-covered rampart in front of the wall. Although the besieged, who relied solely on their fortifications, showed great endurance and skill in the arts of war, a picked force of their opponents, chafing at the long delay, carefully surveyed the entire environs in the hope of finding a spot where they could force a way into the city either by direct assault or by their artillery. But when the difficulties proved insuperable they began to prosecute the siege with less energy. Those in reserve, leaving only sentries and pickets on duty, took to plundering the country about, which was rich in supplies of every kind. Most of the loot they gathered they shared with their comrades, and overindulgence in stuffing and drinking led to loss of morale.

When Julian, who was still at Constantinople for the winter, heard from Immo and his colleagues what had happened, he hit on a shrewd way of rectifying the situation, and sent the infantry commander Agilo to Aquileia. Agilo at that time had a great reputation, and it was hoped that the sight of so famous a man and the news which he brought of the death of Constantius would bring the siege to an end.

Meanwhile, since other methods had failed, it was decided to keep up the siege of Aquileia and to overcome the fierce resistance of its defenders by forcing them to surrender through thirst. The aqueducts were cut, but this had no effect on the confidence of the besieged, so with enormous effort the course of the river was diverted. Even this was unsuccessful. Though they no longer had so plentiful a supply of drinking-water, the men who had shut themselves up in the town by their own foolhardiness made do with the scanty amount that they could get from wells.

While this was happening with the result I have mentioned, Agilo appeared on the scene in accordance with his orders. He approached the walls boldly, protected by a thick screen of shields, but his detailed and true account of the death of Constantius and of the establishment of Julian as emperor was rejected with contumely as a pack of lies. No one believed his statement until he was admitted alone to one of the bastions under a safe-conduct and confirmed what he had told them by a solemn oath. Then the inhabitants, overjoyed at their release from their long agony, flung open the gates and poured out to greet the general who brought them peace. They excused themselves by representing Nigrinus and a few others as the authors of their mad act, and begged that the execution of these men should suffice to wipe out the guilt of treason and the woes of the city. A few days later, after a strict inquiry before the praetorian prefect Mamertinus, Nigrinus was burned at the stake as primarily responsible for the war. After him two members of the town council, Romulus and Sabostius, were convicted of having recklessly sown the seeds of discord, and suffered capital punishment. All the rest, who had engaged in this mad conflict from compulsion rather than inclination, escaped unharmed. Such was the equitable decision arrived at by the emperor, who was merciful and not hard to appease.

But all this happened later. While Julian was still at Niš, he had serious grounds for fearing that he might have to face dangers on both sides. Behind him, a sudden attack by the troops besieged at Aquileia might shut the passes of the Julian Alps and deprive him of provinces from which he expected support at any moment. At the same time he was greatly alarmed by the strength of the East; he heard that the forces dispersed over Thrace had been quickly concentrated in the face of his sudden threat and were approaching the neighbourhood of Succi under the command of count Marcian. Nevertheless he took action on his own part proportionate to the urgency of these problems, and brought together the army of Illyricum, which was inured to the dust of war and ready to follow a bold leader into battle.

In spite of his critical situation he did not overlook the interests of individuals, and heard a number of suits, especially those which concerned holders of municipal office, whom he was always disposed to favour and many of whom he invested with public posts above their deserts. He found at Niš two distinguished senators, Symmachus and Maximus, who had been sent by their colleagues on a mission to Constantius and were on their way back. He gave them a gracious reception and, passing over the better man, appointed Maximus prefect of the Eternal City in succession to Tertullus. This was to gratify Rufinus Vulcatius, whose nephew he knew Maximus to be. Under

Maximus' administration there was plenty of food, and the usual frequent murmurings of the populace died down. At this time, too, to inspire confidence at a moment of crisis and encourage his loyal supporters, he nominated Mamertinus, the praetorian prefect of Illyricum, to the consulship with Nevitta as his colleague, although he had lately reproached Constantine in unmeasured terms for being the first to promote barbarians of low birth.

13. Retreat of Sapor. Speech by Constantius.

While Julian was thus occupied with new projects in a mood between hope and fear, Constantius at Edessa was disturbed by differing reports from his scouts. He was torn between two incompatible courses of action; at one moment he was preparing his forces for a pitched battle, and at the next contemplating, if opportunity offered, a second siege of Bezabde, believing with justice that he should not leave his Mesopotamian flank unprotected during the offensive which he was about to mount in the north. Various causes contributed to protract his state of indecision. King Sapor was lingering on the far side of the Tigris, waiting to move until the omens were favourable. If he were to cross the river unopposed he could easily break through to the Euphrates. Another consideration was that Constantius, who had to keep his troops in condition for a civil war, was nervous of exposing them to the perils of a siege, knowing from experience the strength of the fortifications and the energy of the defence.

To keep things on the move, however, and to avoid any charge of inaction, he put into the field strong columns under Arbitio and Agilo, the masters of cavalry and infantry, not to provoke the Persians to battle but to be deployed along our bank of the Tigris and watch to see in what direction their fierce monarch would break out. He gave them both oral and written orders that if the enemy host should begin to cross they must at once withdraw. While these generals were guarding the front assigned to them and trying to read the hidden intentions of that most subtle of all peoples, Constantius himself kept the great part of his army in a state of alert and made occasional sallies to protect the neighbouring towns. From time to time scouts and deserters brought him inconsistent reports. They could not give him any clear forecast because among the Persians knowledge of what is planned is confined to the grandees, who can be trusted not to reveal it and who worship silence as if it were a god. The generals in the field incessantly sent to the emperor with requests for reinforcements and asserted that only a concentration of the whole army could withstand the assault of the ambitious king.

During this anxious time there arrived in quick succession indubitably authentic reports that Julian, after a lightning march through Italy and Illyricum, had seized the pass of Succi and was only waiting for the auxiliaries, which he had summoned from every quarter, to invade Thrace with an armed host. This news plunged Constantius in grief; his only comfort was that he had always come off best in civil wars. The situation made it very difficult to form a plan, but he decided that the best course was to use the public post service to send relays of troops ahead of him to meet this fearful threat as soon as possible. This met with unanimous approval and light-armed men set out in accordance with his orders, but on the next day Constantius heard that king Sapor and all his forces had returned home because bad auspices compelled him to abandon his enterprise. This relieved Constantius' anxiety. He recalled all the troops except those normally stationed in Mesopotamia, and returned at once to Hierapolis.

Once the army was concentrated, Constantius, uncertain of the ultimate outcome, assembled by trumpet-call all the centuries, maniples, and cohorts. When they had crowded on to the field, the emperor, to impress on them the necessity of prompt obedience, took his place on a high platform surrounded by a larger suite than usual, and addressed them with a show of calm and confidence as follows:

'I have always made it my aim to avoid any careless word or action inconsistent with strict honour. Like a cautious pilot I have put my helm up or down in accordance with the motion of the waves. Now, however, my loving subjects, I have to confess a mistake, or, to use a truer word, an act of kindness which I believed would serve the interests of the state. Give me a favourable hearing, I beg you, while I explain in simple terms my reason for convoking this assembly.

'While Magnentius, whom your valour overthrew, was pursuing his mischievous course, I raised my cousin Gallus to the dignity of Caesar and sent him to defend the East. He swerved from the path of justice by many crimes as hateful to relate as to behold, and was punished by the judgement of the law. If only Nemesis, that arch-contriver of trouble, had been content with that, and had left me to recall in anguish but at peace no more than a single past sorrow. But now a second has fallen on me more grievous, I might well say, than the first, for which, however, your native courage will with the help of Heaven provide a remedy. Julian, to whom, while you were fighting the foreign peoples threatening Illyricum, I entrusted the defence of Gaul, has become so madly presumptuous on the score of some trivial victories over half-armed Germans as to recruit from his auxiliaries, for an ambitious design against the state, a small band of desperadoes who will stick at nothing. He has trampled underfoot the rule of law, the nursing-mother of the Roman world, which I am confident from my own experience and from the lessons of the past will take vengeance on his criminal acts and *reduce his pride to ashes*.

What course, then, is left but to meet the storm that has been raised and to act with speed to crush this mad rebellion before it gathers strength? I have no doubt that with the very present help of God most high, under whose eternal judgement the ungrateful stand condemned, these men who, so far from being provoked, have conspired to destroy the innocent after being loaded with favours, will find the sword that they have wickedly drawn turned to their own destruction. Rest assured – I forecast it with confidence and it accords with the promise that Justice will help the righteous – that when we come to close quarters our enemies will be too numb with panic to face the fire flashing from your eyes or the first note of your war-cry.'

This speech won them all to his side. Brandishing their spears angrily, they expressed much sympathy for Constantius and demanded to be led forthwith against the rebel. Their favourable response changed the emperor's fear into joy. Dismissing the assembly he ordered Arbitio, with whose unrivalled success in quelling civil wars he was well acquainted, to go ahead of him with the Lancers and Mattiarii and some companies of light-armed troops. Gomoarius likewise was sent on with the Laeti to oppose the enemy's advance at the pass of Succi. He was chosen because he had a grudge against Julian for the contemptuous treatment that he had received in Gaul.

14. Omens of Constantius' death.

In this storm of trouble Constantius' fortunes began to falter and decline, and it became plain from omens almost as clear as words that the crisis of his life was at hand. He was disturbed by a vision in the night; before he was quite asleep he saw his father's spirit holding out

to him a fine child. He took it and placed it in his lap, where it shook
from his grasp and threw to a distance the orb which he was carrying
in his right hand. This was a sign of an approaching political upheaval,
although the soothsayers gave it a favourable interpretation. Later he
admitted to his closest confidants that he felt abandoned because he
could no longer see a mysterious something which he thought dimly
appeared to him from time to time. This he believed to be a guardian
angel appointed to protect him, and its departure to be a sign that he
was about to leave this world. Divines believe that a particular spirit of
this kind is assigned to every man at birth to direct his course, as far as
the decrees of fate permit, but that it is visible to very few, in fact only
to those of unusual merit. This is the teaching of oracles and of eminent
writers, among them the comic poet Menander, whose works contain
the following couplet:

> A spirit goes along with every man
> From birth, to guide him on the path of life.

Similarly, we are given to understand by the immortal poems of Homer
that it was not the gods of Olympus who spoke to the heroes and stood
by them and helped them in battle, but the familiar spirits which
belonged to them. We are told that it was by their particular support
that Pythagoras and Socrates and Numa Pompilius became famous,
not to mention the elder Scipio and, as some believe, Marius, and
Octavian, who was the first to bear the title of Augustus. There are also
Hermes Trismegistus and Apollonius of Tyana and Plotinus, the last
of whom was bold enough to write on this esoteric subject and to
demonstrate by profound reasoning how it comes about that these
spirits are joined to the souls of men and nurse them as it were in their
bosoms as long as fate allows, initiating them into higher truths if they
find that they are pure and have kept themselves spotless and free from
the pollution of sin during their association with the body.

15. *Constantius dies at Mobsucrenae in Cilicia.*

Constantius made a rapid return to Antioch, eager as always to meet
the challenge of civil war head on. When all was ready he was in
excessive haste to march, and although many of his officials murmured
against his decision no one dared to dissuade or oppose him openly.
Autumn was already far advanced when he set out. In a suburb called

Hippocephalus, three miles from the city, he saw in broad daylight on the right of the road the headless corpse of a murdered man lying with its feet towards the west. In spite of his alarm at this omen of his approaching end he persisted in pushing on, and reached Tarsus, where he contracted a slight fever. Believing that the motion of the journey would help him to shake off this indisposition he pursued his way over difficult country to Mobsucrenae, which lies at the foot of Mount Taurus and is the last post-station in Cilicia as you come from here. Next day he tried to go on but was prevented by the worsening of his condition; the fever in his veins gradually reached such a height that his body burned like a furnace and was too hot to touch. Being now past all medical aid and at his last gasp, he began to lament his death, and we are told that while he was still in possession of his senses he named Julian as his successor. As his last struggle for breath began he fell silent, and finally after a long agony departed this life on the fifth of October. He was forty-four and a few months old and he had reigned for thirty-eight years.

After the last solemn call to the deceased and an outburst of lamentation and grief, the highest officials of the court debated what course to take. A few tentative suggestions were made privately that they should choose a new emperor; this proposal is said to have emanated from Eusebius, who was driven to it by consciousness of guilt. Seeing, however, that any attempt at such a revolution would be frustrated by the near approach of Julian, Theolaif and Abigild, who were then counts, were sent to him to inform him of the death of his cousin and to beg him to come without delay and take possession of the East, which was ready to obey him. Unconfirmed rumour had it that Constantius had left a will, in which, as I said, he made Julian his heir and gave trusts and legacies to his nearest friends. His wife was with child when he died, and his posthumous daughter was called after him and when she grew up was married to Gratian.

16. The good and bad qualities of Constantius.

I propose to draw a clear distinction between Constantius' good and bad qualities, and it will be convenient to deal first with the former. He always maintained the dignity of his position as emperor and thought it beneath him to court popularity. He was exceedingly sparing in the conferment of higher honours; with a few exceptions he allowed no changes which would increase the prestige of his administrators, and he never let the military set themselves up too high. Under him, no general was advanced to the highest rank of nobility; as far as my memory serves, generals were only of the second grade. A master of cavalry was never given an official reception by the governor of his province, and was not allowed any share in civil administration. All officials, both civil and military, looked up to the praetorian prefect with traditional respect as the holder of the highest of all offices. In handling his army Constantius was exceptionally careful and sometimes over-critical in his scrutiny of men's merits. Appointments at court were regulated with scrupulous exactness. No unknown newcomer to the palace was ever entrusted with an important function, and anyone who was to be master of the offices, or treasurer, or anything of that sort, rose to this only after giving thorough evidence of his quality during ten years' service in other posts. It very rarely happened that a military man was transferred to a civil office, and, conversely, only experienced veterans were placed in command of troops.

Constantius was industrious and had aspirations to learning, but he was too dull-witted to make a speaker, and when he turned his mind to versifying produced nothing worth while. His style of living was frugal and temperate, and he ate and drank only in moderation; in consequence his health was so robust that he was rarely unwell, though such illnesses as he had were dangerous. Long experience confirms medical opinion that this is what happens with people who keep clear of dissipation and luxury. When necessary he could do with little sleep, and for long periods of his life he was so exceptionally chaste that *even his most confidential servants* could not so much as suspect him of behaviour which malice invents in those who enjoy the freedom of supreme power, even when it can find no grounds for it. In riding, throwing the javelin, and above all in archery, as well as in the various skills of the infantry, he was thoroughly expert. I will not dwell, because it has been related so often, on the fact that he was never seen in public wiping his face or nose or spitting or turning his head to either side and that he never in his life tasted fruit.

After picking out his good qualities, as far as I could ascertain them, I turn to the description of his defects. Although in most respects he was comparable with other emperors of average merit, yet if he discovered any ground, however false or slight, for suspecting an attempt upon the throne he showed in endless investigations, regardless of right or wrong, a cruelty which easily surpassed that of Caligula and Domitian and Commodus. Indeed, at the very beginning of his reign he rivalled their barbarity by destroying root and branch all who were connected with him by blood and birth. The sufferings of the wretched men accused of infringing or violating his prerogative were increased by the bitter and angry suspicions nourished by the emperor in all such cases. Once he got wind of anything of this kind he threw himself into its investigation with unbecoming eagerness, and appointed merciless judges to preside over such trials. In the infliction of punishment he sometimes tried to prolong the agonies of death, if the victim's constitution could stand it, and showed himself in this respect more savage even than Gallienus. That emperor was the object of many genuine plots by rebels such as Aureolus, Postumus, Ingenuus, Valens surnamed Thessalonicus, and several others, yet on some occasions he punished capital crimes more mildly than they deserved. Constantius, on the other hand, employed excessive torture to give an appearance of authenticity to circumstances which were invented or at best uncertain. In such cases he showed himself the deadly enemy of justice, although his great object was to be thought just and merciful. He was adept at making a mountain of mischief out of a molehill of evidence, just as sparks from a dry wood can be fanned by even a slight breeze into a fire which rushes with irresistible violence on the surrounding countryside. In this he was the antithesis of that blameless emperor Marcus. The latter was engaged in a campaign in Illyricum when Cassius usurped the imperial title in Syria, and a bundle of Cassius' letters to his accomplices fell into his hands by the capture of their bearer. Marcus at once ordered the packet to be burnt unopened in order that he might not know the names of the plotters and be forced against his will to regard certain people as his enemies. Many right-thinking men believed that it would have been much better for Constantius' reputation to renounce his power without bloodshed instead of using such cruel methods to defend it. The same lesson is enforced by Cicero in a letter to Nepos in which he reprobates the cruelty of Caesar. 'Happiness,' he writes, 'is nothing but success in noble actions, or, in other words, the good fortune that brings worthy aims to fruition. The man who has no such aims cannot be happy. It follows that no happiness was to be found in the wicked and criminal designs nursed by Caesar. In my opinion Camillus was happier in exile than Manlius would have been at the same period if he had achieved the object of his wishes and made himself king.' Heracleitus of Ephesus teaches the same truth when he tells us that, though the changes and chances of life have sometimes put outstanding men at the mercy of weaklings and cowards, the truest glory is won when a man in power totally subdues his cruel and savage and angry impulses and erects in the citadel of his soul a splendid memorial of his victory over himself.

Constantius, though he suffered grievous defeats in foreign wars, prided himself on his success in civil conflicts, and bathed in the blood which poured in a fearful stream from the internal wounds of the state. Perverting the normal and honourable grounds for such an action, he erected triumphal arches in Gaul and Pannonia at great expense to commemorate the ruin of the provinces, and inscribed on them the record of his deeds for men to read of him as long as the monuments should last. He was excessively influenced by his wives and his shrill eunuchs and certain court officials, who applauded his every word and were on the watch for opportunities to agree with whatever he asserted or denied.

The sorrows of the age were increased by the insatiable greed of the tax-collectors, whose exactions earned Constantius more hatred than revenue. What made the situation seem even less tolerable in the eyes of many was that he never heard a tax case himself, or took any steps to alleviate the burden of the provinces, which were crushed by a multiplicity of dues and imposts. Moreover, he never found it difficult to take away what he had previously granted.

The plain and simple religion of the Christians was bedevilled by Constantius with old wives' fancies. Instead of trying to settle matters he raised complicated issues which led to much dissension, and as this spread more widely he fed it with verbal argument. Public transport hurried throngs of bishops hither and thither to attend what they call synods, and by his attempts to impose conformity Constantius only succeeded in hamstringing the post service.

As to his appearance and build: he was rather dark, with staring eyes and sharp sight. His hair was soft, and his cheeks regularly shaved to give him a trim and shining look. From the base of the neck to the groin his body was unusually long, but his legs were very short and bowed, which made him a good runner and jumper.

The body of the dead emperor was washed and placed in a coffin, and Jovian, who was still only a staff-officer, was ordered to convey it in royal state to Constantinople to be buried with his family. As he was sitting in the vehicle which carried the remains, Jovian was treated in a way usually reserved for emperors. Samples of the soldiers' rations (which they call 'tastes') were presented to him and the animals of the post service paraded, while the people thronged about him as they commonly do. These and other things of the sort were a sign that imperial power would come to Jovian, though only in an empty and shadowy form, since they occurred while he was directing a funeral procession.

BOOK 22

1. Julian halts in Dacia.

While the turning wheel of fortune was bringing these things about in another part of the world, Julian, among his manifold activities in Illyricum, busied himself with the inspection of the entrails of sacrifices and with observation of the flight of birds. He was eager to discover how things would end, but the answers were ambiguous and obscure and left him in doubt about the future. At last the Gallic rhetorician Aprunculus, a master of this branch of divination, who was later promoted to the government of Narbonese Gaul, announced that he had discovered what was to come by the inspection of a liver, which he had found covered with a double layer of skin. Julian was afraid that this might be an invention designed to flatter his hopes and was in consequence depressed, but he then experienced himself a much more convincing omen, which clearly symbolized the death of Constantius. At the very moment when the latter died in Cilicia the soldier whose right hand was supporting Julian as he was mounting his horse slipped and fell to the ground, whereupon Julian was heard by a number of people to exclaim that the man who had raised him to his high station had fallen. But in spite of these favourable signs his resolve to remain within the borders of Dacia was unshaken. He was still a prey to many fears and thought it rash to put his trust in forecasts which might perhaps be fulfilled in a contrary sense.

2. Entry of Julian into Constantinople.

This period of suspense was ended by the sudden arrival of the envoys Theolaif and Abigild, who announced that Constantius was dead and that with his last breath he had named Julian his successor. The receipt of this news, which delivered him from a sea of troubles and the turmoil of anxiety inseparable from war, elated Julian beyond measure. He now put implicit faith in the predictions he had received, and, knowing from experience that speed had often contributed to his success, he ordered an advance into Thrace. The march began at once, and crossing the pass of Succi he made for Philippopolis, the former Eumolpias, followed with enthusiasm by all the troops under his command. They were aware that the throne which they had been on their way to seize at the hazard of their lives had now beyond all expectation fallen into Julian's hands by way of regular succession. Surprising events are always liable to exaggeration, and from this point Julian seemed almost to fly through the air like a second Triptolemus, who traversed the earth, according to the ancient legend, in a chariot drawn by winged serpents. His approach inspired dread on sea and land alike, and without meeting any delays he entered Heraclea, otherwise known as Perinthus. As soon as this was known at Constantinople the whole population without distinction of age or sex poured out to see him as if he had appeared from the skies. So on 11 December he was welcomed by the respectful greetings of the senate and the unanimous huzzas of the populace, and advanced, escorted by crowds of soldiers and citizens, as if at the head of a line of battle, the object of the unwavering and wondering gaze of all. It seemed like a dream that this man of slight build who had just reached maturity should, after a series of notable exploits and bloody victories over kings and peoples, have flown from city to city with unheard-of speed, acquiring accessions of might and strength wherever he appeared, and that, after seizing everything with an ease that rivalled the flight of rumour, he should finally have received the imperial power by the decree of heaven without the infliction of any loss upon the state.

3. Reprisals on Constantius' adherents.

Shortly after this Julian advanced Secundus Salutius to the praetorian prefecture, and committed to his loyalty the oversight of the trials which were to be instituted. Mamertinus, Arbitio, Agilo, and Nevitta were to be his associates, as well as Jovinus, lately promoted to be master of cavalry in Illyricum. They all crossed over to Chalcedon, and in the presence of the generals and officers of the Joviani and Herculiani examined those brought before them with more prejudice than impartiality, except for a few cases in which the guilt of the accused was indisputable.

The first victim was Palladius, formerly master of the offices, whom they banished to Britain, merely on the suspicion that he had poisoned Constantius' mind against Gallus when he was master of the offices under Gallus as Caesar. Next, Taurus, the former praetorian prefect, was exiled to Vercellae, though judges capable of distinguishing right from wrong might well have thought his behaviour pardonable. What crime did he commit by fleeing to the protection of his emperor from the storm that had arisen? The sentence passed on him was read with great horror, since the official report began as follows: 'In the consulship of Taurus and Florentius, when Taurus was summoned to stand trial ...' Pentadius was in danger of a similar fate. The charge against him was that he had taken notes on Constantius' behalf of the answers given by Gallus, when the latter was being interrogated on several matters just before his execution. But Pentadius defended himself successfully and in the end was acquitted. By a like act of injustice Florentius son of Nigrinian, at that time master of the offices, was deported to the island of Bua off the Dalmatian coast. (The other Florentius, an ex-praetorian prefect and actual consul, was so terrified by the sudden change in the state that he went into hiding with his wife to save himself, and could not return while Julian was alive; he was condemned to death in his absence.) A similar fate befell Euagrius, count of the privy purse, Saturninus, former steward of the palace, and the ex-notary Cyrinus, who were all sent into exile. But the death of Ursulus, count of the sacred largesses, seemed to show such ingratitude in the emperor that Justice herself must have wept. When Julian was sent to the West as Caesar it was intended that he should be kept under the strictest control and deprived of the means of making any present to his troops, so as to leave him more exposed to the danger of mutiny. But this same Ursulus wrote to the official in charge of the treasury of Gaul with orders to pay the Caesar without question any sum he required. When Julian found that the death of Ursulus laid him open to reproaches and curses in many quarters he sought to absolve himself from this unpardonable crime by declaring that it had been committed without his knowledge, and that Ursulus' destruction had been brought about by the anger of the troops, who remembered the remark which I reported him to have made when he saw Amida in ruins.

Julian's lack of confidence, or his ignorance of what was fitting, was demonstrated by his choice of Arbitio, an arrogant and incorrigible double-dealer, to preside over these trials; the others, including the legionary commanders, were associated with him merely to give a show of respectability. He knew that Arbitio had been the chief threat to his own safety, as was to be expected of one who had taken a leading part in the successes of the civil war.

Although the actions which I have mentioned displeased Julian's supporters, he showed in what followed a proper energy and severity. Apodemius, a former member of the secret service, whose mad eagerness to destroy Silvanus and Gallus I have already described, and the notary Paul nicknamed 'the Chain', whose very name is enough to excite a chorus of groans, were burnt alive, and thus met the fate one must have hoped for them. Besides these, Eusebius, Constantius' grand chamberlain, a proud and cruel man, was condemned to death by the judges. He had risen from a mean station to a position of almost imperial power, which made him insufferable. Nemesis, who judges the acts of men, had tweaked him by the ear, as they say, and warned him to moderate his insolence. But he was stiff-necked, so she threw him down headlong from the peak to which he had climbed.

4. Reforms of the court.

The emperor next turned his attention to the staff of the palace, and dismissed all who were or could be comprised under this heading. In doing so he showed a lack of concern for the discovery of truth quite unbecoming in a philosopher. It would have been commendable to keep at least those of good character and proved integrity, few though they were. It must be admitted that for the most part these people constituted such a hotbed of all the vices that they corrupted the state by their evil passions and did even more harm by their bad example than by the impunity with which they offended. Some of them, who had grown fat on the plunder of temples and lost no opportunity of smelling out gain, had risen at a bound from the depths of poverty to enormous riches. They had formed the habit of appropriating the property of others, and bribed, robbed, and squandered without restraint of any kind. Here the seeds of loose living found a fertile soil; men ceased to regard truth or reputation, and mad pride led them to stain their credit by the criminal pursuit of gain. With this went the growth of gluttony and of prodigal expenditure on their bellies. Triumphs in battle were replaced by triumphs at table. Silk and other fine textiles were used more and more lavishly, the kitchen became the object of ever keener attention, and grand sites for luxuriously furnished houses were eagerly snapped up.

The dimensions of these were such that, if the consul Cincinnatus had owned an equivalent area in farmland, he would have lost the reputation of being a poor man even after his dictatorship.

These moral blemishes were accompanied by shameful defects in military discipline. Instead of their traditional chants the troops practised effeminate music-hall songs. The soldier's bed was no longer a stone, as of old, but a yielding down mattress. Their cups were heavier than their swords, since they now thought it beneath them to drink from earthenware, and they expected to be housed in marble, although it is recorded in ancient history that a Spartan soldier was severely punished for daring to appear under a roof at all during a campaign. Moreover, the troops of this period were brutal and greedy in their behaviour to their own people, and weak and cowardly in face of the enemy. In consequence they led an idle life in which they became rich by wire-pulling, and adept at judging the quality of gold and precious stones, a trait foreign to the military character even in recent times. Everyone knows the story of the common soldier in the army of the Caesar Maximian who, finding a Parthian jewel-case full of pearls among the loot of a sacked Persian fort, threw away the contents because he did not know their value, and went off delighted simply with the polished leather of the receptacle.

At this same time there occurred the following incident. A barber who had been sent for to trim the emperor's hair presented himself splendidly dressed. Julian was astonished at his appearance and said: 'I sent for a barber, not a treasury official.' Then he asked what the man earned by his trade, and was told that it brought him in every day twenty men's allowance of bread and a proportionate amount of fodder for his beasts (reckoned by what are commonly called 'heads'), as well as a substantial annual salary and many profitable perquisites. Julian's reaction was to dismiss the whole category of these people, together with cooks and the like, who were in the habit of receiving about the same amount. He declared that he had no use for their services and told them to take themselves off where they pleased.

5. Julian openly professes paganism.

Although Julian from his earliest boyhood had nursed an inclination towards the worship of the pagan gods, which gradually grew into an ardent passion as he grew older, fear of the consequences had kept him from practising its rites except in the greatest possible secrecy. Now, however, that this fear was removed and he saw that the time had come when he could do as he liked, he revealed what was in his heart and directed in plain unvarnished terms that the temples should be opened, sacrifices brought to their altars, and the worship of the old gods restored. To make this ordinance more effective he summoned to the palace the Christian bishops, who were far from being of one mind, together with their flocks, who were no less divided by schism, and warned them in polite terms to lay aside their differences and allow every man to practise his belief boldly without hindrance. His motive in insisting on this was that he knew that toleration would intensify their divisions and that henceforth he would no longer have to fear a unanimous public opinion. Experience had taught him that no wild beasts are such dangerous enemies to man as Christians are to one another. Believing that he was following an example set long before by the emperor Marcus, he would often say: 'The Alamanni and the Franks listened to me, so I expect you to listen.' But he did not observe that the two cases were quite different. Marcus' complaint was uttered when he was passing through Palestine on his way to Egypt and was frequently disgusted by the disturbances made by the filthy Jews. What he is supposed to have said was: 'Oh for the Marcomanni, the Quadi, and the Sarmatians! At last I have found a people more disorderly than they.'

6. *Egyptian litigants sent home.*

At this moment various rumours prompted the arrival of a number of Egyptians. Egyptians are a contentious race, who take delight in the complexities of litigation, and are particularly eager to demand excessive compensation for any payment that they have been constrained to make, so as either to escape their debt altogether or at any rate to have the convenience of postponing its discharge. Another of their tricks is to threaten the rich with a prosecution for extortion which they will be anxious to avoid. Chattering like jackdaws these people thrust themselves in a disorderly crowd upon the emperor himself and the praetorian prefects, demanding the restitution of sums which they declared that they had paid, justly or not, to several persons about seventy years earlier. They brought all other business to a stop, so the emperor published an order that they should all go over to Chalcedon,

promising that he would come himself shortly and settle all their claims.
Once they had crossed, stringent orders were given to the captains of
the ferry-boats not to allow an Egyptian on board. The strict observance
of this ban put an end to this obstinate attempt at blackmail, and they
all went home disappointed of their hopes. As a result a law was passed
under what one can only call the direct inspiration of Justice, which
provided that no patron could be challenged in respect of payments
which it was established that he had fairly received.

7. Julian at Constantinople (A.D. 362).

The new year came, and the names of Mamertinus and Nevitta were
added to the list of those who had held the consulship. The emperor
displayed his condescension by attending their inauguration on foot
with other persons of distinction. This won him credit with some, but
others criticized it as a cheap affectation. This was followed by a show
given by Mamertinus in the circus, at which it was traditional to confer
freedom on a number of slaves. When they were led in by a deputy
master of ceremonies, the emperor himself hastily pronounced the usual
formula: 'Proceed according to law.' When he was reminded that by
doing so on that day he had infringed the rights of another magistrate,
he fined himself ten pounds in gold for the mistake he had made.

He was frequently in the senate-house to settle the numerous disputed
points which arose. One day, when he was hearing cases there, he was
told that the philosopher Maximus had arrived from Asia. He forgot
himself so far as to leap up in undignified haste, run out some way from
the ante-room, kiss Maximus, and bring him into the chamber with
every mark of respect. By this unseemly performance he showed himself
excessively anxious for empty distinction, forgetting the splendid saying
of Cicero, who criticizes such ambition in the following words: 'Those
same philosophers inscribe their own names on the very books which
they write urging men to despise glory; this shows their desire for
reputation and recognition in the very act of preaching contempt for
such distinctions.'

Soon afterwards two members of the secret service who had been
dismissed approached Julian confidentially and offered in return for
their reinstatement to reveal where Florentius was hiding. He rebuked
them and called them informers, adding that it was beneath an emperor
to avail himself of underhand means to detect a man who had gone into

hiding to save his life, and who perhaps would not be allowed to remain long in that condition without hope of pardon. In all these incidents he was attended by Praetextatus, a man of distinguished ability and a dignity reminiscent of times gone by. He happened to be at Constantinople on private business, and Julian on his own initiative appointed him governor of Achaea with the powers of a proconsul.

But although he devoted such attention to the reform of civil abuses, Julian did not on that account neglect military matters. He gave the army commanders of proved experience, strengthened all the cities of Thrace as well as the frontier fortifications, and took particular care that the troops posted along the Danube, of whose watchfulness and energy in the face of barbarian attacks he heard good reports, should not lack either arms and clothing or pay and food. While he was thus engaged and showing that he would not tolerate any slackness, his closest advisers urged that he should attack the neighbouring Goths, who were often unreliable and treacherous. He replied that he was looking for a worthier foe; the Goths could be dealt with adequately by the slave-traders of Galatia, who offered them for sale in all parts without distinction of status.

In these pursuits he gained among foreign peoples a reputation for courage, restraint, military skill, and a host of good qualities, which gradually spread over the whole world. The widespread fear of his coming led both his neighbours and those far away to send delegations to him in unusual haste. From one quarter, the peoples beyond the Tigris and the Armenians sued for peace; from another, Indian peoples as far removed as Ceylon and other islands took time by the forelock and vied with each other in sending grandees with gifts; from the south, the Moors offered their services to the Roman state; from the north and the solitary regions through which the Phasis flows into the Black Sea, the Bosporani and other previously unknown tribes sent envoys with the humble request that on payment of an annual tribute they might be left to live at peace in the land of their birth.

8. (*1–48 omitted.*) *A description of Thrace and the Black Sea littoral.*

One more thing filled Julian's cup of joy to the brim, an event long hoped for but delayed by a complex combination of factors. Agilo and Jovius, who was later quaestor, brought the news that the defenders of Aquileia, sick of the long siege, had opened their gates and surrendered on hearing of the death of Constantius. The ringleaders of the revolt had been handed over and, as I have already told, burnt alive; all the rest had been granted an amnesty and pardon for their offences.

9. *Julian's march to Antioch.*

Such was Julian's elation at these successes that he began to entertain ambitions too high for a mortal. After all the dangers to which he had been exposed the Roman world was now at peace under his sway. He enjoyed all the worldly glory and prosperity that the bounty of a smiling fortune could bestow, and the honours of his former victories were enhanced by the fact that while he was sole emperor no internal disturbance menaced his rule and no barbarian dared to break his proper bounds. All peoples, in fact, abandoning their craving for aggression, which they now realized brought nothing but loss and injury, united with wonderful enthusiasm in singing his praises.

So, after settling with calm deliberation all the problems posed by the various exigencies of the times, and encouraging his troops by frequent speeches and adequate pay to greater keenness in the discharge of their duty, he set out for Antioch at the height of his popularity, leaving Constantinople in much better case than he found it; he had been born there, and he loved and cherished it because it was his native place. Crossing the Bosphorus and passing by Chalcedon and Libyssa, where Hannibal the Carthaginian is buried, he came to the once famous city of Nicomedia, which the lavish expenditure of former emperors had enriched with such a multitude of buildings, both public and private, that discerning critics reckoned it practically a region of the Eternal City. Julian found its walls a pathetic heap of ashes, and silent tears testified to his sorrow as he made his slow way to the palace. The feature of the city's plight which particularly distressed him was that the local senate and people, who had formerly been immensely prosperous, met him dressed in mourning. Some of them he recognized, having been brought up at Nicomedia by the bishop Eusebius, who was distantly related to him. He made a generous contribution, as he had elsewhere, to the cost of repairing the damage done by the earthquake, and went on past Nicaea to the borders of Galatia. Here he made a detour to the right to visit the ancient shrine of the Great Mother at Pessinus. This is the town from which her image was brought to Rome by Scipio Nasica during the second Punic War, in obedience to an injunction found in the Sibylline books. I have included a short digression on her arrival in Italy, together with some other relevant matter, in my account of the reign of the emperor Commodus. Authorities disagree on the origin of the name Pessinus. Some hold that the town is so called because the image of the goddess fell from heaven ('pesein' being the Greek for 'to fall'). Others maintain that it was Ilus, son of Tros and king of Dardania, who gave the place this name *after a war in which many fell.* Theopompus, however, says that it was not Ilus but Midas, the once mighty king of Phrygia.

After worshipping the goddess and soliciting her favour by sacrifices and prayers Julian returned to Ankara (Ancyra). As he was leaving it he was beset by a huge mob. Some demanded the return of property of which they had been forcibly deprived; others complained that they had been unfairly conscripted into the local council; a number showed such insane disregard for their own safety as to level charges of high treason against their opponents. Julian, however, weighed every case with more than the strictness of a Cassius or a Lycurgus, and gave each man his due. He never deviated from the truth and showed particular severity towards slanderers, whom he hated because he had himself been the object of their madly impudent attacks while he was still a humble private citizen, and they had almost cost him his life.

There are many instances of the patience which he showed in matters of this kind, but a single illustration will suffice. A man was pressing a charge of treason in intemperate language against a personal enemy, with whom he was on terms of bitter hostility. The emperor turned a deaf ear, but the accuser went on with the same story day after day. At last Julian asked who was the object of this attack, and was told that he was a wealthy citizen. 'What makes you think him guilty?' said Julian with a smile. 'He is making himself a purple robe out of a silk cloak.' Thinking him a worthless creature making a serious charge against another of his own kidney, Julian told him to hold his tongue and take himself off out of harm's way, but he still persisted. The emperor grew sick of the whole matter. He turned to the count of the largesses whom he saw standing near, and said: 'Have a pair of purple shoes given to this lousy chatterbox to take to his enemy, who, so I am given to understand, has made himself a robe of the same colour. That will teach him what cheap rags are worth without great power.'

But although such behaviour was praiseworthy and deserves to be imitated by good rulers, it was nevertheless harsh and reprehensible that in Julian's time anybody whom a town council wished to co-opt could hardly obtain fair treatment, even if he was entitled to exemption by special privileges, or by length of service in the army, or by the clearest evidence that he was of totally alien extraction. This went so far that many people bought themselves off by clandestine payments from the vexatious burdens which terrified them.

Julian pursued his journey, and when he reached the gates which divide Cappadocia from Cilicia he greeted the governor of the latter with a kiss, gave him a seat in his carriage, and took him with him to Tarsus. The governor's name was Celsus and he had been known to Julian since they were students together at Athens. He was now in a hurry to see Antioch, the magnificent jewel of the East. He approached the city by the usual stages and was received by the worshipping populace as if he were a god. The cries of the great crowd shouting that a lucky star had risen over the East filled him with wonder. As it happened, his arrival coincided with the annual celebration of an ancient rite in honour of Adonis. According to the legend Adonis was the darling of Venus and was fatally wounded by a boar, an event which symbolizes the reaping of the crops at harvest. It seemed a sad omen that the emperor should make his first entrance into the great city, where princes dwelt, to the accompaniment of general wailing and sounds of grief.

At Antioch he gave a proof of his mild and patient temper which was trivial in itself but nevertheless remarkable. He hated a certain Thalassius, a former deputy master of petitions, because he had intrigued against his brother Gallus. Thalassius was consequently forbidden to take his place among the notables who greeted the emperor, and next day some enemies of his, with whom he had a law-suit, gathered a crowd of supporters and came to Julian, shouting: 'Your majesty's enemy has forcibly seized our property.' Julian saw that this was a chance to destroy the man, but answered: 'I realize that the man you speak of has given me just cause of offence. Nevertheless, you would do well to keep quiet until he has given satisfaction to me, who am his principal enemy.' He then gave instructions to the prefect in attendance that the case should not be heard until he himself was reconciled to Thalassius, which soon after came about.

10. Julian at Antioch.

The winter was passed at Antioch in accordance with Julian's wishes, but he remained proof against all the temptations to sensuality which Syria offers in such abundance. He appeared to find his recreation in judicial business, which presented him with a variety of problems no less difficult than those of war. He was admirably patient in weighing evidence, so as to give every man his due and reach a just decision, whether it was a question of inflicting moderate punishment on the guilty or protecting the innocent from inroads upon their property. Although in examination he sometimes showed lack of tact, asking at an inappropriate moment what religion each of the parties professed, one cannot point to any decision by him which flew in the face of the evidence, nor could he ever be accused of having deviated from the path of strict equity because of a man's religion or for any other reason. A right and acceptable judgement is one which *draws the line* between what is just and unjust after a minute examination of all the facts, and Julian was as careful to steer a straight course as a sailor anxious to avoid running on a rock. He owed his success in this to the fact that he was conscious of the excitability of his disposition and allowed his prefects and close associates freedom to curb his impetuosity by timely advice when it led him astray. On many occasions he made it clear that he regretted his mistakes and that he was glad to be put right. When advocates for the defence praised him to the skies for his perfect uprightness, he is said to have replied with much feeling: 'I should certainly be glad and proud if I knew that this praise came from people who were also in a position to blame me for anything that I had said or done amiss.'

Of the many instances of his mild behaviour on the bench it will be enough to mention one, which is neither irrelevant nor without point. A woman was once brought before him who was surprised to see that her adversary, one of the palace staff who had been dismissed, was still wearing his belt of office. When she complained loudly of this act of impudence, the emperor said: 'Go on, woman, if you think that you have been wronged. As for this man, he is only wearing his belt to get through the mire more easily. It can do no harm to your cause.'

Incidents such as these led people to believe, as he himself constantly asserted, that the ancient goddess of Justice, who, according to Aratus, fled to heaven in disgust at the wickedness of mankind, had returned to earth during his reign. This would be easier to accept if Julian had not sometimes followed his own inclination rather than the letter of the law, and dimmed the lustre of his many glorious acts by occasional errors. It is true that among other things he reformed certain laws by pruning them of ambiguities and making it perfectly clear what they enjoined or forbade. But he was guilty of one harsh act which should be buried in lasting oblivion; he banned adherents of Christianity from practising as teachers of rhetoric or literature.

11. Riots at Alexandria.

At this same period the notary Gaudentius, who, as I have told, had been sent by Constantius to oppose Julian in Africa, and another Julian, a former vice-prefect, who had been very active on the same side, were brought back under arrest and put to death. Artemius also, who had commanded the troops in Egypt and who was charged by the people of Alexandria with a mass of outrageous crimes, paid the supreme penalty. Next, the son of Marcellus, at one time master of both cavalry and infantry, was publicly executed on the ground that he had plotted to seize the throne. Beside these, Romanus and Vincentius, tribunes of the first and second divisions of Scutarii, were convicted of nursing designs above their stations and sent into exile.

After a brief interval the people of Alexandria heard of the death of Artemius. They had been afraid that he would return, as he threatened, with his power restored and take revenge on the many people who had injured him. Now, however, they turned their rage upon their bishop George, a human snake who had often made them suffer from his poisonous fangs. George was born, they say, in a fuller's shop in the Cilician town of Epiphania, and rose in the world to be the instrument of many people's ruin. Finally, against his own interest as well as the state's, he was consecrated bishop of Alexandria, a city given to frequent spontaneous and unmotivated outbreaks of violence. George himself acted as a powerful irritant to the savage temper of the populace by proceeding to denounce a number of people to Constantius, who was always ready to listen, on the ground that they had disobeyed his commands. In doing this he forgot the faith he professed, which preaches only justice and mercy, and descended to the abominable trade of an informer. Among other pieces of malicious information which he fed to Constantius, he was said to have told him that all the buildings on the soil of the said city which had been erected by its founder Alexander at great public expense ought in consequence to be a source of profit to the treasury. All these mischievous deeds were crowned by another, which in a short time brought him to utter destruction. On his way back from the emperor's court, attended as usual by a large crowd, he looked in passing at the fine temple of the city's protecting deity and remarked: 'How long shall this sepulchre stand?' Many of his hearers were thunderstruck by these words, and, fearing that he would attempt to destroy the temple, devoted all their energies to plotting his downfall. Suddenly there arrived the glad tidings that Artemius was no more. The whole population went wild with joy at this unexpected piece of good news. They fell upon George, howling and yelling, beat him about, trampled on him, and finally spread-eagled him *and finished him off.*

Dracontius, the superintendent of the mint, and a certain Diodorus, who was thought to be in league with him, had ropes tied to their legs and were killed at the same time. The former had overturned an altar recently set up in the mint which he controlled, and the latter, while directing the building of a church, had taken the liberty of cropping the curls of some boys, because he thought that long hair was a feature of the worship of the heathen. Not content with this, the brutal mob loaded the mutilated bodies on camels and took them to the beach, where they burned them and threw their ashes into the sea, for fear that the remains might be collected and have a church built over them. This had happened in other cases, when men persecuted for their religion endured torture till they met a glorious death with their faith unspotted, and are now called martyrs. The wretched victims of these cruel sufferings might have been saved by the help of their fellow-Christians had not the whole population been inflamed by universal hatred of George.

When news of this outrage reached the emperor his anger was roused and he was on the point of exacting the supreme penalty from the authors of this abominable crime, but he was pacified by those nearest to him, who urged him to be lenient. So he issued a proclamation in which he expressed his horror in sharp terms, and threatened extreme measures if any similar breach of law and order were committed in future.

12. Preparations for war with Persia.

Meanwhile preparations went on for war with Persia, which had long been part of Julian's lofty designs. He was passionately eager to avenge the past, knowing from experience as well as report that for almost sixty years this fierce people had stamped cruel evidence of carnage and rapine upon the East and had often utterly annihilated our armies. Two causes intensified his longing for war. In the first place he was tired of inactivity and dreamed of trumpets and battles, and in the second he was on fire to add the title of Parthicus to the glorious record of his exploits. In the first flower of his youth he had had to encounter the arms of savage peoples, and the recollection that he had received supplications from kings and princes who had been expected to resist to the last rather than surrender was still warm in his mind.

Seeing the scale and speed of his preparations, his idle and malicious detractors put it about that it was shameful and disastrous that the change of a single person should lead to so untimely an upheaval. They made every effort to get the campaign postponed, and kept saying in the hearing of those whom they believed to be in a position to report it to the emperor that if he did not show more restraint in the use of his extraordinary prosperity his very advantages would bring him to grief, like a plant which outgrows its strength in too fertile a soil. But their long and loud agitation achieved nothing. Julian was a man impervious to insults behind his back, and no more affected by the barking of his critics than Hercules by the Pygmies or by Thiodamas the yokel of Lindus. His great spirit put him in a different class from other men; he was as determined as ever on this grand campaign and pushed on all the necessary preparations with the utmost energy.

Nevertheless, the victims with whose blood he drenched the altars of the gods were all too numerous. On occasion he sacrificed a hundred bulls and countless flocks of other animals, as well as white birds, for which he combed land and sea. The result was seen in the intemperate habits of the troops, who were gorged with meat and demoralized by a craving for drink, so that almost every day some of them were carried through the streets to their quarters on the shoulders of passers-by after debauches in the temples which called for punishment rather than indulgence. Conspicuous in this respect were the Petulantes and Celts, whose indiscipline at this time passed all bounds. Ceremonial rites too were performed with increased and excessive frequency, at a heavy cost hitherto quite unheard of. Anyone who professed a knowledge of divination, whether qualified or not, was allowed to consult oracles and examine entrails, which sometimes reveal the future, all this without any sort of restriction or the observance of any prescribed rules. Ostentatiously varied methods were employed. The notes and flight of birds and omens in general were studied in the hope that reliable information about the future could somehow be obtained.

In the midst of this, Julian's omnivorous curiosity led him to embark on a new mode of inquiry. He thought of re-opening the prophetic springs of the Castalian fount, which the Caesar Hadrian is said to have blocked with a huge mass of stone; he himself had learnt from the oracular waters that he would become emperor and he did not want anyone else to receive the same message. *After invoking the god* Julian decided that the bodies buried round the spring should be moved elsewhere, with the same ritual as that used by the Athenians when they purified the island of Delos.

13. Christians blamed for the burning of the temple of Apollo.

At this same period, on 22 October the superb temple of Apollo at Daphne, which was built by that choleric and cruel king Antiochus Epiphanes, together with the statue of the god, which equalled in size that of Zeus at Olympia, was suddenly set on fire and burnt to the ground. The unexpected destruction of the shrine by so fearful an accident roused the emperor to such rage that he ordered an unusually strict investigation and the closure of the great church at Antioch. He suspected that the fire was an act of spite by the Christians, because they could not bear to see the temple enclosed by a magnificent colonnade. It was rumoured, however, though on very slight grounds, that the philosopher Asclepiades, whom I have mentioned in my account of Magnentius, was responsible for the fire. He had come to Daphne from abroad to visit Julian, and the story went that, after placing a silver image of the Great Mother which he took with him everywhere at the feet of the sublime statue, he had lit some wax tapers, as is customary, and gone away. After midnight, when there was no one about to help, flying sparks from these tapers alighted on some very old woodwork. The flames fed on this dry fuel and burnt up everything they could reach, however high from the ground.

In this year also, just as winter was setting in, there was a fearful drought. Some streams dried up, and even springs which previously had a copious head of water ceased to flow, though later they regained their usual strength. On 2 December, towards evening, what was left of Nicomedia and no small part of Nicaea were destroyed by an earthquake.

14. Julian's reaction to his critics at Antioch.

These events caused the emperor sorrow and anxiety, but he did not neglect the urgent problems that remained to be solved before he could gratify his longing for war. But, among all the important and serious steps which he took, one seemed unnecessary. Without any adequate reason and simply to gain popularity he engaged in the regulation of the price of commodities, a course whose injudicious adoption sometimes results in want and famine. Though the senate of Antioch clearly pointed out the impossibility of carrying out his orders at that time, he refused to be diverted from his plan. In this he showed all the obstinacy, though not the cruelty, of his brother Gallus. He gave vent to his fury at the obstinacy of his critics by composing a satire on them called the 'Antiochian' or 'Misopogon' ('Beard-hater'), in which he enumerated the defects of the city in no friendly terms and in some respects went beyond the truth. They retaliated by circulating a number of jests at his expense which for the moment he had to pretend to take in good part, though in fact he was boiling with suppressed wrath. He was caricatured as a monkey, or as a dwarf who tried to impress by squaring his narrow shoulders, wearing a goatee beard, and taking big strides like a brother of Otus and Ephialtes, who were Homeric giants of enormous height. The number of his sacrifices earned him the nickname of axe-man instead of priest, and he was justly criticized for the ostentatious delight which he took in carrying the sacred objects himself instead of leaving the task to the inferior priesthood, and in being attended by companies of women. But in spite of his anger at insults of this sort he held his peace, kept his temper under control, and went on with his solemnities.

Finally, on the appointed feast-day he ascended the rounded slopes of Mount Casius, a hill clothed in woods from which one can get one's first sight of the sun at second cock-crow. As he was sacrificing to Jove he suddenly saw a man lying prostrate on the ground begging for life and pardon. Julian asked his name and was told that he was Theodotus the former governor of Hierapolis, who among other nobles had escorted Constantius from that town and had flattered him shamefully in the belief that he would undoubtedly emerge the victor. Shedding crocodile tears, he had begged Constantius to send them the head of the ungrateful rebel Julian to be paraded about in the same way as he remembered happening with the head of Magnentius. This elicited the following reply from Julian: 'A number of people have already told me this story, but put aside all fear and go home in peace. You owe this to the mercy of a prince who has taken to heart the words of the sage and is eager to lessen the number of his enemies and increase that of his friends.'

When he left at the conclusion of the ceremony, a letter was brought him from the governor of Egypt announcing that after a long and laborious search they had at last been able to find a new Apis bull. The inhabitants of those parts believe that this is a lucky sign which portends a good harvest and various other blessings.

This calls for a brief explanation. Of the animals traditionally held sacred, Mnevis and Apis are the best known. Mnevis is sacred to the sun, and nothing of special note is reported of him; Apis belongs to the moon. He is a bull distinguished by various birth-marks, in particular by the shape of the crescent moon on his right flank. After living his appointed span, which is prescribed by the obscure authority of certain occult books and may not be exceeded, he is killed by drowning in a sacred pool, and with the same ritual a heifer, also marked in a particular way, which has been found and presented to him. His death is followed by public mourning and the search for another Apis. If one can be found which perfectly meets the criteria he is brought to Memphis, a city famous for the frequent visits of the god Aesculapius. A hundred priests welcome him and escort him to his stall. From that moment he is an object of worship and is said to give clear indications of coming events. Sometimes he gives an unfavourable response by repulsing those who approach him. We are told, for example, that on one occasion he turned away from Germanicus Caesar, who was offering him food, and thus gave a sign of what soon afterwards came to pass.

Chapter describing Egypt and its fauna, the Nile, and the Pyramids (15) is omitted.

16. (1–5 omitted.) The provinces and cities of Egypt.

Egypt itself, which ever since it has formed part of the Roman empire has been ruled by prefects, is adorned by the great cities of Athribis, Oxyrrhynchus, Thumis, and Memphis, not to mention many lesser towns.

But the crown of all cities is Alexandria, which is enriched by many splendid features through the ingenuity of its founder and his architect Dinocrates. The latter, when laying out the long circuit of its fine walls, found that there was a temporary shortage of lime and used flour instead to mark its boundary; this accident was a sign that the future city would enjoy an ample supply of food. Healthful breezes blow there, the air is calm and mild, and the experience of many generations has shown that there is hardly a day on which the inhabitants do not see a cloudless sky.

The approach by sea is treacherous and brought many early navigators to grief. This led Cleopatra to erect in the harbour a high tower, which takes its name of Pharos from the place itself. This made it possible to show a light to ships arriving in darkness. Before that, vessels coming from the Parthenian or Libyan sea, with no landmark of mountain or hill on the broad curved shore to guide them, ran aground on the soft, sticky sand and broke up. This same queen built with almost incredible speed the extraordinarily massive mole known as the Heptastadion. The emergency which inspired it is well known. The island of Pharos, where Homer in somewhat pompous language places Phocus and his herds of seals, lay a mile from the city on the mainland and was subject to a payment of tribute to the Rhodians. One day, when the collectors arrived from Rhodes with an exorbitant assessment, the queen, who was never lacking in resource, took them with her to a place outside the city on the pretext of a religious celebration, and gave orders that the work should go on without a pause till it was finished. In seven days, by building a causeway out into the sea, as many furlongs were reclaimed for the land. The queen drove to the spot and laughed at the Rhodians for their blunder in demanding tax for what was not an island but part of the mainland.

There are also many temples with lofty roofs, chief among them the Temple of Serapis. Its splendour is such that mere words can only do it an injustice, but its great halls of columns and its wealth of lifelike statues and other works of art make it, next to the Capitol, which is the symbol of the eternity of immemorial Rome, the most magnificent building in the whole world. It contained two priceless libraries. Ancient records are unanimous in their evidence that 700,000 volumes, brought together by the sleepless energy of the Ptolemies, went up in flames under the dictator Caesar, when the city was sacked in the Alexandrine war.

Twelve miles from Alexandria is Canopus, which tradition says is named after Menelaus' steersman, who was buried there. It is an exceptionally delightful place, well supplied with agreeable inns and fanned by soft airs. The climate is healthy, and a visitor to that region, listening to the murmur of the breeze in that sunny atmosphere, might well think himself transported to another world.

Alexandria itself has not grown gradually like other cities, but has covered a wide area from its very foundation. For a long time it was a prey to bitter internal dissension, till finally, during the reign of Aurelian, the quarrels of the citizens reached the proportions of a civil war. The walls were destroyed and it lost the greater part of the district called Bruchion, which for a long time had been the chosen abode of outstanding men. Here dwelt Aristarchus, who excelled in the thorny topic of grammar, Herodian, who investigated the minutiae of learning, Ammonius Saccas, the teacher of Plotinus, and many other writers in various branches of humane studies. Among these Didymus Chalcenterus was pre-eminent; he owed his reputation to his encyclopedic knowledge, although in six books of generally unsuccessful criticism of Cicero, in which he imitates the scurrilous writers of satirical verses, he sounds to the ears of the learned like a puppy-dog feebly yelping from a safe distance at a grimly roaring lion.

These that I have mentioned and many others flourished in the early days of the city, but even now the voice of learning in its various branches is not silent. Teaching in different disciplines still somehow survives; the mathematician's rule brings hidden truths to light; music is not wholly dried up among them or harmony dumb; some, though not many, still keep warm the study of the movements of the earth and the stars; and there are others who are skilled in the science of number. Besides these, there are a few who are expert in divination. The study of medicine too, whose help is often needed in a society which is neither frugal nor sober, advances every day; for a doctor to be able to say that he received his training at Alexandria is sufficient recommendation of his skill. No practical demonstration is needed, though in fact everything that he does smacks of his medical school.

So much for that subject. But anyone who cares to engage in a brisk review of the multifarious books on knowledge of the divine and the origin of prognostics will find that the source from which learning of this kind has spread throughout the world is Egypt. It was there that men, long before others, discovered various religions in what may be called their cradle, and now carefully preserve the origins of worship in their esoteric scriptures. Training in this sphere taught Pythagoras to worship the gods in secret, gave unquestioned authority to whatever he said or ordained, and caused him often to exhibit his golden thigh at Olympia and to be frequently seen in colloquy with an eagle. Egypt taught Anaxagoras to foretell a rain of meteorites and to predict earthquakes by the feel of mud in a well. Solon too was helped by the dicta of the priests of Egypt in framing his legal code, which has given Roman law its strongest support. Plato drew on this source, and it was after a visit to Egypt that he achieved his highest flights in language whose sublimity rivalled Jove himself, and served with glory on the field of wisdom.

The people of Egypt are for the most part rather swarthy and dark, and have a gloomy cast of countenance. They are lean and have a dried-up look, are easily roused to excited gestures, and are quarrelsome and most persistent in pursuing a debt. It puts a man to the blush if he cannot exhibit a number of weals incurred by refusing to pay tribute. And nobody has yet been able to devise a torture harsh enough to compel a hardened robber from that country to reveal his name against his will.

Everybody knows from early histories that the whole of Egypt was formerly ruled by kings who were friendly to Rome. But after the defeat of Antony and Cleopatra at the battle of Actium it was occupied by Octavian and given the status of a province. We acquired the dry part of Libya by the last will of king Apion; Cyrene and the other cities of Libya-Pentapolis came to us through the generosity of Ptolemy. After this long digression I will resume my main theme.

BOOK 23

1. Attempted restoration of the temple at Jerusalem (A.D. 363).

These in broad outline were the events of that year. But Julian, who had already been consul three times, now entered on his fourth tenure of the highest magistracy, taking as his colleague Sallustius, the prefect of Gaul. The association of a private citizen with the emperor was a novelty; the last recorded instance was that of Aristobulus with Diocletian. In spite of his extreme eagerness to push on the multifarious preparations for his campaign and his anxiety to be forearmed against all contingencies, Julian none the less extended his activity into every field. His desire to leave a great monument to perpetuate the memory of his reign led him to think in particular of restoring at enormous expense the once magnificent temple at Jerusalem, which, after much bitter fighting during its siege first by Vespasian and then by Titus, had finally been stormed with great difficulty. Alypius of Antioch, who had once governed Britain as the praetorian prefects' deputy, was placed in charge of this project. He set to work boldly, assisted by the governor of the province, but repeated and alarming outbursts of fire-balls near the foundations made it impossible to approach the spot. Some of the workmen were burnt to death, and the obstinate resistance of the fiery element caused the design to be abandoned.

At the same period the emperor conferred various honours on envoys sent to him from the Eternal City, men of distinguished family and approved worth. Apronian was appointed prefect of Rome and Octavian proconsul of Africa. The governorship of Spain was entrusted to Venustus, and Rufinus Aradius was promoted to be count of the East in place of the emperor's uncle Julian, who had recently died. After making these arrangements Julian was alarmed by an omen which subsequent events proved to be all too accurate. Felix, count of the largesses, had died suddenly of a haemorrhage and had been followed to the grave by count Julian. The populace, taking their cue from the emperor's official titles, uttered them in the order Felix, Julian – Augustus. There had also been another unlucky incident. On the very first day of January, when the emperor was ascending the steps of the temple of the Genius of the Roman people, one of the priests in attendance, who was older than the rest, suddenly fell, though no one pushed him, and died a totally unexpected death. The bystanders, either from ignorance or from a desire to flatter Julian, insisted that the omen applied to the older of the two consuls, that is to Sallustius. But events showed that it pointed to the approaching death not of the senior in age but of the senior in rank.

Besides these, other less important signs indicated on various occasions what was to ensue. At the very start of the preparations for the Parthian war it was reported that Constantinople had been shaken by an earthquake, and the experts announced that this was not a happy omen for a ruler who was intent on invading the territory of another. So they tried to persuade Julian to abandon this ill-timed enterprise and to convince him that signs of this sort could be neglected with propriety only in face of a foreign invasion, when to defend the safety of the state by every possible means with unremitting energy is the one fixed law which supersedes all others. At the same time Julian was told by letter that a consultation of the Sibylline books that he had ordered had elicited the definite answer that the emperor must not advance beyond his frontiers that year.

2. *Crossing of the Euphrates.*

Meanwhile envoys from many races presented themselves giving promises of help. They were warmly received, but their offers were declined, the emperor declaring with a fine show of confidence that it was beneath the dignity of Rome to rely on foreign aid for its defence; on the contrary, it was Rome that should support its friends and allies if they had any need to beg its assistance. An exception was made in the case of Arsaces king of Armenia, who was warned to collect a strong force and wait for orders, and told that he would learn shortly where to march and what steps to take. Then, seizing the first opportunity consistent with prudence, Julian hastened to occupy enemy territory before any rumour of his coming could precede him. Spring had hardly arrived when he sent marching orders to the units of his army and ordered them all to cross the Euphrates. All hurried from their winter quarters, crossed the river in accordance with their instructions, and awaited the arrival of the emperor in various cantonments. He himself, on the eve of leaving Antioch, appointed one Alexander of Heliopolis to the government of Syria. Alexander was a violent and cruel man, and Julian remarked that he did not merit the post, but that such a magistrate was what the greedy and rebellious people of Antioch deserved. At his departure he was escorted by a heterogeneous crowd praying for a successful outward march and a glorious return, and begging that he would then show himself milder and less intransigent. But his anger at their abuse and insults had not abated, and he replied in bitter terms, declaring that he had no intention of visiting them again. He told them that he had made his plans for the winter; at the end of the campaign he would return to Tarsus in Cilicia by the shortest route, and he had already written to Memorius, the governor of Tarsus, to make all necessary preparations for his reception. This in fact was what happened not long afterwards; his body was brought back to Tarsus with the minimum of parade or fuss and buried in accordance with his own instructions in a suburb of the city.

On 5 March he set out under a sunny sky and came to Hierapolis by the usual route. As he entered the gates of that great city a colonnade on his left suddenly collapsed; its beams and timbers crushed fifty soldiers who were camping under it, as well as wounding a large number of others. Then, concentrating all his forces, he made a rapid march towards Mesopotamia. His object was to seize Assyria by surprise, and he had taken the strictest precautions against any rumour of his movements preceding him. Finally, he crossed the Euphrates on a bridge of boats and arrived with his army and his Scythian auxiliaries at Batnae, a town in Osdroene. Here he encountered a sinister omen. A great throng of grooms assembled by an immensely high hayrick of the type constructed in those parts. They came to get fodder as usual, but so many seized on it at once that the rick tottered and collapsed, and in its fall the huge mass buried fifty men, who were all killed.

3. March through Mesopotamia. Arrival of the fleet.

Julian left Batnae in a state of gloom, and advanced by forced marches to Carrhae, an ancient town memorable as the scene of the disaster of the Roman army under Crassus and his son. At Carrhae two royal roads to Persia fork. The left goes through Adiabene and over the Tigris, the right through Assyria and along the Euphrates. Julian stayed at Carrhae some days to complete his preparations, and sacrificed according to the local rite to the moon, which is worshipped in that region. There is a story that, while he was standing before the altar and no third party was present, he handed his purple cloak in conditions of complete secrecy to his kinsman Procopius, with orders that he should boldly seize the throne if he learned that Julian had fallen in the Parthian war. Julian was disturbed here in his sleep by a dream, which gave him a foreboding of some approaching calamity. So he and the interpreters of dreams reviewed the circumstances and concluded that a careful watch must be kept on the following day, which was 19 March. In fact, however, as was afterwards learnt, it was on this same night that the temple of Palatine Apollo in the Eternal City went up in flames during the prefecture of Apronian, and if help of various sorts had not been at hand the books of the Cumaean Sibyl also would have been consumed by the raging fire.

After dealing with these matters, Julian was organizing his column of march and supplies of all kinds when he received a report from scouts, who arrived panting for breath, that some squadrons of enemy horse had suddenly violated the frontier nearby and carried off booty. Stung by this outrage Julian at once put into execution a plan already formed. He put 30,000 picked troops under the joint command of Procopius and count Sebastian, formerly commander in Egypt, with orders to stay for the time being on the nearer side of the Tigris and keep their eyes open for any unexpected attack on his unguarded flank, of a kind which experience taught him often occurred. They were also to effect a junction if possible with king Arsaces, march with him through Corduene and Moxoene, lay waste in passing a rich region of Media called Chiliocomum and other districts, and finally meet Julian while he was still operating in Assyria to reinforce him if he needed their help.

When this was settled Julian made a feint of setting out himself by the Tigris route, along which he had purposely ordered supply dumps to be placed, but in fact wheeled to the right. After a quiet night he called next morning for his usual mount, which was called Babylonius. When it was brought it rolled on the ground in an attack of colic, and in its agony damaged its harness, which was studded with gold and precious stones. This portent caused Julian to exclaim triumphantly, amid the applause of his suite: 'Babylon lies low, stripped of all her

finery.' After a short halt to make a sacrifice which would confirm the
favourable omen, he reached the fortified camp of Davana at the source
of the river Belias (Balikh), a tributary of the Euphrates. Here the troops
fed and rested, and next day reached Callinicum, a strongly walled
place and a rich centre of trade. Here on 27 March, the day on which a
procession in honour of the Mother of the Gods is held annually at
Rome and the carriage which conveys her image is washed, we are told,
in the waters of the Almo, he celebrated her festival according to the
ancient ritual and slept peacefully through the night in a glow of joy
and confidence.

Next day he kept on with his escort along the high bank of the river,
whose waters were swollen by affluents from all directions, and reached
an outpost, where he bivouacked. Here some sheikhs of the Saracen
tribes offered on their knees a crown of gold and paid him homage as
lord of the world and its peoples. He gave them a gracious reception
because of their usefulness in guerilla warfare. While he was addressing
them a fleet as large as that of the mighty Xerxes arrived under the
command of the tribune Constantian and count Lucillian. It covered
the whole width of the broad Euphrates, and consisted of a thousand
transport vessels of various types carrying abundant supplies of food,
weapons, and siege-engines, fifty ships of war, and an equal number of
pontoons for bridge-building.

Chapter describing various types of siege-engine (4) is omitted.

5. Crossing of the Khabur (Abora) at Cercusium.

After incorporating with his army the auxiliaries so willingly offered by
the Saracens the emperor made a rapid march to Cercusium, which he
entered at the beginning of April. Cercusium is a strong and cunningly
constructed fortress; its walls are washed by the rivers Khabur (Abora)
and Euphrates, which form what is practically an island. In earlier times
it was a small and insecure place, but Diocletian, when he was organizing
defences in depth on our actual frontier with the barbarians, surrounded
it with walls and high towers *to prevent the Persians making an inroad*
into Syria of the kind that had occurred *some years before* and inflicted
great damage on our provinces. What happened on that occasion was
this. One day at Antioch, while a comedian and his wife were on the
stage performing some scenes from common life before a hushed and

admiring audience, the woman said: 'Unless I am dreaming, the Persians are here.' The spectators all turned their heads and then fled in confusion to escape the missiles raining down upon them. The city was set on fire, and many people who were strolling at large, as one does in time of peace, were cut down. The neighbourhood was burned and ravaged, and the enemy returned home without loss and laden with spoil. Mareades, who had rashly guided them to destroy his fellow-citizens, was burnt alive. This incident took place in the reign of Gallienus.

While Julian was waiting at Cercusium for the construction of a bridge of boats to enable his army and all its hangers-on to cross the Khabur, he received a gloomy letter from Sallustius the prefect of Gaul, begging him to defer the campaign against the Parthians and conjuring him not to expose himself to inevitable destruction since he had failed so far to obtain the approval of heaven. Julian ignored this prudent advice and pushed on confidently, for no human strength or merit has ever availed to prevent what has been ordained by the decree of destiny. As soon as he had crossed he ordered the bridge to be destroyed, so that no one should lag behind his unit in the belief that he could go back. Here too he encountered an unfavourable omen in the shape of the outstretched corpse of a commissary who had fallen by the hand of the executioner. Salutius, the praetorian prefect in attendance, had condemned him to death because, after promising to furnish additional provisions before a certain day, he had been prevented by circumstances from fulfilling his undertaking. But on the day following the wretched man's execution another fleet arrived, as he had promised, with plentiful supplies.

Setting out from here we reached a place called Zaitha, which means olive-tree. Here we saw, while we were still at a distance, the tomb of the emperor Gordian, whose history from his earliest boyhood, successful campaigns, and treacherous murder I have described in their proper place. Julian with his innate piety sacrificed to the deified emperor, and was on his way to the deserted town of Dura when he saw a troop of soldiers in the distance and came to a halt, wondering what they were bringing him. It turned out to be a huge lion, which had attacked their unit and been dispatched by a rain of weapons. Julian was overjoyed by what he regarded as a certain omen of success and pursued his course, but there is no trusting the fickle winds of fortune and the event was far otherwise. The death of a king was foreshadowed, but it was not clear of which king. In fact, history tells us of other ambiguous oracles whose meaning became clear only from subsequent events. There is, for example, the prediction from Delphi that if Croesus crossed the Halys he would destroy a great empire, and another which darkly indicated that the Athenians should choose the sea as the theatre of war against the Medes. A third, later than these, was true but nevertheless ambiguous: 'You, son of Aeacus, I say, the Roman people can vanquish.'

The Etruscan soothsayers, however, who accompanied the other experts on prodigies, finding that their frequent attempts to stop the campaign met with no success, brought out their manuals of divination in time of war and demonstrated that this sign constituted a prohibition against the invasion of another's territory by a ruler, even if right were on his side. This warning met with contemptuous dismissal from the philosophers, who had much influence at that moment, though they were often wrong and apt to put up a dogged fight about matters of which they knew little. On this occasion they advanced as a plausible argument why they should be believed the experience of the former Caesar Maximian. The dead bodies of a lion and a huge wild boar were brought to him when he was on the point of joining battle with the Persian king Narses, and he came back safe after defeating the enemy. But they left out of account the fact that such an omen signified the destruction of an aggressor, and that Narses had in fact begun the conflict by seizing Armenia, which was under Roman jurisdiction.

A further omen occurred on the following day, 7 April. Towards sunset a cloud, which was at first quite small, suddenly spread over the darkening sky and obscured the light. An alarming storm followed with frequent thunder and lightning, in the course of which a soldier called Jovian and two horses which he was bringing back from watering in the river were struck dead by a thunderbolt. The interpreters of such things were sent for and questioned; they declared with confidence that this omen too was against the campaign. The thunderbolt was of the type known as 'advisory', the name they give to an omen which either prohibits or prescribes a particular course. In this case caution was especially needed because the soldier killed with the chargers bore so exalted a name, and the books on the subject say that one should not look or tread on spots struck by lightning. The philosophers, on the other hand, maintained that there was no particular significance in this sudden flash of fire from heaven; it was merely a violent blast of wind pushed down from the upper air by some force. If it portended anything it was an increase of honour for the emperor at the outset of his glorious enterprise, since it is common knowledge that fire naturally flies upward if there is nothing to check it.

So when all had crossed and the bridge, as I said, had been broken down, the emperor thought it his first duty to address his troops, who were inspired in their bold advance by belief in themselves and in their commander. In answer to a trumpet-call all the centuries, cohorts, and maniples assembled, and the emperor, standing on a mound of earth and surrounded by a suite of high-ranking officers, delivered with an air of calm confidence the following speech, which was received by all with enthusiastic approval.

'Seeing you, my gallant men, full of such energy and eagerness, I have decided to address you, and I mean to demonstrate to you by more than one example that this is not, as some scandal-mongers suggest, the first time that Romans have invaded the kingdom of Persia. To say nothing of Lucullus or of Pompey, who after traversing the lands of the Albani and Massagetae, whom we now call Alans, broke into this country also and set eyes on the Caspian Sea, we know that Antony's lieutenant Ventidius gained countless bloody victories in these parts. Passing on, however, from early times, I will run over events in more recent history. Trajan and Verus and Severus came back from this country crowned with the laurels of victory, and the younger Gordian, at whose tomb we have just done reverence, would have returned with equal glory after defeating the Persian king at Resaina and putting him to flight, had he not fallen victim at the spot where he now lies buried to a wicked conspiracy hatched by the praetorian prefect Philip and a few accomplices in crime. But his spirit did not long wander unavenged. Justice weighed his enemies in her scales and all who plotted Gordian's destruction met an agonizing death. And whereas these emperors were impelled by ambition to embark on their memorable enterprises, the driving force behind our undertaking is the wretchedness of recently captured cities, the unavenged shades of our slaughtered armies, the immense damage we have suffered, and the loss of our standards. We are all united in our desire to remedy past disasters and to strengthen the Roman state on this flank, so that posterity may have a glorious account to give of us.

'With the help of the eternal godhead your emperor will be with you everywhere. The front ranks as well as the cavalry shall see him among them, and the omens, I believe, are good. But if fickle fortune should lay me low in battle I shall be content to have sacrificed my life for the Roman world, like the Curtii and Mucii and the noble family of the Decii in early times. Our task is to wipe out a most pernicious people, on whose swords the blood of our kin is not yet dry. It took our ancestors many generations to uproot the obstacles in their path. Carthage was defeated in a long and confused war, but its great conqueror was afraid to let it survive his victory. After enduring the manifold accidents of a siege Scipio razed Numantia to the ground. Rome overthrew Fidenae lest she should become her rival, and in the same way crushed Falerii and Veii, so that even reliable ancient records have a task to convince us that these cities were ever powerful.

'These examples I have given you from my knowledge of history. It remains for you to check the greed for loot which has often been the bane of Roman troops. Keep in strict formation as you advance, and, when the moment comes to fight, stick to your own unit; you may be sure that any man who lags behind will be left hamstrung. I fear nothing but the trickery and guile of our wily foe. Finally, I give you all a solemn promise that once this business is brought to a successful end I will waive the privilege of emperors to use their authority as sufficient warrant for the rightness of their orders and decisions, and will make myself accountable to anyone who requires it for the correctness of my actions or the reverse. So now, I beg you, summon up your courage, summon it up in full expectation of success, knowing that I shall take an equal share in any hardship you may undergo and remembering that a just cause always triumphs.'

These words made a most acceptable peroration. The warriors, glorying in the reputation of their chief and fired by hope of success, raised their shields aloft and cried out that they would find nothing dangerous or difficult under a leader who imposed more toil on himself than on the common soldiers. The Gallic units in particular demonstrated their feelings by shouts of joy. They remembered how often when Julian was in command and moving among their ranks they had seen some peoples destroyed and others compelled to sue for mercy.

6. (1–74 omitted.) A long and confused digression on the regions of the Persian empire from west to farthest east, designed perhaps to stress the magnitude of Julian's undertaking. It contains the following generalized and largely imaginary description of Persian society.

Among all these peoples of various tongues there are differences of physical type as well as of situation. But if I am to give a general description of their appearance and character, I would say that they are almost all slight in build with a darkish or livid and bloodless complexion. Their eyes are like goats' eyes and have a grim expression. Their eyebrows are arched in a semicircle and meet in the middle. They have handsome beards and wear their hair long. All without distinction carry swords in their girdles even at banquets and on public feast-days. This is a custom which we have the unquestioned authority of Thucydides for saying that the Athenians were the first of the Greeks of antiquity to lay aside.

Most Persians are inordinately addicted to the pleasures of sex, and find even a large number of concubines hardly enough to satisfy them; they do not practise pederasty. A man has many or few wives according to his means, and his affections, being divided between a number of objects, are lukewarm. The luxury of an elegant table and especially indulgence in drink they shun like the plague. Only the king has a set hour for dining. Apart from him every man times his meals by his stomach. When this gives the signal he eats whatever is available, and once he has satisfied his hunger no one loads his digestion with superfluous food. Their restraint and caution are so extraordinary that sometimes they march through the vineyards and gardens of an enemy without attempting to touch anything for fear of poison and black arts. They are also most careful to avoid any violation of modesty; you will hardly ever see a Persian make water standing, or step aside to answer a call of nature. They are so careless and undisciplined in their movements and slouch about so sloppily that you might think them effeminate, but in fact they are most active warriors, crafty rather than courageous, and particularly formidable at long range.

They are full of empty words and talk madly and extravagantly. They are tiresomely and disgustingly boastful, and given to threats whether things are going well or ill. They are cunning, proud, and cruel, and claim the power of life and death over slaves and humble plebeians. They flay men alive, either completely or bit by bit. No servant who waits on them at table is allowed to open his mouth, speak, or spit; once the cloth is spread everyone's lips are sealed.

They are greatly in awe of their laws; those dealing with ingrates and traitors are especially grim, and they have other detestable statutes which provide that a whole family should be put to death for the guilt of a single member. They appoint as judges men of experience and integrity who have no need of others to advise them. In consequence they laugh at our custom of giving unlearned judges eloquent assessors who are thoroughly versed in public law. But the story that a judge was made to take his seat on the skin of another judge who had been convicted of corruption is an ancient fiction, or, if such a custom ever existed, it has gone out of use.

Their military training and discipline, and their constant practice of manoeuvres and arms drill, which I have often described, make them formidable even to large armies. They rely especially on their cavalry, in which all their nobility and men of mark serve. Their infantry are armed like gladiators, and obey orders like soldiers' servants. These people follow behind their masters in a mass, condemned as it were to perpetual servitude and never remunerated either by pay or presents. This nation, so bold and well exercised in martial arts, would have set its yoke on many peoples beside those which it has fully subdued, had it not been constantly harassed by domestic and foreign wars.

Most of them are dressed in garments of various gleaming colours, which are open in front and at the sides and flutter in the wind, but never expose any part of their bodies from head to heel. After their victory over Lydia and Croesus they acquired the habit of wearing gold armlets and necklaces, and particularly pearls, which they possess in great abundance.

An account of the origin of pearls (85–8) is omitted.

BOOK 24

1. Julian invades Assyria

After thus testing the morale of his troops, who evinced their unanimous enthusiasm by their customary acclamation, and by calling God to witness that so successful a prince was invincible, Julian decided that things should be brought rapidly to a head. So he *cut short* the night's rest and ordered the trumpets to sound the march. He had made every preparation needed for so difficult a campaign, and in the dazzling light of dawn set foot in Assyria, riding about the ranks in a mood of supreme confidence and inspiring all with a desire to rival him in deeds of valour. Being a commander versed in both the practice and the theory of war, and fearing that his ignorance of the terrain might expose him to a surprise, he began his march in battle order. He arranged that 1,500 skirmishers should precede the main body at a slow pace and advance cautiously, keeping watch against any sudden attack on both flanks as well as in front. The infantry of the centre, which was the flower of his whole army, was under his immediate command, but on the right Nevitta with several legions was ordered to skirt the bank of the Euphrates. The left wing with the cavalry he entrusted to Arintheus and Hormisdas, with orders to lead them in close column over the easy country of the plain. The rear was commanded by Dagalaif and Victor, and last of all came Secundinus, who had been general in Osdruene. Then, in order that the enemy, should they appear at any point, might be alarmed by an exaggerated idea of his numbers even from a distance, he caused men and animals to march at wider intervals, so that there were almost ten miles between the rear and the standard-bearers in the van. This is a stratagem said to have been often employed with wonderful skill by Pyrrhus king of Epirus, who was thoroughly expert not only in choosing suitable places to camp but also in expanding or contracting his forces so as to make them appear more or less numerous as it suited him. The baggage, servants, non-combatant staff, and stores of every kind were placed between two flanking divisions of regular troops so as not to leave them unprotected and liable to be carried off by a sudden attack, as often happens. The fleet, though it had to cope with the frequent windings of the stream, was not allowed either to fall behind or to get ahead.

After marching for two days we approached the deserted town of Dura, which lies on the river bank. Here we found several herds of deer. Some beasts were shot and others knocked over by heavy oars, and these provided more than enough food for all. But deer are rapid swimmers, and most of them leapt into the river and escaped to their usual solitary haunts before they could be caught.

Then, after four more days of easy marching, count Lucillian was sent at nightfall with a thousand light-armed men in boats to take the fortress of Anatha, which, like many others, is surrounded by the waters of the Euphrates. In accordance with the emperor's orders the boats took station at suitable points to blockade the island, which a misty night enabled them to approach unseen. But when it was clear day a man who went out to fetch water suddenly caught sight of them, and gave a loud yell which roused the garrison to arms. The emperor, who had been reconnoitring the fort from some high ground, at once crossed the river with an escort of two ships followed by a multitude of vessels carrying siege-engines. When he got near the walls he realized that a fight would be very risky, so he attempted by a mixture of cajolery and threats to persuade the garrison to surrender. They asked to speak with Hormisdas, and were induced by his sworn promise to hope great things from the mercy of the Romans. Finally they came humbly down from their walls driving before them a garlanded ox, a symbol with them of the acceptance of terms of peace. The whole fort was immediately burnt, and its commander Pusaeus, who was later general in Egypt, was awarded the rank of tribune. The rest received kind treatment and were sent with their families and belongings to the city of Chalcis in Syria. Among them was a soldier who had been left behind sick at the place when Maximian invaded Persia. He told us that at that time he was hardly more than a beardless boy. He had married several wives after the custom of the country and was now a bent old man with numerous descendants. He was the moving spirit behind the surrender and was overjoyed when he was brought to our lines, where he declared before witnesses that he had known and foretold long before that when he was nearly a hundred years old he would be buried in Roman soil. After this the Saracens delighted the emperor by bringing in some skirmishers belonging to an enemy corps. They were rewarded and sent back to repeat their exploit.

The following day saw a calamity. A tornado arose and the whirling gusts of wind caused such havoc that many tents were torn to pieces and numbers of men, finding it impossible to keep their feet in the gale, were hurled on their faces or their backs. On the same day another equally dangerous incident occurred. The river suddenly burst its banks and a number of supply vessels were sunk, because the stone sluices which control the flow of water for irrigation collapsed. Whether this was an act of sabotage or was caused by the volume of water could not be discovered.

After the capture and burning of this first enemy city and the removal of the prisoners the army was filled with greatly increased confidence and broke into loud acclaim of the emperor, believing that henceforth they would be the object of heaven's peculiar care.

The hidden dangers involved in an advance over unknown country required particular caution, and the many forms of deception likely to be practised by the wily foe gave grounds for fear. In consequence the emperor kept changing his station. At one moment he was in the van of the army and at the next bringing up the rear. He had with him a troop of light-armed men with whom he scoured the rough scrub of the valleys for hidden traps, and he checked any tendency to straggle away from the main body partly by his natural powers of persuasion and partly by threats. But he allowed the burning of the enemy's rich agricultural land together with their crops and huts on condition that every man first took plenty of what he needed to supply himself. In this way the enemy suffered substantial damage before they were aware of it. Our warriors were glad to make use of the spoil won by their own hands. They felt that their own valour had opened fresh magazines to them, and were delighted to have ample subsistence without having to draw on the supplies carried by the ships. It was here that a drunken soldier, who had been rash enough to cross to the opposite bank without orders, was seized and put to death by the enemy before our eyes.

2. Surrender of Pirisabora.

After these incidents we reached a fortress called Thilutha, which stands in the middle of the river. It rises to a dizzy height and its natural fortifications are as strong as any built by human hands. Since its lofty crags made attack impossible, we naturally had recourse to soft words to induce the inhabitants to surrender. They answered that this was not the right moment for defection, but went so far as to add that when the advance of the Romans reached the interior of the country they would go with the kingdom to which they belonged and adhere to the winning side. After this exchange they watched in respectful silence without moving while our ships passed under their very walls. Leaving them behind we came to another fortress called Achaiachala, which is protected by the surrounding river and difficult to scale. Here we were rebuffed in similar terms and went on. Next day we burned and left behind us another fort which had been abandoned owing to the weakness of its walls. In the next two days we covered some twenty-five miles and reached a place called Baraxmalcha. Here we crossed the river and seven miles further on broke into the city of Diacira, which we found deserted by its inhabitants but well stocked with grain and rock salt. We burned a lofty temple which crowned the citadel, and killed a few women whom we found there. Then, after passing a spring from which bitumen was welling, we seized the town of Ozogardana, which also had been abandoned by the inhabitants in fear of our approach. Here we were shown a tribunal dating from the reign of Trajan.

After burning this place too we were given two days' rest. Towards the end of the second night the Surena, who in Persia is the functionary next in rank to the king, together with the emir Podosaces, sheikh of the Assenite Saracens, a notorious brigand who had long ravaged our frontier with the utmost ferocity, laid a trap for Hormisdas. They had learnt somehow or other that he was about to set out on a reconnaissance, but their attempt failed because the river at this point was too narrow and deep to be fordable.

At daybreak the foe were in view, and we had our first sight of them in their gleaming helmets and stiff coats of mail. Our men rushed at the double to the attack and fell upon them most bravely. Their opponents bent their bows with might and main, and the flash of steel added to the Romans' alarm, but our courage was whetted by rage and our ranks covered by a dense wall of shields, and we pressed them so hard that they could not loose their shafts. Inspirited by these first-fruits of victory the army reached the village of Macepracta, where the remains of crumbling walls could be seen. We were told that in early times they were of great extent and protected Assyria from foreign invasion. Here

the river divides and one branch diverts a great volume of water
into the interior of Babylonia for the benefit of the farms and the
neighbouring cities. Another canal, called Naarmalcha, which means
'the king's stream', flows past Ctesiphon, and a high tower like the
Pharos of Alexandria stands at its mouth. All the infantry crossed this
on carefully constructed bridges. But the cavalry in full armour and
the baggage animals swam over where a bend in the stream made
the current less powerful; some were drowned, and others suddenly
came under heavy enemy fire. A troop of auxiliaries, however,
specially trained as runners, disembarked, put the foe to flight,
and following hard on their heels struck them down like birds of
prey.

　After this further successful affair we reached the large and populous
city of Pirisabora, which is surrounded by water on all sides. The
emperor reconnoitred its walls and the whole position on horseback,
and took the first tentative steps towards a siege, hoping that this would
be enough to deter the people of the town from any thought of resistance.
When, however, after several parleys they still remained proof against
both promises and threats, the siege began in earnest. A triple line of
armed men was drawn round the walls, and fighting went on at long
range from dawn to nightfall. Then the besieged, whose courage
equalled their strength, spread curtains of goats' hair loosely over the
battlements to cushion the impact of missiles, and from behind their
shields, which were made of the toughest wicker covered with a thick
layer of raw hide, put up a most obstinate resistance. They looked
entirely made of iron, because the plates of their mail exactly followed
the contours of their bodies and provided full protection for the whole
man. More than once they earnestly demanded to speak with Hormisdas,
who was their fellow-countryman and of royal birth, but when he came
near they attacked him with abuse and insults as a traitor and a deserter.
This prolonged exchange of gibes took up most of the day, but in the
silence which came with nightfall engines of various kinds were brought
up and men set to work to fill up the ditches.

　The doubtful light of first dawn revealed these operations to the
watchful eyes of the besieged, and when in addition a violent blow from
a ram made a breach in a corner tower they abandoned the double walls
of the city and retired to the adjoining citadel. This stood at the top of
a rugged hill which rose steeply from the level ground. Its central part
rose high in the air, and its regular shape presented the appearance of

an Argive shield, except on the north, where a gap in its outline was protected by cliffs which fell sheer to the stream of the Euphrates. There were high battlements built of bitumen and baked brick, a type of construction well known to be stronger than any other. Our men, whose rage had risen after traversing the city and finding it empty, now embarked on a fierce struggle with the townspeople, who rained down missiles of all kinds from the citadel. Finding themselves hard pressed by our catapults and artillery, these same defenders on the heights above raised their bows and bent them with all their might. The curved horns of these weapons which extend on both sides of the stock were so pliable that, when the strings were released after being drawn back by the brute strength of the fingers, they despatched iron-tipped arrows which crashed into the bodies in their path and stuck there with fatal results. No less energy was displayed by both sides in hurling showers of stones by hand. The struggle was evenly balanced, fierce fighting went on obstinately from dawn to dusk, and when it was broken off neither side had gained an advantage.

Next day the assault was renewed with great violence. There were many casualties on both sides and parity of strength kept the issue in suspense. While this mutual slaughter went on, the emperor, who was eager to accept any odds, placed himself in the middle of a wedge of troops, whose close-packed shields protected him from arrow-shots, and charged with his brave escort at one of the gates, which was heavily reinforced with iron. He and his companions in danger had to encounter volleys of stones, bullets, and other missiles, but he kept cheering them on as they tried to break down the leaves of the gate and force an entrance, and did not desist till he saw that he must be overwhelmed by the rain of missiles which poured down from above. However, he came off safe with all his men, a few of whom were slightly wounded. He himself was unhurt, but his face was suffused with a blush. He had read that Scipio Aemilianus with the historian Polybius, a native of Megalopolis in Arcadia, and thirty others, had demolished a gate at Carthage by an attack of this sort. But the admittedly truthful account given by the early authorities in fact justifies Julian's more recent exploit. Whereas the gate approached by Scipio was covered by an arch of stone under which he could shelter in safety before breaking into a city which he found devoid of defenders because they were engaged in trying to shift the massive stones of the arch, the place where Julian attacked was exposed, and it was only when the face of heaven was

darkened by fragments torn from mountains and other missiles that he
was with great difficulty forced to withdraw.

All this took place in haste and confusion, but when it became clear
that the laborious business of mantlets and ramps was being greatly
hindered by the pressure of events Julian gave orders that a machine of
the type known as 'helepolis' ('city-taker') should be put together with
all possible speed. This, as I have said before, was used by Demetrius,
whose many successes in capturing towns earned him the name of
Poliorcetes ('the Besieger'). When the besieged fixed their gaze on this
huge object, which would overtop their highest battlements, and took
into account also the determination of the besiegers, they suddenly
betook themselves to entreaties. Lining their walls and towers and
stretching out their arms, they begged to be taken under the protection
of Rome and granted life and pardon. When they saw that work on the
machine was at a standstill and that the engineers had downed tools –
a sure sign of peaceful intentions – they asked for an opportunity of
conferring with Hormisdas. This was granted, and Mamersides, who
commanded the garrison, was let down on a rope and conducted, as he
asked, to the emperor, from whom he obtained a firm promise of life
and immunity for himself and his comrades, together with a safe-
conduct. As soon as it became known to the besieged that all their
conditions had been met peace was ratified with solemn religious
ceremonies, and the whole population of both sexes poured out from
the gates shouting that a guardian angel had appeared to give them light
in the person of the great and merciful Caesar. Those who surrendered
numbered only 2,500; the rest of the inhabitants had anticipated the
siege by crossing the river in small boats and making off. Great store
of arms and provender was found in this citadel. From this the victors
took what they needed and burned the rest along with the place itself.

3. Discontent of the Roman troops pacified.

On the following day, while the emperor was peacefully taking his
dinner, he received the unwelcome news that the Persian commander
called the Surena had unexpectedly attacked three squadrons of our
scouts. Our casualties had been very slight, but a tribune had been
killed and a standard captured. Furiously angry, Julian flew in person
to the spot with an armed force – the speed of the operation guaranteed
its safety – and completely routed the marauders. The two surviving

tribunes were cashiered for cowardice and neglect of duty, and ten men out of those who had run away were discharged and put to death in conformity with ancient Roman practice.

After burning the town, as I have said, Julian mounted a platform built for the purpose and publicly thanked the assembled troops. He called on them to repeat their exploit and promised each a hundred pieces of silver. Realizing that the smallness of this sum was provoking something not far from mutiny, he spoke as follows in words of deep indignation:

'Look at the Persians, who are wallowing in wealth of every kind. The treasures of this people can enrich you, if we act in harmony and behave like men. I would have you know that the Roman state has been reduced from prodigious prosperity to dire penury through the activities of men who have feathered their own nests by persuading emperors to spend their gold on buying peace from the barbarians. The treasury has been plundered, cities fleeced, provinces pillaged. I myself, in spite of my noble birth, have neither means nor family connections, nothing in fact but a heart entirely devoid of fear. There is no disgrace in an emperor who values the cultivation of the soul above all else making a public admission of honourable poverty. The Fabricii too, whose estate was poor, directed momentous wars and were rich in glory.

'All these blessings can be yours in abundance if you cast fear aside and are more amenable, and allow yourselves to be guided by God and by me, who will direct you with all the foresight that is humanly possible. But if you are stiff-necked and disgrace yourselves by a return to the mutinous temper of earlier times, so be it. I, by myself, will crown my career by meeting death on my feet, as becomes an emperor, setting no store by a life which a slight bout of fever can snatch from me. Or else I will abdicate, since I have not lived in such a way that I cannot return to a private station. And I am proud and glad to say that we have generals among us whose ability has been thoroughly tested and who are perfectly skilled in all the arts of war.'

This sober speech by the emperor, who steered a middle course between indulgence and severity, quieted the troops for the time being. Hope of an improvement in their condition restored their confidence. They promised to be tractable and obedient, and with common consent lauded his authority and heroic spirit to the skies in a demonstration which, when it comes from the heart, is usually accompanied by a slight clashing of arms. Then they returned to their tents and recruited their strength by a night's rest and such food as was available. They were encouraged by the fact that Julian's words of cheer took the form of solemn oaths not by the lives of those dear to him but by the magnitude of the affairs he had in hand. 'As I hope to make the Persians submit', he would say, or, 'As I hope to restore the tottering Roman world'. Trajan is said to have often emphasized his statements by similar phrases, such as: 'As I hope to see Dacia reduced to a province', or, 'As I hope to bridge the Danube *as well as the Euphrates*'.

Next, after a march of fourteen miles, we came to a place where the country is copiously irrigated. The Persians, learning in advance what route we should take, had broken down the sluices and allowed the streams to spread into a flood. The ground over a wide area being thus waterlogged, the emperor gave the army another day's rest and went ahead himself to construct little bridges with the aid of bladders *and small boats* and planks from palm trees. In this way he got his men across, though not without difficulty.

In this region many fields are planted with vines and fruit-trees of different sorts. Immense palm groves also cover a wide expanse and extend as far as Mesene and the Great Sea (Persian Gulf). Wherever you go you see branches cut from palms, some with their fruit, from which honey and wine are made in great quantities. We are told that palms themselves mate, and that the sexes may easily be distinguished. It is said too that female trees conceive when they are smeared with the seeds of the male, and that they take delight in mutual love, which is shown by the fact that they lean towards each other and cannot be separated even by a strong wind. If the female is not smeared with the seed of the male in the usual way, she miscarries and loses her fruit before it is ripe. If it is not known with what male tree a female is in love her trunk is smeared with her own nectar, and nature arranges that another tree senses the sweet smell. This is the evidence on which belief in a kind of copulation is based.

The army satisfied its appetite with ample food from this source, and whereas men previously dreaded a dearth there was now a serious fear that they would overeat. Several islands were passed and finally, after suffering an attack from ambush, which did not go unpunished, we reached a place where the main stream of the Euphrates splits into a number of channels.

4. Storming and sack of Maozamalcha.

In this area a town deserted by its Jewish inhabitants because of its low walls was burnt down by the angry troops. Then the emperor continued his advance in higher spirits, believing himself to be under the gracious protection of Heaven. Arriving at Maozamalcha, a large city defended by strong walls, he pitched camp, and took precautions against any sudden attack by the Persian horse, whose daring in open country inspires unspeakable dread in all peoples. After seeing to this he took a few light-armed men and went with them on foot himself to make a careful reconnaissance of the city, but fell into a dangerous trap from which he barely escaped with his life. Ten armed Persians emerged from a hidden postern, crawled along the bottom of the slope on hands and knees, and suddenly threw themselves on our men. The emperor's dress made him conspicuous, and two of them attacked him with drawn swords, but he protected himself by raising his shield. From under its cover he plunged his sword into the side of one with superb courage, while the other was despatched by repeated blows from his escort. The rest, some of whom were wounded, scattered in flight. Both the dead men were stripped of their arms, and Julian, without suffering any loss, brought back the spoils to the camp, where he was welcomed with universal delight. Torquatus once took a gold collar from a prostrate foe, and Valerius, afterwards known as Corvinus, overcame an insolent Gaul with the aid of a raven. Both have earned the praise of posterity for their glorious deeds. We do not grudge it them, but this fine exploit of Julian should also be added to the records of the past.

Next day bridges were built and the army crossed over to occupy a camp in a better position. It was fortified by a double rampart because, as I said, Julian was nervous of the empty open plains. Then he began the siege of the town, believing that it would be dangerous to advance further and leave a formidable enemy in his rear.

During these arduous preparations the Surena, who commanded the enemy forces, attacked our baggage-animals, which were grazing in a palm-grove. He was frustrated by some units of camp-guards and retired with the loss of a few men. The inhabitants of two towns entirely surrounded by water lost confidence in their power to resist and fled in panic to the fortifications of Ctesiphon. Some pushed through the thick woods, others made use of dugout canoes to cross the neighbouring marshes, thinking that these offered the best, indeed the only, hope of accomplishing their long trek in safety and reaching the country which lay beyond. Some of them after resistance were killed by our troops, who themselves also scoured the country in skiffs and boats and sometimes brought in prisoners. The emperor, after weighing up the situation, had arranged that while the infantry attacked the walls the cavalry in small parties should concentrate on pillage. In this way the army was kept fed on the vitals of the enemy without any cost to the people of our own provinces.

And now the emperor, having drawn a triple line of shields round the town, which was protected by double walls, threw all his strength into the attack which was to achieve his end. But though the undertaking was necessary its successful accomplishment was very difficult. On every side high, steep rocks which involved winding detours made the approach dangerous and the town inaccessible, especially as there were many formidable towers rising as high as the rocky eminence on which the citadel stood, and strong battlements guarding the sloping plateau overlooking the river. A further not less serious embarrassment was that the large garrison of picked men was proof against all inducements to surrender. They seemed resolved either to conquer or not to survive the reduction of their native place to ashes. On our side the troops could hardly be restrained from rushing impetuously to the assault. They clamoured for a pitched battle in an open field, and even when the recall was sounded were still consumed with a passionate desire to harass the enemy.

Better judgement, however, prevailed over this violent uproar. Duties were assigned, and every man set about his allotted task with alacrity. Some were building high ramps, others filling up ditches; elsewhere long passages were being driven into the bowels of the earth, and the artillery-men were setting up their engines, ready to burst out into deadly noise. Nevitta and Dagalaif were in charge of the mines and the sheds which covered them, but the emperor himself directed the opening of the assault and the protection of the artillery from fire and sorties.

When all these various tasks preparatory to the destruction of the city had been completed and our men were spoiling for the fight, the general named Victor returned. He had reconnoitred the roads as far as Ctesiphon and reported that he had met with no opposition. This news sent all our men wild with joy. Their confidence was reinforced, and they stood to arms waiting for the signal to attack.

Then, as the trumpets sounded their martial note, both sides burst into uproar. The Romans took the initiative and launched repeated assaults full of sound and fury. The enemy put their trust in their coats of mail; the plates of this were like the thin feathers of a bird, and our missiles rebounded from their smooth iron surface. On our side the interlocked shields which exactly covered our men *like moving arches* sometimes gaped apart under the strain of incessant motion. The Persians for their part clung obstinately to their walls and used every effort to baffle and frustrate our deadly assaults. But when the assailants, carrying frames of wicker in front of them, were pressing hard upon the defence, slingers and archers, aided by others who even rolled down huge stones, tried to keep their foe at bay with flares and fire-bombs. Then there was screeching of ballistas being wound up; they were adapted for firing wooden arrows, and showers of missiles were discharged, while scorpions hurled round stones wherever they were aimed by expert hands. The fight was renewed again and again, but towards noon the growing heat of the day under a blazing sun forced us all to withdraw, worn out and dripping with sweat, in spite of our eagerness to perfect the siege-works and continue the fray.

The same determination was shown on the following day, when both parties carried on the struggle fiercely in various ways, and finally separated without either having gained an advantage. But for the emperor, who maintained the closest contact with his troops in the face of every danger, the destruction of the town was a matter of urgency, since if he were detained too long about its walls he might have to abandon his more important objectives. But in times of extreme crisis nothing is too trivial to tip the scales, sometimes with grave and unexpected results. At one of the many moments when the fighting slackened and was about to be broken off, a tower taller than all the rest and strongly built of baked brick was demolished by an exceptionally powerful blow from a ram just brought into action, and in its fall brought down the adjacent section of wall with a tremendous crash. This at once transformed the situation, and the energy of besiegers and besieged alike manifested itself in splendid feats of arms. Nothing seemed too hard for our men, who were in a fury of rage and resentment, nothing too terrifying or awful for their opponents, who were fighting for their lives. The struggle swayed this way and that with great bloodshed on both sides, and it was not till nightfall brought it to an end that the exhausted combatants thought of rest.

While this action was still going on in the broad light of day, the emperor, who was always on the alert, received a report that the legionaries detailed for the mines had completed their task. Underground passages supported by props now reached beyond the foundations of the walls, and they were ready to break out when he gave the word. So when night was well advanced the trumpets again sounded the assault and all rushed to arms. The plan was to mount an attack on the walls on both sides, so that, while the besieged were running hither and thither to repel these threats, their attention would be distracted from the clinking of iron tools close at hand, and the sappers, suddenly emerging, would not encounter any resistance. These arrangements answered their purpose, and while the garrison was fully occupied the mine was opened and out sprang Exsuperius, a soldier of the regiment called Victorious, followed by the tribune Magnus and the notary Jovian, at whose heels came the whole intrepid band. They first dispatched those they found in the building through which they reached the surface, and then, advancing on tiptoe, cut down all the sentries, who in their native manner were singing songs in praise of the justice and good fortune of their king.

There was once a belief that Luscinus was aided in his attack on the camp of the Lucanians by Mars himself (if it is consistent with the majesty of the gods to associate with mortals). What gave rise to this was that in the heat of battle an armed figure of terrific stature was seen carrying a scaling-ladder, but next day, when the army was reviewed, he could not be found in spite of a special effort to discover him. If he had been a soldier, consciousness that he had performed a notable exploit would have caused him to reveal himself. But whereas then the hero of a splendid feat remained quite unknown, on the present occasion those who had now shown such heroism received the distinction of a siege crown and a public citation in accordance with ancient usage.

At last the town, stripped of its defenders and with its walls full of breaches, which made its fall inevitable, was overrun by our troops, who in their fury destroyed all that came in their path without distinction of age or sex. Some, panic-stricken at the approach of death and finding themselves caught between fire and sword, threw themselves headlong from the walls bewailing their fate. Maimed in every limb they prolonged for a short time a life worse than death, until someone finished them off. Nabdates, however, who commanded the defence, was taken alive with eighty followers, and when he was brought before the emperor the latter in a serene and merciful mood gave orders that he and the rest should be kept unharmed.

There followed a division of the spoils in accordance with each man's service and deserts. Julian, who was easily satisfied, took for himself only a dumb boy who was adept at conveying with graceful gestures all that he knew in sign language, *together with three gold pieces*; this he considered a pleasant and acceptable reward for the victory he had won. He would not touch or even look at any of the lovely young girls who were captured, though Persian women are renowned for their beauty. In this he followed the example of Alexander and Africanus, who would not allow themselves to succumb to desire after showing themselves invincible by hardship.

In the course of these operations one of our engineers, whose name escapes me, happened to be standing behind a scorpion when a stone, carelessly fitted to its sling by the artillerymen, was hurled backwards. His breast was crushed, and he was thrown on his back and killed. His whole body was so mangled as to defy recognition.

The emperor had just set out from this place when he was reliably informed that a party of the enemy was lying in wait near the walls of the fallen town in some dark and treacherous pits, of which there are many in those parts. Their intention was to rush out unexpectedly and take our army in the rear. A detachment of infantry of tried courage was at once sent to dislodge them. Finding that they could neither force their way in nor induce those inside to come out and fight, they collected straw and brushwood and piled them at the mouths of the caves. The smoke, which became thicker as the passages narrowed, killed some by suffocation; others were scorched by the flames and forced out to meet a swift death. When all had perished by fire or sword our men rapidly rejoined their units. Thus a great and populous city was destroyed by the strength of Roman arms and reduced to dust and ruins.

After this glorious achievement we crossed a network of streams by a series of bridges and came to two forts with *blind* walls. Here a son of the Persian king, advancing from Ctesiphon with some grandees and a large force, tried to prevent count Victor, who was in front of our main body, from crossing a river, but when he saw the regiments of troops behind Victor he withdrew.

5. *Another fortress stormed and burnt.*

Continuing our advance we came to woods and a smiling countryside planted with various crops. We found a royal lodge built in the Roman style and left it untouched in accordance with orders. In this same region there was also a large circular park enclosed by a fence, where wild animals were preserved for the king's enjoyment. There were lions with long manes, bristly wild boars, bears of the extraordinarily savage type peculiar to Persia, and other choice beasts of enormous size. Our cavalry broke down the bars of the gates and slaughtered them all with hunting spears and a hail of missiles.

From this richly cultivated place *it is only a few miles* to Coche, otherwise known as Seleucia. An extempore camp was pitched and for two days the army took advantage of the food and water available. Meanwhile the emperor went ahead with a party of skirmishers to survey the ruins of the city once destroyed by the emperor Carus, where a never-failing spring forms a vast pool which empties into the Tigris. Here he saw many corpses on gibbets, the remains of the family of the man who surrendered the town of Pirisabora. Here too Nabdates, who, as I said, had been dragged from hiding with eighty others after the storming of his town, was burnt alive. He had put up a most obstinate resistance after giving a secret promise at the beginning of the siege to betray the town, and, though he received a pardon for this which he could not have hoped for, he subsequently became so insolent as to assail Hormisdas with all manner of abuse.

After proceeding some distance we were shocked by a sad mishap. While three cohorts of our skirmishers were engaged with a Persian detachment which made a sudden sally from the gates of a town, another enemy force from the opposite bank of a stream intercepted and cut to pieces the baggage train which was following us, together with a few foragers who were roaming at large. The emperor left the place grinding his teeth with rage, and was approaching the environs of Ctesiphon when he came upon a high and strongly walled fort. Believing that he would not be recognized he rode with a few companions about the walls to reconnoitre, but when he was rash enough to get within range he could not escape detection. He at once became the target of a rain of missiles and would have met his death from an engine on the walls had he not been protected by a strong screen of shields. His armour-bearer was wounded close beside him, but he himself escaped from this desperate peril and got away unhurt.

In a frenzy of rage he decided to besiege the fort, which its garrison was resolutely determined to defend, relying on its almost inaccessible situation, and believing also that the king, who was rapidly advancing with large forces, would appear at any moment. The mantlets and all the other paraphernalia of a siege were all ready when towards midnight a bright moon made everything clear to the watchers on the battlements. Gathering in one mass they suddenly threw open the gates and sallied out, took one of our squadrons by surprise, and killed a large number, among them a tribune who fell attempting to repel the attack. Meanwhile the Persians on the opposite bank repeated their previous tactics and attacked a part of our forces, killing a number and taking some prisoners. At first our men showed little spirit; they were alarmed and had an exaggerated idea of the enemy's strength. But then they recovered their courage and armed themselves as best they could in the confusion, while the rest of the army, roused by the call of the trumpets, hastened to the spot with defiant shouts, so that in the end the attackers were thrown back in a panic, though without loss. The emperor was in a fury, and punished the survivors of the squadron which had lost its nerve in the face of the marauders by transferring them with loss of rank to serve as infantry, which is more laborious. He was now on fire to destroy the fort where he had encountered such danger, and flung himself heart and soul into the task, never leaving the front rank, where he could set an example by his personal courage and see and judge the conduct of his men. At last, after long exposure on his part to extreme peril, the fort could no longer hold out against the united resolve of the assailants with their various siege-engines and missiles, and was captured and burnt. After this, in view of the hard tasks it had already performed and those which were still in store, the army, which was exhausted by its toils, was allowed a rest and received a generous distribution of victuals. But from that time greater care was taken to strengthen the camp with a close palisade and a deep ditch, to guard against sudden sallies and other surprises from Ctesiphon, which was now close at hand.

6. A successful engagement outside Ctesiphon.

Then we came to a man-made channel called Naarmalcha, 'the king's canal', which at that time was dry. In earlier days Trajan and subsequently Severus had taken great pains to have the earth dug out to make a large canal, through which water could be diverted from the Euphrates and convey shipping to the Tigris. In all the circumstances it seemed safest to clean out this channel, which the Persians, fearing a repetition of the design, had blocked with a great mass of stones. Once the channel had been cleared and the dams removed, a great head of water carried our fleet in safety a distance of some three miles into the Tigris. Bridges were at once built and the army crossed and advanced towards Coche. Hoping to enjoy a welcome respite from our fatigue we encamped in a rich region full of smiling orchards, vineyards, and green groves of cypress. In their midst was a shady and delightful hunting lodge decorated throughout with pictures in the native style of the king killing his quarry in various types of blood-sport. Among this people painting and sculpture are entirely confined to various forms of slaughter and scenes of battle.

So far everything had gone as the Augustus wished. He was now ready to meet all difficulties with greater confidence and conceived such hopes from his hitherto consistent good fortune that he often pushed his luck to the verge of rashness. He unloaded the strongest of the vessels carrying food and artillery and embarked eighty armed men on each. Then, forming the fleet into three squadrons and keeping the main part with him, he decided to send count Victor at nightfall with one squadron to make a swift crossing and seize the bank occupied by the enemy. His generals were greatly alarmed by this plan and tried unanimously to dissuade him, but they could not turn him from his purpose. The signal was given in accordance with his orders and five vessels suddenly vanished from sight. When they reached the opposite bank they came under fierce attack from fire-bombs and every sort of combustible, and they would have gone up in flames with all on board had not the emperor shown astonishing presence of mind. He shouted that our men had, as instructed, given the agreed signal that they had made a successful landing, and ordered the whole fleet to join them at full speed. By this device our ships were saved, and the rest of our troops, in the face of a hail of stones and other missiles from above, succeeded after a fierce struggle in scaling the high, steep bank and holding the position they had gained. History finds it wonderful that Sertorius managed to swim across the Rhône in arms and breastplate, but on this occasion some soldiers who were in disorder and afraid of being left behind when the signal was given took to the water clinging face downwards to their broad, curved shields, and, though their steering was clumsy, kept up with the ships in their passage over the eddying river.

The Persians opposed us with squadrons of cuirassiers drawn up in such serried ranks that their movements in their close-fitting coats of flexible mail dazzled our eyes, while all their horses were protected by housings of leather. They were supported by detachments of infantry who moved in compact formation carrying long, curved shields of wicker covered with raw hide. Behind them came elephants looking like moving hills. Their huge bodies threatened destruction to all who approached, and past experience had taught us to dread them.

On our side the emperor followed the Homeric tactic of placing his weakest infantry units between lines of other troops, not in the van, where if they disgraced themselves by giving way they might carry the whole army with them, nor yet in the rear behind all the centuries, where they could turn tail with no one to stop them. He himself with the light-armed auxiliaries kept galloping between front and rear.

So, when both sides were in full view of each other, the Romans in their gleaming crested helmets advanced slowly swinging their shields, as if to the beat of an anapaestic rhythm. After a preliminary discharge of missiles by the skirmishers, whirling clouds of dust covered the whole field. Shouting their traditional war-cries and inspired by the blare of trumpets, both sides fought hand-to-hand with spears and drawn swords; the quicker our men forced themselves into the enemy's line the less were they exposed to danger from arrows. Meanwhile Julian, who took an active share in the fighting as well as directing it, was busy in reinforcing weak points and hounding on laggards. In the end, the front line of the Persians gave way and retreated, slowly at first and then at a rapid pace, to the neighbouring city. Our troops, though likewise exhausted by fighting on a scorching plain from dawn to dusk, followed hard on their heels, hacking at their calves and backs, and drove the whole army with its best generals, Pigranes, the Surena, and Narses, in headlong flight to the very walls of Ctesiphon. In fact, they would have broken into the city along with the routed enemy, had not their commander Victor restrained them with hand-signals and shouts.

He himself had been hit in the shoulder by an arrow, and he feared that if our men in their mad rush got within the circuit of the walls and could find no way out they would be overwhelmed by weight of numbers.

The old poets may sing of Hector's battles and extol the courage of the Thessalian chief; age after age may tell of Sophanes and Aminias and Callimachus and Cynegirus, the crowning glories of the Persian wars; but it is universally admitted that the courage of some of our men on that day shone no less bright.

Having lost all their fears and trampled on the bodies of their foes, our men, still stained with blood righteously shed, gathered by the emperor's tent, and gave him praise and thanks for his victory in a battle in which no one could tell whether he had been more of a general or a common soldier. So successful had he been that the Persians lost approximately 2,500 men to our seventy. Julian addressed by name several whose undaunted valour he had personally witnessed, and rewarded them with naval, civic, or camp crowns.

Fully convinced that similar successes lay before him he prepared to offer a number of victims to Mars the Avenger. Ten fine bulls were brought for this purpose, but before they reached the altar nine of them sank to the ground in a sorry state. The tenth, which broke its halter and escaped, was recovered with difficulty, and when it was slaughtered the omens it gave were unfavourable. At the sight of them Julian cried out in high indignation, and swore by Jupiter that he would never sacrifice to Mars again. Nor did he ever revoke his vow, since soon afterwards he was carried off by death.

7. *Burning of the fleet and retreat from the river.*

At a conference of the general staff about the siege of Ctesiphon, the day was carried by those who were sure that it would be a rash and foolish undertaking, first, because the very situation of the city made it impregnable, and, second, because it was believed that the king would soon make his appearance with a formidable host. So the better opinion prevailed, and its expediency was recognized by the sagacious emperor, who sent Arintheus with a body of light-armed foot to lay waste the rich pastures and cornfields of the neighbourhood. He was also actively to pursue the enemy who had recently scattered and taken cover in hide-outs known only to themselves amid a network of overgrown paths.

A considerable lacuna has been plausibly suspected here (cf. p. 463).

Julian, however, whose ambition was never satisfied, rejected all warnings and charged with cowardice and love of ease the generals who were urging him to abandon the kingdom of Persia when it was all but won. He decided to leave the river on his left and to march rapidly into the interior under the conduct of guides who turned out to be guides to disaster. And one would think that Bellona herself must have lit the fatal flame when he gave orders that all the ships should be burnt, except for twelve smaller ones which were to be carried on wagons to serve in bridge-building. In taking this step he believed that he was acting with prudence; the enemy would be denied the use of his fleet, and he would no longer have nearly 20,000 of his troops occupied in towing and manoeuvring the ships, as they had been from the beginning of the campaign.

When our men grasped the self-evident truth that if they were turned back by drought or the height of the mountains they would not be able to return to the water, they were in fear of their lives and began to complain. At the same time the deserters openly confessed under torture that they had misled us. So orders were given that all hands should turn to and put out the flames. But most of the ships had already been consumed by the fury of the fire, and only the twelve which had been set apart to be kept could be saved intact. In this way the fleet was needlessly lost, but Julian, relying on the fact that his forces were concentrated now that none of the troops were required for other duties, advanced with superior numbers into the interior over a rich region which provided food in abundance.

Hearing of this, the enemy set fire to the vegetation and standing crops in order to expose us to the torments of starvation. The fire made it impossibe for us to move, and we were kept stationary in our camp till the flames should die down. The Persians also began to make game of us from a distance, at one moment spreading themselves out and at the next halting in close order, to give the impression to those watching from afar that the king's forces had arrived, and to make us believe that this accounted for their bold sallies and unusual tactics. The emperor and the army, however, were in gloom. Now that they had rashly lost their ships they had no means of making a bridge, nor could they check the movements of the approaching enemy, whose presence was betrayed by the bright gleam of their close-fitting mail. A further serious misfortune was the failure of Arsaces and our generals to appear with the reinforcements we were expecting. The reasons for this have already been given.

8. Attempt to return through Corduene.

To alleviate the anxiety of the troops on this score the emperor ordered some prisoners to be put on show. They were of slight build, like almost all Persians, and by now emaciated as well. Julian turned towards our men and said: 'Look at the creatures that you brave warriors take for men, filthy, loathsome little nanny-goats who, as experience has often shown us, throw away their arms and take to flight before battle is joined.' The prisoners were then removed and the general situation discussed. Much was said on both sides; the ignorant rank and file clamoured to return by the way we had come, but the emperor firmly resisted this suggestion, and many others supported him, pointing out that this was impossible, since fodder and crops had been destroyed over the whole extent of the plain and the ruined villages we had burnt were in a state of hideous destitution. Besides, the melting of the winter snows had turned the whole area into a quagmire, and the rivers had burst their banks and become raging torrents. What added to the difficulty was that when that region is exposed to the heat of the sun it is entirely covered by such swarms of flies and gnats as to veil the light of day and the twinkling stars at night.

Since human wisdom was of no avail, it was decided after much doubt and hesitation to build altars and offer sacrifice, so as to ascertain whether it was the will of the gods that we should return through Assyria or whether we should march slowly along the base of the mountains and surprise and pillage Chiliocomum on the borders of Corduene. But inspection of the entrails showed that neither alternative would do. Nevertheless it was decided, since no better course was available, to seize upon Corduene, and on 16 June we struck camp. The emperor had set out at daybreak when we saw what seemed to be smoke or a whirling cloud of dust, which led us to believe that a herd of wild asses, which abound in those parts, was moving in a dense pack to frustrate a savage attack by lions. Some, however, thought that it was Arsaces and our generals, stirred into action by the news that the emperor was attacking Ctesiphon in great force, and some insisted that the Persians had intercepted us. To avoid any mishap in this uncertain situation the marching troops were halted by trumpet-call, and we rested in safety in a grassy valley by a stream, where our camp was protected by a circle of shields arranged in depth. The atmosphere remained thick till evening and we could not make out what it was that we saw through the gloom.

BOOK 25

1. Persian attacks repulsed.

No star relieved the darkness of the night, which we spent as one does in moments of doubt and difficulty; no one dared to sit down or close his eyes for fear. But as soon as day broke the distant appearance of gleaming breastplates and glittering corslets edged with iron showed that the king's forces were at hand. This sight roused our troops, who were separated from the enemy only by a shallow stream. They were in a hurry to join battle, but were checked by the emperor. However, a fierce struggle took place not far from our rampart between our skirmishers and the Persians, in which Machamaeus, who commanded one of our units, fell. His brother Maurus, later to command in Phoenicia, tried to protect him; he slew the man who had killed his brother and struck fear into all he encountered, and though he was wounded himself in the shoulder managed by a great effort to drag off Machamaeus, whose face was already drained of colour by approaching death.

Finally, when both sides were exhausted by the almost intolerable heat and repeated encounters, the enemy squadrons scattered after suffering a serious reverse. As we were withdrawing from this place the Saracens, who were following us at a distance, were compelled to retreat from fear of our infantry. Shortly afterwards, however, they joined the main body of the Persians and were able to attack in greater safety, hoping to capture the Roman baggage, but when they saw the emperor they fell back upon the squadrons held in reserve. Leaving this region we came to a domain called Hucumbra, where we found supplies of all that we needed and abundance of grain. We halted for two days to enjoy this unhoped-for relief, and then moved on, after first burning everything except what we could carry with us.

Next day, as we were moving more peacefully, the Persians suddenly attacked the troops whose turn it was that day to bring up the rear.

They would have had little trouble in killing them had not our nearest cavalry, though widely extended over the shallow valleys, quickly grasped the situation and averted this grave danger with loss to the authors of the surprise. Among those who fell in this fight was a satrap of high birth called Adaces, who had once been sent as an envoy to the emperor Constantius and kindly received. The man who killed him brought his armour to Julian and was duly rewarded. On the same day the cavalry corps called Tertiaci were accused by the legionaries of having undermined the morale of almost the entire army by gradually giving way at a moment when the legions themselves had broken into the enemy's front. Julian, in a fit of righteous indignation, deprived them of their standards, broke their spears, and condemned all who were charged with flight to march among the baggage-train with the prisoners. Their leader, who alone had shown courage, was given the command of another troop, whose tribune was convicted of cowardice in the face of the enemy. Four other tribunes of cavalry detachments were also cashiered for similar misconduct. The emperor contented himself with this comparatively mild punishment in view of the difficulties which faced him.

During a further march of some eight miles our supplies of all kinds began to run out owing to the burning of the crops and vegetation, and every man had to snatch for himself from the very flames whatever grain and forage he could carry. Leaving this place in turn the whole army had reached a district called Maranga, when about dawn an immense host of Persians appeared with Merena, the master of the horse, two of the king's sons, and many other grandees. All their troops were clad in mail; their bodies were covered with plates so closely fitting that the stiff joints of the armour conformed to the articulation of the limbs beneath, and representations of human faces were so skilfully fitted to their heads that the whole man was clothed in metal scales. The only spots where a weapon could lodge were the tiny holes left for the eyes and nostrils, which allowed some degree of vision and a scanty supply of air. Those of them who were to fight with pikes stood so still that they might have been fixed to the spot by metal ties. Close by, the archers, practised from the very cradle in a skill in which that people especially excels, were bending their flexible bows. Their arms stretched so wide that while the point of the arrow touched their left hand the string brushed their right breast. By highly skilful finger-work the shafts flew with a loud hiss, dealing deadly wounds.

Behind them were gleaming elephants, whose awful aspect and gaping jaws inspired almost unbearable fear, and whose noise, smell, and strange appearance terrified our horses even more than ourselves. The mahouts mounted on them had knives with hafts tied to their right hands. The Persians had not forgotten the disaster which befell them at Nisibis, when the elephants turned upon their own side and crushed the rank and file. If a beast ran amok and could not be controlled by its driver, he severed with all his strength the vertebra between the head and the neck. Hasdrubal the brother of Hannibal discovered long ago that this is the quickest way of destroying this type of monster.

Our men felt no little fear at the sight which met their eyes, but the emperor was full of confidence. Surrounded by his escort of men-at-arms and accompanied by his principal officers, he drew up his forces to meet the enemy in a crescent formation with curved wings, as the desperate nature of the situation required.

To prevent the preliminary volleys of the archers from disrupting our ranks he advanced at the double and so ruined the effect of their fire, and, when the formal signal for battle was given, the Roman foot in close order made a mighty push and drove the serried ranks of the enemy before them. When the fight was at its hottest the clash of shields, the shouts of the combatants, and the dreary hiss of whirring missiles went on without pause, and blood and bodies covered the field. The Persians fell in greater numbers because they often lack spirit in a clash of arms and are at a grave disadvantage in hand-to-hand combat. Their forte is fighting at long range, and if they see their forces giving ground they deter the enemy from pursuit by discharging a rain of arrows backward as they withdraw. So the Parthians were driven back by sheer force, and when the recall was sounded our men, exhausted by long exposure to the fiery heat of the sun, returned to their tents in a mood to perform even greater exploits. As I said, the Persian losses in this engagement were clearly the greater and ours very light. But one conspicuous event among the varied incidents of the fight was the death of the warrior Vetranio, who commanded the legion of the Zianni.

2. *Alarming portents of disaster.*

After this there was an armistice for three days, during which everyone attended to his own or his neighbour's wounds. But we were now destitute of food and tormented by intolerable pangs of hunger. Crops and fodder had been burnt and men and beasts were at their last gasp, so a large part of the food carried by the baggage-animals of the tribunes and counts was distributed to relieve the pressing needs of the rank and file. Instead of delicacies fit for a royal table, the emperor, who was to take his frugal meal under the poles of a tent, had prepared for him a scanty ration of porridge which even a common soldier would have spurned. Regardless of his own comfort he caused to be distributed among the famished masses all the victuals required for his personal service.

At dead of night Julian, after a short period of restlessness and troubled sleep, had roused himself, as was his habit, and was writing in his tent, after the example of Julius Caesar. He was lost in the profound thoughts of some philosopher when he saw in the gloom, as he admitted to his intimates, the shape of the Genius of the Roman people, which appeared to him in Gaul when he rose to the dignity of Augustus. Now it was departing in sadness through the curtains of his tent with its head and horn of plenty veiled. For a moment Julian remained in a state of stupor; then he rose above all fear and committed the future to the will of Heaven. The night was far spent and he was fully awake, so he left his bed, which was on the ground, and betook himself to prayer, using the ritual appropriate to avert evil. Then he thought he saw a blazing light like a falling star, which clove its way through part of the air and vanished. He was horror-struck by the thought that the star of Mars had appeared to him in this manifestly threatening form. In fact this fiery object was what we Greeks call a shooting star, which never falls or touches the earth. Anyone who thinks that bodies can fall from the sky must be set down as an ignoramus or a fool. This phenomenon has been explained in various ways, of which it will be enough to mention a few. Some think that glowing sparks torn from the active ether are extinguished when they are no longer strong enough to continue their flight; others that fiery rays encountering thick clouds give out sparks through the violence of the shock. A third theory is that when some light comes in contact with a cloud it takes the form of a star and moves downward as long as the strength of the fire sustains it. Finally, however, the vast space it has traversed causes it to disintegrate, and it loses itself in the airy element, turning back into the substance by whose excessive friction it was ignited.

The Etruscan diviners were sent for in haste before first light and asked what this novel kind of star portended. They answered that the greatest care must be taken to avoid any new enterprise for the moment, and gave as their authority the Tarquitian books, which in the section on signs from heaven forbid engaging in battle or any similar operation when a fiery object is seen in the sky. Julian made light of this as he had of many other warnings, but the diviners begged him at least to put off his departure for some hours. They could not obtain even this concession, *although they brought to bear their entire knowledge of divination*, and as soon as day dawned we struck camp.

3. Death of Julian after a wound.

When we set out again the Persians, who had conceived from their frequent defeats an aversion to pitched infantry battles, adopted the tactics of ambuscade, and dogged our steps without showing themselves. They kept the marching troops under observation from high hills on either side, and our men, haunted by consciousness of this, passed the entire day without building a rampart or protecting themselves by a palisade. Our flanks were strongly guarded and the army was moving in battle formation, though with some raggedness owing to the nature of the ground, when the emperor, who had gone ahead unarmed to reconnoitre, was told that our rearguard had been suddenly attacked from behind. Shocked by this disaster he forgot his breastplate, and in his hurry simply laid hold of a shield, but as he was rushing to bring support to those in the rear he was recalled by the fearful news that the van which he had just left was in a similar plight. He was hastening to restore the position there, regardless of danger to himself, when in another quarter a troop of Parthian cuirassiers attacked our centre, overran its left wing, which gave way because our men could not stand the smell and noise of the elephants, and tried to force a decision with pikes and showers of missiles. The emperor flew from one danger-spot to another, and our light-armed troops took the offensive, hacking at the backs and legs of the Persians and their monstrous beasts as they turned tail. Julian, throwing caution to the winds, thrust himself boldly into the fight, shouting and waving his arms to make it clear that the enemy had been routed and to encourage his men to a furious pursuit. His escort of guards, who had been scattered in the mêlée, were crying out to him from all sides to avoid the mass of fugitives as he would the collapse of a badly built roof, when suddenly a cavalry spear, *directed no one knows by whom*, grazed his arm, pierced his ribs, and lodged in the lower part of his liver. He tried to pull it out with his right hand, but both sides of the spear were sharp and he felt his fingers cut to the bone. He fell from his horse, there was a rush to the spot, and he was carried to the camp, where he received medical treatment.

A temporary remission of pain relieved his fears. Fighting against death with all his great spirit, he called for his horse and arms, wishing to return to the fight to restore the confidence of his men and to make it apparent that it was concern for others' safety, not his own, that most deeply affected him. He showed the same spirit, though in different circumstances, as the famous general Epaminondas, who, when he was fatally wounded at Mantinea and carried out of the fight, asked with particular anxiety after his shield. When he saw it near him he died happy; the man who could lay down his life unafraid dreaded the loss of his shield. But Julian's strength was not equal to his spirit, and he was weak from loss of blood. So he lay still, and when he was told in answer to his question that the place where he fell was called Phrygia he abandoned all hope of recovery, for he had been told that he was destined to die there.

After the emperor had been taken back to camp his troops in a frenzy of rage and grief flew upon the enemy with incredible eagerness to wreak their revenge, clashing their spears against their shields and resolved to die if that were their lot. Their eyes were blinded by dust, which rose high in the air, and their energy was impaired by the growing heat, yet they rushed recklessly on the enemy's swords, released, as it were, from discipline by the loss of their leader. On the other side the Persians, plucking up heart, shot arrows in such dense clouds as to hide them from the sight of their opponents, and the elephants, who came on slowly in front of them, struck terror into man and beast by their immense size and the plumes crowning their awful heads. The din, compounded of the clash of men-at-arms, the groans of the fallen, the snorting of horses, and the clang of weapons, carried to a distance, till at last, when both sides had had their fill of slaughter, the exhausted combatants parted after night had fallen. Fifty Persian grandees and satraps fell, besides a great number of the rank and file; among them were the leading generals Merena and Nohodares. Early writers may marvel in high-sounding terms at the twenty battles fought by Marcellus in divers places; they may add Sicinius Dentatus, who won a host of military crowns; beside these they may extol Sergius, who is said to have been wounded twenty-three times in various battles, and whose

latest descendant Catiline tarnished this glorious record with an indelible stain. But our joy in our success was marred by sorrow. While this
fight went on after the removal of the emperor, the right wing of our
army succumbed to exhaustion, and Anatolius, the master of the offices,
was killed. The prefect Salutius was saved from imminent destruction
by the help of his aide-de-camp and came off safe, though his assessor
Phosphorius, who happened to be with him, was lost. *A number of
court officials* and soldiers managed to make a hazardous escape to the
safety of a neighbouring fort, and were able to rejoin the army two days
later.

Meanwhile Julian, lying in his tent, addressed the sad and dejected
company around him. 'My friends, the time has come – and there could
not be a better – for me to depart this life. Nature is calling in my debt,
and like an honest debtor I shall repay it gladly, not, as some might
expect, in affliction and sorrow, because I share the common conviction
of philosophers that the soul's bliss is of a higher order than the body's,
and believe that when the better is separated from the worse one should
rejoice rather than grieve. I bear in mind also that in some instances
the gods themselves have bestowed death as the supreme reward on
certain men of outstanding merit. Besides, I am quite sure that the duty
assigned to me is not to succumb to difficulties or to humiliate or abase
myself, for I have learnt from experience that afflictions triumph over
the unmanly but give way before the resolute. I do not regret what I
have done, nor am I troubled by the consciousness of any serious
wrongdoing, either when I was relegated to an obscure corner or since
I have enjoyed imperial power. *This* came to me as a gift from the gods
to whom I am akin, and I have kept it, to the best of my belief, free
from stain, showing moderation in the conduct of civil matters, and
waging war, whether offensive or defensive, only after mature deliberation. But well-conceived plans are not always attended by success,
since the ultimate outcome of any enterprise is in the hands of the
powers on high. Believing that the aim of a just ruler should be the
welfare and safety of his subjects, I have always, as you know, been
inclined to peaceful courses and have banished from my actions all lack
of restraint, which corrupts conduct as well as character. I depart gladly,
knowing that whenever, in obedience to the imperative commands of
my parent, the state, I have deliberately exposed myself to danger, I
have stood my ground unshaken, having trained myself to trample
underfoot the storms of chance. And I am not ashamed to admit that I

learned long ago from a prophecy in which I put faith that I should fall in battle. I give thanks to the everlasting god that I am not dying through secret conspiracy or from a painful and lingering disease or as a condemned criminal, but have been found worthy to take so honourable a departure from the world in the midst of a successful and glorious career. Fairly considered, the man who seeks to escape death when his hour is come is as base a coward as the man who seeks it when it is his duty to avoid it. My strength is failing, and these words must suffice. I deliberately refrain from speaking of the choice of my successor. I might either pass over a worthy candidate from inadvertence, or by naming one whom I think suitable expose him to extreme danger if another is perhaps preferred. I will only, as a dutiful child of the state, express the hope that a good ruler may be found to succeed me.'

After speaking to this effect in a calm tone he asked for Anatolius, the master of the offices, intending to express his last wishes for the distribution of his personal possessions among his closest friends. The prefect Salutius told him that Anatolius was happy. Julian understood from this that he had fallen, and grieved bitterly for the fate of his friend, though he had shown such unconcern for his own. Meanwhile everybody present was in tears, and Julian rebuked them with all his usual dignity, saying that it was beneath them to mourn for a prince who was restored to heaven and numbered with the stars. This kept them silent, while Julian engaged in a deep discussion with the philosophers Maximus and Priscus on the sublime nature of the soul. Suddenly the wound in his side gaped wide, and swelling in the veins obstructed his breath. He asked for and drank some cold water, and then at dead of night expired peacefully. He was in his thirty-second year. He was born at Constantinople and was left an orphan in childhood by the death of his father Constantius (who lost his life with many others in the troubles about the succession which followed the death of his brother Constantine) and of his mother Basilina, who came from an old and noble family.

4. Character of Julian.

Julian must be reckoned a man of heroic stature, conspicuous for his glorious deeds and his innate majesty. Philosophers tell us that there are four cardinal virtues: self-control, wisdom, justice, and courage; and, in addition to these, certain practical gifts: military skill, dignity, prosperity, and generosity. All these Julian cultivated both singly and as a whole with the utmost care.

To begin with, he was so spectacularly and incorruptibly chaste that after the loss of his wife he never tasted the pleasures of sex, but kept in mind what we read in Plato about the tragedian Sophocles. When Sophocles was asked in extreme old age whether he still had intercourse with women he answered 'No', and added that he was glad to have escaped from slavery to so mad and cruel a tyrant as love. To strengthen this resolve Julian was in the habit of repeating a saying of the lyric poet Bacchylides, one of his favourite authors, to the effect that chastity adds lustre to a life of high ideals just as a good painter enhances the beauty of a face. In his mature manhood he avoided this weakness so rigidly that even his closest attendants never so much as suspected their master, as such people often do, of the slightest indulgence in lust.

This kind of self-control was strengthened in him by his sparing use of food and sleep, a habit to which he adhered obstinately both at home and in the field. In time of peace the frugality of his regimen and of his table excited the wonder of good judges; he seemed on the point of re-assuming the dress of a philosopher. On his various campaigns he was to be seen partaking of poor and scanty fare, which he often ate standing, like a common soldier. His frame was inured to fatigue, and when he had refreshed himself with a short allowance of sleep he would, on waking, personally superintend the relief of sentries and pickets, and after this important task betake himself to his studies. And if the lamps by which he worked at night could have spoken they would without doubt have testified to the difference between him and some other emperors, since they knew that he refrained from indulging even in such pleasures as human nature requires.

Evidence of his wisdom is abundant and a few examples will suffice. He was highly skilled in the arts of both war and peace. He set great store by citizenly behaviour, and made only such claims for himself as he thought necessary to preserve a mean between abjectness and insolence. In the qualities that make a man he was older than his years. He showed keen interest in all legal inquiries, and was sometimes an inflexible judge. He was a very strict censor of conduct. He displayed a calm contempt for riches and looked down on all worldly things, maintaining that it was shameful for a wise man to seek to be honoured for his physical endowments when he possessed a soul.

Of his excellence in the administration of justice there is ample proof.

For one thing, he took into account the circumstances of a case and the persons involved, and he could inspire fear without being cruel. Next, he chose to check wrongdoing by making an example of a few, and preferred the threat of the sword to its actual use. Finally, to be brief, it is common knowledge that in dealing with some open enemies who conspired against him he was so merciful that he allowed his native mildness to mitigate the severity of the law's demands.

His courage is shown by the number of his battles and his conduct in war, as well as by his endurance of extremes of cold and heat. In contrast to the physical efforts required of the common soldier the work of a commander is mental, but Julian on one occasion boldly met and dispatched a savage foe, and often stemmed the retreat of our men single-handed by putting himself in their path. In his destructive campaigns against fierce German kings and on the burning sands of Persia, he would give his men confidence by fighting in the front rank.

His skill in military matters can be illustrated by many well-known facts, such as his sieges of towns and strongholds, his ability to draw up a complex line of battle even at moments of crisis, his cautious choice of safe places for a camp, and his well-thought-out arrangements for frontier-posts and pickets in the open fields.

His authority was so well established, and the fear in which he was held by his men so tempered by the affection inspired by his sharing their hardships and dangers, that he could punish slackness even in the midst of a fierce engagement. Moreover, while he was still Caesar, as I related a long way back, he kept his hold on his troops though they were without pay and at grips with savage tribes, and once, when he was faced by a mutiny, he threatened that he would retire into private life if they did not return to their duty. Lastly, this single example will serve as well as many. Simply by addressing them he persuaded his Gallic troops, accustomed to the frosts of their native Rhine, to follow him on a long march over strange countries, and brought them through the torrid plains of Assyria to the very borders of Media.

His success was so remarkable that for a long time he seemed to ride, as it were, on the shoulders of Fortune, by whose favour and guidance he overcame enormous difficulties in his victorious career. And after he had left the West all its peoples remained in perfect peace as long as he was on earth, as if Mercury's magic wand had put the world to rest.

Of his generosity there are countless well-authenticated instances. He imposed very light tribute, remitted the accession money, cancelled long-standing accumulations of debt, made a fair settlement of disputes between the treasury and individuals, and restored their revenues and lands to certain cities, with the exception of property lawfully sold by previous officials. Finally, there is the fact that he was never anxious to increase his wealth, because he thought that it was in better keeping with its present owners. He was often heard to repeat an anecdote of Alexander the Great, who, on being asked where he kept his treasure, generously answered: 'In the hands of my friends.'

Having listed his good qualities to the best of my knowledge, let me turn to an account of his faults, though these have already been dealt with piecemeal as occasion arose. His temperament was impulsive, but he compensated for this by the excellent habit of allowing himself to be corrected when he went wrong. He was a copious talker and very seldom silent. He was too much given to divination, and seemed in this respect to rival the emperor Hadrian. He was superstitious rather than genuinely observant of the rites of religion, and he sacrificed innumerable victims regardless of expense; it was reckoned that if he had returned from Parthia there would have been a shortage of cattle. In this he resembled the great Caesar Marcus, who, we are told, was the subject of the following epigram:

> Greetings to Marcus from the oxen white.
> We're done for if you win another fight.

He liked the popular applause of the mob, and was excessively eager to be praised for the most trivial reasons, and his desire for popularity often led him to converse with unworthy persons.

But in spite of all this his claim that during his reign the ancient goddess of Justice came down again to earth might be regarded as sound (according to Aratus she had fled to heaven in disgust at men's sins), had he not sometimes acted arbitrarily and in an uncharacteristic way. The laws which he enacted were not oppressive, and what they enjoined or prohibited was precisely stated, but there were a few exceptions, among them the harsh decree forbidding Christians to teach rhetoric or grammar unless they went over to the worship of the pagan gods. An equally intolerable grievance was that he allowed some persons to be wrongfully conscripted into town councils, though they were either foreigners or entirely exempt by privilege or birth from liability to serve on such bodies.

His personal appearance and physique were as follows. He was of middle height, his hair was smooth as if it had been combed, and he wore a bristly beard trimmed to a point. He had fine, flashing eyes, the sign of a lively intelligence, well-marked eyebrows, a straight nose, and a rather large mouth with a pendulous lower lip. His neck was thick and somewhat bent, his shoulders large and broad. From head to foot he was perfectly built, which made him strong and a good runner.

His critics allege that it was he who stirred up war afresh to the destruction of the common weal, but I would have them know that the plain truth is that it was Constantine, not Julian, who kindled the Parthian conflagration, because his greed led him to accept the lies of Metrodorus, of which I gave a full account earlier. It was this that caused the scandalous loss of our armies, the capture of some of our units, the destruction of cities, the seizure or demolition of fortresses, and the exhaustion of our provinces by the burdens imposed on them, when the Persians, putting their threats into effect, aimed at extending their dominion as far as Bithynia and the shores of the Propontis. In Gaul the insolence of the barbarians had grown apace. The Germans, having overrun our territory, were on the point of forcing the Alps and devastating Italy, and the inhabitants, after unspeakable sufferings, were reduced to tearful panic; the past was full of bitter memories, and they could look forward only to an even gloomier future. Our hero, who was sent to the West as a Caesar only in name, retrieved this situation with almost miraculous rapidity, driving kings before him like the lowest slaves. With the same passionate eagerness to put things right in the East he attacked the Persians, from whom he would have won a triumph and an addition to his titles, if his designs and glorious deeds had been seconded by the favour of Heaven. We know that some people are so rash that they fly in the face of experience, and renew war after being defeated or go to sea again after shipwreck, returning to the difficulties to which they have so often succumbed. And yet there are those who blame an emperor who, after a career of unbroken victory, sought an opportunity to repeat his success.

5. Accession of Jovian.

After this there was no room for mourning or tears. Such steps as the situation and the time allowed were taken for the preservation of Julian's body, so that it might be buried in the place which he had once appointed himself, and at dawn of the next day, which was 27 June, while we were surrounded on all sides by the enemy, the generals called together the commanders of the legions and cavalry regiments to confer about the choice of an emperor. This caused violent disagreement. Arintheus and Victor and the survivors of Constantius' household looked for a suitable successor in their own party, whereas Nevitta and Dagalaif and the leaders of the Gauls wanted one of their comrades-in-arms. After much discussion which changed no one's opinion the choice fell unanimously on Salutius, but he pleaded illness and old age. Seeing that his resolution could not be shaken a soldier of high rank said to them: 'What would you be doing if the emperor had entrusted you with the conduct of the war in his absence, as has often happened? Would you not put everything else aside and save the army from the disaster which hangs over it? Do the same now, and if we see Mesopotamia again the united votes of both armies will then proclaim a lawful emperor.'

During this delay, which was not long for a matter of such importance, and before the various opinions had been weighed, the hasty action of a few men, which is often decisive in a crisis, resulted in the election of Jovian. He was the senior staff-officer and a passable candidate on account of his father's services, being the son of Varronian, a count of great reputation, who had recently retired from the army into private life. Hurriedly dressed in the imperial robes, Jovian suddenly emerged from his tent, and made a rapid tour round the army as it was getting ready to march. The column was four miles long, and those in the van, hearing shouts of 'Jovian Augustus!', took them up more loudly, misled by the similarity of names, which were only one letter different, into thinking that Julian had recovered and was being received with the usual applause. But when the bent and lanky figure of the new emperor came into sight they guessed what had happened, and all burst into tears of grief.

Any scrupulous lover of legality who finds fault with the rashness of a step taken when the army was at its last gasp might with greater justice blame a ship's company which has lost its pilot in a storm, and in the common peril entrusts the helm to a member of the crew chosen at random.

These events were decreed by fortune in what one may call a moment of blindness. But the standard-bearer of the Joviani, once under the command of Varronian, had been on bad terms with the new emperor while he was still a private citizen because he had mischievously slandered Jovian's father. Now that his enemy had risen above the common level he feared for his life and deserted to the Persians. He told Sapor, who was not far away and gave him an audience, that the foe he feared was dead and that Jovian, till then a staff-officer, a passive and spineless character, had been proclaimed a shadow emperor by an unruly throng of camp-followers. The king, *who had hardly dared to hope for such news*, was overjoyed by this unexpected stroke of luck. He reinforced the troops opposed to us with a large number of royal cavalry, and decided to hasten his advance and fall upon the rear of our army.

6. *Rearguard actions during the Roman retreat.*

While these steps were being taken on both sides, victims were sacrificed on behalf of Jovian and their entrails inspected. On the strength of this it was announced that ruin would ensue if he persisted in his plan of staying within the rampart, but that if he marched out he would prevail. Just as we were beginning to move the Persians attacked with elephants in front. At first their smell and *the horror of their approach* threw horses and men into confusion, but the Joviani and Herculiani killed a few of the brutes and put up a stout resistance against the mail-clad horse. Then the legions Jovii and Victores came to the aid of their distressed comrades and killed two elephants and a considerable number of the enemy. On our left wing three gallant officers fell, Julian, Macrobius, and Maximus, tribunes of the best legions in our army. They were buried as well as the difficulties of the moment allowed, and we were pressing on towards a fortress called Sumere when towards nightfall we recognized the corpse of Anatolius lying in the road and hastily committed it to the earth. Here too we were rejoined by sixty soldiers and some court officials who, as I said earlier, had taken refuge in a deserted fort.

Next day the best place we were able to choose for our camp was a valley protected by natural walls, except for one broad exit. We fortified our position with a palisade of stakes with points as sharp as swords. Seeing us there, the enemy assailed us from the woods above with missiles of various kinds and a storm of abuse, calling us traitors who had murdered an admirable prince. They too had heard from deserters of a vague rumour going about that Julian had been killed by a Roman weapon. Finally some troops of horse succeeded in breaking through the principal gate of the camp and got near the emperor's very tent, but they were firmly repulsed with severe losses in killed and wounded.

The next night we set out again and took possession of a place called Charcha. Here we were safe because the bank of the river had been artificially raised by dykes as a precaution against Saracen raids into Assyria, and no one harassed our lines as they had previously. From here on 1 July we marched some four miles to the town of Dura. Our beasts were worn out, and their riders were consequently marching on foot in the extreme rear, when they were surrounded by a throng of Saracens and would have perished instantly if some squadrons of light horse had not come to their rescue. The reason for the hostility of the Saracens was that Julian had put a stop to their receiving payments and numerous gifts as in the past, and had answered their complaints simply by saying that a warlike and watchful emperor possessed only steel, not gold. The persistence of the Persians made us spend four days at Dura. When we tried to move they followed us, and forced us to withdraw by their incessant charges. If we halted to fight they gave way gradually, and inflicted on us long and agonizing delays. When men fear the worst any fiction gains credit, and a rumour spread that we were not far from our own frontier. This caused wild excitement among the troops, who demanded to be allowed to cross the Tigris. The emperor and his generals tried to restrain them. He pointed out that they were now in the dog-days, when the river was in flood, and begged them not to trust themselves to its dangerous eddies, adding that many of them could not swim and that parties of the enemy were in possession of both banks of the swollen river. Finding, however, that they were deaf to his repeated warnings and that the worst was to be expected from the loud clamour of the soldiers, he at last reluctantly consented that a mixed party of Gauls and northern barbarians should take to the water first. If they were swept away by the force of the stream the obstinacy of the rest would be broken, and if they got over in safety the crossing could be attempted with more confidence. Men were picked for this business who had been used from early boyhood in their own country to cross even the largest rivers. When nightfall made it possible to carry out the plan unseen, they shot off in a body like men at the start of a race and seized the opposite bank more quickly than one would have thought possible. A number of Persians had been posted to guard various spots, but they were peacefully asleep, believing that there was no danger. Our men trampled on them and cut them to pieces, and then raised their hands and waved their cloaks to show that their attempt had succeeded. When this was seen from our bank the whole army was on fire to cross, and it was restrained only by a promise by the pioneers to construct bridges with the inflated skins of dead animals.

7. A shameful peace concluded by Jovian.

While these fruitless efforts were being made, king Sapor, both before and after his arrival, was kept informed by reliable reports from scouts and deserters of the brave exploits of our troops, who had inflicted humiliating losses on his forces, with greater slaughter of elephants than he had ever known in his reign. He was told too that the Roman army, hardened by continual exertion, was set upon avenging its illustrious chief rather than upon self-preservation, and intended to extricate itself from its pressing difficulties by either complete victory or a glorious death. This caused him much anxious thought. He knew that it would be a simple matter to mobilize the troops dispersed in great numbers throughout the Roman provinces, and that his own people were in a state of abject terror owing to the great losses among the rank and file, and he also learned that we had left in Mesopotamia an army not much smaller than that which faced him. What particularly disturbed him, however, was that 500 of our men had crossed the swollen river in a body, massacred his guards, and encouraged the rest of their comrades to make a similar attempt.

Meanwhile, however, the force of the stream made it impossible to construct bridges, and our men spent two miserable days. They had consumed everything that could serve for food, and hunger and rage together inspired a mad desire to fall by the sword rather than perish by starvation, the most ignominious of all deaths. But the eternal providence of God was on our side, and the Persians belied our expectations by making the first overture. They sent the Surena and another grandee to negotiate terms of peace, because they too were in a state of despondency. The Romans had the upper hand in almost all the fighting, and this shook the Persians ever more severely as the days went by. Nevertheless, the proposals they brought were intricate and difficult to accept. They took the line that their merciful king would allow the remnants of our army to return home on grounds of humanity if the emperor and his principal officers complied with his demands. We responded by sending Arintheus and the prefect Salutius, and while detailed discussion went on about the final settlement we passed four days in agonizing starvation and despair worse than death. If, before sending his representatives, the emperor had employed this period to effect a gradual withdrawal from enemy territory he could undoubtedly have reached the refuge of Corduene, a fertile region which was in our hands and only a hundred miles from the scene of these events.

The king stuck obstinately to his demands for what he called his own possessions, the territory, that is, seized long before by Maximian. In the course of the negotiation it emerged that he required as our ransom five regions on the far side of the Tigris, Arzanene, Moxoene, and Zabdicene together with Rehimene and Corduene, and fifteen forts, as well as Nisibis and Singara and the Moors' Fort, a strongpoint of critical importance. It would have been better to fight ten times over rather than surrender any of these. But the faint-hearted emperor was under pressure from a clique of flatterers, who planted in his mind the dreaded name of Procopius, and declared that if, on hearing the news of Julian's death, Procopius returned with the forces under his command intact he could easily engineer a revolution that would meet with no resistance. The constant repetition of this fatal suggestion excited the emperor's fears. He accepted all the king's demands without hesitation, obtaining, though only with difficulty, the concession that Nisibis and Singara should be transferred to the Persians without their inhabitants, and that the Roman garrisons in the forts to be surrendered should be allowed to return to our territory. A further disastrous and shameful condition was that once the treaty was signed we should never give any help against the Persians to our consistently faithful friend Arsaces. This had a double object, first, to punish the man who had laid Chiliocomum waste on the emperor's orders, and second, to leave open the possibility of subsequently invading Armenia at will. The ultimate consequence was that Arsaces was taken prisoner, and that in the quarrels and confusion that ensued Artaxata with a great tract of Armenia bordering on Media was seized by the Parthians.

On the conclusion of this shameful treaty men of distinction were exchanged as hostages to be a surety against any breach of the conditions during the armistice. *Ours were Nevitta, Victor, and two tribunes* of famous units; theirs were Bineses, one of their grandees, and three other satraps of note.

So, after peace had been made for thirty years and ratified by solemn oaths, we returned by another route, avoiding the rough and broken ground by the river and suffering from lack of food and drink.

8. Return to Mesopotamia.

This peace, which was ostensibly granted on grounds of humanity, resulted in loss of life on a large scale. Many of our men, who were at their last gasp from starvation and had therefore gone ahead unnoticed, were either drowned in the depths of the river because they could not swim, or else, if they succeeded in reaching the opposite bank, were seized by the Saracens or Persians (who, as I said just now, had been routed by the Germans), and were either slaughtered like cattle or transported to a distance to be sold as slaves. But, when the trumpets sounded to give the official order to cross, the eagerness with which men embraced danger was prodigious; everyone strove to get ahead of the rest in his haste to escape from a frightful situation. Some embarked on hastily constructed rafts, keeping hold of their animals, which swam beside them; others, by using bladders and various other expedients under the pressure of necessity, took an oblique course across the opposing current. The emperor himself with a small suite crossed in the little craft which I said were left intact when the fleet was burnt, and ordered these boats to go backwards and forwards till we were all ferried over. At last we all reached the further bank, except those who were drowned, and by the favour of heaven made a hair's-breadth escape.

While we were still oppressed by fear of trouble to come we learned from our scouts that the Persians were building a bridge out of our sight, supposing, now that the storm of war had been lulled by a firm treaty of peace, that we should march more carelessly and that they would be able to fall upon our sick and our exhausted beasts. Finding, however, that they had been discovered they desisted from their wicked design. Relieved of this fresh anxiety we arrived by forced marches in the neighbourhood of Hatra, an old town lying in the wilderness and long since abandoned. On various occasions the warrior emperors Trajan and Severus had attacked it and themselves almost perished with their armies; I have described these incidents in my account of their reigns. We learned that for a distance of seventy miles over the arid plain we should find no water that was not salt and stinking, and nothing to eat but southernwood, wormwood, dragonwort, and other bitter herbs. All the receptacles we had with us were filled with fresh water, and food of a sort, however unwholesome, was provided by slaughtering camels and baggage-animals. After we had marched for six days and could no longer find even grass, the last resource of the destitute, Cassian, the commander in Mesopotamia, who had been sent on some time before for this purpose with the tribune Mauricius, met us at the Persian fortress of Ur and brought us food from the stores which the army left with Procopius and Sebastian had saved by strict rationing.

From this place a notary also called Procopius and the military tribune Memoridus were sent to the regions of Illyricum and Gaul to announce the death of Julian and the elevation of Jovian to the imperial throne. The emperor also instructed them to give his father-in-law Lucillian, who had gone into retirement after laying down his command and was then living at Sirmium, a commission appointing him master of horse and foot, and to urge him to hurry to Milan to consolidate the position there and to oppose any attempt at revolution which it was feared might be made. The official document was accompanied by a private letter telling Lucillian to take with him certain people of tried energy and loyalty, whose help he could use as circumstances required. A prudent step was to send Malarich, who was then in Italy on business of his own, a commission to succeed Jovinus, the commander-in-chief in Gaul. This had two advantages. It removed from the scene a general whose high standing made him suspect, and the promotion of a man with humbler prospects would bind him to use all his energies to strengthen the still uncertain position of his patron. The men who were sent on these missions were instructed to represent what had happened in the best possible light and to spread an agreed report, wherever they went, that the Parthian campaign had ended in success. They were to travel by night as well as day and communicate the new emperor's message to the provincial governors and commanders. After secretly sounding the opinions of all they were to hurry back with their answers, so that mature and careful plans for strengthening the emperor's power might be based on knowledge of what was happening in distant regions.

The errand of these messengers was forestalled by rumour, the quickest transmitter of disastrous news. It flew through provinces and people and struck the inhabitants of Nisibis in particular with bitter grief. They learned that their city had been surrendered to Sapor, whose wrath and enmity they feared, recalling what losses he had suffered in his repeated attempts to take it by storm. It was generally held that the eastern world could have fallen into the hands of Persia but for the resistance of this well-placed and strongly fortified town. The wretched inhabitants, in spite of their fears for the future, were yet sustained by one slight hope; the emperor, either spontaneously or in response to their entreaties, would surely keep in its present state the city which was the strongest bulwark of the East.

While different reports of what had happened were being disseminated, the army, having exhausted the scanty supplies whose arrival I have mentioned, would have been reduced to the necessity of feeding on human flesh had not the meat of the slaughtered animals lasted a little longer. But famine caused most of our arms and packs to be thrown away. The hunger which consumed us was so fearful that if, as rarely happened, a single peck of meal was found it commanded a price of ten gold pieces, and that was thought a bargain.

Setting out from Ur we reached Thilsaphata, where we were met, as duty required, by Sebastian and Procopius with the tribunes and officers of the troops entrusted to them for the defence of Mesopotamia. They were cordially received and went with us. Finally, after forced marches, the welcome sight of Nisibis met our eyes. The emperor formed a standing camp outside the city and obstinately resisted the earnest entreaties of a huge throng that he would enter and occupy the palace like his predecessors. It put him to the blush that an impregnable city should be handed over to an angry foe while he was within its walls. Here in the gloom of evening Jovian the chief notary, the man who, as I related, had been one of those who sprang out of the mine at the siege of Maozamalcha, was seized while he was at dinner, taken to a lonely place, thrown headlong into a dry well, and pelted to death with stones. The reason was that after Julian's death a few people had spoken of him as a suitable candidate for the throne, and when Jovian was elected he did not behave discreetly; he was heard muttering about the matter and from time to time he invited some of the officers to his table.

9. Surrender of Nisibis, Singara, and five regions.

Next day Bineses, a Persian whose high standing I have mentioned, hastened to carry out the king's orders and urgently demanded the implementation of our promises. With the permission of the Roman emperor he entered the city and planted the standard of his nation on the citadel, thus confirming the lamentable news that the inhabitants must leave their native place. At this order for a sudden and complete evacuation they begged with outstretched arms and tears in their eyes that they should not be compelled to go, declaring that they were strong enough to defend their homes by themselves without support from the state in provisions and men, and that they were sure that justice would come to their help in their fight for their birthplace, as so often in the past. But these entreaties by council and people might have been addressed to the winds; the emperor refused to incur the guilt of perjury. This at least was his pretext, though in fact what he feared was something quite different. Then Sabinus, who stood high among his fellow-citizens on account of his wealth and birth, burst into a flood of words. Constantius, he said, after several defeats by the Persians in the course of a cruel war had finally been driven to take refuge with a few others in the defenceless fort of Hibita, where he lived on a crust of bread begged from an old peasant woman. Yet to his last day he never surrendered anything, whereas Jovian was beginning his reign by abandoning the barrier protecting his provinces, behind which they had remained unharmed from the earliest times. But it was no good; the emperor persisted in sheltering behind the sanctity of his oath. For some time he refused the crown that was offered him, and at last accepted it only under pressure. This caused an advocate called Silvanus to exclaim boldly: 'May your majesty be crowned thus in the cities that remain.' This angered the emperor, and in spite of their protestations he ordered all the inhabitants to leave the town within three days.

So the word was given to apply compulsion and to threaten all those who delayed with death. The city was filled with lamentation and grief; nothing was to be heard but one universal wail. Married women tore their hair at the prospect of being driven into exile from the homes in which they had been born and brought up; mothers who had lost their children or been widowed were forced away from the tombs of those they loved; the weeping throng embraced the doorposts and thresholds of their homes in floods of tears. The different roads were crowded with refugees dispersing as best they could. In their haste many people smuggled away such of their goods as they thought they could carry; the rest of their property, however extensive and valuable, they disregarded, being compelled to abandon it for lack of transport.

At this point we may well reproach the goddess who controls the fortunes of the Roman world. At a time when storms were battering the state she struck the helm from the hands of an experienced captain, and entrusted it to a raw young man who had never in his life won distinction in business of this kind, and who therefore cannot fairly be either blamed or praised. But what cut patriots to the very heart was that fear of a rival, and the thought that ambitious designs had often had their beginnings in Gaul or Illyricum, led him in his eagerness to outstrip the news of his coming to commit an act unworthy of an emperor, and on the pretext of avoiding the guilt of perjury to betray Nisibis, which from the time of king Mithridates had struggled with all its might to prevent the East falling into the hands of the Persians. Nowhere, I believe, in the history of the city from its foundation can we find an instance of territory being surrendered to an enemy by emperor or consul. On the contrary it was only an extension of our realm, not even the recovery of anything lost, that earned the glory of a triumph. That is why triumphal honours were refused to Publius Scipio, who recovered Spain, to Fulvius, who overcame Capua after a long struggle, and to Opimius, who after a war of shifting fortunes compelled our deadly enemies, the people of Fregellae, to surrender. History also tells us that, when in extreme necessity a shameful treaty was concluded and both sides had sworn to it in set terms, it was at once invalidated by a renewal of hostilities. This happened in early days when our legions were made to pass under the yoke at the Caudine Forks in Samnium, and also when Albinus had contrived an infamous peace in Numidia. A third instance occurred when Mancinus, the author of a treaty made in disgraceful haste, was repudiated and given up to the people of Numantia.

So, after the expulsion of the citizens and the surrender of the city, the tribune Constantius was sent to hand over the fortresses and the regions about them to Persian grandees. At the same time Procopius was dispatched with Julian's remains to be buried in accordance with his own directions in the suburb of Tarsus. Procopius set out on his errand, and as soon as the funeral was over disappeared. Every effort was made to trace him, but in vain, until long afterwards he suddenly appeared at Constantinople, dressed in the purple.

10. Death of Jovian on his journey westward.

After these events and a hurried march we reached Antioch. There for days on end there was a series of dreadful portents which seemed to indicate the anger of God, and the interpreters of prodigies declared that their outcome would be disastrous. The statue of the Caesar Maximian in the vestibule of the palace lost the bronze celestial sphere which it carried, the beams in the council hall creaked horribly, and comets were seen in broad daylight.

A short digression on comets is omitted.

The emperor stayed but a short time at Antioch. He was bowed down by the weight of his anxieties and consumed by an extraordinary eagerness to leave the place. So he set out in mid-winter, in spite of the many unfavourable omens I have mentioned. Sparing neither beasts nor men he entered Tarsus, the famous city of Cilicia whose foundation I have already described. Here too he was in a fever to depart, but he gave orders for the embellishment of Julian's tomb, which lay on the outskirts of the city on the road which leads to the passes over Mount Taurus. If proper consideration had then been given to the matter Julian's ashes should not lie within sight of the Cydnus, beautiful and limpid though it is. To perpetuate the memory of his exploits they should have been laid where they might be lapped by the Tiber, which intersects the Eternal City and skirts the monuments of earlier deified emperors.

After leaving Tarsus Jovian came by forced marches to Tyana, a town in Cappadocia, where the notary Procopius and the tribune Memoridus met him on their return. They gave him an account of what had happened in proper order, beginning at the point when Lucillian entered Milan. Here Lucillian heard that Malarich had refused the command, so he set off at full speed for Reims with the tribunes Seniauchus and Valentinian, whom he had taken with him. Then, however, he went off the rails, to use a slang expression, and behaved as if profound peace prevailed. Although the situation was very uncertain he devoted himself most unseasonably to examining the accounts of a former financial officer, who knowing that he was guilty of fraud, fled to the army with a story that Julian was still alive and that a nobody had attempted a revolution. These falsehoods provoked a storm of excitement among the troops, and Lucillian and Seniauchus were killed. Valentinian, who soon after became emperor, did not know where to turn, but was removed to a place of safety by his friend Primitivus. These gloomy tidings were followed by another item of a cheering kind to the effect that a number of what soldiers call 'brass hats' were on their way from Jovinus to announce that the army in Gaul cordially welcomed Jovian as emperor.

When this was known Valentinian, who had returned with these people, was given command of the second division of the Scutarii, and Vitalian, who served in the Eruli and who was later raised to the rank of count and came to grief in Illyricum, was promoted to the guards. Arintheus was at once sent to Gaul with a letter to Jovinus urging him to act with resolution and maintain his position. He was also ordered to punish the originator of the trouble, and to arrest the ringleaders and send them to the court. When these steps had been taken to meet the situation the officers from Gaul were seen by the emperor at Aspuna, a small town in Galatia. The news they brought was warmly welcomed in a formal audience, and they were rewarded and told to return to their posts.

When he reached Ankara the emperor had such preparations made for the ceremony as circumstances permitted, and assumed the consulship (*A.D. 364*), taking as his colleague his son Varronian, who was still a small child. Varronian cried and struggled obstinately to escape being carried in the curule chair in accordance with tradition, and this was an omen of what happened soon afterwards.

From this point fate drove Jovian rapidly on to meet his appointed doom. After arriving at Dadastana, on the border between Bithynia and Galatia, he was found dead in his bed. There are a number of conflicting accounts of the circumstances of his death. It was said that he was overcome by the noxious smell of fresh plaster in his bedroom, or that the fumes of a huge fire brought on cerebral congestion, or that he died of indigestion after eating to excess. He died in his thirty-third year. His death was like that of Scipio Aemilianus, and I have not yet heard of a serious investigation into either case.

He had a dignified gait and a cheerful expression. His eyes were grey, and he was enormously tall, so tall that for some time no royal robe could be found to fit him. He modelled himself upon Constantius, and sometimes continued with serious business till after mid-day, and he was in the habit of jesting in public with his suite. He was an adherent of the Christian faith and took some steps to exalt it. He was no more than moderately well educated, but he was of a kindly disposition, and careful in his choice of officials, as was clear from the few appointments that he made. But he was greedy and given to wine and women, faults which regard for the dignity of his position might have led him to correct.

It was said that his father Varronian had previous intimation of what would happen from a dream, which he confided to two close friends, adding that he himself would also wear the consular robe. Part of his prophecy came true, but he was disappointed of the rest. He heard of his son's elevation, but death carried him off before he saw him again. As for what the old man was told in his dream about the highest magistracy falling to one of his name, it was Varronian, his grandson, still a small child, who was proclaimed consul with his father Jovian, as I have related.

BOOK 26

1. Valentinian chosen emperor (A.D. 364).

Having spared no pains in relating the course of events up to the beginning of the present epoch I had thought it best to steer clear of more familiar matters, partly to escape the dangers which often attend on truth, and partly to avoid carping criticism of my work by those who feel injured by the omission of insignificant detail, such things, for example, as the emperor's table-talk or the reason for the public punishment of soldiers. Such folk also complain if in a wide-ranging geographical description some small strongholds are not mentioned, or if one does not give the names of all who attended the inauguration of the urban prefect, or passes over a number of similar details which are beneath the dignity of history. The task of history is to deal with prominent events, not to delve into trivial minutiae, which it is as hopeless to try to investigate as to count the small indivisible bodies we Greeks call atoms which fly through empty space. Fears of this kind led some older writers not to publish in their lifetime eloquent accounts they had composed of various events within their knowledge. For this we have the unimpeachable testimony of Cicero in a letter to Cornelius Nepos. Now, however, I will proceed with the rest of my story, treating the ignorance of the vulgar with the contempt it deserves.

This dreadful period of uncertainty came to a sad end with the death of these emperors in so brief a space. Jovian's body was embalmed and sent to Constantinople to be interred with the bodies of his predecessors, and the army marched to Nicaea, the metropolis of Bithynia. Here the leading civil and military officials, some of whom entertained vain hopes for themselves, were constrained by their responsibility for the general good to look for a ruler of tried ability and dignity.

The name of Equitius, tribune of the first division of Scutarii, was faintly hinted at by a small party, but failed to obtain the approval of the more influential, who thought him too much of a rough diamond.

Their fickle thoughts then turned towards Januarius, the chief commissary in Illyricum and a relation of Jovian. But he too was rejected on the ground that he was too far away. Finally, by divine inspiration, Valentinian was unanimously chosen as a man who possessed the necessary qualifications. He commanded the second division of the Scutarii, and had been left behind at Ankara to follow later in accordance with orders. It was agreed nem. con. that his election would best serve the interests of the state, and messengers were sent to hasten his arrival. For ten days the empire was without a ruler, a state of affairs which the soothsayer Marcus announced at Rome after inspecting the entrails of a sacrifice.

In the interval Equitius took steps to ensure that no attempt should be made to overturn this decision, and that the favour of the troops, which is always uncertain, should not be diverted to the choice of someone on the spot. He was supported by Leo, who was still serving as military treasurer under Dagalaif the master of cavalry, and was later to be a disastrous master of the offices. These two did everything in their power to uphold the decision of the whole army, being themselves Pannonians and partisans of the emperor-designate.

When Valentinian arrived in response to the summons *he delayed* the implementation of his election, either from a presentiment, as was generally thought, or under the influence of repeated dreams. He would not be seen or appear in public next day because it happened to be the intercalary day of February, which he had heard was sometimes unlucky for the Roman state.

A digression on the bissextile (or leap) year is omitted.

2. Valentinian's accession.

When the day which some think unlucky for the beginning of great enterprises had passed and evening was coming on, everyone readily accepted a proposal by the prefect Salutius that no one who held high office or had been thought to nurse ambitious designs should appear in public next morning on pain of death. After a night passed in chagrin by many who were tormented by empty hopes, the whole army was assembled at dawn. Valentinian appeared on the parade-ground and was allowed to mount the high platform which had been erected. His claims as a man of substance were most cordially received, and he was proclaimed ruler of the empire by a form of popular election. Wearing the imperial robes and a crown, he was hailed as Augustus with all the applause to be expected from men's delight at this new development, and made ready to address the audience in a prepared speech. But as he stretched out his arm to command a hearing, a deep murmur arose. The centuries and maniples began to heckle, and the whole body of cohorts obstinately insisted that a second emperor should at once be nominated. Some thought that a few men had been hired to mount this demonstration in favour of disappointed candidates, but there are strong grounds for rejecting this supposition. The cries which were heard did not come from a hired claque but expressed the unanimous wish of the whole throng, which had learnt from recent experience how precarious is the position of those in high places. It looked as if what began as a murmur among the dissatisfied army would end in violence, and the insolence of the troops, which sometimes breaks out into acts of outrage, excited alarm. But Valentinian, who feared this more than anything, quickly raised his right hand, and ventured with all the vigour of an emperor whose confidence was unshaken to reprimand some of them as obstinate mutineers. Then he delivered his projected speech without further interruption.

'Gallant defenders of our provinces, it is and will always be my pride and boast that I owe to your courage the rule of the Roman world, a position which I neither desired nor sought but for which you have judged me to be the best qualified. While the empire lacked a governor the responsibility was yours. You have discharged it splendidly in the general interest by raising to the summit of power a man who you know by experience has lived from his earliest youth to his present mature age with honour and integrity. Now I must ask you to listen to me quietly while I explain in simple words what I think the welfare of the state requires. I do not doubt nor dispute that there are cogent reasons for the co-option of a colleague with equal status to meet all contingencies. I am only human, and I dread the accumulated responsibilities and the various uncertainties that await me. But above all we must strive for harmony, which brings strength out of weakness, and we shall easily attain it if you will be patient and fair-minded, and allow me the free exercise of my proper power. I shall use my best efforts, and fortune, which attends on wise plans, will, I trust, reward my careful search with a man of steady character. It is a sound maxim, not only in affairs of state, where the risks are greatest and most numerous, but also in private and everyday matters, that a prudent man should not admit a stranger to his friendship till he has tested him, rather than testing him after he has taken him into his confidence. I promise you this with every hope of a happier future. For your part you must maintain your discipline and recruit your spirit and strength while your winter rest gives you the opportunity. You shall receive without delay what is due to you for my nomination as emperor.'

By this speech, which gained force from its unexpected firmness, the emperor won over his whole audience. Even those who shortly before had most clamorously demanded another course adopted his advice and escorted him to the palace, surrounded by eagles and standards and a splendid retinue of various ranks. He was already an object of fear.

3. The urban prefecture of Apronian.

While fate was giving this turn to events in the East, Apronian was in charge of the Eternal City. He was an upright and strict official, and, among all the responsibilities which fall on the urban prefect, made it his prime concern to arrest sorcerers, who at that time were becoming *more numerous*. Those who after trial were found plainly guilty of inflicting harm on others he punished with death after they had revealed their accomplices, his intention being to make an example of a few and to flush out, through fear of a similar fate, any who remained in hiding. He is said to have been particularly active in this matter for the following reason. He had been appointed by Julian while the latter was still in Syria, and on his way to take up his post had lost an eye, an injury which he ascribed to the practice of black magic. His resentment, though justifiable, was exceptionally strong, and led him to inquire into these and other crimes with great energy. Some thought him savage, because on occasion he investigated the gravest offences even while the people were thronging into the amphitheatre for the races. Finally, after several crimes of this sort had been visited with punishment, a charioteer called Hilarinus was convicted on his own confession of having apprenticed his young son to a sorcerer to be taught black arts forbidden by law, so that his father could have help available at home and no one need be the wiser. Hilarinus was condemned to death, but owing to the slackness of the executioner suddenly escaped and took refuge in a Christian chapel, from which he was dragged out and immediately beheaded. But though at this period measures were taken for the prompt suppression of crime of this kind, and none or very few of its practitioners dared to defy the vigour of the authorities, at a later time monstrous wickedness throve on long-continued impunity, and licence went so far that a certain senator, who followed Hilarinus' example and was convicted of having made what amounted to a contract with a teacher of black magic for the instruction of his slave in these abominable mysteries, bought himself off from execution by payment of a large sum, according to common report. And this same man, after escaping in the way described, so far from being ashamed of his wicked life, has taken no pains to wipe out the stain, but behaves as if he were the only innocent man in a vicious society. He rides about the streets on a horse with splendid trappings, and is followed to this day by a train of slaves, claiming the attention of curious eyes by a new sort of distinction. He might in fact be a second Duillius, who, we are told, after the glorious outcome of his sea-fight assumed the privilege of having a flautist play soft music before him as he returned home after dinner.

But under the rule of Apronian there was such a constant abundance of commodities that not the faintest murmur ever arose, as it frequently does at Rome, about any scarcity of provisions.

4. Valens chosen by his brother as co-emperor.

Valentinian, having, as I said, been proclaimed emperor in Bithynia, gave orders to march on the next day but one. Then, summoning his chief officers with the apparent intention of being entirely guided by their advice rather than by his own wishes, he asked whom they thought he should take as his colleague in the empire. All were silent till Dagalaif, then commander of cavalry, made this bold answer: 'Your highness, if you love your kin you have a brother, but if you love the state look carefully for a man to invest with the purple.' Valentinian was ruffled by this reply, but held his peace and dissembled his intentions. After a forced march he entered Nicomedia, and on 1 March appointed his brother Valens supervisor of the stables with the rank of tribune. Then on 28 March, when he had reached Constantinople, after much heart-searching and in the belief that he was unequal to the pressure of urgent business and that there was no time to be lost, he conducted Valens outside the walls and with the approval of the whole army, for no one dared to object, proclaimed him Augustus. He dressed Valens in the imperial robes, placed a diadem on his head, and, sharing the same carriage, took him back to the city as his legitimate partner in power. In fact, however, Valens proved more like an obsequious lieutenant, as the subsequent narrative will reveal.

All this went off without any disturbance, but then both emperors were seized by violent fever. When after a long illness their recovery was assured, being more apt to set inquiries on foot than to ensure tranquillity they commissioned Ursatius, master of the offices, a raw Dalmatian, and Viventius of Siscia, then quaestor, to conduct a strict investigation into what they suspected to be the cause of their ailment. A rumour persisted that the suggestion that they were the victims of black magic was made in order to discredit the memory of the emperor Julian and his friends. But this insinuation was easily disposed of, since not a shred of evidence could be found for the existence of a plot.

During this period practically the whole Roman world heard the trumpet-call of war, as savage peoples stirred themselves and raided the frontiers nearest to them. The Alamanni were ravaging Gaul and Raetia simultaneously; the Sarmatians and Quadi were devastating Pannonia; the Picts, Saxons, Scots, and Attacotti were bringing continual misery upon Britain; the Austoriani and other Moorish peoples were attacking Africa with more than usual violence; and predatory bands of Goths were plundering Thrace *and Moesia*. The king of Persia was laying unlawful hands on Armenia and sparing no effort to bring that country once more under his rule. His pretext was that, since Jovian, with whom he had made a treaty of peace, was dead, nothing ought to stand in his way and prevent him recovering what he claimed had formerly belonged to his ancestors.

5. *Division of functions between the two emperors.*

After a quiet winter the two emperors, one of whom had been formally elected and the other co-opted as his colleague, though more in appearance than reality, crossed Thrace in perfect harmony and reached Niš (Naissus). There in a suburb called Mediana, three miles from the city, they shared the commanders between them in view of their coming parting. Jovinus, who had previously been promoted by Julian to the command in Gaul, and Dagalaif, who had been advanced to the same rank by Jovian, fell to the lot of Valentinian, whose wishes in the matter were decisive. Victor, however, who also owed his promotion to the last-named emperor, was to accompany Valens to the East together with Arintheus. Lupicinus, also promoted master of cavalry by Jovian, was in charge of the defence of the eastern provinces. At the same time Equitius, who was not yet a master of troops but only a count, was given the command in Illyricum, and Serenian, who had left the service but was now recalled because he was a Pannonian, was allotted to Valens to command his bodyguard. These arrangements were accompanied by a division of the troops between the two emperors.

The brothers then entered Sirmium. The court officials were shared in accordance with the wishes of the senior, and Valentinian departed to Milan, Valens to Constantinople. Salutius governed the East as praetorian prefect, Mamertinus Italy with Africa and Illyricum, Germanian the provinces of Gaul. During their stay in their respective capitals both brothers assumed for the first time the consular robes. The whole year which followed inflicted heavy losses on the Roman state.

The Alamanni violated the German frontier. The reason for their exceptional hostility was that the envoys whom they sent to Roman headquarters to receive the regular gifts that they had come to expect were fobbed off with smaller and cheaper presents, which they thought unworthy of them and threw away in a rage. After rough handling by Ursatius, master of the offices, a cruel and passionate man, they went home with an exaggerated account of the matter and roused their savage countrymen to revenge the insulting treatment they had received.

About the same time, or soon after, Procopius set on foot a revolution in the East, and news of both these events reached Valentinian on the same day, as he was approaching Paris about 1 November. He at once sent Dagalaif to encounter the Alamanni, who had retired to a distance without loss after devastating the places nearest to them. But he was in much doubt how best to suppress Procopius' coup before it gathered strength, especially since he did not know whether Valens was still alive or whether Procopius' attempt was the result of Valens' death. The tribune Antonius, who commanded in central Dacia, had sent Equitius a report which contained only a vague account of what he had heard, and Equitius in turn had passed this on to the emperor in bald terms before he had ascertained the whole truth. On receipt of this news Valentinian promoted Equitius to the rank of master and decided to return himself to Illyricum, in case the rebel should overrun Thrace and invade Pannonia with an already formidable force. His fears were greatly increased by an example from the recent past; he remembered how Julian, thinking nothing of the opposition of an emperor who had always been successful in civil war, had surpassed all hopes and expectations by the incredible speed with which he flew from city to city. But his burning anxiety to return was modified by the opinions of those closest to him, who advised and begged him not to expose Gaul to the barbarians who threatened it with destruction or to let this be a reason for abandoning provinces which were much in need of support. Their pleas were seconded by deputations from cities of note, imploring him not to leave them unprotected in times of such doubt and difficulty; his presence could save them from extreme peril and his mighty name would strike fear into the Germans. At last, after much consideration, he gave in to the views of the majority, saying more than once that Procopius was merely his own and his brother's enemy, whereas the Alamanni were enemies of the whole Roman world. So he decided to make no move for the moment outside the boundaries of Gaul. He advanced as far as Reims, but he was anxious about the possibility of a sudden invasion of Africa and decided to send Neoterius, at that time a notary but afterwards consul, and Masaucio, a member of the general staff, to defend it. Masaucio was chosen because he had been trained in Africa under his father the former count Cretio, and knew the weak spots. To these two he joined Gaudentius, an officer of the Scutarii, whom he knew and trusted from of old.

Seeing, then, that sad storms broke out at one and the same time on both fronts, I shall arrange the details of each separately in due order, dealing first with the East and afterwards with the campaign against the barbarians. Most of the events in East and West occurred during the same months, and to dart suddenly from one place to another would be totally confusing and plunge the course of events into utter obscurity.

6. *Procopius' career and usurpation.*

Procopius came of a noble family and was born and bred in Cilicia. Since he was related to Julian, who was afterwards emperor, he attracted attention from his first entry into public life, and being of unblemished character, though reserved and silent, served with distinction for a long time as notary and tribune. His prospects of obtaining an important position were about to be realized when the changes which followed the death of Constantius made him a kinsman of the emperor. He was promoted to the rank of count and began to entertain loftier ambitions, and it became clear that if he had the chance he would disturb the public peace. When Julian invaded Persia he left Procopius in Mesopotamia with Sebastian, who was to share with him the command of a strong force. There was a dark rumour, never confirmed by any reliable evidence, that he was told by Julian to be guided by the course of events and to take immediate steps to have himself proclaimed emperor if the worst came to the worst. Procopius carried out his orders with loyalty and prudence, but when he heard that Julian had been fatally wounded and Jovian raised to power, and a false report got about that in his last moments Julian had expressed a wish that Procopius should take the helm, he feared that this would be enough to bring him to death without a trial, and disappeared from sight. His alarm reached its height after the death of the other Jovian, the chief notary, who, he learned, had been nominated by a few soldiers as a worthy candidate for the empire after Julian's death, and had come to a frightful end because from that moment he was suspected of revolutionary designs. Hearing that great efforts were being made to find him, Procopius determined to avoid incurring an even heavier load of ill-will and withdrew into the most remote seclusion, but he found that the emperor was trying still harder to discover his whereabouts. He had fallen from a lofty position and was tired of living the life *of a wild beast* and skulking in rough country where he was actually in need of food and cut off from human society. So under the pressure of extreme necessity he made his way by a roundabout route to the neighbourhood of Chalcedon. Here he believed that he could find safe refuge by hiding in the house of Strategius, a senator who had been an officer in the palace and who was his firm friend. From this base he made excursions in the greatest possible secrecy to Constantinople; this emerged from the evidence of the same Strategius when the accomplices in the plot were subjected to repeated examination. Procopius, who concealed his identity by his unkempt and emaciated appearance, collected like a clever spy the gossip that was flying about. Men are always discontented with the existing state of affairs, and many accused Valens of an inordinate desire to enrich himself at the expense of others. The harshness of the emperor found a deadly stimulus in his father-in-law Petronius, a former commander of the legion Martenses, who had been advanced at a bound to the rank of patrician. He was as twisted morally as physically, and consumed with sadistic eagerness to strip one and all of their possessions. After exquisite tortures he exacted penalties four-fold from innocent and guilty alike, hunting out debts as far back as the time of the emperor Aurelian and grievously upset if he let anyone escape unharmed. A further odious feature of his insufferable character was that, while battening on the woes of others, he was deaf to all prayers and ferociously cruel. His heart was of stone and he was incapable of either speaking or listening to reason. He was more hated than Cleander, Commodus' prefect, who we are told ruined the fortunes of many by his insane arrogance, more oppressive than Plautian, who held the same office under Severus, and whose overweening pride would have brought all to ruin if he had not perished by the avenging sword. The disastrous events inspired by Petronius, which caused the closure of many houses both rich and poor under Valens, together with the fear of worse to come, made a deep impression on both provincials and soldiers, who had equal cause to complain. Though no one expressed it openly, the hope that providence would bring about a change was universal.

All this came to the ears of Procopius while he was in hiding. Thinking that a lucky turn of events could easily bring him to the top, he lay low like a beast of prey, ready to pounce as soon as he saw a possible opening. While he was eagerly maturing his plans chance presented him with an exceptionally favourable opportunity. The winter was over, and Valens had already crossed the frontier of Bithynia on his way to Syria when he heard from his generals that the Goths, who had been left undisturbed and were consequently very wild, were combining to violate the borders of Thrace. In order not to interrupt his own journey Valens ordered a sufficient force of horse and foot to the area threatened by the barbarians. Procopius, worn out by hardships and thinking that even a cruel death would be better than the misery he was suffering, resolved to hazard everything on a single throw. The emperor was at a distance, and the troops allotted to the campaign in Thrace would in the usual course of events spend two days in Constantinople. Among them were the Divitenses and the Junior Tungricani, and Procopius, dismissing all fear of the consequences, embarked in desperation on a deed of the utmost audacity. His plan was to seduce these legions from their allegiance through the agency of some acquaintances among them; it would be dangerous and difficult to address the whole body, and he therefore confided only in a few. These few succumbed to the lure of a huge reward and took a solemn oath to do everything he wished. They guaranteed a favourable reception by their comrades, with whom their long and meritorious service gave them commanding influence. So at break of day Procopius, a prey to conflicting emotions, went to the baths of Anastasia, so called after Constantine's sister, where he knew that the legions were stationed, and where he was told by his confidants that at a nocturnal meeting all had united in his support. His safety was unhesitatingly guaranteed and he was received by a throng of venal soldiers, who treated him with respect but kept him practically a prisoner. Like the praetorians who took up the cause of Didius Julianus when he made a bid for the empire after the death of Pertinax, these men, keen not to lose any chance of profit, defended Procopius on his first steps towards his unlucky reign.

There he stood, a shrunken figure which might have risen from the grave. No purple robe was available, and he was dressed in a gold-spangled tunic like a court official, though from the waist downwards he looked like a page. He wore purple shoes and carried a spear, with a shred of purple cloth in his left hand. Altogether he was a grotesque object such as might suddenly appear on the stage in a satirical farce. Elevated in this ridiculous way to an honour rooted in dishonour, he addressed his supporters in tones of servile flattery, promising them ample wealth and high promotion as the first-fruits of his rule. When he appeared in public escorted by a throng of armed men with raised standards he held himself more confidently. All about him was the dismal din of clashing shields held by the troops in a dense mass over the very crests of their helmets, in case they should be pelted from the rooftops with stones or broken tiles.

As he advanced more boldly he met with neither resistance nor favour from the populace. Nevertheless it was stirred by the pleasure naturally aroused in vulgar minds by novelty, and what contributed to excite it further was the detestation in which, as I said, Petronius was held because of his persecution of people of all classes by resurrecting long-buried transactions and shadowy debts.

Ascending the tribunal amid general stupefaction, Procopius was alarmed by the gloomy silence which greeted him. It looked to him as if he had merely found a quicker road to death. He trembled all over, could not find his voice, and stood for a long time without uttering a word. Finally he began with a few broken phrases, like a dying man, justifying himself by his relationship to the imperial family. These were received with a gentle murmur of approbation by a hired claque, and then by the tumultuous shouts of the people, who impetuously acclaimed him emperor. He went at once to the senate-house, where he found nobody of rank but only a few nonentities, and then hastened to the palace, another step on his ill-starred path.

If some feel surprise that a reign rashly and thoughtlessly begun in such ridiculous circumstances should have brought such lamentable disaster on the state, it is because they are ignorant of previous history and suppose that this was the first time such a thing happened. In fact, it was in this way that Andriscus of Adramyttium, who was of the meanest origin, acquired the title of Pseudophilip and was the cause of a third serious war with Macedon, and that Elagabalus Antoninus sprang up at Emesa when the emperor Macrinus was at Antioch. Similarly the unexpected attack of Maximin resulted in the murder of Alexander Severus with his mother Mamaea. So too the elder Gordian was rushed to the throne in Africa, but in panic at the dangers which threatened him ended his life by hanging himself.

7. Further success of Procopius.

So dealers in cheap luxuries, servants and ex-servants in the palace, and veterans who had retired from the army to a more peaceful life were recruited, whether they were willing or not, for this extraordinary and hazardous adventure. Some, however, to whom anything seemed better than the present state of affairs, slipped out of the city unobserved and made as fast as they could for the emperor's camp. They were all outstripped by the exceptional speed of the notary Sophronius, afterwards prefect of Constantinople, who met Valens as he was about to leave Caesarea in Cappadocia for Antioch at the end of the hot season in Cilicia. Valens was naturally shocked and amazed at Sophronius' report, and was persuaded to go to Galatia to take things in hand before they had gone too far.

While Valens was making this hurried march Procopius was spending days and nights of strenuous activity. He suborned a number of people who pretended to have come some from the East and some from Gaul, and who unblushingly asserted that Valentinian was dead and that nothing now stood in the way of the new and universally popular emperor. Impudent seizure of power is often fortified by rapid action, and nothing which could inspire dread was left undone. Nebridius, who at the instance of Petronius' party had recently succeeded Salutius as praetorian prefect, and Caesarius, urban prefect of Constantinople, were at once arrested and imprisoned; Phronimius and Euphrasius, both Gauls highly regarded for their intellectual accomplishments, were appointed urban prefect and master of the offices respectively. Gomoarius and Agilo were recalled to the service and charged with the military administration, an unwise step, as their later treachery proved. It was feared that count Julius, who commanded the forces in Thrace, was near enough to be able to crush the rebels if he heard of their doings, and an effective scheme was devised to forestall this danger. Nebridius from his prison was forced to write a letter apparently on the orders of Valens, summoning Julius to Constantinople for an important conference on the movements of the barbarians, and when he arrived he was put under close arrest. By this clever trick the warlike tribes of Thrace were won over without bloodshed, and proved a strong reinforcement to the rebel cause.

After these successful steps Araxius obtained the praetorian prefecture by court favour, ostensibly because he was supported by his son-in-law Agilo. Many others were appointed to various offices at court and in the provincial administration, some against their will, but others because they put themselves forward and bought their promotion. As usual in times of civil strife, desperation and blind ambition brought some of the dregs of the populace to the top, while others of noble birth crashed from the highest eminence into death or exile.

Once Procopius' party had firmly established itself by these and similar measures, it remained to collect a sufficient military force. This, which in times of public disorder has sometimes been an obstacle to bold initiatives even in a just cause, presented no difficulty on this occasion. Some units of cavalry and infantry were passing by on their way to the campaign in Thrace, and received a warm and generous welcome. Collected into a single body they already looked like an army, and in their greed for the rich rewards dangled before them they swore allegiance to Procopius with the most fearsome oaths and vowed to fight to the death in his defence. Procopius hit upon a particularly effective way of winning their support by personally carrying about in his arms the small daughter of Constantius, whose memory they cherished, and stressing his relationship with that emperor and Julian. Another favourable circumstance was that Faustina, the child's mother, happened to be present when he received certain items of the imperial insignia.

Another plan, which required great promptitude if it was to succeed, was to select agents foolhardy enough to run any risk and send them to take possession of Illyricum. Their only resource was their own impudence; they took with them gold coins minted with the head of the new emperor, and other inducements. But Equitius, who commanded in those parts, seized them and put them to a variety of deaths. Then, fearing a repetition of such an attempt, he blocked the three narrow approaches to the northern provinces, the first through Dacia Ripensis, the second and best known through Succi, and the third, called Acontisma, through Macedonia. These precautions frustrated the unlawful usurper in his vain hope of seizing Illyricum, and denied him much material of war.

Meanwhile Valens, appalled by the dreadful news, was on his way back through Galatia, moving timidly and hesitatingly, when he heard what had happened at Constantinople. Sudden terror affected his judgement, and he fell into such despair that he thought of casting off the heavy burden of his imperial robes, and would no doubt have done so had he not been deterred from this disgraceful course by his closest associates. Encouraged, however, by better men than himself, he sent forward two regiments called Jovii and Victores to make a sudden assault on the rebel camp. As they approached, Procopius, who had returned from a visit to Nicaea, hurried to Mygdus, a place on the banks of the Sangarius, taking with him the Divitenses and a mixed rabble of deserters which he had collected in the course of a few days. The legions were about to join battle and were already exchanging volleys when Procopius rushed forward alone into the intervening space as if to challenge the enemy. By a stroke of luck he appeared to recognize a man called Vitalian in the opposing ranks (whether he really knew him is uncertain), greeted him warmly in Latin, and asked him to step forward. Then he offered his right hand and kissed him, and to the astonishment of both sides spoke as follows: 'So this is the traditional loyalty of Roman troops, this is the way in which you observe your solemn oaths. Can it be your wish, my brave fellows, that our people should draw their swords in such numbers for a stranger, that you and we should have to suffer grievous wounds to enable a degenerate Pannonian to carry all before him and win a throne for which he never dared to entertain the faintest hope? Follow instead the representative of your imperial house, who has taken up arms in a just cause, not to seize what is another's but to establish himself in possession of the power which is his by inheritance.'

These calm words pacified them all. Though they had come prepared for a fierce struggle, they lowered their standards and eagles and gladly went over to Procopius. Instead of raising the fearful war-cry which barbarians call 'barritus', they acclaimed him emperor. Crowding about him in the traditional way they escorted him back to camp in complete harmony, swearing by Jupiter, the usual soldier's oath, that Procopius would be invincible.

8. Procopius gains the provinces of Bithynia and Hellespont.

This piece of good fortune was followed by another rebel success. The tribune Rumitalca, who had come over to Procopius and been put in charge of the palace, crossed the sea with his troops after careful preparation, landed at Helenopolis, the former Drepanum, and unexpectedly occupied Nicaea. Vadomar, the former leader and king of the Alamanni, was sent to besiege Nicaea with a force trained for this kind of operation, while Valens himself proceeded to Nicomedia. Leaving this he threw all his strength into an attack on Chalcedon, where he was received with a chorus of insults from the walls and the derisive name Sabaiarius ('beer-swiller'). ('Sabaia' is the poor man's drink in Illyricum and is a kind of beer made from barley or some other grain.) Valens was about to abandon the siege owing to lack of supplies and the obstinacy of the defence when the garrison of Nicaea suddenly opened their gates and sallied out under the bold leadership of Rumitalca. They routed a great part of the besiegers and hurried on to take Valens in the rear. The latter had not left the environs of Chalcedon, and the attempt would have succeeded had he not received warning of the destruction which threatened him and eluded the pursuit of his foes, who were close on his heels, by a hasty retreat by way of the Sunonensian lake and the winding river Gallus. By this reverse Bithynia also fell into the hands of Procopius.

Valens returned with all speed to Ankara. There he heard that Lupicinus was approaching from the East with a respectable force, and plucking up heart sent his best general Arintheus to encounter the enemy. When Arintheus reached Dadastana, the scene of Jovian's death, he suddenly saw Hyperechius with some troops in his front. Hyperechius had formerly served in the court kitchens, but being a friend of Procopius had now been put in command of a body of auxiliaries. Arintheus thought it beneath him to defeat so mean an opponent, and relying on his authority and his imposing stature called out to the enemy to put their commander in irons themselves. Thus this mere shadow of a general was arrested by his own men.

Meanwhile an official of Valens' treasury called Venustus, who had been sent some time before to Nicomedia with money to pay the troops stationed in the East, heard of the disaster that had occurred, and judging the moment unpropitious for his errand betook himself hastily to Cyzicus with what he had with him. There he happened to find Serenian, at that time commander of the household troops, who had been sent to guard the treasury. He had hurriedly collected a garrison and was trying to hold the city, which was famous for its ancient monuments and protected by impregnable walls. Procopius had detached a strong force to storm it in the hope of adding the province of Hellespont to his gains in Bithynia. Success, however, was delayed by two factors. Arrows, sling-shot, and other missiles inflicted heavy losses on the besieging forces, and to prevent the entrance of enemy warships the defence had skilfully barred the mouth of the harbour with an iron chain of immense strength fastened at either end to the land. Finally, after officers and men had exhausted themselves in fierce fighting, a tribune called Aliso, a *tried* and skilful warrior, broke the boom in the following way. He fastened together three ships and protected their decks by a covering of shields arranged thus. In front men stood on the thwarts with their shields closely interlocked above their heads; behind them were others who stooped a little; and behind these again a third party who bent lower still in descending order, so that the rearmost squatted on their hams and the whole looked like the side of an arched building. The object of this formation, which is used in assaulting walls, is that missiles and stones may glide down the slope which it presents and run off like so much rain. By this device Aliso was protected for a time from the enemy's fire, and, being a man of prodigious physical strength, was able to hold a block of wood beneath the chain while he struck it great blows with an axe and at last succeeded in bursting it asunder. A broad entrance was thus cleared, and the city lay open to attack. When later the author of the whole rebellion was killed and savage punishment inflicted on those who had taken part in it, the life of this same tribune was spared on account of this brilliant exploit and he was retained in the service. Long afterwards he met his death in Isauria at the hands of a band of brigands.

This feat of war having put Cyzicus at his disposal, Procopius hurried thither. He pardoned all who had resisted him except Serenian, whom he ordered to be put in irons and removed to strict imprisonment at Nicaea. Immediately afterwards he conferred on Hormisdas, a man of maturity beyond his years and son of the royal prince of that name, the rank of proconsul, with authority in both civil and military affairs as in earlier times. Hormisdas acted with characteristic mildness. But finding that he was about to be seized by a party of troops sent by Valens through the back country of Phrygia he showed great energy in effecting his escape. He embarked on a ship which he had ready in case of emergency, and carried off with him his wife, who narrowly escaped capture as she was following but whom he saved by a heavy discharge of arrows. She was a woman of wealth and high birth whose spotless reputation and heroic resolution later saved her husband from extreme danger.

After this victory Procopius' confidence knew no bounds; he forgot that before the day is out a turn of fortune's wheel may plunge any man from happiness into the depths of misery. Hitherto he had spared the house of Arbitio as if it were his own, because he believed that Arbitio was on his side, but now he ordered it to be completely cleared of all its priceless furniture. He was aggrieved because on several occasions Arbitio had failed to come when he was sent for, pleading sickness and the infirmities of old age. The usurper feared that this might have serious consequences. Yet, although there was now nothing to prevent him from overrunning the eastern provinces with the free consent of their inhabitants, who were chafing at the harshness of the existing regime and eager to see a change, he wasted time trying to win over some cities in Asia and recruit experienced fund-raisers, who he thought would be useful in the many great battles that he expected. He was in fact a sword that had lost its cutting edge. In this he was like Pescennius Niger, who dawdled in Syria, deaf to the frequent appeals of the people of Rome to rescue them in their dire need, and was defeated by Severus at the gulf of Issus, the place in Cilicia where Alexander routed Darius. After being put to flight, Niger perished in a suburb of Antioch at the hands of a common soldier.

9. Procopius betrayed and executed (A.D. 366).

These were the events of mid-winter in the consulship of Valentinian and Valens. But when spring came, and Gratian, who was as yet unknown to public life, succeeded to the highest magistracy with

Dagalaif for colleague, Valens mobilized his forces, joined Lupicinus and his strong army of auxiliaries, and marched quickly to Pessinus, a town formerly in Phrygia but now in Galatia. Leaving a garrison to guard against any surprise in that area he advanced over difficult country along the foot of Mount Olympus towards Lydia, intending to attack Gomoarius, who was lazing away there. He met, however, with widespread and obstinate resistance, chiefly because his enemy carried about with him in a litter Constantius' small daughter and her mother Faustina, not only on the march but even into line of battle, and in this way excited his men to fight more resolutely for the imperial family, with which he claimed to be himself connected. Just so the Macedonians on the eve of one of their battles with the Illyrians placed their infant king in his cradle behind their line, and from fear that he might be captured crushed their opponents with all the greater energy.

To counter this clever move and bolster his tottering cause the emperor adopted a wise expedient. He urged the ex-consul Arbitio, who had long been in retirement, to come to him, in the hope that respect for one of Constantine's generals would abate the insolence of the rebels. He was not disappointed. Arbitio was everybody's senior in age and rank. He showed his venerable white head, calling Procopius a public enemy, but addressing his deluded followers, among whom were many potential deserters, as his own sons and partners in his early labours. He begged them to follow him, whom they knew to be successful, like a father, rather than obey a worthless profligate who deserved to be abandoned and must shortly fall. When he heard of this, Gomoarius, who might have given his enemies the slip and returned unharmed to his base, preferred to take advantage of the proximity of the emperor's camp to desert to him, pretending that he had been surprised by the sudden appearance of a large force and had been taken prisoner.

Heartened by this Valens advanced into Phrygia, and the two armies joined battle near Nacolia. *While the issue was still undecided* Agilo turned the scale by suddenly changing sides. He was followed by many others who in the very act of brandishing their pikes and swords deserted to the emperor, holding their standards and shields reversed, which is a sure sign of defection.

This totally unexpected event robbed Procopius of any hope of safety. He took to flight and hid in the recesses of the surrounding woods and mountains accompanied by Florentius and the tribune

Barchalba, who had won renown in the fiercest wars from the time of Constantius, and had been led into treason by necessity rather than inclination. The greater part of the night had passed, lightened by a moon which shone brightly from its first rising till dawn and intensified Procopius' fears. All chance of escape was cut off; he was at his wits' end and sunk in despair. While he was bitterly reproaching fortune for his troubles, as men do in such straits, he was suddenly seized by his companions. At daybreak they took him to the camp and handed him over, silent and stupefied, to the emperor. He was immediately beheaded, and so stilled the rising storm of civil war. His fate was that of Perperna, who killed Sertorius at table and enjoyed a brief spell of power, but was then dragged from the thickets where he was hiding, brought before Pompey, and put to death at his orders.

In the prevailing mood of anger, which allowed no time for reflection, Florentius and Barchalba, who had surrendered Procopius, were also at once put to death. If they had betrayed their lawful emperor, Justice herself could have found no fault with their execution, but, since their victim was generally acknowledged to be a rebel who had disturbed the peace of the realm, they ought to have been generously rewarded for a notable service.

Procopius was forty years and ten months old when he died. He was tall and not bad-looking, though he *stooped* and kept his eyes on the ground as he walked. His austere and reserved character was like that of the Crassus who, according to Lucilius and Cicero, only once laughed in his life. A remarkable thing about him was that he went through life innocent of bloodshed.

10. Punishment of Procopius' adherents.

About the same time Marcellus, a staff-officer and a kinsman of Procopius who commanded the garrison of Nicaea, hearing of the death and betrayal of Procopius, suddenly fell upon Serenian, who was confined in the palace, and dispatched him at the dread hour of midnight. Serenian's death saved many lives. He was a boor of savage temper who loved inflicting harm, but his similarity of character and the fact that they came from the same neighbourhood made him welcome to Valens. He had too an insight into Valens' propensity to cruelty. If he had survived the victory he would have brought destruction on many innocent folk.

After killing Serenian, Marcellus hastened to get possession of Chalcedon, and with the support of a few worthless desperadoes embarked on a fatal career as a shadow emperor. He was under a double delusion. For one thing he thought that he could buy for a small sum the loyalty of the 3,000 Goths whom their kings, now reconciled to Rome, had sent to help Procopius because he based his claim on his kinship to Constantius. In the second place he was as yet unaware of what had happened in Illyricum.

While things were still in confusion Equitius, learning from reliable reports that the weight of the whole war had now shifted to Asia, crossed the pass of Succi and made a great effort to break into Philippopolis, the former Eumolpias, which was held by a hostile garrison. He had not yet heard what had happened at Nacolia, and Philippopolis was well placed to thwart his plans if he had to hurry to Haemimontus to bring help to Valens and left it untaken in his rear. But when soon afterwards he heard of Marcellus' futile presumption he at once sent a body of bold and active men, who seized Marcellus like a guilty slave and kept him in custody. A few days later he was brought out and flogged to death; his accomplices received the same treatment. The only thing to his credit is that he made away with Serenian, who was as cruel a persecutor as Phalaris *on the flimsiest pretexts*.

The death of the rebel leader put an end to the horrors of war, but many were punished more severely than their errors or crimes deserved. This was particularly true of the defenders of Philippopolis, who were most reluctant to surrender themselves and their city and only did so when they were shown the head of Procopius, which was being taken to Gaul. Some, however, who had influential friends, got off lightly. Araxius was a notable example. Though he had obtained the prefectship by wire-pulling at the moment when the conflagration was hottest, his son-in-law Agilo succeeded in limiting his punishment to deportation to an island, from which he soon escaped. Phronimius and Euphrasius were sent to the West to be dealt with at Valentinian's discretion. Euphrasius was released, but Phronimius banished to the Crimea. Their cases were identical, but Phronimius was more harshly treated because he had been a favourite of the late emperor Julian, whose conspicuous merits both the imperial brothers disparaged, though they were not his equals or anything like it.

A generalized account of atrocities committed under Valens is omitted.

The usurper whose complex career and death I have described was still living when on 21 July in the first consulship of Valentinian and his brother a frightful disaster, surpassing anything related either in legend or authentic history, overwhelmed the whole world. Day had just dawned when, after a thunderstorm of exceptional violence, the solid frame of the earth shuddered and trembled, and the sea was moved from its bed and went rolling back. The abyss of the deep was laid open; various types of marine creatures could be seen stuck in the slime, and huge mountains and valleys which had been hidden since the creation in the depths of the waves then, one must suppose, saw the light of the sun for the first time. Many ships were stranded on what was now dry land, and a host of people roamed at large in the shallows that were left to pick up fish and similar objects. Then, however, the roaring sea, as if indignant at its repulse, turned back, and rushed over the seething shoals to burst in fury upon islands and wide tracts of the mainland. Innumerable buildings in towns or wherever they were standing were levelled to the ground, and the whole face of the earth was changed by this mad conflict of the elements, and revealed wonderful sights. The sudden return of the vast sea when it was least expected drowned many thousands; when the watery element again subsided many ships had been destroyed by the force of the tidal wave, and the dead bodies of their shipwrecked crews were left lying on their backs or faces. Other great vessels, hurled along by the raging winds, landed on the roofs of buildings, as happened at Alexandria, and some were carried nearly two miles inland, like the Laconian ship which I saw myself during a journey near Mothone, gaping at the seams from long decay.

BOOK 27

Chapters describing renewed attacks by the Alamanni and successful reprisals by the Romans under Jovinus (1 and 2) are omitted.

3. Events at Rome.

At this time, or a little earlier, a new type of portent appeared in Annonarian Tuscany, and even those skilled in the interpretation of omens could not tell what it portended. In the town of Pistoia (Pistoria) about nine in the morning a donkey mounted the tribunal before a crowd of witnesses and brayed persistently, to the astonishment of all who were present or heard of it. No one could guess what was to happen, but afterwards the meaning of the portent became clear. Terentius, a Roman of low birth and a baker by trade, was rewarded with the governorship of this same province for accusing the ex-prefect Orfitus of embezzlement. This emboldened him to stir up trouble in a big way, but finally he was convicted of fraud in some business with a guild of shippers – that at any rate was the story – and perished by the hand of the executioner during the urban prefectship of Claudius.

Long before this, however, Apronian was succeeded by Symmachus, a man of the most exemplary learning and discretion. Through his efforts the Holy City enjoyed peace and plenty to an unusual degree, and can boast of a splendid and solid bridge which he *restored* and dedicated, to the great joy of the citizens, who, nevertheless, some years later demonstrated their ingratitude in the plainest way. They set fire to his beautiful house across the Tiber, enraged by a story, invented without a shred of evidence by some worthless ruffian, that Symmachus had said that he would rather use his wine to quench lime-kilns than sell it at the reduced price that the people hoped for.

Symmachus was succeeded in the government of the city by Lampadius, a former praetorian prefect. His vanity was such that he took it very ill if even his manner of spitting was not extolled for its unique adroitness, but nevertheless he was sometimes strict and honest. When he gave a magnificent show as praetor and distributed largesse on a most generous scale, he could not bear the clamorous demands of the populace that he should make gifts to its undeserving favourites, and in order to demonstrate both his liberality and his contempt for the mob summoned needy folk from the Vatican and bestowed rich presents on them. Of his vanity I will avoid further digression by giving a single instance, slight in itself but a warning to high officials. In all parts of the city which had been beautified by the generosity of various emperors he had his own name inscribed, not as the restorer of ancient buildings but as their founder. This is a fault under which the emperor Trajan is said to have laboured, and it earned him the satirical nickname of 'wallflower'.

Lampadius' term of office was disturbed by frequent riots. The worst occurred when a mob of the lowest canaille attacked his house near the baths of Constantine with torches and firebrands, and would have set it alight if his neighbours and servants had not rushed to the spot and repelled the attackers by pelting them from the roof with stones and tiles. Lampadius himself had fled in panic at the first sign of trouble to the Mulvian bridge, which is said to have been built by the elder Scaurus. There he waited till the tumult should subside. A serious grievance had given rise to it. In preparing to erect new buildings or restore old he did not provide for the expense from the usual public funds. If iron or lead or bronze or the like were needed, minor officials were sent in the guise of purchasers to carry off the various materials without payment. His rapid flight barely saved him from the fury of enraged and impoverished people who had continual losses to deplore.

Lampadius' successor was Viventius, a former quaestor of the palace, an upright and wise Pannonian, under whose quiet and peaceful administration there was general plenty. But he too had to endure an alarming outbreak of violence by the turbulent populace, which arose as follows. Damasus and Ursinus, whose passionate ambition to seize the episcopal throne passed all bounds, were involved in the most bitter conflict of interest, and the adherents of both did not stop short of wounds and death. Viventius, unable to end or abate the strife, was compelled by force majeure to withdraw to the suburbs. The efforts of his partisans secured the victory for Damasus. It is certain that in the basilica of Sicininus, where the Christians assemble for worship, 137 corpses were found on a single day, and it was only with difficulty that the long-continued fury of the people was later brought under control.

Considering the ostentatious luxury of life in the city it is only natural that those who are ambitious of enjoying it should engage in the most strenuous competition to attain their goal. Once they have reached it they are assured of rich gifts from ladies of quality; they can ride in carriages, dress splendidly, and outdo kings in the lavishness of their table. They might be truly happy if they would pay no regard to the greatness of the city, which they make a cloak for their vices, and follow the example of some provincial bishops, whose extreme frugality in food and drink, simple attire, and downcast eyes demonstrate to the supreme god and his true worshippers the purity and modesty of their lives. But enough of this digression; let me now return to my narrative.

Chapter describing the provinces and cities of Thrace (4) is omitted.

5. *Valens makes war on the Gothic allies of Procopius* (A.D. 367–9).

Once Procopius had been crushed in Phrygia and the occasion of civil strife removed, Victor, the master of cavalry, was sent to the Goths to ask, without beating about the bush, why a people friendly to Rome and bound by a long-standing treaty of peace had helped a usurper to make war upon the lawful emperors. The Goths, believing that they had a strong case, produced a letter from Procopius asserting that he had merely assumed the throne which was his due as a close kinsman of the house of Constantine. They claimed that they had fallen into a pardonable error. On receiving Victor's report Valens brushed aside this empty excuse and took the field against the Goths, who had advance information of his movements. In early spring he concentrated his army, established his base near a fort called Daphne, and crossed the Danube on a bridge of boats without encountering any resistance. His confidence grew as he scoured the country without finding an enemy to defeat or overawe, since the whole body, alarmed by the approach of so formidably equipped a force, had made for the high mountains of the Serri, which are inaccessible to anyone not acquainted with the terrain. Not wishing, however, to waste the whole summer and return empty-handed, Valens despatched the infantry commander Arintheus with some raiding parties. Some of the families of the Goths were seized while they were still wandering over the plains and before they could reach the steep and winding mountain tracks. After this meagre success, which he owed merely to chance, Valens returned with his troops without having either inflicted or suffered any serious damage.

In the following year an equally vigorous attempt to invade the enemy's territory was frustrated by the flooding of the Danube over a wide area, and Valens had to remain inactive in a standing camp near a village of the Carpi till the end of autumn. Then he retired to winter quarters at Marcianople, since nothing could be done in view of the extent of the floods.

For a third year in succession Valens still persevered. Crossing the river by a bridge of boats at Noviodunum he broke into the territory of the barbarians and made a forced march to attack the remote and warlike tribe of the Greuthungi. After some skirmishing he defeated Athanaric, at that time their most powerful ruler, who dared to resist with what he believed to be an adequate force but was compelled to flee for his life. Valens himself returned with his whole army to Marcianople, the most suitable place for winter quarters to be found in that region.

The events of these three campaigns created a favourable climate for ending hostilities. The enemy were alarmed by the emperor's long stay in their neighbourhood, and the interruption of trade had reduced the barbarians to such want that they sent a number of delegations to beg for pardon and peace. The emperor decided that the best policy was to grant their request. In spite of his inexperience his judgement was still sound; it was only later that he succumbed to the fatal lure of flattery and inflicted on the state disasters that we can never cease to deplore. So he in turn despatched Victor and Arintheus, commanders of the cavalry and infantry respectively, and when they sent a reliable report that the Goths were ready to agree to his terms a suitable place was chosen for concluding the treaty. Athanaric declared that he was bound by a tremendous oath taken at the behest of his father never to set foot on Roman soil. Since he could not be persuaded to do so, and it would be undignified and degrading for the emperor to cross over to him, the sensible decision was reached to conclude the treaty in mid-stream, the emperor with his guard being conveyed from one bank and the tribal chief with his attendants from the other. When this had been settled and hostages exchanged Valens returned to Constantinople, where at a later date Athanaric, driven from his country by a domestic conspiracy, died and was buried with splendid rites conducted in the Roman manner.

6. *Gratian co-emperor with Valentinian.*

Meanwhile Valentinian fell dangerously ill and was at the point of death. The Gauls in attendance on him held a clandestine meeting and proposed as his successor Rusticus Julianus, master of the records, a man whose bestial thirst for human blood verged upon madness, as he showed in his government of Africa as proconsul. As urban prefect, the office in which he died, he was forced to appear milder and more lenient because of the precarious standing of the despot who had raised him to that high position, presumably owing to a dearth of deserving candidates. The Gauls were opposed by some with higher aims who put forward Severus, then master of infantry, as a suitable candidate. Although he was rough and inspired fear he was easier to bear than the other and in every way preferable.

These plans, however, were hatched in vain. The emperor recovered by the application of various remedies and, realizing that he had had a narrow escape from death, decided to confer the insignia of empire on his son Gratian, who was approaching manhood. When all was ready and steps had been taken to secure the approval of the troops, Gratian arrived, and Valentinian, attended by a splendid suite of high officials, proceeded to the parade-ground and ascended the dais. Taking the boy by the right hand he led him forward, and presented the future emperor to the army in a formal speech.

'The imperial robe which I am wearing is a happy token of the goodwill which led you to prefer me to many distinguished rivals. You then should share my plans and promote my wishes, now that the time has come for me to take in hand my duty as a father, relying for a happy outcome on the promises of God, by whose eternal aid the Roman state will stand unshaken. I beg you, my gallant men, to give a favourable reception to my desire, bearing in mind that I wish an act sanctioned by natural affection not merely to be brought to your knowledge but to receive your approval as befitting us and likely to be beneficial to the state. You see before you my son Gratian, who has long lived among your own children and whom you love as a pledge of the bonds which unite us. He is now grown, and I intend for the preservation of public peace to take him as my colleague in the empire, provided that the will of heaven and your sovereign power support the promptings of a father's love. He has not, like us, had a harsh upbringing from his very cradle and been inured to the endurance of hardship, nor, as you see, is he yet fit to encounter the dust of battle, but before long, in conformity with the reputation of his family and the glorious deeds of his forebears, he will, if I may say so without presumption, achieve distinction. Close observation of his character and inclinations, immature though he is, leads me to think that when he becomes a man the training which he has acquired from a liberal education will enable him to form an impartial judgement of right and wrong. He will conduct himself in such a way that good men will realize that he knows their value. He will be eager to perform noble deeds, and will never desert the standards and eagles of his men. He will endure heat, snow, and frost, thirst and lack of sleep. He will fight to defend his camp, should he ever need to do so. He will risk his life for his comrades, and above all, which is the first and highest duty, he will love the state as he loves the home of his father and his ancestors.'

Before Valentinian had finished his speech, which was received with enthusiastic applause, the soldiers, each in the way appropriate to his rank, strove to outdo one another in their haste to proclaim Gratian emperor and to play their part in this joyful and propitious event, accompanying their loud shouts with an approving clash of arms. Valentinian, encouraged and elated by this reception, put a crown on Gratian's head, invested him with the imperial robes, and kissed him. Then he addressed him as follows, while the boy, who made a brilliant figure, listened attentively:

'The hopes of us all, my dear Gratian, are fulfilled by your assumption of the imperial robes, conferred on you under the happiest auspices by my will and that of our comrades. Prepare yourself to act as the colleague of your father and your uncle as the pressure of events requires. Accustom yourself to make your way boldly with the infantry over the frozen Rhine and Danube, to stand shoulder to shoulder with your men, to shed your blood without hesitation for those under your command, and to treat nothing with indifference that concerns the welfare of the Roman empire. Enough by way of admonition for the moment; I shall not fail to advise you hereafter. The rest of you, who constitute the chief bulwark of the state, I beg and beseech to defend with steady affection the growing emperor committed to your care.'

These words from the emperor were received with profound respect. Then Eupraxius, a native of Mauretania Caesariensis, who was master of the records, gave a lead by shouting: 'The family of Gratian deserves this honour.' He was at once promoted to the quaestorship, an office in which he set an example of noble independence which wise men should follow. He never departed from his native fearlessness, but was always as firm and consistent as the law itself, which as we know speaks with one and the same voice to all in the most varied circumstances. His loyalty to the cause of justice became even more steadfast when the emperor rejected his good advice and tried to intimidate him with intemperate threats.

Eupraxius' lead was followed by a general outburst of praise for both the elder and the boy emperor, and particularly for the latter, who was recommended by a bright gleam in his eye, a most agreeable face and figure, and a noble character. This would have made him a ruler comparable to the best of his predecessors if fate had permitted, and if the corrupt actions of his intimates had not cast a cloud over his good qualities before they were firmly rooted.

In this matter Valentinian went beyond the long-established custom, in that his generosity led him to promote both his brother and his son to the rank of Augustus instead of Caesar. No one before had taken a colleague with power equal to his own except the emperor Marcus, who made his adopted brother Verus his partner without any inferiority of status as an emperor.

7. *Valentinian's irascibility, savagery, and cruelty.*

After this business was settled in accordance with the will of the ruler and the army, only a few days elapsed before the praetorian prefect Mamertinus, on his return from Rome, which he had visited to correct certain abuses, was accused of peculation by Avitian, a former vice-prefect. He was therefore replaced by Vulcatius Rufinus, a man perfectly qualified in every respect. To all appearance this was the crown of his long and honourable career; nevertheless he never let pass any chance of enriching himself if he could hope to do so undetected. As soon as he gained the emperor's ear he obtained the release from banishment of Orfitus, the former urban prefect. By Rufinus' agency his confiscated property was restored to him and he returned to his home.

Valentinian was generally known to be a cruel man, but at the beginning of his reign he strove to modify his reputation for harshness by taking some pains to control his savage impulses. But this insidious vice grew on him though its appearance was deferred, and gradually broke out without restraint to the destruction of several persons; it gained strength from his liability to passionate outbursts of anger. Anger is defined by philosophers as a long-standing and sometimes incurable mental ulcer, usually arising from weakness of intellect. In support of this they argue with some plausibility that this tendency occurs more in invalids than in the healthy, more in women than in men, more in the old than in the young, more in those in trouble than in the prosperous.

Among the executions of others of lower rank, what attracted most attention at that time was the death of Diocles, former treasurer of Illyricum, whom the emperor ordered to be burnt at the stake for trivial offences, and also of Diodorus, a former agent, and three officials of the vice-prefect of Italy. These latter all suffered a cruel death because the commander of the forces complained to the emperor that Diodorus had brought a civil action against him, and that the three officials had had the audacity to summon him on the judge's orders to appear as defendant as he was setting out on a journey. The memory of these men is cherished to this day by the Christians in Milan, who call the spot where they are buried 'The Place of the Innocents'.

Later, in the affair of one Maxentius from Pannonia, whom the judge had very properly ordered to be immediately executed, Valentinian commanded that the local senators of three towns should be put to death. The quaestor Eupraxius intervened, saying: 'Show more restraint, your highness. These men who are to be executed as criminals on your orders will be honoured by the Christians as martyrs.' Eupraxius' salutary boldness was imitated by the prefect Florentius, when he heard that the emperor, in a fit of passion over some venial offence, had ordered the execution of three senators in each of a number of cities. 'What happens,' he said, 'if some town does not have as many as three? A rider will have to be added that they shall be put to death when the town has enough.'

Another feature of his ruthless behaviour is as horrible to relate as it was in actual fact. If anyone, in order to avoid appearing before a powerful enemy, asked that his case should be transferred to another judge, the request was refused and he was sent back to the man he feared, however sound his plea might be. Another frightful thing which was much discussed was that when Valentinian heard that a debtor was in such straits that he could pay nothing he pronounced a sentence of death upon him.

The reason why some emperors are so arrogant as to commit these and similar acts is that they give their friends no opportunity of setting them right when they go wrong in thought or deed, and that their enormous power frightens their enemies into silence. There is in fact no way of correcting wrongdoing in those who think that the height of virtue consists in the execution of their will.

8. *Theodosius in Britain.*

After setting out from Amiens on a rapid march to Trier, Valentinian was shocked to receive the serious news that a concerted attack by the barbarians had reduced the provinces of Britain to the verge of ruin. Nectaridus, the count of the coastal region, had been killed, and the general Fullofaudes surprised and cut off. Greatly perturbed by these events the emperor sent Severus, still at this period count of the household troops, to retrieve the situation if he found a suitable opportunity. Shortly afterwards Severus was recalled, and *Jovinus set out for the island, but sent an appeal for* strong reinforcements, which the pressing needs of the moment required. Finally, in response to the alarming reports which constantly arrived, Theodosius was selected for the task and ordered to proceed to Britain without delay. He had a great reputation as a soldier, and, getting together a tough force of horse and foot, he set out on his mission with every prospect of success.

In my account of the reign of Constans, I have described to the best of my ability the ebb and flow of the tides and the geography of Britain. It seems superfluous therefore to repeat what has already been dealt with; Ulysses in Homer shrinks in the same way from the hard task of repeating his adventures to the Phaeacians. It will suffice to say that at that time the Picts, of whom there were two tribes, the Dicalydones and Verturiones, together with the warlike people of the Attacotti and the Scots, were roving at large and causing great devastation. In addition the Franks and Saxons were losing no opportunity of raiding the parts of Gaul nearest to them by land and sea, plundering, burning, and putting to death all their prisoners.

In the hope that a favourable turn would enable him to put a stop to these outrages our energetic commander set out for the ends of the earth. He reached the coast at Boulogne, which is separated from the opposite shore by a narrow strait, where the sea by turns is swollen to a dreadful height and then sinks again to the level of a plain, when it presents no danger to navigation. From Boulogne Theodosius made a calm crossing to Richborough, a quiet harbour on the opposite coast. On the arrival of his troops, which consisted of the Batavi and Heruli together with the Jovii and Victores, a sufficiently strong force, he disembarked and marched towards the old town of London, since called Augusta. Dividing his men into several detachments, he attacked the roving parties of freebooters, who were hampered by the weight of their spoils and driving before them prisoners and cattle. He quickly routed them and wrested from them the plunder which the wretched provincials had lost. He restored everything to its owners except for a small part which he distributed to his exhausted troops, and then entered the town in triumph. Hitherto it had been plunged in the deepest distress, but it was now re-established almost before it could have hoped for rescue.

This success encouraged Theodosius to undertake operations on a larger scale, but he waited for a time in some doubt about his safest course. He had learnt from the confessions of his prisoners and the information given by deserters that the scattered and wildly ferocious peoples of the various tribes could be subdued only by a strategy of stealth which took them unawares. Finally he issued a proclamation promising immunity to deserters who returned to the colours and summoning many others who were dispersed in various places on furlough. This secured the return of the majority. Theodosius' anxiety was relieved, and he asked that Civilis, a man of fiery temper but uncompromising integrity, should be sent to him to govern Britain as pro-prefect. He asked also for the services of Dulcitius, a general distinguished for his military skill.

9. Events in Africa. Praetextatus as urban prefect.

This is what was happening in Britain. But Africa, from the very beginning of Valentinian's reign, was victim to the fury of the barbarians, who made audacious raids to satisfy their constant thirst for blood and booty. The mischief was increased by the slackness of the troops and their eagerness to enrich themselves at the expense of others, traits which were particularly evident in their commander Romanus. This officer, who could see what was in the wind and was adept at shifting unpopularity on to others, was detested for his brutality, and especially for his keenness to outdo the enemy in ravaging the provinces. He relied on the support of his kinsman Remigius, the master of the offices, who sent in false and conflicting reports, so that the emperor, who prided himself on his watchfulness, was left for a long time in ignorance of the lamentable losses of the Africans.

I shall give a full account of events in this region, including the deaths of the governor Ruricius and the envoys, and other disasters, when the course of my work requires it. And since I am now free to express my own opinion I will say openly that Valentinian was the first emperor to foster the arrogance of the military to the detriment of the state by advancing them notably in standing and wealth. In addition he pursued a policy, which is to be deplored on both public and private grounds, of punishing the offences of common soldiers with inflexible severity while treating their superiors leniently. The latter in consequence assumed that they had a licence to sin, and were encouraged to the commision of frightful crimes, and since that time have had the audacity to believe that the fortunes of all men alike depend on their will and pleasure. The legislators of earlier times, in an attempt to humble their pride and influence, were of opinion that sometimes even innocent people must be sentenced to death. This often happens when the wrongdoing of a large number unfairly involves the punishment of some who are not guilty, a thing which has sometimes applied even in the trials of private persons.

A short passage on Isaurian brigands is omitted.

At this period Praetextatus distinguished himself as urban prefect. His many acts of uprightness and honesty, for which he had acquired a reputation from his early years, earned him an unusual distinction. He was feared by the citizens without forfeiting their affection, which is generally weaker towards officials who inspire dread. Praetextatus' authority and his support of the cause of truth and justice quieted the disturbance caused by the quarrels of the Christians. After the banishment of Ursinus profound peace reigned, a state of affairs extremely welcome to the citizens of Rome, and the fame of their excellent governor was enhanced by a number of salutary measures. He had all projecting galleries removed; these were the invention of Maenius, and their erection had also been banned in the early laws of Rome. He had the walls of private houses demolished where they had been built on to temples without regard for their sanctity. He instituted standard weights in all parts of the city as the only way of dealing with the greed of many shopkeepers who rigged their scales to suit themselves.

In trying legal cases he achieved to a unique degree what Cicero speaks of in his eulogy of Brutus; though he did nothing to court favour, everything that he did was favourably received.

Chapter on a successful campaign by Valentinian against the Alamanni (10) is omitted.

11. Career and character of Probus (A.D 368).

During this period Vulcatius Rufinus died in office, and Probus was recalled from Rome to succeed him as praetorian prefect. Probus was known all over the Roman world for his high birth, powerful influence, and vast riches; he owned estates in almost every part of the empire, but whether they were honestly come by or not is not for a man like me to say. In his case Fortune, who, to use the language of poetry, carried him on her swift wings, took a double form. Sometimes she exhibited him as a benevolent man engaged in promoting the careers of his friends; at others he appeared as a pernicious schemer who worked off his deadly grudges by inflicting injury. Throughout his life he exercised enormous influence owing to the gifts he bestowed and the constant succession of offices he filled. There were times when he showed fear of those who stood up to him, but he took a high line with those who were afraid of him. When he felt that he was on strong ground he hectored in the elevated style of tragedy, but in panic he could be more abject than any down-at-heel comedian. Probus languished like a fish out of water if he was not in office. This he was driven to seek by the lawless behaviour of his countless dependants, whose excessive greed could never be satisfied in an innocent way, and who thrust their master into public life so as to be able to gain their ends with impunity. It must be admitted that he had sufficient principle never to order a client or slave to break the law, but if he heard that any had committed a crime he would defend him in the teeth of justice itself, without any investigation of the matter or regard for right and honour. This is a fault reprobated by Cicero when he says: 'What is the difference between prompting a deed and approving it when it is done? Or what difference does it make whether I wished it to happen or am glad that it has happened?'

Probus was by nature suspicious and petty. He could wear a sour smile, and sometimes employed flattery when he meant to injure. He had a common defect of characters of his type that is conspicuously bad, especially when its possessor believes that he can conceal it: he was so implacable and inflexible that once he had decided to injure a man he was deaf to all entreaties. Nothing could induce him to pardon an offence, and his ears seemed stopped with lead rather than the proverbial wax.

Even at the height of wealth and honour he was nervous and worried, and in consequence always subject to slight ailments. This was the course of events in the western part of the empire.

12. *Struggles with the Persians over Armenia and Hiberia.*

For a short time after the death of the emperor Julian and the conclusion of that shameful treaty, the great Sapor, now an old man, who had been addicted to the delights of rapine from the very beginning of his reign, seemed with his people to be on friendly terms with us. Then, however, he trampled upon the pact made under Jovian and laid hands on Armenia, intending to incorporate it in his dominions as if the agreement were no longer in force. At first he confined himself to various stratagems and inflicted only slight losses on this populous country, suborning some of the grandees and satraps and surprising others by unexpected raids. Next, by a calculated mixture of flattery and perjury he entrapped king Arsaces himself. He was entertained at a banquet, and then taken by Sapor's orders to a concealed door. His eyes were put out, and he was loaded with chains of silver, which in that country is regarded as a consolation, empty though it is, for the sufferings of persons of rank. Finally he was exiled to a fortress called Agabana, where he was tortured and despatched by the sword of the executioner.

After this, that nothing might be lacking to complete the tale of treachery, Sapor drove out Sauromaces, who had been placed by Rome on the throne of Hiberia, and conferred the rule of this people on one Aspacures, on whom he also bestowed a crown to demonstrate his contempt for the authority of our rulers. Having effected these infamous designs he entrusted Armenia jointly to a eunuch called Cylaces and to Arrabannes, both of whom had earlier defected to him; the former was reported to have been prefect of that people and the latter commander-in-chief. They were told to spare no effort to destroy Artogerassa, a strongly held and fortified town which sheltered the treasure of Arsaces as well as his wife and son. The siege was begun in accordance with Sapor's orders. The fortress stood on a rugged height and could not be approached in the prevailing snow and frost. So Cylaces, who, being a eunuch, was good at wheedling a woman, obtained a safe-conduct and came quickly up to the very walls with Arrabannes. His request to be allowed to enter with his colleague was granted, and with a certain amount of browbeating he urged the besieged and their queen to surrender at once and thus soften the temper of Sapor, the most merciless of men. There was much argument on both sides, and lamentation from the woman over the sad fate of her husband; this moved the two zealous advocates of surrender to pity and they changed their plan. Setting their sights higher, they arranged in a private meeting that at a given time in the night the gates should be suddenly flung open and a strong force sally out to surprise the enemy's camp, and they vowed to see that this plan was kept secret. This promise was sealed with an oath and they left the city, and reported back that the besieged begged to be allowed two days to make up their minds. The besiegers were thus lulled into inactivity, and at the time of night when men are relaxed and snoring most deeply the city gate was unbarred and a band of warriors issued swiftly out. Creeping along with noiseless footsteps and with daggers in their hands, they broke into the camp of the unsuspecting foe and slaughtered numbers in their sleep without opposition. The unexpected defection of this pair and the unforeseen massacre of the Persians led to fearful bad blood between us and Sapor, and this was aggravated by the fact that Arsaces' son Pap had left the fortress with a few followers at his mother's instance and been welcomed by the emperor Valens. Neocaesarea, a well-known town in Pontus Polemoniacus, was appointed to be his temporary residence, and generous arrangements were made for his support and upbringing. This act of kindness encouraged Cylaces and Arrabannes to send envoys to Valens to ask for aid, and to beg that Pap might be given them as their king. For the moment actual aid was refused, but Pap was sent back to Armenia through the agency of the general Terentius to rule his people without the insignia of royalty for the time being. There was a good reason for this arrangement; it protected us from the charge of violating the treaty and breaking the peace.

When he heard what had happened Sapor's rage knew no bounds. He collected a larger force and set about the devastation of Armenia without disguise. His arrival terrified Pap as well as Cylaces and

Arrabannes. No help was available, and they took refuge in the high mountains which divide our territory from Lazica. There they remained concealed in the deep forests and ravines for five months, eluding every attempt of the king to find them. The latter, seeing that he was wasting his time to no purpose under the frosty winter sky, burned all the fruit-trees and the forts and strongholds which he had captured by force or fraud, and surrounded Artogerassa with all the weight of his forces. After some indecisive fighting the city was laid open by the exhaustion of its defenders. Sapor set it on fire and carried off the wife and treasure of Arsaces. This led to the dispatch of count Arintheus with an army to those parts to help the Armenians if the Persians attempted to harass them in a second campaign.

Meanwhile Sapor, that monster of guile, who was conciliatory and overbearing by turns as best suited him, sent a secret message to Pap suggesting a future alliance, and reproaching him for being so careless of his own interests as to be the tool of Cylaces and Arrabannes in spite of his appearance of royal power. Pap fell headlong into the trap of these soft words; he killed them both and sent their heads to Sapor as a token of submission.

The news of this disaster got abroad, and Armenia would have perished defenceless if the Persians had not been deterred by the arrival of Arintheus. This caused them to defer a second invasion and to content themselves with sending a mission to the emperor asking him to observe the treaty made with Jovian and to withdraw his protection from Armenia. The request was rejected, and Sauromaces, who as I said had been driven from the throne of Hiberia, was sent back there with Terentius and twelve legions. When he had nearly reached the river Cyrus, Aspacures suggested that as they were cousins they should reign jointly; he declared that he could not give way completely or go over to Rome because his son Ultra was still a hostage with the Persians.

Learning of this the emperor acquiesced in the division of Hiberia, thinking it a sensible way of allaying the troubles likely to be caused by this affair. The Cyrus was to be the boundary between the two domains, Sauromaces keeping the region bordering on Armenia and Lazica, and Aspacures the parts adjoining Albania and Persia.

This arrangement enraged Sapor, and he protested that he was being shamefully treated. The Romans had broken the treaty by sending help to the Armenians, and his mission of remonstrance had come to nothing. Moreover, the decision to divide the kingdom of Hiberia had been taken without his knowledge or consent. So he slammed the door on friendship, collected auxiliary troops from the neighbouring peoples, and mobilized his own army, intending at the opening of the warm season to undo all the measures taken by the Romans to protect their interests.

BOOK 28

1. Trials and executions at Rome for sorcery, fornication, and adultery. (Some incidents towards the end of this chapter are omitted.)

While in Persia, as I have described above, the bad faith of the king was causing unexpected trouble, and hostilities were being renewed on the eastern front, at Rome, rather more than sixteen years after the death of Nepotian, Bellona (the goddess of war) was raging through the Eternal City and setting it ablaze. Small beginnings culminated in fearful disasters, which one could wish buried in total oblivion. I pray that there may be no such outrages hereafter to do more harm by the example they set than by their actual effects. I reflected deeply on the various circumstances, and felt that I had good grounds for fearing the consequences if I gave a minute account of this bloody business, but the better moral climate that now prevails encourages me to touch on the things worth recording. I do not, however, feel at all reluctant to explain briefly the episode in ancient history which caused me alarm.

In the first war against the Medes, the Persians after seizing Asia laid siege to Miletus in overwhelming strength. The besieged were threatened with an agonizing death and brought to such a pass by their miseries that they killed their nearest and dearest, made a bonfire of their movables, and vied with one another in their haste to consign themselves to the flames and perish on the common pyre of their country. Soon afterwards Phrynichus used this disaster as the plot of a tragedy and produced it on the stage at Athens. At first it was well received by the audience, but as the sad story unfolded in high tragic style their indignation was aroused and they punished the author, whose object, they thought, was not to console but to reproach. A lovely city had perished without any help from its founders, and Phrynichus had had the bad taste to make a stage play of its sufferings. Miletus was a colony of Athens, founded with other Ionian cities by Nileus, son of

Codrus. (Codrus is said to have laid down his life for his country in war with the Dorians.)

But let me come to my subject. Maximin, formerly vice-prefect of Rome, was a man of very humble origin from Sopianae, a town in Valeria. His father was a clerk in the governor's office and came of Carpian stock. (The Carpi were a tribe which Diocletian expelled from their original homes and transferred to Pannonia.) After a superficial education and an undistinguished career at the bar Maximin became governor, first of Corsica, then of Sardinia, and finally of Tuscany. From this he was promoted to the charge of the corn supply of Rome, but, owing to a delay in the arrival of his successor, still retained the governorship of Tuscany. To begin with he behaved with caution, for three reasons. In the first place he had a vivid memory of a prediction by his father, who was expert in the interpretation of the flight and song of birds, to the effect that he would reach a high position but perish later at the hand of the executioner. Next, he had got hold of a man from Sardinia who had the power to raise evil spirits and elicit prognostications from the dead. Rumour had it that he later betrayed this man to his death, but while he survived he was milder and more amenable for fear of being betrayed himself. Lastly, while he was still worming his way through inferior posts like a snake in the earth he was not strong enough to cause mischief on a large scale.

His first chance to enlarge the area of his operations arose as follows. Chilo, a former vice-prefect, and his wife Maxima complained to Olybrius, who was then urban prefect, that an attempt had been made on their lives by poison, and secured the immediate arrest and imprisonment of the suspects, Sericus, an organ-maker, Asbolius, a wrestler, and Campensis, a soothsayer. The case was held up by the long and serious illness of Olybrius, so to expedite matters the plaintiffs petitioned that their suit should be heard by the prefect of the corn supply. To save time their request was granted. Maximin thus won an opportunity to do harm, and gave free scope to the innate cruelty of his savage heart, like wild beasts in the amphitheatre when they escape by breaking through the bars of their cages.

While the matter was still at an early stage and various preliminary investigations were being made, cruel scourging elicited from some witnesses the names of a number of nobles, who were alleged to have secured the services of professional criminals through the agency of dependants and other creatures who were notorious informers. Then the hellish judge went beyond his last, to use the proverbial phrase, and reported to the emperor out of pure malice that frightful crimes committed by several people at Rome could be investigated and punished only by using harsher methods. At this the emperor, who was passionate rather than rigorous in his antipathy to wrongdoing, issued in a rage a general ordinance to cover cases of this kind, which he arbitrarily identified with the crime of treason, and decreed that all who were exempted from torture by early legislation and the decrees of former emperors should be put on the rack if circumstances required it. And to multiply misery by doubling and exalting the authority which could inflict it, Valentinian empowered Maximin to act as pro-prefect of Rome, and associated Leo with him in the prosecution of inquiries set on foot to destroy a large number of people. Leo was then a notary and later master of the offices, a grave-robbing brigand from Pannonia, slavering like a wild beast in search of prey and as thirsty for human blood as Maximin. The arrival of a like-minded colleague and the charm of a commission which gave him high rank were a stimulus to Maximin's persistent propensity to inflict injury. His delight would not let him keep still, his gait was more of a dance than a walk, and he seemed bent on copying the Brahmins, who some say levitate in the air about their altars.

The tocsin which heralds internal calamities was now ringing, and people were numb with horror at the frightfulness of the situation. Among many other brutal and merciless acts, too various and numerous to relate, the death of the advocate Marinus stood out. He was accused of having employed black art to win the hand of one Hispanilla, and Maximin after a perfunctory survey of the evidence condemned him to death.

It occurs to me that some readers who examine my account in minute detail may perhaps object that I have sometimes transposed the order of events or passed over things which came under their own observation. To them I can only say that not everything that happened among obscure individuals is worth relating, and that in any case there would not be adequate material in the public archives to meet such a requirement. Too great a mass of mischief was on the boil, and low and high were confounded in a new wave of unbridled madness. It was quite clear that men's chief fear at that time was not a trial at law but a complete suspension of legal proceedings.

The senator Cethegus was accused of adultery and beheaded.

Alypius, a young man of good birth, who had been banished for a venial offence, and others of low rank were put to death. Every man saw in their wretched fate a picture of what he might expect himself, and torture, imprisonment, and a dark lodging haunted his dreams.

The same period saw the trial of Hymetius, a man of outstanding ability. The circumstances, to my certain knowledge, were these. During his government of Africa he sold to the people of Carthage, who were suffering from famine, grain from the supplies set aside for the people of Rome. Soon afterwards there was a good harvest, and he at once restored in full what he had taken. Since, however, he had sold ten bushels for one gold piece to those in need and was now able to purchase thirty for the same sum, he sent the profit accruing from the difference in price to the imperial treasury. Valentinian suspected that he had not sent as much as he should as a result of this transaction, and confiscated part of his property. At the same time Hymetius' troubles were compounded by another incident equally fatal in its consequences. A particularly celebrated soothsayer of the day called Amantius was accused by some unknown informer of having been suborned by Hymetius to offer a sacrifice for some nefarious purpose, a charge which he steadfastly denied even when bent double upon the rack. As an admission could not be wrung from him, his private papers were brought from his house and a memorandum in Hymetius' hand was found asking him to carry out a solemn rite of intercession that God would soften the emperors' hearts towards the writer. The last part of the document contained some criticism of the greed and cruelty of Valentinian. This was represented by the judges to the emperor in the worst light, and Valentinian ordered them to pursue the matter with the utmost rigour. Frontinus, a member of the accused's staff, was charged with helping to draw up the form of prayer. He confessed after a scourging and was banished to Britain; Amantius was later condemned to death and executed. After these transactions Hymetius was taken to Ocriculum to be tried before the urban prefect Ampelius and his deputy Maximin. Seeing that he was on the verge of destruction, he seized an opportunity of appealing to the emperor, and by invoking his protection saved his life. When Valentinian's pleasure was consulted he referred the matter to the senate, which after mature deliberation banished Hymetius to Boae in Dalmatia. By this it incurred the wrath of the emperor, who was deeply affronted when he heard that a man whom he had intended to be condemned to death had been given a milder sentence.

These and many similar incidents made men fear that what was happening in a few cases would be the fate of all. To pass over such outrages in silence would encourage their gradual proliferation, so, to check the increase of misery, the nobility resolved to send a deputation to the emperor. It consisted of Praetextatus, formerly urban prefect, Venustus, a former vice-prefect, and Minervius, who had been a consular governor. They were to ask that punishments should not be out of proportion to the offence and that no senator should be subjected to torture, a proceeding which was neither customary nor legal. When they were admitted to an audience and discharged their errand, Valentinian denied that he had made any such decree and complained that he had been slandered. But the quaestor Eupraxius tactfully contradicted him, and his frankness brought about the repeal of the cruel edict, which was of unexampled frightfulness.

About the same time Lollianus, son of the ex-prefect Lampadius, who was little more than a beardless youth, was convicted after a strict examination by Maximin of having written a book on the black arts at an age when he was still too young to know better. It was expected that he would be banished, but on his father's advice he appealed to the emperor and was taken to Valentinian's court. But this was a jump from the frying-pan into the fire. He was handed over to Sphalangius, the governor of Baetica, and perished at the hands of the executioner.

In addition, Tarracius Bassus, afterwards urban prefect, his brother Camenius, and two others, Marcianus and Eusaphius, all men of senatorial rank, were brought to trial. They were alleged to be the patrons of a charioteer called Auchenius and his accomplice in sorcery, but the evidence was doubtful and they were acquitted. There was a widespread rumour that they owed their acquittal to the influence of Victorinus, a crony of Maximin.

Even women were not exempt from afflictions like these. Many of high birth were found guilty of adultery or fornication and put to death. The most conspicuous cases were those of Claritas and Flaviana. When the latter was on her way to death her clothing was torn from her, and she was not allowed to keep even enough to cover her nakedness. For this monstrous outrage the executioner was burnt alive.

The senators Paphius and Cornelius, who both confessed that they had disgraced themselves by the practice of poisoning, were sentenced by the same Maximin and executed. The head of the mint also suffered the same fate. Sericus and Asbolius, mentioned earlier, who had been solemnly assured by Maximin, in an attempt to induce them to mention any names they pleased, that no one would be punished at the stake or on the block, were dispatched by violent blows from an instrument loaded with lead. The soothsayer Campensis, however, was consigned to the flames, since in his case Maximin was bound by no such promise.

(*30–35*) *omitted*.

By these and other equally deplorable acts, which were a blot on the fair face of the Eternal City, this man, whose very name provokes groans, pursued his violent path amid the wreck of many fortunes, overstepping the limits set by the law. He is said to have kept a cord hanging from a remote window in his official residence, to the end of which *anonymous charges could be attached*, unsupported by evidence but designed to injure many innocent people.

(*37–40*) *omitted*.

Later a successor to Maximin was appointed, and the latter was summoned to the imperial court, to which Leo had preceded him. There he was promoted praetorian prefect. His cruelty was unabated, and he continued to do harm at long range like a basilisk. At that time, or a little earlier, the brooms used to sweep the chamber in which the nobility met burst into leaf, a sign that some people of the lowest sort would rise to high offices of state.

It is time for me to return to my narrative, but in order not to disrupt the sequence of events I will linger over a few of the outrages in the city committed through the wickedness of the vice-prefects, who served as the agents, or rather the mere instruments, of Maximin's will and pleasure. His immediate successor was Ursicinus. He was inclined to milder courses, and to demonstrate his caution and respect for the law referred to higher authority a statement that Esaias, with others who were in prison for adultery with Rufina, was endeavouring to bring a charge of treason against her husband Marcellus, a former agent. This brought Ursicinus into contempt for his inactivity; he was regarded as unfit for the vigorous prosecution of these matters, and his appointment as vice-prefect was terminated. His place was taken by Simplicius of Emona, a confidant of Maximin, who had been a teacher of literature. He had not been proud or arrogant *in his provincial administration*, but his sidelong glances excited alarm, and his studiously moderate language was a veil for the ruin he was plotting against a number of people. He first put Rufina to death along with all those who had been her partners or abettors in adultery (this case, as I said, had been referred by Ursicinus to the court), and after that several others, regardless of their guilt or innocence. Having enlisted under Maximin, he became his rival in the business of butchery and strove to outdo him in hamstringing noble families. In this he followed the example set in ancient times by Busiris and Antaeus and Phalaris of Agrigentum, and all he seemed to lack was the bull of the last-named.

In the course of these and similar horrors a married woman called Hesychia, who was detained in the house of a court official on a criminal charge, was in such terror of savage treatment that she pressed her face into a feather bed on which she was lying and killed herself by suffocation.

(48–56) omitted.

But the curses uttered by the victims in their last moments did not sleep. As I shall tell in due course, Maximin, who behaved with insufferable arrogance during the reign of Gratian, fell by the sword of the executioner and Simplicius was beheaded in Illyricum. Doryphorian (*his successor*) was also condemned to death and thrown into the prison called Tullianum. The emperor, however, removed him from there at his mother's instance, and when he got home had him put to an agonizing death. Now let me return to the point from which I digressed. This, if I may say so, was the state of affairs at Rome.

Chapter (2) describing Valentinian's fortification of the entire left bank of the Rhine is omitted.

3. Theodosius in Britain.

The general Theodosius, bearer of a famous name, set out full of confidence from London, now called Augusta, with a force which he had re-formed with energy and skill. This was of the greatest service to the defeated and harassed Britons. He forestalled the barbarians by seizing positions suitable for guerilla warfare, and imposed no duties on his troops which he himself was not the first to undertake with alacrity. Combining in this way the duties of an active soldier with the responsibilities of high command, he routed and put to flight various tribes, whose burning eagerness to attack anything Roman was fanned by a belief that they could do so with impunity. He completely restored towns and forts which had suffered a series of calamities, but which were now strengthened to secure a long period of peace.

But while he was thus employed a fearful development took place, which would have led to grave danger if it had not been nipped in the bud. One Valentinus from the Pannonian province of Valeria, a man of arrogant temper and a brother-in-law of Maximin, the pernicious vice-prefect who later became praetorian prefect, had been banished to Britain for a serious offence. Like the beast of prey he resembled he could not keep quiet, but embarked on a fresh career of mischief, nursing a particular grudge against Theodosius, whom he looked upon as the only obstacle to his wicked designs. After a good deal of open and clandestine reconnaissance his insatiable ambition led him to tamper with other exiles and such troops as he was in a position to seduce by the bribes he promised. The time for his coup was approaching when the commander-in-chief learned from his intelligence what was going on. Firmly resolved to grasp the nettle and to punish the plot that had been uncovered, he sent Valentinus with a few of his closest associates to the general Dulcitius to be put to death. But his pre-eminent skill in military matters led him, with an eye to the future, to forbid further inquiry into the conspiracy. He was afraid that by spreading alarm among a large number he might reawaken the troubles in the provinces that had been laid to rest.

After the removal of this danger, which conclusively showed that in all his undertakings fortune never deserted him, Theodosius put in hand many necessary reforms. He restored cities and garrison towns, as I have said, and protected the borders with guard-posts and defence works. The recovery of a province which had fallen into the hands of the enemy was so complete that, to use his own words, it now had a lawful governor, and the emperor, treating the matter as a triumph, decreed that henceforth it should be called Valentia.

These were the most important events. The members of the so-called 'Secret Service', a body of long standing of which I gave some account in my history of Constans, had gradually become corrupt and were removed from their posts by Theodosius. They were clearly convicted of having been bribed by gifts or promises of large rewards to pass to the barbarians regular information about what we were doing. Their function was to circulate over a wide area and report to our generals any threatening movements among the neighbouring tribes.

After his brilliant management of these and similar matters, Theodosius was recalled to the court. Like Furius Camillus or Papirius Cursor he had rendered distinguished service to the state by a series of victories, and he left the provinces dancing for joy. Such was his popularity that he was escorted by a large crowd to the straits, over which he had a smooth crossing. He was received at the emperor's headquarters with joy and warm praise, and promoted to the command of the cavalry in place of Jovinus, who was thought to be slack.

4. The vices of Roman society (A.D. 369–72).
(Corruption of the text necessitates some omissions.)

The profusion of events abroad has kept me too long from the affairs of the city. I shall now return to a brief account of these, beginning with the prefectship of Olybrius, which was very quiet and peaceful. He never deviated from a humane policy, and took great pains to ensure that no word or act of his should be accounted harsh. He punished slander severely, pruned the profits of the treasury wherever he could, drew a sharp distinction between right and wrong, and all in all was an admirable judge and very mild towards those he governed. Nevertheless, these good qualities were overshadowed by a defect, which did little harm to the community but was discreditable in a high official. His private life verged on the luxurious and was almost entirely devoted to the stage and to women, though his liaisons were not criminal or incestuous.

Ampelius, also a pleasure-seeker, succeeded him in the government of the city. He was a native of Antioch and previously master of the offices. He had ruled two provinces as proconsul and at a much later date reached the height of praetorian prefect. Though in other respects well fitted to win popularity, he was nevertheless capable of occasional firmness, and I could wish that he had stuck to his principles. He could have done something, however little, to correct the prevailing gluttony and gross immorality if he had not relaxed his strictness and thus lost his chance of winning lasting glory. He ordained that no tavern should open and no ordinary citizen heat water before mid-morning, that victuallers should not display cooked meat for sale before a prescribed hour, and that no respectable person should be seen chewing in public.

These and even more disreputable habits had taken such a hold through continued neglect that even Epimenides of Crete, if he could have been brought back to us from the dead like some legendary hero, could not have cleaned up Rome single-handed. So gross were the incurable vices to which most people had succumbed.

I will deal first with the faults of the nobility, as I have done before as far as space allowed, and then with those of the common people, confining myself to a brief digression on the various points. Some plume themselves on what they consider distinguished forenames, such as Reburrus, Flavonius, Pagonius, and Gereon, or trace their descent from the Dalii or Tarracii or Ferasii or some other high-sounding family. Some, dressed in gleaming silk, go about preceded by a crowd of people, like men being led to execution or, to avoid so unfortunate a simile, like men bringing up the rear of an army, and are followed by a throng of noisy slaves in formation. When such people, each attended by a train of some fifty, enter the public baths, they shout in a peremptory voice: 'What has become of our girls?' If they hear of the sudden appearance of some obscure strumpet, some old street-walker who has earned her living by selling herself to the townsfolk, they vie in courting and caressing the newcomer, and praise her in such outrageously flattering terms as the Parthians used to Semiramis, the Egyptians to their Cleopatras, the Carians to Artemisia, or the people of Palmyra to Zenobia. Such is the behaviour of men among whose ancestors a senator was thought to have behaved improperly and to deserve a reprimand from the censor because he kissed his wife in the presence of their own daughter.

If one tries to greet these people with an embrace they turn their head to one side like a bad-tempered bull, though that is the natural place for a kiss, and offer their knee or their hand instead, as if that should be enough to make anyone happy for life. As for strangers, even those to whom they are under an obligation, they think they have done everything that politeness requires if they ask what bath or spa they frequent or where they are putting up. Though they are so solemn and think themselves so cultured, the news that someone has announced the arrival of horses or drivers, no matter from where, causes them to pester him with knowing questions, and to show him as much respect as their ancestors did to the twin sons of Tyndareus when they spread universal joy by bringing tidings of those famous victories in old times.

Their houses are the resort of idle gossips, who greet every word uttered by the great man with various expressions of hypocritical applause, like the toady in the comedy who inflates the pride of the boastful soldier by attributing to him heroic exploits in sieges and in fights against overwhelming odds. In the same way our toadies admire the beauty of columns in a high façade or the brilliant sight presented by walls of coloured marble, and extol their noble owners as more than mortal. Sometimes too at their dinner-parties scales are called for to weigh the fish, birds, and dormice that are served. The guests are bored to death by repeated expressions of wonder at the unheard-of size of the creatures, especially when some thirty secretaries are in attendance with writing-cases and notebooks to take down the statistics, and all that is wanting to complete the appearance of a school is the schoolmaster.

Some of them hate learning like poison, but read Juvenal and Marius Maximus with avidity. These are the only volumes that they turn over in their idle moments, but why this should be so is not for a man like me to say. Considering their claims to distinction and long descent, they ought to read a variety of books. They should be aware that Socrates, when in prison and under sentence of death, asked a musician who was giving a fine rendering of a lyric by Stesichorus to teach him to do the same while there was still time. The musician asked what good this would be to him, seeing that he was to die next day, but Socrates answered: 'It would give me some new knowledge before I depart.'

A few of them treat offences with such severity that a slave who is slow in bringing hot water will be ordered 300 lashes. But if he should have deliberately killed someone and there is a general demand for his punishment, his master will merely exclaim: 'What else can you expect of such a worthless rascal? If he does anything like this again he shall pay for it.'

Their notion of the height of good breeding is that it is better for a stranger to kill someone's brother than to refuse an invitation to dinner. A senator feels that he has suffered a severe personal loss if a man, whom he has made up his mind after mature reflection to invite once, fails to appear.

A journey of fair length to visit their estates or to be present at a hunt where all the work is done by others seems to some of them the equivalent of a march by Alexander the Great or Caesar. If they sail in their smart yachts from Lake Avernus to Puteoli, *they might be going after the golden fleece*, especially if they undertake the adventure in hot weather. If flies settle on the silk fringes of their garments as they sit between their gilded fans, or if a tiny sunbeam finds its way through a hole in the awning over them, they wish that they had been born in the land of the Cimmerians. When they leave the bath of Silvanus or the spa of Mamaea, each of them as he emerges from the water dries himself with a fine linen towel. Then he has his presses opened and makes a careful inspection of his shimmering robes, of which he has brought enough with him to dress eleven people. Finally, he makes his choice and puts them on, takes back from his valet the rings which he has left with him to avoid damage from the water, and goes his way.

(20) *omitted*.

Some of these people, though not many, dislike the name of gamblers and prefer to be called dice-players, though the distinction is no more than that between a thief and a robber. It must be admitted, however, that, while all other friendships at Rome are lukewarm, those between gamblers are as close and are maintained with as much steadfast affection as if they had been forged by common effort in a glorious cause. You will find members of these sets so harmonious that they might be the brothers Quintilius. On the same principle you may sometimes see a man of low origins but great expertise at dice, who has been placed below a proconsular at some great dinner or reception, walking about with an expression of dignified sorrow, like Porcius Cato after his totally unexpected defeat for the praetorship.

Some lay siege to men of means – it makes no matter whether they are old or young, childless or unmarried, or even if they have wives and children – and employ extraordinary tricks to induce them to make their will. When their victims have finally set their affairs in order and left something to the people whom they have humoured by doing so, they forthwith perish, as if death were merely waiting for them to discharge this duty ...

Another, who has won some promotion, however humble, stalks about, swollen with pride and looking askance on his old acquaintances; he might be Marcellus returning from the capture of Syracuse.

Many, who deny the existence of providence, nevertheless neither appear in public nor eat nor think it safe to take a bath without a minute study of the almanac to discover, for example, the position of Mercury or what degree in the constellation of Cancer the moon has reached in her course through the sky.

Another, if he finds himself harassed by the importunity of a creditor, resorts to a charioteer – a man of this class will undertake any dirty business – and suborns him to prosecute the creditor for sorcery, a charge from which he cannot free himself without giving a bond and incurring heavy costs. In addition the accuser has the voluntary debtor shut up as if he were his chattel, and will not set him free till he acknowledges the debt.

Elsewhere a wife harps day and night on the same string, to use the old proverbial phrase, in order to drive her husband to make a will, and the husband exerts equal pressure on the wife to do the same. Lawyers are brought in on both sides to give contradictory advice; one sits in the bedroom while his rival occupies the dining-room. These are joined by opposing readers of horoscopes; one makes profuse promises of high office and foretells the deaths of rich ladies, while the other urges that all necessary arrangements should be made for the husband's approaching end ... As Cicero says, 'the only earthly good that they recognize is gain. They treat their friends like cattle and value most those from whom they hope to get the greatest return.'

When these people want a loan you will find them cringeing like Micio or Laches. When they are asked for repayment they take such a high and mighty line that they might be the tragic heroes Cresphontes and Temenus. So much for the senate.

Let me now turn to the idle and lazy proletariat. Among these are some who have no shoes but are the proud bearers of such distinguished names as Messor ('mower'), Statarius ('stroller'), Semicupa ('hogshead'), Serapinus, Cicymbricus, Gluturinus ('gobbler'), Trulla ('ladle'), Lucanicus ('sausage'), Porclaca ('pig's belly'), Salsula ('pickle'), and so on. They devote their whole life to drink, gambling, brothels, shows, and pleasure in general. Their temple, dwelling, meeting-place, in fact the centre of all their hopes and desires, is the Circus Maximus. You may see them collected in groups about the squares, crossings, streets, and other public places, engaged in heated argument on one side or the other of some question. Those who have drained life to the dregs and whose age gives them influence often swear by their white hair and wrinkles that the country will go to the dogs if in some coming race the driver they fancy fails to take a lead from the start, or makes too wide a turn round the post with his unlucky team. Such is the general decay of manners that on the longed-for day of the races they rush headlong to the course before the first glimmering of dawn as if they would outstrip the competing teams, most of them having passed a sleepless night distracted by their conflicting hopes about the result.

To turn now to the vulgarity of the stage. The players are hissed off unless the favour of the mob has been purchased by a bribe. If there is no demonstration of this sort they follow the example of the savages of the Chersonese, and clamour for the expulsion of foreigners from the city, though they have always been dependent on the help of these same foreigners for their livelihood. Their language is foul and senseless, very different from that in which the commons of earlier times expressed their feelings and wishes, and of which many witty and elegant examples are preserved by tradition.

  (33) omitted.

Most of these people are addicted to gluttony. Attracted by the smell of cooking and the shrill voices of the women, who scream from cockcrow like a flock of starving peacocks, they stand about the courts on tip-toe, biting their fingers and waiting for the dishes to cool. Others keep their gaze fixed on some revolting mess of meat till it is ready. They look like Democritus and a party of anatomists poring over the guts of a slaughtered beast, and demonstrating how future generations can avoid internal pain.

Enough for the present of the affairs of the city. Now let me return to the events which various causes brought about in the provinces.

5. *A Saxon attack on Gaul ends in a truce, but the Saxons are subsequently destroyed by an act which even Ammianus calls treacherous. Valentinian encourages the Burgundians to attack the Alamanni, but leaves them in the lurch. (Omitted.)*

6. *The disasters of the province of Tripolis (A.D. 363–77).*

From here let us move into what is almost another world, and come to the troubles of the African province of Tripolis. These must have drawn tears, I would think, from Justice herself, and the causes from which the conflagration arose will become clear when I have finished my story.

The Austoriani, who border on those parts, are savages always ready to make a sudden raid and accustomed to live by rapine and slaughter. After a brief period of quiescence they relapsed into their natural state of lawlessness, on the pretext of what they called a genuine grievance. One of their number, called Stachao, availing himself of peaceful conditions to travel freely in our territory, committed some unlawful acts, of which the most serious was to stir up unrest in the province by every trick in his power. The evidence against him was incontrovertible, and he was burnt to death at the stake.

To avenge the death of a man who they claimed was their countryman and had been unjustly condemned, the Austoriani rushed from their haunts like mad beasts. This happened while Jovian was still emperor. They were afraid to approach the populous and strongly fortified town of Lepcis, but encamped for three days in the fertile region round it. They slaughtered the peasants, of whom those who were not paralysed by panic were driven to take refuge in caves, burned a quantity of household goods which they could not carry off, and withdrew with a huge load of booty, taking with them as their prisoner a leading local councillor of Lepcis called Silva whom they had caught with his family in his country house.

The inhabitants of Lepcis were terrified by this sudden disaster, and, to forestall any further mischief from the insolent barbarians, begged the protection of Romanus, who had lately been promoted to command in Africa with the rank of count. But when he arrived with his troops and was asked to help the town in its distress, he replied that he would not take the field unless he were furnished with abundant supplies and 4,000 camels. The wretched citizens were stunned by this answer. They declared that after all that they had suffered from burning and looting they could not meet such prodigious demands, even to recoup their tremendous losses. So, after bamboozling them for about forty days, the count departed without having made any effort to do anything whatever.

The hopes of the people of Tripolis were thus disappointed, and they feared the worst. Accordingly, at the next annual meeting of the provincial assembly it was resolved to send Severus and Flaccian as envoys to Valentinian. They were to greet him on his accession with golden statuettes of the goddess of victory and give him an unvarnished account of the lamentable condition of the province. Hearing of this, Romanus sent a horseman at top speed to the master of the offices Remigius, a kinsman of his and his partner in extortion, telling him to see that the investigation of the matter was referred by imperial decree to himself and the vice-prefect Dracontius. The envoys reached the court, had an audience with the emperor, and made a verbal report of their sufferings, supported by an official document setting out the whole course of the affair. The emperor read it, but refused to give credence either to the report of the master of the offices, who sought to put Romanus' misconduct in a favourable light, or to that of the envoys, who asserted the opposite. He promised a full inquiry, which, however, was put off, as such things often are, when advantage is taken of their being occupied with more important business to hoodwink the holders of supreme power.

While the Tripolitans were kept waiting in anxious suspense for some relief from the emperor's headquarters they were again attacked by bands of barbarians, whose confidence was raised by their previous exploit. They overran the territories of Lepcis and Oea, killing and plundering, and then withdrew with enormous quantities of spoil. Many local officials lost their lives, of whom the best known were the former high-priest Rustician and the aedile Nicasius. The reason why this raid could not be averted was that the conduct of military matters, which at the earnest request of the envoys had been entrusted to Ruricius the governor of the province, was soon afterwards transferred to Romanus. A further envoy was now sent to Gaul with news of this fresh calamity, which greatly angered the emperor. Accordingly the tribune and notary Palladius was sent to discharge the arrears of pay due to the troops stationed in Africa and to make a reliable report on events in Tripolis.

While time was being wasted in long deliberations and in waiting for answers, the Austoriani, rendered still more insolent by their double success, flew upon their victims again, like birds of prey roused to frenzy by the taste of blood. They killed all who did not manage to make their escape, and, after cutting down the trees and vines, carried off all the spoil that they had previously left behind. On the outskirts of the town they captured a well-born and influential citizen called Mychon. He gave them the slip before he could be shackled, but lameness prevented him from getting clear away. So he threw himself into an empty well, from which the barbarians pulled him out with a broken rib, and brought him before the town gates, where he was ransomed at the urgent entreaty of his wife. He was lifted up to the battlements by a rope, but died two days later. On this occasion the marauding savages showed greater persistence, and assailed the very walls of Lepcis, which echoed with the doleful screams of the women, who had never experienced a siege before and were prostrated with terror. After keeping up the siege for eight days, during which some of them were wounded without effecting anything, the enemy returned to their own domains somewhat disappointed.

The townspeople were now in fear for their lives. The earlier envoys had not returned, and as a last resource they sent Jovinus and Pancratius to give the emperor a true account of what they had seen and suffered personally. They met the previous envoys Severus and Flaccian at Carthage, and learned on inquiry that these had been told to report to the vice-prefect and the count. Immediately afterwards Severus fell seriously ill and died. In spite of what they had been told, Jovinus and Pancratius hurried to the court with all possible speed.

After this Palladius reached Africa. Romanus was acquainted in advance with the purpose of his mission, and to secure his own safety sent instructions through confidential agents to the commanders of units to leave to Palladius the greater part of the pay he had brought, since he was a person of influence and very close to the highest officials of the court. This was done, and Palladius, thus enriched, proceeded to Lepcis. To get to the bottom of things he took with him to the devastated area two eloquent burghers of high standing, Erechthius and Aristomenes, who informed him unreservedly of their own troubles and those of their fellow-citizens and neighbours. They showed him everything, and, after surveying the deplorable ruin to which the province was reduced, he returned and reproached Romanus for his inactivity, threatening to give a true account of all he had seen to the emperor. Romanus in a furious passion retorted that he too would shortly make a report to the effect that the supposedly incorruptible notary had diverted to his own pocket all the money intended for the troops. The result was that Palladius, with such a load on his conscience, acted thenceforth in concert with Romanus, and when he returned to the court misled Valentinian by a wicked lie to the effect that there was no substance in the complaints of the people of Tripolis. He was sent back to Africa with Jovinus, the most recent envoy, Pancratius having died at Trier, and with instructions to look into the credentials of the second mission also. In addition, the emperor gave orders that Erechthius and Aristomenes should have their tongues cut out for having uttered what Palladius intimated were libels.

The notary followed the vice-prefect, as had been arranged, and reached Tripolis. Hearing of this, Romanus lost no time in sending thither one of his personal attendants together with Caecilius, a native of that province, whose advice he relied on. By their agency all the townspeople were induced, whether by bribery or fraud is not clear, to lay all the blame on Jovinus, and assert positively that they had given him no instructions to report as he had to Valentinian. So iniquitous, indeed, were these proceedings that Jovinus himself was driven by fear for his life to confess that he had lied to the emperor.

When this news reached him through Palladius on his return, Valentinian, who was always prone to harshness, decreed that Jovinus as the prime mover, with Caelestinus, Concordius, and Lucius as partners in his fraud, should suffer capital punishment, and that the governor Ruricius, whose lies were aggravated by his having apparently used intemperate language, should also be put to death. Ruricius was executed at Sitifis, but the others were delivered up to be sentenced by the vice-prefect Crescens at Utica. Before the death of the envoys, however, Flaccian was brought before the vice-prefect and the court. He defended himself with energy, but was almost finished off by the furious troops, who rushed at him shouting abuse, and claiming that the reason why it had been impossible to protect the Tripolitans was that they refused to provide the supplies necessary for the operation. He was therefore thrown into prison until the emperor could be consulted and decide what should be done with him. But he made his escape to Rome, by bribing his guards, it was generally believed, and there he went into hiding and died a natural death.

By this remarkable outcome Tripolis, the victim of both domestic and external calamities, was reduced to silence. But she was not left without champions. The ever-open eye of Justice was on the watch, and the last curses uttered by the envoys and the governor had their effect, as became clear at a much later date. Palladius was dismissed from his post and retired into private life, with his pride utterly humbled. And when that superb general Theodosius came to Africa to check the pernicious designs of Firmus, and in accordance with his instructions examined the effects of the outlawed Romanus, he found a letter from one Meterius addressed to his 'lord and patron Romanus', which contained among other matters not here relevant the following sentence: 'The disgraced Palladius sends you his greetings, and wishes you to know that the only reason for his disgrace was that in the affair of Tripolis he uttered a lie to the sacred ear of majesty.' This letter was sent to the court and read. Meterius was arrested at Valentinian's order and admitted that he was the writer. Orders were then given for the production of Palladius, but he, conscious of the mass of crimes that he had committed, one evening at a halt on the way took advantage of the absence of his guards, who were at church attending an all-night celebration of a Christian feast, to knot a noose about his neck and hang himself. When it became public knowledge that things had taken a turn for the better by the destruction of the author of these sad troubles, Erechthius and Aristomenes emerged from the distant hiding-place in which they had taken refuge on hearing that their tongues were to be cut out for their allegedly extravagant words. The emperor Gratian, who had now succeeded Valentinian, was reliably informed of the wicked fraud that had been perpetrated, and Erechthius and Aristomenes were sent to have their case heard by the proconsul Hesperius and the vice-prefect Flavian, whose impartiality was as unimpeachable as their authority. They extracted from Caecilius under torture a full confession that it was he who had persuaded the citizens to accuse the envoys of lying. There followed a report which set out the whole course of events in an unquestionably reliable form, and to this no reply was made.

Even so, to complete the full tragic effect of this frightful drama, an epilogue was added after the fall of the curtain. Romanus set off for the court with Caecilius to accuse the judges of prejudice in favour of the province. He had a favourable reception from Merobaudes, and asked that further persons whom he needed for his case should be produced. They were brought to Milan, but were able to show conclusively that they had been sent for unnecessarily on grounds of personal hostility. They were therefore discharged and returned home. But even before the death of Valentinian, Remigius, after the events I have narrated above, retired into private life, and finally hanged himself, as I shall relate in its proper place.

BOOK 29

1. Trial of Theodorus and others for treason at Antioch. (A short account of an inconclusive campaign in Mesopotamia opens this chapter.)

While Valens was at Antioch, free for the moment from anxiety about his foreign foes, he narrowly escaped death from domestic treachery, as the following account will make clear.

A restless character called Procopius, always keen to make trouble, charged two courtiers Anatolius and Spudasius, who had been summoned to pay amounts of which they had defrauded the treasury, with an attempt on the life of count Fortunatian, who was notoriously oppressive in pursuing such claims. This maddened Fortunatian, a man of naturally choleric temper, and in accordance with the rules defining his authority he handed over to the court of the praetorian prefect a man of the lowest origin called Palladius, who he alleged had been ordered to poison him by the aforesaid courtiers, together with a reader of horoscopes called Heliodorus, in order that they might be forced to reveal what they knew of the matter. In the course of a strict investigation of the crime or attempted crime, Palladius had the effrontery to assert that the point at issue was trivial and negligible. If he were allowed to speak he could tell of a more momentous and fearful plot for which elaborate preparations had been made, and which, unless precautions were taken, would create universal havoc. He was offered immunity in return for his information and proceeded to unroll a long string of charges to the effect that the ex-governor Fidustius, together with Pergamius and Irenaeus, had used the abominable art of divination in secret to discover the name of Valens' successor. Fidustius, who happened to be about, was at once seized and privately examined. When he was confronted by the informer he made no attempt to deny or conceal what had already been disclosed, but revealed the details of the whole sinister affair. He admitted unreservedly that with the assistance of Hilarius and Patricius, who were adepts at divination (the former

had held a post in the administration), he had held a seance about the
succession, and that the outcome of their inquiries was a prediction that
an excellent prince would be named but that the inquiries themselves
would come to a sad end. They discussed who there was at that time of
outstanding character, and came to the conclusion that the best of all
was Theodorus. He had already risen to the second place among the
notaries, and was in fact just such a man as they thought him. He came
of an old and distinguished family in Gaul, had received a liberal
education from earliest boyhood, and was highly regarded for his
moderation, wisdom, refinement, charm, and learning. He always
seemed too good for the office or rank he was holding and was the
favourite of high and low alike. His was almost the only mouth which
could not be shut for fear of consequences, though he kept a bridle on
his tongue and never spoke without reflection. After being tortured
almost to death, Fidustius added that he had informed Theodorus of
these predictions through the agency of Euserius. The latter was a man
of remarkable literary attainments and highly thought of, who had
recently governed Asia as pro-prefect. He was arrested, and the record
of the proceedings was read to the emperor in the usual way. The result
was that the monstrous ferocity of Valens spread everywhere like a
blazing fire, and was fed by the shameful flattery of many of his court,
in particular of Modestus the praetorian prefect. This man was racked
with daily-increasing anxiety about the succession, and, though he
veiled his skilful adulation by covertly sneering at Valens, who was
something of a dunce, used various devices to win his favour. He called
his rough, crude language 'Ciceronian flowers of speech', and flattered
his vanity by promising that the very stars could be made to shine if
Valens commanded it.

In consequence, orders were given that Theodorus should be brought
with all speed from Constantinople, which he was visiting on private
business. While he was on the way various preliminary inquiries were
pursued day and night, which resulted in many people of high rank and
birth being fetched from widely separated places. The public prisons
were full to overflowing, and even when private houses were requi-
sitioned the numbers under arrest could not be properly lodged. They
were confined in crowded and stifling conditions, most of them in chains
and all in fear for their own fate and that of their relatives. At last
Theodorus himself arrived, dressed in mourning and as good as dead.
He was kept hidden in a remote part of the territory of Antioch, and

when everything was ready for the coming trials it was as if a trumpet sounded to herald domestic disaster.

Since it is as misleading knowingly to conceal facts as it is to invent fictitious incidents, I do not deny the undisputed truth that the life of Valens, which had often before been the object of conspiracies, was now plunged into extreme danger. The military had a sword almost at his throat, and it was turned aside only by destiny, which was reserving him for deplorable disasters in Thrace. While he was enjoying a quiet afternoon nap in a wooded spot between Antioch and Seleucia, he was attacked by the targeteer Sallustius, and many attempts were made on his life at other times. He escaped these monstrous outrages only because he had not yet completed the span of life allotted to him at birth. The same thing often happened in the reigns of Commodus and Severus, whose lives were frequently attempted with great violence. The former, after surviving many domestic dangers, received an almost fatal dagger wound from the hand of the senator Quintian, a man of lawless ambition, as he was traversing a passage in the amphitheatre to attend the games. The latter at the very end of his life was surprised in his bed by the centurion Saturninus at the instigation of the prefect Plautian, and would have been stabbed if he had not been rescued by his young son. Valens therefore had every reason to take precautions to preserve his life, which traitors were eager to take from him. What was inexcusable was that in his tyrannical pride he maliciously pursued and persecuted innocent and guilty alike under one and the same law, without making any distinction between their deserts. While the charge was still unproved the emperor had decided upon the sentence, and some learned that they had been condemned before they knew that they were suspected. His own greed and that of his courtiers acted as a spur to this rigid policy; they were always opening their mouths for fresh gains, and on the rare occasions when mercy was suggested they called it slackness. The flattery of these bloodsuckers fatally corrupted the character of a man who had death at the tip of his tongue, and the untimely storm which they raised in their haste to destroy the richest houses blew down everything. Valens had two fatal defects which put him at the mercy of intriguers; he was liable to intolerable fits of rage just at the moments when he should have been ashamed to be angry, and his princely pride did not allow him to sift the truth of what he allowed people to whisper to him in the freedom of private conversation; he took it all as true and certain. As a result many innocent people were thrust from their homes by what purported to be an act of mercy, and driven headlong into exile. Their property was collected by the treasury and used by the emperor for his own purposes, while the condemned were ground down by fearful poverty and reduced to beg their bread, a fate which the wise old poet Theognis advises us to avoid, if necessary by hurling ourselves into the sea. Even if one allows that these decisions were just, the severity with which they were executed was hateful. It has been truly observed that no sentence is more cruel than one which veils its harshness under an appearance of mercy.

When the notables, to whom the conduct of these trials was entrusted, had assembled under the presidency of the praetorian prefect, the racks were set up, and leaden weights, cords, and scourges put in readiness. The air was filled with the appalling yells of savage voices mixed with the clanking of chains, as the torturers in the execution of their grim task shouted: 'Hold, bind, tighten, more yet.' The victims that I have seen hauled away after agonizing torments are so numerous that everything is confused in my recollection and I am left in the dark. Since the details of all that happened escape me, I will give a brief account of what my memory retains.

After a few trivial preliminaries Pergamius was brought in first. He, as I said, had been betrayed by Palladius for inquiring into the future by the forbidden practice of sorcery. He was a fluent speaker and liable to endanger people by letting his tongue run away with him. While the judges were debating the order of their interrogation he burst boldly into speech, pouring out an endless list of accessories and demanding that some people should be fetched from the ends of the earth to stand trial on serious charges. This was setting the court too hard a task, and he was punished with death. After him, others were executed in droves till at last the case of Theodorus was reached, the Olympic event, so to speak, which crowned the series. The same day saw the following sad event among many others. Salia, who shortly before had been count of the treasury in Thrace, was being brought from prison to be tried and was just putting his foot into his shoe, when he collapsed suddenly under the stress of overwhelming terror and breathed his last in the arms of his guards.

The court was constituted and the judges announced the rules which were to govern its procedure, but in the event they manipulated the outcome of the cases in accordance with the wishes of their master. This caused universal horror. Valens had entirely abandoned the path of equity and learned the trade of persecution; so he broke out into the most furious anger, like a wild beast in the arena when anyone who has come near its place of work escapes.

Patricius and Hilarius were brought in and told to give a full account of what had occurred. Their first statements differed a little, but, after a savage flogging and the production of the tripod which was their instrument, they were reduced to such straits that they revealed the truth of the whole business from the beginning. Hilarius spoke first:

'My lords, in an unlucky moment we put together out of laurel twigs in the shape of the Delphic tripod the hapless little table before you. We consecrated it with cryptic spells and a long series of magical rites, and at last made it work. The way in which it did so, when we wished to consult it about hidden matters, was this. It was placed in the middle of a room thoroughly fumigated with spices from Arabia, and was covered with a round dish made from an alloy of various metals. The outer rim of the dish was cunningly engraved with the twenty-four letters of the alphabet separated by accurately measured intervals. A man dressed in linen garments and wearing linen sandals, with a fillet round his head and green twigs from a lucky tree in his hand, officiated as priest. After uttering a set prayer to invoke the divine power which presides over prophecy, he took his place above the tripod as his knowledge of the proper ritual had taught him, and set swinging a ring suspended by a very fine cotton thread, which had been consecrated by a mystic formula. The ring, moving in a series of jumps over the marked spaces, came to rest on particular letters, which made up hexameters appropriate to the questions put and perfect in scansion and rhythm, like the lines produced at Delphi or by the oracle of the Branchidae. On this occasion, when we asked who would succeed the present emperor – we had already learnt that whoever it was would be excellent in every way – the ring lightly touched the letters making the two syllables THEO, and when it came to the following letter one of those present cried out that the finger of fate inevitably pointed to Theodorus. So we left the matter there, being entirely satisfied that he was the man we were looking for.'

After putting the whole affair before the court in so clear a light, Hilarius was good enough to add that Theodorus was entirely ignorant of it all. He and Patricius were next asked whether the method of sorcery they had used with such confidence had foretold their own present sufferings. In reply they uttered the notorious lines which clearly foretold that this act of inquiry into the supernatural would be fatal to those who engaged in it, but that nevertheless the Furies, breathing fire and slaughter, were in wait also for the emperor himself and his judges. Of these lines it will be enough to quote the last three:

> Your blood shall be avenged; Tisiphone
> For them too has an evil fate in store,
> When Ares waxes wroth on Mimas' plain.

After reciting these lines both the accused were fearfully mangled by the torturers' hooks and taken away unconscious.

Later, in order to expose the whole machinery of the projected crime, a group of men of rank were put on trial. These comprised the actual heads of the conspiracy. Each thought only of his own safety and tried to shift his own ruin on to another, till finally by permission of the court Theodorus began to speak. At first he lay prostrate begging for pardon, but when he was forced to come more to the point he declared that when he heard of the matter through Euserius he made several attempts to report it to the emperor. Euserius, however, had prevented this by assuring him that what they were waiting for would not come about by an unlawful bid to usurp the throne, but by the inevitable workings of fate. Euserius, when interrogated under torture, confirmed this statement, but Theodorus was convicted by a letter of his own to Hilarius. Its terms were indirect and tortuous, but its purport was that Theodorus, encouraged by the prediction, felt no hesitation about the matter and was only waiting for the right moment to attain his desire.

When these facts were established the accused were removed, and Eutropius, who then held the proconsular post of governor of Asia, was charged with complicity in the plot. But he was rescued by the philosopher Pasiphilus and escaped unharmed. Pasiphilus was cruelly tortured to induce him to ruin Eutropius by false evidence, but all efforts to overcome his stubborn resistance failed. There was also another philosopher called Simonides, who was still quite young but a man of the strictest principles I have ever known. He was accused of having heard of the plot through Fidustius. Realizing that the outcome of the trial would not depend on the truth but on the will of a single man, he said that he had heard of the prediction, but felt bound as a man of honour to keep the secret.

After scrutinizing all these matters with a keen eye the judges consulted the emperor. In response he issued a comprehensive decree for the execution of all the accused. In the presence of a countless throng which could hardly view the fearful sight without a shudder, and which filled the air with laments, since the sufferings of individuals seemed likely to be the common fate, they were all brought out and pitifully beheaded. The single exception was Simonides. The author of this savage sentence had been maddened by his unshaken firmness and commanded him to be burnt alive. Simonides, however, to whom death was an escape from the grim tyrant life, and who laughed at sudden disastrous turns of fate, stood unmoved amid the flames, like the famous philosopher Peregrinus, nicknamed Proteus. He, having decided to leave the world, mounted a pyre which he had built himself at the quinquennial celebration of the Olympic games, and was consumed by fire while the whole of Greece looked on. In the days following the execution of Simonides a crowd of people of all ranks, who had been caught in the snare of slander and whom it would be a hard task to enumerate by name, gave the arms of the executioners no rest, after their strength had first been exhausted by rack, lead, and scourge. Some were put to death without a moment's delay, while the question of their guilt was still being debated, and the whole scene resembled a slaughterhouse.

Then innumerable books and whole heaps of documents, which had been routed out from various houses, were piled up and burnt under the eyes of the judges. They were treated as forbidden texts to allay the indignation caused by the executions, though most of them were treatises on various liberal arts and on jurisprudence.

Not so very long afterwards, Maximus, a famous philosopher with a great reputation for learning, from whose fruitful discourses the emperor Julian acquired such a store of knowledge, was accused of having heard the lines of this same oracle. He admitted that he had heard them, but had kept them to himself out of professional etiquette; he added, however, that he had volunteered the prediction that those who consulted the oracle would themselves perish at the hands of the executioner. He was taken to his native city of Ephesus and beheaded, learning by this last fatal experience that an unjust judge is worse than any accusation. Diogenes too was entrapped by a wicked lie. He was a man of noble stock and outstanding ability combined with great eloquence and charm, who had once been governor of Bithynia. He was put to death so that his ample estate might be plundered. Worse still, the arm of iniquity stretched so far that even Alypius, the ex-governor of Britain, a gentle and amiable man who was living quietly in retirement, was plunged into extreme misery and accused with his son Hierocles, a young man of good character, of practising sorcery. The only evidence came from a low creature also called Diogenes, who was mangled mercilessly to cause him to utter what the emperor, who was the real author of the charge, wished to hear. When there was nothing of Diogenes left to torture he was burnt alive. Alypius had his property confiscated and was condemned to exile, but recovered his son, who was reprieved by a stroke of luck after being actually led out to suffer a miserable death.

2. Further trials for magic and treason in the East.

During all this time Palladius, the fomenter of all these troubles, who, as I said earlier, had been arrested by Fortunian and whose mean condition led him to stop at nothing, piled one disaster on another and caused universal grief and tears. Having once got the chance of naming whom he liked, whatever their station in life, as dabblers in forbidden arts, he entangled many people in his fatal snares like an expert hunter following the obscure track of his prey. Some he charged with having disgraced themselves by the practice of magic, some with being accessory to the treasonable ambitions of others. Even wives were left no time to bewail the misfortunes of their husbands; men were sent immediately to seal up their houses, and, in the course of examining the possessions of the condemned paterfamilias, to smuggle in among them old wives' spells and absurd love-charms designed to endanger innocent folk. When these were read in court, where no law or scruple or sense of justice prevailed to distinguish truth from falsehood, young and old were indiscriminately deprived of their property without any opportunity of defence, although they were quite guiltless, and after suffering wholesale torture were taken off in litters to execution. The result was that throughout the eastern provinces whole libraries were burnt by their owners for fear of a similar fate; such was the terror which seized all hearts. In a word, we all crept about at that time in a Cimmerian darkness, filled with the same fear as the guests of Dionysius of Sicily. While they were stuffing themselves with a meal more dreadful than any degree of hunger, swords hung over their heads suspended by horse-hairs from the ceiling of the room in which they were sitting, and kept them in a state of continual terror.

At this time too, Bassian, a man of distinguished family and a notary of the highest class, was charged with attempting to obtain foreknowledge of matters beyond his sphere, though he maintained that his inquiries were merely about the sex of a child that his wife was expecting. The influence exerted by his relations saved him from death, but he was stripped of his inherited wealth.

While so much was crashing in ruin Heliodorus, the hellish contriver with Palladius of all this misery, and himself by popular report an astrologer who had been induced by secret overtures from the court to pledge his services, put out his deadly fangs. Every kind of flattery and cajolery was employed to induce him to reveal what he knew or had fabricated. He was solicitously pampered with the choicest viands, and large sums of money were contributed for him to bestow on his whores. His twisted features were to be seen here, there, and everywhere, an object of universal dread, and his confidence was enhanced because in his capacity of chamberlain he had free access to the women's quarters, which he visited at his pleasure, displaying warrants from the Father of his People which were to bring many to grief. By his means Palladius (?) was instructed like an advocate at the bar what to put at the beginning of a speech in order to ensure success and what rhetorical figures to employ to achieve a brilliant effect. It would be tedious to narrate all the exploits of this gallows-bird, but I will give one example of the way in which his bold-faced impudence shook the patriciate to its very foundations. His secret confabulations with courtiers had, as I said, made him outrageously arrogant, and he was so worthless that there was no crime that he could not be hired to commit. He accused that admirable pair of consuls, the brothers Eusebius and Hypatius, connections by marriage of the former emperor Constantius, of planning to exalt themselves and of using divination to further their designs on the empire, and to make this fabrication more plausible he added that imperial robes had actually been got ready for Eusebius. All this was eagerly swallowed by the dangerous lunatic, whose belief in his right to commit any wrong showed him to be unfit to wield authority of any kind. Anyone whom the informer, who was free from all legal restraint, had the sublime assurance to assert ought to be sent for was inexorably hailed even from the furthest corners of the empire, and the emperor ordered a trial on a criminal charge to be set in motion. For a long time Justice was tightly bound and trampled underfoot, while the abandoned scoundrel persisted in his string of falsehoods. But severe torture failed to extort a confession, and merely demonstrated that the distinguished defendants were utterly devoid of any guilty knowledge. Nevertheless, their false accuser continued to be treated with the same respect as before, while they were visited with exile and pecuniary penalties. Shortly afterwards, however, their fines were remitted and they were recalled to the unimpaired enjoyment of their rank and dignity.

Even after these deplorable proceedings Valens' behaviour showed no more restraint or sense of shame than before. Excessive power leaves no room for the thought that a man of sound principles should not plunge wittingly into wrongdoing even in order to inflict harm on his enemies, and that nothing is uglier than supreme authority combined with a cruel nature. When Heliodorus died, whether from natural causes or violence I would not like to say (and I could wish that the circumstances did not speak for themselves), his funeral was marshalled by the undertakers, and several men of rank, including the two consular brothers, were ordered to precede the corpse dressed in mourning. This act of stupidity clearly revealed the utter rottenness of the emperor's rule. Although he was earnestly entreated to refrain from inflicting such an irreparable insult, nothing could move him; he was as deaf as if he had blocked his ears with wax to sail past the rocks of the Sirens. All that could be wrung from him was the great concession that they should accompany the unhallowed bier of the sacrilegious wretch bare-headed and bare-foot, and that certain persons should precede the body with clasped hands. One shudders to think of the humiliation inflicted during this period of mourning on so many men of the highest distinction, and especially on the ex-consuls, who had been honoured with rods of office and robes of state and won for themselves a place in the history of the world. Conspicuous among them was my fellow-countryman Hypatius, whose noble qualities had earned him praise from his earliest youth. He was a man of calm and cool judgement, whose mild and honourable character never deviated from the upright. His career gave fresh lustre to his distinguished forebears, and the admirable way in which he administered his two prefectures conferred fame on his posterity.

At this same time, it must be counted among Valens' other glorious exploits that, although in other cases he was so implacably cruel that he could hardly bear that the torments he inflicted should be terminated by death, he spared Numerius, a man of incomparable wickedness. Numerius was convicted on his own confession of cutting open the womb of a living woman and removing her embryo child in pursuit of a design to raise the dead and question them about a change in the empire. But Valens looked on him with a friendly eye, and, in spite of the murmurs of all classes, let him go free and keep not only his life but his enviable wealth and his rank in the service.

How happy are they on whom Heaven has bestowed the glorious gift of wisdom, which has often ennobled even vicious natures. How much might have been put right in those dark days if Valens had been taught by wisdom the lesson of the philosophers that sovereign power is nothing if it does not care for the welfare of others, and that it is the task of a good ruler to keep his power in check, to resist the passions of unbridled desire and implacable rage, and to realize that, as the dictator Caesar used to say, the recollections of past cruelty is a wretched provision for old age. If a ruler is going to pass judgement on the life and existence of a man, who is part of the world and makes up the number of living beings, he ought to reflect long and earnestly, and not be carried away by passion to commit an act that cannot be undone. Of this truth there is a well-known instance in ancient times. A woman of Smyrna confessed before Dolabella, the proconsul of Asia, that she had poisoned her husband and her son because she had discovered that they had murdered another son of hers by a previous husband. She was remanded for two days, and then, because the body to which the matter was referred was in doubt where to draw the line between revenge and crime, she was sent before the Areopagus, the strict Athenian court which is said to have decided disputes even between the gods. After hearing the case the Areopagus decided that she should appear before it again in a hundred years' time, so as to escape the dilemma of either absolving a poisoner or punishing a person who had avenged her kindred. People think that that never comes too late which is the last of all things.

Such were the iniquitous deeds committed, and the shameful marks of torture branded on the bodies of free men, even if they managed to survive. But the sleepless eye of Justice, the eternal witness and judge of all things, was ever on the watch. The curses uttered by the victims with their dying breath were so plainly justified that they roused the eternal godhead and kindled the flames of war, thus confirming the truth of the oracle which had foretold that no crime would go unpunished.

The events which I have described created widespread internal trouble at Antioch during a lull in the Parthian storm, but, after heaping these manifold disasters one upon another, the grim troop of Furies left that city and settled on the neck of the whole of Asia. These are the circumstances. Fate ordained that one Festus of Trent (Tridentum), a man of the lowest and most obscure origin, whom Maximin loved like a brother because he was a comrade who had grown up with him, should cross over to the East, where as governor of Syria and master of the records he left behind him a good reputation for mildness and respect for the law. From this he was promoted to govern Asia with the status of proconsul, and the wind was set fair, as they say, to waft him to honour. Hearing that Maximin was set on the destruction of all respectable people, he decried his behaviour thenceforth as dangerous and disgraceful. But when he heard that the deaths of his victims had helped to advance his undeserving friend to a prefectship, he was on fire to imitate his conduct and conceived similar hopes. Having adopted this pernicious policy, he suddenly changed masks like an actor, and stalked about with a grim and watchful look, confident that a prefectship would shortly be his if he too defiled himself with the blood of the innocent. Of all the various actions on his part which, to put it mildly, were excessively harsh, it will be enough to give a few examples which were matters of common knowledge and deliberate imitations of what had taken place at Rome. The principles governing good and bad actions are the same everywhere, however much the circumstances may differ in importance.

He executed a philosopher named Coeranius, a man of no small merit, who held out under the most savage torture, because in a private letter to his wife he had added in Greek: 'Take note of what I say and put a wreath on the door.' This is a proverbial expression signifying to the hearer that something of unusual importance is on foot.

A simple-minded old woman, who was in the habit of using a harmless spell as a remedy for intermittent fevers, was put to death as a criminal, even though she had been called in to treat Festus' own daughter with his full concurrence.

Among the papers of a respectable citizen which came to be examined in the course of business the horoscope of a certain Valens was found. The man in question was asked why he had cast the nativity of the emperor; his defence against the false charge was that the Valens mentioned was his brother, who had long been dead. But though he undertook to prove this fully by irrefragable evidence, his judges would not wait to find out the truth, and he was scourged and slaughtered.

A young man in the public baths was noticed touching the marble of the bath and his own breast alternately with the fingers of both hands, reciting the seven Greek vowels as he did so. He believed that this would relieve a stomach complaint, but he was dragged into court, tortured, and beheaded.

3. The cruelty and brutality of Valentinian in the West.

At this point I turn my pen to Gaul, where there is much confusion about the order of events. Maximin, now prefect, is found at the centre of the cruel scene. His authority was extensive, and he exercised a sinister influence on the emperor, in whom unbounded caprice was united with supreme power. The reader who reflects on what I say must also bear in mind what I pass over in silence, and be understanding enough to pardon me if I do not include all the instances in which deliberate wickedness exaggerated the gravity of alleged offences. Valentinian had naturally a savage temper, and passion, which is the enemy of sound reason, grew stronger in him after the arrival of Maximin. There was no one to give him better advice or to act as a restraining influence, and he allowed himself to drift on a stormy sea, as it were, from one act of cruelty to another. His very voice and expression, his gait and his complexion, changed when he was in a rage. Of this there are various indubitable examples, of which it will suffice to mention a few.

A young man of the class known as pages was posted with a Spartan hound in leash to watch for game. He let the dog slip before the proper moment because the animal, in a struggle to get free, leapt upon him and bit him. For this he was cudgelled to death and buried the same day. The manager of a workshop brought the emperor a breastplate of most cunning workmanship for which he expected to be paid. Valentinian, in an outburst of rage, ordered him to be put to death because the finished product weighed slightly less than had been specified. An elder of the Christian church from Epirus *was executed because he failed to surrender the former proconsul Octavian, who had taken refuge with him*, whereas the prime mover in the offence was sent back, though after some delay, to his home. Constantian, a riding-master, who had been sent to Sardinia to inspect cavalry mounts, took the liberty of exchanging a few of them, and was stoned to death at Valentinian's command. Athanasius, a popular charioteer, was an object of such suspicion to the emperor on account of his light-hearted jests that orders were given that he should be burnt alive if there was any more trouble. Shortly afterwards he was accused of practising sorcery and condemned to death at the stake; no indulgence was granted to a man who had given such general pleasure. Africanus, a busy Roman advocate and a provincial governor, aspired to the rule of another province. His request was supported by the master of cavalry Theodosius, who received this rough answer from the gracious emperor: 'Go, count, and change his head for him, since he wants to have his province changed.' By this pronouncement a practised speaker lost his life, simply because he shared the common ambition for preferment. Two officers of the Joviani, Claudius and Sallustius, who had reached the rank of tribune, were accused by a fellow, whose mean origin was enough in itself to make him contemptible, of having spoken in favour of Procopius when he was a pretender to the throne. Although repeated inquiries brought nothing to light, the emperor ordered the masters of cavalry who were hearing the case to send Claudius into exile and to pronounce sentence of death on Sallustius, coupling this, however, with a promise to reprieve the latter on the way to execution. These orders were obeyed, but Sallustius did not escape death, and Claudius was not relieved from the misery of exile till after the decease of Valentinian ...

I shudder to recount all that took place, and I am afraid also of appearing deliberately to stress the defects of an emperor who was in other respects admirable. One thing, however, it would be wrong to pass over or suppress. He had two savage man-eating she-bears called Gold-dust and Innocence, to which he was so devoted that he had their cages placed near his bedroom, and appointed reliable keepers to see that nothing was allowed to impair the destructive fury of the brutes. In the end, after seeing many people buried whom Innocence had torn to pieces, he rewarded her services by returning her safe to the wild, in the hope that she would produce cubs like herself.

4. Valentinian in Germany. The opening sentences are an important testimony to the general success of his policy on the Rhine. (The rest of the chapter, which describes an unsuccessful attempt to capture Macrianus, king of the Alamanni, is omitted.)

These are indubitable indications of Valentinian's character and bloodthirsty disposition. But even his harshest critic cannot find fault with his unfailing shrewdness in matters of state, especially if he bears in

mind that it was a greater service to keep the barbarians in check by
frontier barriers than to defeat them in battle.

> *Chapter giving a long and complicated account of operations in Africa
> by Theodosius against a rebel Moorish chieftain called Firmus (5) is
> omitted.*

6. *Invasion of Pannonia by the Quadi and Sarmatians.*

While Theodosius was labouring through the dust of his campaigns in
Mauretania and Africa, the Quadi, who had long been quiet, suddenly
caused an upheaval. They are a people who nowadays inspire little fear,
but were formerly immensely warlike and powerful. This is shown by
the sudden raids that they made, by the siege of Aquileia, in which they
were joined by the Marcomanni, by the destruction of Opitergium, and
by many bloody feats in the course of a lightning campaign when they
crossed the Julian Alps, and the emperor Marcus, of whom I have
spoken earlier, was hardly able to withstand them. On this occasion
they had what for barbarians was a just ground for complaint.

Valentinian from the very beginning of his reign was burning with a
glorious resolve to protect his frontiers. But he went too far when he
ordered the erection of a fortress on the further side of the Danube and
in the actual territory of the Quadi, which he treated as subject to the
authority of Rome. This infringement of their rights was resented by
the inhabitants, but for the moment they did nothing beyond sending
a delegation and grumbling. Maximin, however, always on the look-
out for a chance to do wrong and unable to bridle his natural arrogance,
which was further swollen by his promotion to prefect, blamed Equitius,
the commander-in-chief in Illyricum, for obstinacy and slackness in
not completing the work which he had orders to hurry on. He added,
with an appearance of public spirit, that if his own son Marcellian were
made general in Valeria the fortress would rise from the ground without
any further shilly-shallying. Both his wishes were soon fulfilled. The
newly appointed general arrived on the scene and acted with the
untimely presumption to be expected of his father's son. Without
making any attempt to placate the people who were being driven from
their country to further a novel and illusory scheme, he took in hand
the works that had been recently begun, but then suspended to allow
opportunity for protest. Finally, when king Gabinius made a modest

request that no further steps should be taken, he gave the impression that he would agree, and with feigned friendliness invited Gabinius and others to dinner. But as his unsuspecting guest was leaving he had him murdered, a most infamous violation of the sacred laws of hospitality.

The news of this outrage at once got abroad, and roused the Quadi and the neighbouring tribes to fury. Mourning the death of their king, they got together and sent out parties to devastate our territory. They crossed the Danube and fell upon the country folk, who were busy with their harvest and had no thought of an enemy. Most of them they killed, and the rest they carried off home together with a large quantity of livestock. An irreparable atrocity was narrowly averted, which would have found a place among the most shameful episodes in Roman history. The daughter of Constantius, who was on her way to be married to Gratian, was nearly captured while she was taking a meal on a crown estate called Prista, but by the mercy of Heaven the governor of the province, Messala, was at hand. He put her in an official carriage and conveyed her at a gallop to Sirmium, twenty-six miles away.

By this lucky chance the princess was saved from the danger of slavery. If she had been captured and it had proved impossible to ransom her, deep disgrace would have been branded on the state. After this the Quadi together with the Sarmatians, both peoples addicted to rapine and brigandage, extended their depredations, carrying off men, women, and livestock, and gloating over the ashes of burnt farms and the sufferings of the murdered inhabitants, whom they took by surprise and slaughtered without mercy. Fear of a similar fate spread over the neighbouring districts. The praetorian prefect Probus, who was quite unused to the horrors of war and was then at Sirmium, was so overcome by this novel and melancholy experience that he could hardly raise his eyes from the ground and was long in doubt what to do. He had a team of swift horses got ready, and decided to fly the following night, but then thought better of it and stayed where he was. He realized that everybody within the walls would follow him and make for a handy place of refuge, and that if this happened the town would be left defenceless to fall into the enemy's hands. So he mastered his fears and roused himself by a strong effort to meet the crisis. He cleared out the moats, which were choked with rubbish, and indulged his native taste for building by raising the greater part of the walls, which had been neglected and allowed to decay owing to the long peace. Even high towers with battlements were now erected, and the works were quickly finished, because he found that materials collected some time before to build a theatre would suffice for his purpose. This admirable plan was supplemented by another useful measure. He sent for a detachment of archers from the nearest post to help in the siege, if this should take place.

These obstacles were enough to discourage the barbarians from attacking the city. They were unskilled in this sophisticated type of warfare and hampered by their loads of booty. So they turned instead to the pursuit of Equitius. They learned from some of their prisoners that he had withdrawn into the remotest part of Valeria, and hurried after him. What particularly enraged them and made them eager to cut his throat was a belief that he was responsible for entrapping their innocent king. When this became known, two legions, the Pannonica and the Moesiaca, were sent in all haste to bring them to battle. They constituted an adequate force and would undoubtedly have come off victorious if they had acted in concert. But their efforts to come to grips with the plunderers separately were frustrated by a quarrel which arose between them over points of honour and precedence. This did not escape the keen eyes of the Sarmatians, who, without waiting for the customary signal, attacked the Moesiaca first. In the confusion our men were slow to get their weapons in order and suffered heavy losses. Then with increased confidence the enemy broke through the line of the Pannonica. Our whole force was thrown into disorder and would have been almost entirely annihilated by repeated assaults if some had not saved themselves from imminent death by flight.

While fortune was inflicting these sad losses on us our general in Moesia, the younger Theodosius, who later proved a most admirable emperor but at that time had barely reached manhood, inflicted several defeats on the Free Sarmatians (so called to distinguish them from their rebellious slaves), who were invading our territory on the other side. Though their converging hosts put up an obstinate resistance, he crushed them so completely in one fight after another that birds and beasts of prey were surfeited by a regular banquet on the bodies of the slain. In consequence the remainder lost heart. They were afraid that a general of such obvious promptitude and valour would overwhelm or rout their invading bands on the very frontier, or else ambush them from the cover of the woods. So after many vain attempts to break through they abandoned hope of success, and sued for pardon and forgiveness of their past offences. For the time being they were conquered and did nothing to violate the terms of the peace granted to them. What particularly alarmed them was the arrival of a strong force of Gallic troops for the defence of Illyricum.

While all these disturbances were taking place, the Tiber, which intersects the Eternal City and receives the effluent of many drains and streams before it empties into the Tyrrhenian Sea, was swollen by excessive rainfall during the prefecture of Claudius. It no longer looked like a river, and flooded almost the entire neighbourhood. All the districts of the city which extend over low-lying ground were under water; only the hills and the higher blocks of dwellings were out of danger. The height of the flood made movement on foot impossible, but many deaths from starvation were averted by the conveyance of abundant supplies of food in boats and wherries. But when the weather moderated and the river which had broken its banks returned to its normal bed, men's fears were banished and no further trouble was expected. The term of office of this prefect passed in complete quiet and was free from any disturbance that went beyond the bounds of reasonable complaint. He restored many old buildings, and among other projects erected a large colonnade near the baths of Agrippa. This was called the colonnade of Good Success because there is a temple to that deity to be seen nearby.

BOOK 30

1. Pap's escape from Roman custody and subsequent murder.

In the midst of the disturbances arising from the atrocious murder of the king of the Quadi by a perfidious general, a dreadful crime was committed in the East, where Pap the king of Armenia was the victim of a treacherous plot. I have ascertained the origin of the iniquitous design, which was this. Some cunning men, who had often enriched themselves at the expense of the public, patched together and brought to Valens' notice in a wickedly exaggerated form a number of charges against Pap, who was still in his early manhood. Among them was the general Terentius, a man who always went about with a humble and dejected look, but was all his life a keen instigator of discord. He allied himself with a few of Pap's countrymen, who lived in dread of punishment for their crimes, and wrote constantly to the court harping on the deaths of Cylaces and Arrabannes and stressing the arrogant behaviour of the young king and his cruelty to his subjects. So, on the pretence that he was needed to take part in a conference on the current situation, Pap was invited to court in terms befitting his dignity, but kept in custody at Tarsus in Cilicia by what was ostensibly a guard of honour. He could not obtain access to the emperor or learn why he had been sent for so urgently, since all about him were silent on the matter. Finally, however, he discovered through a private channel that Terentius was urging the Roman ruler by letter to lose no time in sending another king to Armenia; otherwise hatred of Pap and fear of his return might cause a people serviceable to us to go over to the Persians, who were on fire to seize Armenia by force or threats or cajolery.

Once he knew that he had been tricked Pap realized that a sad end awaited him and that his only hope of escape lay in rapid flight. On the advice of friends he could trust he got together 300 men with fast horses who had accompanied him from his own land. Then, acting with more boldness than discretion, as men often do in dangerous and alarming situations, he set out with the whole troop in the late afternoon and hastened away undaunted. The governor of the province, alerted by a message from the officer on guard at the gate, hurried after Pap and overtook him in the suburbs. His earnest entreaties that Pap should stay went unheeded, and he had to turn back in fear of his life. Nor was this all. When a little later a legion followed and overtook him, Pap himself headed a charge of his best men back upon them. Directing a shower of arrows deliberately wide of the mark, he routed his pursuers so thoroughly that the whole body with its commander retreated in panic to the walls a good deal more smartly than it had set out. Pap's fears were now dispelled, and after an exhausting march of two days and nights he reached the Euphrates. He had no boats and so could not cross the river, which is too deep to be forded. Most of his followers could not swim and were terror-struck, and the king himself was more perplexed than any. He would have had to remain there if, among all the various suggestions made to him, he had not hit upon an expedient which seemed the safest in this desperate situation. He took the beds to be found in the farmhouses and fastened each upon two inflated skins, of which there was an abundance in that country of vineyards. The prince himself and his leading men had one of these rafts apiece, and led their horses behind them. By taking an oblique course they avoided having to contend with the current and its choppy waves, and after encountering extreme danger succeeded in reaching the opposite bank. All the rest clung to their swimming mounts. They were tossed about and frequently submerged by the swirling river, but finally thrown on to the opposite bank exhausted by their wetting and its attendant dangers. There they took a short rest and then went on more rapidly than on the preceding days.

The emperor was deeply disturbed by the news of Pap's flight, believing that now that he had escaped from the snare he would repudiate his allegiance. So he sent count Daniel and Barzimeres the tribune of the Scutarii with a thousand lightly equipped bowmen to bring him back. Their local knowledge enabled them to take short cuts through the valleys and head off the king, who, being a stranger and ignorant of the country, was taking a meandering and circuitous route. Dividing their forces they blocked the two nearest roads, which were three miles apart, so that whichever he took he would be caught unawares. But this plan was frustrated by an accident. A traveller who was hurrying westwards had seen both roads blocked by troops, and in order to avoid them had taken an intermediate track overgrown with bushes and brambles. He fell in with the exhausted Armenians and was brought to the king, to whom he revealed privately what he had seen. He was detained but suffered no harm. The king hid his anxiety, and secretly sent a horseman by the right-hand road with orders to secure lodging and food. A little later a second was sent post-haste by the road to the left with identical orders, quite unaware of the errand of the first. After these salutary precautions the traveller, retracing his steps, showed Pap and his men a rough path almost too narrow for a pack-animal, by which the king left the troops behind and made his escape. The soldiers captured his messengers, who had been sent merely to confuse them, and were expecting his own arrival with open arms like hunters waiting for their quarry. But in the meantime he was restored safe to his kingdom, where he received a rapturous welcome. Thereafter his loyalty remained unshaken, and he digested in silence the wrongs he had suffered.

Daniel and Barzimeres returned baffled, to be loaded with insults and reproaches for their slackness and lack of spirit. Like poisonous snakes whose teeth have been blunted in an initial attack, they sharpened their deadly fangs anew, intending to take the first opportunity of doing all the harm in their power to the man who had eluded them. To mitigate their guilt, or rather to explain away the trick that had been played on them by superior intelligence, they bombarded the emperor, whose ears were most retentive of gossip, with false accusations against Pap. They concocted a story that, like Circe, he was wonderfully adept at transforming and weakening men's bodies by spells; these arts had enabled him to pass through their ranks by wrapping himself in darkness and changing the shapes of himself and his men, and if he were allowed to get away with this trick he would be a source of sad trouble.

By these means the emperor's implacable hatred of Pap was intensified. Every day a fresh scheme was devised to take away his life either by force or fraud, and secret instructions to this effect were sent to Trajan, who at that time was commanding in Armenia. This man employed a confidence trick to insinuate himself into the king's favour, occasionally showing him a letter from Valens as proof that the emperor was kindly disposed towards him, and at other times making himself at home at the king's table. Finally, when his plans were matured, he invited Pap in the most respectful terms to a banquet. The king came, quite unsuspecting, and was seated in a place of honour. The choicest food was set before him, and the great building rang with vocal and instrumental music. When drinking was well under way the host left the room ostensibly to answer a call of nature, and a wild barbarian guardsman was sent in, glaring ferociously and brandishing a drawn sword, to kill the young man. Every way of escape had already been barred. The prince, who happened to be leaning forward from his place, drew his dagger and jumped up to defend himself as best he could, but he was run through the heart and fell a hideous victim foully slaughtered by repeated blows. By this act of treachery, simple credulity was wickedly abused. Under the very eyes of the god who protects guests, and at a banquet whose sanctity would be respected even by the dwellers by the Black Sea, the blood of a stranger was spilt over the fine table-linen. This gory sight was more than enough for the guests, who scattered in the utmost horror. If those who have departed from life can feel grief, this outrage might well draw a groan from the great Fabricius Luscinus as he recalls with what magnanimity he rejected the proposal made to him in secret by Demochares (or, as some say, Nicias), the servant of king Pyrrhus. Pyrrhus was laying Italy waste with fire and sword, and Demochares vowed that he would poison him by means of his drink. But Fabricius warned the king by letter to be on his guard against his personal attendants. Such was the sanctity which in those good old times attached to the convivial table even of an enemy. It is true that some flatterers attempted to justify this recent unheard-of and shameful crime by the example of the assassination of Sertorius. Presumably they did not know that a wrongful act is not justified by the fact that another similar act has gone unpunished. For this we have the authority of Demosthenes, the eternal glory of Greece.

2. Negotiations between Valens and Sapor.

Such were the extraordinary events in Armenia. But Sapor was deeply afflicted by the news of Pap's death, coming as it did after his own earlier reverse. He had been making strenuous efforts to win over Pap, and his alarm was increased by the activity of our army. So, by way of preparation for a greater undertaking, he sent Arraces on a mission to the emperor, urging him completely to abandon Armenia, which was a perpetual source of trouble. If this was not acceptable he proposed as an alternative that the division of Hiberia should be cancelled, the garrisons of the Roman sector withdrawn, and Aspacures, whom he had himself made king of that people, allowed to rule alone. Valens replied that he could not deviate from an arrangement made by common consent, and that he would spare no pains to maintain it. Towards the end of winter this haughty answer provoked a counterblast from the king full of empty verbiage. He maintained that the root causes of disagreement could not be extirpated without the participation of the witnesses to the treaty with Jovian, some of whom he knew to be dead.

These exchanges made matters worse, and the emperor, who was better at choosing between different options than at devising them, decided that the best policy was to order Victor, master of cavalry, and Urbicius, the commander in Mesopotamia, to go at once to the Persians with a quite unambiguous message to the effect that it was criminal in a king who prided himself on being upright and content with his own possessions to covet Armenia, whose inhabitants had been left to choose their own way of life. Unless the troops assigned for the protection of Sauromaces were allowed to return unhindered at the beginning of the following year in accordance with the agreement, Sapor would have to do under compulsion what he had omitted to do voluntarily. This was frank and straightforward enough, but the envoys went astray in one particular: they exceeded their commission by taking under their protection some small districts of Armenia which offered themselves to them. On their return the Surena, whose position is inferior only to the king's, came and offered to the emperor these same districts that our envoys had been rash enough to accept. He was given a magnificent reception but went away empty-handed. Great preparations were then made for war. The emperor's intention was to invade Persia in three columns as soon as the weather moderated, and with this in mind he lost no time in hiring auxiliaries from Scythia.

Sapor, finding his hopes unfulfilled and exasperated beyond his wont by the news that the emperor was preparing for a campaign, defied Valens' anger and entrusted to the Surena the task of retrieving, by force if necessary, the territories accepted by count Victor and Urbicius. He was also to do all he could to harass the troops detailed to protect Sauromaces. These instructions were at once carried out, and there was nothing that we could do to counter them or exact retribution, because another danger now threatened the Roman state. The entire Gothic people was overrunning Thrace as they pleased, a catastrophe of which I will give a brief account in its proper place.

Such were the events in the East. In the course of them the unfailing energy of Justice exacted retribution for the disasters in Africa, and avenged at last the restless ghosts of the envoys from Tripolis. For Justice, though she is sometimes slow, is a rigorous judge of good and bad actions. What happened was this.

Remigius, who, as I related earlier, had supported count Romanus in his depredations on the provinces, was succeeded as master of the offices by Leo, and in retirement devoted himself to country pursuits in his native place near Mainz. His return to a carefree private life excited the contempt of the praetorian prefect Maximin, who made it his object to injure him in any way he could, like the abominable mischief-maker he always was. Hoping to bring further secrets to light he subjected Caesarius, a former servant of Remigius and later an imperial notary, to a savage interrogation, inquiring about Remigius' conduct, and asking how much he had got for abetting the infamous behaviour of Romanus. This came to Remigius' ears while he was, as I said, in retirement, and, either from consciousness of guilt or because fear of his enemy's intrigues got the better of his reason, he put his neck in a noose and hanged himself.

3. *Valentinian makes peace with Macrianus.*

Next year Gratian became consul, with Equitius as his colleague. Valentinian devastated several districts in Germany, and was in the act of building a fort near Basel (called Robur by its neighbours) when he received from the prefect Probus a report of the disasters in Illyricum. He gave this the attention of a cautious commander, and in a state of considerable anxiety sent the notary Paternian to make a searching investigation. As soon as he received through him a true account of the affair he was eager to set out at once, intending to crush at the first onset the barbarians who had dared to violate our frontier. But, since autumn was almost over and the project was attended by many difficulties, all the leading men at court did everything in their power to prevail upon him to postpone operations till the beginning of spring. They urged that the roads were frost-bound and that grass fit for fodder and other supplies would be unprocurable. They reminded him too of the savage temper of the kings on the borders of Gaul, and especially of Macrianus, who was an object of dread at that time, and who, if he were left unpacified, would undoubtedly attack even fortified cities. By these representations and other helpful advice the emperor was won over to a better course, and, as the interests of the state required, a courteous invitation to come to the vicinity of Mainz was sent at once to the aforesaid king, who was himself clearly inclined to come to terms. He arrived in a mood of prodigious self-confidence, expecting that he would have the last word in the negotiations. On the day appointed for the conference he stood majestically erect on the very bank of the Rhine, while his countrymen clashed their shields around him. From the other side the emperor, also attended by a host of officers of various ranks amid a display of gleaming standards, embarked in some river-boats and came to a safe distance from the shore. When the frantic gesticulations and chatter of the barbarians at last died down, there was much exchange of talk from both sides, and a pact of friendship was concluded and confirmed by solemn oaths. The king who had been such a source of trouble then withdrew mollified. From that time he was to prove our ally, and up to the very end of his life gave ample proof of his steadfast loyalty by his noble behaviour. At a later date he perished in the land of the Franks, where he advanced too rashly in the course of a sanguinary raid and fell into a trap set by the warlike king Mallobaudes. After the solemn ratification of the treaty Valentinian retired to winter quarters at Trier.

4. A discussion of the practice of advocacy.

Such were the events in Gaul and on the northern flank of the empire. But in the East, where our foreign enemies were quiescent, the ruin of the state from within was hastened by the friends and intimates of Valens, who subordinated honour to their own advantage. They exerted all their influence to deter the emperor, whose stern nature made him more than willing to try law-suits, from his desire to sit as a judge. They were afraid that, as in the time of Julian, innocence might find a new defender and a check be placed on the arrogance of the powerful, who had taken advantage of their freedom from control to enlarge the field of their activities. For these and similar reasons many people united in an attempt to dissuade the emperor. Prominent among them was the praetorian prefect Modestus, who was the creature of the court eunuchs and whose artificial manner concealed a philistine nature unpolished by any study of ancient literature. He declared that the details of private suits were beneath the emperor's notice, and Valens, believing that the duty of examining swarms of cases had been designed to humble the imperial dignity, took Modestus' advice and entirely abandoned the practice. This opened the door to acts of robbery, which grew more outrageous day by day through the criminal collusion of judges and advocates, who sold the interests of the poor to military commanders or persons of influence in the palace, and thereby won for themselves riches and high position.

The profession of forensic oratory is defined by the great Plato as a 'counterfeit branch of the art of government' or as 'the fourth kind of pandering'. Epicurus too calls it a 'bad skill' and regards it as a mischievous activity. Tisias calls it the creator of persuasion, and Gorgias of Leontini agrees with him. The art which early authorities defined in such terms has been made hateful in the eyes of respectable people by the cunning of certain men in the East, and that is why it is restrained by the imposition of a time-limit on speakers. Before returning to my main theme I will give a brief account of its vileness, which I experienced when I lived in those parts.

There was a time when tribunals were adorned by pleadings in the refined style then in use, when passionately eloquent speakers who had made a special study of rhetoric rose to eminence by their intellect and probity, and by the fluency and richness of their diction. Such were Demosthenes, who, as we learn from the records of Athens, could always draw a crowd from all over Greece to hear him speak; Callistratus, whose noble speech on the affair of Oropus caused Demosthenes to abandon Plato and the Academy and follow him; Hyperides, Aeschines, Andocides, Dinarchus, and the famous Antiphon of Rhamnus, who, according to tradition, was the first person ever to accept a fee for defending a case. It was the same at Rome. Rutilius and Galba and Scaurus were men of outstandingly upright character, and in later generations a number who had been censors or consuls or enjoyed triumphs, Crassus and Antony, Philippus and Scaevola, and a host of others, after a career in the field crowned by victories and trophies gained distinction by serving the state in a civil capacity, won laurels by spectacular forensic exploits, and enjoyed the highest possible reputation. After them came Cicero, the greatest of them all. The irresistible flood of his eloquence often rescued the oppressed from the fiery ordeal of a trial, and he was the author of the dictum: 'It is perhaps possible to escape reproach for not defending a man, but it is criminal to defend him carelessly.'

But now all over the East are to be found various types of violent and rapacious men who flit from court to court and haunt the houses of the rich, keeping their noses to the scent like sagacious Spartan or Cretan hounds till they find the place where a potential law-suit is lurking.

The first of these types consists of those who employ themselves in sowing the seed of discord by causing people to enter into a host of recognizances. They besiege the doors of widows and the thresholds of the childless, and, once they have found a pretext for a quarrel, however slight, they create bitter hatred between friends or relations or connections who are in disagreement. Their vicious passions do not cool with advancing years, as happens in other cases; on the contrary, they grow stronger and stronger. Their insatiable appetite for plunder still leaves them poor, and they use their talent like a dagger, making cunning speeches to corrupt the integrity of judges, whose very title is derived from justice. With these obdurate people impudence masquerades as freedom, reckless audacity as steadfastness, and a sort of empty verbiage as eloquence. As Cicero declares, it is a scandal that a conscientious judge should be deceived by such egregious ploys. 'Nothing in the state,' he says, 'ought to be freer from corruption than the vote and verdict of a judge; so I do not understand why a man who bribes a judge with money should be thought criminal, whereas one who perverts him by a speech may even be praised for it. In my opinion the man who corrupts a judge's mind by a speech does more harm than the man who does so with money, since no one can influence a man of sense by a bribe, but may do so by words.'

The second class comprises those who profess a knowledge of jurisprudence, a subject which the conflict of mutually contradictory statutes has entirely vitiated. These men keep a bridle on their tongues and preserve an unbroken silence like mere shadows of themselves. They compose their features to an expression of solemnity like casters of horoscopes or interpreters of the Sibylline books, and make a profit out of their very yawns. To give an impression of the profundity of their learning they quote Trebatius and Cascellius and Alfenus and laws of the Aurunci and Sicani which have long been obsolete, buried centuries ago with the mother of Evander. If you allege that you have deliberately murdered your mother, they promise that there are many recondite precedents which will secure you immunity, provided that they are assured that you are a man of substance.

Thirdly, there are those who, in order to win distinction in their mischievous trade, whet their venal tongues to attack the truth, and often gain a hearing wherever they choose by their brazen impudence and disgraceful clamour. When the court is already deeply perplexed they add complications which cannot be disentangled, and make it their business to prevent any peaceful outcome by raising knotty questions to embarrass the judges. When courts are properly conducted they are temples of justice, but when they are corrupt they are blind and treacherous pitfalls. Anyone who falls into them will not escape till many years have elapsed and he has been sucked dry to the very marrow.

The fourth and last class is shameless, headstrong, and ignorant. It consists of people who, after prematurely leaving their elementary school, hang about street corners composing comic verses rather than speeches which could be of service in a trial. They haunt the doors of the rich and angle for the delights of a choice table. Abandoning themselves to the pursuit of shady gain and hankering for money from any source, they encourage harmless citizens to engage in futile litigation. On the rare occasions when they are allowed to plead, they learn their client's name and the scope of his business only when they are in the actual presence of the judge and the issue is already joined. Then they burst into such a flood of ill-digested irrelevance that their vile outpourings remind one irresistibly of the howls of Thersites. When they find themselves unable to substantiate their submissions they take refuge in sheer abuse, and they are sometimes prosecuted and convicted for constantly reviling persons of standing. Some of them are so totally uneducated that they cannot remember ever having possessed a law book, and if the name of an early writer is mentioned in cultivated company they think it is a foreign name for a fish or some other comestible. If some stranger inquires after an advocate hitherto unknown to him, Marcian, let us say, they all rush to pretend that their name is Marcian. There is no regard for right before their eyes; they have sold themselves without hope of redemption into slavery to greed, and to employ their innate insolence in the pursuit of gain is all their skill. Once they have a man in their toils they entangle him in a web of complications, deliberately holding up his case by taking it in turns to plead sickness. The citation of a single well-known authority requires the preparation of seven catchpenny preambles; this is a way of creating interminable delays. Finally, when after the passage of days and months and years the parties have been stripped bare and the actual case comes on when it is already long out of date, these leading lights appear with a crowd of ghost advocates in their train. Once they are at the bar and the property or life of their client is in danger, their task should be to save an innocent man from death or disastrous loss. Instead, the opponents confront one another for an age with wrinkled brows and histrionic gestures – all that seems lacking is the flute player kept by Gracchus at his back to time his delivery – till at last by previous arrangement the more confident speaker utters a sort of sugary prologue which promises to rival the speeches for Cluentius or Ctesiphon. Everybody is longing for it to end, and finally he reaches the conclusion that after three years of this mockery of a trial the advocates must plead that they are not yet fully briefed. So an adjournment is granted, and the advocates clamour to be paid for all the toil and danger they have undergone in their Herculean labours.

All the same, an advocate is liable to a number of disadvantages which an honest man would find it hard to bear. Tempted by the gains to be made from their inglorious calling they quarrel bitterly among themselves, and, as I have said, offend many people by the outbursts of violent abuse in which they indulge when they have no solid arguments to fortify a weak case. Besides, they sometimes have to do with judges who have been trained in the wisecracks of Philistion or Aesop rather than in the school of Aristides the Just or Cato. Such men, who have paid good money for their official posts, are like troublesome creditors, and try to recoup their outlay by prying into everybody's resources and wresting from others the spoil they have won. In addition, there is one other serious drawback to the practice of advocacy. It is an inborn characteristic of almost all litigants to think it the fault of their advocate if they lose their case, though this may happen through any of a thousand accidents. It is always their advocate, never the weakness of their case or, as often happens, the partiality of the court, that is responsible for the result, and their anger is concentrated upon him alone. But now let me return to the point from which I digressed.

5. *Valentinian and the Quadi* (A.D. 375).

When spring was on its way Valentinian moved from Trier and marched rapidly over a familiar route. As he approached his destination he was met by envoys from the Sarmatians. They fell at his feet, begging in propitiatory terms that he would be gracious and merciful, and assuring him that he would find none of their countrymen accessory or privy to any atrocity. In response to their repeated assertions the emperor replied after mature consideration that these outrages must be investigated and punished in the light of the most reliable evidence in the actual places where they were said to have occurred. He then entered the Illyrian town of Carnuntum, which is now abandoned and in ruins but was then very conveniently placed for the commander of an army. Here, whenever chance or design gave him an opening, he was able to check the attacks of the barbarians from a position in their immediate neighbourhood.

Before his coming his reputation for violent temper made him an object of terror to all, and it was expected that he would at once punish the officers whose disloyalty or withdrawal had exposed the flank of Pannonia. Once he arrived, however, he became so lukewarm that he made no inquiry into the murder of king Gabinius, and took no serious steps to discover whose neglect or slackness it was that had led to the infliction of such wounds on the Roman state. It was in fact his way to show great severity in punishing the rank and file, but to be more lenient towards persons of high rank, even when they deserved a severe reprimand. The only man whom he pursued with active hatred was Probus. From the moment he set eyes on him he never ceased to threaten him remorselessly, and he had obvious strong grounds for doing so. Probus had then achieved the prefectship – not for the first time – and was eager to prolong his tenure. If only the various means which he employed to this end had been respectable! Instead, however, of following the exalted traditions of his family, he proved more of a toady than a man of honour. Realizing that the emperor's settled policy was to find means of getting money from every quarter without regard for right or wrong, he made no attempt to bring his misguided master back to the path of justice, as prudent statesmen have often done successfully; on the contrary he followed him in the same tortuous and mistaken course. In consequence those whom he ruled were grievously distressed. The imposition of ruinous taxes fatally sapped the resources of rich and poor alike. Long practice in oppression suggested a series of pretexts, each more powerful than the last. Finally, the burden of tribute and repeated increases in taxation caused such alarm that some members of the upper classes changed their place of residence. Others, squeezed by the harsh demands of the officials to a point where they could pay no more, became permanent inmates of prisons; and some of these grew tired of the light of day and found a welcome relief by hanging themselves. The corruption and ruthlessness of these proceedings were a matter of common and persistent report, but Valentinian's ears might have been stopped with wax, so little notice did he take. He was greedy of the most trivial gain, no matter from what source, and gave his attention only to what lay immediately before his eyes. Yet he might perhaps have spared Pannonia if he had heard earlier of these deplorable methods of raising money, which came to his notice only when it was much too late. The people of Epirus, like the rest of the provincials, were compelled by Probus to send a message to the emperor expressing their gratitude to the prefect, and a philosopher called Iphicles, a man of proven strength of mind, was forced, much against his will, to undertake this errand. When he came before the emperor, Valentinian recognized him and asked the nature of his mission. Iphicles answered in Greek and showed himself true to his philosophical principles. In reply to an explicit question whether those who sent him genuinely thought well of the prefect, he answered: 'They sent me with groans and with great reluctance.' These words cut Valentinian to the heart, and he set about tracking the course of the prefect like a keen-scented hound, inquiring in his native tongue about people he knew. Where was so-and-so, for example, who enjoyed a great reputation among his countrymen, or such-and-such, who was a rich man, or some other leading character? When he was told that one had perished by the hangman's rope, that another had gone overseas, and that a third had killed himself or expired under the knout, he burst into a blaze of anger, to which fuel was added by Leo, master of the offices. Leo himself, I shudder to say, had designs on the prefectship, so that he might have further to fall. If he had obtained that office he would have committed such excesses that in comparison the administration of Probus would have been praised to the skies.

The emperor remained at Carnuntum for three summer months, preparing equipment and supplies and intending to seize a favourable moment to attack the Quadi, the originators of this violent commotion. In this town Faustinus the nephew of the praetorian prefect Viventius, who was serving as a notary, was tortured and executed after a trial presided over by Probus. He was charged with having killed a donkey to further some magical operation. That was what his accusers alleged, but he maintained that he was merely manufacturing a specific to check the falling-out of his hair. A further accusation designed to ruin him was that in answer to one Nigrinus, who was asking for an appointment as notary, he had laughingly replied: 'If you want that you must first make me emperor.' The worst interpretation was placed on this jest, and Faustinus himself together with Nigrinus and others were put to death.

Merobaudes was sent ahead with the infantry under his command and with count Sebastian as his colleague to ravage the country of the barbarians with fire and sword. Meanwhile Valentinian himself quickly moved his camp to Budapest (Aquincum), where without loss of time he improvised a bridge of boats on which he crossed at a second point into the territory of the Quadi. The latter watched his approach from the rugged hills to which they had retired with their families. They had been uncertain what would happen, but were rooted to the spot in amazement when they saw the imperial standards actually on their soil. Valentinian marched rapidly forward as far as circumstances allowed, burning the dwellings and massacring regardless of age all whom his sudden onslaught caught still wandering at large. Then he returned without the loss of a man, and again spent some time at Aquincum. But autumn was passing quickly, as it does in a region usually frozen in the cold season, and he looked about for winter quarters. No suitable place presented itself except Savaria, though that too was in a weak state after a series of disasters. So, setting the matter aside for the moment, important though it was, he set off with unabated energy and marched along the river. Leaving adequate garrisons for the forts and camps on his way he reached Bregetio, where the fate long since ordained to put him to rest announced his approaching end by a series of portents.

Very shortly before his arrival comets blazed in the sky; these are a sign of the death of great persons, and I have already given an account of their origin. Previously, at Sirmium, there was a sudden crash of thunder, and part of the palace, the council-house, and the forum were struck by lightning. While he was still at Savaria an owl perched on the top of the royal bath uttering its fatal hoot, and could not be brought down by arrows and stones, though there was great competition to hit it. Further, when he was leaving the aforesaid city to take the field, he wished to do so by the gate by which he had entered, to obtain an omen that he would soon return to Gaul. But rubbish had been allowed to accumulate, and when this was cleared away the united efforts of a large team could not shift an iron door which had fallen and blocked the entrance. To avoid wasting a day the emperor had to leave by a different gate. On the night before the day which was to be his last he had a dream, as sleepers often do; he saw his absent wife sitting with dishevelled hair and dressed in mourning, and it was not hard to deduce that this gloomily-clad figure was his good fortune, which was about to desert him. Next morning he came out frowning and depressed. The horse that was brought him would not let him mount, but reared on its hind legs, which it had never done before. Valentinian in a fit of his congenital fury gave the savage order that the groom, whose support he had used in the usual way as he mounted, should have his right hand struck off. The innocent young man would have suffered this agonizing fate if Cerialis the tribune of the stables had not deferred the execution of this frightful sentence at the risk of his own life.

6. Death of Valentinian.

After this the envoys of the Quadi appeared, humbly begging for peace and an amnesty for their past offences, and endeavouring to clear every obstacle from their path by promising to provide recruits and other services to the Roman state. Since lack of supplies and the unfavourable time of year made it impossible to harass them further, it was decided to receive them and to send them away with the armistice they were seeking. On the advice of Equitius they were admitted to an audience, and stood in a submissive attitude paralysed with fear. When asked their errand they produced excuses of the usual type, which they swore were genuine. They declared that the wrongs we had suffered had not been the result of any common resolve on the part of their leaders, and that it was bands of foreign brigands living near the river who were to blame for any hostile behaviour. They added, however, as a sufficient justification for what had happened that the rage of the country folk had been aroused by the wrongful and untimely attempt to build a fort. This brought on a paroxysm of anger in Valentinian, and he began his answer boiling with fury. In noisy and abusive language he accused the whole nation of ingratitude and forgetfulness of past favours. He gradually grew calmer and was adopting a milder tone when he was struck as if by lightning. His breathing and speech were obstructed, and a fiery flush overspread his face. Then his pulse failed and he was drenched in a deadly sweat. To save him from falling to the ground before the eyes of the vulgar his personal attendants rushed up and carried him to his private room. There he was laid on a bed. Though his breathing was very shallow he did not lose consciousness. He recognized all the bystanders whom the chamberlains had hastily collected in order to forestall any suspicion of foul play. His body was feverishly hot, and it was necessary to open a vein, but no medical man could be found to do this; they had all been sent by the emperor to various places to attend the troops who were suffering from the plague. At last, however, a surgeon was found, but though he made several incisions he could not extract a drop of blood. Either the organs were burnt up by excessive heat, or else, as some thought, his body was dehydrated because some passages, which we now call blood-vessels, were blocked and clotted by the bitter cold. Valentinian realized from the fearful severity of the attack that his last moment had come. He tried to speak or give some order; this was clear from the gasps that racked his sides, and from the way in which he ground his teeth and made movements with his arms as if he were boxing. Finally, he could do no more. His body was covered with livid spots, and after a long struggle he breathed his last. He was fifty-four years old, and had reigned for a hundred days short of twelve years.

7. *The parentage and reign of Valentinian.*

It is now the moment to recapitulate, as I have in other cases, and to give a brief summary of the history of this emperor from his father's birth to his own death. I shall not fail to distinguish his good and bad qualities, which his high station placed in a strong light. Such a position always reveals a man's true nature.

The elder Gratian was born of humble stock at Cibalae, a town in Pannonia. From early boyhood he was nicknamed 'Rope Man', because while still young he successfully resisted the strenuous efforts of five soldiers to wrest from him a rope which he was carrying round for sale. He was in fact a second Milo of Croton, who would often hold an apple in his right or left hand, from which no degree of force availed to wrench it. Gratian's physical strength and his skill at wrestling in the soldiers' fashion made him widely known, and after serving successively as staff-officer and tribune he commanded the army in Africa with the rank of count. He left this post under a cloud, having incurred a suspicion of theft, but much later he was commander-in-chief in Britain with the same rank, and finally received an honourable discharge and returned home. While he was living quietly in retirement his property was confiscated by Constantius, on the alleged ground that during the civil war he had hospitably entertained Magnentius, when the latter crossed his land on his way to his objective.

His father's services caused Valentinian to be favourably regarded from his early years, and his own merits contributed to enhance his reputation. In consequence he was invested with the imperial purple at Nicaea and took as his colleague his brother Valens, who was very close to him in sentiment as well as in blood. Valens' character, as I shall demonstrate in due course, exhibited a mixture of good and bad qualities. Valentinian before he was emperor had encountered many dangerous situations, and at the beginning of his reign he made for Gaul, to *strengthen* the fortresses and cities lying near the rivers. Gaul was exposed to the attacks of the Alamanni, who took new heart when they heard of the death of the emperor Julian, the only commander since Constans of whom they were afraid. Valentinian, however, also made himself deservedly dreaded. He strongly reinforced the army, and fortified the high ground on both banks of the Rhine with strong-points and castles, so that no assault on our territory could be launched unobserved.

I will pass over a number of measures taken by Valentinian once his authority was established, either in person or through the agency of efficient subordinates. After taking his son Gratian as his partner in power he caused Vadomar's son Vithicab, the king of the Alamanni, to be assassinated, since he could not bring about his death openly. Vithicab was in the first bloom of manhood and was inciting his peoples to unrest and war. In a fight with the Alamanni near Solicinium, Valentinian fell into an ambush and almost lost his life, but he would have destroyed the enemy to a man if a few had not saved themselves by swift flight under cover of darkness.

Another instance of his prudent conduct of war was this. The Saxons in a mood of appalling fury overran *the coastal region*; it was their way to make sudden descents on impulse in any direction. On this occasion they had almost got away with a rich haul of booty, but Valentinian by a perfidious yet successful stratagem destroyed them and stripped the vanquished brigands of their spoil.

Again, when the Britons were unable to resist the hordes of enemies infesting their country, he gave them hope of a better future and restored peace and freedom, allowing hardly any of the aggressors to return home.

With like vigour he nipped in the bud the attempt of the exiled

Pannonian Valentinus to disturb the public peace in that province. He also saved Africa from great danger at a time when it had been struck by a sudden calamity, Firmus having raised a rebellion of the Moorish tribes, which are susceptible to the least breath of sedition, because he could not endure the greed and arrogance of the military. He would have shown similar resolution in avenging the lamentable disasters in Illyricum had not death supervened and compelled him to leave that important task unfinished.

The successes I have mentioned were admittedly the work of his excellent generals, but the personal exploits of a man of such quick understanding and long military experience were undoubtedly numerous. Among these none would have been more glorious than to take that formidable figure king Macrianus alive. Valentinian made great efforts to do this when he heard to his distress and sorrow that Macrianus had escaped from the Burgundians, whom he had himself put in motion against the Alamanni.

8. Valentinian's cruelty, greed, jealousy, and timidity.

This is a brief summary of the emperor's achievements. Now in the belief that posterity, being free from the constraints of fear and shameful servility, is an impartial judge of the past, I will enumerate Valentinian's defects and follow them by an account of his good qualities. He occasionally feigned mildness, although his naturally hot temper made him more prone to severity; he forgot that the ruler of an empire should shun all extremes like a precipice. He was never content with a slight punishment, and often ordered a proliferation of bloody trials, in which some people were brought to death's door by grim tortures. His propensity to inflict injury was so excessive that he never commuted the sentence of anyone condemned to death, though even the cruellest rulers have occasionally done so. Both at home and abroad he could have found many past examples of humanity and compassion to imitate, qualities which philosophers call kindly sisters of the virtues. Of these it will be enough to cite the following. Artaxerxes the great king of Persia, called 'Long-hand' because of the length of one limb, was so mild-tempered that he modified the various punishments which that rude people was in the habit of inflicting. In the case of some criminals he cut off their turbans instead of their heads, and instead of cropping men's ears for their offences in the regular royal way he sheared off the strings hanging from their fur caps. This merciful behaviour won him such acceptance and respect from his subjects that with their unanimous support he performed a number of wonderful feats which are chronicled by the writers of Greece. In one of the Samnite wars a magistrate of Praeneste, who had been slack in obeying an order to hurry to his post, was brought out to expiate his offence. Papirius Cursor, who was then dictator, caused the lictor to make ready his axe, and then, when the panic-stricken officer had abandoned all hope of reprieve, ordered a bush nearby to be cut down. By this practical joke the praetor was both punished and exonerated, but, far from being despised for it, Papirius got the upper hand in a long, hard war inherited from his fathers, and was reputed to be the only man who could have resisted Alexander the Great if he had set foot on Italian soil. Perhaps it was because he was ignorant of these precedents and failed to reflect that a merciful disposition in a ruler is always a comfort in distress that Valentinian reinforced his punishments by the use of fire and sword, which to virtuous minds are the last resort in adversity. Isocrates makes this point in a fine passage, in which he maintains in imperishable words that a defeated commander is sometimes more worthy of pardon than one who does not know what is right. It was this thought, I believe, that inspired Cicero's noble statement in his defence of Oppius: 'To be strong enough to save another has often been thought honourable, but it has never been a disgrace to be too weak to destroy him.'

Greed for gain, regardless of right and wrong, and eagerness to find new ways of enriching himself by the ruin of others welled up in this emperor and burned ever fiercer. Some tried to justify this by the example of the emperor Aurelian, who, finding the treasure exhausted after the deplorable events of the reign of Gallienus, fell upon the rich like a tidal wave. In the same way, they argued, Valentinian, after the disasters of the Parthian campaign, had to find immense sums to reinforce and pay his troops. This accounted for the mixture of greed and cruelty with which he amassed great resources, affecting not to know that there are some things which one ought not to do even though one has the power. In this he was very unlike Themistocles. The latter, after the battle with the Persians and the destruction of their army, was strolling over the battlefield when he saw some golden bracelets and a collar lying on the ground. He turned to one of his companions and said: 'You may take them, since you are not Themistocles', implying that personal gain was beneath the dignity of a self-respecting commander.

Examples of similar restraint can be found in abundance in Roman generals. These I will pass over. They are not proofs of perfect virtue, since after all it is not particularly praiseworthy to keep one's hands off the property of others. I will, however, give one instance among many of the honesty of common folk in early times. When Marius and Cinna left the rich dwellings of the proscribed to be plundered by the commons of Rome, the mob, which for all its roughness had a respect for human rights, forbore to touch the fruits of other men's labours; even among the poor and people of the lowest class no one could bring himself to take advantage of permission to enrich himself by the miseries of his countrymen.

Furthermore, this emperor in his inmost heart was consumed with envy, and, knowing that most vices can generally masquerade as virtues, was apt to say that jealousy is the inseparable associate of the severity inherent in lawful power. Men in supreme positions, believing that they are above the law, are inclined to suspect those who oppose them and to remove from their neighbourhood anyone better than themselves. So Valentinian hated the well-dressed, the educated, the rich, and the highly born, and disparaged the brave, wishing to monopolize all good qualities himself, a fault which we are told was glaringly apparent in the emperor Hadrian.

This same prince was in the habit of abusing timid persons, calling them dirty rascals for whom no degradation was bad enough. Yet he himself sometimes turned abjectly pale at the thought of imaginary terrors and was inwardly afraid of nonexistent bogies. The master of offices Remigius was well aware of this, and when he saw that something had put the emperor in a passion used to throw out a casual hint of a rising among the barbarians. The mere mention of this caused Valentinian such alarm that he became as mild and merciful as Antoninus Pius.

He never deliberately appointed brutal officials, but if he heard that some of his nominees were behaving with cruelty he would boast that he had found men to rival Lycurgus and Cassius, those pristine pillars of justice, and would constantly urge them in writing to visit even trivial offences with severity. Those who fell on hard times found no refuge in the kindness of the emperor, though in the past this had always offered a welcome haven to life's shipwrecked mariners. For, as philosophy tells us, the goal of a just reign should be the safety and welfare of its subjects.

9. Valentinian's good qualities.

It is fitting to turn next to those of his actions which deserve the approval and imitation of right-thinking men. If he had regulated the rest of his conduct by the same standard his life would have been like those of Trajan and Marcus Aurelius. He treated the provincials indulgently and everywhere lightened the burden of tribute. He met a longstanding need by building towns and fortifying frontiers. He was admirably strict in enforcing military discipline; his only defect was that, while he punished even trivial offences in the rank and file, he allowed grave faults in their superiors to grow unchecked, and often turned a deaf ear to the complaints brought against them. This led to disturbances in Britain, disaster in Africa, and devastation in Illyricum.

He was entirely chaste in his personal life both at home and abroad, and kept himself unspotted by any taint of obscenity or impurity. In consequence he kept a tight rein on the wantonness of the imperial court, which he was able to control the more easily because he never showed indulgence to his own relations. They were either kept in retirement or given posts of no great importance. The sole exception was his brother, whom the exigencies of the time compelled him to take as his colleague in supreme power.

He was most careful in making appointments to high positions. In his reign no one engaged in finance governed a province, and no office was put up for sale except in his early days, a period when some crimes are often committed in the hope that the emperor will be too busy to punish them.

In wars both offensive and defensive he showed great skill and caution, being steeled to endure the dust of battle. He was prudent in urging the right course and deprecating the reverse, and he kept a keen eye on all ranks in the service. He wrote a good hand, was an accomplished painter and modeller, and invented new weapons. His memory was good, and his speech vigorous, though it seldom approached eloquence. He loved elegant simplicity and took pleasure in tasteful but not profuse entertainments.

In the last place, his reign was distinguished for religious tolerance. He took a neutral position between opposing faiths, and never troubled anyone by ordering him to adopt this or that mode of worship. He made no attempt to fasten his own beliefs on the necks of his subjects, but left the various cults undisturbed as he found them.

His frame was strong and muscular, and he had gleaming hair and a high complexion. His eyes were grey, with a stern sidelong glance. He was of a good height and perfectly well built, and all in all presented a splendid figure as an emperor.

10. *The younger Valentinian is proclaimed emperor.*

When the last tributes of grief had been paid, the emperor's body was prepared for burial and dispatched to Constantinople to lie among the remains of his predecessors. The impending campaign was postponed, and anxious fears were felt about the attitude of the Gallic troops, who were not always loyal to the lawful princes and regarded themselves as arbiters in the choice of an emperor. It was thought that they might take the opportunity of attempting a coup, especially as they had the additional inducement that Gratian, who knew nothing of what had happened, was still at Trier, where his father had stationed him when he set out on his own campaign. While things were in this critical state there was general alarm. All felt that they were in the same boat, and likely to share in any danger that arose. Finally, the highest-ranking officers decided that the bridge erected by Valentinian for his invasion of the enemy's territory should be dismantled, and that Merobaudes should be immediately recalled in Valentinian's name, as if he were still living. Merobaudes was shrewd enough to guess what had happened, or possibly was informed by the courier who summoned him. Suspecting that the Gallic troops would break their oaths of loyalty, he pretended that he had received a signal to return with the bearer to guard the banks of the Rhine against a growing barbarian threat. In accordance with secret instructions he removed Sebastian, who was still unaware of the emperor's death, to a distant post. He was a quiet and peaceful man but very popular with the troops, and needed therefore to be closely watched.

On Merobaudes' return and after the most careful deliberation it was proposed that young Valentinian, the four-year-old son of the deceased, should be sent for and co-opted emperor. He was a hundred miles away, living with his mother Justina in a country house called Murocincta. The proposal met with unanimous assent, and Cerealis, the boy's uncle, was sent to fetch him at once. He was put in a litter and brought to the camp, and six days after his father's death was formally proclaimed emperor. At the time it was thought that Gratian might take it amiss that another emperor had been installed without his permission, but later this anxiety was dispelled and peace of mind returned. Gratian, who was a kindly and dutiful man, treated his kinsman with great affection and supervised his upbringing.

BOOK 31

1. Omens of the death of Valens and of the imminent Gothic disaster.

Meanwhile a rapid turn of fortune's wheel, which is perpetually alternating adversity and prosperity, was arming Bellona and her attendant Furies and bringing sad calamity upon the East. Its approach was plainly foreshadowed by omens and portents. Besides many true predictions from seers and augurs, dogs howled in answer to wolves, night-birds burst into doleful shrieks, and gloomy dawns dimmed the bright light of morning. At Antioch, where quarrels and riots among the populace were common, it became the habit for anyone who thought himself wronged to shout boldly: 'Burn Valens alive.' Criers could be heard constantly urging people to collect combustibles to set fire to the Baths of Valens, which had been built at the instance of the emperor himself. This indicated almost in so many words the manner of his death. In addition, the ghostly likeness of the king of Armenia and the pathetic shades of the victims in the recent affair of Theodorus made the night hideous with dirge-like howls, and inspired dire terror. A heifer was found lying dead with its throat cut, and this was a sign of widespread misery and death among the public. Lastly, when the old walls of Chalcedon were being taken down to provide material for a bath at Constantinople, the removal of the stone revealed a square block hidden in the fabric, on which were inscribed in Greek the following verses, a clear indication of what was to come:

> When through the city's street with garlands crowned
> Fresh maidens whirl rejoicing in the dance,
> And what was once a city wall shall serve –
> O what a mournful change – to guard a bath,
> Then countless hordes of men from lands afar
> Shall cross fair Ister's river, lance in hand,
> And lay all Scythia and Mysia waste;

Next on Paeonia turn their mad career,
To spread there likewise nought but death and strife.

2. The nature of the Huns and Alans.

The seed-bed and origin of all this destruction and of the various
calamities inflicted by the wrath of Mars, which raged everywhere with
unusual fury, I find to be this. The people of the Huns, who are
mentioned only cursorily in ancient writers and who dwell beyond the
Sea of Azov (Palus Maeotis) near the frozen ocean, are quite abnormally
savage. From the moment of birth they make deep gashes in their
children's cheeks, so that when in due course hair appears its growth is
checked by the wrinkled scars; as they grow older this gives them the
unlovely appearance of beardless eunuchs. They have squat bodies,
strong limbs, and thick necks, and are so prodigiously ugly and bent
that they might be two-legged animals, or the figures crudely carved
from stumps which are seen on the parapets of bridges. Still, their
shape, however disagreeable, is human; but their way of life is so rough
that they have no use for fire or seasoned food, but live on the roots of
wild plants and the half-raw flesh of any sort of animal, which they
warm a little by placing it between their thighs and the backs of their
horses. They have no buildings to shelter them, but avoid anything of
the kind as carefully as we avoid living in the neighbourhood of tombs;
not so much as a hut thatched with reeds is to be found among them.
They roam at large over mountains and forests, and are inured from
the cradle to cold, hunger, and thirst. On foreign soil only extreme
necessity can persuade them to come under a roof, since they believe
that it is not safe for them to do so. They wear garments of linen or of
the skins of field-mice stitched together, and there is no difference
between their clothing whether they are at home or abroad. Once they
have put their necks into some dingy shirt they never take it off or
change it till it rots and falls to pieces from incessant wear. They have
round caps of fur on their heads, and protect their hairy legs with
goatskins. Their shapeless shoes are not made on a last and make it hard
to walk easily. In consequence they are ill-fitted to fight on foot, and
remain glued to their horses, hardy but ugly beasts, on which they
sometimes sit like women to perform their everyday business. Buying
or selling, eating or drinking, are all done by day or night on horseback,

and they even bow forward over their beasts' narrow necks to enjoy a deep and dreamy sleep. When they need to debate some important matter they conduct their conference in the same posture. They are not subject to the authority of any king, but break through any obstacle in their path under the improvised command of their chief men.

They sometimes fight *by challenging their foes to single combat*, but when they join battle they advance in packs, uttering their various war-cries. Being lightly equipped and very sudden in their movements they can deliberately scatter and gallop about at random, inflicting tremendous slaughter; their extreme nimbleness enables them to force a rampart or pillage an enemy's camp before one catches sight of them. What makes them the most formidable of all warriors is that they shoot from a distance arrows tipped with sharp splinters of bone instead of the usual heads; these are joined to the shafts with wonderful skill. At close quarters they fight without regard for their lives, and while their opponents are guarding against sword-thrusts they catch their limbs in lassos of twisted cloth which make it impossible for them to ride or walk. None of them ploughs or ever touches a plough-handle. They have no fixed abode, no home or law or settled manner of life, but wander like refugees with the wagons in which they live. In these their wives weave their filthy clothing, mate with their husbands, give birth to their children, and rear them to the age of puberty. No one if asked can tell where he comes from, having been conceived in one place, born somewhere else, and reared even further off. You cannot make a truce with them, because they are quite unreliable and easily swayed by any breath of rumour which promises advantage; like unreasoning beasts they are entirely at the mercy of the maddest impulses. They are totally ignorant of the distinction between right and wrong, their speech is shifty and obscure, and they are under no restraint from religion or superstition. Their greed for gold is prodigious, and they are so fickle and prone to anger that often in a single day they will quarrel with their allies without any provocation, and then make it up again without anyone attempting to reconcile them.

This wild race, moving without encumbrances and consumed by a savage passion to pillage the property of others, advanced robbing and slaughtering over the lands of their neighbours till they reached the Alans. The Alans are the ancient Massagetae, and at this point it is relevant to discuss their origin and situation. This is a problem that has perplexed geographers, who have, however, *after much discussion found a reliable solution.*

The Danube, swollen by the waters of a number of tributaries, flows past the territory of the Sarmatians, which extends as far as the river Don (Tanais), the boundary between Europe and Asia. Beyond this the Alans inhabit the immense deserts of Scythia, deriving their name from the mountains. By repeated victories they gradually wore down the people next to them, and, like the Persians, incorporated them into a single nation bearing their own name. Of these the Nervi occupy the interior of the country near high peaks whose steep sides are frozen hard and swept by north winds. Next to them are the savage tribes of the Vidini and Geloni, who flay the skin from their dead enemies and make coverings of it for themselves and their chargers. On the borders of the Geloni are the Agathyrsi, who tattoo their bodies and colour their hair with a blue dye; the common people display only small spots widely spaced, but in the nobles they are larger and closer together. Beyond them, we are told, roam the Melanchlaenae and Anthropophagi, who live on human flesh. On account of this abominable habit all their neighbours have given them a wide berth and removed to distant regions. In consequence the entire north-eastern tract as far as China has remained uninhabited. In another direction, near the country of the Amazons, the Alans approach the East and form populous and widespread communities. These stretch into Asia, and I have been told that they reach as far as the Ganges, the river which intersects India and empties into the southern sea.

Thus the Alans, whose various tribes there is no point in enumerating, extend over both parts of the earth (*Europe and Asia*). But, although they are widely separated and wander in their nomadic way over immense areas, they have in course of time come to be known by one name and are all compendiously called Alans, because their character, their wild way of life, and their weapons are the same everywhere. They have no huts and make no use of the plough, but live upon meat and plenty of milk. They use wagons covered with a curved canopy of bark, and move in these over the endless desert. When they come to a grassy place they arrange their carts in a circle and feed like wild animals; then, having exhausted the forage available, they again settle what one might call their mobile towns upon their vehicles, and move on. In these wagons the males couple with the women and their children are born and reared; in fact, these wagons are their permanent dwellings and, wherever they go, they look upon them as their ancestral home.

They drive their cattle before them and pasture them with their flocks, and they pay particular attention to the breeding of horses. The plains there are always green and there are occasional patches of fruit-trees, so that, wherever they go, they never lack food and fodder. This is because the soil is damp and there are numerous rivers. Those whose age or sex makes them unfit to fight stay by the wagons and occupy themselves in light work, but the younger men, who are inured to riding from earliest boyhood, think it beneath their dignity to walk and are all trained in a variety of ways to be skilful warriors. This is why the Persians too, who are of Scythian origin, are such expert fighters.

Almost all Alans are tall and handsome, with yellowish hair and frighteningly fierce eyes. They are active and nimble in the use of arms and in every way a match for the Huns, but less savage in their habits and way of life. Their raiding and hunting expeditions take them as far as the Sea of Azov and the Crimea, and also to Armenia and Media. They take as much delight in the dangers of war as quiet and peaceful folk in ease and leisure. They regard it as the height of good fortune to lose one's life in battle; those who grow old and die a natural death are bitterly reviled as degenerate cowards. Their proudest boast is to have killed a man, no matter whom, and their most coveted trophy is to use the flayed skins of their decapitated foes as trappings for their horses.

No temple or shrine is to be found among them, not so much as a hut thatched with straw, but their savage custom is to stick a naked sword in the earth and worship it as the god of war, the presiding deity of the regions over which they range. They have a wonderful way of foretelling the future. They collect straight twigs of osier, and at an appointed time sort them out uttering a magic formula, and in this way they obtain clear knowledge of what is to come. They are all free from birth, and slavery is unknown among them. To this day they choose as their leaders men who have proved their worth by long experience in war. Now I must return to what remains of my main theme.

3. *The Huns and Alans expel the Goths from their homes.*

The Huns, overrunning the territory of those Alans who border on the Greuthungi and are commonly called the Don Alans, killed and stripped many of them, and made a pact of friendship with the survivors. This success emboldened them to make a sudden inroad on the rich and extensive realm of Ermenrich, a warlike king whose many heroic exploits had made him a terror to his neighbours. Ermenrich was hard hit by the violence of this unexpected storm. For some time he endeavoured to stand his ground, but exaggerated reports circulated of the dreadful fate which awaited him, and he found release from his fears by taking his own life. He was succeeded as king by Vithimir, who resisted the Alans for a time, relying on the help of other Huns whom he had hired to support him. But after many defeats he was overwhelmed by superior force and lost his life in battle. The guardianship of his young son Videric was undertaken by Alatheus and Saphrax, experienced commanders of proved courage, but their plans were frustrated by circumstances, and they had to abandon any hope of successful resistance. So they prudently withdrew to the line of the river Dniester (Danastius), which waters the wide plains between the Danube and the Dnieper (Borysthenes).

Athanaric the chief of the Thervingi, against whom, as I have already said, Valens had recently taken the field to punish him for sending help to Procopius, heard of these unexpected events and attempted to maintain his ground, being resolved to put forth all his strength if he should be attacked like the rest. Accordingly he took up his position in a good spot near the banks of the Dniester but some distance from the defensive works of the Greuthungi, and sent Munderic, who later commanded on the Arabian frontier, together with Lagariman and some other notables twenty miles ahead to watch for the approach of the enemy, while he himself marshalled his army undisturbed. But things turned out very differently from what he expected. The Huns, who are good guessers, suspected that there was a larger force further off. So they paid no attention to the troops they had seen, who had lain down to rest as if they had no enemy near them. Then the Huns forded the river by moonlight, and took what was undoubtedly the best course. They forestalled the possibility of any warning reaching the enemy by making a rapid assault on Athanaric himself, and before he could recover from the surprise of their first onset drove him with some losses on their own part to take refuge in rugged mountain country. This new situation and the fear that there was worse to follow constrained him to erect a high rampart extending from the Pruth (Gerasus) to the Danube and skirting the territory of the Taifali. He believed that this hastily but carefully constructed barrier would ensure his security. But while he was pushing on this important work he was hard pressed by the rapid advance of the Huns, who would have overwhelmed him if the weight of booty they were carrying had not forced them to desist.

A report, however, now spread widely among the other Gothic tribes that a hitherto unknown race of men had appeared from some remote corner of the earth, uprooting and destroying everything in its path like a whirlwind descending from high mountains. Weakened by lack of the necessities of life the greater part of the people abandoned Athanaric, and looked for a dwelling far from all knowledge of the barbarians. After much debate where to settle they fixed upon Thrace as the most eligible refuge for two reasons, first, because of its fertility, and second, because it is separated by the broad stream of the Danube from the regions exposed to the thunderbolts of the alien Mars. This decision met with unanimous support.

4. The Goths cross the Danube.

So led by Alavivus the Thervingi spread themselves over the bank of the Danube, and sent agents to Valens, humbly begging to be admitted to his dominions, and promising that they would live quietly and supply him with auxiliaries if the need arose. While this was going on outside our frontiers, terrifying rumours got about of a new and unusually violent commotion among the peoples of the North. Men heard that over the whole area extending from the Marcomanni and Quadi to the Black Sea a savage horde of remote tribes, driven from their homes by unexpected pressure, were roaming with their families in the Danube region. Our people paid little attention to this at first, because news of wars in those parts generally reaches distant hearers only when they are already over or at least quiescent. Gradually, however, the story gained credence, and it was confirmed by the arrival of the foreign agents begging and praying that the host of refugees might be allowed to cross to our side of the river. Even so, the affair seemed matter for rejoicing rather than dread, and the practised flatterers in the emperor's entourage extolled in exaggerated terms the good fortune which unexpectedly presented him with a large body of recruits drawn from the ends of the earth. Combined with his own troops they would give him an invincible army, and there was the further advantage that a vast amount of gold would accrue to the treasury by way of the levy paid each year by the provinces in lieu of troops. With these high hopes various officials were sent to transport this wild host, and the greatest care was taken to ensure that, even if he were suffering from mortal illness, none of those destined to overthrow the Roman empire should be left behind. Once the emperor's permission to cross the Danube and settle in parts of Thrace had been granted, the work of transportation went on night and day. The Goths embarked by troops on boats and rafts and canoes made from hollowed tree-trunks. The crowd was such that, though the river is the most dangerous in the world and was then swollen by frequent rains, a large number tried to swim and were drowned in their struggle against the force of the stream.

Thus the tumultuous eagerness of those who urged on these proceedings led to the destruction of the Roman world. One thing at least is clear and certain; the unlucky officials responsible for the operation tried several times to calculate the numbers of the barbarians but had to give up the attempt as hopeless. In the words of our greatest poet,

> To try to find their number is as vain
> As numbering the wind-swept Libyan sands.

This event may well give a new lease of life to the old stories about the Persian invasion of Greece. These include a description of the bridges over the Hellespont, the cutting of an artificial channel for the sea through the isthmus of Athos, and the numbering of the army by companies at Doriscus, and have all been dismissed as fables by the unanimous verdict of posterity. The credibility of the old accounts is now strengthened by this fresh instance of a countless swarm of peoples pouring over the provinces, spreading themselves over the wide plains, and occupying every region and every mountain range. The first to be received were Fritigern and Alavivus, who by the emperor's orders were given food for their immediate needs and land to cultivate.

The critical situation resulting from the opening of our frontier and the eruption of armed men from the barbarian lands like lava from Etna called for generals of the highest distinction, but by some unfavourable dispensation of providence men of flawed character were collected and put in command. At their head were Lupicinus and Maximus, the one commander in Thrace and the other a disastrous general, both equally reckless. Their sinister greed was the source of all our troubles. To say nothing of other crimes committed for the worst motives by these men or others with their permission against the hitherto innocent newcomers, one action must be recorded so revolting and incredible that even judges prejudiced in their own favour could not pardon it. The barbarians

after crossing the river were distressed by want of food, and these
loathsome generals devised an abominable form of barter. They collected all the dogs that their insatiable greed could find and exchanged
each of them for a slave, and among these slaves were some sons of
leading men.

At the same period Videric, king of the Greuthungi, accompanied
by his guardians Alatheus and Saphrax together with Farnobius, also
approached the bank of the Danube, and sent envoys in haste to beg
the emperor to receive him with similar kindness. This request was
rejected as not being in the public interest, and while they were in doubt
what to do Athanaric, fearing a like fate, took himself off. He recalled
that he had treated Valens with some contempt at the time of the treaty,
when he declared that he was bound by a solemn vow not to set foot
on Roman soil and forced the emperor in consequence to conclude
negotiations in mid-stream. Fearing that this had caused a lasting
grudge, he retired with all his men to Caucalanda, an inaccessible
region of deep woods and high mountains out of which he drove the
Sarmatians.

5. The Thervingi revolt from Valens and rout Lupicinus.

It was now some time since the Thervingi had been allowed to cross
the river, but they were still roaming about in its vicinity. Two
difficulties beset them. In the first place they were not supplied with
the means of subsistence owing to the scandalous neglect of the generals,
and in the second they were deliberately kept there to maintain the
shameful trade that I have mentioned. When they realized this they
grumbled that the only way out of their pressing troubles was to break
their agreement, and Lupicinus, fearing a revolt, brought up troops to
compel them to move on speedily.

The Greuthungi, seeing that our men were engaged elsewhere, and
that the boats which patrolled the river to prevent their crossing had
ceased to operate, took advantage of the opportunity to slip over on
roughly made rafts, and pitched their camp a long way from Fritigern.
The latter, however, whose native shrewdness served to protect him
against any eventuality, found a way both to obey his orders and at the
same time unite himself with these powerful kings. He advanced at a
leisurely pace and in due time reached Marcianople. Here another
fearful event occurred, which fanned to a blaze the firebrands prepared

by the Furies for the general ruin. Lupicinus invited Alavivus and Fritigern to dinner, but placed troops to keep the mass of the barbarians from the walls of the town. The latter made repeated requests to be allowed to enter to buy victuals, seeing that they were our subjects and allies, and finally quarrels broke out between the inhabitants and those excluded on such a scale that fighting became inevitable. The barbarians, roused to madness by seeing some of their kindred carried away by force, killed and stripped of their arms a large contingent of troops. News of this was secretly brought to Lupicinus, who, after a long sitting at an extravagantly luxurious meal followed by a noisy floor-show, was muzzy and dropping with sleep. Guessing the outcome, he put to death the whole guard of honour which was waiting for the two princes outside his headquarters.

The people surrounding the walls heard of this with great indignation; uttering savage threats they gradually thronged together to avenge their kings, whom they supposed to be prisoners. Fritigern, fearing that he might be kept as a hostage with the rest, was resourceful enough to cry out that there would be no avoiding a regular battle unless he were allowed to go with his companions to pacify his countrymen, whose riotous conduct he ascribed to the belief that their chiefs had been done to death under a show of hospitality. This request was granted; they emerged to be greeted with cheers of joy, and then took horse and hurried away to kindle the flame of war in various places.

When common report, the spiteful nurse of rumour, noised abroad what had happened, the whole people of the Thervingi was on fire to fight. Amid fearful scenes which heralded the gravest danger they raised their standards in their accustomed manner to the trumpets' dismal bray. Already bands of looters were rushing hither and thither, robbing and burning homesteads and spreading devastation wherever they could find an opportunity.

Lupicinus mustered his forces to meet them in tumultuous haste, and advanced with more temerity than discretion nine miles from the city, where he halted ready to give battle. When they saw him the barbarians hurled themselves recklessly on our lines, dashing their shields upon the bodies of their opponents and running them through with spears and swords. In this furious and bloody assault our standards were snatched from us and our tribunes and the greater part of our men perished, all but their luckless commander. While others were fighting his one aim was to get away, and he made for the city at a gallop. After this the enemy armed themselves with Roman weapons and roamed at large unresisted.

Having reached this stage in my complex story, I earnestly beg my readers, should I have any, not to demand minute details or the exact number of the slain, which there was no way of discovering. A truthful and unvarnished summary of the main points will suffice; scrupulous honesty is the duty of every writer of history. Those who are ignorant of ancient times say that this was the darkest disaster which ever fell upon the state, but they are led astray by the horror they feel at this latest catastrophe. A review of earlier or even quite recent history will show that such melancholy events have often happened.

The Teutones and Cimbri came from the furthest shores of ocean and flooded over Italy, but after inflicting enormous losses on the Roman state they were finally overcome by our great generals and destroyed root and branch, learning from a fight to the death what can be achieved in war by a combination of might and good judgement. Again, in the reign of Marcus, a number of discordant peoples combined in mad fury, and after prodigious commotion and the infliction of great suffering on the cities they captured and sacked *seemed likely to leave but a small part of our territory intact*. But after these calamitous losses the situation was restored. This was because our old, sober morality had not yet been undermined by the temptations of a laxer and more effeminate way of life; there was no craving for ostentatious banquets and ill-gotten gain. High and low alike were of one mind, and eager to meet a glorious death for their country as if it were a peaceful and quiet haven.

Again, hordes of Scythian tribes burst the barrier of the Bosphorus and the Sea of Marmora in 2,000 ships, and inflicted bitter defeats on us by land and sea, but they lost the greater part of their number and had to retreat. The two emperors Decius, father and son, fell fighting against the barbarians. The cities of Pamphylia were besieged, many islands laid waste, and the whole of Macedonia set on fire. For a long time their host lay encamped around Thessalonica and Cyzicus. Anchialus was taken, and also Nicopolis, which had been founded by the emperor Trajan as a memorial of his victory over the Dacians. After many cruel calamities on both sides Philippopolis was destroyed, and, if the records are to be trusted, 100,000 people were slaughtered within its walls. Foreign foes ranged at will over Epirus, Thessaly, and the whole of Greece. But when the celebrated general Claudius became emperor, and after his noble death was succeeded by Aurelian, an active commander and a ruthless revenger of injuries, the enemy were driven back and kept quiet for very many years, except that occasionally bands of robbers raided the parts nearest to them and brought destruction upon themselves. But I must now pursue the topic from which I digressed.

6. Sueridas and Colias rebel.

The news of these events was spread by a series of messengers, but the Gothic chieftains Sueridas and Colias, who had been admitted into our territory with their followers much earlier and assigned to Adrianople for winter quarters, thought their own safety more important than anything else, and refused to let themselves be disturbed by what had happened. Suddenly, however, a letter came from the emperor ordering them to remove to the province of Hellespont. They respectfully asked for journey-money, food, and a postponement of two days, but this request was very ill-received by the chief magistrate of the city, who bore them a grudge for damage done to his property in the suburbs. Collecting the dregs of the populace along with the workers in the arsenal, who are there very numerous, he put arms in their hands, ordered the trumpets to sound, and threatened the Goths with the most dire consequences if they did not depart at once in accordance with the emperor's command. The Goths, bewildered by this unexpected ill-treatment, and alarmed by the prospect of an attack by the citizens more impromptu than deliberate, stood stock still, till at last a storm of curses and abuse, accompanied by an occasional missile, drove them into open revolt. They killed a large number who had been misled by their own rashness into launching an assault, and compelled the rest to retire wounded in all sorts of ways. Then, equipping themselves with Roman arms stripped from the dead, they put themselves under the orders of Fritigern, whom they saw in the neighbourhood, blockaded the city, and threatened it with the horrors of a siege. They were, however, in difficulties themselves. Their attacks on the city were disorderly and unconcentrated. They lost some men of outstanding valour whom they were unable to avenge, and arrows and sling-stones accounted for many of them. Fritigern realized that it was pointless for men without experience of siege-works to fight at such a disadvantage. He suggested that the siege should be abandoned and a sufficient force left behind to contain the enemy. He had no quarrel, he said, with stone walls, and he advised them to attack and pillage in perfect safety rich and fruitful regions which were still unguarded. They approved of this plan, in which they knew that they would have the king's active support, and advanced cautiously in small parties over the whole of Thrace. Some of their prisoners, or others who had surrendered voluntarily, pointed out to them rich districts, particularly those where food was said to be abundant. Their natural confidence was much increased by the fact that every day their numbers were augmented by a host of their own people who had been sold into slavery at an earlier date, together with many who, at the first crossing of the river, had been exchanged for a little thin wine or mouldy bread by men half dead from starvation. They were joined too in no small numbers by expert prospectors for gold, who were unable to bear the heavy burden of taxation. These were warmly welcomed, and proved to be of great service as they traversed this strange country by directing them to concealed stores of grain and hidden corners where people had taken refuge. Under their guidance only the most inaccessible and out-of-the-way places were left untouched. Everything was consumed in an orgy of killing and burning that paid no regard to age or sex. Infants were snatched from the very breast and put to death, mothers ravished, and married women widowed by seeing their husbands killed before their eyes. Boys of tender years or past adolescence were dragged away over the corpses of their parents. Many older men, who had lost their possessions and their lovely wives, were marched into exile with their arms tied behind them, crying out that they had lived too long and weeping over the ashes of the homes of their fathers.

7. An inconclusive battle with the Goths.

The emperor Valens heard with great sorrow of this news from Thrace, which multiplied his anxieties. The threatening state of affairs required some agreement about Armenia, and he at once sent the master of cavalry Victor to Persia to arrange this. He decided to leave Antioch himself, and wait for a time at Constantinople, sending on in advance Profuturus and Trajan, both men of high ambition but poor generals. In the region where they had to operate the right policy was to wear down the enemy piecemeal by guerilla warfare, but this pair took the untimely and dangerous course of engaging the barbarians, who were still raging like madmen, with the legions from Armenia. These had often shown to advantage in battle, but they were no match for the huge numbers which had spread themselves over the high mountains as well as the plains.

These units, which had never experienced what can be achieved by a combination of despair and wild fury, drove the enemy beyond the rugged Balkan range (Mount Haemus) and forced them into its steep defiles, a barren wilderness from which it was hoped that they would be unable to find a way out and so ultimately perish from hunger. Meanwhile our men were to wait for the arrival of the general Frigeridus, who was on the way with reinforcements drawn from the Pannonian and Transalpine troops. Gratian, in response to an appeal from Valens, had ordered him to take the field and succour the forces of his uncle, which were facing utter destruction. Frigeridus was followed by Richomer, commander of the household troops, who, also at Gratian's orders, moved from Gaul and hurried towards Thrace. The regiments that he brought with him were regiments only in name; most of their number had deserted at the instance, it was alleged, of Merobaudes, who feared that, if Gaul were stripped of its defences, it would be wide open to raids from across the Rhine. Since, however, Frigeridus was disabled by gout, or, as his detractors asserted, pretended to be so to avoid the heat of battle, Richomer by common consent took command of the whole force, and joined Profuturus and Trajan, who were encamped near the town of Salices. Not far away was a countless horde of barbarians, who had drawn up their numerous wagons in a circle, inside which they were taking their ease and enjoying their rich plunder as comfortably as if they were protected by city walls.

Hoping that things would take a turn for the better and that the opportunity for a glorious feat of arms would present itself, the Roman generals watched carefully for any move by the Goths. The plan was that if they were to shift their camp, as they very often did, the Romans would fall on their rear, run many of them through, and carry off a large part of their spoils. The enemy saw through this design, or heard of it from deserters, who kept them informed of everything. So they remained stationary for a long time, but in the end fear of the opposing army and the expectation that it would receive reinforcements drove them to summon by their tribal call the raiding parties scattered in the vicinity. These obeyed the orders of their chiefs and returned like lightning to what they call their wagon-fort, where their presence

stimulated their countrymen to greater daring. After that neither side
had any rest except for brief periods of truce. Once those whom it had
been necessary to detach had returned, the whole host was crowded
together inside its ring fence in noisy commotion and fierce excitement,
eager to encounter any danger and meeting with no discouragement on
the part of its leaders. It was now, however, late in the day, and nightfall
compelled them reluctantly and sullenly to rest. So they took some food
at their leisure, but remained awake. When they learned what was going
on the Romans on their part were equally sleepless. The enemy and
their crazy leaders were as dangerous as so many wild beasts, but though
our inferior numbers made the outcome doubtful our men awaited it
intrepidly, trusting for success in the greater justice of their cause.

Day had hardly dawned when the trumpets on both sides gave the
signal for battle. The barbarians, after taking their customary oath to
stand by one another, attempted to reach some hilly ground from which
they could rush down as if on wheels and carry all before them by the
impetus of their attack. In view of this our men hurried to their stations
and stood fast; no one strayed about or left the ranks to make a sally.
When both sides had advanced cautiously and halted, the opposing
warriors glared at each other with mutual ferocity. The Romans raised
their morale by striking up their battle-cry; this begins on a low note
and swells to a loud roar, and goes by the native name of 'barritus'. But
the barbarians roared out rude chants in praise of their forefathers,
and, while this discordant clamour in divers tongues was going on,
skirmishing began. After an exchange of javelins and other missiles at
long range, the opposing sides clashed and fought foot to foot with their
shields locked in tortoise formation. The barbarians with their usual
nimbleness and alacrity hurled at our men huge clubs hardened in the
fire, plunged their daggers in the breasts of those who put up a stout
resistance, and broke through our left wing. This gave way, but a strong
body of reserves made a fierce counter-attack from close by and rescued
our men from the very jaws of death. As the fighting grew hotter there
was great slaughter. All the most active rushed into the thick of the
fight and met their death either by the hail of missiles or by the sword.
The fugitives on either side were pursued by cavalry, who hacked at
their heads and backs with all their strength, while at the same time
men on foot hamstrung those who had got away but were checked by
fright. The whole field was strewn with corpses, among whom were
some only half dead who still nursed a futile hope of survival. A number

had fallen by sling-shot or had been transfixed by shafts tipped with metal. In some cases the head had been split in two by a sword-stroke through crown and forehead, and hung down on both shoulders, a most gruesome sight.

Stubborn though the conflict was, neither side gave way to exhaustion and neither gained the upper hand. The fight was kept up without any abatement of resolution on either part as long as men's strength and spirit held out. But at last day gave place to evening, which put an end to the murderous struggle. Both sides withdrew in disorder as best they could, and the survivors returned in gloom to their camps. Some of the dead who were men of note received such burial as time and place allowed. The bodies of the rest were devoured by birds of prey, which were accustomed to feast on corpses at that period; the proof of this is that the battlefield is still white with bones. It is certain that the Romans, who were far fewer, suffered great losses in this fight against superior numbers, but in spite of that they inflicted severe distress on the barbarian host.

8. The Goths break out and devastate Thrace.

After the lamentable termination of this battle our troops returned to the neighbouring city of Marcianople. The Goths crowded of their own will within the narrow circuit of their waggons and did not dare to emerge or show themselves for seven days. This gave our forces the opportunity to build high barriers to confine the other huge hordes of barbarians in the defiles of the Balkan range, hoping, of course, that this destructive enemy host, penned between the Danube and the wilderness and unable to find a way out, would perish from lack of food, all the necessities of life having been removed to the fortified towns, none of which the barbarians even then attempted to besiege owing to their total ignorance of operations of this kind. After this Richomer returned to Gaul to fetch fresh troops for the greater battles which were expected. All this took place towards the beginning of autumn when Gratian, with Merobaudes for his colleague, was consul for the fourth time.

Meanwhile Valens, on receiving these sad tidings of war and devastation, put Saturninus in temporary command of the cavalry and sent him to the aid of Trajan and Profuturus. At the same time the barbarians, having consumed everything edible in the regions of Scythia and

Moesia, were compelled by hunger as much as their native ferocity to make frantic efforts to break out. After several attempts had been frustrated by the energy of our troops, who put up a stout resistance on the rugged terrain, the enemy were driven by sheer necessity to seek the alliance of some of the Huns and Alans by dangling before them the prospect of immense booty. News of this caused Saturninus, who by this time had arrived and was arranging a system of outposts and pickets, gradually to concentrate his forces and prepare to withdraw. He had good reason to do so. There was a danger that the barbarian host might suddenly burst through like a river in spate, and sweep away without difficulty all who were keeping a close watch on the points of danger. Once the passes were left open by the timely withdrawal of our men, the enemy escaped from their confinement in a disorderly rush, as each man found his way clear, and set about creating havoc. They spread devastation over the whole breadth of Thrace from the banks of the Danube to the range of Rhodope and the strait which separates the two great seas. Everything was involved in a foul orgy of rapine and slaughter, bloodshed and fire, and frightful atrocities were inflicted on the bodies of free men. Sights as fearful to relate as to behold met men's sorrowing eyes; women driven along under the lash distraught with fear and carrying the burden of infants yet unborn, on which horrors had fallen even before they came into the light of day; small children too, clinging to their mothers. One could hear the cries of boys and girls of high birth whose hands were tied by their cruel captors, and see grown maidens and chaste wives led along with drooping heads bewailing their fate, longing to escape violation by any death, however agonizing. Here a man of good birth, who not long before had been rich and free, was being dragged like a wild beast, railing at the cruelty and blindness of Fortune, which in a moment had stripped him of his wealth and family, driven him from his home which he saw reduced to dust and ashes, and placed him at the mercy of a brutal conqueror either to be torn limb from limb or to endure the blows and tortures of slavery.

The barbarians poured over the wide extent of Thrace like wild animals escaping from their cage, and made for the town of Dibaltum, where they found Barzimeres, tribune of the Scutarii and a veteran commander. They fell upon him as he was pitching his camp with his own men and the Cornuti and some other infantry units. Finding himself in imminent danger of destruction he ordered the trumpets to sound, strengthened his flanks, and charged at the head of his men in full battle order. His brave resistance would have brought him off undefeated, had he not been surrounded by a strong force of cavalry when he was breathless from exhaustion. So he fell after causing the barbarians serious casualties, whose numbers were concealed by the size of their forces.

9. Frigeridus defeats the Goths and Taifali.

After this exploit the Goths were in doubt about their next move, but decided to seek out and destroy Frigeridus, who was a formidable obstacle in their path. After a short pause for sleep and something better than their usual food, they set out to hunt him down like wild beasts on the trail. They had heard that he had returned to Thrace at Gratian's orders and fortified a position near Beroea, where he was waiting to see how things would develop. But while they were hurrying to execute their plan, Frigeridus, a general who knew how to conserve as well as how to employ his forces, either guessed what they had in mind or received clear information from his scouts, and returned over high mountains and through thick forests to Illyricum, elated by a great piece of good fortune which unexpectedly befell him on the way. As he was slowly advancing with his men in close order he came upon the Gothic chief Farnobius, who was roaming at large with his bands of brigands and had with him the Taifali, who had recently joined him. I hardly like to mention that the latter had taken advantage of our men having scattered in fear of these unknown tribes to cross the river and ravage the region we had left defenceless. When the cautious Frigeridus suddenly caught sight of them he got ready for a hand-to-hand fight, and launched an attack upon the marauders of both peoples *before they could do more than utter fierce threats*. He could have destroyed them to a man, so that no one would have been left to tell the tale. But when many had fallen including Farnobius, who had been a formidable troublemaker, he yielded to the survivors' urgent entreaties for mercy, and banished those whose lives he had spared to the Italian towns of Modena, Reggio, and Parma to work on the land. I have been told that this people of the Taifali are so sunk in gross sensuality that among them boys couple with men in a union of unnatural lust, and waste the flower of their youth in the polluted embraces of their lovers. But if a young man catches a boar single-handed or kills a huge bear, he is exempt thereafter from the contamination of this lewd intercourse.

10. *Gratian's generals defeat the Lentienses.*

Such was the storm of destruction which swept over Thrace as autumn turned to winter. But the frenzy that prevailed at that time spread abroad and extended also to distant regions, as if the whole world were at the mercy of the Furies. The Lentienses, an Alamannic tribe on the border of Raetia, made treacherous raids on our frontier in violation of a longstanding agreement. The origin of this disastrous event was as follows. One of that tribe who was serving as a member of the imperial guard returned home on personal business, and being a chatterbox told those who asked him what was happening at court that Gratian had been sent for by his uncle Valens and would shortly march to the East, to double the forces available to repel the people on our frontiers who had conspired to destroy the Roman state. This information was greedily swallowed by the Lentienses, who saw that they were themselves in a similar position relative to us. With their usual speed and impulsiveness they formed themselves into raiding parties, and in February crossed the Rhine upon the ice. The Celts, however, who were encamped nearby with the Petulantes, were strong enough to inflict a severe defeat upon them, though not without loss to themselves. But, although the Germans were forced to withdraw, the knowledge that most of the army had gone ahead to Illyricum to await the emperor heightened their war-fever, and they conceived the idea of a greater exploit. Gathering together the inhabitants of all their districts they burst into our territory in a mood of sublime confidence. Their armed men numbered 40,000, though some, to magnify the triumph of the emperor, put them at 70,000.

This news caused Gratian great alarm. He recalled the units which he had sent ahead into Pannonia, mobilized the others, which he had wisely retained in Gaul, and put the business in the hands of a brave but prudent general called Nannienus, joining, however, with him in the command Mallobaudes, the count of the household troops and king of the Franks, who was always spoiling for a fight. So, while Nannienus kept in mind the fickleness of fortune and counselled caution, Mallo-baudes, who could brook no delay, was driven by his habitual consuming eagerness for battle into attacking the enemy. A terrific din arose on the other side, the trumpets sounded, and battle was joined at Argentaria (*near Colmar*). Both sides suffered casualties from arrows and javelins. But when the fighting was at its hottest our men, realizing that the enemy's numbers were inexhaustible, avoided open combat by dispersing as best they could over broken country covered with trees. Then they stood their ground firmly, and the imposing spectacle of their gleaming arms seen in the distance inspired the barbarians with fear that the emperor was approaching. They suddenly turned tail, and in spite of sporadic attempts to fight to the last were so thoroughly cut to pieces that it was estimated that out of the number I mentioned not more than 5,000 escaped under cover of the woods. Among a number of other bold and brave men they lost their king Priarius, the author of this disastrous war.

Gratian, who was already on his way to the East, was so elated by this success that he made a left turn and crossed the Rhine unobserved, in the confident expectation that, if his luck held, he would be able utterly to destroy this treacherous and turbulent people. A series of messengers brought news of this to the Lentienses, who were already almost annihilated by the losses their people had suffered. Stunned by the sudden approach of the emperor, they were at their wits' end. Not a moment's respite was to be had to organize resistance or concert a plan; so they made a rush for some heights, which were defended by impassable crags. Here they took up their position on the encircling cliffs and prepared to fight to the last in defence of their possessions and families, which they had brought with them. In the face of this difficulty, 500 veterans were picked from each legion to force a barrier as strong as a city wall. Their resolve was strengthened by seeing the emperor playing an active part among the foremost, and they set about scaling the cliffs as if a hunted animal awaited easy capture when they reached the top. The fight began before mid-day and was still going on at nightfall. Both sides suffered heavy losses. Our men slew and were slain in considerable numbers, and the gilded and brightly coloured armour of the imperial guard was shattered by a hail of heavy missiles.

After a long conference with his senior officers Gratian decided that it was dangerous and pointless to persist with ill-timed obstinacy against these rugged and towering heights. Many different views were naturally put forward, but the final decision was to give our men a respite and starve the barbarians out by a blockade in view of the unfavourable nature of the terrain. But the Germans still held out as doggedly as ever, and were enabled by their local knowledge to retreat to other hills higher than those that they had previously occupied. So the emperor turned his army in that direction with unabated courage, and began to look for paths leading to the heights. Then the Lentienses, realizing that he was inflexibly resolved not to relax his grip on their throats, humbly begged for terms and surrendered. As one of the conditions their able-bodied young men were enrolled among our recruits, and the rest were allowed to return home unharmed.

This timely and profitable victory, which crippled the western tribes, was by the blessing of heaven achieved by Gratian in a display of unbelievable energy at a time when he was marching at top speed in another direction. He was a young man of remarkable talent, eloquent, controlled, warlike, and merciful, and seemed likely to rival the best of his predecessors while the down of youth was still spreading over his cheeks. But he had an innate tendency to play the fool which his intimates made no attempt to check, and this seduced him into the frivolous pursuits of the emperor Commodus, though he was never bloodthirsty. Commodus was in the habit of dispatching with javelins a host of wild animals before the eyes of the populace, and used a variety of weapons to slaughter, without the need for a second blow, a hundred lions let loose together in the amphitheatre, an exploit which gave him prodigious delight. Similarly, Gratian amused himself by shooting at beasts of prey enclosed in what are called game preserves, and neglected many matters of serious importance. This was at a time when even Marcus Antoninus, had he been emperor, would hardly have been able to remedy the lamentable state of public affairs without colleagues like himself and a most prudent policy.

After taking such steps as the situation in Gaul required, and punishing the treacherous targeteer who had revealed to the barbarians that the emperor was on his way to Illyricum, Gratian made forced marches by way of the forts at Felix Arbor and Lauriacum to bring help to the parts where it was most needed. At the same moment Frigeridus, who among other useful contributions to the general welfare was hurrying to fortify the pass of Succi so as to prevent bodies of light-armed marauders spreading at will over the northern provinces like rivers in spate, was superseded by one count Maurus, whose bold exterior masked a corrupt nature and who was in every respect shifty and unreliable. This was the man who, while serving in the bodyguard, had, as I related earlier, the presumption as well as the wit to take the chain from his own neck and offer it to the Caesar Julian, when the latter was in doubt what to use as a diadem. So at the very moment when we were reeling under disasters a cautious and careful general was dismissed, who, even if he had been long retired, ought to have been recalled to duty in such a grave crisis.

11. Victory of Sebastian at Beroea.

At about the same time Valens accomplished the long march from Antioch and reached Constantinople, where his stay, which lasted very few days, was disturbed by a minor outbreak of popular discontent. Sebastian, a notably wide-awake general, who had recently been sent from Italy at Valens' request, was put in command of the infantry in succession to Trajan. Valens himself moved to the imperial estate of Melantias, and tried to put the troops in good humour by pay, rations, and much flattering talk. He then gave orders to march to a fort called Nike, where he heard from scouts that the barbarians had returned laden with booty from the region of Rhodope to the neighbourhood of Adrianople, but, on learning that the emperor was on the move with a large force, were now hurrying to join their countrymen in a fortified camp near Beroea and Nicopolis. This gave an opening which was not to be lost. Three hundred men were picked from each unit, and Sebastian was directed to march with this force and perform his promise to do the state some service. He advanced at speed till he was seen near Adrianople, where the gates were tight shut and he was forbidden to come near. Its garrison were afraid that he might have been captured and suborned by the enemy, and that this would have fatal consequences for the city, such as occurred when *a commander* was caught in a trap by the troops of Magnentius and used by them to open the passes of the Julian Alps. In the end, however, Sebastian was recognized and admitted to the city. He gave his men such food and rest as he could, and next day sallied out again secretly and in haste. Towards evening he suddenly caught sight of some Gothic raiding parties near the river Maritza (Hebrus). He concealed himself for a while behind dykes and bushes, and then crept forward on tiptoe under cover of night to attack them in their sleep. His success was so complete that all perished except for a few who saved themselves by speed of foot. An immense quantity of booty was retrieved, more than the city and the wide area about it could hold.

Fritigern was stung by this disaster. Fearing that this general, of whose reputation for success he was well aware, might surprise and destroy his separated parties while they were scattered at large and intent on pillage, he recalled them all to the vicinity of Cabyle and then quickly evacuated that area, intending to keep his people in open country where they could not be surprised or suffer from lack of food.

During these events in Thrace, Gratian, who had informed his uncle by letter of his hard-won victory over the Alamanni, sent on his baggage-train overland while he himself with a light-armed force descended the Danube to Bononea and entered Sirmium. After four days' stay he went on by water to the Camp of Mars, though he was suffering from an intermittent fever. In that region he was unexpectedly attacked by some Alans and lost a few of his men.

12. Valens decides to fight without waiting for Gratian.

Two things vexed Valens at this period; first, the news that the Lentienses had been defeated, and, second, the exaggerated accounts of his achievements sent from time to time by Sebastian. So he marched from Melantias, eager to put himself on a level with his nephew, whose exploits irked him, by some glorious deed of his own. He had with him a force made up of various elements. It was active and by no means to be despised, seeing that it contained a large number of veterans and, among other officers of high rank, Trajan, recently commander-in-chief, who had been recalled. Careful reconnaissance showed that the enemy intended to intercept our lines of supply with a strong force, but this threat was effectively met by dispatching a body of archers on foot together with a squadron of cavalry to secure the adjacent passes. During the next three days the barbarians advanced slowly over difficult country expecting to be attacked, keeping fifteen miles from the city and making for the post at Nike. Through some mistake Valens was assured by his skirmishers that the part of the enemy's host that they had seen was only 10,000 strong, and this filled him with a rash craving to encounter them. Advancing in close formation he took up a position near the outskirts of Adrianople, and fortified it with a palisade and ditch. While he was impatiently waiting for Gratian, the count of the household troops, Richomer, arrived; he had been sent ahead with a letter anouncing that Gratian would soon be there himself. The letter contained an urgent plea that Valens would wait a short time till Gratian arrived to share the danger, and would not rashly commit himself to the risks of a decisive action single-handed. Valens called a council of war of various senior officers and canvassed their opinions. Some, under the influence of Sebastian, urged him to give battle at once, but the master of cavalry Victor, who, though a Sarmatian, was a prudent and cautious man, found much support when he recommended that Valens should wait for his colleague in the empire, since the additional strength provided by the army of Gaul would make it easier to crush the fiery insolence of the barbarians. But the fatal obstinacy of the emperor and the flattery of some of his courtiers prevailed. They urged immediate action to prevent Gratian sharing in a victory which in their opinion was already as good as won.

While the necessary preparations for battle were being made, a Christian presbyter (to use their own title) was sent by Fritigern with some other envoys of low rank to the emperor's camp. He was received with courtesy and presented a letter from his commander, asking openly that he and his people, who had been driven from their homes by the migrations of wild savages, should be allowed to settle in Thrace with all its corn and cattle, and promising perpetual peace if this request were granted. This same Christian, who was apparently a trusted confidant of Fritigern, gave Valens also a private letter from his master, who was an old hand at any kind of deception. In this he addressed Valens as his future friend and associate, and informed him that he would not be able to tame the fierce spirit of his countrymen and induce them to make terms favourable to the Romans unless he could at once give them a sight of Valens' troops close at hand and ready for battle. The fear of the emperor's name would then damp their fatal passion for war. The envoys, however, did not inspire confidence and were sent away empty-handed.

When dawn came on the day marked in the calendar as 9 August, the army was put in rapid motion. All its impedimenta and baggage were left near the walls of Adrianople under an adequate guard, and the praetorian prefect and members of the consistory remained inside the town with the treasure-chests and the imperial insignia. After a march of eight miles over rough country under a burning mid-day sun our troops came within sight of the enemy's waggons, which, as our scouts had reported, were drawn up in a regular circle. While the enemy in their usual way were raising a wild and doleful yell, the Roman generals marshalled their line of battle. The cavalry on the right wing were furthest advanced, and the greater part of the infantry were some way to their rear. But the cavalry of our left wing were still straggling along the road, making what speed they could but under serious difficulties. While they were deploying without as yet encountering any opposition, the barbarians, alarmed by the dreadful din of clattering arms and the ominous beating of shields, and bearing in mind that part of their force under Alatheus and Saphrax had not yet come up, though it had been summoned, again sent envoys to ask for peace. The emperor was not prepared to treat with people of such low rank, and demanded that persons of suitable standing should be sent to make a firm agreement. But the enemy deliberately wasted time so that their own cavalry, which they expected at any moment, might have a chance to get back while this sham armistice lasted, and also to ensure that our men, who were already exhausted by the summer heat, should be parched with thirst. With this in view they had fired the countryside over a wide area, feeding the flames with wood and other dry material. A further fatal circumstance was that both men and beasts were tormented by severe hunger.

In the meantime Fritigern, who had great foresight and dreaded the uncertainties of battle, on his own responsibility sent a private soldier as herald to suggest that if some picked persons of high rank were at once sent as hostages *he would come himself without fear to conduct the necessary negotiations.* This proposal from so formidable a commander met with warm approval, and the tribune Equitius, a kinsman of Valens and marshal of the court, was unanimously chosen to go at once as a surety. When he objected, on the ground that he had escaped as a prisoner-of-war from Dibaltum and therefore feared the irrational anger of the Goths, Richomer offered to take his place, and gladly undertook what he regarded as a glorious and heroic mission. He was on his way to the enemy's rampart with evidence of his rank and birth, when the archers and Scutarii commanded by Cassio and by the Iberian Bacurius impulsively launched a hot attack and engaged the enemy. Their retreat was as cowardly as their advance had been rash, a most inauspicious start to the battle. This untimely proceeding not only thwarted the errand of Richomer, who was forbidden to go at all, but also brought on an attack by the Gothic cavalry under Alatheus and Saphrax, who had now arrived supported by a party of Alans. They shot forward *like a bolt from on high* and routed with great slaughter all that they could come to grips with in their wild career.

13. *Gothic victory and death of Valens.*

Amid the clashing of arms and weapons on every side, while Bellona, raging with more than her usual fury, was sounding the death-knell of the Roman cause, our retreating troops rallied with shouts of mutual encouragement. But, as the fighting spread like fire and numbers of them were transfixed by arrows and whirling javelins, they lost heart. Then the opposing lines came into collision like ships of war and pushed each other to and fro, heaving under the reciprocal motion like the waves of the sea. Our left wing penetrated as far as the very waggons, and would have gone further if it had received any support, but it was abandoned by the rest of the cavalry, and under pressure of numbers gave way and collapsed like a broken dyke. This left the infantry unprotected and so closely huddled together that a man could hardly wield his sword or draw back his arm once he had stretched it out. Dust rose in such clouds as to hide the sky, which rang with frightful shouts. In consequence it was impossible to see the enemy's missiles in flight and dodge them; all found their mark and dealt death on every side. The barbarians poured on in huge columns, trampling down horse and man and crushing our ranks so as to make an orderly retreat impossible. Our men were too close-packed to have any hope of escape; so they resolved to die like heroes, faced the enemy's swords, and struck back at their assailants. On both sides helmets and breast-plates were split in pieces by blows from the battle-axe. You might see a lion-hearted savage, who had been hamstrung or had lost his right hand or been wounded in the side, grinding his clenched teeth and casting defiant glances around in the very throes of death. In this mutual slaughter so many were laid low that the field was covered with the bodies of the slain, while the groans of the dying and severely wounded filled all who heard them with abject fear.

In this scene of total confusion the infantry, worn out by toil and danger, had no strength or sense left to form a plan. Most had had their spears shattered in the constant collisions, so they made do with their drawn swords and plunged into the dense masses of the foe, regardless of their lives and aware that there was no hope of escape. The ground was so drenched with blood that they slipped and fell, but they strained every nerve to sell their lives dearly, and faced their opponents with such resolution that some perished at the hands of their own comrades. In the end, when the whole field was one dark pool of blood and they could see nothing but heaps of slain wherever they turned their eyes, they trampled without scruple on the lifeless corpses.

The sun, which was high in the sky (it was moving into the house of the Virgin after traversing Leo), scorched the Romans, who were weak from hunger, parched with thirst, and weighed down by the burden of their armour. Finally, our line gave way under the overpowering pressure of the barbarians, and as a last resort our men took to their heels in a general sauve qui peut.

While all were scattering in flight over unfamiliar paths, the emperor was in a situation of frightful peril. He picked his way slowly over the heaps of bodies and took refuge with the Lancearii and Mattiarii, who stood firm and unshaken as long as they could withstand the pressure of superior numbers. His bodyguard had left him, and when Trajan saw him he cried out that all was lost unless he could be protected by the foreign auxiliaries. At this count Victor rushed off to bring up the Batavi to the emperor's assistance. They had been placed in reserve not far off, but not one of them was to be found. So Victor retired and left the field. Richomer and Saturninus saved themselves in the same way.

The barbarians' eyes flashed fire as they pursued their dazed foe, whose blood ran cold with terror. Some fell without knowing who struck them, some were crushed by sheer weight of numbers, and some were killed by their own comrades. They could neither gain ground by resistance nor obtain mercy by giving way. Besides, many lay blocking the way half dead, unable to endure the agony of their wounds, and the carcasses of slaughtered horses covered the ground in heaps. At last a moonless night brought an end to these irreparable losses, which cost Rome so dear.

Soon after nightfall, so it was supposed, the emperor was mortally wounded by an arrow and died immediately. No one admitted that he had seen him or been near him, and it was presumed that he fell among common soldiers, but his body was never found. A few of the enemy were hanging about the field for some time to strip the dead, so that none of the fugitives or local people dared to approach. The Caesar Decius is said to have met with a similar fate. During a hot fight with the barbarians he lost control of his horse, which stumbled and threw him into a bog. He could not get out and his body was never found. According to another account, Valens did not expire on the spot, but was taken with a few of his guards and some eunuchs to a farmhouse nearby, which had a fortified second storey. While he was receiving such rude treatment as was available he was surrounded by the enemy, though they did not know who he was. But he was spared the shame of being taken prisoner. His pursuers tried to break down the doors, which were bolted, but came under arrow-fire from the overhanging part of the building. In order not to let this delay rob them of their chance of spoil, they piled up bundles of straw and faggots, set fire to them, and burned the house with all who were in it. One of the guards escaped through a window and was taken prisoner. He told them what they had done, which greatly vexed them, because they had lost the glory of taking the ruler of Rome alive. This same man later escaped and rejoined the army, and gave this account of what had occurred. A similar disaster befell one of the Scipios after the recovery of Spain. He was burnt to death by the enemy, we are told, in a tower in which he had taken refuge. One thing is certain. Neither Scipio nor Valens was given the final honour of burial.

Among all the distinguished men who perished, Trajan and Sebastian were outstanding. With them fell thirty-five tribunes, either in command of units or supernumerary, together with Valerian and Equitius, marshals of the stable and the palace respectively. Among them was also Potentius, tribune of the Promoti, who died in the flower of his youth. He was greatly respected by all good men, both on his own account and on that of his father Ursicinus, a former commander-in-chief. It is certain that hardly a third of our army escaped. *No battle* in our history except Cannae was such a massacre, though more than once the Romans have been the playthings of fortune and suffered temporary reverses, and many disastrous struggles are recorded with grief in the legendary sagas of Greece.

14. Character of Valens.

Such was the death of Valens at the age of almost fifty after a reign of a little less than fourteen years. I will now speak of his good qualities, which are well known, and of his defects.

He was a faithful and reliable friend, and repressed ambitious intrigues with severity. He maintained strict discipline in the army and the civil service, and took particular care that no one should gain preferment on the score of kinship with himself. He was extremely slow both to appoint and to remove officials. In his dealings with the provinces he showed great fairness, protecting each of them from injury

as he would his own house. He was especially concerned to lighten the
burden of tribute, and allowed no increases in taxation. He was mild in
his assessment of what was due, and a harsh and bitter enemy of
embezzlers and of officials detected in corrupt practices. In matters of
this kind no emperor is more kindly remembered in the East. He also
combined liberality with restraint; of this, one example out of the many
available will suffice. Courts always contain people eager to enrich
themselves at the expense of others. When anyone put in a claim to
lapsed property or something of that kind, he drew a clear line between
right and wrong, and gave anyone who wished to protest an opportunity
to state his case. If he allowed the claim he often added the names of
three or four absentees as sharers in the grant. As a result, men of
restless greed behaved with more restraint, seeing that the profit they
had their eye on was diminished by this device. To avoid tedium, I will
pass over the buildings which he restored or ordered to be newly erected
in various towns and cities, and will leave these works to speak for
themselves. In all these respects he set an example, in my opinion, to
all right-minded people. Now let me enumerate his defects.

He was insatiable in the pursuit of wealth and unwilling to endure
fatigue, though he affected enormous toughness. He had a cruel streak,
and was something of a boor, with little skill in the arts of either war or
peace. He was quite willing to gain advantages for himself from the
sufferings of others, and his behaviour was particularly intolerable when
he construed ordinary offences as lèse-majesté. Then his rage could be
satisfied only by blood and the spoliation of the rich. What was also
unendurable was that, although he pretended to leave all suits and trials
to the operation of the law, and put their investigation into the hands
of judges appointed for the purpose, he in fact allowed nothing to be
done contrary to his own pleasure. In other ways too he was unjust and
passionate, always ready to lend an ear to the charges of informers
without sifting truth from falsehood. This is a shameful fault, and
greatly to be dreaded even in private and everyday matters.

He was dilatory and sluggish. His complexion was dark, and the sight
of one eye was impaired, thought this was not apparent at a distance.
He was well-made, neither tall nor short, bow-legged, and with a
somewhat protruding stomach.

This is a sufficient account of Valens, and it is amply confirmed by
the evidence of my contemporaries. But one circumstance must not be
omitted. He had heard from the oracle of the tripod, operated, as I

described, by Patricius and Hilarius, those three prophetic lines, of which the last ran:

> When Ares waxes wroth on Mimas' plain.

Being uncultivated and ignorant he at first thought nothing of it, but as his troubles multiplied he became abjectly nervous, and the recollection of this prophecy made him tremble at the mention of Asia; he had heard from men of learning that Homer and Cicero had written of a mountain called Mimas, rising above the town of Erythrae. We are told that after his death and the departure of the enemy a stone monument was found near the spot where he was believed to have fallen, on which was a tablet with a Greek inscription to the effect that in early times a worthy called Mimas had been buried there.

15. The siege of Adrianople.

When dark night covered the earth after the fatal battle, the survivors scattered to right and left in whatever direction panic took them. Everyone was looking for his comrades and thought only of his own safety, fancying that an enemy's sword was about to descend on his head. At a distance could be heard the pathetic cries of those left behind, the sobs of the dying, and the agonized groans of the wounded.

At daybreak, however, the victors, like wild beasts maddened by the taste of blood, made for Adrianople in dense hordes, resolved to take it at any cost. What roused their hopes, though to no purpose, was the information they had received from traitors and deserters that the highest officials of the empire, together with the imperial insignia and the treasury of Valens, had been left there for safety in what was thought an impregnable fortress. For fear that the slightest delay might cool their ardour they surrounded the walls by mid-morning, and a most bitter struggle ensued. The attackers with their native savagery rushed headlong to destruction, while on the other side the defence was roused to a most resolute resistance. A large number of soldiers and their servants, who had been refused admission to the city with their beasts, stood with their backs to the walls and the houses which joined them, and put up a stout fight, considering the disadvantage of their low position. The mad fury of the attack had lasted till the afternoon, when suddenly 300 infantry of those near the actual parapet formed into a wedge and went over to the enemy, who seized them in a frenzy of excitement and for some unknown reason slaughtered them on the spot. From that moment it was remarked that no one thought of imitating them, however desperate his plight.

While this accumulation of horrors was at its worst, torrents of rain accompanied by thunder poured from the black clouds and dispersed the milling hordes. They returned to the circular rampart of their waggons, and went so far in their appalling arrogance as to send an envoy with a threatening letter, ordering our troops to surrender the city on condition that their lives should be spared. The envoy did not dare to come within the walls, and the message was brought by a Christian, and read. It was received with the contempt it deserved, and the rest of the day and all the following night were spent in preparations for resistance. The gates were blocked on the inside with huge rocks, the weak sections of the walls were strengthened, and engines were placed in suitable spots to discharge javelins or stones. A sufficient supply of water was also collected. On the previous day some of the combatants had been so distressed by thirst as to endanger their lives.

On their side the Goths, reflecting on the uncertainties of war and dismayed by seeing their bravest warriors killed or wounded and their strength gradually eroded, formed a shrewd plan, which Justice in person brought to light. They suborned some members of the imperial guard who had gone over to them on the previous day to pretend to escape and to return to their comrades. They were thus to gain entrance to the city, and having done so to set fire to a designated area. This would serve as a signal, though the besieged would not know its meaning, and, while the greater part of them were busy in extinguishing the flames, the city would be left defenceless and might be broken into. The guardsmen carried out the plan and advanced to the ditch, begging with outstretched arms to be admitted to the city as Romans. There was no ground for suspicion and they were let in, but when they were questioned about the enemy's plans they gave inconsistent answers. They were put to the torture and beheaded, after openly confessing what they had come to do.

So after extensive preparations the barbarians, putting behind them the anxiety caused by previous reverses, poured about midnight in enormous numbers against the blocked gates and *strove to break the resolution of the defence*. But the provincials and court officials joined with the soldiers in a spirited attempt to crush them, and the numbers were so great that their missiles even when discharged at random could not fail to inflict injury. Our men noticed that the barbarians were making use of the same weapons as had been hurled at them. So an order was given that the thongs binding the arrow-heads to the shafts should be partially cut through before shooting. This did not affect them while in flight, and if they found their mark they were as effective as ever, but if they missed they at once fell to pieces.

While the fight was at its hottest a quite unexpected incident had serious consequences. A piece of artillery called a scorpion, but known in common parlance as a 'wild ass', which was sited opposite a dense mass of the enemy, hurled a huge stone. This crashed harmlessly to the ground, but the novelty of the spectacle put such terror into the foe that they shrank back and were in a mind to run. Their chiefs, however, ordered the trumpets to sound, and the battle was renewed. The Romans continued to get the better of it, and hardly a javelin or sling-shot missed its mark. The chiefs, who filled the front ranks, were on fire to lay hands on Valens' ill-gotten riches, and they were closely followed by the rest, eager to be seen to share the danger of their betters. Some were writhing on the ground in a death-agony, crushed beneath heavy weights or run through the body by a missile; others who were carrying ladders and preparing to scale the wall in many places were buried under their loads, and stones and fragments and drums of pillars were pushed down on them. But in spite of the ghastly carnage it was not till late in the day that any of these madmen desisted from his heroic efforts. They were encouraged by the glad sight of the many casualties suffered by the defence, and the fierce struggle for and against the walls went on without intermission. No kind of order was now observed by the enemy, who rushed forward in small groups, a sign of utter desperation. Finally, as evening came on they all withdrew in dejection to their own camp, accusing one another of reckless folly in not listening to the advice of Fritigern and avoiding the woes of a siege.

16. Vain attempt on Constantinople.

The whole short summer night was taken up in giving the wounded such medical treatment as they practise. At dawn they discussed their next step, and after much argument decided to seize Perinthus and *then other rich cities in the vicinity*. They had full information of these from deserters, who were acquainted with the contents of individual houses, let alone cities. In pursuit of this policy, which seemed the best available to them, they advanced slowly, robbing and burning as they went, without meeting any resistance.

After the Goths had departed in the nick of time, the defenders of Adrianople, finding from reliable scouts that the enemy had vacated the neighbourhood, marched out at dead of night, and took their way by unfrequented routes through the woods, avoiding the highways. Some made their way to Philippopolis and thence to Serdica, others to Macedonia. They took with them such valuables as had escaped damage, and made the best possible speed in the hope of finding Valens in those parts. They were quite unaware that he had died in the battle or, alternatively, taken refuge in a hut where he was presumed to have been burnt to death.

The Goths, however, in conjunction with some Huns and Alans, brave and warlike peoples inured to hardship, whom Fritigern had shrewdly won to his side by the prospect of wonderful rewards, pitched their camp near Perinthus. Warned by their earlier mishap they did not dare to approach or attack the city itself, but utterly devastated the wide area of fertile country round it, and either killed the farmers or took them prisoner. Then they made a rapid march to Constantinople, keeping in a regular formation for fear of surprise. Its enormous accumulation of wealth aroused their greed, and they meant to make a mighty effort to destroy this famous city. But when their furious onrush had brought them so far that they were almost knocking at the gates, divine providence gave them a check. A body of Saracens, a people of whose origin I have given a full account in various places, had been summoned to the city. They are more at home in the tricks of guerilla warfare than in a formal battle, but on the sudden appearance of the host of barbarians they made a bold sally from the city to attack it. After a long and obstinate fight they parted on equal terms. But an incident of an utterly unheard-of sort gave the warriors from the East the upper hand. One of them, a man with long hair wearing nothing but a loin-cloth, drew his dagger and hurled himself with blood-curdling yells into the midst of the Gothic host. He cut a man's throat, then put his lips to the wound and sucked the streaming blood. This appalling sight terrified the barbarians, who lost their habitual confidence and advanced only with hesitation. Their spirit was further damped when they contemplated the long circuit of the walls and the huge extent of the blocks of buildings within them, the beauties of the city beyond their grasp, its vast population, and the strait nearby which separates the

Black Sea from the Aegean. After suffering greater losses than they inflicted they dismantled the works that they were constructing, and left the neighbourhood to spread themselves over the northern provinces, which they traversed as far as the foot of the Julian (or, as they were formerly called, Venetic) Alps.

At this time Julius, who commanded beyond the Taurus, distinguished himself by a swift and salutary deed. Learning of the disasters in Thrace, he sent secret orders to those in charge of the Goths who had been transferred earlier to Asia, and dispersed in various cities and fortresses. These commanders were all Romans, an unusual thing at the present time. The Goths were to be collected quite unsuspecting outside the walls in the expectation of receiving the pay that they had been promised, and at a given signal all put to death on one and the same day. This wise plan was carried out without fuss or delay, and the provinces of the East saved from serious danger.

This is the history of events from the reign of the emperor Nerva to the death of Valens, which I, a former soldier and a Greek, have composed to the best of my ability. It claims to be the truth, which I have never ventured to pervert either by silence or a lie. The rest I leave to be written by better men whose abilities are in their prime. But if they choose to undertake the task I advise them to cast what they have to say in the grand style.

NOTES ON THE TEXT

There is no historical commentary on Ammianus in English apart from the footnotes to the Loeb edition by J. C. Rolfe. In French there are excellent notes to the Budé series by J. Fontaine and others, covering to date Books 14–19 and 23–8. In German there are brief notes on all the books by W. Seyfarth, *Ammianus Marcellinus: Römische Geschichte*, 4 volumes (1968–71). On Books 20–21 a full commentary is being published by J. Szidat (as *Historia Einzel-schriften* 31 (1977) and 38 (1981)). The commentary of P. de Jonge (1935–80) is mostly directed to linguistic points. There is a valuable selection of chapters with commentary by Roger Blockley (Bristol Classical Texts (1980)). The following notes offer no more than orientation on basic points. They are gathered together in the form of a running commentary by chapters or groups of chapters.

NOTE: Where titles of publications are given in full in the Further Reading section (pp. 36–7), a shortened form is used here.

BOOK 14

1. For the historical background, see Introduction, § 14. Gallus was in his mid-twenties when Constantius released him from confinement at Macellum and made him Caesar. He was given Constantius' sister Constantina in marriage on the same occasion. Her previous husband Hannibalian was the son of Constantine's half-brother Delmatius and had been made king of Pontus, lesser Armenia, and Cappadocia by Constantine, but was one of the victims of the massacre of 337. The account of treason trials at Antioch covers the period 351–4 (cf. below, 29.1, for a later wave of trials). Amphiaraus the seer (p. 42) was one of the Seven against Thebes; Marcius was supposed to have foretold the Roman defeat at Cannae. Nothing further is known of the wife of Maximin (p. 42), described in one of the lost books. In roaming the streets in disguise (p. 43), Gallus imitated not only Gallienus (258–68), always a villain for A., but (more significantly in Antioch) king Antiochus Epiphanes.

5. 10 October 354 marked the beginning, not the end, of Constantius' thirtieth year of rule, calculated from his proclamation as Caesar under

445

Constantine. Paul 'the Chain' incurs odium equally for his treatment of the adherents of the usurper Magnentius and for later investigations: see Notes on Persons.

6. Memmius Vitrasius Orfitus was prefect of Rome 353–5 and again 357–9. A. takes his prefecture as the opportunity for the first of two memorable satires on the inhabitants of Rome (cf. 28.4). The image of the four ages of Rome goes back to Seneca; but A. is the first to treat the city's old age as something meriting veneration. The unusual image of the Caesars as the children of Rome allows for a positive point of view: no longer the centre of power, Rome ought at least to enjoy respect as a symbol. It is this that makes the conduct of its inhabitants so regrettable. His account appears to be coloured by personal experience, especially if he was among the men of learning expelled (probably in 384 in the prefecture of Symmachus; see Introduction, §§ 6–7). The 'examples' of republican characters, like numerous such examples in his text, seem to be taken from the collection made by Valerius Maximus in the early first century A.D.: Valerius Publicola (the early consul), Regulus (victim of the Carthaginians), and Scipio Africanus are all among Valerius' examples of poverty (4.4); he also records Acilius Glabrio's gilded statue (2.5.1) and the theatre awnings of Catulus, consul in 78 B.C. (2.4.6). Further details on these and all other examples in A.'s history are readily accessible in the *Oxford Classical Dictionary*; but A. himself did not necessarily know much more than he tells. The comic poet alluded to (p. 48) is Terence (*Eunuchus*, 780). The poet of Ascra (p. 46) is Hesiod (*Works and Days*, 289). Semiramis (p. 48) was a legendary queen of Nineveh. For lotus-eaters (p. 49), cf. *Odyssey*, 9.84.

7. Food shortages were a recurrent problem at Antioch, as Julian discovered (below, 22.14); A. here underplays the difficulties. The clash of authority between Gallus and his praetorian prefect was a product of the ambiguity of their positions, since each derived authority directly from the emperor (cf. 17.3, below, for a similar clash involving Julian). The praetorian prefect was at this date the senior civil official (but without troops under his command). The Caesar since Diocletian's reforms was strictly a subordinate of the Augustus: as we are reminded later (14.11), Diocletian had emphasized the subordination of his Caesars. For the importance of purple cloth to a pretender, see below, 15.8, on Julian's proclamation.

9. A., who must have been present at this judicial inquiry in the suite of Ursicinus, is anxious here as elsewhere to exculpate his patron: see Thompson, *The Historical Work of Ammianus*, 42ff. On A.'s own position, see Introduction, § 3. The heroic philosopher who supposedly

spat out his tongue at the tyrant Nearchus (p. 55) was Zeno of Elea, not the Stoic Zeno.

10. For geographical details of the Alamannic campaigns, see Map B.

11. The imaginative account of Gallus' fall draws on the techniques and language of tragedy and epic with its allusions to Virgil (*Aeneid*, 6.480, for the proverbial pallor of Adrastus, while the corpse of the once-feared Gallus recalls that of Priam at *Aeneid*, 2.556f.), as also in its allegorical personification of the figure of just retribution, Adrastia. These distinctly pagan reflections on the mutability of fortune close with a battery of examples from hellenistic Greek and republican Roman history (pp. 63f.): Agathocles and Dionysius were tyrants of Syracuse, Andriscus and Perseus kings of Macedon; Mancinus (in 137 B.C.), Veturius (in 334), Claudius (in 226), and Regulus (in 256) were generals whom the Romans handed over to the enemy rather than accept terms of surrender; Eunus (136–2), Viriathus (147–39), and Spartacus (73–2) led revolts against Rome.

BOOK 15

1. The preface on historical method marks the beginning of a new section of the work (15–25), grander in theme (below, 9) because dominated by Julian. Contrast the opening of 26.1, where excessive detail is criticized. The pride of Constantius is a recurrent theme, used to set off Julian's modesty. 'Our Eternity' and similar expressions were normal in the chancellery style of the period, though Julian tried to reverse the trend. Vetranio (p. 65) had been proclaimed Augustus in 350 on the death of Constans, but abdicated in favour of Constantius (cf. 21.8).

2. The poisoning of the emperor's ear by whispers at court is a leitmotif of the history. A. builds up sympathy for the injured innocence of Ursicinus by comparison with the Tacitean hero Corbulo, victor in the Armenian campaigns under Nero (*Annals*, 13–15: the account of his death is lost). Julian here makes his first entry in the surviving portion, also as an innocent victim; he narrates the anxieties of his early years in his *Letter to the Athenians* (271–4).

3. Constantius takes on the colours of Verres, the notorious governor of Sicily, as his agents are compared with Verres' henchmen Tlepolemus and Hiero (Cicero, *Verrines*, 4.13.30). The 'learned' story that the people of the Atlas do not dream (p. 68) stems from Herodotus (4.184).

4. The Lentienses (modern Lenze preserves their name) and another tribe whose name is lost in a lacuna lived north of Lake Constance, which formed the frontier. The brief digression on Lake Constance is

characteristically enhanced by reference to the myth of Arethusa, the famous spring in Syracuse. The Campi Canini were at the far end of the province, above the Italian lakes (modern Bellinzona); A. thus shows Constantius far from the field of action. He also deprives the hated Arbitio of credit for success by highlighting the personal valour of three junior officers and comparing them with heroes of the early republic.

5. The Frank Silvanus had received his command in Gaul as a reward from Constantius for deserting the usurper Magnentius at the battle of Mursa in 351 (narrated in a lost book). The episode is notable as the first appearance of the author, together with his friend Verinian (cf. 18.8). Despite the dubious role played by his patron Ursicinus and himself, A. represents Silvanus as an innocent victim, blaming his disloyalty on the machinations of sycophants, as does Julian (*Letter to the Athenians*, 273d). Constantius' arrogance in success finds a model in that of Domitian (p. 77): like Constantius (cf. above, 15.1) he was criticized for ascribing divinity to himself. The corrupting influence of flattery upon a tyrant was a standard topic of Greek essays on kingship: A.'s illustrations (p. 78) perhaps derive from one of these.

6. The persecution of Silvanus' associates is put in the worst light; an emperor was supposed to exercise clemency towards defeated opponents. The Poemenius incident (p. 78) occurred in a lost book: but Trier was loyal to Constantius against Decentius, Caesar to the usurper Magnentius, in 352/3, and Poemenius therefore might have merited pardon.

7. The city prefecture of Leontius fell in 355–6, after that of Olybrius (14.6). Liberius was bishop of Rome from 352–6, and supported the Catholic leader Athanasius, condemned by synods at Arles (353) and Milan (355), against the Arian Constantius. Liberius was sent into exile. A. ignores doctrinal controversy, as elsewhere, and so 'secularizes' what was for ecclesiastical historians an important issue: see H. Chadwick, *The Early Church*, 136ff.

8. The importance of the elevation of Julian is underlined by the fulsome description of the ceremonial and the use of speeches (cf. the elevation of Gratian, 27.6). Julian's modest rejection of pomp (p. 83) is typified by his quotation of Homer (*Iliad*, 5.83): the same line is said to have been used in criticism of the pomp of Alexander the Great (Athenaeus, *Deipnosophists*, 540a). In Homer, purple simply refers to blood. With the account of the significance of clashing shields (p. 82), contrast the incompatible account at 20.5, below.

9–12. The allusion (p. 84) to the famous words with which Virgil introduces the second and more martial half of the *Aeneid* (7.44–5) signals the importance which A. attaches to the approaching campaigns of Julian. The long digression on Gaul provides, despite the author's claims, little orientation for the narrative, but again helps to magnify its impact. Ethnographical excursuses were typical in the classical historians, and Timagenes of Alexandria (first century B.C.) is unlikely to have been his only source. (A large part has been omitted in the translation.) The citation from Cicero's defence of Fonteius (p. 85) is, as so often, from a work no longer surviving.

BOOK 16

1. A. admits that in his account of Julian he will almost (but not quite) cross the conventional dividing line between history and panegyric (cf. Introduction, §19), and proceeds to employ some of its characteristic tricks of embellishment, particularly comparison of the hero with past emperors and heroes. Julian records his own opinion of his predecessors and his admiration for Marcus in his *Caesars*. The reference to Cicero (p. 88) is a paraphrase of *Orator*, 43.147. Erechtheus (p. 88) as a mythical king of Athens was a suitable comparison with Julian, who had studied in the city; the tradition of his upbringing by the patron goddess of culture goes back to *Iliad*, 2.546.

2–4. Julian in his own account of the campaigns of 356 (*Letter to the Athenians*, 277d) stresses his subordination to other generals and his lack of troops. He apparently lacked the normal imperial escort of Scutarii and Gentiles (4, cf. above, 14.7); the heavy-armed cuirassiers who escort him (2) are the *clibanarii* described below (10).

5. A panegyrical interlude illustrates Julian's possession of the Platonic virtues of self-discipline, wisdom, and justice (the fourth, courage, is demonstrated by the narrative); on these virtues see below, 25.4. That the numerous sumptuary laws of the late Republic, limiting expenditure particularly at table, had anything to do with Lycurgus of Sparta (p. 92) is fantasy, though Spartan austerity was also legendary. The cult of Mercury (p. 92), better known as Hermes Trismegistus, was an important component of paganism in the late empire. Julian's measures on taxation (p. 93) are described more fully at 17.3; the claim that he never remitted arrears is seemingly contradicted at 25.4.

6–8. Court intrigues make a dim contrast with Julian's heroism. The eulogy of the eunuch Eutherius (pp. 95f.) is exceptional in the extensive late Roman and Byzantine literature on eunuchs: see K. Hopkins, *Conquerors and Slaves* (1978), 172ff. Since Eutherius retired to Rome, it is very likely that A. knew him and used him as a source (cf. Introduction, § 8). Menophilus, eunuch of Mithridates VI of Pontus

(111–63 B.C.), is not otherwise known. Dionysius I of Syracuse (405–367 B.C.), with whom Constantius is compared (p. 98), served as the archetype of the tyrant haunted by insecurity: Cicero, *Tusculans*, 5.58f. and Valerius Maximus, 9.13.4, give the same example. For A.'s hostility to the family of the Anicii, cf. below, 27.11, on Petronius Probus. Note that the prefect Rufinus, criticized at the end (p. 98), is distinct from the informer whose activities are described immediately before.

9. The thread of Persian affairs is picked up from 15.13, and continued below at the end of 10 with the return of Ursicinus and A. himself to the eastern front. In their absence the narrative is played down.

10. An imperial visit to Rome was at this period a great rarity; this marked Constantius' *vicennalia*, twenty years of rule, calculated from 337 (cf. 14.5). An imperial entry (*adventus*) to any city was a ceremonial occasion: see S. MacCormack, *Art and Ceremony in Late Antiquity* (1981), 17ff. A.'s celebrated description is built round the contrast between the false pomp of Constantius and the true pomp of Rome. The ceremonial aspect of Constantius' bearing is described in words that echo Xenophon's picture of Persian royal ceremonial (*Cyropaedia*, 8.1.40f.). To Roman eyes such pomp was hollow, and A. makes disapproval explicit in the contrast with the warlike conduct of Julius Caesar, Claudius Gothicus, and Galerius (pp. 99–100). One should also contrast the 'citizenly' conduct of Julian (22.7). The enumeration of the magnificent sights of Rome reveals not only the author's own enthusiasm for the Eternal City but also Constantius' growing awareness of his own inability to match such true glory (for the location of the sights mentioned, see Monuments of Rome, p. 500). Note that A. fails to mention among these sights the Christian churches of Constantine, notably his Basilica, let alone record the controversial removal of the Altar of Victory from the Senate. The criticism that Constantius enjoyed no genuine success in foreign as opposed to civil war (p. 99) is much repeated (cf. 21.16); the Temple of Janus was only closed on the successful termination of all foreign wars. The departure of Hormisdas, son of the Persian king (p. 102), was described in a lost book; he later assisted in Julian's invasion of Persia. The allegation against Eusebia is remarkable in view of A.'s favourable picture of her elsewhere (21.6).

11–12. Julian's campaigns of 357, culminating in the battle of Strasbourg, sealed his claim to heroic stature. A. drew on the emperor's own memoir of the campaign. His narrative is rhetorically overblown, but not necessarily inaccurate: see Crump, *Ammianus Marcellinus as a Military Historian*, 85ff. Chnodomar's defeat of the usurper Decentius (p. 106) in 352 will have been narrated in the lost portion. After the victory, attention returns to the corrupt and arrogant imperial court. Why Julian was belittled as Victorinus (p. 115) is unclear: perhaps the reference is to the Gallic usurper of 260–74, or perhaps the point lies in the diminutive form of Victor.

BOOK 17

1–2. Hyperbolic comparison with the Punic and Teutonic Wars (the latter presumably refer to Marius' victories) elevates the status of this minor and somewhat obscurely narrated campaign. The area invaded was the former Roman territory of the Agri Decumates. Trajan's fort (p. 118) is hard to identify; but Julian follows here in the footsteps of the great soldier-emperor (cf. 16.1), just as he does in Persia (24.2, 3 and 6).

3. A. is generally critical of over-taxation under Constantius (cf. 21.16) and praises here as elsewhere (16.5, 25.4) Julian's attempts to alleviate the burden. For the crisis caused by taxation under Valentinian in Illyricum, see 30.5. On taxation in this period see Jones, *Later Roman Empire*, 462ff. The second Belgic province centred on Reims.

4. It was a considerable gesture of respect for Rome, which A. scarcely allows, that Constantius there erected the obelisk apparently intended by his father for Constantinople. 'Hundred-gated' Thebes is confused by A. with Hecatompylus in Libya, captured at a much later date by Carthage. A. is, however, right about Gallus, first governor of Egypt and first love-elegist of Latin literature. The obelisks of Rome have all been subsequently moved. Constantius' is now in front of St John Lateran. A. goes on to cite at length a Greek translation of the hieroglyphic inscription from one of Augustus' obelisks. This is the only occasion on which a Roman historian writing in Latin quotes Greek at length. It appears to be irrelevant.

5. The diplomatic exchange between Constantius and Sapor is (in conformity with the practice of ancient historians and unlike the documents in the previous chapter) the historian's own composition, not original documentation. Since, however, both the praetorian prefect Musonian and the notary Spectatus were friends of Libanius, A. could have had access to reliable information.

7. The destruction of Nicomedia was also lamented by Libanius (*Oration*, 61), who was a friend of the governor Aristaenetus. It is ironical that Nicomedia was the city for which the younger Pliny requested, and Trajan refused, a fire brigade (*Letters*, 10.33–4).

8–10. Julian's campaigns of 358 secured the lower Rhine so that the route was open to supplies from Britain (cf. 18.2). A. emphasizes not the strategy but the heroism of Julian. The books of Tages and Vegoe (p.

129) were those of Etruscan haruspicy, in high repute among pagans in the fourth century; see 21.1 for A.'s views on divination.

11.   More backbiting at court. Cimon and Scipio (pp. 131–2) are similarly coupled by Plutarch as examples of victims of slander (*To an uneducated prince*, 782).

12–13. These chapters cover Constantius' successful campaigns of 358 against trans-Danubian tribes, especially the Sarmatians. The account helps to put Julian's campaigns in perspective: his role was to hold the Gallic frontier secure while the Augustus dealt with the more serious threat. Two groups of Sarmatians are involved in these chapters: the 'Free Sarmatians' (often simply 'Sarmatians') and the Limigantes, supposedly their former slaves. Constantius accepts the surrender of the 'Free Sarmatians', endorses the authority of their leader Zizais, and uses their complaints against their 'former slaves' to subject the Limigantes to genocide. Roman policy was to exploit divisions between tribes where possible.

14.   The mission of Eustathius to Persia (above, 17.5) returns empty-handed. It is described by Eunapius in his *Lives of the Sophists* (465–6), who asserts that the pagan philosopher nearly succeeded in converting Sapor and persuading him to abdicate. For Procopius' rebellion under Valentinian, see below, 26.6–9.

BOOK 18

1.   For Julian's emphasis on the administration of justice, cf. below, 22.10. On the importance Ammianus attached to jurisdiction, see Introduction, § 39.

2.   The towns re-fortified by Julian are old frontier posts on the lower Rhine between Mainz and the Netherlands (Fort Hercules lay between Leiden and Nijmegen). The tribes he attacked occupied the area across the Rhine south of Mainz in the old Roman territory of the Agri Decumates. The crossing-point was possibly at Speyer. The tribune Hariobaudes and the German king Hariobaudus should not be confused.

3.   The Barbatio scandal presumably took place while he was at Constantius' court at Sirmium. Arbitio, inveterate intriguer, doubtless hoped to replace him as master of infantry (an office senior to that of master of cavalry). In fact Ursicinus was appointed (below, 18.5). Valentinus (p. 148) had been promoted from the corps to which A. belonged, the *protectores*. The Alexander example (p. 148) may be taken from Valerius Maximus (7.2.11); Callisthenes was Alexander's court historian and was executed for his freedom of speech. The story about geese (p. 148) was a widespread fable.

4. On A.'s horror of eunuchs, cf. 16.7 above (also 14.6). Gibbon nicely alludes to the 'sarcasm of an impartial historian' according to which Constantius 'possessed some credit with his haughty favourite' (vol. 2, ch. 19, p. 246f.). Ursicinus' possession of a house at Antioch may be significant for his link with A.

5. A. tends to exculpate the renegade Antoninus as a victim of fiscal oppression (cf. below, 18.8). He is compared with Zopyrus (p. 150) who, according to Herodotus (3.153ff.), betrayed Babylon to Darius (Libanius, *Oration*, 12.74, compares him with Demaratus of Sparta, also in Herodotus). The battle of Hileia or Singara (p. 151) belongs to the 340s, perhaps 348: 'forty years' is more appropriate to A.'s viewpoint in the 380s.

6. The most autobiographical part of A.'s narrative now starts. He should not always be taken too literally. He hardly gathered the details of the cross-examination of a prisoner while at full gallop (p. 154), nor saw the companions of the Persian king at a distance of fifty miles (p. 155); these details he presumably discovered by inquiry. It seems likely that Jovinian was a fellow-student at Antioch. The allusion to Doriscus (p. 156) invites a comparison with the Persian wars in Herodotus. Xerxes reviewed his troops at Doriscus (7.59), but A., though better informed than Herodotus, gives no catalogue.

7. Nineveh is to the north of the Anzaba (see Map C); Sapor passed it after, not before, crossing the stream. A.'s memory of geographical detail is not perfect (cf. below, 18.9). Edessa was a centre of Christian martyr cult, and Sabinian was possibly only offering prayers. The accusation of watching dancing in time of war was also levelled against the emperor Verus. Constantina (p. 157) is the Antoninupolis, rebuilt by Constantius, mentioned at 18.9.

8. Describing his own entry into Amida, A. sacrifices clarity to the sensational. Why does he mention his friend Verinian (who was with him on the Silvanus mission, 15.5)? What happened to him? How can Romans and Persians, alive and dead, have spent the night jammed in the approaches? It is the narrowness of his own escapes that A. constantly advertises.

9. It is hard to see how A.'s description of Amida can be accurate. The town is south, not north, of the river; Mesopotamia lies to the south, not east; and the river Nymphaeus is to the east rather than the north. The author works from a memory of circumstances thirty years past, not from a map. The progress of Aelian (p. 160) from *protector* to tribune to count is typical – the path that A. himself did not follow.

10. For the romantic tale of Craugasius, see 19.9 and 20.6. Christian convents were common in the area. A.'s reasons for not calling a nun

a nun (p. 161) *may* be purely stylistic; see A. and A. Cameron, *Classical Quarterly* n.s. 14 (1964), 306ff. and Introduction, § 36.

BOOK 19

1. The allusion to the battle over Patroclus' corpse (p. 164) in *Iliad*, 17 is the first of a series of epic touches which enhance the Amida narrative. For a similar reference to the Adonis myth, cf. 22.9.

2. A. truly has a horror of elephants: cf. 19.7. The cross-reference (p. 165) indicates that he also voiced his horror in one of the lost books. The spear-throwing ritual of the Roman fetial priests, with which the gesture of Grumbates is compared (p. 165), was long since obsolete. A legion (p. 166) had a paper strength of 1,000 at this date, so of the 20,000 besieged up to 7,000 were troops: see Jones, *Later Roman Empire*, 681f. Note, here and throughout, the extreme generality of A.'s descriptions of carnage.

3. For Sabinian's graves, see above, 18.7. Note the theme of individual advantage versus the advantage of the state (Introduction, § 40).

4. A mild plague (perhaps no more than marsh fever) gives A. the opportunity to compare his siege (p. 168) with the classic depictions of plague in the *Iliad* (Book 1) and Thucydides (Book 2). Learned digression substitutes for hard fact.

5. The northern, not the southern, wall of Amida (p. 169) looks down on the Tigris: see above, 18.9.

6. Another episode assimilated to epic by comparison with the *Iliad* (p. 172): in Book 10 Odysseus and Diomedes attack the tents of the Trojan ally Rhesus and kill him in his sleep. The night before the new moon would have been 27 September.

8. Amida is sacked and A. narrowly escapes (cf. above, 18.8). As an officer and a gentleman ('of free birth') he was more used to riding than to running. His observations (p. 175) on the 'earth-born' men of mythology (as in the story of Cadmus) shows the same rationalizing approach as his treatment of the Adonis myth (above, 1) or of Apollo in the *Iliad* (above, 19.4). The fate A. escaped emerges in the next chapter: the other *protectores* were led off into captivity.

9. The constellation of the Kids rises on 6 October; Amida fell, to judge by the state of the moon (above, 19.6) on 4 October, after a seventy-three-day siege since 24 July. Craugasius nicely illustrates the ambiguous loyalties of the inhabitants of this border territory: cf. above, 18.10. The Virgilian tag (p. 176) is from the foot-race at *Aeneid*, 5.320.

10. The prefect of Rome regularly celebrated games for Castor and Pollux at Ostia on 27 January; as a pagan, Tertullus did it with a good will.

For A.'s belief in Rome's eternity, cf. above, 14.6 and Introduction, § 38.

11. The story of Constantius' Sarmatian campaigns picks up from 17.13. On the importance A. attaches to lightening the burden of taxation, cf. Introduction, § 39. Anatolius is praised on the same grounds by Aurelius Victor, *Caesars*, 13. For the later troubles indicated (p. 178), see 30.5. The temptations and dangers of supplying the shortage of manpower by naturalizing barbarians which this episode illustrates recur on a grander scale in the disaster of Adrianople (cf. 31.4).

12. Renewed trials for sorcery and treason, linked to earlier trials by the person of Paul (last met persecuting the adherents of Silvanus, 15.6), and with the trials of 371 at Antioch (29.1–2) by the unattractive figure of Modestus. Since so few victims of injustice are named, it is hard, as elsewhere, to judge whether A.'s lurid colouring is justified. The treason laws of Sulla (p. 183) had been redefined subsequently; it is only in the late empire that torture becomes the legal norm. A.'s complaint of the neglect of prodigies (pp. 183–4) was also made by Livy (43.13.1); regular expiation of prodigies went out with the empire. On Daphne (p. 183), cf. 22.13. The quotation from Cicero (p. 183) is, as often, not found in the surviving works; A. certainly knew works now lost, but perhaps also relied on an imperfect memory.

BOOK 20

1. Britain offered Julian an important source of corn-supply: cf. above, 18.2. The British expedition of Constans (p. 185) had been in 343. For the problems of the province, see S. S. Frere, *Britannia* (2nd ed., 1978), 376ff.

2. The loss of seven legions at Amida was a major setback and questions were inevitably asked. A. assumes, as elsewhere, the innocence of his chief.

3. The solar eclipse of 28 August 360 provokes a scientific excursus on eclipses, here omitted. By interrupting the narrative, it draws attention to the importance of Julian's proclamation in the next chapter.

4. Julian's proclamation is described by Julian himself (*Letter to the Athenians*, 281ff.), by Libanius in several orations, and by other historians. Like Julian and Libanius, A. depicts it as a spontaneous move on the part of the troops: the hasty attempts to improvise a diadem emphasize the unplanned nature of the occasion. Yet to invite the officers to dinner was a clear sign of subversive intentions, and the historian Eunapius saw it as a planned attempt and attributed to Julian's doctor Oribasius, who wrote a memoir of Julian, a leading role in

455

5.   seducing the troops. Barbarian troops formed the core of Julian's support, and the king-making ritual has one distinctively barbarian element – the elevation of the chief on a shield (p. 189). The barbarian auxiliary regiments, Celts and Petulantes (p. 189), remained Julian's favoured troops (cf. 22.12) and the barbarian Nevitta was rewarded with the consulship.

5.   A formal address to the troops (*adlocutio*) was an imperial prerogative (16.12, p. 110) and this adloction formally marks Julian's elevation in status (though A. could not resist the temptation to put a speech into his mouth earlier, before the battle of Strasbourg, 16.12). The practical proposal Julian makes (p. 191) is to stop improper promotion. Offices were awarded on the basis of the recommendation of superiors (*suffragium*), which often amounted to sale of office. Already Constantine had legislated against the award of military rank through influence to civilians, since it frustrated promotion. See further below, 22.6, and Jones, *Later Roman Empire*, 392ff. The clashing of shields and spears (p. 191) in approval contradicts his account of the matter above (15.8). The vision of the Genius of Rome (p. 191) here corresponds to the vision of its disappearance immediately before his death (25.2). The representation of the Genius as a young man with a cornucopia was normal on imperial coinage until 326. A.'s account is very reminiscent of Suetonius' account of the appearance and disappearance of Fortune in his *Life of Galba* (4.3, 18.2). Julian himself had a quite different account of signs from the gods (*Letter to the Athenians*, 284).

6–7.   Sapor follows up his success at Amida in 359 with further sieges in 360. He had besieged Nisibis without success in 337, 350 and 359. Bezabde was a Christian stronghold, and its bishop (Heliodorus) naturally acted as spokesman. A. goes out of his way to rebut an anti-Christian rumour.

8–9.   Though A. may well have been able to read the correspondence between Julian and Constantius, it is unlikely that he here preserves the authentic wording. Despite Julian's protestations of innocence, his treatment of Constantius' reply shows that he knew how to manipulate popular opinion.

10–11.   Further success by Julian against the barbarians is juxtaposed with Constantius' lack of success. A. lingers over the fruitless siege of Bezabde, and underlines its importance with a digression (on rainbows, here omitted), in order to point the often-repeated moral that Constantius, successful in civil war, had no luck in barbarian wars (cf. 14.10). Ablabius (p. 202) was a favourite of Constantine, murdered on Constantius' instigation in 337; his daughter Olympias was subsequently poisoned by the displaced wife of Arsaces.

BOOK 21

1.   At the start of a book which describes the open conflict between Julian and Constantius, A. digresses on the practice of divination. It was an element of paganism unacceptable to Christianity and banned under Constantius. In defending its rationale, A. defends Julian's use of the practice (though he thought Julian went too far; see 25.5), and makes his own pagan beliefs and debt to Neoplatonism explicit. He describes four main branches of divination: augury, haruspicy (on the books of Tages, cf. above, 17.10), prophecy, and dream-interpretation. He omits oracles and astrology. He concludes with an appeal to the authority of Cicero (*De natura deorum*, 2.12) – extraordinarily, since Cicero *On Divination*, Book 2, is a devastating attack on the intellectual basis of the practice.

2.   The chapter summarizes signs given to Julian up to the present moment in the narrative. From now on A., who approves this old-fashioned historian's practice (19.12), includes signs and portents in the narrative. By his description of Epiphany (pp. 209f.) he clearly distances himself from Christianity. The astrological prediction (Zeus is the planet Jupiter, Cronos Saturn) refers to a rare conjunction of stars that occurred in late 361 or early 362; Constantius in fact died in November 361. Julian's pretence of Christianity in this period may be linked with an attempt to win the support of Western bishops after Constantius' failure to achieve agreement at the Council of Rimini in 359.

3–4.   The affair of Vadomar allowed Julian to move his troops to the edge of Constantius' area without alerting suspicion. A. admits, unlike Julian himself or Libanius, that there was doubt whether Constantius actually incited Vadomar. Philagrius was surely A.'s informant for this episode; note that as count of the East he will have been in Antioch.

5.   Another formal speech for Julian marks another important step. Oath-taking was a Roman military custom, but this ceremony appears to be barbarian in form.

6.   A. was presumably an eyewitness for events in Antioch. His praise for Eusebia (pp. 214–15) is remarkable in view of the allegation that she procured the miscarriage of Julian's children (16.10); her brothers were residents of Antioch and surely known to A. (cf. 29.2). The 'highest magistracy' to which Florentius is promoted (p. 215) is the consulship.

7.   Africa's importance lay in supplying grain and oil to Rome and the West. Since Gaudentius had already offended Julian (17.9) he could be relied upon by Constantius not to desert. In fact Julian executed him (22.11).

8.   Julian's appointment of the praetorian prefect is the final mark of

independence. Julian is compared with Alexander elsewhere (16.5, 24.4).

9–12. The highlight of the narrative of Julian's march is a siege; such is A.'s inexhaustible appetite for siege narratives that the chronology of the main narrative is sacrificed to anticipation of the outcome of the siege. Victor (p. 219) is the Aurelius Victor who wrote the surviving epitomized history terminating with Julian; his appointment was a reward. A. certainly read his work, but surely derived more from him as an oral source. Symmachus (p. 224) is the father of the famous letter-writer. A.'s description of him as 'the better man' has been taken as an indication of friendship with the family; but Symmachus had been vice-prefect of Rome immediately before, whereas Maximus left little other trace (see *Prosopography of the Later Roman Empire*, vol. 1, Maximus, 17).

13. Constantius in his last speech claims that Justice or Nemesis will bring Julian low as it did Gallus (cf. 14.11); A.'s unspoken implication is that Justice in the event vindicated Julian. Arbitio had proved his worth in civil war against Magnentius.

14. The account of the portents of the death of the Christian Constantius and especially of his 'guardian angel' (*genius*) is distinctly pagan. It culminates with allusion to three notable pagan 'holy men': Hermes Trismegistus (a hellenized version of the Egyptian Thoth, supposed author of a body of philosophical–religious writing, the 'Hermetic corpus'), Apollonius of Tyana (a wonder-worker of the first century A.D., whose life was written by Philostratus), and the great Neoplatonic philosopher Plotinus, with whose thought A. appears to be acquainted. Pythagoras, Socrates, and Numa (supposedly a Pythagorean) were also often treated as holy men. It is unclear what Scipio, Marius, and Octavian are doing in this company, apart from keeping up the batting for the Roman side; all three, however, laid claim to divine help.

15. Constantius was born on 7 August 317, appointed Caesar in 324, and became Augustus in 337. The manuscripts of A. give 5 October as the date of his death; other authors give 3 November. Cf. below, 29.6, for the marriage of Constantia to Gratian.

16. The scores on which Constantius is praised are much the same as for Valentinian (30.8–9). On the preservation of imperial dignity, and abstention from spitting, etc., which open and close the good points, cf. 16.10 on the entry into Rome. Praise for not advancing generals to the highest grade (the clarissimate) is anachronistic: it was only under Valentinian and Valens that the great inflation of senatorial honours took place (Jones, *Later Roman Empire*, 527f). None of the good points emerge clearly in the course of the narrative. By contrast, the bad

points have been dinned in: merciless and unjust condemnations (15.3 and 6, 16.8, 19.12, etc.), failure in foreign as opposed to civil wars (14.10, 20.11, etc.), and oppressive taxation (17.3, 19.11). The criticism of Constantius' ecclesiastical politics explains why he says so little on this important topic (cf. 15.7). The sermon against imperial cruelty is one A. never tires of preaching (cf. 29.2, 30.8); for Marcus and Avidius Cassius, see the life of the latter in the *Historia Augusta* (*Lives of the Later Caesars*) with similar sentiments; the citation from Cicero (p. 231), if genuine, is from a letter not extant.

BOOK 22

1. After looking forward in time to the surrender of Aquileia and then the death and burial of Constantius, A. takes the narrative back to the moments of anxiety for Julian before Constantius' death.

2. Julian is seen as either like a god or acting with the support of the gods. Triptolemus (p. 235) was worshipped in Attica, in association with Demeter, at the Eleusinian mysteries into which Julian had himself been initiated. The picture of all ages and sexes greeting one as if descended from the skies is borrowed from Cicero's panegyric of Pompey (*De imperio Cn. Pompei*, 41, also used for Julian's obituary, 25.4).

3. Contrast the trials of Julian's opponents with those of the adherents of Gallus (15.3) and Silvanus (15.6). A. condemns the abuse of justice, but omits lurid colouring. On Nemesis or Adrastia (p. 237), see above, 14.11. For judges and victims, see Notes on Persons; Palladius, Euagrius, and Cyrinus are not met elsewhere in A. For Ursulus at Amida (p. 236), cf. 20.11 (p. 202).

4. The moralizing against luxury and the use of Cincinnatus the dictator as an example of poverty (p. 238) are traditional. Salaries normally were paid in kind at this period (Jones, *Later Roman Empire*, 396ff.).

5. A. evidently approves of Julian's edict of toleration. For his disapproval of doctrinal controversy, cf. above, 21.16, on Constantius' encouragement, and on its bloody consequences, below, 22.11 and 27.3. Julian made plain his admiration for the philosopher-emperor Marcus in his own writings, notably the *Caesars*.

6. The monies the Egyptian litigants were attempting to recover were paid to influential men for their patronage. Julian had already attempted to discourage payment for patronage (above, 20.5). By refusing clients any protection at law for the recovery of their money, he made payment more perilous and thus less tempting. See T. D. Barnes, *Classical Philology* 69 (1974), 288ff.

7. Julian's conduct at the ceremony is extolled in the surviving speech of thanks by Mamertinus; A. is less enthusiastic (cf. 25.5). The relationship between Julian and Maximus of Ephesus, philosopher and wonder-worker (p. 240), is fully related in Eunapius' *Lives of the Sophists*, 47ff.; A. is not sympathetic. The Cicero quotation (p. 240) is from *Pro Archia*, 26. The mention of Vettius Agorius Praetextatus (p. 241) has suggested to some that he was A.'s informant, direct or ultimate; on the pagan 'circle' in Rome and A.'s links with it, see Introduction, § 7. On the Indian embassies (p. 241) Gibbon remarks (Vol. 2, ch. 24, p. 481, n.7), 'Ammianus, who unwarily deviates into gross flattery, must have forgotten the length of the way, and the short duration of the reign of Julian.'

8. The omitted geographical excursus is long, learned, confused, and of no apparent relevance. Its function (apart from display of learning) is presumably to pad out Julian's reign.

9. On the earthquake at Nicomedia, see above, 17.7. Julian's visit to the shrine of the Great Mother (Cybele) was connected with his recent publication of an essay interpreting her cult. Julian's attitude to service on local councils constituted one of A.'s main criticisms (cf. 25.4); for the bearing of this on A.'s own position, see Introduction, § 2. With Julian's reaction to the manufacture of a purple robe (p. 243), contrast that of Gallus (14.9). Julian's arrival in Antioch (p. 244) recalls his arrival in Vienne (15.8).

10. A.'s praise for Julian's justice (cf. 18.1, 22.6) is now tempered by sharp criticism of his treatment of Christians (repeated at 25.4). The return of Astraea or Justice from the stars (pp. 245–6) was a standard symbol in imperial panegyric for the return of the Golden Age.

11. The riot at Alexandria was the worst of a whole rash of anti-Christian riots provoked by Julian's declaration of approval for paganism. Bishop George (confused by medieval hagiography with the patron saint of England) was an Arian, bitter enemy of Athanasius. Julian knew, and confiscated, his fine classical library. It is possible that his death preceded that of Artemius (i.e. in 361, not 362). Despite disapproval of lynching, A. distances himself from Christianity by his elaborate explanation of martyr cult. For paganism in Alexandria, cf. below, 22.16.

12–13. 'Sixty years' of Persian carnage (p. 248) dates from the successes of Galerius Maximian in 298, often alluded to in the narrative (cf. 24.1); this assertion, however, conflicts with the claim that Constantine was responsible for starting the war (below, 25.4, p. 299). The futile attacks on Hercules (p. 248) are somewhat obscure myths, perhaps derived from Philostratus, *Imagines*, 2.22 and 24. This is the first A. says of the extravagant sacrifices Julian had in fact performed throughout the course of his progress from Gaul. The account of the temple at Daphne (p. 249) is unclear. The Castalian spring was an oracle at Daphne; it was particularly the remains of St Babycas, enshrined there by Gallus, that Julian had cleared away, so incensing the Christian community. He also had the temple restored. That its burning was Christian retaliation is more than likely; the rumour blaming the pagan philosopher Asclepiades would be a Christian invention.

14. Julian's visit to Antioch was a triple disaster: he failed to discourage Christianity, to stop the corn shortage, and to boost the local council: see G. Downey, *A History of Antioch in Syria* (1967), 380ff. Libanius was one of few who remained loyal; A. himself was less than enthusiastic. The *Misopogon* (p. 250) survives.

16. The omitted part of the excursus on Egypt is highly derivative. But A. reveals himself in his enthusiasm for Alexandria and its two main products, learning (note how many of the branches he mentions are subjects of his own digressions) and religion. The silence about Christianity in Alexandria (cf. above, 22.11) is indicative. Note by contrast the mention of the founder of Neoplatonism, Ammonius Saccas (p. 253). The Temple of Serapis (p. 252), object of wonder to A., and the library it contained, were burnt in anti-pagan riots in 391; A. published too soon to know this (see Introduction, § 9). The details of his account are unreliable: Cleopatra built neither Pharos nor the causeway, and the number of books burnt by Caesar is inflated.

BOOK 23

1. Sallustius was a pagan, and either he or more probably Julian's friend Salutius was author of a surviving work of pagan theology (see Notes on Persons). In fact the last private citizen to share a consulship with an emperor (p. 255) was Pomponius Januarius with Maximian in 285. The attempted rebuilding of the temple at Jerusalem (p. 255) was a calculated blow against Christians, perhaps designed to frustrate the prophecy of Christ. The unfavourable omens reported here and in the following narrative act as counterweight to Julian's own incessant search for favourable signs; for A. such omens are an essential part of history since they reveal the actual will of the gods (cf. above, 19.12, 21.1). The imperial titulature reversed by the populace (p. 256) was Julianus Pius Felix Augustus.

2. For Julian's bad relations with the people of Antioch, see above, 22.14; for his funeral, see below, 25.9.

3. Carrhae (modern Harran) was the site of the defeat of the triumvir

Crassus in 53 B.C. when three legions were lost. The Sibylline books, recently consulted (23.1), which now escaped burning (p. 258), succumbed to a later fire early in the fifth century under Stilicho. That Julian promised the throne to his kinsman Procopius (p. 258) seems unlikely in view of his subsequent refusal to designate a successor (25.4); the story sounds like an attempt to legitimate his later proclamation as Augustus (26.6).

4. The omitted excursus on siege-engines is one of the two great digressions which bulk out a quarter of the narrative on the Persian expedition and add to its epic proportions. For a translation and full technical commentary, see E. W. Marsden, *Greek and Roman Artillery, Technical Treatises* (1971).

5. Antioch was twice occupied by the Persians, in 256 and 260 under Gallienus and Valerian. The story (pp. 259f.), also known to Libanius, would derive from local knowledge. The reappearance of 'we' at this point in the narrative implies that A. himself joined the expedition at Cercusium (cf. Introduction, § 4). The ambiguity of oracles was an old chestnut, and A. takes two of his examples from Herodotus (p. 261), who is much in his mind throughout the Persian narratives. The Roman example, a verse of Ennius referring to Pyrrhus, was cited by Cicero, *On Divination*, 2.116. The death of Jovian (p. 261) was ill-omened since his name recalled Jove (Jupiter), and Jovius was an element in the imperial titulature. In a formal adlocution to the troops, Julian backs his plans by examples which are not wholly apposite (p. 262); neither Lucullus, Pompey, nor Ventidius in fact invaded Persia. All these examples, however, underline A.'s conception of Julian as standing in the great old Roman military tradition. For the personification of Justice, see above, 14.11.

BOOK 24

1. It is only after Julian enters Persia that A. names his commanders. The majority came with him from the West, but Hormisdas, son of a Persian king, was a notable exception. The anecdote of the old soldier (p. 267) is presumably from A.'s own experience: since the campaign of Galerius was in 296–8, the man must have been at least eighty-five years old.

2. The tribunal (p. 269) was a stone construction either put up by Trajan or named after him. A. likes to note where Julian follows in Trajan's footsteps in Germany (17.1) and in Persia (cf. below, 24.6). The capture of Pirisabora (the name means Victorious Sapor) is written up with much epic, and specifically Virgilian, colour: note especially the 'Argive shield' (p. 271), a comparison borrowed from *Aeneid*, 3.637, where it

refers to the Cyclops' eye. The comparison (for the better) with Scipio Aemilianus (p. 271) is an encomiastic touch, turning a failure into a personal triumph; the episode described is not found in the surviving text of Polybius. Julian is welcomed, as often before, as a 'guardian angel' (cf. 15.8).

3. The ancient practice that the traditionalist Julian revives (p. 273) is presumably decimation, though this involved execution of every tenth soldier, not simply of ten. In his speech Julian compares himself with a standard example of poverty, C. Fabricius Luscinus (p. 273), hero of the war with Pyrrhus (who is cited again in the next chapter). Julian is linked by a further anecdote with Trajan, conqueror of Mesopotamia. A.'s account of the love-life of palm trees (p. 274) is, curiously, most closely paralleled in a sermon of St Basil.

4. Frequent *exempla* give the siege of Maozamalcha ('king's town') heroic status. Manlius Torquatus and Valerius Corvinus (p. 275) were famous for their single-handed duels with barbarians: Julian's exploit was hardly in the same class. The three heroes of the mining operation (p. 278) are a little oddly compared with an episode from the Pyrrhic war (on Fabricius Luscinus, see above, 24.3). One of them, Magnus, has been identified with Magnus of Carrhae who wrote a history which included a first-hand account of this Persian expedition; if this is right, A. himself makes no comment. Another, Jovian, soon met an unpleasant end (25.8). The restraint of Alexander and of Scipio Africanus towards female captives (p. 279) was famous, and this comparison is more apt.

5. Coche and Ctesiphon were sacked in 283 by the emperor Carus who died shortly after. Coche and Seleucia were distinct sites, though A. treats them as identical. The gibbeted family (p. 280) was that of Mamersides (above, 24.2).

6. The Naarmalcha, which flows from Pirisabora to Ctesiphon, is confused with Trajan's canal, cutting across to the Tigris north of Ctesiphon (see Map C). With this chapter Roman success reaches a climax, marked by the *exempla* of Sertorius who distinguished himself in the campaign against the Cimbri and Teutones in 105 B.C., and above all by reference to the heroes of the *Iliad*, Hector and Achilles, and four valiant fighters from the battles of Plataea, Salamis, and Marathon who were singled out by Herodotus (p. 284). But the sacrifice to Mars Ultor (whose temple in Rome contained the standards retrieved from the Persians by Augustus) introduces the first note of disaster to come.

7. We now reach the turning-point of the invasion. Up to Ctesiphon all has gone well for Julian; but from now on his luck changes. Our understanding of what went wrong is obscured by the loss of what must be assumed to be a large section of the text. From parallel

narratives (e.g. Libanius, *Oration*, 18.257ff.) we learn that at this point Julian was approached by a Persian embassy offering terms, which he rejected out of hand. It is possible that, like Alexander, he decided to advance into the heart of the kingdom in pursuit of the Persian king; the decision to burn the boats would make sense in this context. Persian 'deserters' encouraged him in this decision by misinformation, presumably about the movements of the king and the main body of the army. Julian also counted on making a junction with the division under Procopius and Sebastian, together with the Armenian troops of Arsaces (cf. 23.3 for the plan). With hindsight, the decision to burn the ships was fatal, and A. here sees the agency of Bellona, goddess of destructive war, as in the last disaster of Adrianople (31.13).

8. The return march to Corduene starts. The book ends with a magnificent cliff-hanger. The total ignorance of the Romans as to the movements of enemy troops is striking.

BOOK 25

1. A. never tires of describing the Persian armed cavalry (cf. above, 24.6) or the terror inspired by their elephants (above, 19.2). Perhaps, as one accustomed to ride a horse (19.8), he was especially vulnerable. The Persians suffered their setback at the siege of Nisibis (p. 290) in 350.

2. Omens mark Julian's approaching end, as they mark every important stage in the expedition. On the vision of the Genius, see 20.5. One must question whether Julian himself could possibly have been the source of this vision. Constantius too is supposed to have seen his Genius departing (21.14). The mini-excursus on shooting stars (p. 291) gives the flavour of some of the longer scientific digressions here omitted. The Tarquitian books (p. 292) on which the Etruscan diviners rely are the same as those of Tages and Vegoe (above, 17.10, 21.1).

3. A. says nothing of the part he played in this battle: one suspects he was in the centre, panicking at the smell and noise of the elephants. Other sources have various explanations for Julian's extraordinary lack of armour (the heat, or a conviction of invincibility): none can bring themselves to suggest that he was courting death as a way out of the disastrous situation into which he had led the Roman army. It is notable that A. does not here so much as mention the version of Julian's death favoured by pagans, that he was struck by a Christian within his own ranks; later he alludes to this version as an unfounded rumour made known to the Persians by deserters (25.6). Epaminondas of Thebes (p. 293) is an appropriate *exemplum* for a hero's death; less obvious is the relevance of the republican heroes listed, all of whom appear in the

elder Pliny's list of Romans with exceptional records in war (*Natural History*, 7.92, 101–6). Julian dies, after the fashion of Socrates, discoursing on the soul. This is doubtless authentic, but the speech attributed to him is hardly so, and tells us more about A.'s own evaluation of Julian.

4. The balanced assessment of Julian should be compared with those of Constantius (21.16) or Valentinian (30.7–9). A. had predicted his account of Julian would 'not fall far short of a panegyric' (16.1). Here he adopts the panegyrist's technique of enumerating virtues, starting with four standard philosophical ones, and adding four more practical ones derived directly from Cicero's encomium of Pompey. Under these heads he summarizes good points already brought out in the course of the narrative: see especially 16.5 (self-control), 22.7 (citizenly conduct), 18.1 and 22.10 (justice), 24.3 (authority), 22.9 (fortune), 16.5 (generosity). In sharp contrast to the formal arrangement of the praise stand the points of criticism, briefly but tellingly summarized: see especially 22.10 (impulsiveness), 22.12 (superstition), 22.9–10 (injustice), 22.14 (pursuit of popularity). The effect of this contrast is extraordinary. The formality of the panegyric emphasizes Julian's claim to be seen as an ideal philosopher-king. But it seems almost wooden when set against the sober and realistic criticisms A. has to make. The resulting impression is not of heroisation, but of ambivalence. For a full discussion of A.'s assessment of Julian, see Blockley, *Ammianus Marcellinus*, 73ff. The lies of Metrodorus (p. 299) which misled Constantine must have been described in the lost books: he was a philosopher who told Constantine that the gifts he was bringing him back from India had been seized by Sapor.

5. Jovian is chosen as emperor by the officers (and civil authorities), as was Valentinian soon after (26.1). A. was surely himself present, and Gibbon shrewdly suggested (vol. 2, ch. 24, p. 518, n.104) that the unnamed officer was A. himself. (This has been doubted.) His words undoubtedly represent A.'s own views (cf. 25.8, below). Jovian was the senior officer (*primicerius*) among the *protectores domestici*, A.'s own corps (cf. Introduction, § 3).

6. Pagan sacrifices continue, though Jovian was in fact a Christian. Anatolius, whose corpse is found (p. 301), was reported killed in the battle above (25.3).

7. In criticizing Jovian, A. greatly understates the distance to Corduene, and underestimates the number of days the retreat would have taken and the actual safety this disputed area would have offered. The surrendered areas, all north-east of the Tigris, had been acquired by

Galerius Maximian in 298. The identity of the Roman hostages is uncertain (p. 304), but they may have been Nevitta and Victor.

8. Jovian suppresses potential rivals. Jovinus was suspect for the same reason that Constantius distrusted Ursicinus. It was the murder of the notary Jovian that alarmed Procopius into going into hiding (below, 26.6). Thilsaphata (p. 307) is called Thebeta by other sources.

9. A.'s point is that if Jovian had stayed and put up a fight for Nisibis, as he ought, he might have been challenged by a usurper like Jovinus in the West. A. believes that the interests of the state should be put before those of the individual (see Introduction, § 40). A. takes his examples of triumphs refused (p. 309) from Valerius Maximus' collection (2.8.4), but confuses with them Scipio Africanus, whose triumph was refused on quite different grounds.

10. With the safe return of the army to Antioch, A. himself (as revealed by 'we') again disappears from the narrative. The account of Julian's tomb (p. 310) is emotionally charged and borrows the moving language in which Virgil spoke of the tomb of Marcellus, washed by the Tiber (*Aeneid*, 6.873f.). Libanius thought Julian should have been buried at Athens; A.'s sentiments reflect his feelings for Rome (Introduction, § 7). On A.'s account, Jovian's death was accidental. Others spoke of poison, and it is possible that the comparison with Scipio Aemilianus (p. 311), who was widely supposed to have been assassinated, carries an allusion to this suspicion. If so, A. rebuts it. Odd though the story is of poisonous fumes in a newly plastered room, a similar accident befell Julian, by his own account (*Misopogon*, 341c–d).

BOOK 26

1. A preface defending brevity contrasts with that at 15.1 defending fullness, and introduces a new section at a much faster tempo (see Introduction, § 13). Cicero's letter to Nepos (p. 313) does not survive, but we hear elsewhere of a secret work, *On his own councils*. With the election of Valentinian, compare that of Jovian (25.5): the candidates are remarkably junior. The omitted observations on the leap year are, as Gibbon puts it (vol. 3, ch. 25, p. 8, n. 25), 'long because unseasonable'.

2. A formal adlocution marks the elevation of Valentinian, as of Julian (15.8) and Gratian (27.6), but not of Jovian or Valens.

3. Apronian's prefecture fell in 362–4 and has already been mentioned (23.3). A. postpones his account to 364 rather than interrupt his narrative on Julian. Valerius Maximus (3.5.4) gives Duillius (p. 317) as an example of extravagant behaviour.

4. Valens was crowned at a suburb called Hebdomon, suitable for a

gathering of the army, where eastern emperors were regularly crowned thereafter. Accusations of black magic are a leitmotif of the later books: for the underlying causes, see Brown, *Religion and Society*, 119ff.

5.   The new emperors surrounded themselves with fellow-Pannonians, whom A. regularly regards as brutal. As A. indicates, the following books have a multiple story-line following theatres of war, in contrast to the Julian narrative.

6–9.   A. underlines the farcical character of Procopius' revolt, but admits the strength of anti-Pannonian feeling, and the dangers of rebellion however ill-conceived. Here, as at 31.5, he uses historical examples to make a historical point (contrast his panegyrical examples in the Julian narrative). He gathers a series of examples of successful rebels (pp. 322–4, 329); Andriscus has already been used to demonstrate the unpredictability of fortune (14.11). He is particularly aware of Roman usurpations: in the course of the narrative he mentions Didius Julianus (A.D. 193), Elagabal (218–22), Maximin (235–8), Gordian I (238), and Pescennius Niger (193). These cases, as of the favourites Cleander (who fell in 189) and Plautian (d. 205), come from the same period. The comparison (p. 331) of Procopius with Crassus (an ancestor of the triumvir) is merely a learned allusion to Cicero (*De finibus*, 5.92). On A.'s handling of this episode, see Blockley, *Ammianus Marcellinus*, 55ff.

10.   A. treats the punishment of the rebels with the same horror as he does that of the adherents of Gallus (15.3) or Silvanus (15.6). Omitted here is a moralizing account of Valens' use of torture and punishment, totally lacking in specific evidence. A.'s account of earthquakes (p. 333) is used by Gibbon (vol. 3, ch. 26, p. 69, n.1), who, somewhat unjustly, castigates him: 'Such is the bad taste of Ammianus that it is not easy to distinguish his facts from his metaphors. Yet he positively affirms that he saw the rotten carcase of a ship, *ad secundum lapidem*, at Methone, or Modon, in Peloponnesus.' The eyewitness account incidentally betrays the historian's travels, which seem to have been extensive (see Introduction, § 6).

BOOK 27

3.   The chapter rounds up events at Rome 364–7: Symmachus was prefect 364–5, Lampadius 365–6, Viventius 366–7. Terentius was governor of Tuscany 364–5; the portent (p. 334) pointed doubly towards him since Pistoria recalled the Latin for baker (*pistor*) and bakers' mills were worked by asses. Symmachus (p. 334) is the father of the letter-writer (Introduction, § 7): Valentinian ordered the price of wine to be

reduced in his prefecture. Lampadius' restorations (p. 335) were the consequence of a ban on new buildings by the emperor. The anecdote about Trajan (p. 335) is garbled; Constantine was supposed to have dubbed him 'Wallflower', but his numerous buildings were his own. The vivid account of rioting over the bishopric of Rome characteristically suppresses the crucial doctrinal background: Ursinus was the Arian candidate, Damasus was Orthodox and a supporter of Liberius (15.7). A.'s point of view is close to that of the pagan aristocrat Praetextatus, who teased Damasus: 'Make me bishop of Rome and I will turn Christian at once.' Damasus was notorious for courting rich women for their money, and Valentinian legislated against the practice in 370.

4–5. Valens' Gothic campaigns, introduced appropriately by a description of Thrace, here omitted, are gathered together for the years 366–70. This theatre of war is then passed over until it becomes of all-embracing importance in Book 31. These Goths inhabited the mountains of Dacia (Rumania). The mountain range of the Serri is the south Carpathian; Noviodunum was near the mouth of the Danube. Athanaric was notable for his persecutions of Christians, including the missionary Wulfila. For the sequel, see 31.3.

6. Rusticus Julianus was prefect of Rome in 387 under the usurper Magnus Maximus, a 'despot' (p. 338) because he deposed Gratian and was put down by Theodosius. The formal adlocution is appropriate for the elevation of an Augustus or a Caesar; cf. 15.8 for Constantius' elevation of Julian. It was of course this precedent which deterred emperors from creating Caesars of junior rank. Gratian is first of a string of 'child-emperors', but the way was paved by Jovian's promotion of the baby Varronian to the consulship (25.10). A. alludes (p. 340) to Gratian's murder in 383.

7. A. returns to the theme of Valentinian's cruelty in 29.3 and 30.8. This may be the product of anti-Pannonian prejudice: see Alföldi, *A Conflict of Ideas*, especially 41ff. But his highly irascible disposition is beyond doubt.

8. Since Severus had been promoted from count to master *before* the elevation of Gratian (above, 27.6) the chronology of this chapter must be confused. On it, see R. Tomlin, *Britannia* 5 (1974), 303ff. Notable is the panegyrical treatment of Theodosius, father of the emperor reigning at the time of publication. This point is underlined by Thompson in *The Historical Work of Ammianus*, 87ff.

9. For the sequel to the misconduct of Romanus and Remigius, see 28.6. The criticism of Valentinian (p. 344), repeated at 30.5, is challenged

by Alföldi in *A Conflict of Ideas*, 45f. Praetextatus' prefecture fell in 367–8. Cicero's commendation of Brutus (p. 345) is in *Orator*, 34.

10. At 30.9, A. rightly praises Valentinian as a vigorous defender of the frontiers. His campaigns against the Alamanni are omitted in this selection (also 28.2, 29.4, 30.3), but are summarized, with due acknowledgement of their importance, at 30.7.

11. On the great Petronius Probus, A. clearly had sharply conflicting reports from friends and enemies. Probus was a patron of Ambrose; but it is not for his Christianity that A. criticizes him but for abuse of power and fiscal oppression (cf. 30.5). Probus was linked by marriage to the family of the Anicii, against whose avidity A. had already registered a protest (16.8). The citation from Cicero is from *Philippics*, 2.29.

12. Here and in the sequel (30.1), A. ignores a crucial dimension of the Armenian problem, the anti-Persian intrigues of the Christian church in Armenia, described by Faustus of Byzantium. See Blockley, *Ammianus Marcellinus*, 62ff. Sapor had come to the Persian throne as a child in 310, so was now probably in his sixties. The pact made with Jovian (25.7) had excluded the Romans but not the Persians from military interference in Armenia.

BOOK 28

1. A.'s account of affairs at Rome becomes difficult to follow. The last notice was of the prefecture of Praetextatus in 367–8 (27.9). Below at 28.4, A. opens with an apology for his long silence about Rome, as if the present chapter did not exist, and records the prefectures of Olybrius (369–70) and Ampelius (371–2). There is no notice in the subsequent books of the prefectures of Bappo and Principius (372–3) nor of the much-praised Eupraxius (374), but there is one final notice of Claudius Caesarius in 374 (29.6). The present account of sorcery and treason trials, particularly under Maximin, is, as A. admits, chronologically confused. Maximin was prefect of the corn-supply under Olybrius, appointed vice-prefect during Olybrius' illness in 370 and continued in office under Ampelius, 370–71, until his promotion to prefect of Gaul (371–6), when he was succeeded by Ursicinus – not the general – (371–3), Simplicius (374–5), and Doryphorian (376). Nepotian (p. 350), nephew of Constantine, had set up as Augustus in Rome sixteen years before, in 350, in opposition to the usurper Magnentius, surviving only a month; evidently A. gave a dramatic narrative of this in a lost book. The account of the dramatist Phrynichus (p. 350), who according to Herodotus (6.21) upset the Athenians by

staging his 'Sack of Miletus' in 494 B.C., underlines A.'s consciousness of the dangers of writing about so sensitive a topic, even under the 'better moral climate' of Theodosius. This may also explain other obscurities and silences, such as the fact that the victim Alypius (pp. 352–3) was brother of the prefect Olybrius, that Petronius Probus, who refused to take information against Maximin (31–3), was son-in-law of Olybrius, and all were connected with the Anicii. Note also that Lollianus, Tarracius Bassus (prefect of Rome in 375), and Camenius all belonged to the Caeionii. What was at issue in this furore remains obscure: see Alföldi, *A Conflict of Ideas*, 65ff., and Matthews, *Western Aristocracies*, 56ff. (Omitted in this selection is the complex episode of Aginatius and Anepsia, sections 30–35, 48–56.)

3.   Picks up from 27.8, from which it continues directly. The panegyrical tone is sustained, and the comparisons with the republican heroes Camillus and Papirius Cursor enhance Theodosius' glory. Thompson, *The Historical Work of Ammianus*, 93ff., suggested that Maximin was responsible for the mysterious death of Theodosius in 377: if so, the affair of his brother-in-law may have some bearing.

4.   On the prefectures of Rome, see above, 28.1. Here A. says nothing of sorcery trials, but returns to the subject of 14.6 and satirizes the aristocracy and people of Rome. There is considerable overlap in topics, and the viewpoint of a visitor and man of learning again emerges. What is humorous about the aristocratic names (p. 359), which are mostly not met elsewhere, is no longer apparent; the plebeian names largely suggest foodstuffs. The contemporary nobility are contrasted with the old republican nobility: Cato the censor is supposed to have expelled a senator for kissing his own wife; the younger Cato was famous for his grim dignity; Claudius Marcellus may have been known for pride. Castor and Pollux ('sons of Tyndareus', p. 359) legendarily announced various victories in Rome, especially that of Lake Regillus; it may be relevant that, like charioteers, they were represented as horsemen. The brothers Quintilius (p. 361) were famed for mutual affection, held office together, and were executed together by Commodus. Marius Maximus (p. 360) wrote imperial biographies; it is relevant that the surviving *Lives of the Caesars* (*Historia Augusta*) probably have a publication date close to that of Ammianus' history. The mention of Juvenal (p. 360) is remarkable, in view of A.'s own debt to him in the Roman digressions. The passage is rich in literary allusions (and demonstrates A.'s own wider reading): Epimenides of Crete (p. 359) was supposed to have purified Athens after a plague; the comedy with a boastful soldier (p. 360) is Plautus' *Miles Gloriosus*; the Socrates anecdote (p. 360) comes from Cicero (*De Senectute*, 26); the Cimmerians

(p. 361) in the *Odyssey* (11.14ff.) live in a land never seen by the sun; Cicero (p. 362) is cited (from *De Amicitia*, 79); Micio and Laches (p. 362) are characters from new Comedy and Terence, Cresphontes and Temenus probably from Euripides; and the savages of the Chersonese (p. 363) are Euripides' Tauri from his *Iphigeneia in Tauris*.

6.   The account of the troubles of Tripolis is the sequel to 27.9, above; and it leads in its turn to the graver episode of the rebellion of Firmus, narrated in terms highly complimentary to the father of the emperor Theodosius (29.5, omitted). The present episode reveals with unusual clarity the workings of imperial government; the mechanisms by which officials found themselves drawn into corruption, and the difficulty for the emperor in penetrating the conflicting reports of his subordinates. In the sequel at 29.5, Romanus and Remigius again combine to prevent true reports from reaching the ear of the emperor. On the latter episode, see the analysis of J. F. Matthews, 'Mauretania in Ammianus and the Notitia', in R. Goodburn and P. Bartholomew (eds.), *Aspects of the Notitia Dignitatum* (1976), 157ff. Remigius in the end commits suicide (30.2).

BOOK 29

1–2.   Sorcery trials at Antioch (371–2) echo the similar terror at Rome (28.1). A. explicitly signals that this is an eyewitness account and testifies to his share in the sense of terror; 'Cimmerian darkness' (p. 376) is a Homeric allusion (see above, 28.4). The possibility ought to be considered that he himself was driven into exile by a purported act of mercy or at least burnt his library in fear. A., like all the participants, assumes that the powers of magic are real. Implicit in the Theodosius story is the assumption that the letters THEOD correctly pointed to Theodosius. He later explains (31.14) how the verse prediction associated with it was proved right. It is uncertain whether the affair reflects a specifically pagan opposition to Valens; but it did bring the ruin of some pagan supporters of Julian, notably the philosopher Maximus, and another source alleges a general persecution of pagan philosophers. Simonides (p. 375), the philosopher martyr-figure, is compared with the Cynic Peregrinus whose life was written by Lucian.

2.   The warmth of A.'s language about Hypatius and Eusebius (p. 377) suggests that they (and particularly the former) were contacts of A.: see Introduction, § 8. Little is known of any of the other victims named. Eutropius is the author of the surviving abbreviated history down to the death of Jovian; present on Julian's Persian expedition, later prefect of Illyricum and consul 387, he was surely known to A. The reflections

Valens provokes on the proper role of the emperor (p. 379) are in line with A.'s reflections elsewhere: see Introduction, § 39.

3. On A.'s views of Valentinian's cruelty, see above, 27.7. The lurid anecdote about the pet bears (p. 382) is not reliable: Lactantius has a similar horror-story about the emperor Galerius (*De mortibus persecutorum*, 21.5–6).

6. The Quadi had last given trouble under Constantius (17.12). The narrative shows up two of A.'s favourite villains, Maximin and Petronius Probus, and permits the introduction of praise for the reigning emperor Theodosius. Constantia (p. 384), who married Gratian in 374, had also been exploited for her dynastic connections by Procopius (26.7 and 9).

BOOK 30

1. The story of Pap is the sequel to 27.12. A. suppresses the information that Pap had quarrelled with the Armenian church, and had murdered its primate Narses at a banquet, so meriting by poetic justice his own fate: see Blockley, *Ammianus Marcellinus*, 62ff. The vivid escape story (pp. 388–9) recalls A.'s own escapes (18.6, 19.8) and must derive from an eyewitness. The example of Perperna's murder of Sertorius (p. 390) has already been adduced (26.9); the Demosthenes quotation (p. 390) is a paraphrase of *Against Androtion*, 7.

2. Sapor still harks back to Jovian's treaty (25.7). Victor was probably involved in the treaty, hence his choice on this occasion was suitable. For the episode of Remigius (p. 392), see above, 28.6.

4. A. assigns great importance to the emperor's role in jurisdiction: see Introduction, § 39. The satirical excursus on advocacy, like those on Rome, reflects personal experience; one might guess that A. lost his family property under Valens after a protracted private suit. The four classes of advocates distinguished are hard to separate and appear to run into each other. Plato's views on rhetoric (p. 394) are cited from the *Gorgias*, 463B. The names of great orators, Greek and Roman, presumably came from a rhetorical handbook: the Greek names are standard, the Romans are among those mentioned by Cicero in the *Brutus*. Of the two Cicero citations, the first (p. 394) is unknown; the second (p. 395) is assigned by modern editors to the *Republic* (5.11). Trebatius, Cascellius, and Alfenus (p. 395) were jurists of the first century B.C., but the Arunci, Sicani and Evander's mother have nothing to do with the law and merely symbolize the obsolete. The comparison of the advocate to the Homeric Thersites (p. 396) suggests that he is not fit to speak among the well-born. Gaius Gracchus' flautist (p. 397)

helped him modulate his pitch according to Cicero (*De oratore*, 3.225). The defences of Cluentius and Ctesiphon (p. 397) were famous speeches by Cicero and Demosthenes. Aristides and Cato the elder (p. 397) are models of justice; Philistion and Aesop are obscure, but perhaps stand for farce on the stage.

5. The chapter is the sequel to 29.6, where Maximin and Probus are blamed. The complaints about Probus' extortionate taxes are also registered by Jerome in his *Chronicle* (372); for the grave effects of over-taxation, see Jones, *Later Roman Empire*, 1043f. Portents foretell the death of Valentinian as of all other emperors: note that like Constantius (21.14) and Julian (25.2) he sees the figure of departing Fortune. The excursus on comets is at 25.10, omitted in this selection.

6. This incomparable scene, based obviously on eyewitness accounts, is enriched by touches from death-scenes in Virgil (*Aeneid*, 4.643, Dido; 9.415, a victim of Nisus and Euryalus).

7–9. The obituary of Valentinian, unlike those of Constantius (21.16) and Julian (25.4), includes a summary of his military achievements as related in the foregoing narrative; this reflects A.'s view of the importance of his contribution to defence. Consideration of his central vice of cruelty (cf. 27.7) leads to another sermon on clemency (cf. 29.2, apropos Valens): the examples could be drawn from numerous ancient essays on this subject – the Papirius Cursor anecdote (p. 405) occurs in Livy (9.16), and note that the elder Theodosius was compared to this republican hero (28.3). Isocrates (p. 405) wrote several essays on kingship including similar sentiments (the reference here is to *Panathenaikos*, 185). Cicero's speech for Oppius (p. 405) does not survive. On one point the chapters on vice and virtue apparently conflict: Valentinian's handling of taxes. The same contradiction is perhaps implicit in the chapter on Probus' abuses (30.5), where Probus extorts money from the provincials to placate the emperor, but provokes his fury when his conduct is discovered. See further Blockley, *Ammianus Marcellinus*, 41ff. Note that by taking virtues after vices A. keeps his praise for religious toleration to the last. It had sharp contemporary relevance.

10. The elevation of the child Valentinian II followed the precedent of Gratian (above, 27.6). Some argue that Books 26–31 must have been published after his death in 392: see Introduction, § 10. A. avoids saying anything of the reigns of Gratian or Valentinian II, and moves directly to the end of Valens.

BOOK 31

1.   The mention of Bellona (p. 410) is a sure sign of impending disaster
      in A. (cf. 24.7). The omens serve a dramatic function. By implication
      the ghosts of Pap (30.1) and the victims of the terror (29.1–2) are about
      to take revenge. The prophecy (pp. 410–11) points to a barbarian
      crossing of the Danube (Ister) into the Danubian provinces of Thrace,
      Moesia, and Pannonia – the disguise is transparent, though the Greek
      names properly belong to other areas.

2.   The striking ethnographical digression on the Huns and Alans derives,
      unlike most other such digressions, from contemporary evidence
      rather than book-learning (contrast 15.9). The Huns were previously
      unknown, and made a powerful impression on the Romans: see O. J.
      Maenchen-Helfen, *The World of the Huns* (1973). Even so, some details
      are the product of stereotyping of nomad savages: see Introduction,
      § 23. The (erroneous) idea that the Huns eat half-raw meat (p. 411)
      occurs in very similar words in a work published by Jerome in 393;
      this is a possible pointer to the latest publication date of this book (see
      A. Cameron, *Journal of Roman Studies* 61 (1971), 259, and Introduction,
      § 10).

3.   For the earlier story of Athanaric, see 27.5. An alternative form of the
      name Ermenrich is Hermanarich. The names Alatheus and Saphrax
      are non-Gothic; it has been suggested that they were Huns or Alans.
      The Thervingi and Greuthungi are distinguished as Visigoths and
      Ostrogoths respectively.

4.   A. shows the same prudent restraint in estimating large armies as
      with the Persian army (18.6), where he makes the same reference to
      Herodotus' account of Xerxes' army. Another source guesses at 200,000
      men. The Virgilian quotation (p. 417) is from *Georgics*, 2.105f. The
      numbers vastly exceeded the possible food supply, irrespective of the
      honesty of the Roman officials.

5.   Lupicinus is A.'s scapegoat for the disaster; correspondingly he implies
      by his examples that a great general can retrieve such a situation, as
      Marius defeated the Teutones (102 B.C.) and Cimbri (101), Marcus the
      Marcomanni (A.D. 180), Claudius and Aurelian the Goths (270). His
      optimism was misplaced.

6.   The assistance given to Fritigern by locals, apparently labourers in the
      mines (gold was mined in northern Moesia), is one of several signs that
      the peasantry felt little loyalty to the state against barbarians: see
      G. E. M. de Ste Croix, *The Class Struggle in the Ancient Greek World*
      (1981), 479ff.

7.   Ad Salices ('The Willows') was near the mouth of the Danube, twenty-
      five Roman miles north-west of Constanza. The description of the field

'white with bones' (p. 425) has been taken to imply that A. had been there, but the phrase is a reminiscence of Virgil (*Aeneid*, 12.36) and need not imply autopsy (Introduction, § 6). The phrase here translated as 'like lightning' provoked Gibbon to remonstrate (vol. 3, ch. 26, p. 104, n. 83): 'I have used the literal sense of real torches or beacons: but I almost suspect that it is only one of those turgid metaphors, those false ornaments, that perpetually disfigure the style of Ammianus.'

10. For the Lentienses, cf. above, 15.4. Gratian died in 383 so that A. had no need to adopt a panegyrical tone. This is the only notice on his reign he includes. On the crowning of Julian by Maurus (p. 430), see 20.4.

11. The civil war incident, when a commander (Actus or Acacius) was trapped (p. 431), was doubtless described in a lost book. It is not otherwise heard of.

12–13. The campaign and battle of Adrianople are discussed by N. J. E. Austin in *Acta Classica* 15 (1972), 77–83, and by T. S. Burns in *Historia* 22 (1973), 336ff. A.'s preoccupation with the creation of mood leaves the military details obscure. In describing the mission of the Christian presbyter (p. 433) A. omits to mention that the Goths and Valens shared adherence to the Arian faith. Valens persecuted Catholics, and the Catholic Orosius (7.33) blames the disaster on this. A. offers historical parallels for both versions of Valens' death (pp. 436–7): Decius' death in action in 251 (cf. 31.5) and that of Scipio Calvus in 211 B.C. These and the final allusion to Cannae, the great disaster of the Hannibalic war, reinforce the attempt at 31.5 to put this catastrophe in historical perspective. A.'s personal link with Ursicinus explains the mention of Potentius (p. 437).

14. After a wholly negative account of his reign, it is a surprise to find A. conceding 'well-known' good qualities to Valens. The prediction of his death (p. 439) picks up the account at 29.1.

16. The Saracens were described at 14.4 (omitted) in terms similar to the description of the Huns. The concluding paragraph, like the final paragraph of Eutropius' history, repeats the conventional contrast between impartial history and panegyric (cf. 15.1). No historian could safely touch on the present reign; for this reason Gratian's elevation of Theodosius after the death of Valens is not mentioned.

NOTE ON OFFICIALS
AND THEIR TITLES

The governmental structure of the late empire, established in its essentials by Diocletian and Constantine, was complex and not wholly rigid. It is fully described in Jones, *Later Roman Empire*, 321ff. The following is a simplified account of the bare bones of the structure. Latin technical terms are given in brackets, though it should be noted that Ammianus does not always use technical language.

COURT

The emperor held court in a variety of cities round the empire (Milan, Sirmium, Constantinople, Antioch, etc., but never Rome) and was accompanied by a variety of officials (the *comitatus*): the household establishment of chamberlains (*cubicularii*) under the grand chamberlain (*praepositus sacri cubiculi*), the marshal of the court (*curator palatii*), and the superintendent of the stables (*tribunus stabuli*); administrative officials, particularly notaries (*notarii*) under the master of offices (*magister officiorum*), and his subordinates like the masters of petitions (*libellorum*) and of records (*memoriae*); treasury officials (*rationales*) under the count of the privy purse (*comes rei privatae*), and the treasurer (*comes sacrarum largitionum*); the quaestor (*quaestor sacri palatii*) in charge of legislation; together with the senior army commanders and the senior civil official, the praetorian prefect in attendance (below). The consistory (*consistorium*), the highest decision-making body, drew upon these officials. A military presence was provided by the household or palatine troops (*scholae palatinae*) under the master of offices, and the elite corps of *protectores domestici* used as staff-officers.

PROVINCES

The empire was divided into four prefectures, Gaul (including Spain), Italy (including the Alpine area and Africa), Illyricum, and the East; each was under the civil authority of a praetorian prefect (*praefectus praetorio*) who would attend the court if an emperor or Caesar was in his area. Under his authority came his vice-prefects or vicars (*vicarii*) in charge of groups of provinces, and provincial governors with a variety of grades and titles (*consulares*, *correctores*, *praesides*, etc.). Their prime concern was the administration of justice. Rome had its separate system: its own urban prefect (*praefectus urbi*), his vice-prefect (*vicarius*), and other subordinates like the prefect of the corn supply (*annonae*).

ARMY

The military system was where possible kept separate from the civil. Troops fell into three main types: the emperor's household or palatine troops (above); the field armies (*comitatenses*) and the frontier troops (*limitanei*). The senior command was provided by the masters of infantry and cavalry (*magistri peditum* or *equitum*) of whom a number were distributed round the prefectures; the division of function between horse and foot was notional, and might be combined in a master of troops (*magister militum* or *armorum*). Next to them ranked the counts (*comites*). At provincial level, frontier troops were under commanders (*duces*). Junior ranks included tribunes (*tribuni*). Staff-officers for the high command were supplied by detaching *protectores domestici* from the court (above). A quasi-military group was that of the security agents (*agentes in rebus*).

NOTES ON PERSONS

For full details on persons in Ammianus, consult A. H. M. Jones, J. R. Martindale and J. Morris, *Prosopography of the Later Roman Empire*, vol. 1 (1971). For ease of identification where there are several persons of the same name in *PLRE*, the appropriate number is given in brackets below; where the name is not the one used for the entry in this list, the *PLRE* alternative is printed in **bold** type. Minor characters and those not mentioned in more than one chapter are not generally admitted; emperors are also excluded.

AGILO   Officer of Alamannic origin, falls under suspicion in scare (14.10); promoted to replace Ursicinus (20.2) and takes over duties (21.13); helps bring over Aquileia for Julian (21.12); sits on Chalcedon commission (22.3); joins Procopius, but deserts in time (26.7, 9 and 10).

ALATHEUS   Ostrogothic leader with Saphrax in 378 (31.3 and 4); at Adrianople (31.12).

ALYPIUS (4)   Educated at Antioch, friend of Julian, pagan. Governor of Britain in 358; appointed by Julian to rebuild temple of Jerusalem (23.1); later with son Hierocles, a pupil of Libanius, condemned in treason trials of 371/2 but reprieved (29.1).

ALYPIUS (**Faltonius Probus A.** 13)   Roman aristocrat, brother of Olybrius, linked with Anicii; as young man banished in 370/71 under inquisition of Maximin (28.1.16); later prefect of Rome 391. Possible informant of A.

AMPELIUS (3)   Antiochene, former master of offices and proconsul, prefect of Rome 371–2; a voluptuary, but tried to control taverns (28.4); prefect during trials conducted by Maximin (28.1).

ANATOLIUS (3)   Native of Beirut, governor of Syria in 349 and friend of Libanius; refused city prefecture of Rome in 355. Prefect of Illyricum 357–60, praised by A. for lightening tax burden (19.11); died in office (21.6).

ANATOLIUS (5)   Pagan and close friend of Julian; appointed by him master of offices (20.9); with Julian on Persian expedition, killed in same battle (25.3); body later found and buried (25.6).

ANICII   Prominent Roman aristocratic family, criticized for greed (16.8). *See also* Probus and Olybrius.

APODEMIUS (1)   Agent of Constantius, seen as an inveterate troublemaker;

arrests and executes Gallus (14.11); reports execution to Constantius (15.1); fails to summon Silvanus (15.5); executed by Chalcedon commission (22.3).

APRONIAN (L. Turcius A. Asterius 10)   Son of city prefect of 339; sent on embassy to Julian by senate and appointed city prefect (23.1); during his prefecture (362–4) temple of Apollo burned down (23.3) and sorcerers punished (26.3).

ARBITIO   Rose from ranks to master of cavalry; schemes against rival Ursicinus (14.11, 15.2); tries accomplices of Gallus (15.3); campaigns ineptly against Alamanni (15.4); schemes against Silvanus (15.5); consul 355 (15.8); farcical escape from prosecution (16.6); venal and unjust (16.8); schemes against Barbatio (18.3); investigates Ursicinus' conduct at Amida (20.2); sent East, then against Julian (21.13); chairs commission of Chalcedon (22.3); persuades troops to desert Procopius (26.8–9).

ARINTHEUS   Distinguishes himself as tribune (15.4); commander under Julian in Persia (24.1 and 7); looks for successor to Julian (25.5); used on missions by Jovian (25.7 and 10); serves Valentinian (26.5); defeats Procopius (26.8); master of infantry under Valentinian (27.5 and 12). Consul 372, baptized and died 378. Name frequently coupled with that of Victor; surely known to A.

ARSACES   King of Armenia c. 350–64 or 339–69; loyal to Rome under Constantius (20.11, 21.6); supports Julian in Persian campaign (23.2, 24.7–8); abandoned by Jovian (25.7); captured by Sapor and killed (27.12). Father of Pap.

ATHANARIC   Chief of Visigothic Thervingi, defeated by Valens 367–9 (27.5); defeated by Huns (31.3 and 4). Later surrendered to Theodosius; died in Constantinople in 381 and magnificently buried (cf. 27.5).

BAINOBAUDES   Tribune of Scutarii sent by Constantius to watch Gallus (14.11); later in 357 cashiered, together with future emperor Valentinian, on false charge (16.11).

BARBATIO   Commander of household troops of Gallus, instrumental in his fall (14.11); replaces Silvanus as master of infantry in 355 and is obstructive to Julian (16.11); defeats Juthungi in 358 (17.6); executed with wife for treason (18.3).

BARZIMERES   Tribune of Scutarii, fails to recapture Pap (30.1); killed by Goths at Dibaltum in 377 (31.8).

BASSUS (Iunius Bassus Theotecnius 15)   City prefect of Rome 359, died after entering office (17.11). Father a praetorian prefect under Constantine; a baptized Christian.

CASSIAN (2)   Commander of army in Mesopotamia; provides information on Persia in 356 (16.9); destroys supplies when Persians invade (18.7); at Nisibis suspects Craugasius (19.9); brings supplies to Jovian (25.8).

CELLA Tribune of Scutarii, causes future emperor Valentinian to be cashiered by false report (16.11); killed in battle in 359 (19.11).

DAGALAIF Promoted count by Julian in 361, accompanies him East from Gaul (21.8 and 9); commander under Julian in Persia (24.1 and 4); with Gallic officers searches for successor to Julian (25.5); promoted master of cavalry by Jovian; warns Valentinian against appointing Valens (26.1, 4 and 5); serves Valentinian in West (26.5, 27.2); consul 366 with Gratian; presumably barbarian, as Nevitta with whom his name is linked, and known to A.

DOMITIAN (3) Prefect of East 353/4, insults Gallus and is lynched by troops (14.7, cf. 15.13).

EQUITIUS Pannonian officer; candidate for throne in 364, backed Valentinian (26.1); promoted count, then master of infantry (26.5); resists Procopius (26.7 and 10); in 373 put to flight by Quadi (29.6); consul 374; introduces embassy to imperial council (30.6). Backed election of Valentinian II. Distinct from the kinsman of Valens and marshal of the palace killed at Adrianople (31.12–13).

EUPRAXIUS Promoted quaestor for timely praise (27.6); as such repeatedly deflects Valentinian's anger (27.7, 28.1). Prefect of Rome in 374, still alive 384; highly praised by A., and surely an informant.

EUSEBIA Wife of Constantius, sister of Eusebius and Hypatius; stands up for Julian (15.2 and 8) but allegedly caused his baby to be killed (16.10); died before 361. A. praises her for beauty and kindness (21.6).

EUSEBIUS (11) Grand chamberlain of Constantius, intrigues against Gallus (14.11) and Ursicinus (15.3, 18.4, 20.2); present at Constantius' deathbed (21.15); executed by Chalcedon commission (22.3). Also an Arian and enemy of Athanasius.

EUSEBIUS (40) Brother of Hypatius, q.v.

EUTHERIUS (1) Chamberlain of Constantius 356–60; defends Julian against accusations (16.7); negotiates on his behalf with Constantius (20.8); recalled to court in 361, then retires to Rome (16.7). A very likely informant of A., who praises him warmly.

FLAVIAN (Virius Nicomachus Flavianus 15) As *vicarius* of Africa in 377 investigates Lepcis scandal and writes report exonerating the city (28.6), which honoured him as patron. Prefect of Italy probably 390–92 and, under usurper Eugenius, 393–4. Close friend of Symmachus, leading pagan, author of *Annales*. Committed suicide 395. Possible source of A.

FLORENTIUS (3) Antiochene, as deputy master of offices reveals Silvanus' innocence (15.5); master of offices 359–61, inquires into loss of Amida (20.2); condemned to exile under Julian by Chalcedon commission (22.3).

FLORENTIUS (5) Praetorian prefect of Gaul (357–60), comes into conflict with Julian (16.12, 17.3, 18.2); withdraws to Constantius on Julian's proclamation as emperor (20.4 and 8); made prefect of Illyricum 360, consul 361 (21.6); condemned by commission of Chalcedon and goes into hiding (22.3).

FRIGERIDUS Count in Illyricum and Thrace in 377, appointed by Gratian at Valens' request (31.7); pursued by Goths (31.9); defeats Gothic bands, but is replaced (31.10). A. laments dismissal of a cautious commander.

FRITIGERN Gothic chief, rival of Athanaric, supported by Valens became Arian. Leads Goths across Danube in 376 (31.4); escapes assassination (31.5); leader of Goths in Adrianople campaign (31.6, 11 and 12).

GAUDENTIUS As security agent reports on treasonable talk in 355 (15.3); promoted notary and sent to spy on Julian (17.9); then sent to Africa to oppose Julian (21.7); executed on Julian's orders in 362 (22.11).

GOMOARIUS Supposed to have betrayed usurper Vetranio as tribune (21.8); appointed master of cavalry in 360 by Constantius (20.9), but dismissed by Julian (21.8); opposes march of Julian (21.13); appointed to command by usurper Procopius (26.7), but betrays him (26.9).

GRUMBATES King of Chionitae, invades with Sapor (18.6); assists in siege of Amida, loses son (19.1 and 2).

GUNDOMAD Alamannic chief, brother of Vadomar, attacked by Constantius in 357 (14.10); assassinated (16.12).

HORMISDAS Son of Persian king Hormisdas II, and brother of Sapor, fled to Roman empire. Accompanies Constantius on visit to Rome (16.10); one of Julian's commanders on Persian expedition, used to bring over Anatha (24.1), but reviled as traitor by garrison of Pirisabora (24.2 and 5). Father of Hormisdas appointed proconsul by usurper Procopius (26.8).

HORTAR (1) Alamannic king at battle of Strasbourg (16.12); makes peace with Romans in 358 (17.10); cooperates with Romans in 359 (18.2).

HYPATIUS Brother-in-law of Constantius. Consul with brother Eusebius in 359 (18.1); both residents of Antioch and victims there of treason trial in 371, but subsequently exculpated (29.2). City prefect of Rome 379, prefect of Italy 382–3. Praised highly by A., and a possible informant.

JOVIAN (1) The senior notary, distinguished himself on Julian's Persian campaign at siege of Maozamalcha (24.4); considered for throne after Julian's death, and assassinated (25.8).

JOVINUS (6) Master of cavalry 361–9, commands one group on Julian's march eastwards (21.8 and 12); member of commission of Chalcedon (22.3); sent to Gaul; Jovian nervous of him and tries to supersede him (25.8), but eventually confirms him (25.10); serves under Valentinian (26.5) against Alamanni (27.2); consul 367; sent briefly to Britain (27.8); fights again against Alamanni (27.10). Became Christian under Valentinian and built church.

JULIUS (2) Count in Thrace; arrested by Procopius (26.7); master of cavalry and infantry in East 371–8; massacred Gothic recruits after Adrianople (31.16).

LAMPADIUS (C. Ceionius Rufius **Volusianus** L. 5)   Member of powerful clan of Caeionii; prefect in Gaul 355, incriminates Silvanus by forgery (15.5); prefect of Rome 365, notable for building operations (27.3). A pagan.

LEO   Pannonian, brutal, backed election of Valentinian (26.1); assists in treason trials at Rome (28.1); appointed master of offices; intrigues against Probus (30.5). A. never mentions his name without horror.

LEONTIUS   Appointed quaestor to Gallus in 354 to keep watch on him (14.11); prefect of Rome 355–6, and deposed Pope Liberius (15.7).

LUCILLIAN (3)   Defended Nisibis against Sapor in 350. Appointed to keep watch on Gallus (14.11); sent on mission to Persia in 358 (17.14, 18.6); master of cavalry in Illyricum in 361; caught by Julian and deposed (21.9); promoted master of infantry and cavalry by son-in-law Jovian in 363 (25.8), but killed in mutiny (25.10).

LUPICINUS (3)   Served bravely against Alamanni (27.10); count in Thrace, profiteers in supplying Goths (31.4); fails to assassinate Gothic leaders (31.5).

LUPICINUS (6)   Master of cavalry in Gaul 359–60 (18.2), sent to Britain (20.1 and 4); Julian fears he might rebel (20.9); master of cavalry in East under Jovian and Valens (26.5); resists Procopius (26.8–9), consul 367. Criticized by A. for arrogance, praised by Libanius for patronage of literature.

MACRIANUS   Alamannic chieftain, brother of Hariobaudus, defeated by Julian in 359 (18.2); attacked successfully by Burgundians (28.5, omitted); attacked and displaced as chief by Valentinian (29.4, omitted); makes peace with Valentinian (30.3).

MALARICH   Frankish officer in command of Gentiles in 355, defends fellow-countryman Silvanus against charges of plotting (15.5); offered post of master of cavalry in Gaul by Jovian (25.8), but refuses (25.10).

MALLOBAUDES   A Frank, sent as tribune to try Gallus (14.11); protests at intrigue against the Frank Silvanus (15.5); count of household troops and king of Franks, defeats Macrianus (30.3) and Alamanni (31.10).

MAMERTINUS (2)   Put in charge of treasury by Julian in 361 (21.8), promoted prefect of Illyricum and consul for 362 (21.10 and 12); Julian makes much of ceremonial of his consulship (22.7); tries Julian's opponents at Aquileia (21.12) and Chalcedon (22.3); still prefect of Italy, Africa and Illyricum in 365 (26.5); dismissed on charge of peculation (27.7).

MARCELLUS (3)   Master of cavalry and infantry in Gaul 356–7 after Ursicinus (16.2); refuses to cooperate with Julian (16.4); discharged by Constantius and accuses Julian (16.7); retires home to Serdica (16.10); his son executed under Julian for treason (22.11).

MAVORTIUS (**Lollianus** M. 5)   Roman aristocrat, city prefect 342. Prefect of Illyricum and consul 355 (15.8); hears treason charges (16.8). A pagan, dedicatee of the astrological text of Firmicus Maternus.

MAXIMIN (7)   Pannonian, rose through advocacy to governorships; 369–71 as prefect of corn supply, then as vice-prefect of Rome, conducts sorcery trials; promoted prefect of Gaul but still operates in Rome through agents (28.1); encourages cruelty of Valentinian (29.3); responsible for invasion of Quadi (29.6); inquires into conduct of Remigius (30.2). Executed by Gratian.

MAXIMUS of Ephesus (21)   Philosopher, thaumaturge, teacher of Julian. Summoned to Constantinople, with excessive ceremony (22.7); accompanies Persian expedition, presumably leader of philosophers who misread the omens (23.5); attends Julian's deathbed (25.3); victim of treason trials of 371 (29.1).

MEROBAUDES (2)   Master of infantry in West c. 375 (30.5); responsible for proclamation of Valentinian II (30.10); retains in Gaul troops ordered to Thrace in 377 (31.7); at court in Milan shields Romanus (28.6). Later consul 383. Died supporting usurper Magnus Maximus.

MODESTUS (Fl. Domitius M. 2)   Count of the East 358–62, in charge of judicial inquiries into sorcery and treason (19.12); prefect of Constantinople 362–3 under Julian; praetorian prefect in East 369–77; takes part in treason trials at Antioch and flatters Valens (29.1); instrumental in deterring Valens from exercising jurisdiction (30.4). Consul 372. A pagan under Julian, but an Arian under Valens.

MUSONIAN (Strategius M.)   Able linguist, Christian, helped Constantius investigate Manichees; praetorian prefect in East 354–8, conducts trial under Gallus (15.13); negotiates with Persians (16.9 and 10). Regarded by A. as cultured but venal; a friend of Libanius.

NEBRIDIUS   Count in the East 354–8 (14.2); quaestor to Julian in Gaul in 360, promoted to praetorian prefect in Gaul (20.9, 21.1); refuses to support Julian's march, nearly lynched (21.5 and 8); praetorian prefect in East 365, but captured by Procopius (26.7).

NEVITTA   Commander of barbarian origin; distinguishes himself in battle against Juthungi in 358 (17.6); promoted master of horse by Julian and accompanies him to East (21.8 and 10); tries associates of Constantius (22.3); commander under Julian in Persia (24.1 and 4); with Gallic officers searches for successor to Julian (25.5). Though barbarian, appointed consul in 362 by Julian, to A.'s disapproval (21.10 and 12, cf. 22.7); brutal, uncultivated; name linked with Dagalaif.

NOHODARES   Persian general, invades Mesopotamia in 354 (14.3), again in 359 (18.6 and 8); killed in battle in 363 (25.3). In fact his name is Iranian title for 'governor'.

OLYBRIUS (Q. Clodius Hermogenianus O. 3)   Christian aristocrat, married into Anicii, father-in-law of Petronius Probus, brother of Alypius; prefect of Rome 369–70, mild and just (28.4), falls ill in office, deputized for by Maximin (28.1). Later prefect of Illyricum, of Orient, consul 379; died between 384 and 395.

ORFITUS (Memmius Vitrasius Orfitus 3)   Roman aristocrat, city prefect 353–5 (14.6) and 357–9 (16.10); during his office Constantius erects obelisk (17.4); exiled for peculation (27.3), but restored (27.7). Prominent pagan and father-in-law of Symmachus.

PAP (Papa)   Son of Arsaces III of Armenia; escapes attacks of Sapor, restored by Romans (27.12); summoned by Valens, escapes back to Armenia and is murdered at banquet (30.1).

PAUL 'THE CHAIN' (4)   Notary under Constantius, conducts bloody investigations of supporters of Magnentius (14.5), Gallus (15.3), and Silvanus (15.6); supervises Julian in Gaul, then sent East for inquiry (19.12) where he punishes opponents of Bishop George of Alexandria; condemned by Chalcedon commission and burnt alive (22.3). Hated by Julian and A.

PENTADIUS   Notary involved in execution of Gallus (14.11); master of offices of Julian in Gaul, sent as envoy to Constantius (20.8–9); acquitted by Chalcedon commission (22.3).

PRAETEXTATUS (Vettius Agorius P. 1)   Zealous pagan aristocrat and man of learning, witness of events at Julian's court in Constantinople, appointed governor of Achaea (22.7); prefect of Rome 367–8, quells Christian rioting (27.9); member of senatorial embassy to Valentinian (28.1); later prefect of Italy; died 384. Highly praised by A. and indicated as a source of information.

PROBUS (Sex. Claudius Petronius P. 5)   Roman aristocrat, outstanding for wealth, power, and connections; prefect of Illyricum 364, Gaul 366, Italy 368–75 and again in 383. Sketched (27.11); ignores criticism by Maximin (28.1); resists invasion (29.6); escapes condemnation for fiscal oppression (30.5). Among his clients was Ambrose.

PROCOPIUS (4)   Tribune and notary in 358, sent on mission to Persia (17.14, 18.6); rose as kinsman of Julian to count, and put in command of detachment of troops (23.3, 25.8, 26.6) after supposed secret promise of throne; entrusted with burial of Julian (25.9); falls under suspicion from Valentinian and Valens, goes into hiding and proclaims himself emperor (26.5–6); executed in 366 (26.9).

PROSPER   Deputy of Ursicinus in East (14.11), and Gaul (15.13); cowardly and corrupt; sent on mission to Persia (17.5 and 14).

REMIGIUS   Financial official under Silvanus in 355, questioned about Ursicinus (15.5); master of offices 367–371/2; colludes in African scandal (27.9, 28.6; also 29.5, omitted); later exposed and commits suicide (30.2); had deflected anger of Valentinian by talk of barbarian attacks (30.8).

RICHOMER (Flavius R.)   Commander of household troops under Gratian 377–8, fights Goths (31.7); returns to Gaul (31.8); joins Valens at Adrianople (31.12); survives battle (31.13). Later master of troops and consul (384), served Theodosius against Magnus Maximus; uncle of rebel commander of pagans Arbogast; died 393.

RUFINUS (2)   Senior official under prefect of Illyricum 355–6; lays information against governor (15.3); executed for slander and adultery (16.8).

RUFINUS (Vulcacius Rufinus 25)   Maternal uncle of Gallus, prefect in Illyricum, then Gaul, but falls out of favour with Gallus (14.10); prefect of Italy under Valentinian 365–8, dies in office (27.11). Criticized for feathering nest under Constantius (16.8) and later (27.7).

SABINIAN (3)   Old and wealthy man appointed master of cavalry in East to replace Ursicinus (18.5); inept as military commander (18.6); wastes time in Christian devotions (18.7); fails to relieve Amida (19.3), exonerated by inquiry (20.2).

SALLUSTIUS (5)   Appointed praetorian prefect in Gaul by Julian (21.8); shares consulship of 363 with Julian (23.1); writes urging against Persian expedition (23.5). A pagan, not to be confused with Salutius (below).

SALUTIUS (Saturninius **Secundus** S. 3)   Cultivated pagan assigned as adviser to Julian as Caesar, becoming close personal friend. Appointed praetorian prefect in East by Julian 361 and made president of commission of Chalcedon (22.3); in charge of commissariat for Persian expedition (23.5); present at Julian's deathbed (25.3); refuses throne (25.5); sent by Jovian to negotiate with Persians (25.7); involved in election of Valentinian (26.2); serves Valens as prefect (26.5), temporarily replaced as result of intrigue (26.7); retired in 367, keen on history. Probably he (not Sallustius) is the Saloustios who dedicated to Julian a pagan theology in Greek, *On the Gods and the Universe*.

SAPOR II   King of Persia 309/10–379, made king while very young, warred with Rome 336–78. *Passim.*

SATURNINUS (10)   Steward of palace to Constantius, exiled by commission of Chalcedon (22.3); master of cavalry under Valens at Adrianople (31.8 and 13). Later consul 383, still active in 390s.

SAUROMACES   King of Hiberia, installed by Romans, but expelled by Sapor, restored by Romans 370 (27.12); expelled again by Sapor in 377/8 (30.2).

SEBASTIAN   As count, shares command of detachment with Procopius in Julian's Persian expedition (23.3, 25.8, 26.6); campaigns with Valentinian against Alamanni (27.10, omitted), and Quadi (30.5); popular enough with troops to be regarded as threat to throne (30.10); master of infantry in Gothic war, killed at Adrianople (31.11–13).

SENIAUCHUS   Distinguishes himself in command of squadron against Alamanni in 355 (15.4); as tribune, killed by soldiers with Lucillian (25.10).

SERENIAN (2)   Pannonian, exonerated by Gallus (14.7) yet takes part in his execution (14.11); recalled to office by Valens (26.5); resists Procopius (26.8) but killed, to A.'s relief (26.10).

SEVERUS (8)   Master of cavalry in Gaul 357–8 in succession to Marcellus (16.10); commands well (16.11); fights at Strasbourg (16.12); meets raiding

Franks (17.2); defeats Salii (17.8); loses heart against Alamanni (17.10); succeeded by Lupicinus (18.2).

SILVANUS   Of Frankish descent, as tribune in 351 deserted Magnentius for Constantius before Mursa; master of infantry in Gaul 352/3–5; attempts usurpation in 355 but is killed (15.5); his accomplices put on trial (15.6); part of his property granted to Barbatio (18.3).

TAMSAPOR   Persian commander; negotiates with Musonian in 356–7 (16.9, 17.5), active in invasion of 359 (18.5 and 8, 19.9).

TAURUS (3)   As quaestor sent on mission to Armenia (14.11); prefect of Italy 355–61, flees on Julian's proclamation (21.9); consul 361, yet condemned by Chalcedon commission (22.3). Still alive in 390s, but not politically active again.

THALASSIUS (father and son)   Father served against Magnentius; prefect of East 351, reports on Gallus (14.1); dies in 353 (14.7). Son hated by Julian as enemy of Gallus like father, but forgiven (22.9). Both Christians and friends of Libanius.

TRAJAN (2)   Count in East 371–4 (29.1); kills king Pap (30.1); master of infantry defeated at battle of ad Salices (31.7–8); replaced in 378 (31.11) but recalled and killed at Adrianople (31.12). A Catholic, critical of Valens' persecutions.

URSICINUS (2)   Commander and patron of A., master of cavalry in East 349–59; tries treason charges at Antioch (14.9); recalled to court (14.11); object of Eusebius' intrigues (15.2); sent against Silvanus (15.5); master of cavalry in Gaul under Julian (15.13), but superseded (16.2); sent back East in 357 (16.10); master of infantry in East 359–60 (18.4), but replaced by Sabinian (18.5); recalled, then sent back, faces Persian invasion (18.6–8); not allowed to relieve Amida (19.3); withdraws to Antioch (19.8); scapegoat for fall of Amida (20.2). Father of Potentius, killed at Adrianople (31.13).

URSULUS   Treasurer under Constantius; stops calumnies at court in 356–7 by outspokenness (16.8); earns hatred of military by remark on fall of Amida (20.11); despite putting funds at Julian's disposal in Gaul, condemned by commission of Chalcedon (22.3).

VADOMAR   King of Alamanni on Upper Rhine, attacked by Constantius (14.10); his subjects invade Gaul in 357 (16.12); makes peace with Julian in 359 (18.2); attacks Gaul in 361, suspected of acting on Constantius' orders and arrested (21.3–4); later governs Phoenicia (21.3); sent by Valens against Procopius (26.8); skirmishes with Persians in 371 (29.1). Father of Vithicab (30.7).

VENUSTUS (Volusius V. 5)   Of noble birth, on senatorial embassy to Julian and appointed governor of Spain (23.1); on senatorial embassy to Valentinian and persuades him senators should not be tortured (28.1.24–5). Father of famous pagan Nicomachus Flavianus (Flavian).

VERINIAN   Colleague of Ammianus as *protector domesticus*, accompanies him on Silvanus mission in 355 (15.5); left wounded by A. in flight to Amida (18.8).

VICTOR (4)   Commander under Julian in Persia (24.1, 4 and 6); looks for successor to Julian (25.5); promoted master of cavalry by Jovian (26.5); serves Valens (26.5, 27.5, 30.2); helps Valens at Adrianople (31.12 and 13). Consul 369. Friend of Libanius, Catholic of Sarmatian origin; name often coupled with Arintheus. Presumably known to A.

VICTOR (Sex. Aurelius V. 13)   Author of history of Rome from Augustus to Julian (360), published *c.* 361; appointed governor of Pannonia by Julian and much honoured; later (389) city prefect at Rome (21.10). Surely known to A. and an informant.

VIVENTIUS   Pannonian, quaestor 364, conducts investigations into magic (26.4); prefect of Rome 365, fails to quell Christian riots (27.3); prefect of Gaul 368–71 (cf. 30.5).

DATES OF EMPERORS

Augustus	d. A.D.14	Gordian III	238–44
Tiberius	14–37	Philip	244–9
Gaius	37–41	Decius	249–51
Claudius	41–54	Trebonianus Gallus	251–3
Nero	54–68	Volusian	251–3
Galba	68–9	Aemilian	253
Otho	69	Valerian	253–60
Vitellius	69	Gallienus	253–68
Vespasian	69–79	*Postumus	259–68
Titus	79–81	*Victorinus	267–8
Domitian	81–96	Claudius Gothicus	268–70
Nerva	96–8	Quintillus	270
Trajan	98–117	Aurelian	270–75
Hadrian	117–38	Tacitus	275–6
Antoninus Pius	138–61	Florian	276
Marcus Aurelius	161–80	Probus	276–82
Lucius Verus	161–9	Carus	282–3
Commodus	176–92	Carinus	283–5
Pertinax	193	Numerian	283–4
Didius Julianus	193	Diocletian	284–305
Septimius Severus	193–211	Maximian	286–305
*Clodius Albinus	193–7	Constantius I	305–6
*Pescennius Niger	193–4	Galerius	305–11
Caracalla	198–217	Severus	306–7
Geta	209–11	Maxentius	306–12
Macrinus	217–18	Constantine I	307–37
Diadumenian	218	Licinius	308–24
Elagabal	218–22	Maximin	308–13
Severus Alexander	222–35	Crispus (Caesar)	317–26
Maximin	235–8	Constantine II (Caesar)	317–37
Gordian I	238	(Augustus)	337–40
Gordian II	238	Constantius II (Caesar)	324–37
Balbinus	238	(Augustus)	337–61
Pupienus	238		

Constans (Caesar)	333–7	Valentinian I	364–75
(Augustus)	337–50	Valens	364–78
Delmatius (Caesar)	335–7	*Procopius	365–6
*Magnentius	350–53	Gratian	367–83
*Decentius (Caesar)	351–3	Valentinian II	375–92
*Vetranio	350	Theodosius I	379–95
*Nepotian	350	*Magnus Maximus	383–8
Gallus (Caesar)	351–4	*Eugenius	392–4
Julian (Caesar)	355–60	Arcadius	383–408
(Augustus)	360–63	Honorius	393–423
Jovian	363–4	Theodosius II	402–50

* Indicates usurpers, i.e. those who failed to establish their claims to power. Usurpers are given selectively. No distinction is made between Caesars and Augusti except for the family of Constantine.

GEOGRAPHICAL KEY

Name	Location (*modern equivalent*)	Map
Abarne	village of Mesopotamia (Çernik)	C
Abora, R.	tributary of Euphrates (Khabur)	C
Abydos (1)	city on Hellespont	D
Abydos (2)	city of Egypt	Gen.
Achaiachala	fort on Euphrates (Al Haditha)	C
Acimincum	city in Pannonia	B
Acontisma	pass between Thrace and Macedonia (at Kavalla)	B
Adiabene	district of Assyria	C
Adrianople	city of Thrace (Edirne)	B
Ambiani	city of Belgica (Amiens)	A
Amida	city on Tigris (Diyarbakir)	C
Amudis	fort in Mesopotamia (Amouda)	C
Anatha	fort on Euphrates (Anah)	C
Ancyra	city of Galatia (Ankara)	D
Antennacum	city of Germany (Andernach)	A
Antioch	capital of prefecture of East	C
Anzaba, R.	tributary of Tigris (Great Zab)	C
Aquileia	city at head of Adriatic (near Udine)	B
Aquincum	city of Valeria (Budapest)	B
Arelate	city of southern Gaul (Arles)	A
Argaeus, Mt	mountain near Kayseri (Erciyas Daği)	D
Argentaria	town on Rhine (Horburg)	A
Argentorate	city on Rhine (Strasbourg)	A
Artaxata	city of Armenia (near Yerevan)	C
Artogerassa	city of Armenia	C
Arzanene	region north of Tigris	C
Aspuna	small town in Galatia	D
Assyria	Persian province in Mesopotamian plain	C
Athribis	city of Egypt	Gen.
Augst	*see* Rauraci	
Augustodunum	city of Gaul (Autun)	A
Autessiodurum	city of Gaul (Auxerre)	A
Autun	*see* Augustodunum	
Auxerre	*see* Autessiodurum	
Axius, R.	river of Macedonia (Vardar)	B
Baraxmalcha	town on Euphrates	C
Barzalo	fortress in Mesopotamia on Euphrates	C
Batnae	city of Osdroene (Seruç)	C

Name	Location (*modern equivalent*)	Map
Bebase	village in Mesopotamia (Tel Beş, south of Mardin)	C
Belias, R.	tributary of Euphrates (Balikh)	C
Beroea	city of Thrace (Stara Zagora)	B
Besançon	*see* Vesontio	
Bezabde	fortress on Tigris (Çizre)	C
Bonna	city on Rhine (Bonn)	A
Bononea	city of Pannonia near Sirmium	B
Bononia	city of Belgica (Boulogne)	A
Boulogne	*see* Bononia	
Bregetio	city of Pannonia on Danube	B
Brotomagum	city of Gaul (Brumath)	A
Busan	fortress of Mesopotamia	C
Cabyle	town of Thrace (near Iambol)	B
Cabyllona	city of Gaul (Châlon-sur-Saône)	A
Caesarea	city of Cappadocia (Kayseri)	D
Callinicum	town of Mesopotamia (Raqqa)	C
Campi Canini	area round modern Bellinzona	B
Canopus	suburb of Alexandria	Gen.
Capersana	town of Assyria on Euphrates	C
Carnuntum	city of Pannonia (Petronell)	B
Carrhae	city of Mesopotamia (Harran)	C
Casius, Mt	mountain near Antioch (Jebel Akra)	C
Cercusium	city of Mesopotamia on Euphrates (Buseire)	C
Chalcedon	city on Propontis (Usküdar)	D
Chalcis	city of Syria (Qinnesrin)	C
Châlon-sur-Saône	*see* Cabyllona	
Chamavi	tribe near mouth of Rhine	A
Charcha/Reman	fortress on Tigris near Amida (Kerk)	C
Charcha (2)	fortress on Tigris near Sumere (Karkh Samarra?)	C
Chiliocomum	region of Media	C
Cibalae	city of Pannonia (Vinkovci)	B
Claudias	fortress of Mesopotamia on Euphrates	C
Coche	city near Seleucia (but identified by Ammianus)	C
Cologne	*see* Colonia Agrippina	
Colonia Agrippina	city of lower Germany (Cologne)	A
Concordia	fort in Germany near Strasbourg	A
Confluentes	city of Gaul (Koblenz)	A

Name	Location (*modern equivalent*)	Map
Constantina	town of Mesopotamia on R. Abora (Viranşehir)	C
Cora	small town in Gaul near Autun (? St Moré)	A
Corduene	region north of Tigris (north-east Hakkari)	C
Ctesiphon	city on Tigris	C
Cydnus, R.	river of Cilicia passing Tarsus (Tersus Çay)	D
Cyzicus	city on Propontis (near Erdek)	D
Dacia	*former* Roman province, north of Danube	B
Dacia Ripensis	*actual* Roman province, south of Danube	B
Dadastana	city of Bithynia	D
Daphne (1)	suburb of Antioch	C
Daphne (2)	fort on Danube in Moesia	—
Davana	town of Mesopotamia on Belias R. (Ain Arous)	C
Decem Pagi	district of Belgica (Dieuse)	A
Diacira	town on Euphrates (Hit)	C
Dibaltum	city of Thrace (Burgas)	B
Dnieper, R. (Borysthenes)	river north of Black Sea	Gen.
Dniester, R. (Danastius)	river north of Black Sea	Gen.
Don, R. (Tanais)	river north-east of Black Sea	Gen.
Drave, R. (Dravus)	tributary of Danube	B
Drepanum	*see* Helenopolis	
Dura (1) (Europus)	town of Mesopotamia on Euphrates	C
Dura (2)	town of Assyria on Tigris (Dur Arabaya)	C
Edessa	city of Osdroene (Urfa)	C
Ephesus	city of Asia	D
Epiphania	city of Cilicia	D
Felix Arbor	fortress on L. Constance (Arbon)	A/B
Fort Hercules	fortress on lower Rhine (Druten?)	A
Greuthungi	Ostrogothic tribe east of Dniester	Gen.
Gumathena	area of Mesopotamia	C
Haemus, Mt	Thracian mountain range (Balkan)	B

Name	Location (modern equivalent)	Map
Hatra	city of Mesopotamia (el Hadr)	C
Hebrus, R.	river in Thrace (Maritza)	B
Helenopolis/ Drepanum	city of Bithynia (Karamürsel)	D
Hiaspis	town on upper Tigris	C
Hiberia	kingdom east of Black Sea (Georgia)	Gen.
Hierapolis	city of Euphratensis (Membij, south of Mardin)	C
Horren/Lorne	small town of Mesopotamia	C
Hucumbra	estate on lower Tigris (Akbara)	C
Istria	district of Dalmatia	B
Iuliacum	city of upper Germany (Juliers)	A
Izala, Mt	plateau in north Mesopotamia (Tur Abdin)	C
Juthungi	Alammanic tribe near Raetia	B
Koblenz	see Confluentes	
Lacotena	city of Armenia	C
Lauriacum	city of Noricum (Lorch)	B
Lazica	area east of Black Sea = Colchis	Gen.
Lentienses	tribe near L. Constance	B
Lepcis	city of Tripolitana	Gen.
Lorne	see Horren	
Lugdunum	city of Gaul (Lyons)	A
Macepracta	village of Assyria near Euphrates	C
Main, R. (Moenus)	river of Germany	A
Mainz	see Moguntiacum	
Maozamalcha	town of Persia near Ctesiphon	C
Maranga	village of Persia near Ctesiphon	C
Marcianople	city of Moesia (Devnja)	B
Marcomanni	tribe north of Noricum	B
Maride	fortress of Mesopotamia (Mardin)	C
Mars, Camp of	fortress in Dacia (Kula)	B
Massa Veternensis	town in Etruria (Massa)	B
Mediolanum	city of north Italy (Milan)	A/B
Mediomatrici	city of Belgica (Metz)	A

Name	Location (*modern equivalent*)	Map
Meiacarire	village of Mesopotamia (Ziyaret Sultan Çeikmun)	C
Melitene	city of province of Armenia (Malatya)	C
Memphis	city of Egypt	Gen.
Mesene	region near Persian Gulf	C
Mesopotamia	Roman province *excluding* lower plain	C
Metz	*see* Mediomatrici	
Meuse, R. (Mosa)	river in Belgica	A
Moguntiacum	city of Gaul on Rhine (Mainz)	A
Moors' Fort (Castra Maurorum)	town of Mesopotamia, north-east of Nisibis	C
Moxoene	region north of Tigris	B
Mursa	city of Pannonia (Osijek)	B
Mygdus	city of Phrygia	D
Naarmalcha	'King's Canal' between Euphrates and Tigris	C
Nacolia	city of Phrygia (Seitgazi)	D
Naissus	city of Moesia (Niš)	B
Natesio, R.	river passing Aquileia (Natisone)	B
Nemetae	city of Germany (Speyer)	A
Neocaesarea	city of Pontus	D
Nicaea	city of Bithynia (Iznik)	D
Nicomedia	city of Bithynia (Izmit)	D
Nicopolis	city of Thrace (Nikyup)	B
Nike	town of Thrace near Adrianople	B
Nineveh	city of Adiabene on Tigris	C
Nisibis	city of Mesopotamia (Nusaybin)	C
Nomentum	town of Italy	B
Novesium	city of Germany on Rhine (Neuss)	A
Noviodunum	city of Scythia (in the Dobrudja)	B
Nymphaeus, R.	tributary of Tigris (Batman Su)	C
Ocriculum	town of Umbria on Tiber (Otricoli)	B
Odrysae Mts	range in Thrace known after tribe (Strandza)	B
Oea	city of Tripolitana (Tripoli)	Gen.
Olympus, Mt	mountain probably in Bithynia (Ulu Dağ)	D
Opitergium	city at head of Adriatic (Oderzo)	B
Osdroene	region of Mesopotamia	C
Oxyrrhynchus	city of Egypt	Gen.

Name	Location (modern equivalent)	Map
Ozogardana	city of Assyria on Euphrates	C
Palas/Capellatii	name given to old Roman frontier	A/B
Perinthus	city of Thrace (Marmara Ereğlisi)	B
Pessinus	city of Phrygia	D
Phaenicha	fortress on Tigris (Finik) confused with Bezabde	C
Phasis, R.	river east of Black Sea	Gen.
Philippopolis	city of Thrace (Plovdiv)	B
Phrygia	place on Tigris	C
Pirisabora	city of Persia (Al-Ambar)	C
Pistoria	city of Tuscany (Pistoia)	B
Pola	city of Istria (Pula)	B
Pruth, R. (Gerasus)	river north of Black Sea	B
Quadi	tribe north of Pannonia	B
Quadriburgium	city of Germany (Qualburg ?)	A
Rauraci	city on upper Rhine (Augst)	A/B
Rehimene	region north of Tigris	C
Reims	see Remi	
Remagen	see Rigomagum	
Reman	see Charcha	
Remi	city of Belgica (Reims)	A
Resaina	town of Osdroene (Ras El Ain)	C
Rhodope Mts	range in Thrace	B
Rigomagum	city of Germany on Rhine (Remagen)	A
Salices (ad)	city of Scythia (in the Dobrudja)	B
Saliso	city of upper Rhine (Seltz)	A
Salona	city of Dalmatia (Split)	B
Samosata	city of province of Armenia on Euphrates (Samsat)	C
Sanctio	city on upper Rhine (Säckingen)	A
Sangarius, R.	river of Asia Minor (Sakarya)	D
Savaria	city of Pannonia (Szombathely)	B
Save, R. (Savus)	tributary of Danube	B
Scythia	Roman province (the Dobrudja)	B
Scythopolis	city of Palestine on L. Tiberias	C
Sedelaucum	city of Gaul (Saulieu)	A

Name	Location (*modern equivalent*)	Map
Seleucia	city of Persia on Tigris	C
Senones	city of Lugdunensis (Sens)	A
Sens	*see* Senones	
Serdica	capital of diocese of Dacia (Sofia)	B
Serri Mts	range in old Dacia (Carpathians)	B
Singara	city of Mesopotamia (Beled Sinjar)	C
Sirmium	capital of prefecture of Illyricum (Sremska Mitrovica)	C
Sisara	fortress of Mesopotamia	C
Sitifis	city of Mauretania (Sétif)	Gen.
Solicinium	place in Germany (Schwetzingen)	A
Sopianae	city of Valeria (Pécs)	B
Speyer	*see* Nemetae	
Spoletium	city of Italy (Spoleto)	B
Strasbourg	*see* Argentorate	
Strymon, R.	river of Thrace (Struma)	B
Succi	pass between Thrace and Dacia (Ihtiman pass)	B
Sumere	fortress on Tigris (Samarra)	C
Sunonensian Lake	lake in Bithynia	D
Tabernae	city of Germany (Rheinzabern)	A
Tarsus	capital of Cilicia	D
Taurini	city of north Italy (Turin)	B
Taurus Mts	range in Cilicia	D
Thebes	city of Egypt	Gen.
Theiss, R. (Parthiscus)	tributary of Danube	B
Thervingi	Gothic tribe east of R. Pruth	B/Gen.
Thilsaphata	town of Mesopotamia	C
Thilutha	fortress on island in Euphrates	C
Thumis	city of Egypt	Gen.
Ticinum	city of north Italy (Pavia)	B
Tongres	*see* Tungri	
Toxiandria	area of Belgica (approx. Brabant)	A
Trent	*see* Tridentum	
Tres Tabernae	town of Germany (Saverne)	A
Treveri	city of Gaul (Trier)	A
Tricasae	city of Lugdunensis (Troyes)	A
Tricensima	fortress on lower Rhine (Xanten)	A

Name	Location (modern equivalent)	Map
Tridentum	city of north Italy (Trent)	A/B
Trier	see Treveri	
Tungri	city of Germany (Tongres)	A
Tyana	city of Cappadocia	D
Ur	city of Assyria	C
Utica	city of Africa	Gen.
Valence	see Valentia (1)	
Valentia (1)	city of Gaul (Valence)	A
Valentia (2)	province of Britain	Gen.
Valeria	province of Pannonia	B
Vangiones	city of Germany (Worms)	A
Vesontio	city of Gaul (Besançon)	A
Vienna	city of Gaul (Vienne)	A
Vienne	see Vienna	
Vingo	city of upper Germany (Bingen)	A
Virta	city of Mesopotamia on Euphrates (Birecik)	C
Worms	see Vangiones	
Zabdicene	region north of Tigris	C
Zaitha	city on Euphrates	C
Zeugma	city on upper Euphrates (Balkis)	C
Ziata	fortress of Mesopotamia on upper Tigris (Ammaneh)	Gen.

The Later Roman Empire

LYDIA	Names of Provinces
ITALIA	Names of Dioceses
▬▬▬	Prefecture boundaries
ALANI	Tribal names

0   100   200   300 miles
0 100 200 300 400 500 km

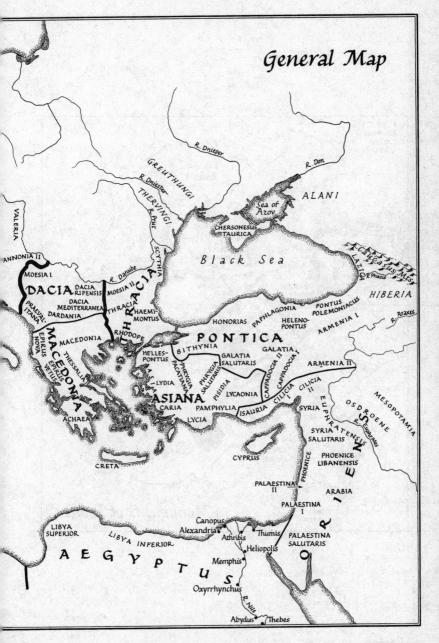

General Map

R. Dnieper

R. Don

GREUTHUNGI

R. Dniester

THERVINGI

R. Prut

ALANI

Sea of
Azov

VALERIA

CHERSONESUS
TAURICA

SCYTHIA

ANNONIA II

Black Sea

R. Danube

CAUCASUS Mts.

MOESIA I

LAZICA

DACIA
RIPENSIS

R. Phasis

DACIA

DACIA
MEDITERRANEA

MOESIA II

THRACIA

HIBERIA

PRAEVAL·
ITANA

DARDANIA

HAEMI-
MONTUS

HONORIAS

PAPHLAGONIA

PONTUS
POLEMONIACUS

ARMENIA I

R. Araxes

EPIRUS
NOVA

MACEDONIA

RHODOPE

HELENO-
PONTUS

EPIRUS
VETUS

THESSALIA

PONTICA

BITHYNIA

HELLES-
PONTUS

GALATIA

MACEDONIA

PHRYGIA
PACATIANA

GALATIA
SALUTARIS

ARMENIA II

LYDIA

PHRYGIA
SALUTARIS

CAPPADOCIA II

CAPPADOCIA I

EUPHRATENSIS

MESOPOTAMIA

ACHAEA

ASIANA

PISIDIA

LYCAONIA

CILICIA

CILICIA
II

OSDROENE

R. Euphrates

CARIA

PAMPHYLIA

ISAURIA

SYRIA I

LYCIA

CYPRUS

SYRIA
SALUTARIS

PHOENICE

PHOENICE
LIBANENSIS

CRETA

PALAESTINA
II

ARABIA

PALAESTINA
I

ORIENS

LIBYA
SUPERIOR

LIBYA INFERIOR

Canopus

Alexandria

Athribis

Thumis

Heliopolis

PALAESTINA
SALUTARIS

AEGYPTUS

Memphis

R. Nile

Oxyrrhynchus

Abydus

Thebes

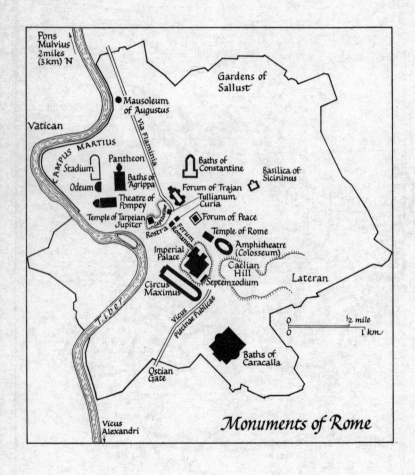

Pons
Mulvius
2 miles
(3 km) N

Gardens of
Sallust

Vatican

Mausoleum
of Augustus

CAMPUS MARTIUS

Via Flaminia

Stadium

Pantheon

Baths of
Constantine

Basilica of
Sicininus

Odeum

Baths of
Agrippa

Theatre of
Pompey

Forum of Trajan

Tullianum
Curia

Temple of
Jupiter

Tarpeian

Forum of Peace

Temple of Rome

Rostra

Forum Romanum

Capitoline

Imperial
Palace

Amphitheatre
(Colosseum)

Caelian
Hill

Lateran

Circus
Maximus

Septemzodium

Vicus
Piscinae Publicae

0 ½ mile
0 1 km

Ostian
Gate

Tiber

Baths of
Caracalla

Vicus
Alexandri

Monuments of Rome

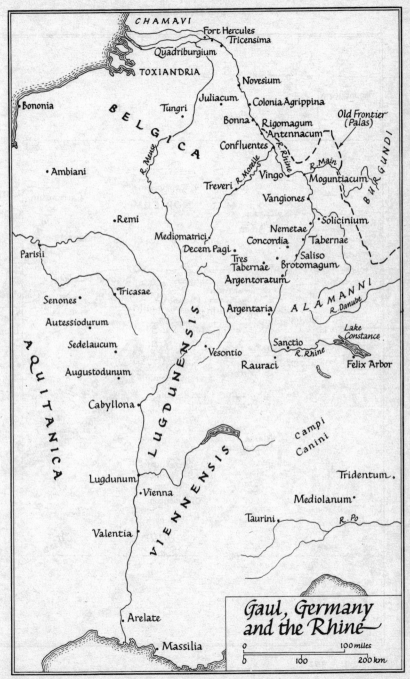

CHAMAVI
Fort Hercules
Tricensima
Quadriburgium
TOXIANDRIA
Novesium
•Bononia
Tungri
Juliacum
•Colonia Agrippina
BELGICA
Bonna•
Rigomagum
Old Frontier
(Palas)
Antennacum
Confluentes
R. Rhine
R. Meuse
BURGUNDI
R. Main
•Ambiani
Vingo•
Moguntiacum
Treveri
R. Moselle
•Remi
Vangiones
•Solicinium
Mediomatrici
Nemetae
•Tabernae
Parisii
Decem Pagi•
Concordia
Tres
Saliso
Tabernae•
Brotomagum
Senones•
Argentoratum
•Tricasae
ALAMANNI
Autessiodurum
Argentaria•
R. Danube
AQUITANIA
•Sedelaucum
Lake
Constance
LUGDUNENSIS
Vesontio•
Sanctio•
Augustodunum•
Rauraci
R. Rhine
Felix Arbor
Cabyllona•
campi
Canini
Tridentum•
Lugdunum
•Vienna
Mediolanum•
VIENNENSIS
Valentia•
Taurini•
R. Po
•Arelate
Gaul, Germany
and the Rhine
0   100 miles
•Massilia
0   100   200 km

The Danube, Italy and Thrace

0   100   200 miles

0   100   200   300 km

R. Theiss

R. Pruth

THERVINGI

R. Dniester

FREE SARMATIANS

OLD DACIA

Noviodunum

SCYTHIA

R. Tibiscus

Serri

Salices

Tomi

Bononea

Acimincum

LIMIGANTES

TAIFALI

Sirmium

MOESIA II

Black

PANNONIA II

MOESIA I

R. Danube

Camp of Mars

Marcianople

Nicopolis

DACIA

Cabyle

Sea

Naissus

Haemus

Beroea

Dibaltum

Serdica

THRACE

Succi Pass

R. Hebrus

Odrysae

R. Strymon

Philippopolis

R. Axius

Rhodope

Adrianople

Constantinople

MACEDONIA

Perinthus

Acontisma Pass

Aegean

Sea

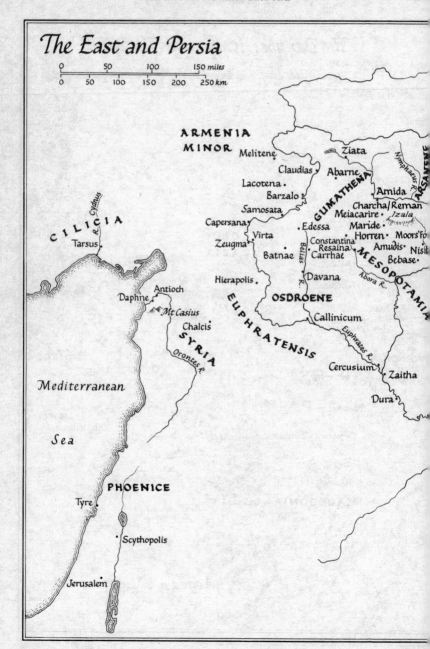

The East and Persia

0   50   100   150 miles

0   50   100   150   200   250 km

ARMENIA
MINOR

Melitene
Ziata
Claudias · Abarne
Lacotena ·
Barzalo
GUMATHENA
Amida
ARSANENE
Nymphaeus R.
Charcha/Reman
Samosata
Meiacarire ·
Izala
Capersana ·
· Edessa
Maride ·
Virta
Constantina
Horren ·
Moors'Fo
Zeugma ·
Resaina
Amudis ·
Nisil
Carrhae
Bebase ·
MESOPOTAMIA
Batnae ·
Belias R.
Abora R.
Hierapolis ·
Davana
CILICIA
Cydnus R.
Tarsus ·
OSROENE
Antioch
EUPHRATENSIS
Daphne
Mt Casius
Callinicum
Chalcis
SYRIA
Orontes R.
Euphrates R.
Cercusium · Zaitha
Mediterranean
Dura ·
Sea
PHOENICE
Tyre ·
· Scythopolis
Jerusalem

MAP C

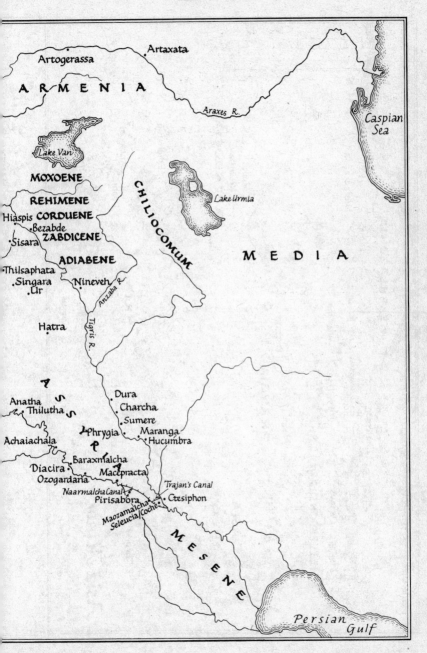

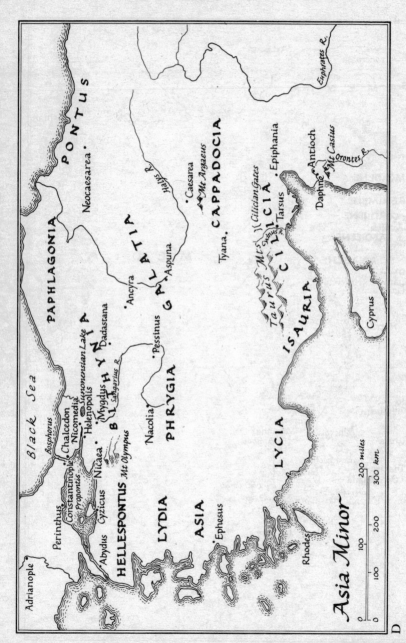

Asia Minor

READ MORE IN PENGUIN

In every corner of the world, on every subject under the sun, Penguin represents quality and variety – the very best in publishing today.

For complete information about books available from Penguin – including Puffins, Penguin Classics and Arkana – and how to order them, write to us at the appropriate address below. Please note that for copyright reasons the selection of books varies from country to country.

In the United Kingdom: Please write to *Dept. EP, Penguin Books Ltd, Bath Road, Harmondsworth, West Drayton, Middlesex UB7 0DA*

In the United States: Please write to *Consumer Services, Penguin Putnam Inc., 405 Murray Hill Parkway, East Rutherford, New Jersey 07073-2136.* VISA and MasterCard holders call 1-800-631-8571 to order Penguin titles

In Canada: Please write to *Penguin Books Canada Ltd, 10 Alcorn Avenue, Suite 300, Toronto, Ontario M4V 3B2*

In Australia: Please write to *Penguin Books Australia Ltd, 487 Maroondah Highway, Ringwood, Victoria 3134*

In New Zealand: Please write to *Penguin Books (NZ) Ltd, Private Bag 102902, North Shore Mail Centre, Auckland 10*

In India: Please write to *Penguin Books India Pvt Ltd, 11 Community Centre, Panchsheel Park, New Delhi 110017*

In the Netherlands: Please write to *Penguin Books Netherlands bv, Postbus 3507, NL-1001 AH Amsterdam*

In Germany: Please write to *Penguin Books Deutschland GmbH, Metzlerstrasse 26, 60594 Frankfurt am Main*

In Spain: Please write to *Penguin Books S. A., Bravo Murillo 19, 1°B, 28015 Madrid*

In Italy: Please write to *Penguin Italia s.r.l., Via Vittorio Emanuele 45la, 20094 Corsico, Milano*

In France: Please write to *Penguin France, 12, Rue Prosper Ferradou, 31700 Blagnac*

In Japan: Please write to *Penguin Books Japan Ltd, Iidabashi KM-Bldg, 2-23-9 Koraku, Bunkyo-Ku, Tokyo 112-0004*

In South Africa: Please write to *Penguin Books South Africa (Pty) Ltd, P.O. Box 751093, Gardenview, 2047 Johannesburg*

READ MORE IN PENGUIN

A CHOICE OF CLASSICS